Afghanistan from the Cold War through the War on Terror

Afghanistan from the Cold War through the War on Terror

BARNETT R. RUBIN

OXFORD
UNIVERSITY PRESS

OXFORD

UNIVERSITY PRESS

Oxford University Press is a department of the University of Oxford.
It furthers the University's objective of excellence in research, scholarship,
and education by publishing worldwide.

Oxford   New York
Auckland   Cape Town   Dar es Salaam   Hong Kong   Karachi
Kuala Lumpur   Madrid   Melbourne   Mexico City   Nairobi
New Delhi   Shanghai   Taipei   Toronto

With offices in
Argentina   Austria   Brazil   Chile   Czech Republic   France   Greece
Guatemala   Hungary   Italy   Japan   Poland   Portugal   Singapore
South Korea   Switzerland   Thailand   Turkey   Ukraine   Vietnam

Oxford is a registered trade mark of Oxford University Press
in the UK and certain other countries.

Published in the United States of America by
Oxford University Press
198 Madison Avenue, New York, NY 10016

Library of Congress Cataloging-in-Publication Data
Rubin, Barnett R.
Afghanistan from the Cold War through the War on Terror / Barnett R. Rubin.
p. cm.
Includes bibliographical references and index.
ISBN 978-0-19-979112-5 (hardback : alk. paper) 1. Afghanistan—Politics and government—
1989–2001. 2. Afghanistan—Politics and government—2001– 3. Afghan War, 2001–
4. War on Terrorism, 2001–2009. 5. Afghanistan—Foreign relations—21st century.
6. Postwar reconstruction—Afghanistan. 7. Local government—Afghanistan.
8. Taliban. 9. Islamic fundamentalism—Afghanistan. I. Title.
DS371.3.R83 2013
958.104—dc23

2012046996
9780199791125

1   3   5   7   9   8   6   4   2

Printed in the United States of America on acid-free paper

To Lakhdar Brahimi and Richard Holbrooke: thanks for the opportunity to serve.

CONTENTS

PART THREE: BACK TO WAR

FOREWORD

For almost three decades, Barnett Rubin has been a most acute observer of Afghanistan's iterated wars, as well as an activist in the protracted search there for justice and peace. For the past dozen years, his perch for that work was the NYU Center on International Cooperation, where I have the privilege of being his colleague.

Barney is not your average scholar. Like the best academics, he is deeply versed in the literature and theory of conflict, in the methods of empirical research, and in the region that has now been most of his life work. Unlike most academics, he has the kind of in-depth knowledge of the culture, history, and people of Afghanistan and its neighborhood that often surprises Afghans themselves. I got a glimmer of how unusual is his expertise when I was given an account of a meeting he attended along with an Iranian diplomat in Dubai (this at a time when only a handful of Americans had any contact with official Iran), conducted partly in terms of trading refrains from Iqbal, the Indo-Pakistani poet-philosopher—in Farsi. Barney's insight into the relationships that shape the local and subregional dynamics of the Afghan wars is unparalleled.

After September 11, and through 2008, Barney was called on by the UN's Lakhdar Brahimi, by the Afghan authorities, and by the NATO allies with increasing frequency—and with increasing despair about the missed opportunities, errors in misunderstanding, and mistakes of strategy that characterized much of the coalition effort. Barney was never content to carp on the sidelines, though, but took every flight and invitation to publish, brief, or advise to help shape, wherever he could, a more productive engagement.

One person who saw Barney's unique value was Richard Holbrooke. They had worked together when Barney ran the Council on Foreign Relations's groundbreaking project on preventive action in the mid-1990s, when Barney was also writing his seminal books *The Fragmentation of Afghanistan* and *Blood on the Doorstep*. When Holbrooke became chair of the board of the Asia Society, he called on Barney to work on their Afghanistan program, culminating in an influential study, "Back from the Brink," cochaired by Barney and master diplomat Tom Pickering. When President Obama and Secretary Clinton tapped Holbrooke to serve as special envoy for Afghanistan and Pakistan, he again turned to Barney for advice. For two years, Barney gave frequent and always richly informed advice to Holbrooke and the secretary.

One of the things that distinguish CIC from many academic centers is the understanding that policy advice is conveyed most effectively through people, not papers. We recruited highly talented people such as Jake Sherman, Rahul Chandran, and Tom Gregg to complement Barney's work on Afghanistan, enabling him to devote a substantial portion of his time to advising Holbrooke, as well as maintaining his unique dialogue with the Afghans and their neighbors. I am very grateful to our donors—especially the Norwegian Ministry for Foreign Affairs—for supporting our Afghan program generously, but more important, flexibly. Through and around Barney's effort, CIC, Norway, and the U.S. government have become partners in the search for an end to this long episode of the Afghan wars. We were together in Dubai for a joint CIC/Norwegian workshop on the regional dynamics of a potential Afghan peace, whose outcome Holbrooke was anticipating, when he was suddenly and tragically felled by an aortal aneurysm.

All wars shape their protagonists, but some wars shape more than just those who fight them. The U.S. war in Afghanistan is one such war. The U.S. effort to eliminate or at least contain the threat posed by al-Qaeda, the allied effort to rebuild Afghanistan after this and previous wars, NATO's role in both military and civilian operations, and the regional and international effort to stem the flow of opium from Afghanistan all have reshaped the way international security is perceived and managed. For readers who want a richer understanding of the Afghan war, or of how that war has shaped the broader international system, this compilation of Barney's writings provides both evidence and insight. For those who wish to understand what comes next, it's an essential read. The critical reader will notice that most of the ideas that now shape U.S. and international approaches to Afghanistan found an airing in Barney's writing well before they came to fruition in policy. Most important, Barney was an early—and frequently lonely—voice for reconciliation when many in Washington preferred to believe that military strategy alone could prevail. Presidents Obama and Karzai have come around to Barney's view—not least because Barney was dogged in explaining the rationale for reconciliation to Holbrooke, notwithstanding its costs and its discomfort, and strategies for achieving it. When Marc Grossman took over as U.S. special envoy, he too sought Barney's help and advice, and reconciliation has been a central theme of the U.S. effort since. As I draft this introduction, new agreements among the Taliban, President Karzai, and the United

States herald the first public step in a move toward a political settlement to end this round of Afghanistan's long war.

That first step is tentative and fragile, and there will inevitably be reversals and crises—probably several of them—before real progress is recorded. In time, though, and with patience, the United States can help forge a political process that preserves essential gains in freedom and rights but accommodates those Afghan forces never included in the Bonn accords. If such an agreement is eventually negotiated, credit will go to those political actors who had the courage to stand firm on core principles and the equal courage to make necessary compromises to avoid another generation of bloodshed. History rarely gives credit to those who think the issues through and agitate behind the scenes. But if Afghanistan does reach a reasonable peace, Barney's ideas and his tireless agitation and advice on behalf of Afghanistan will have played a crucial role.

Bruce Jones
Director and Senior Fellow, NYU Center on International Cooperation
Director, Managing Global Order Project, the Brookings Institution
January 2012

ACKNOWLEDGMENTS

I wrote the chapters of this book over a period of more than a decade, while I was employed by the Council on Foreign Relations and then the Center on International Cooperation at New York University. For much of that time I worked as an official or unofficial consultant to the United Nations mission to Afghanistan. Les Gelb, president of the Council on Foreign Relations, regarded the works included here that I wrote during 1996–2000 as distractions from the job he was paying me to do as director of the Center for Preventive Action, but he tolerated my behavior for as long as he could. Since the premature death of our mutual friend Richard Holbrooke (about whom more later), we have had many conversations on the wars in Afghanistan, which have outlived not only Holbrooke but both of our jobs at CFR.

Shepard Forman, founder and director (now emeritus) of the Center on International Cooperation, first allowed me the time to complete the book I would have finished at CFR had I not spent so much time on Afghanistan, *Blood on the Doorstep* (2002). Just as I finished that, the events of September 11, 2001, destroyed, among other things, our plans for the future of CIC, but together we pivoted with events to create the Afghanistan Reconstruction Program, which continues today as the Afghanistan Regional Program (ARP), and which sponsored most of the work collected here. He and his successor as CIC director, Bruce Jones, managed to use my obsession to add a new program to CIC's multiple activities, an arrangement from which I have benefited enormously. I hope they feel the same way. Bruce, who has written a foreword for this book, gave support over the past few years without which I could not have assembled this work.

When Lakhdar Brahimi became the UN Secretary-General's personal representative for Afghanistan in 1997, he reached out to me, starting a relationship that has endured and deepened. Originally I helped him convene an informal advisory group, including Ashraf Ghani, Ahmed Rashid, Olivier Roy, and

William Maley. After September 11, he brought Ghani and me into the team that organized the UN Talks on Afghanistan in Bonn. Lakhdar's support throughout his tenure as UN special representative for Afghanistan and long after made much of this work possible. If this work shows any of the wisdom I have tried to learn from him, all the credit is his.

The friendship of Brahimi's predecessor as head of the UN Special Mission for Afghanistan, Francesc Vendrell, who later served as the European Union's special representative to Afghanistan, provided many chances for reflection over the years. Brahimi's successor as SRSG, Jean Arnault, enabled me to continue the work I had done on the Bonn Agreement through the Afghanistan Compact and the Afghan National Development Strategy. At UNAMA I benefited from the friendship and collaboration of Chris Alexander, Rina Amiri, Anders Fänge, Ameerah Haq, Talatbek Masadykov, Janan Musazai, Mervyn Patterson, Thomas Ruttig, Eckart Schiewek, and Michael Semple among others. I owe them and many other UN colleagues a lot of gratitude. In Kabul I appreciated the hospitality and insights of Kate Clark and Andrew Wilder.

Although I never worked for the U.S. government until 2009, officials of all the administrations spanning the years in which I wrote these chapters were willing to talk and help test my ideas against their experience. They included Richard Boucher, Ryan Crocker, James Dobbins, Karl Eikenberry, Robert Finn, Rick Inderfuerth, Doug Lute, Ronald Neumann, Ann Patterson, Robin Raphel, William Wood, and my University of Chicago classmate Zalmay Khalilzad.

Ashraf Ghani's vision led to a partnership that inspired much of the work here. Our joint work as unofficial advisors to Brahimi led Ashraf to propose that we establish the ARP; we drafted the first proposal in a hotel room in Washington on October 1, 2001, just before we were both called by Brahimi to serve as official advisors. I owe him an intellectual debt greater than can be acknowledged in scholarly notes.

All of this work required funding, and I have had good fortune in finding support. I am grateful to the donors to CFR's Center for Preventive Action who unwittingly subsidized my work, especially to the Carnegie Corporation of New York and David Hamburg, then of the Carnegie Commission for Preventing Deadly Conflict, and the Century Foundation, led by Richard Leone until his retirement in 2011.

Since September 11, the government of Norway has supported CIC's work on Afghanistan practically without interruption. The donor relationship with Norway has added an important dimension to both my work and my life. I benefited in particular from the support of Vidar Helgesen, Kai Eide, and Kåre Aas. During Eide's tenure as UN SRSG and especially Aas's tenure as ambassador to Afghanistan and then political director of the Norwegian Foreign Ministry, this relationship deepened into a true partnership.

At ARP's inception, George Soros, Aryeh Neier, and Anthony Richter of the Open Society Institute offered the quick and flexible funding that enabled us to get off the ground. This collaboration later led to establishment of OSI's programs in Afghanistan. The UK, both the Department for International Development (DfID) and the Foreign and Commonwealth office, quickly saw potential in our work; I appreciated in particular the help of Mukesh Kapila and Tom Phillips.

Canada provided strategic assistance to CIC's work on the Afghan Constitution. At various times the work published here benefited from support from the Ford Foundation, the Rockefeller Foundation, the Carnegie Corporation of New York, and the Government of Japan, for which I owe Sadako Ogata particular gratitude. The World Bank, the UN High Commissioner for Human Rights, the Swedish Committee for Afghanistan, and the Friedrich Ebert Foundation all helped make this book possible.

I could never have done all of this without the many colleagues who became friends. Several of these chapters were coauthored with some of my colleagues at CIC. Helena Malikyar helped launch ARP in the fall of 2001 and went on to carry out the revelatory field research that formed the foundation for our study of the debate over the form of the state in Afghanistan. Abby Stoddard, in addition to her work as head of CIC's program on humanitarian action, constructed a pioneering database on donor contributions to Afghanistan. Humayun Hamidzada and I collaborated through all of the work on the Afghan constitutional process and much more. He accompanied me on several visits to Afghanistan and provided help on the ground both during and after his tenure at CIC. CIC and I had the good fortune of benefiting from Abubakar Siddique's collaboration during the Fulbright fellowship that enabled him to graduate from NYU's school of journalism, though we had already decided to write together on Afghanistan-Pakistan relations after several conversations we had while he was covering the Constitutional Loya Jirga in Kabul in December 2003. Malalai Wassil Wardak's help was indispensable in the work that Patricia Gossman and I did in 2004 for the UN High Commissioner for Human Rights on the "mapping report" on human rights violations in Afghanistan.

Compiling this book out of scattered fragments of text, all in different formats, would have been beyond my own capacities. Parnian Nazary of CIC worked assiduously and independently to format text, obtain rights and permissions, list tables and figures, and encourage me to finally get the job done. Her work for ARP has entailed far more than that, but she deserves special thanks for her patience nonetheless with these painstaking details. Darcy Courteau's outstanding editorial skills were also essential for transforming all of these documents into a coherent manuscript.

I have heard that Afghans hate foreigners, and perhaps someday they will feel comfortable enough with me to express their xenophobia. Thus far they have concealed it behind an impenetrable façade of hospitality and friendship. I could not possibly acknowledge all the relationships that have come to form so much of my life since this work started, and an attempt to explain them would turn this prefatory note into a memoir. I can do little here other than list names, while emphasizing that none of them is implicated in what I have written. In addition to those mentioned previously, I relied on my relationships with Abdullah Abdullah, Anwar-ul-Haq Ahady, Hidayat Amin-Arsala, Abdullah Arsala, Orzala Ashraf, Muhammad Haneef Atmar, Umer Daudzai, Muhammad Eshaq, Adib Farhadi, Fatima Gailani, Ali Ahmad Jalali, Sayyid Tayeb Jawad, Kawun Kakar, Mujahid Kakar, Massoud Karokhail, Hamid Karzai, Hekmat Karzai, Qayum Karzai, Fawzia Koofi, Jawed Ludin, Ahmad Wali Massoud, Ahmad Zia Massoud, Saad Mohseni, Muhammad Muhaqqiq, Janan Musazai, Wakil Ahmad Mutawak-kil, Nader Nadery, Ishaq Nadiri, Ghulam Jilani Popal, Yunus Qanuni, Ahmad Idrees Rahmani, Zalmai Rassoul, Daud Saba, Nilofar Sakhi, Amrullah Saleh, Seema Samar, Hamid Siddiq, Dadfar Rangin Spanta, Massoum Stanekzai, Humayun Tandar, Abdul Hakim Taniwal, Wahid Waissi, Faruq Wardak, Abdul Salam Zaeef, and Omar Zakhilwal. I wish I could tell how each contributed, and I wish I could mention many more.

Afghanistan is forever twinned with Pakistan, and my friends east of the Durand Line were equally important. Ahmed Rashid belongs to a special cate-gory: as already mentioned, we worked together to advise Brahimi, and our friendship developed into a true partnership, including but exceeding coauthor-ship. All members of Ahmed's extended clan of friends expect to be awakened at any time by a phone call starting with his trademark greeting—"It's a disaster!"—and he and I have experienced quite a few disasters together. With him, even that has been a pleasure.

Asma Jehangir, in addition to providing me with her clear-eyed vision of Pakistan, also gave me an important opportunity in her role as the UN special rapporteur on extra-judicial killings. In 2004 she asked me to help draft a "map-ping report" of major human rights violations in Afghanistan from 1978 to 2001. Perhaps someday that still-secret report—based entirely on public documents—will be released.

Aisha Ahmad (actually a Canadian) organized a door-opening trip to Islam-abad for me in 2008. That trip introduced me to people I would otherwise not have met. I continue to learn from her. Mushahid Hussain provided me with the unique opportunity to address a gathering in a Sufi shrine in Rawalpindi on the occasion of the eight hundredth birth anniversary of Mawlana Jalaluddin Rumi (known to Afghans as "Balkhi"). He also offered a window into the thinking of the Pakistani establishment. Maleeha Lodhi, whom I first met in Mushahid's office in 1985, has provided invaluable insights and introductions and continues to do so. Afrasiab Khattak has been an inspiration for years, as we met on both sides of the Durand Line, in Kabul, Peshawar, and Islamabad. He enabled Ahmed Rashid and me to attend the Pakhtun Peace Jirga in Peshawar in November 2007. Khalid Aziz's hospitality also opened many doors. I must also thank Salman Bashir, Asad Durrani, Tariq Fatemi, Husain Haqqani, Abida Husain, Fakhr Imam, Sughu Imam, Riaz Muhammad Khan, Rustam Shah Mohmand, Muhammad Saad, and Rahimullah Yusufzai.

Several Iranians have helped me over the years, but under current circumstances it might not be an act of friendship to thank them by name. They know who they are. Shahrbanou Tadjbakhsh helped open that gate during my first visit to Iran in 1994, when she was still a Ph.D. student at Columbia. Since then we have collaborated on much more in Central Asia and Afghanistan.

I am sad that Richard Holbrooke will never have the chance to see this book. I'm even sorrier that he won't be around to make people buy it. We first met in 1995, when I was preparing a mission to Serbia, Kosovo, Macedonia, and Albania for CFR's Center for Preventive Action. Even during that frenetic time, just after the signing of the Dayton Accords, he took time out to get us a meeting with Slobodan Milosevic. Thus began a unique friendship that ended abruptly on December 13, 2010, when Richard died in a hospital in Washington of a ruptured aorta, while I was in Dubai helping CIC and Norway organize a meeting of regional stakeholders in Afghanistan.

This book ends when our closest partnership started: the day after the inauguration of Barack Obama as president, when Richard sent me a text message at 6:00 A.M., asking if I was still interested in the job we had discussed, advising him as U.S. special representative for Afghanistan and Pakistan. From April 2009, when I got my security clearance (something for which Richard claimed personal credit), until his death twenty months later, and after, the incomparable opportunity he gave me has required me to observe public silence. It has been worth it. Though I missed the chance to thank him on his deathbed for that opportunity and for all I learned from him, I will do so in print here, where he can scrawl his edits in the eternal unseen margins of history.

September 11 blew apart the plans I had made for a somewhat calmer life, and no one knows better what that has meant than my wife, Susan Blum. Through these years of constant travel and distraction, we have grown closer than I thought two people could be. We both have struggled with the pains of separation. Eventually we both gave up on—or at least postponed—the dream of a calmer life, as I became a government official and Sue transformed herself with immense commitment and dedication into a skilled and caring psychotherapist. An old friend, a linguist from Transylvania, recently characterized our lives as "eventful and dynamic," and that is equally true of our love.

CONTRIBUTORS

Andrea Armstrong

Andrea Armstrong joined the Loyola University New Orleans College of Law faculty in 2010. Her research and teaching interests include criminal procedure, criminal law, civil rights, domestic and international human rights, law and poverty, and race and the law. Professor Armstrong is a graduate of Yale Law School and the Woodrow Wilson School of Public and International Affairs at Princeton University, where she completed her M.P.A. in international relations.

Prior to law school, Armstrong researched regional conflict dynamics at the Center on International Cooperation at NYU and transitional justice strategies at the International Center for Transitional Justice. She has also examined conflict prevention for the United Nations Department of Political Affairs; the denial of citizenship in Central Asia and the Caucasus for the Commission on Human Security; and human rights and refugee protection for the International Rescue Committee. She has also taught policy modules on democratization at the Junior Summer Institute at Princeton University.

Ashraf Ghani

Ashraf Ghani, chairman of the Institute for State Effectiveness, was named among the twenty most influential global thinkers of 2009 and 2010 for his work on fragile states. As adviser to the UN secretary-general, he advised on the Bonn Agreement for Afghanistan, and then as Afghanistan's finance minister between 2002 and 2004, he is credited with a series of successful reforms in Afghanistan, including reform of the treasury, customs, budget, and the currency. He prepared Afghanistan's first National Development Framework and

Securing Afghanistan's Future, a $28 billion reconstruction program for the country. In 2010, he developed and facilitated the successful Kabul Conference and Process to build internal consensus and external alignment on priorities in Afghanistan. Ghani was named best finance minister in Asia by *Emerging Markets*, a publication of Euromoney Institutional Investor plc, in 2003 and was previously nominated for the posts of UN secretary-general and the president of the World Bank.

Trained in political science and anthropology at the American University of Beirut and Columbia University. Ghani served on the faculty at Johns Hopkins from 1983 to 1991 and has taught at Kabul University, Aarhus University, and Berkeley. He was chief anthropologist at the World Bank from 1991 to 2001, working on large-scale development and institutional projects in East Asia, South Asia, and Russia, and global issues of strategy and development. Ghani is involved on the advisory boards for a number of activities supporting the reform of global institutions, including the Commission on the UN High-Level Panel on Legal Empowerment of the Poor, the UN Democracy Fund, the Asian Development Bank, the Inter-American Development Bank, IDEA, the Brookings Institution's project on global insecurity, the Atlantic Council, and the World Justice Project of the American Bar Association. He is a former chair of the World Economic Forum's Global Agenda Council on Fragile States and a Senior Non-Resident Fellow at the Brookings Institution. He is author (with Clare Lockhart) of *Fixing Failed States* (2008) and a *Window to a Just Order* (in Pushtu and Dari, 2009).

Humayun Hamidzada

Humayun Hamidzada is an independent scholar and consultant based in Toronto, Canada. He served as Afghanistan's deputy minister of finance for policy between 2009 and 2011. Previously, Hamidzada served the president of Afghanistan as his chief spokesman and director of communications from 2007 to late 2009.

Prior to his period of service in the Presidential Palace, Hamidzada served as founding director of the Center for Policy and Human Development (CPHD), an independent policy research institute at Kabul University. Hamidzada received his master's degree from the Fletcher School of Law and Diplomacy at Tufts University. Hamidzada has previously worked in senior research and management roles for the Center on International Cooperation at New York University, the United Nations Office for Coordination of Humanitarian Affairs in New York, and the United Nations Development Program in Kandahar, Kabul, and Islamabad.

Bruce Jones

Bruce Jones is director and senior fellow of the NYU Center on International Co-operation, and senior fellow and director of the Managing Global Order Program at the Brookings Institution. He has served as senior external advisor for the World Bank's World Development Report 2011 on Conflict, Security, and Development; as a member of the Secretary-General's Senior Advisory Group to guide the Review of International Civilian Capacities (2010–11); as the lead scholar on the International Task Force on Global Public Goods (2007); and as deputy research director for the UN High-Level Panel on Threats, Challenges, and Change (2004–05). He is coauthor with Carlos Pascual and Stephen Stedman of *Power and Responsibility: Building International Order in an Era of Transnational Threats* (2009); coeditor with Shepard Forman of *Cooperating for Peace and Security* (2009); author of *Peacemaking in Rwanda: The Dynamics of Failures*; series editor of the *Annual Review of Global Peace Operations* and author of several book chapters and journal articles on U.S. strategy, global order, the Middle East, peace keeping, postconflict peace building, and strategic coordination. He is consulting professor at Stanford University, adjunct faculty at the NYU Wagner School of Public Service, and professor by courtesy at the NYU Department of Politics.

William Maley

William Maley is professor and director of the Asia-Pacific College of Diplomacy at the Australian National University. He is a member of the Order of Australia (AM) and a fellow of the Academy of the Social Sciences in Australia (FASSA). He is author of *Rescuing Afghanistan* (2006) and *The Afghanistan Wars* (2002, 2009); coauthor of *Regime Change in Afghanistan: Foreign Intervention and the Politics of Legitimacy* (1991) and *Political Order in Post-Communist Afghanistan* (1992); and editor of *Fundamentalism Reborn? Afghanistan and the Taliban* (1998, 2001).

Helena Malikyar

Helena Malikyar is an independent researcher and writer based in Kabul. Since 2001, she has worked on numerous governance-related projects with the UN and USAID, as well as the Center on International Cooperation's Afghanistan Regional Project. She was an aide to the former Afghan king, Mohammad Zahir Shah, in Rome. Malikyar holds an M.A. from New York University with concentration on the history of state building in Afghanistan.

Ahmed Rashid

Ahmed Rashid is a Pakistani journalist based in Lahore who has covered Afghanistan, Pakistan, and Central Asia for a variety of publications since 1979. He is the author of the best-selling *Taliban*, which in April 2010 was reissued on its tenth anniversary with an updated version. His later book is *Descent into Chaos: The US and the Disaster in Afghanistan, Pakistan and Central Asia*. His other books include *Jihad* (2002) and *The Resurgence of Central Asia* (1994). His fifth and latest book is *Pakistan on the Brink: The Future of America, Pakistan and Afghanistan*. He writes for the *Financial Times*, the *New York Times*, the *New York Review of Books*, Spain's *El Mundo*, *BBC Online*, and Pakistani publications.

In 2001, he won the Nisar Osmani Courage in Journalism Award, given by the Human Rights Society of Pakistan. In 2008 he won Spain's prestigious Casa Asia prize for contributing most about Asia to the Spanish people. The following year he was presented with the prize for best columnist in the Spanish press by King Juan Carlos at a dinner honoring him. In December 2009 he was appointed a member of the board of New York's Committee to Protect Journalists, while *Foreign Policy* magazine chose him as one of the world's most important 100 Global Thinkers in 2009 and 2010. He has also served on the board of advisers for the International Committee of the Red Cross for five years. His books have won numerous prizes.

Olivier Roy

Olivier Roy is presently professor at the European University Institute (Florence); he heads the Mediterranean program at the Robert Schuman Centre for Advanced Studies and the ReligioWest research project (funded by the European Research Council). He has been a senior researcher at the French National Center for Scientific Research (since 1985), professor at the Ecole des Hautes Etudes en Sciences Sociales (since 2003), and visiting professor at Berkeley University (2008–09). He headed the OSCE's Mission for Tajikistan (1993–94) and was a consultant for the UN Office of the Coordinator for Afghanistan (1988). His fields of study include Afghanistan, political Islam, Middle East, Islam in the West, and comparative religions. Roy received an Agrégation de Philosophie and a Ph.D. in political science. He is the author of *The Failure of Political Islam* (1994), *Globalized Islam* (2004), and more recently *Holy Ignorance* (2010).

Jake Sherman

Jake Sherman is the Afghanistan/Pakistan regional team leader for the U.S. Agency for International Development's Office of Transition Initiatives, a position he has held since May 2012. Previously, he held various positions at the Center on International Cooperation at New York University, most recently as deputy director for conflict programs. At CIC, Sherman's research focused on United Nations peace keeping and preventive diplomacy, as well as on counternarcotics and private security companies in Afghanistan. From 2003 to 2005, Sherman was a political officer for the United Nations Assistance Mission in Afghanistan.

Abubakar Siddique

Abubakar Siddique is a senior correspondent covering Afghanistan and Pakistan for Radio Free Europe/Radio Liberty's Central Newsroom. He has spent the past decade researching and writing about security, political, humanitarian, and cultural issues in Pakistan, Afghanistan, and the Pashtun heartland along the border region where he was born. He is writing a book on the future of extremism in Pakistan and Afghanistan. Siddique has contributed to eurasianet.org, Pakistan's *Friday Times* and *Newsline* magazines, as well as the *Central European Journal of International and Security Studies*, the National Defense University's Global Strategic Assessment 2009, and the Barcelona Center for International Affairs. He has also contributed to edited volumes on stabilization and regional studies. He holds master's degrees in journalism and anthropology. He was a Fulbright Scholar at New York University from 2005 to 2006, and while at NYU he also worked at the Center on International Cooperation. He speaks English, Pashto, Urdu, and several other languages of Afghanistan and Pakistan.

Abby Stoddard

Abby Stoddard is a partner with the independent research group Humanitarian Outcomes and a senior program advisor for humanitarian affairs at New York University's Center on International Cooperation. Her past professional experience includes ten years in program positions with international humanitarian organizations, and she currently serves as board president for Doctors of the World (Médecins du Monde USA). She is the author of *Humanitarian Alert: NGO Information and Its Impact on US Foreign Policy* (2006), along with numerous articles and book chapters on humanitarian action, nongovernmental organizations, and the U.S. foreign aid architecture. She holds a Ph.D. in politics from New York University and a master's in international affairs from Columbia University.

Introduction

On my first day back from a late vacation, on September 11, 2001, I was supposed to appear on the dais of the Council on Foreign Relations along with UN Secretary-General Kofi Annan. Annan was to present his report on preventing violent conflict to a meeting chaired by retired General John W. Vessey, chairman of the Council's Center for Preventive Action. As CPA's founding director, I was to offer a few comments on the subject.

The previous day, as I was driving with my wife, Susan Blum, to the airport in Nice, a brief report on the radio announced, "En Afghanistan, le commandant Massoud, chef de l'alliance du nord anti-taliban, a été légèrement blessé dans un attentat" ("In Afghanistan, Commander Massoud, head of the anti-Taliban Northern Alliance, has been lightly wounded in an attack"). That afternoon, as soon as I arrived at my apartment in New York, journalists calling from Kabul, London, and Washington told me that Massoud was most likely dead. They asked me what would happen in Afghanistan.

A few days earlier, still on vacation, I had finished checking the page proofs of *Blood on the Doorstep*, the book I had written about preventing violent conflict, based on my experience as the director of CPA. The title came from a poem by the classical Persian poet Saadi, which I had memorized when I started learning that language in order to study Afghanistan:

> I said, with tricks and spells I will hide my inmost secret.
> It will not stay hidden, for blood flows over the doorstep.

The poem expressed the overflow of suffering beyond the confines where we try to keep it. "The world has become so linked," I argued, "that no threat to human security is unconnected to our own." Written between the fall of the Berlin Wall and the fall of the Twin Towers, this book argued that global security depended on preventing and managing armed conflicts seemingly on the margins of great strategic issues. For most of those concerned with foreign policy in the United

States, these wars, the prevention of which was the goal of the report Kofi Annan was to present on September 11, seemed to be:

> Marginal diversions from the big business at hand—managing the breakup of the Soviet Union and the decline of Russia, integrating or deterring China as it becomes an economic and military power, creating a new North Atlantic relationship between the United States and a uniting Europe, reaffirming and strengthening the security relationship with Japan, creating a financial and trading architecture to safeguard prosperity, and defending the nation's land and people from the terrorism or ballistic missiles of outlaw regimes and movements.[1]

Neither the public nor the foreign policy establishment intuitively understood the causes or the potential consequences of these "spectacles of atrocity that appeared intermittently on the television screen." Were these due to eruptions of irrational fanaticism, or to "the manipulations of a few evil men—Saddam Hussein, Slobodan Milosevic, Usama Bin Laden?" My research and experience not only in Afghanistan but in Central Asia, Central Africa, West Africa, and the Southern Balkans had led me to a different conclusion:

> What is most difficult to convey about foreign conflicts is not the foreign cultures, beliefs, or hatreds that make others different from us; it is rather the radically different circumstances that make people just like us behave differently. It is those situations—desperate impoverishment, fear for one's life, collapse of institutions that once made sense of existence and gave a sense of security, the threat that not using violence will leave one prey to the violence of others—that propel people into bloody conflict. And these situations are not as far from us as we sometimes think. Often enough, when tracing back the links that lead to violence, one finds global institutions—arms dealers, banks, markets, corporations, intelligence agencies, governments, international organizations—whose immense power and resources form the context for the decisions of local actors. Opportunism and evil exist, but they find their openings when people become desperate and lack alternatives.[2]

I had planned to present such ideas about the sources of violence in my comments on the secretary-general's report. I had developed them by extending the work I had done on Afghanistan to other parts of the world. A few years before I had summarized my previous conclusions as I finished the manuscript of *The Fragmentation of Afghanistan*. At that time, in 1994, the country had again descended into civil war, even as the United States, the UN, and the entire "international community" abandoned any effort to stabilize or rebuild it. In early January 1994, I was supposed to travel from Islamabad to Kabul on a UN flight, which was then considered the only relatively safe way to reach the capital. As the warlords who controlled the capital shifted their allegiances and launched new attacks, the flight was canceled. Instead I drove with a few companions up the Khyber Pass from Peshawar.

An hour into Afghanistan, as we approached Jalalabad, we found six hundred families who had fled fighting in Kabul camped by the road:

> Across the road, a chalkline marks the ground. Men in olive fatigues move methodically along the rectangles with metal detectors, searching for mines and unexploded munitions (they have already found two thousand pieces) before expanding the refugee camp. Something disturbed by the wind that sweeps down from the mountains explodes in the middle distance, raising a pillar of white smoke beyond the deminers.
>
> On a plot of barren ground by the camp, men unload a truck that has just arrived from Kabul. Brightly dressed women with children in rags squat in the sun with small bundles of belongings. They swarm around us recounting their stories. I record these fragments:
>
> Twenty-five families from Kabul came here by private car. It cost Af 10,000 per person. We left the houses with all our property still in them. Families left the bodies of their family members killed in the fighting. The bodies are still there. If you can help us, then give us help. Otherwise, don't write anything. We spent last night in the cold with no shelter. For one week the children have had no food. We left the bodies and locked the doors. There is no protection for our property. What are we doing here? What should we do here? We have no way to get food. They were attacking on the ground and from the air. There were many kinds of ammunition. Everyone who had a Kalashnikov took what he wanted. Last Saturday, the first day of fighting, the fighting was inside the houses. They fired on and bombarded the houses. People were asleep when the fighting started. They were just taking property, and they had no other purpose. All the big stores and markets were looted. Shahzada market, the big money bazaar, was first looted and then burned.
>
> The parties attacked the houses and even took the food from the houses by force. One family was kicked out of their house, and the house was occupied. You see all we have taken with us. We have nothing with us but the children. No medicine, no shelter. We never had to leave our houses while the communists and Soviets were there, but now we do. When the Soviets were there, there was no fighting.

The aircraft were bombing. I hid underground. My niece here was injured. Her whole body was injured, because she was buried when the bombs fell. Four members of my family were martyred. Please pay attention to our lives here. . . .[3]

Not far from there, eleven months earlier, two European UN officials and two Afghan UN employees had been found murdered, probably by some of the Arab extremists who had come to fight the Soviets and stayed on to help the radicals fighting the government at the behest of Pakistan. On my first visit to this area, in January 1989, with mujahidin who were debating what to do on the eve of the end of the Soviet occupation a month later, I had heard a lot about these Arabs. In a short note published by Human Rights Watch, I tried to pass on the warnings from the Afghans but found little interest.[4]

The mujahidin then felt many pressures. The Soviet-supported communist government still held the city of Jalalabad. The mujahidin were in contact with the garrison, hoping, according to Afghan tradition, to reach an agreement to end the fighting. Pakistani officers supported by the CIA, however, were pressing them to launch a conventional frontal attack on the city, for which these guerrilla fighters were ill prepared. Though as we sat in the Ghaziabad State Farm in January 1989 we did not know it, U.S. and Pakistani officials had already decided on this offensive at a meeting in Islamabad. Among those eager for the fight were the radical Arabs who had established several bases in the border region. As the Soviets withdrew, the Afghans increasingly protested about these Arabs, who slaughtered Afghan civilians living in government-controlled areas and condescendingly tried to teach the Afghans, who had lost a million martyrs, to be better Muslims.[5] Many of them, including Usama Bin Laden himself, later participated in the battle of Jalalabad, a major military and political defeat for the mujahidin.

A few months later, in Jeddah, Saudi Arabia, a reporter named Jamal Khashoggi gave me copies of his articles about these Arab "mujahidin." Khashoggi later became the media advisor to Prince Turki al-Faisal, when the former intelligence chief was the Saudi ambassador to the United States. Subsequently he became a reformist newspaper editor who lost his job for his outspoken articles. Khashoggi showed me a photo published in the English-language paper *Arab News* in 1988. It depicted him inside Afghanistan, standing with a tall, young, Kalashnikov-wielding Saudi named Usama Bin Laden.

A few months after my 1994 visit to Jalalabad, thinking back over these and other scenes, I composed the final section of *The Fragmentation of Afghanistan*, entitled, "The Ruins of Empire":

The day the Berlin Wall fell, in November 1989, I had dinner with other fellows and officers of the United States Institute of Peace at the home of a senior State Department official in the Washington suburbs. Each of us spoke in turn on the heretofore unimaginable events of the day. Among the well justified rejoicing, I remembered a line from the Urdu poet Ghalib, who witnessed the final days of the Mughal Empire: "Because of my tears, I was expelled from your feast."

I certainly did not mourn the fall of the Soviet and Russian empires. I had seen Afghan men and women break down and weep as they relived the tortures of KhAD [the Soviet-trained Afghan secret police]. I had seen children without arms and legs, paralyzed and burned by Soviet bombs and mines. But I had also seen a photograph of the bloodied corpse of Sayd Bahauddin Majrooh, my teacher and mentor, assassinated with weapons U.S. taxes may have purchased, weapons that were supposed to defend our security. . . .

The great powers showered weapons, cash, and attention on the protagonists of this struggle. The principals in neither Washington nor Moscow could make "their" Afghans into reliable agents, but the resources they supplied shattered much of what the peoples of Afghanistan had preserved from their past. The Afghans had to find new ways to survive and interpret their often devastated environment.[6]

With the breakdown of the political agreement that had led both the United States and the USSR to support the Afghan state until 1978, that state itself shattered. Armed networks linked to the intelligence agencies of neighboring countries, drug traffickers, and radical movements took their place, as the global establishment, the "international community," treated Afghanistan as a charity case, a humanitarian emergency. I concluded:

Without a global struggle to give strategic value to corners of the world where some of its poorest people live, those people seem to be left to fend for themselves with the legacies of colonialism and superpower competition. But the international impact of domestic conflicts can be as far-reaching as the domestic impact of international conflicts. The continued turmoil in Afghanistan has already contributed to the civil war in Tajikistan, to authoritarianism in Uzbekistan, to growing Russian aggressiveness prompted by fear of Islam along Russia's southern frontier, and to the dissemination of military skills to radical Islamists in South Asia and the Arab world. If the international community does not find a way to rebuild Afghanistan, a floodtide of weapons, cash, and contraband will escape that state's porous boundaries and make the world less secure for all.[7]

By the morning of September 11, 2001, I already knew that Massoud had been killed by two of these radical Islamists from the Arab world. One of Massoud's oldest companions, Muhammad Eshaq, who had helped Massoud organize an abortive uprising in Panjshir in 1975, was representing the Northern Alliance government in Washington. When I had called him the evening before to offer my condolences, he accepted them, despite his superiors' attempt to keep the news from leaking out. The next morning, I forced myself to vote in the primary election for mayor of New York, thinking that at least it was better to choose leaders this way than by assassinating your opponents.

I got on the downtown subway at 96th and Broadway and transferred to the N train at Times Square. Just before 9:00 a.m., the train reached Union Square, the northern edge of downtown Manhattan. As the doors opened, an announcement came over the loudspeaker: "If you are traveling below Fulton Street, please transfer at Canal Street to the J, M, or Z trains. This train will not travel below Fulton Street, because of a plane crash at the World Trade Center."

On Thursday, September 20, I received a terse e-mail from Craig Karp, an old friend and Afghan hand in the State Department: "Subject: URGENT. Can you come to a meeting in DC at State at 5PM on Monday? Future of Afghanistan."

My worst fear had not come to pass. Late in the morning of September 11, soon after the collapse of both towers, I was standing on the roof of an apartment house in Greenwich Village with a friend from graduate school and an acquaintance of hers. We watched the burning wreckage send a pillar of smoke over Manhattan and speculated on how many people's deaths we were watching. Unaware at that point of the heroic work of the NYPD and FDNY in hurrying people out of the buildings before they collapsed, I thought the toll might be ten thousand, even twenty thousand. I said that Usama Bin Laden was probably responsible, and that I feared reprisals against Afghanistan, like a carpet bombing of Kandahar. As far as my new acquaintance was concerned, however, "they" should all be bombed as thoroughly as possible.

A few days after September 11, when I was able to concentrate enough to think, I put together some thoughts on this subject in an article that appeared on the *New York Times* Op-Ed page on September 22 under the title "Afghans Can Be Our Allies" (the article introduces Part II of this volume). I argued that Afghans would accept a U.S. and international presence as long as they saw it was there to help them, to rescue them from misgovernment, nongovernment, and destitution. We could not just use their country to pursue our own objectives.

I had seen both the destruction of the country and Afghans' desire for a way out firsthand in 1998, when I traveled across southern and eastern Afghanistan and visited both Kandahar and Kabul. Lakhdar Brahimi, then the personal representative of the UN secretary-general for Afghanistan, asked me to examine what the UN was doing in Afghanistan. In June I spent several days in the Taliban's center, Kandahar, not realizing that I was nearly crossing paths with Prince Turki al-Faisal, then the head of the Saudi intelligence agency, who was trying to convince Taliban leader Mullah Muhammad Umar to hand over Usama Bin Laden.

With just my driver and no security, I drove west from Kandahar, past the vineyards of Panjwai, stopping in tea houses in Dil Aram (Heart's Rest) and Girishk, where the road crossed the Helmand River. I proceeded to Lashkargah, center of Helmand Province, where I spent the night in the UN High Commissioner for Refugees (UNHCR) guest house, a 1950s-style suburban residence built for the American engineers who designed the Helmand Valley Project. When I asked the elderly cook what was for dinner, he pulled himself erect to his full six feet and announced, "Spaghetti and meatballs." To my amazement, it was just what Harriet might have served to Ozzie and Rickie Nelson during the Eisenhower administration.

The next day I proceeded through the Registan Desert to Farah in the far southwest, where I spent another night. The UN flight from Farah to Islamabad was canceled, as the plane was needed for earthquake relief in the far northeast, so I drove back to Kandahar. During our stopover in Lashkargah, my driver and I ate kebabs in the bazaar and watched local youths play soccer. Back in Kandahar, I took the UN flight to Islamabad. The eight-seater plane, on which I was the only passenger, was diverted to Kabul for an emergency medical evacuation. We had to land outside the "window," a few hours per day when all sides promised the UN not to attack the airport. Red Cross personnel loaded an unconscious Afghan deminer whose leg had been blown off while clearing unexploded ordinance from a destroyed neighborhood in Kabul. His bare chest heaved above his mutilated lower body, entirely wrapped in bandages, as his nurse (bearded, like all Afghan men under the Taliban) adjusted the IV. We dropped them in Peshawar to be hurried to the hospital of the International Committee of the Red Cross, and I returned to Islamabad.

A few days later I flew to Kabul, where I saw the wreckage visited on the city by the militias. My flight back was canceled again, as the earthquake emergency worsened. I therefore had to drive back to Islamabad by way of Jalalabad and Peshawar, retracing the route I had taken in 1994. I got a fuller look at the country's devastation this time. I could hardly find words to describe the destruction of what Michael Ignatieff later called the "Dresden of post-Cold War conflict." In a *Newsweek* article that now introduces Part I of this volume, I wrote, "Exhausted after two decades of war, Afghans longed to end the fighting, reunite their nation, rejoin the international community, and invest in their future."

In a report I wrote for the UN, I recounted:

> While it might be wrong to generalize from a few conversations with UN Afghan national staff, people encountered in teahouses, and a few others (all male), it is quite striking the extent to which continued war appears to lack a constituency, even in core areas of Taliban support. Conversations continually returned to the theme "everything has been destroyed" in twenty years of war, that there was no reason to fight with Afghans in other regions of the country, that the war continued because of foreign interference, and that energy and resources should be spent on reconstruction. People encountered in teahouses spontaneously offered ideas for development projects (e.g., building new irrigation works on the Helmand river to cultivate fruit and vegetables) that could be carried out if resources were not wasted on war. People constantly criticized Afghans for fighting with each other and destroying the nation's resources. The lack of education for children—including girls, though this distinction was not always made—was also a constant preoccupation. Everywhere Afghans are pursuing private courses, home schooling—whatever they can do to assure education for their children, with or without the consent of the authorities. It appears, strangely enough, that Kabul University has even managed to award 10 Ph.D.s in the past year. . . .
>
> Equally strong appears to be the sense of Afghan national identity, over and above ethnic group, that was emphasized by all interlocutors. When speaking to foreigners Afghans (like others) do tend to play down signs of disunity, especially ethnic, or blame any problems on foreign manipulation or evil leaders. Whatever sense of unity and national identity Afghans express does not negate the reality of a conflict largely structured on ethnic lines and characterized by some ugly inter-ethnic violence. Nonetheless, the sense of national identity, and the belief that Afghan national identity is inherently both Islamic and multi-ethnic, seems sincere, widespread, and deeply rooted.

The Taliban leaders could not satisfy these aspirations, which were shared by many who were working with their regime on September 11. The Taliban leaders were intent on pursuing the war, defeating and even terrorizing Afghans in the north and the Central Highlands, and limiting education and development to what they could keep under their strict control. In my *New York Times* Op-Ed I tried to explain to an American audience, traumatized by violence and hungry for action against the "evildoers," that all those now with the Taliban need not be our enemies.

Some Taliban members and allies were trying to protect themselves by joining with the winning side. Afghans and others in the region saw how the United States and other major powers had turned away from Afghanistan, while Pakistan used whatever resources it could to establish a weak, pro-Pakistani government in Kabul by supporting the Taliban. As the world, looking with renewed interest to Afghanistan, turned against the Taliban, Afghans' perception of who was the winning side could shift.

Pakistan, I argued, "terrified by the consequences to itself of a possible American attack on Afghanistan," has said it would withdraw support, leading some Taliban supporters to put "their fingers to the wind." In a speech to the nation on September 19, General Pervez Musharraf, who had taken power in a coup in October 1999, announced that the United States had asked for intelligence, use of airspace, and logistical support. In his speech, Musharraf made clear that he was acting mainly to protect Pakistan from India, which had offered all facilities to the United States and wanted Pakistan to be declared a "terrorist state." Therefore, to secure Pakistan and retain the ability to pursue its objectives in Kashmir, Pakistan would help the United States. Nonetheless, Musharraf argued that he was "more concerned about Taliban and Afghanistan" than those who demanded that he resist the United States. He had argued against sanctions and for engagement, saying: "I would like to ask how we can save Afghanistan and Taliban from being harmed or how we can reduce their losses. Can we do it by isolating ourselves from the international community or by moving along with them?"

Many did not perceive this ambiguity in Pakistani policy and thought that Islamabad had turned against the Taliban, but I continued to receive reports from UN officials, journalists, and NGO workers in the field of movements of weapons and fighters from Pakistan to the Taliban.

Mindful of the dangers of foreign occupation of Afghanistan, I warned against "actions that stir up Afghan nationalism that will only bolster the Taliban leadership and the foreign extremists to whom it has given safe harbor." A purely military approach would fail to close the bargain with the Afghan people. An Afghan-led political transition backed up with credible commitments to reconstruction could attract defecting Taliban and work with "two other focal points of Afghan politics: the United Front, the armed resistance led by Ahmed Shah Massoud until his recent assassination, and exiles working with the former king, Zahir Shah, now in Rome, who are trying to convene a loya jirga, or a traditional Afghan assembly." Though the UF, commonly known as the Northern Alliance, was mainly non-Pashtun, some of Zahir Shah's supporters might be able "to raise troops, including recruits from the predominant Pashtun ethnic group in whose territory Mr. Bin Laden's followers are largely based."

I had doubts about both of these groups. Although some Afghans, especially Pashtuns, did long for the return of the king at least as a symbolic transitional leader, neither he nor the group of mostly elderly exiles, long resident in the West, who formed the factionalized court around him in Rome had shown much aptitude for governance even when they were in power. The king had come to the throne at the age of nineteen when his father, a formidable autocrat, was assassinated in 1933. First his uncles and then his cousin Daoud ruled the country in his name until 1963. During the next ten years, the king presided over an experiment in constitutionalism, so-called New Democracy, during which the government changed hands four times, inflation and unemployment spiraled up, and rival groups of leftists and Islamists took to the streets. When Daoud ousted him in a coup in 1973, while the king was relaxing at an Italian resort, crowds greeted the change in the streets. No one in the country lifted a finger to protest. Only one person died in the coup, a luckless soldier whose tank overturned in the Kabul River. Daoud was killed in the communist coup in 1978, and for most of the time since then the king had stayed on the sidelines, issuing occasional statements. Some of his advisors had drawn up plans for a loya jirga (great council), but, as Pakistan refused the former king and his family access to its territory for most of the time right up to September 11, and most of his advisors showed little initiative in countering those strictures, he had little presence on the ground.

The Northern Alliance commanders had stayed and fought, most in the jihad against the Soviets, some as militias for the communist government, and some, of course, as both. Some had also done double duty for the Taliban. Their best-known leader, Ahmad Shah Massoud, commander of the Panjshir Valley, and founder of the Supervisory Council of the North, was a gifted guerrilla strategist and a charismatic and media-savvy leader who had gained a considerable following in the West. But inside Afghanistan his charisma never extended far beyond his fellow Panjshiris and some other Tajiks. He seized Kabul in 1992 when the communist regime fell to an internal mutiny launched by unpaid regime militia commanders led by Abdul Rashid Dostum, an Uzbek from Jauzjan Province in the north. Iran brokered the original "Northern Alliance" among the disparate non-Pashtun groups that took control of the capital, with Massoud in the lead. Rather than support a UN plan for a technocratic transitional government, Massoud invited the exiled leaders of the mujahidin parties to take power in Kabul.

Pakistan supported the ethnic Pashtun extremist, Gulbuddin Hikmatyar, and his Arab allies, who made an alliance of convenience with Pashtun former communists to stage a failed offensive against Massoud and then keep him under attack. In the ensuing years of ethnically and regionally fueled civil war, Massoud, against his own inclination, remained a Tajik and Panjshiri leader, hated by many for his role in the destruction of Kabul, the killing of thousands of civilians, and, to many, the humiliation of Pashtuns. Ismail Khan, who ruled Herat in the West, had brought a degree of security and relative prosperity to the area, but he was often embroiled in feuds with factional rivals and commanders outside the city, who eventually brought about his downfall. The other leaders were worse. Afghans had hoped that the fall of the communists would lead to a stable national government, but they were bitterly disappointed. Most remembered the period of mujahidin and militia rule as a reign of thieves and a time of war and chaos.

I witnessed the difference between Taliban time and mujahidin rule. In January 1994, I rode from Peshawar to Jalalabad, through territory "controlled" by the former mujahidin. We passed a post where the UN staff had been murdered the previous year. We saw masses of people displaced by the furious warfare in Kabul, and most told of being robbed and expelled by Massoud's men. Our Afghan hosts would not let us walk outside the door of our compound in the city of Jalalabad without a security escort. There was too great a danger of a kidnapping or killing, whether by a greedy criminal or an extremist fanatic, perhaps an Arab "Wahhabi," as the Afghans then called the members of al-Qaeda.

In January 1996, together with Anthony Richter of the Open Society Instute, the writer David Rieff, and the photographer Susan Meiselas, I took a ferry across the Panj river from Tajikistan to mujahidin-ruled northern Afghanistan, where we visited camps of refugees from Tajikistan. We stayed in the compound of the UNHCR in the city of Kunduz, where we met Amrullah Saleh, later the head of Afghanistan's intelligence agency. He was then a young emissary from Massoud. All UN international staff had been evacuated under threats from the Arab radicals who were training guerrillas for Tajikistan in the refugee camp we visited outside the city. The Afghan officials would not let us leave the compound without an armed guard. Signs of recent fighting between the local shura, or council, and Dostum's forces were visible in rocket craters by the road to the airport. Driving in a UN vehicle for hours past villages leveled by Soviet bombing, we passed unidentified groups of armed men. Fortunately, none of them disturbed us. One evening, we drove north from Baghlan toward Mazar-i Sharif, along a road that passed through a narrow defile lined with the wreckage of Soviet armored vehicles. As darkness fell, Richter asked our Soviet-trained driver in Russian if he was afraid. "Nyet problema," came the answer. "Nobody's out here at this time of night. It's much too dangerous."

The contrast in security in the Taliban heartland was remarkable. Afghan UN staff in Farah recounted instances of highway robbery and death threats they had experienced during the mujahidin period. Now, however, I could go anywhere with just a driver. The guards at Taliban checkpoints, festooned with flags made of unwound cassette tapes of banned music confiscated from drivers whose puritan religiosity fell short of official standards, waved us through. Overloaded trucks piled high with vehicle parts imported from Dubai for sale in smugglers' markets in Pakistan slowly bumped across the rutted roads and the nearby (and flatter) deserts. They lined up to refuel at petrol stations along the way. Fields of poppy stalks harvested a few weeks earlier dried by the side of the road. In Farah and Helmand, good rains—the last for four years—had left the wheat fields green, though farmers rushed to show me the low yields from each stalk, and asked for improved varieties.

In my report to the UN, I analyzed the sources of this achievement:

> The Taliban are the only group that appears to have an effective national state building strategy. The areas under the domination of the Taliban are controlled, though unevenly, by a single central authority that enjoys something close to a monopoly of armed force in those areas. While the Taliban are as driven by factionalism, personal rivalries, and disagreements as any other group, these differences have so far been pursued within a unitary, centralized structure. This gives them a decisive advantage in mobilizing the resources under their control. The groups composing the northern alliance, however, have each maintained their own military formations and commands, and factional disputes have led to their split into competing military groups. . . . The Taliban have developed a surprisingly strong national project and organizational framework for carrying it out, and outsiders have consistently underestimated them.

Later that summer, the Taliban's superior organization, together with support from Pakistan delivered in a more coherent and effective way than the Northern Alliance's aid from Iran, Russia, India, and Central Asian countries, enabled them to capture much of northern and central Afghanistan. In those areas, inhabited by Tajiks, Uzbeks, and Hazaras (a Shia group), the Taliban not only favored the Pashtuns who had been settled in the area by the Afghan monarchy but carried out ethnic massacres and expulsions in some areas. In part these were reprisals for the massacres of Taliban prisoners in Mazar-i Sharif in May 1997. Uzbek commander Abdul Malik Pahlawan had plotted to bring the Taliban to Mazar-i Sharif to take revenge on Abdul Rashid Dostum, who he believed had assassinated his brother. A Pakistani delegation led by Foreign Minister Gohar Ayub flew to Mazar to proclaim complete Taliban victory and ask the world to recognize the regime. They barely escaped before Malik turned on his Taliban allies. He and the Shia militia, Hizb-i Wahdat, then massacred hundreds of Taliban soldiers whom they took prisoner. UN special envoy Lakhdar Brahimi pressed the UN High Commissioner for Human Rights, Mary Robinson, to investigate these killings, which would have demonstrated the UN's evenhandedness and helped open a dialogue with the Taliban at a time when the country was divided more or less in half. Although Robinson sent an expert to do a preliminary survey, she never focused on the issue, and the opportunity was lost. The arguments made by Usama Bin Laden, that the international community was inherently biased against an Islamic organization, were becoming more and more convincing.

When the Taliban returned to the north, they took the harshest measures against the Shia, whom they considered heretics. They killed thousands of both Hazaras and Uzbeks in the north. A Pakistani Sunni extremist group fighting under Taliban command massacred Iranian diplomats captured in Mazar-i Sharif, nearly provoking a war, which was averted only by Brahimi's preventive diplomacy.

In 2002, when I returned to Afghanistan, I was able to see how the Taliban had destroyed areas where their opponents were based. As a guest of the new government for the first Nawruz (March 21, the Persian Solar New Year) after the Taliban's defeat, I visited the Shamali plain north of Kabul. The well-watered rich land of this plain and the hills around it have for centuries been a garden and orchard, where mainly Tajik peasants tended vineyards watered by poplar-lined streams and canals. Orchards of almond, pomegranate, apples, pears, apricots, walnuts, mulberries, and other fruits lined the hills that led up to scenic resort of the village of Istalif, famous for its blue-glazed pottery. Here the Taliban, together with al-Qaeda, had tried to create a ruin as desolate as the neighborhoods of Kabul leveled in fighting among militias. They burned every building and removed the roofs, beams, and windows. They forced Hazara prisoners to labor in the vineyards and orchards, cutting each vine at the root and each tree at the trunk. The people of the area, some of whom were summarily executed, fled in all directions, some to Pakistan, some to the resistance bastion of Panjshir, and some to Kabul, where they huddled in the wreckage of the former Soviet Embassy.

For the United States after September 11, the problem was, I thought, how to eliminate the haven the Taliban had granted to al-Qaeda without returning Afghanistan to the chaos it had known before, under rule by the same commanders the United States was about to fund and arm. One approach would have been to negotiate with the Taliban, placing them under as much pressure as possible, until Pakistan made them deliver al-Qaeda or orchestrated an internal coup to remove Mullah Umar and the small group of leaders closely allied to the foreign extremists. This approach might make possible gradual transformation of the Taliban state to one more inclusive and open to development, without destroying its capacity to maintain a degree of public order. Treating the issue as one of law enforcement held no hope for redress, however, as the Taliban would not recognize the non-Islamic legal grounds under which the United States would seek extradition of al-Qaeda leaders and members. No one knew what other attacks might be planned in the near future, and no U.S. leader could risk delay in preventing them. There was little or no scope for patience and no penalty for what might turn out in retrospect to be overly hasty action.

The UN Special Mission had been working on this problem. Under Lakhdar Brahimi in 1997–1999, it had focused on trying to develop a consensus among the neighboring countries, the United States, and Russia on how to stabilize the country through the so-called six-plus-two process. Brahimi suspended his actions in July 1999, when Pakistan openly backed a Taliban offensive while Brahimi was in Islamabad to follow up on a just concluded "six-plus-two meeting" in Tashkent, where all Afghanistan's immediate neighbors, plus the United States and Russia, had pledged to work for a peaceful solution and use their influence to convince the Afghan parties to refrain from warfare. Brahimi's successor, Francesc Vendrell, had also worked to support restoration of the former king and the loya jirga process. He had worked to bring the factionalized Rome group together and to bridge the gaps between the former king's camp and the Northern Alliance.

Of course, not only foreign experts and diplomats worried about how to remove the Taliban without destabilizing Afghanistan. So did Afghans. After his 1996 retreat from Kabul, Massoud had realized he needed to create alliances with others. He worked to form a government led by a Pashtun prime minister, Abdul Rahim Ghaffurzai, a diplomat who had denounced the Soviet invasion in the UN General Assembly and then sought refugee status in the United States. Ghaffurzai's death in a plane crash along with forty of his colleagues in August 1997 effectively ended that effort. The Rome group, supported by Vendrell, was working to create a political framework for a national transition through the institution of the loya jirga, or great council. Some of the younger members of the Rome group who were trying to organize support for a loya jirga inside Afghanistan, in particular commander Abdul Haq and Hamid Karzai, had started contacts with the United States after the August 1998 bombings of U.S. embassies in Kenya and Tanzania. Karzai's father, Abdul Ahad, had been assassinated in Quetta in July 1999, not long after his son and I had testified in the U.S. Senate together. At that hearing, Hamid Karzai memorably said that what Afghanistan needed was not a "broad-based government," a coalition of armed factions, but a "national government," a political authority to control and build the much-weakened state as the representative of the people.

Abdul Haq, a mujahidin commander whom I met in the 1980s, and with whom I had testified before the Joint Congressional Task Force on Afghanistan in January 1985, had left Pakistan for Dubai after losing part of his foot to a landmine and falling out with Pakistan's intelligence agency, which did not like commanders having their own strategic vision. Like Karzai, Abdul Haq had worked with Zahir Shah's group in favor of a loya jirga; unlike Karzai, he saw himself as a competitor with Ahmad Shah Massoud and wanted the former king to designate him his military chief. Most of Abdul Haq's immediate family had been murdered in a still-unexplained incident in Peshawar during the Taliban period.

The CIA helped the Rome group establish contacts with Massoud, who managed his external relations through the Afghan embassy in Dushanbe, Tajikistan. When I met Massoud's foreign minister, Dr. Abdullah, in New York in July 2001, he told me rather sarcastically that members of the Rome group had come to Dushanbe and said that "now they were really serious." What were they before? Still, Rome was split between those who wanted to form a partnership with the Northern Alliance, as Massoud proposed, and those who insisted that such an alliance would reduce the king to merely another faction, rather than an overarching symbol of national unity and continuity.

Given the geography of landlocked Afghanistan, and the relations between the United States and Iran, after September 11 Pashtun leaders such as Abdul Haq and Karzai could work to replace the Taliban and in favor of a loya jirga process only through the territory of Pakistan. I therefore argued in my Op-Ed that the United States should press Pakistan "to guarantee full freedom of action to Afghan leaders who appear capable of establishing a stable government that will meet minimal international standards." I emphasized "minimal" international standards, because I knew firsthand how damaged, divided, and destitute the country was. Once involved, the "international community" seemed to have no way to define achievable goals in Afghanistan, instead piling on objectives, though not the resources to achieve them.

Soon after September 11, Hamid's brother, Qayum, a Baltimore-area businessman with whom I kept in regular contact, told me that Pakistan had refused to renew Hamid's visa, forcing him to choose between removing himself from the scene and entering Taliban-controlled Afghanistan without adequate preparation. Abdul Haq had returned to Peshawar, where he was trying to raise forces to take on the Taliban and opposing any campaign of bombing by the United States.

For Pakistan to support anti-Taliban Afghans would require a reversal of long-standing Pakistani policies. I did not think that pressure alone, no matter how aggressively applied, could bring about a durable change in Pakistan's policy, which was based not on support for anti-American terrorism but on durable national interests. President Musharraf had spelled out Pakistan's interest in preventing "a change in Afghanistan and the establishment of an anti-Pakistan government there." I therefore advocated incentives for Pakistan that lessened the likelihood of Pakistan perceiving a post-Taliban government to be its enemy. I wrote: "Afghans should acknowledge Pakistan's concerns by, for instance, settling the two countries' longstanding border dispute. The United States could also accede to Pakistani requests for economic aid and debt relief in exchange for agreeing to these and other conditions, like those relating to American military access."

More important than aid to Pakistan, I noted later while appearing on the *Charlie Rose* show, would be quotas for the import of Pakistan-made textiles into the United States, which would create employment and show we were trying to help the people in Pakistan, not just strike a deal with the military, receiving basing rights in return for selling them F-16 fighter planes. Still, I vastly underestimated the complexity and difficulty of transforming Pakistan's relations to Afghanistan.

Thus far I had seen no recognition by the administration that Afghanistan was a nation, not just a terrorist base. The discussions of the Afghan groups were all oriented around how to assemble a coalition to eliminate al-Qaeda and topple the Taliban, not how to build a stable Afghanistan that would give Afghans—and their neighbors, first of all Pakistan—a real stake in guaranteeing that such threats would not return. The revelations of high-level discussions published since that time have borne out that for at least two weeks after September 11, more than a week after approval of the war plan, the NSC had not considered any plan for political succession and reconstruction of Afghanistan.

The evening of Thursday, September 20, when I received the email inviting me to the State Department, the president issued an ultimatum to the Taliban in his speech to the Congress:

> Deliver to United States authorities all the leaders of al Qaeda who hide in your land. (Applause.) Release all foreign nationals, including American citizens, you have unjustly imprisoned. Protect foreign journalists, diplomats and aid workers in your country. Close immediately and permanently every terrorist training camp in Afghanistan, and hand over every terrorist, and every person in their support structure, to appropriate authorities. (Applause.) Give the United States full access to terrorist training camps, so we can make sure they are no longer operating.
>
> These demands are not open to negotiation or discussion. (Applause.) The Taliban must act, and act immediately. They will hand over the terrorists, or they will share in their fate.

The President assured the Afghans that the United States did not consider them targets:

> Afghanistan's people have been brutalized—many are starving and many have fled. Women are not allowed to attend school. You can be jailed for owning a television. Religion can be practiced only as their leaders dictate. A man can be jailed in Afghanistan if his beard is not long enough.

The United States respects the people of Afghanistan—after all, we are currently its largest source of humanitarian aid—but we condemn the Taliban regime. (Applause.) It is not only repressing its own people, it is threatening people everywhere by sponsoring and sheltering and supplying terrorists. By aiding and abetting murder, the Taliban regime is committing murder.

The president said nothing about what the United States would offer the Afghans other than humanitarian aid. Perhaps, I hoped, this was because, until he decided the moment had come to move from ultimatum to war, he could not discuss the postwar plans in public.

But it turned out that there wasn't any postwar plan. Richard Haass was trying to come up with one. That's why he asked Craig Karp to organize the meeting.

On the afternoon of September 24, I took the train to Washington. Most airports had reopened, but the shuttle flights between New York and Washington were still grounded. After meeting us in the lobby of the State Department, where a new level of security had been hastily erected, officials ushered us visitors into a windowless conference room on the seventh floor, near the office of the secretary of state and his policy planning staff. Besides me, the outside advisors included Thomas Gouttierre, an outgoing and affable Midwesterner, head of the Center for Afghanistan Studies (and dean of the Center for International Studies) at the University of Nebraska at Omaha. Tom had coached the Afghan national basketball team as a Peace Corps volunteer in the 1960s and later earned an M.A. in anthropology. His Center for Afghanistan Studies had won lucrative contracts from the CIA-USAID program of cross-border aid to the mujahidin in the 1980s, producing school textbooks that praised jihad and used Kalashnikov rifles in arithmetic lessons. In the 1990s Tom had spent six months serving with the UN Special Mission for Afghanistan based in Islamabad, a job that took advantage of his personal diplomacy skills and fluent Dari. Another participant had also worked for UNSMA: Arnold Schaffenburger, a retired Foreign Service officer who had worked on Afghan issues in the U.S. mission to the UN during the early Clinton administration. Haass had also invited Daoud Yaqub, a young Afghan-American lawyer who had worked for the Afghanistan Foundation and was now coordinating relations with the U.S. government for Zahir Shah in Rome.

As I looked around the room, I saw some familiar faces: people like Karp; Marvin Weinbaum, a University of Illinois specialist on South Asia who had become an intelligence analyst for the State Department after retirement; and the South Asia team. I recognized David Champagne, an army Special Forces officer I had met in the 1980s who trained the Special Forces at Fort Bragg in the cultural and political knowledge they would need to operate on the ground in Afghanistan.

Others came from the National Security Council (NSC), Department of Defense (DoD), or other government agencies.

The meeting opened with Haass telling us that the meeting was off the record, and that he didn't want to read about it in the newspapers. Although Yaqub, representative of an Afghan group, did not stay for the discussion about U.S. policy, Haass asked him to start the meeting with a report on discussions between the Rome Group and the Northern Alliance. Yaqub, a strong supporter of Rome's cooperation with the Northern Alliance, told us that Massoud's last words after being wounded by his suicide assassins were "Work with Zahir Shah." Amrullah Saleh, who was present at the killing, later told me that Massoud had died instantly, but this myth served a function at that tense moment. The two groups had reached agreement in principle on forming a Supreme Council of Afghanistan with about 150 members, with half appointed by each. The Supreme Council would in turn elect a transitional government.

Despite this general agreement that Yaqub reported, Zahir Shah's followers and the Northern Alliance were deeply divided. Rather than explore these political problems, however, we spent several minutes listening to a State Department official query Yaqub on when the U.S. would receive the accounts for $800,000 that it had granted to Zahir Shah's office.

As we were sitting in Washington, other agencies of the U.S. government were disbursing money in Afghanistan in a quite different manner. The day after our meeting in Washington, CIA operative Gary Schroen carried $3 million in cash into the Panjshir Valley. That evening, he met with Engineer Arif, the late Massoud's intelligence chief. Schroen informed Arif of the U.S. intention to overthrow the Taliban. In order to act as an "honest broker in a post-Taliban Afghanistan," Schroen claimed, the United States would disburse money directly to commanders, rather than work through the more centralized structures that Massoud had painstakingly established in the years since 1998, when I had reported on the Northern Alliance's inability to coordinate strategically. Just as the ISI had done in the 1980s, the CIA would control the purse strings to ensure that Afghans followed a strategy made in Washington. Schroen recounts:

> Arif reluctantly accepted that fact, but the issue would return to plague our relationship for weeks to come.
>
> As promised, I produced the backpack in which I had placed the $500,000 and passed it to Arif. He hefted the bag but did not look into it, then handed it to Mumtaz. I told him the amount and said that this money was the first payment I would make to the Northern Alliance.... I said I was sure that General Fahim would utilize some of the money to secure supplies for his forces, but I asked Arif to stress to Fahim that much more money was available for purely military purposes.

The next day General (later Marshall) Muhammad Qasim Fahim, who had succeeded Massoud as military commander, arrived, together with Dr. Abdullah. In anticipation of the meeting, Schroen "went back to the black suitcase and got $1 million wrapped and ready." Schroen recounts a discussion in which he insisted on the U.S. policy of funding and arming commanders separately through small CIA teams, effectively placing them under U.S. command. Finally:

> I produced the backpack with the $1 million and explained to Fahim that these funds were to assist in preparing his military forces for the coming battle. I said I had given Arif $500,000 the night before and hoped those funds would be used primarily to strengthen Arif's organization [intelligence]. I stressed that other money was available if and when specific needs were identified. I placed the money on a small table in the center of our semicircle of chairs, but no one made a move to pick it up. When the meeting ended, and we stood with handshakes all around, still no one made a move to pick up the backpack, even as we all began to leave the room. For a second I had the foolish thought that they might not take the money. Then Arif motioned to Mumtaz, who casually picked up the backpack with one hand, then strained against its weight, almost dropping the bag. He looked at me and smiled, and I said, "Yes, a million dollars is heavier than you think."

According to one participant in the meeting, Fahim and Dr. Abdullah told Schroen they would use the funds to build a stable Afghanistan under a multiethnic, national government including the former king, rather than seek power for themselves, but Schroen did not mention such a discussion in his memoir.

A few days later, Schroen traveled to Charikar, just outside the southern end of Panjshir, and gave $100,000 in cash to Abdul Rabb Rasul Sayyaf, who had been close to Usama Bin Laden in the 1980s: "Unlike the money I had passed to the Northern Alliance, I had left this bundle in the original clear plastic wrapping so that Sayyaf could see what it was." Sayyaf handed the money to an aide. Schroen soon was running short, and the CIA's Counterterrorist Center delivered $10 million more a few days later. Schroen left the four cardboard boxes containing the cash in a corner of the office that Arif gave him. He had a good laugh with Arif one time when he gave him $22,000 for two trucks of helicopter fuel that somehow never arrived.

The total amount of cash given to commanders by the CIA in this manner ultimately amounted to several hundred million dollars. Commanders, or those they paid with the money, had to change the hundred-dollar bills into local currency rapidly in order to obtain usable denominations, and as they did so and more CIA dollars flooded the money market, the value of dollars fell rapidly. The exchange rate of the dollar with Afghanistan's currency was halved in two months, according to statistics gathered by the International Monetary Fund. The rapid devaluation of the dollar created incentives to unload the greenbacks as quickly as possible, first into other currencies and then into profitable investment, for which there were few outlets in Afghanistan. As the price of opium had increased tenfold as a result of the Taliban ban on cultivation, and as the U.S. offensive occurred during the opium planting season, many of the dollars were quickly recycled by commanders and money changers into loans to farmers to finance the next spring's poppy crop, enabling the farmers to rebound quickly and profitably from the losses suffered because of the Taliban ban.

In Washington, however, the day before Schroen arrived in Panjshir with the first black bag of $3 million in cash, the State Department was demanding receipts from the office of the former king. When Daoud Yaqub finally promised that the required financial reports would be produced, the State Department let him go, so we could proceed to deliberate on the "Future of Afghanistan."

Haass first asked the outside experts how the U.S. government should follow up on any military victory in Afghanistan. As we each spoke, a clear consensus emerged: the United States had helped create the current situation by its actions after the withdrawal and collapse of the Soviet Union. We claimed a victory and walked away. We treated Afghanistan as a humanitarian issue and provided no leadership or support for stabilization or reconstruction. The reaction after the embassy bombings was similarly one-dimensional: we focused on al-Qaeda, the direct security threat to the United States, not on the problems of Afghanistan. If we did not want to repeat the same mistakes, the United States had to engage, mobilize the United Nations, and lead an effort to establish legitimate government and reconstruct the economy.

Haass asked for reactions. Two people from the National Security Council staff, whom I did not recognize, immediately objected, "That's nation-building! We don't do nation-building." They were correctly representing the position on which President Bush had run. In the second debate with Vice President Al Gore, he had said, "I don't think our troops ought to be used for what's called nation-building. I think our troops ought to be used to fight and win war." The moderator followed up:

MODERATOR: Some people are now suggesting that if you don't want to use the military to maintain the peace, to do the civil thing, is it time to consider a civil force of some kind that comes in after the military that builds nations or all of that? Is that on your radar screen?

BUSH: I don't think so. I think what we need to do is convince people who live in the lands they live in to build the nations. Maybe I'm missing something here. I mean, we're going to have kind of a nation building corps from America? Absolutely not. Our military is meant to fight and win war. That's what it's meant to do. And when it gets overextended, morale drops.[8]

The young conservative activists from the White House understood what their boss wanted. But there were other people in the room with different experiences. David Champagne took the floor. I remembered him over the years as a military professional well versed in Afghanistan. Like me, he was in his fifties. He had gone through the experience of supporting the U.S. aid to the mujahidin in the 1980s and witnessed the collapse of the country afterward.

He said, "We did this to the Afghan people." He looked around the room, catching several people by the eye. "Nearly everyone here was involved." He concluded: "And we have a responsibility to assure that this never happens again."

At least in that room, that was the end of the discussion as to whether the United States should do as President Bush had advocated in the debate less than a year before.

At the end of the meeting, I became concerned that an overly ambitious agenda was developing, focused on making Afghanistan into a democracy. The central task was helping Afghans reestablish a state that could provide security to eliminate the hole in the global social fabric that threatened both the Afghans and us. I said, "We're not saying that we should turn Afghanistan into a stable democracy in two years. We are just saying that we need to help Afghans establish a legitimate state that can police the territory to provide security for both them and us. Then an Afghan political process can continue, with all the problems it will entail, but without posing a threat."

Haass seemed to like that formulation. "OK," he responded with a small smile, "Nation building lite!"

With that the meeting adjourned, and I spent the subsequent decade commuting between New York and Kabul, with many other stops. As the works collected in this book attest, I oscillated between protesting against the inadequacy of the resources allocated to Afghanistan and the excessive ambition of the goals enunciated. I was swept up into events and practice to the extent that I never wrote the comprehensive book I promised to so many. Instead, in the course of my work for the UN, the Afghan government, and my home institution, the Center on International Cooperation of New York University, I produced both analysis and advocacy. I have collected some of these works here, editing them for anachronisms but trying not to conceal my differences of opinion with myself, my changes of views, and my errors.

In 2009, after the inauguration of President Barack Obama, Ambassador Richard Holbrooke became the U.S. special representative for Afghanistan and Pakistan and asked me to join him in the State Department as a senior advisor. The responsibilities of that post, which I continue to hold under Holbrooke's successor, Ambassador Marc Grossman, preclude me from writing about U.S. policy toward Afghanistan since I joined the government. Nonetheless the views presented in this collection have informed my work and defined how I have tried to shape U.S. policy. The results on the ground are sufficiently humbling that I do not need to make any claims for this work, other than that I tried, and sometimes managed, to devote my best efforts to bringing a measure of peace to Afghanistan. Only God knows the whole truth.

Notes

1. Barnett R. Rubin, *Blood on the Doorstep: The Politics of Preventing Deadly Conflict* (New York: Century Foundation Press, 2002), p. 3.
2. Ibid., p. 8.
3. *The Search for Peace in Afghanistan: From Buffer State to Failed State* (New Haven, CT: Yale University Press, 1995), p. 5.
4. "Policies of the Pakistani Military Toward the Afghan Resistance: Human Rights Implications," *News from Asia Watch,* February 27, 1989.
5. Ibid.
6. Barnett R. Rubin, *The Fragmentation of Afghanistan: State Formation and Collapse in the International System* (New Haven, CT: Yale University Press, 1995), pp. 278–79.
7. Ibid., p. 280.
8. Second Gore-Bush presidential debate, October 11, 2000, http://www.debates.org/pages/trans2000b.html.

PART ONE

PRELUDE: AFGHANISTAN BETWEEN TWO WARS, 1989–2001

Helping Afghanistan

New York—Just outside Lashkargah, a town in southwest Afghanistan, stands a great brick arch overlooking the remains of a city that flourished before Genghis Khan. Driving to the monument over a rutted desert track, by empty cotton warehouses (opium poppy earns more), I cannot always distinguish what was destroyed by Soviet bombs, what by local factions, and what by the Mongol hordes.

Returning home, I find it almost impossible to convey the extremity of destruction in what was already one of the world's poorest countries. And the destruction continues, not only in the civil war but in daily acts of violence. A country that can no longer produce even a bar of soap has been flooded with sophisticated weapons by foreign countries struggling for power and wealth.

It started with the Cold War. The Soviet Union invaded to prop up a failing Communist regime. The United States, Saudi Arabia, and Pakistan funded the Islamic resistance (the mujahidin) in the largest covert operation in history. The Pakistani secret service funneled weapons to their favored groups—including Islamic extremists. Thinking Moscow would dig in for good, the United States gave little thought to the consequences, as long as the fighters killed Soviet troops.

When the Soviet Union dissolved, the Afghan regime it had propped up crumbled. But the mujahidin, along with the remnants of the army, turned into feuding warlords and ethnic militias. The Soviets had devastated villages that sheltered mujahidin; the victors made ruins of Kabul, the national capital, and other towns.

New strategic stakes emerged: access to the oil and natural gas of the newly independent, landlocked, states of Central Asia. Would Russia control new pipelines, as it had the old, or would new routes open? And if new routes went south, would they go through Iran, the object of U.S. sanctions, or to Pakistan via Afghanistan?

Originally published as "Helping Afghanistan," *Newsweek*, July 13, 1998.

Pakistan saw its future in imposing a friendly—or subservient—government in Afghanistan and linking its economy to Central Asia via pipelines and roads through Afghanistan. Together with its nuclear weapons, such ties would offset the threat posed by its massive neighbor, India. Iran, however, determined to break the U.S. embargo by blocking pipeline routes that did not cross Iran.

When Pakistan's former Afghan allies failed to gain power, it found a new one, the Movement of Islamic Taliban (students). This ultraconservative group started as a revolt against the warlords in southern Afghanistan, dominated by the Pashtun ethnic group. Some in the U.S. government hoped it would unify the country and guard the pipeline route.

With Pakistani aid, the Taliban captured the capital and two-thirds of the country's territory. The remainder, which contains nearly half the country's population, is controlled by various armed factions drawn from other ethnic groups. Iran supplies them, as do Russia and Central Asian states, fearful of the Taliban's approach to their borders.

The Taliban have outraged much of the world by banning women from schools, jobs, and hospitals—temporarily, they say, until proper Islamic arrangements can be made. And although international agencies struggle to help Afghans and respect basic principles in Taliban areas, they have fled most of the rest of the country after repeated looting by undisciplined fighters.

Despair about Afghanistan may be intellectually respectable, but we cannot walk away from a civil war in a region with new nuclear powers, bordering on the world's major sources of energy. And the United States has a special responsibility: we paid for many of the weapons that have destroyed Afghanistan, and we helped put them in the wrong hands.

After decades of war and division, Afghanistan cannot be reassembled in a day. Before Afghans can reach agreement, their neighbors must stop fueling the battle. The United States must press on all fronts—diplomatic and economic— to back up a recent UN protest against foreign military and logistical supplies to Afghanistan. The nuclear tests in South Asia should not remove Afghanistan from our agenda with Pakistan.

And as long as we can, the UN and other agencies must stay engaged with the Afghan people, helping them survive and build grassroots institutions that will outlive the war. In their different ways, both the Taliban and their opponents make this task a formidable one. But the Afghan people, who suffered more than anyone to end the Cold War, have not had an easy time either.

1

Afghanistan in the International System

The conflict in Afghanistan is the core of a struggle over the reconstitution of political and economic relations in southwest Asia in the aftermath of the collapse first of the British and then of the Russian empires. Given the long-standing and regional character of the conflict, it would be a mistake to analyze it solely or even primarily in terms of the political differences between the current [2001] protagonists, the Taliban, led by Mullah Muhammad Umar, and the forces of the United Front, led by Ahmad Shah Massoud. It is unlikely to be settled by a negotiated agreement between these forces. The fact that this conflict has continued for over twenty years, despite repeated changes in the identity of the antagonists and the issues apparently at stake, indicates that its causes transcend such transient manifestations.

Nor should one analyze the policy objective simply as "peace" or "ending the war." A more appropriate policy goal would be reconstructing the country as part of the interstate and economic structure of an entire region. The usual notion of a peace process in a civil war within a national framework includes an end to outside interference; a negotiated cease-fire perhaps monitored by peace-keepers; an interim government; a process for establishing long-term governance; and, finally, reconstruction. Such a process will not suffice in a case such as Afghanistan. The war is not a civil war but a transnational one. The transnational links are too deep to be untangled and will have to be transformed.

If the situation remains unchanged, this entire region (Afghanistan, southern Central Asia, Pakistan, Kashmir, maybe parts of Iran) could become a battleground for decades. Central Asia will then be the home to expanding global

Note: This chapter is a reedited compilation of material first published in "Afghanistan: The Forgotten Crisis," *Refugee Survey Quarterly*, v. 15, n. 2 (1996), pp. 1–35; "Afghanistan: The Last Cold-War Conflict, the First Post-Cold-War Conflict," in *War, Hunger and Displacement: The Origins of Humanitarian Emergencies*, eds. E. Wayne Nafziger, Frances Stewart, and Raimo Väyrynen (Oxford: Oxford University Press, Vol. II, 2000), pp. 23–52; and with Ashraf Ghani, William Maley, Ahmed Rashid, and Olivier Roy, "Afghanistan: Reconstruction and Peacebuilding in a Regional Framework," *KOFF Peacebuilding Reports 1/2001*, Swiss Peace Foundation, Berne, 2001.

terrorist groups. The effect on Pakistan could lead sympathizers of these terrorist groups to gain access to nuclear weapons.

Afghanistan and the End of the Cold War

Since the intensity of the conflict in the 1980s owed so much to the Cold War that ended in 1989, many hoped that the United States and USSR could cooperate to end this as well as other conflicts. In Afghanistan as in some other places, however, the new situation transformed rather than ended the conflict. The events of 1989–1991 that transformed world politics included three distinct though closely related transformations: the end of the central conflict (the Cold War properly speaking) between the European-centered alliance systems led by the United States and USSR, symbolized by the fall of the Berlin Wall; the end of the communist system in the USSR; and the breakup of the USSR itself, which President Mikhail Gorbachev announced on December 25, 1991.

These transformations had different effects. During the period between the fall of the Berlin Wall and the breakup of the USSR, leaders of both superpowers hoped that the United States and an intact USSR could cooperate to resolve conflicts and manage the international system. In Afghanistan such cooperation took the form of a U.S.-Soviet dialogue that supported a UN-mediated solution that would lead to a cease-fire, the end of arms supplies to both sides, the establishment of an interim government that would hold elections, and the start of peaceful reconstruction. Variations of this strategy, in accord with a nascent international regime for the resolution of regional conflicts, more or less worked in El Salvador, Nicaragua, Cambodia, and Namibia.

The end of the Cold War, however, also allowed the major powers, and in particular the United States, to distinguish among interests that had all been lumped together under the Cold War. The United States continued to have an interest in Central America, on its borders, but not in distant Afghanistan. A greatly weakened Russia could not replace the USSR as a hegemonic power in Central Asia.

The end of the bipolar strategic structure also spelled the end of the alliance systems that had participated in it. The loss of a common threat meant that regional powers—some previously existing, like Pakistan and Iran, some newly independent, like the Central Asian states—could define and pursue their interests much more autonomously. Where these interests supported peace agreements, as in Southern Africa or Southeast Asia, they eventually were implemented. Where they reinforced conflict, as in Afghanistan, it proved impossible to agree on or implement a peace agreement. Instead the changes in the international system transformed the war into what became known as a "post–Cold War" conflict.

The new pattern of conflict not only extended the life of the previous "humanitarian emergency" but restructured it in ways that have become sadly familiar:

- Dissolution of the foreign supported state. The process of state collapse in Afghanistan was already well advanced when the USSR broke up. With the end of the Soviet effort to sustain it, the Afghan state's most basic institution, the army, split along factional and ethnic lines. The only political organizations were militarized networks of men joined by some ethnic or regional links. The incapacity of the state made impossible any comprehensive reconstruction program.
- Ethnic and opportunistic multipolar rather than ideological bipolar structure of the conflict. Whereas previously actors had allied mainly around the two ideological poles of the Cold War, immediately after the breakup of the USSR and the end of aid flows from the United States and USSR, the actors formed new alliances based on ethnic and regional considerations. These alliances proved unstable and shifted several times under the impact of changes in the domestic and regional balance of power. One of the stereotypical characteristics of the post–Cold War world, of course, is the prevalence of ethnic conflict. The increased salience of ethnic cleavages in Afghanistan is consistent with this trend, but it also illustrates that it may be deceptive. Ethnic conflict is more the effect than the cause of the current pattern of cleavages.
- Greater freedom of action of regional powers, unregulated by global alliance systems. The war seemed no longer to have global ideological or strategic implications. One superpower dissolved, and the other disengaged. For two years (1992–1994) there was no UN-sponsored effort to negotiate peace in Afghanistan. Regional powers (Pakistan, Iran, the Central Asian states, Saudi Arabia, India, and eventually Russia) stepped in. By 1994 a new strategic stake emerged: control over trade and potential pipeline routes from Central Asia to the international market. Pakistan supported the Taliban to secure key trade and potential pipeline routes to Central Asia, which would compete with Iran's attempt to enjoy a monopoly of such routes. Russia took advantage of the threat of Afghanistan as well as of the civil war in neighboring Tajikistan to reestablish itself as a power in Central Asia. Iran also opposed Pakistan's moves, which ran counter to its regional economic interests and which it saw as part of the U.S. strategy of encirclement. Transnational coalitions developed. Pakistan's military, with its large group of Pashtun officers, as well as Pakistani drug traders, many of whom operate in the Pashtun tribal areas, collaborated with the mainly Pashtun Taliban. Massoud received direct aid from Russia through a base in Kulab, Tajikistan, the home of that country's ruling faction. The opium producers of northeast Afghanistan, in the area then controlled by Massoud, allied with those who marketed and exported

their product in Tajikistan, Kyrgyzstan, Uzbekistan, and Russia. Until his defeat by the Taliban in August 1998, Abdul Rashid Dostum developed close links to Uzbekistan, which feared both the Pakistani advance and the Russian-Iranian effort to counter it.

- Increased importance of unofficial flows of resources. During the Cold War there were two principal, officially sponsored flows of resources. Now there were multiple flows, and more of them involved nonstate actors. Money from smuggling of drugs and other goods took on increased importance as opium production expanded more quickly than before. International Islamist extremists established more bases in this unpoliced territory and brought more money with them. Oil and gas companies such as the U.S.-based UNOCAL, the Saudi company Delta, and the Argentine company Bridas entered the area with plans for pipelines through Afghanistan. Arms and ammunition were purchased on the international black and gray markets, in addition to some officially sponsored deliveries.[1] In addition, after the Taliban established security of travel on most roads, smugglers brought consumer goods estimated at more than US$2 billion per year from the Persian Gulf free port of Dubai to Pakistan via Afghanistan. Taxes on this transit trade became an important source of revenue for the Taliban.

- Shift of war to the capital city. As there was not even a residual central state to protect the capital, the war shifted to Kabul, which had been a relatively safe haven during most of the conflict. The resulting damage apparently exceeded that done to Sarajevo or Mogadishu. As regionally based militias fought over Kabul, however, much of the countryside grew calmer. Hence it became easier for some rural refugees to return home, as an estimated 3.84 million did by the end of 1996.[2] After the capture of Kabul by the Taliban in September 1996, security also increased there, though the Taliban religious police harassed citizens over their veils, beards, and other Taliban requirements.

- Increased dependence on humanitarian organizations. Returning refugees, of course, received no assistance from the virtually nonexistent Afghan state. Any aid they received came from international humanitarian organizations or NGOs. The end of both Soviet aid to Afghanistan's cities and U.S.-led support for refugee-warrior communities in Pakistan, combined with the continuing shortage of agricultural production, led international humanitarian organizations to take over increasing responsibility for feeding urban populations in Afghanistan.

- War-induced inflation. This trend continued as successive authorities in Kabul had even fewer resources than the last Soviet-supported president, Najibullah. For instance, bread prices in Kabul rose 400 percent in the first four months of 1996. The regime of Tajik mujahidin leaders President

Burhanuddin Rabbani and Defense Minister Ahmad Shah Massoud continued to distribute new currency printed in Russia, as it was even more dependent on this source of revenue than Najibullah. After they retreated from Kabul, they continued to distribute new banknotes, even flooding the market in areas controlled by the Taliban, who printed no notes themselves. Before the Taliban capture of Kabul, repeated blockades by the regime's foes of the roads linking Pakistan to Kabul periodically sent the cost of food and fuel skyrocketing out of the reach of many Kabulis.

- Exclusion of women from public space. Women always played a limited role in public politics in Afghanistan, but some had served as ministers and in the professions. Years of war brought the militarization of the society as well as the destruction of many of those productive activities that had given women access to resources and made them valuable to the male-dominated community. As resources became scarcer, males (the only armed gender) gained ever more disproportionate access to whatever was available. The unprecedentedly strict Taliban regulations on female education and employment were the culmination of previously existing trends but codified them and enforced them with harsh coercion. Furthermore, the pervasive male feeling of dishonor as a result of the war led to harsher attempts to control women, who, as in most patriarchal societies, are seen as the repositories of the honor of their families.

A state once sustained by foreign aid was torn apart by a proxy war, leaving a heritage of massive stocks of weapons and destruction of productive capacity. Humanitarian aid, on which warlords and the Taliban counted to free them to pursue military goals, sustained a large portion of the population. Women were totally excluded from the public sphere. Drug trade, smuggling, links to international terrorist networks, and covert actions by neighboring countries sustained the war, while an entire generation came to maturity with little education, most of it rudimentary and heavily ideological, and no professions but arms for the men and silent seclusion for the women.

The final element of the post–Cold War syndrome, of course, was the indifference of those with resources that could help. The Taliban arose in order to combat warlordism and establish an Islamic order whose harshness was proportionate to the disorder that reigned before. Pakistan made them into a military force for its own security requirements without regard for the effect of its policies on the Afghan population. For the developed world it was far easier and reassuring to stigmatize the Taliban for support of terrorism and "gender apartheid" than to find the means to bring Afghanistan, a member of the League of Nations and a founding state of the United Nations, back into the global community.

Interests of States

Pakistan

The state with the closest ties and strongest links to Afghanistan was Pakistan. The partition of the British Empire in South Asia left behind Pakistan as an existentially insecure state. Pakistan's extreme insecurity results from its confrontation with its much larger neighbor, India; the loss of over half its population when its eastern province became the independent country of Bangladesh after the 1971–72 civil war (which ended with Indian intervention); and Afghanistan's historic challenge to the incorporation of the Pashtun areas into Pakistan— Afghanistan was the only country to vote against Pakistan's admission to the United Nations.

Pakistan sees its main security task as obtaining parity with India, a country almost eight times larger, which has resulted in the ruination of Pakistan's economy due to excessive military spending, the accumulation of the world's fastest growing nuclear arsenal, the use of "asymmetric strategies" such as support for insurgencies and extremist groups (capacities augmented by U.S. assistance during the Afghan war), and the quest for "strategic depth"—links and alliances with parts of the Muslim world to the West. Pakistan's military rulers saw the war in Afghanistan as an opportunity to reverse Pakistan's antagonistic relations with Afghanistan over Pashtunistan. Hence successive governments, regardless of ideology, supported Islamist rather than nationalist groups in Afghanistan, as the former opposed ethnonationalist claims against a fellow Muslim state, or at least did not raise them so loudly.

The deep involvement of Pakistan in the war also helped incorporate many ethnic Pashtuns more firmly into key military and civilian elites there. As a result, the Pashtun question changed for Pakistan. Previously, Afghan nationalist governments had used Pashtun border tribes to raid or exert pressure on Pakistan, which had consequently been hostile to Pashtun nationalism. Now, however, Pakistani Pashtun elites, well integrated into the Pakistani state, could exercise control or influence over religiously oriented Pashtun groups in Afghanistan, while nationalist groups and their tribal base became weakened. Pashtun rule of the "right" kind in Afghanistan thus became an instrument of Pakistani influence, rather than a security threat through the Pashtunistan question. The opening of Central Asia led some in Pakistan also to see trade and pipeline routes through Afghanistan to Central Asia as a key to the country's future security and well-being. These would add yet greater strategic depth.

Until more than two years after the fall of Najibullah, in April 1992, support for Gulbuddin Hikmatyar's Hizb-i Islami remained the main means through which Pakistan pursued the goal of installing a Pashtun-dominated client regime in Kabul. In mid-1994, however, the government of Prime Minister Benazir Bhutto shifted support to the Taliban. Originally the goal seems to have been limited to clearing the road from Quetta to Kandahar and the Kandahar-Herat highway of tribal militias who had regularly extorted tolls from traders and terrorized travelers. The Taliban developed their own ambitions, however, and Pakistan eventually threw the full weight of its support behind them as the future government of Afghanistan. Pakistani Foreign Minister Gohar Ayub Khan signaled a new level of public support in May 1997 when he flew to Mazar-i Sharif with a large delegation immediately after the Taliban's initial, short-lived capture of the city, recognized the Taliban government, and announced that all others should follow suit, as the civil war was now over. Pakistan was supported in this policy by Saudi Arabia and the United Arab Emirates.

The government and military of Pakistan provided comprehensive assistance to the Taliban, including military supplies, training, assistance with recruitment of Pakistani and Afghan madrasa students, seconding of military advisers, financial support, diplomatic representation and advocacy, and regular military units for key offensives. The Pakistani Directorate of Inter-services Intelligence (ISI) also used bases in Afghan territory for training Pakistani extremist groups who supplied fighters in Kashmir.

Saudi Arabia

Saudi Arabia funded much of Pakistan's policy in Afghanistan through both official and unofficial channels. Until mid-1998, Saudi Arabia supplied heavily subsidized fuel to the Taliban through Pakistan and also provided general funding. Saudi Arabia felt some affinity to the Taliban interpretation of Islam, and support for the Taliban was consistent with its rivalry with Iran and long-term strategic cooperation with Pakistan. Some Saudi companies and individuals also had interests in the pipeline proposals under consideration. Thus Saudi policy toward the Taliban was initially a continuation of its previous support for extremist Sunni groups to block Iranian influence.

A specific Saudi concern, however, which pushed the Kingdom in a different direction, was the activities of Usama Bin Laden, the wealthy businessman who funded militant Islamist groups in Afghanistan, Saudi Arabia, and elsewhere. The United States charged him with responsibility for the bombings of the United States embassies in Kenya and Tanzania in August 1998.

Bin Laden was one of the first Arabs to join the mujahidin's struggle against the Soviet Union, and he stayed throughout the war. He funded much of the participation of Arab and other international volunteers. Throughout that time he worked in collaboration with the Saudi intelligence agency and its Pakistani and U.S. counterparts. He turned against his erstwhile sponsors at the time of the Persian Gulf War, when he opposed the invitation of U.S. troops to Saudi Arabia. After being deprived of his Saudi citizenship in 1994, he lived for a time in Sudan, which expelled him under pressure from Egypt and the United States. He returned to Afghanistan in May 1996. Pakistani intelligence agencies assisted his entry to Afghanistan, in return for his agreement to help train fighters for Kashmir. Most of those killed in the U.S. August 1998 raids were Kashmiris and Punjabis trained to fight in that region. Bin Laden, together with a group of his followers, was living under the protection of the Jalalabad shura until the Taliban captured the area in September 1996. He moved to Kandahar in 1997.

The Taliban promised Saudi Arabia that Bin Laden would not use his refuge to support any acts of violence abroad, but in mid-1998 the Saudis seemed to have become skeptical that this agreement was being observed. In a June 1998 meeting in Kandahar Mullah Umar promised Saudi intelligence chief Prince Turki al-Faisal that he would transfer Bin Laden to Saudi custody. When Turki returned to Afghanistan in September 1998 to take custody of Bin Laden, however, Mullah Umar reversed his position, leading Saudi Arabia to withdraw its diplomats and terminate its aid to the Taliban.

Iran

Iran's links to Afghan groups changed and deepened over time. Iran's policy was dictated by a combination of solidarity with the Shia in Afghanistan (and in Pakistan) and strategic concerns over the U.S. embargo, access to Central Asia, and rivalry with Saudi Arabia.

Iran originally became involved through its links to revolutionary Shia groups that took control of the Central Highlands region of Hazarajat, including Bamiyan and portions of all the neighboring provinces, from the more traditionalist formations established in 1979. As it emerged in 1988 from its war with Iraq and adjusted to the changes in the Soviet Union, which coincided with the death of Ayatollah Ruhollah Khomeini in 1989, Iran's policy became more assertive. It united most of the Shia parties into the Hizb-i Wahdat in 1988 and pressed for the Wahdat's inclusion in international negotiations, which had been dominated by the Sunni parties supported by the United States, Pakistan, and Saudi Arabia. From the Soviet troop withdrawal in February 1989 until the fall of President Najibullah in April 1992, Iran saw the Soviet-backed Kabul government as the main force blocking the takeover of Afghanistan by Sunni Wahhabi parties backed by these three countries. Although it continued to support Shia parties politically, it did not support their making war on the Najibullah government.

The breakup of the Soviet Union and the rise of the Taliban led Iran to undertake a more active policy in which it provided economic and military assistance to groups beyond its traditional Shia beneficiaries. As the Najibullah regime collapsed, Iran helped form and arm the "Northern Alliance," including the Jamiat-i Islami-SCN (Supervisory Council of the North), the newly formed Junbish-i Milli-yi Islami-yi Afghanistan (National Islamic Movement of Afghanistan), and Hizb-i Wahdat. It was partly motivated to do so by the desire to block the parties supported by the United States, Pakistan, and Saudi Arabia from coming to power.

Strategically, the opening of Central Asia and the Caucasus—the Caspian basin—was, if anything, more important for Iran than for Pakistan. Bordering on the Caspian itself as well as the newly independent littoral states of Azerbaijan and Turkmenistan, Iran offered the shortest route to the sea for that region's oil and attractive routes to customers such as Turkey for the region's natural gas. Its location as the only state on both the Persian Gulf and the Caspian Sea increased Iran's strategic and international importance and its leverage over U.S. sanctions.

Gas and oil pipelines from Central Asia through Afghanistan and Pakistan would be the only southern route other than through Iran. Construction of such pipelines would enable the United States to promote its goal of linking Central Asia to international energy markets by routes other than through Russia while still bypassing Iran. Iran therefore suspected that support for the Taliban by Pakistan and Saudi Arabia was not merely an attempt to impose an extremist Sunni, anti-Shia regime on Afghanistan but part of the U.S. plan to encircle and isolate Iran. By guaranteeing security for the pipeline route, the Taliban would weaken the leverage that Iran had gained. Hence Iran's efforts to stop the spread and consolidation of Taliban power were dictated by both ideological and strategic considerations.

Since the Taliban's first approach to Kabul in early 1995, when Massoud also crushed the remnants of Hizb-i Wahdat within Kabul city, strategic considerations dominated. Iran became the principal supplier of fuel, weapons, and other equipment to all groups fighting the Taliban, including those, such as Massoud's, that also opposed Hizb-i Wahdat.

The rivalry between Iran and Pakistan thus became the principal external factor fueling the war. It was worsened by one of the war's by-products: increasing Sunni-Shia violence in Pakistan. This took the form of assassinations by small extremist groups, not mass violence.

Hostility to the Taliban and suspicion of Pakistan deepened when forces fighting alongside the Taliban (apparently Pakistanis from Sipah-i Sahaba [a violently anti-Shia Sunni extremist group]) murdered eight Iranian officials and a journalist in Mazar-i Sharif during the August 1998 Taliban takeover. ["Sipah-i Shaba" means "Army of the Companions of the Prophet"; Sunnis accepted this group of "companions"—including the "rightly guided" caliphs Umar and Uthman—as the legitimate successors to Muhammad, while Shia recognized only the prophet's son-in-law, Ali, and his descendants.] This incident, together with the capture of thirty-five other Iranian nationals by the Taliban, led Iran to build up a military presence on the Afghan border and threaten military action. UN special envoy Lakhdar Brahimi negotiated the return of the detainees and the bodies of the slain, defusing the threat of military action.

Iran became a major supplier of arms and ammunition to the United Front (UF) and served as a base for meetings among the UF's various feuding factions. Iran mounted a significant military effort against Afghan drug traffickers. Some forces in Iran, notably the Foundation of the Shrine of Imam Ja'afar in Mashhad, invested in the transit trade and thus economic links with Afghanistan, and indirectly the Taliban. Iran and the Taliban renewed the traditional Afghan-Iran dispute over the Helmand river waters, intensified by the drought of 1998–2001.

Russia

Russia, too, played an important role in supplying the northern groups, especially Massoud's forces. In the immediate aftermath of the Soviet withdrawal from Afghanistan and the breakup of the Soviet Union, Russia, which no longer had a border with Afghanistan, withdrew from the region. The war in newly independent Tajikistan drew Russia back in; it provided about twenty-five thousand troops and border forces to stabilize control of that country by the victors in the 1992–1997 civil war.

Russia saw Pakistan's ambitions in Afghanistan and Central Asia as a threat to its security sphere, which it came to define as the entire former Soviet Union. It found common interest with Iran there, as in the Caucasus, where Turkey and the United States were the main external powers. Russia provided some support to the Rabbani-Massoud government, as well as to General Dostum, in the interest of resisting Hikmatyar.

Moscow and Kabul, however, had a conflict over the Islamic guerrillas from Tajikistan, who found shelter and received aid and training in the predominantly Tajik areas of northeastern Afghanistan. The rise of the Taliban led Russia, Iran (where some exiled Tajik Islamic opposition leaders lived), and the Rabbani-Massoud forces to attempt to liquidate this problem in order to consolidate the rear bases of resistance to the Taliban. Joint pressures by them on the parties in the Tajikistan conflict led to the signing of a peace accord in June 1997 and the subsequent repatriation of most of the refugees and fighters. At the same time, Massoud was granted access to an air base in Kulab, home of Tajikistan's Russian-supported ruling clan. There he received both Russian and Iranian assistance and was able to keep his small air force in repair. Although Tajikistan had few resources of its own to give, it did facilitate the use of its territory in this way, in conjunction with Russia and Iran.

After 1998 Russia took the lead in seeking sanctions against the Taliban in the UN Security Council. Moscow saw the Taliban as central to a network of Islamist groups, including Usama Bin Laden, undermining security in Russia itself, as in Chechnya and Daghestan, and elsewhere in the former Soviet space, in particular Central Asia as through the Islamic Movement of Uzbekistan.

Uzbekistan

Uzbekistan supported resistance to the Taliban but was more strongly attached to Dostum, who helped it with its goals in Tajikistan. It refused to provide assistance to Abdul Malik Pahlawan after the latter ousted Dostum in May 1997. Uzbekistan was also alarmed by the Tajikistan peace agreement, which brought Islamists into the government, excluded the Uzbekistan-sponsored party in northern Tajikistan, and kept Russian forces on Uzbekistan's borders. Threatened both by an Islamic insurgency led by exiles from the Ferghana Valley (IMU) based in Afghanistan and Tajikistan, and by Russia's reassertion in the region, Uzbekistan vacillated between sounding the alarm about the Taliban and trying to reach an accommodation. It hoped to meet the IMU threat without increasing Russian military presence in Central Asia.

Turkmenistan

Turkmenistan alone of the Central Asian states professed to feel no threat from the Taliban and determined its policy solely on the basis of economic interest. Turkmenistan's overriding foreign policy goal was the search for international markets for its oil and natural gas, and the Davlatabad gas field just northwest of Afghanistan could be profitably connected with the Pakistani gas network in Baluchistan via a pipeline through western Afghanistan. Creating conditions for construction of this pipeline was one of the original purposes envisaged for the Taliban by their international supporters. Construction of the gas pipeline (and, to a lesser extent, a complementary oil pipeline along the same route) remained the lodestar of Turkmen policy toward Afghanistan. Though Turkmenistan did not break with the international and Central Asian consensus by recognizing the Taliban's Islamic Emirate of Afghanistan (IEA), it maintained friendly relations and sometimes advocated the Taliban's case in international forums.

China

China played a major though largely unacknowledged role as a (paid) arms supplier to the mujahidin during the Soviet occupation of Afghanistan. Until the Soviet withdrawal, it cooperated quietly with the United States, Pakistan, and

Saudi Arabia in this operation. Since then, in line with its generally realpolitik approach, it lowered its interest, but it later become concerned with possible support for Uyghur separatists and Islamists from international Islamist networks in Taliban-controlled areas. China both held talks with the Taliban and sent a number of warning messages to Pakistan, such as abstaining on the Security Council resolution imposing sanctions on the Taliban. China did not fully use its considerable leverage with Pakistan over this issue, as the difficulties in Xinjiang remained manageable, and other geopolitical factors outweighed it.

United States

During President Bill Clinton's first term, the U.S. government expressed some supportive views about the Taliban. It suggested it might consider reopening the U.S. embassy if security improved in Kabul following a Taliban victory, and it advocated engagement rather than isolation of the Taliban in UN forums. After Madeleine Albright became secretary of state, however, U.S. condemnation of Taliban policies on gender was forthright. The secretary's own views may have influenced this direction, but so did the organization of an influential lobbying network of feminist, human rights, and humanitarian groups, supported by some Afghan women exiles in the United States, who made Taliban gender policies a political issue. This network included key constituencies of President Bill Clinton and the Democratic Party. The link drawn between the Taliban regime and international (non-Afghan) terrorists who have targeted U.S. installations and citizens ensured that no reconciliation or even dialogue was possible.

The region as a whole, including Afghanistan, regained a certain level of importance to the United States. In the spring of 1997, Deputy Secretary of State Strobe Talbott announced a new policy that gave a higher priority to Central Asia. South Asia also received more attention because of India's economic importance, as an offshoot of the interest in Central Asia and pipelines, and because of the security dangers posed by nuclearization and the Kashmir conflict. Hopes for improved relations with Iran after the election of President Muhammad Khatami in May 1997 also sparked interest in Afghanistan as a place where the United States and Iran had common interests and could collaborate. As a result, the United States became somewhat more engaged in Afghanistan in 1998, with U.S. Permanent Representative to the United Nations Bill Richardson making a one-day trip to the country in April. Richardson was the highest U.S. official to visit Afghanistan in more than twenty years.

Until the attacks on its embassies in August 1998, the United States defined its policy mainly as supporting UN efforts at peace making, in the hope that Afghanistan could be reconstructed and pipelines built to Central Asia. The embassy attacks, however, redefined Afghanistan as a one-issue country: terrorism.

U.S. policy toward Afghanistan came to be almost completely dominated by concern over the Taliban's harboring of Usama Bin Laden, whom Director of Central Intelligence (DCI) George Tenet characterized as the single greatest threat to U.S. national security.

International Organizations

The United Nations operated in Afghanistan without the major collaboration of or competition from other intergovernmental organizations. Unlike in Europe, Africa, or Latin America, regional organization has tended to be weak throughout Asia. Alongside the UN were various NGOs, both Western and Islamic. The Western-based NGOs largely worked under the umbrella of the UN system. The International Committee of the Red Cross also performed the full range of its activities throughout the country.

The role of the UN system, like the strategies of states, changed with the transformation of the international system and the war in Afghanistan. Its humanitarian role began with aid by the United Nations High Commissioner for Refugees (UNHCR) to the first flows of refugees, mainly in Pakistan, in 1978, and its political role began in 1981, with the first mission of a personal representative of the UN secretary-general.

During the Soviet occupation, the UN's humanitarian and development activities were politically polarized. The UNHCR led an effort to help the more than three million Afghan refugees in Pakistan in ways that effectively funded a rear base for the U.S.-Pakistani-Saudi effort to support the mujahidin. This was eventually complemented by cross-border "humanitarian" efforts funded by the U.S. Agency for International Development (USAID) that aimed at building the capacity of mujahidin political organizations. The NGOs that participated in this effort largely saw themselves as supporters of the struggle against the Soviet occupation. Islamic NGOs provided support for Arab and other Muslim fighters who joined the mujahidin, Islamic education for refugees, and other activities.

In 1984 the UN Human Rights Commission appointed a special rapporteur on Afghanistan, the first such appointment for a pro-Soviet country. These relatively frank reports, written by Austrian jurist Felix Ermacora, were passed with large majorities in the commission and approved by the General Assembly. On the other side, the UN Development Program led an effort in Kabul that supported development programs of the Soviet-aided Afghan government. Until Soviet leader Mikhail Gorbachev changed the Soviet attitude toward international norms and organizations, the International Committee of the Red Cross was excluded from Afghanistan; it gained access in 1986.

The political efforts of the United Nations during this period led to the signing on April 14, 1988, of the Geneva Accords, which provided for the withdrawal of Soviet troops by February 15, 1989. Virtually none of the other elements of the accords were ever implemented. The United Nations essentially provided diplomatic cover for the Soviet decision to withdraw, which was largely negotiated through direct bilateral channels with the United States.

Until the collapse of the Soviet Union and its client government in Afghanistan, the UN played a complementary role to a United States–Soviet dialogue that tried to reach agreement on an interim regime in Afghanistan. This process was typical of the period at the end of the Cold War, with the United States and the Soviet Union attempting to liquidate their remaining disputes and jointly manage the international system.

The humanitarian effort similarly tried to bridge gaps. Following the signing of the Geneva Accords, a single coordinator was appointed for all humanitarian efforts for Afghans in and outside Afghanistan. The coordination operation, called Operation Salaam by the first coordinator, Sadruddin Aga Khan, negotiated agreements making it possible for humanitarian actors to cross political and military lines to provide assistance anywhere in Afghanistan.

The humanitarian operations continued, but the political effort of the UN lapsed after 1992. Political and strategic stakes were unclear, and humanitarianism emerged as an all-around response to state collapse, ethnic conflict, and other problems. Such an approach failed in Afghanistan as it did in Bosnia, Somalia, and elsewhere.

In December 1993, pursuant to a resolution of the General Assembly, the UN reestablished a political office, the UN Special Mission for Afghanistan (UNSMA). The UN Afghan mission in the field, led by Dr. Norbert Holl of Germany and augmented by seconded officers from the United States, Japan, Britain, and Russia, reported progress toward agreement on a cease-fire and demilitarization of Kabul.[3] Shortly before the fall of Kabul to the Taliban, the UN tried to signal a higher level of commitment to its political efforts in Afghanistan. Under-Secretary-General for Political Affairs Marrack Goulding spent September 10–13, 1996, in Afghanistan meeting leaders and discussing the UN role.[4]

Once the Taliban took Kabul, the humanitarian agencies had to struggle with the new situation. Soon after the Taliban victory, UN Secretary-General Boutros Boutros-Ghali, issued a statement reiterating the UN's commitment to the rights of women.[5] Agencies that had become accustomed to working through quiet, slow pressure now had to confront the challenge to their principles head-on.[6] The Taliban's harsh regulations forced the closure of many programs, including even, in one area, classes for women in landmine awareness. Amid attacks on and arrests of their staff and the impossibility of continuing many programs involving mothers and children or girls' education, many agencies had to consider whether they could continue to work in Afghanistan. UNHCR suspended its programs in

Kabul on November 20, 1996, when the Taliban arrested four members of its Afghan staff.[7] The programs resumed when the staff members were released without explanation three weeks later. The Taliban relented in a number of small ways—allowing women to come out in public to receive food assistance, so long as they waited in lines separate from men, and permitting a small number of female medical staff to work.[8] In early December 1996 Mullah Umar called on the Taliban to treat the people of Kabul less harshly; but the next day Taliban radio announced the punishment of 225 women for violating the dress code.[9]

The UN continued to face some of the harshest dilemmas of humanitarian access. After its offices were sacked and looted during fighting in Mazar-i Sharif in May and again in September 1997, the UN withdrew from all of northern Afghanistan except the Hazarajat. Hence it did not undertake any programs in most areas controlled by forces nominally loyal to the government it recognized. In Taliban areas, however, even though the authorities provided full security for UN personnel and property—except when they arrested or harassed national (Afghan) staff for alleged espionage or violations of Taliban edicts—the UN and NGOs found it difficult to operate for other reasons: Taliban edicts, especially those regarding women, contradicted international principles and made it nearly impossible for many programs to reach their intended beneficiaries.

The conflict between the Taliban and the UN over these issues was punctuated by various incidents. The UN withdrew from Kandahar and southern Afghanistan from mid-April to mid-June 1998 after the governor of Kandahar threw a teapot at the UN regional coordinator for Kandahar. This dispute erupted over a Taliban decree banning the UN from employing foreign Muslim women staff in Afghanistan unless they were accompanied by a mahram, an adult male member of their immediate family. The Taliban also stated that they would henceforth refuse to deal with Alfredo Witschi-Cestari, the UN Development Program resident representative and head of the UN Office of the Coordinator for Humanitarian Affairs in Afghanistan; they apparently regarded his forceful advocacy of international principles as hostile to them.

In response to these conflicts, the UN sought to reach a written understanding with the Taliban on the principles governing humanitarian and development programs. After two weeks of negotiations in Kabul, the two sides agreed on a memorandum of understanding on July 14, 1998. The Taliban said they would respect the privileges and immunities of UN international staff. They conceded that women could work in the health sector. They also agreed to the construction of eleven schools each for boys and girls and to the improvement of some health and higher education facilities for both sexes. There was no agreement on the mahram issue, which was referred to international Islamic scholars. The UN agreed to language stating that women's access to education and health care would be "gradual," a word that provided a target for critics of the memorandum.

Even these conditions seemed difficult for the Taliban, who asked the UN not to publicize the memorandum. Soon after its signing, some elements within the Taliban appeared to be attempting to undermine the agreement by ordering the closure of non-health programs for women and ordering NGOs to move to new common quarters. The new quarters were to be in the Polytechnic, a ravaged former dormitory without water or electricity in a neighborhood of Kabul that was distant from most international offices but close to the front lines. By mid-July 1998, special envoy Brahimi openly speculated that the UN might have to withdraw from Afghanistan entirely. The NGOs in fact left Kabul (though not all of Afghanistan) soon after. Virtually all expatriate personnel, UN and NGOs, left Afghanistan after the killing of a UN officer following the U.S. cruise missile raids in August. Only the International Committee of the Red Cross and a few NGOs (a small minority) remained.

The UN Human Rights Commission repeatedly renewed the appointment of the special rapporteur. In 1997, the UN Human Rights Center in Geneva, upgraded under its recently appointed high commissioner, Mary Robinson, began to explore a new role in Afghanistan: forensic investigation of war crimes accusations. After his return to Afghanistan in September 1997, General Dostum announced the discovery of mass graves holding thousands of Taliban dead. He charged that these had been prisoners captured in Mazar-i Sharif and executed by his rival, Abdul Malik Pahlawan in May 1997. The Wahdat also charged that during the advance on Mazar-i Sharif in September, Taliban (or, more precisely, Pashtun settlers who had sided with the Taliban) had massacred nearly one hundred Hazara civilians in Qizilabad village south of Mazar.

The Taliban and other Afghan parties demanded a UN investigation, and some Afghans began to ask for international war crimes trials of those responsible. The UN Human Rights Center in Geneva sent some investigators to the region for a preliminary inquiry in November 1997. A further mission examined the sites again in May 1998, but the investigation had still not started when the Taliban recaptured Mazar-i Sharif in August 1998. This failure contributed to the environment in which the Taliban carried out the subsequent massacres in Mazar.

Thereafter the UN proposed three investigative or monitoring missions. The Human Rights Center began to prepare to investigate both the mass killings of Taliban in 1997 and those by Taliban in 1998. Following an agreement in principle between the Taliban and UN Special Envoy Brahimi, the secretary-general proposed the stationing of civilian observers in key locations to monitor basic humanitarian standards and prevent further massacres; the Security Council proposed an intergovernmental mission to investigate the killing of the nine Iranians.

The political mission was put on hold. In April 1998, under pressure from Pakistan's Prime Minister Nawaz Sharif, the Taliban agreed to negotiate in Islamabad with a delegation from the United Front. At the insistence of the

Taliban, the negotiations dealt with the naming of a commission of ulama (Islamic scholars) from all sides who would be responsible for resolving the conflict. These negotiations led to a tentative agreement on a nomination procedure and a cease-fire. Nonetheless, all the agreements soon broke down amid recriminations. The Taliban stated that negotiations with the fragmented opposition were a waste of time, while the northerners argued that the Taliban were still intent on a military victory. Time seemed to prove both sides right.

The UN continued to call attention to foreign intervention as an important factor intensifying the conflict. The reports of the secretary-general published in November 1997 and June 1998 spoke in unusually frank terms, describing supplies of arms and military training by foreign countries and explicitly questioning their sincerity in supporting the UN mission. Following a Presidential Statement of the Security Council in July 1998, Special Envoy Brahimi told the press: "The fact is that this war cannot go on unless it receives support from outside. The legend that the Russians have left enough arms for fighting to continue for 50 years is just that—a legend, it is not possible."

It would be difficult to disagree with Brahimi's prognosis. According to a July 1998 press report, he expected "the fighting to worsen in the near future. He [said that] UN Secretary General Kofi Annan has been warning the international community about the deteriorating situation in Afghanistan and it appears his worst fears are now coming true."

UN Peace Efforts

During the first stage, that of the Soviet intervention and the Cold War, the UN secretary-general used his good offices to mediate the Geneva Accords, signed on April 14, 1988, under which Soviet troops withdrew from Afghanistan by February 15, 1989.[10] These accords made no provision for a domestic political settlement within Afghanistan. The text of the accords provided for termination of all assistance to the Pakistan-based resistance, the mujahidin, but the United States claimed the right to continue the provision of aid to parties in Afghanistan, just as the Soviet Union claimed the right to continue aid to the regime it had installed. U.S. determination to gain the maximum advantage over the USSR meant the accords were never implemented. UN mediator Diego Cordovez proposed an interim government under the aegis of neutral officials from Zahir Shah's regime, which would then convene a loya jirga (great assembly). This proposal found no support among the major protagonists, who were bent on winning.[11]

The Geneva Accords intended to reinstate international cooperation over Afghanistan by removing antagonistic flows of power resources: UN mediation would coordinate the withdrawal of Soviet troops with termination of aid to the mujahidin. This agreement, however, failed to provide for an Afghan government able to control the country's territory and population in a way that apportioned influence acceptably among the external powers concerned.

The second stage, from February 1989 to April 1992, was the period of proxy war between the mujahidin, supported by the United States, Pakistan, Saudi Arabia, and other Arab and Islamic sources, and the Soviet-aided regime of Najibullah. Despite the continuing fighting in Afghanistan, this stage corresponded to a period of international cooperation. Between the end of the Cold War and the breakup of the Soviet Union, the United States lost an enemy and seemed to gain a partner in managing the global order. The superpowers conducted a direct dialogue on a range of issues, including Afghanistan, for which they elaborated a plan for a "period of transition."[12] Both superpowers would end aid to their clients, and the UN would preside over an interim authority that would sponsor elections or some other representative procedure to create a permanent government. The UN secretary-general's office continued to mediate between Kabul and the mujahidin, but in a role largely subordinate to that of the superpowers; the UN representative circulated proposals that emerged from the U.S.-Soviet dialogue among the Afghan parties in an attempt to build support for the process.

This finally led to an agreement when Soviet hard-liners were ousted after the failure of their August 1991 coup d'état. The United States and USSR agreed to stop aid at the end of 1991 and support UN efforts to broker a transitional regime.[13] The disintegration of the USSR, however, precipitated the internal collapse of the Najibullah regime just as this plan was about to be implemented.[14] An alliance of some mujahidin groups with fragments of the old regime's armed forces took control of the capital, launching a new round of civil war, mainly among factions of the former mujahidin. Under the Peshawar Accord of April 26, 1992, the Pakistan-based mujahidin groups agreed on an interim presidency leading to elections, but most provisions of the accord were never implemented.

The termination of aid to both sides at the beginning of 1992 was supposed to push them toward accommodation. Instead it led to fragmentation. The coherence of the bipolar conflict was due to the aid flows, not the structure of political cleavages in Afghanistan. The aid-based state had grown without integrating a national society, and that society's fragmentation reasserted itself in the assortment of ethnic, tribal, and factional conflicts—exacerbated by probably the world's highest level of sophisticated personal weapons—that overwhelmed the attempt to create an interim government. The core of the state, the army, collapsed in ethnic-factional mutinies, leaving no core of power for an interim regime to preside over. Armed factions aided by competing regional powers filled the vacuum.

The third stage, after the breakup of the Soviet Union, was a period of strategic vacuum in Afghanistan and, to a considerable extent, in South Asia as a whole. For almost two years after the fall of Najibullah, the UN abandoned any effort to seek a political settlement. The only peace proposal during this time was an effort by Pakistan and Saudi Arabia (with eventual participation by Iran) to broker the Islamabad Accords of March 1993. These accords, broken almost as soon as they were signed, provided for power sharing between what were then the two major military forces around Kabul, the mainly Tajik Jamiat led by Rabbani and Massoud and the mainly Pashtun Hizb-i Islami, led by Hikmatyar, who was named prime minister in the accords.[15]

As the war continued, a number of governments, including the United States, exerted pressure on the United Nations to reactivate its search for a political settlement. The UN started a new good offices mission, led by Tunisian former Foreign Minister Mahmoud Mestiri.[16] Initially, the Mestiri mission tried a new tactic of appealing directly to the people of Afghanistan by convening public meetings in towns and cities in Afghanistan and places of exile. The response— crowds of thousands of people and literally hundreds of peace proposals—left little doubt that the general populace of Afghanistan longed for peace. In the absence of any major power resources to support the initiative, however, a good offices mission was unable to pose a genuine alternative to the warring power holders, among whom Mestiri soon began to mediate. The various proposals he circulated all had the same basic form as the one proposed in 1992: the sitting president (now Rabbani rather than Najibullah) would turn over power to a collective leadership of relatively neutral figures, who would preside over a period of transition.[17] Rabbani avoided Najibullah's fatal step of stating clearly that he would hand over power, and Mestiri's mission was further complicated by the rise of the Taliban, who refused to negotiate. His successor, envoy Norbert Holl, who started his work after the Taliban had taken control of southern Afghanistan, met with the various factions and alienated them all with his penchant for lecturing them.

The mission languished until UN Secretary-General Kofi Annan made Afghanistan a priority in July 1997 by appointing a high-level special envoy, Ambassador Lakhdar Brahimi, the former minister of foreign affairs of Algeria and a long-standing UN diplomat, to oversee the effort. Brahimi took over at a time when the situation was particularly difficult and complex. Since the capture of Kabul by the Taliban in September 1996, the Rabbani government had continued to hold Afghanistan's UN seat, as no member state except Pakistan, Saudi Arabia, and the United Arab Emirates recognized the Taliban. Thus the UN did not recognize the group that controlled the largest amount of territory and population, including the national capital.

Brahimi created some processes of discussion, which led to the Ashqabat talks between the Taliban and United Front/Northern Alliance in 1999. He also engaged all the regional powers in discussion and concentrated much of his work on the clash between Pakistan and Iran over Afghanistan. He succeeded in averting an Iranian attack on the Taliban in the aftermath of their killing of the Iranians in Mazar-i Sharif in August 1998. Brahimi suspended his mission in July 1999, when a Taliban offensive supported by Pakistan, following directly on a meeting in Tashkent that called for a cease-fire, convinced him that his interlocutors were not sincere.

Brahimi was succeeded by UN envoy Francesc Vendrell, who obtained written agreement from both the Taliban and Massoud to engage in an open-ended process of negotiation, which they would pursue until reaching a satisfactory conclusion. Vendrell was trying to draft a broad agenda for this discussion, including the key issues of state building and relations with neighbors, when the February 1999 Security Council sanctions envenomed UN relations with the Taliban and caused them effectively to withdraw from the process. Vendrell also pursued second-track approaches among the key outside countries. The main aim of such approaches was to answer the question that UN envoys kept asking: "What does Pakistan want?" No clear or satisfactory answer was forthcoming, other than "complete victory by the Taliban." Vendrell also recognized that peace would not come under current economic and social conditions, and that the peacemaking process required incentives, not only sanctions. Hence he requested the World Bank to augment its watching brief by starting to plan for reconstruction.

Whatever the strengths and weaknesses of the various envoys, the basic problem of UNSMA was the mandate to mediate negotiations over the formation of a broad-based, representative government in a country without a state. The imagined goal seemed to be some kind of coalition government in which members of opposing factions would share power by gaining different portfolios in the government. But since there was little or no state structure, giving up commanding an armed group in order to become a minister amounted to abandoning power rather than sharing it. The UNGA resolution and "six plus two" mandates thus failed to address the fundamental problems of the country and were based on a mistaken definition of the problem.

Among various options discussed in the "six plus two" group of countries was an arms embargo on all parties. Pakistan claimed to support a Chapter 7 embargo on all arms going to Afghanistan, while the other members of the group claimed to support a political process leading to voluntary ending of arms supplies. Pakistan's position illustrated the fundamental bad faith of the argument. It was much easier to monitor supplies going to the UF, which depended on a few airfields and bridges, than to the Taliban, who could use numerous roads and trails, and who had a much greater stockpile. Pakistan was unlikely to respect any such embargo (as it was then violating the Security Council sanctions against aid to the Taliban, allowing if not instigating madrasa students to cross the border and fight). The United States and Russia at one time produced a joint "nonpaper" on the technical requirements for embargoing arms.

Afghan Exile Peace Efforts

A number of Afghans in exile launched their own peace processes, with the help and support of foreign governments, including the Rome process focused on the former king, Zahir Shah (funded by Italy and indirectly supported by the United States), and the Cyprus process supported by some factions in Iran.

The Rome process was the most serious of these. Since 1983 Zahir Shah periodically articulated the idea of resolving the Afghan conflict through an "emergency loya jirga." The loya jirga (great council) was a traditionalist institution of the Afghan state (i.e., one that reflected a state-constructed tradition) corresponding to a tribal legitimation of the regime. Afghan nationalist intellectuals retrospectively construed gatherings that called the tribes to jihad when there was no functioning legitimate state (as during the two British occupations) as an emergency loya jirga. These plans languished, since Zahir Shah and his advisers had no resources to implement them.

Many Afghans living in Afghanistan appeared to retain a sentimental attachment to Zahir Shah, and the concept of legitimating a new government through a loya jirga still held appeal, but many appeared puzzled as to how an assembly of venerable exiles would seize power from the well-armed groups that controlled Afghanistan. An alliance of the Rome process with Massoud, the emergence of a Pashtun challenger to the Taliban, or a shift in Pakistani policy, might make such an event more likely. It is possible that, in the event of a crisis, an insecure power holder might invoke entities formed through the Rome process to legitimate a new regime. But this would require overcoming Pakistan's resistance, among other obstacles.

Structural Obstacles to Peace Processes

There are several reasons a peace process was so difficult:

- Lack of stalemate. According to one theory, fighters agree to negotiate when they believe they cannot achieve more through war, i.e., when they reach a "hurting stalemate." In transnational wars like Afghanistan, however, access to external aid and international markets (drugs, gems, smuggled consumer goods), international volunteers or recruits from refugees, a diaspora, or allied states, provides replenishable resources. The parties are never exhausted. In this case Pakistan and the Taliban believe they could win, and Massoud believed he could obtain a more advantageous position by building international and domestic political support. Neither side depended on the exhausted Afghan population for any resource other than manpower. Despite economic hardship, the Taliban encountered resistance to recruitment from local communities even in their core areas, but their ability to recruit from the much larger population of Pakistan compensated for this problem. To disrupt such linkages often requires a very high level of determination from powerful states, which may, however, see the theater of conflict as remote from their short-term interests.

- Spoilers with an interest in conflict. Some powerful interests, who may even have lobbies within some governments, may not want to end the war. Some actors (spoilers) can become rich and powerful by exercising violence in a lawless environment, and they will attempt to subvert any peace process. Those benefiting from the drug trade, smuggling, and gem trade could fall into this category. Such spoilers are typically few in number, but they have clear interests and resources to pursue them, while the much larger number of people suffering from the conflict lack resources and organizational capacity.

- Lack of security guarantees. Even when the parties sign an agreement sincerely, it is very difficult to implement without guarantees of security from either law-bound state institutions or third parties. Any negotiated settlement to a civil war involves some disarmament and integration of formerly hostile armed forces and the participation by former combatants in a common political space (e.g., in institutions located in the capital city). Without security guarantees (such as peacekeepers), no one is willing to risk such a transition. The levels of interpersonal trust between key actors are far too low to support the concessions required to transform the nature of the conflict. For instance, try to imagine Massoud taking up a position in a coalition government with the Taliban. Who is responsible for his security in Kabul? There is no national army or security force that is even slightly independent of its leader. No one will trust his security to anyone else's forces, and it will be very difficult to convince third parties without a direct interest to send forces to Afghanistan, though it may become necessary at some stage.

- Conflicting international interests. International actors agree on "peace" as a goal when they care less about the outcome of a conflict than about the process of violence. That is less and less the case in Afghanistan. Pakistan seeks victory by the Taliban. The war increasingly pits Pakistan against all of Afghanistan's other neighbors, as well as, indirectly, the United States and Russia, which increasingly seek to defeat or at least coerce the Taliban.

Although a Taliban victory might seem to bring the country together, it is likely to provoke a strong regional reaction and spark guerrilla warfare. The U.S. missile attack, which was followed by attacks on UN personnel in Kabul and the sacking of the UN office in Jalalabad, has further reduced the possibility that international involvement will bring peace to Afghanistan.

The United States and Russia seek to force the Taliban to change major policies through sanctions against a country whose economy is already almost entirely illegal. A UN-led negotiating process over formation of a "broad-based government" is meaningless in the current environment. The Taliban are seeking to meet those international conditions they have identified as acceptable by pursuing war to gain full control of Afghan territory and forcing peasants to halt opium production. The result of all of these policies, together with the drought (besides genuine reduction in opium growing and, as usual, plenty of killing), is to drive people off the land into internally displaced persons (IDP) camps in Afghanistan, islands in the Panj river (since Tajikistan will not admit them), and camps in Pakistan that are more like concentration than refugee camps.

There is no immediate solution to this crisis. In the absence of an accepted state structure, negotiations cannot lead to a coalition or interim government. The usual sequencing that the UN and others have in mind involves an end to external involvement; a cease-fire; formation of an interim government; an election or constitution-making process, simultaneous with the start of reconstruction; and "return" to normalcy (a state remembered by less than half of the population). But the extensive links between Afghan and Pakistani populations and institutions cannot be broken; at best, they can be transformed.

The composition of a government cannot resolve the problem. The Taliban are not a political group that took over an existing government; they are a movement that is building a weak but centralized state. The Ashqabat talks in 1999 failed over the issue of qiyadi (leadership): the Taliban offered Massoud and his supporters virtually any position in the government, providing they accepted the existing structure of the IEA, and hence the "leadership" of Mullah Umar. From the Taliban's point of view, the alternative is the continued existence of a state within a state with its own separate army; from Massoud's point of view, such an agreement amounted to surrender, not a peace deal. Since there is no autonomous state structure (army, administration, etc.) that both sides accept, there is no purely political mechanism for power sharing.

These efforts, like the previous ones, seem destined to fall short of their proclaimed goal of helping Afghans to establish a stable, legitimate government in their country. Despite frequent shifts in power and the rise of the Taliban, the fundamental reality has not changed. In a situation of such instability and fragility of all alliances and power relations, it is virtually impossible to negotiate stable agreements, especially those long-term ones that form the basis of governments.

The underlying reality of today's Afghanistan remains the same, whoever dominates the scene for a year, a month, or a day. No leader controls a reliable, renew-
able, autonomous flow of resources with which to create and manage a stable
apparatus of power. Each protagonist hopes that by holding out a little longer
and seeking still more foreign aid, opponents can be worn down. Power depends
on transient foreign support, crisscrossing (and double-crossing) networks of
informal ties, and the constant renegotiation of all agreements. No superpower
will impose order (as Britain and the Soviet Union tried to do) or pay an Afghan
to impose order (as Britain ultimately did). Unless Afghanistan's neighbors
reach an agreement, it will remain a legally undivided territory of fragmented
power.

Notes

1. For instance, in August 1995 the Taliban "air force" based in Kandahar intercepted an air-
   plane with a Russian crew flying supplies to the forces of Ahmad Shah Massoud, then based
   in Kabul. The plane, which belonged to the Aerostar Company, registered in Tatarstan (an
   autonomous Republic of Russia), was carrying arms and ammunition purchased in Albania.
2. United Nations Office for Coordination of Humanitarian Affairs in Afghanistan, *Consolidated Appeal for Assistance*, 1997 (Islamabad: UNOCHA, 1996): 11.
3. Reuters, "UN Says New Afghan Ceasefire Plan Drawn Up" (Peshawar, Pakistan), November
   13, 1996.
4. Under-Secretary-General for Political Affairs, United Nations, press briefing (New York,
   September 26, 1996).
5. United Nations Department of Public Affairs, "Secretary–General Restates United Nations
   Policy on Gender Equality in Response to Concerns About Status of Women in Afghanistan" (New York, October 8, 1996); Thalif Deen, "UN-Afghanistan: UN Warns Taliban over
   Treatment of Women," Inter-Press Service (New York, October 9, 1996).
6. Interviews with officials of humanitarian organizations working in Afghanistan, Merges,
   Switzerland, October 4–5, 1996; Karen Byrne, "Aid Agencies Take on the Taliban," UPI (Islamabad), October 13, 1996.
7. *United Nations Assistance for Afghanistan: Weekly Update* no. 187, October 8, 1996, and no.
   193, November 20, 1996; UPI, "UNHCR Suspends Programs in Kabul" (Islamabad).
8. Tim Johnston, "Red Cross Hands Out Food to Disabled Afghan Veterans," Reuters (Kabul),
   November 13, 1996; Johnston, "Despite Taliban, Women Are Back Working," Reuters
   (Kabul), October 30, 1996.
9. Reuters. "Afghan Taliban Asks Members Not to Be Harsh" (Kabul), December 3, 1996.
10. Selig S. Harrison, "Inside the Afghan Talks," *Foreign Policy* 72 (1988): 31–60; Cordovez and
    Harrison, *Out of Afghanistan*; Khan, *Untying the Afghan Knot*; Barnett Rubin, *The Search for
    Peace in Afghanistan: From Buffer State to Failed State* (New Haven, CT: Yale University
    Press), 1995.
11. On this proposal, see Barnett R. Rubin, "Afghanistan: The Next Round," *Orbis* 33 (Winter
    1989): 57–72; Cordovez and Harrison, *Out of Afghanistan,* 368–78.
12. Rubin, *Search for Peace,* 96–111.
13. Communiqué of meeting between Foreign Minister Boris Pankin and Secretary of State
    James Baker, Moscow, September 13, 1991, supplied to the author by the U.S. Department
    of State; David Hoffman, "US, Soviets Sign Afghan Arms Halt: Backing of Combatants
    Abandoned," *Washington Post,* September 14, 1991.
14. Rubin, *Search for Peace,* 126–28.

15. Text of Islamabad Accords supplied to author by Permanent Mission of Afghanistan to the UN.

16. Mestiri's mission was authorized by the UN General Assembly in "Emergency International Assistance for Peace, Normalcy and Reconstruction of War–Stricken Afghanistan," A/RES/48/208 (December 21, 1993).

17. UN Security Council, "Security Council Welcomes Acceptance by Afghan Parties of Phased National Reconciliation Process," S/PRST/77 (November 30, 1994).

2

The Political Economy of War and Peace in Afghanistan

Quid est aliud omnia ad bellum civile hosti arma largiri, primum
nervos belli, pecuniam infinitam? (What is this but to lavish on an
enemy all the weapons for civil war, first of all the sinews of war, unlim-
ited money?)
 —The Fifth Philippic of M. Tullius Cicero against M. Antonius[1]

Introduction

Classical interstate war may be, as von Clausewitz wrote, nothing else but the
pursuit of politics with the admixture of other means, but the pursuit of politics
through both peaceful and violent means requires money. Political leaders speak
in public about their ideals and goals, but much of their activity is devoted to
raising resources to exercise power and reward supporters or themselves. How
political leaders raise and distribute these resources determines the outcome of
their acts, as much as if not more than their stated goals and intentions.

The dominant current form of war is neither Clausewitzian interstate war nor
classic civil war (government versus insurgency), but transnational war involving
a variety of official and unofficial actors, often from several states. Such wars create
conditions for economic activity, though often of a predatory nature, and such
economic returns to the use of violence may both provoke such wars and nourish
interests that perpetuate them. A few actors profit, while most have no say in the
development of their own society. Peace making requires not only political negotiations but transforming the war economy into a peace economy and creating
institutions for accountability over economic and political decision making.[2]

The war economy of Afghanistan exemplifies this phenomenon. Devastated
Afghanistan has become both the world's leading producer of opium (75 percent
of world production in 1999) and a transport and marketing corridor where
armed groups protect a regionwide arbitraging center where profits are made off

Originally published in *World Development* 28 (2000), no. 10, pp. 1789–1803.

policy-induced price differentials. The region in question includes Dubai, the world's largest duty-free shopping mall; Pakistan, a state where the two ISIs—the Directorate of Inter-Services Intelligence and import-substitution industrialization—have created a highly armed and corrupt society where economic interest in evading high tariffs and the imperatives of covert action combine to undermine enforcement of fiscal rules and public order; Iran, where subsidized gasoline sells for three cents a liter; Afghanistan, a barely governed territory that includes the remnants of a road network that links Iran, Central Asia, and Pakistan; Central Asian states opened to the world without institutions to govern markets; and linked wars in Tajikistan, Afghanistan, and Kashmir, plus a growing insurgency in the Ferghana Valley in Uzbekistan.[3]

This economy developed in response to the demands of warlords for resources and of the Afghan people for survival in a country devastated by more than twenty years of war. Illicit activities have become key elements of its people's survival strategies. Though most elements of this war economy had developed before the rise of the Islamic Movement of Taliban, the consolidation by that group of its "Islamic Emirate of Afghanistan" over most of the country has suppressed localized predation, enabling this group to realize what Collier and Hoeffler call "economies of scale" in looting as the war economy has grown.[4] Depending on both decisions by the Taliban and international policy, this development could prove a prelude to state building, with potential for more legitimate governance and development, or to a more rapidly expanding criminalized economy under a stigmatized leadership.

This illicit economy is not confined to Afghanistan. Through the development of an Afghan diaspora linked to neighboring societies, the opening of borders, and absence or corruption of customs enforcement in many areas, the Afghan war economy has generated a pattern of regional economic activity and associated social and political networks that compete with and undermine legal economies and states. This regional economy is in turn linked through the drug and arms trade to globalized crime.[5] Transformation of this war economy is thus essential not only to Afghanistan but to neighboring regions and the world.

Stages of the War Economy's Development

Before the outbreak of war in Afghanistan in 1978, a gradually expanding, foreign-supported state coexisted with a rural sector based on subsistence agriculture and pastoralism. The Communist coup of April 1978, the Soviet invasion of December 1979, and the reaction to these by the United States, Pakistan, Saudi Arabia, China, and others destroyed this system. Both sides of the war depended on military technology and cash provided by foreign sponsors. The pipelines for arms and humanitarian aid supplied capital to build up regional smuggling networks.

After the Soviet withdrawal in February 1989, both Soviet and Western aid decreased, and both ended with the dissolution of the USSR at the end of 1991. Regional powers (mainly Pakistan, but also Iran and Russia) stepped in, but local commanders and some returning refugees pursued new survival strategies in a context of highly fragmented power and no effective central state.[6] Predation by commanders, opium cultivation by peasants, and smuggling to Pakistan and elsewhere constituted adaptations to this high-risk environment.

Predation by commanders imposed heavy costs on commerce, blocked Pakistan's access to Central Asia, and prevented consolidation of an Islamic or any other order. Hence a coalition of Pakistani authorities, Afghan and Pakistani traders, and ultraconservative Afghan and Pakistani religious leaders created the Taliban. The Taliban, a transnational movement benefiting from social capital created in madrasas (Islamic academies) in the Afghan-Pakistan border areas during fifteen years of Afghan dispersion, managed by 1998 to consolidate control over nearly all the country's roads, cities, airports, and customs posts, thereby drastically lowering the cost and risk of transport and consolidating Afghanistan's position at the center of a regional war economy.

Prewar Economy, State, and Society

In the 1970s Afghan society was split between a rural, largely subsistence economy and an urban economy dependent on a state that in turn drew most of its income from links to the international state system and market. About 85 percent of the population lived from the rural economy. As late as 1972, the cash economy constituted less than half of the total.[7] Government expenditure consumed less than 10 percent of the whole, and in the 1960s foreign aid accounted for more than 40 percent of the budget. When aid declined, it was replaced by exports of natural gas from northern Afghanistan to the Soviet Union. Such rentier incomes continued to finance nearly half the budget.[8] Urban society depended on state redistribution. After the introduction of a state-led development model in the mid-1950s, the private sector was largely confined to trade, and the government controlled most urban employment.

Changes in the role of women, including voluntary unveiling, and women's secular education and professional employment were entirely urban phenomena dependent on the state sector. They were decreed by the highest (male) leadership of the state in order to implement a (lightly) imposed vision of modernization. The subsequent collapse and loss of legitimacy of the weakly modernizing state also meant the weakening of the institutional support for women's public roles.[9]

Soviet Occupation and Politically Dependent War Economy

During the Soviet occupation (1979–1989) a number of new phenomena emerged:

—Dependence of competing leaders on opposing flows of politically motivated military assistance;
—Dependence of the population for subsistence on politically motivated
humanitarian aid;
—Destruction of the rural subsistence economy through counterinsurgency;
—Forced urbanization, including internal displacement to Afghan cities and
the flight of millions of mainly rural refugees to camps and cities in Pakistan and Iran;
—Creation of refugee-warrior communities in Pakistan and Iran and of a
regionwide Afghan diaspora; and
—Rapid monetization of the economy.

On one side, the state's dependence on foreign aid and sales of natural gas became even more pronounced, but aid came exclusively from the Soviet bloc. While the state lost access to much of the countryside, more of the swollen urban population came to depend on it. By the Soviet withdrawal, nearly all of Kabul's food and fuel was donated by the USSR and distributed by the govern-ment through coupons. As men under government control were enrolled in the war effort, women's civilian roles expanded.

A different culture of dependency developed on the other side. Food produc-tion fell by half to two-thirds as Soviet counterinsurgency devastated the rural economy.[10] This destruction not only impoverished the rural population but weakened the elites whose power depended on control of rural resources. Much of the rural population fled to Pakistan and Iran, where it entered monetary economies. Islamic parties recognized by Pakistan's Directorate of Inter-Services Intelligence (ISI) as recipients of U.S.- and Saudi-supplied military assistance acted as gatekeepers for distribution of international aid.

In these communities, as well as in rural areas of Afghanistan, patriarchal strictures on women were retained or reinforced. These restrictions resulted from male reaction to both the insecurities of life in exile and reforms associated with the disaster that had overtaken the country.[11]

The infrastructure of support for the resistance poured cash into several social networks. Before reaching its intended beneficiaries, both military and humani-tarian aid passed through many international, Pakistani, and Afghan intermedi-aries, some of whom skimmed off cash and resold arms and commodities. These resources provided capital to expand smuggling and other businesses. While the

Pakistani military delivered arms to mujahidin parties in its own trucks, private teamsters moved the supplies to the border region and into Afghanistan. Many of these trucks were already active in Pakistani-Afghan smuggling derived from violations of the Afghan Transit Trade Agreement (ATTA). Under this agreement, listed goods can be imported duty-free in sealed containers into Pakistan for onward shipment to landlocked Afghanistan. Many if not most of the goods were instead sold in smugglers' markets (bara bazaars) in Pakistan. During the war the trucks used in this lucrative trade were also leased for arms transport, income from which expanded the capital available for investment in smuggling linked to the ATTA, as well as the growing drug trade.

Soviet Withdrawal: Monetization and the Growth of Predation

Within Afghanistan itself, the main economic actors were the commanders, a group mostly drawn from new elites that benefited from U.S., Pakistani, and Saudi policies of supporting only Islamist parties rather than the nationalist former rulers.[12] When the Soviet withdrawal reduced both military pressure and external aid, however, commanders pursued economic strategies to increase their power, wealth, and autonomy, establishing bazaars and providing local security to traders in return for tribute. They also sought aid from Western or Islamic humanitarian organizations engaged in cross-border assistance from Pakistan. Such aid provided services and employment that increased resources under their control.[13]

The Soviet withdrawal also led to a rapid increase in the Afghan money supply. The Soviet-supported government of Najibullah turned to an expensive policy of "national reconciliation," which included increasing the economic dependence of the population on the state, enlarging the local security forces, and offering political recognition and subsidies to defecting commanders. Just as these policies increased expenditures, the government lost income. Soviet aid declined, and natural gas revenues fell with poor maintenance and ended when the Soviet troops left, along with the technicians who ran the gas fields. The government financed the resulting deficit by printing money. From 1987 to the fall of Najibullah in 1992 the value of banknotes in circulation increased by an average of 45 percent per year. Food prices rose by factors of five or ten. The afghani rapidly lost value against the dollar, trading at one thousand to the dollar or about twenty times the official rate, by the summer of 1991.[14] The destruction of agriculture and trading networks created a food deficit. For several months out of the year Afghans had to rely for food on aid or cash purchases at the new high prices.[15]

Such a situation created tremendous incentives for cash-producing activities, mainly smuggling of consumer goods and opium growing. As early as 1987 roads became more secure, and trade and humanitarian assistance that had previously traveled by pack animal over mountain trails could now go by truck.[16] Trade increased, including the drug trade, the import of goods into Afghanistan, and the transit trade, consisting of the export (smuggling) into the neighboring countries of goods imported into Afghanistan from both Dubai (by air or via Iran) and the Far East (via the trans-Siberian railway and links up to the northern Afghan border). In northeast Afghanistan, the gem trade also financed the war, as diamonds do in Angola, Congo, or Sierra Leone: Ahmad Shah Massoud, the ethnic Tajik commander in northeast Afghanistan who built up the most extensive resistance organization inside the country, controlled emerald and lapis lazuli mines in or near his native valley, Panjshir.[17]

Opium, however, became the main expanding source of cash incomes. Opium can be grown in most parts of Afghanistan, and in some regions the yields are the highest in the world. Opium provides cash not only through sale but through credit and demand for labor. Farmers sell the crop to wholesale traders. When faced with cash flow problems or food deficits, especially in the winter months before the harvest, they can obtain loans from traders under a system of futures contracts called salaam. Finally, the opium harvest requires intensive labor, which provides many landless or land-poor young men with earning opportunities.[18]

The fall of the Najibullah government in April 1992 brought mainly non-Pashtun mujahidin groups to power in Kabul. Led by President Burhanuddin Rabbani but dominated by Massoud as military commander, the Islamic State of Afghanistan failed to establish its power over most of the country's territory. Attacks on Kabul by groups supported by Pakistan kept the capital insecure. Those attacks, combined with the unwillingness of Pashtuns to accept a Tajik-led government, kept it from expanding control beyond the capital and its ethnic base in the northeast. Regional warlords developed fiefdoms.

Kabul remained dependent on international aid and printing money. The UN and international humanitarian agencies stepped in to replace the USSR as the supplier of food to the most vulnerable, but they delivered only about half the amount supplied by the Soviets (120,000 tons versus 250,000 tons of wheat per year). Printing currency remained probably the single most important source of state expenditure. Banknotes printed first under contract in Russia and then by other international companies continued to be delivered to the "government." The resulting devaluation of the afghani and inflation were so severe that the government introduced new currency notes of first 5,000 and then 10,000 afghanis (previously the largest note was 1,000). The former communist ethnic Uzbek warlord of northern Afghanistan, Abdul Rashid Dostum, had his own notes printed after breaking with Rabbani in January 1994. By September 1996, when Kabul fell to the Taliban, the afghani, the official rate of which had been 50 to the U.S. dollar under Najibullah, was trading at 17,800 to the dollar in Kabul. The Dostum afghani was worth even less (25,600/dollar) in Dostum's capital, Mazar-i Sharif.[19]

Though road transport was no longer threatened by Soviet bombing, predation along roadways disrupted trade and the national market that had begun to develop with the construction of a highway network in the 1960s. Each region became increasingly integrated with its neighboring foreign market. The war economy, like the political structure, remained fragmented.

Taliban: Toward Predatory Monopoly/Duopoly

In 1994 a number of changes in Afghanistan and the international environment combined to support the growth of the Taliban. Within four years, as the Taliban gained control over the country's main roads, cities, airports, and customs posts, they implemented a transition from localized predatory warlordism to weak rentier state power based on a criminalized open economy. The opposition, which had formerly included Uzbek, Hazara, and Tajik leaders, shrank to a mainly Tajik core, led by Ahmed Shah Massoud in his northeastern mountain bastion.

The breakup of the USSR raised the economic stakes in Afghanistan and pitted Iran and Pakistan against each other in competition for access to the oil- and gas-rich Central Asian states. Pakistan saw commercial and political connections to Central Asia via Afghanistan as key to the development of "strategic depth" in its confrontation with India. The United States defined an interest in the independence and economic diversification of the Central Asian states, without relaxing sanctions on Iran. Pipelines through Afghanistan would reconcile those often contradictory goals. Various companies, including the U.S.-based UNOCAL in alliance with the Saudi company Delta (whose consortium received U.S. government encouragement) and their rival, the Argentine firm Bridas, began negotiations with the Rabbani government and de facto power holders. Traders chafed at the growing insecurity along the major routes crossing the country.

In their first major operation, in October 1994, Taliban freed a Pakistani trade convoy. Led by Col. Imam, a Pakistani intelligence officer who had played a leading role in supporting the mujahidin, this convoy was headed for Turkmenistan via Kandahar and Herat, along the projected pipeline route. [Col. "Imam," whose real name was Sultan Amin Tharar, became an outspoken Taliban supporter. He was killed by a splinter group of Pakistani Taliban while on a still-unexplained mission in Waziristan in 2010.] When it encountered a checkpoint set up by tribal (Achakzai) militia demanding exorbitant tolls, waves of newly armed Taliban flooded across the border to break the blockade. The convoy rolled on to

Turkmenistan as the Taliban marched into Kandahar.[20] This event was emblematic of what the Taliban themselves see as their main accomplishment—"bringing security"—and provided both a model and an economic basis for their nearly nationwide consolidation.

Overcoming predation poses a collective action problem: each predatory actor benefits, while a larger but diffuse constituency would benefit from suppressing predation.[21] Both social capital that strengthens networks of solidarity and investments or side payments from groups benefiting from the suppression of predation can help overcome the obstacles to collective action. The Taliban both mobilized social capital created in madrasas to create a homogeneous leadership group linked to political networks in Pakistan and used assistance from Pakistan and Saudi governments and traders to build up a military force and buy off opponents.

The years of war had destroyed much of Afghanistan's social capital as communities and institutions were dispersed or destroyed. The prevalence of predatory economic activities reflected the fragmentation of social power.[22] During those same years, however, Afghan rural ulama, especially in the traditionalist south, continued to teach or study in either their rural madrasas, away from the centers of war, or in kindred (and much larger) institutions in Pakistan, largely linked to the conservative Deobandi movement.[23] Thousands of Pashtun refugee boys received the only education available in these schools, funded by Pakistani or Saudi donors.

The links among these madrasa students and teachers provided an effective form of social capital. In response to the crisis of anarchy in southern Afghanistan, a group of teachers and students (taliban) from such madrasas formed a movement to overcome warlordism and corruption. They enjoyed the support of their Pakistani colleagues and could recruit troops from madrasa students in both Afghanistan and Pakistan. They were linked across tribes by their common madrasa background, as well as by subethnic solidarity among Kandahari Pashtuns.

Taliban success, however, also required human capital (training), technology (weapons), and finance. For the strategic reasons described above, Pakistan decided in 1994 to provide such assistance to the Taliban, including military training and advisors. Saudi Arabia also provided funds until June 1998, when it ended aid to the Taliban in a dispute over Bin Laden. Hoping that the Taliban would provide security for pipeline routes, stabilize the country, and further isolate Iran, the United States originally did not object to these policies.

Afghan and Pakistani traders, too, were willing to pay for suppression of predation. These cross-border traders form a coherent, organized group with an interest in ending extortion, and they therefore contributed to the Taliban.[24] The Taliban also assessed them when the need arose.

Taliban officials tell visitors, "You can drive from one end of the country to the other even at night with a car full of gold, and no one will disturb you." This expression is hardly a metaphor. Driving across southern Afghanistan from Kandahar to Farah and back in June 1998, I saw many trucks doing just that, though their cargoes consisted of consumer goods and automotive parts rather than gold. In two days' drive I encountered only three, unobtrusive checkpoints. The greater security provided by Taliban also improved the conditions for the trade in opium.[25]

The expansion of Taliban power led to the elimination of all but the strongest opposition. A bandwagon effect combined with the shift in Pakistani support enabled the Taliban quickly to eliminate rivals in the Pashtun areas of southern Afghanistan. They were then opposed by a coalition of non-Pashtun groups, including Uzbeks, Tajiks, and the Shia Hazaras, supported by Iran, Russia, and Central Asian states. By 1998, however, except for occasional pockets of resistance, only Massoud remained. Massoud's areas included a small though expanding opium-growing area, but he appears to have made more money through printing money and the international marketing of gems.[26]

Collier, Hoeffler, and Söderbom argue that ethnic homogeneity enables insurgent groups to coordinate and prolong civil war.[27] In this case subethnic homogeneity of the leadersip of both armed contenders contributed to their endurance: the Taliban leadership is composed exclusively of Kandahari Pashtuns, while Massoud relies almost entirely on Panjshir Tajiks. The use of ethnic and subethnic solidarity to coordinate military and political action has increased ethnic polarization of Afghan society.

The Contemporary War Economy

The projected oil and gas pipelines have been stymied by the continuing war and the Taliban's harboring of Bin Laden. Today's war economy in Afghanistan consists of the transit trade, the drug trade, the gem trade, service industries stimulated by the growth of the three, and the emission of currency. Foreign exchange earned by exports finances Afghanistan's imports of arms as well as food and other necessities.[28] The Taliban control the transit trade, which seems to be the largest of these sectors. Massoud controls the gem trade. Opium production and trade is expanding in regions controlled by both sides, but in 1999 areas controlled by the Taliban produced 97 percent of Afghanistan's poppy.[29]

Control by the Taliban of most of the main road system has cleared a corridor for the smuggling of duty-free consumer goods from Dubai to Pakistan. Until a ban on international flights from Taliban territory imposed under UN Security Council sanctions on November 14, 1999, some goods were flown directly to

Afghanistan from Dubai (the airline's only international destination). Most goods cross the Persian Gulf by ship to Iran, from where truckers haul them through Afghanistan to Pakistan.[30] This trade complements smuggling into Pakistan under cover of the ATTA. In June 1998 I noted that many of the trucks appeared to be carrying automotive vehicle tires and spare parts rather than the electronic appliances I had heard so much about. I later learned that since automotive parts had recently been eliminated from the list of goods eligible for import under the ATTA, they were being imported to Pakistan by this alternate route.[31]

A World Bank study estimated the value of this trade at $2.5 billion in 1997, the first year after the Taliban capture of Kabul, equivalent to nearly half of Afghanistan's estimated GDP and around 12–13 percent of Pakistan's total trade. After the Taliban capture of most of the north in August 1998, the amount increased, according to diplomats in Central Asia. Naqvi estimates that the Taliban derived at least $75 million in 1997 from taxing Afghanistan-Pakistan transit trade.[32] Although this is a significant income in the context of Afghanistan, it is far less than the amount of Pakistani duties that would be owed on these goods, so that the more indirect contraband route is still profitable.

Before the appearance of the Taliban, Afghanistan was already a major opium producer (Table 2.1). About 56 percent of the poppy crop was grown in the areas of southern Afghanistan that the Taliban captured in the fall of 1994, and

Table 2.1 **Estimated Opium Poppy Cultivation in Afghanistan, 1994–1999**

Year	Hectares cultivated	Opium harvested (metric tons)	Average yield (kg/ha)	Districts with reported poppy cultivation	Hectares cultivated in Taliban areas (percentage of total)[a]
1994	71,470	3,416	48	55	(56)[b]
1995	53,759	2,335	43	60	65
1996	56,824	2,248	40	63	65
1997	58,416	2,804	48	60	93
1998	63,674	2,692	42	73	94
1999	90,983	4,581	50	104	97

Notes: [a] Taliban control at time of planting. [b] There was no Taliban control at time of planting in 1994. This figure is the percentage planted in provinces controlled by the Taliban in 1995.

Sources: United Nations International Drug Control Program, Afghanistan Program (UNDCP). (1998a). Annual opium poppy survey 1998. Islamabad: UNDCP. United Nations International Drug Control Program, Afghanistan Program (UNDCP). (1999a). Annual opium poppy survey 1999. Islamabad: UNDCP.

39 percent was grown in eastern Afghanistan, which they took two years later. These remain the principal opium-growing areas, though poppy has also spread to new regions.[33]

Two main factors affect the amount of opium grown in Afghanistan. First, the total has tended to rise through diffusion of a profitable technology and the decrease in risk afforded by Taliban "security."[34] Second, production fluctuates around the trend as a result of weather and price changes, creating a "cobweb" cycle typical of unregulated agricultural commodities. Rains and floods damaged much of the crop in 1998, leading to high prices and indebtedness that encouraged increased production in 1999. Combined with good weather conditions, this resulted in a record crop estimated at 4,581 tons, or about 75 percent of global production. This in turn led to a drop in price and higher labor charges, which may lead to cutbacks in planting for 2000.[35]

Afghans, including the Taliban, earn relatively little from this crop. Superprofits in the global drug market derive from the risk premium of marketing an illegal commodity in wealthy societies. Producers and marketers of the raw material share in these profits only if they develop vertical integration through to the retail markets, as the Colombian cocaine cartels did in the 1980s.[36] Afghan opium traders, however, generally sell only to the border. A few are involved as far as the Persian Gulf, but not in the lucrative retail markets.[37]

Within Afghanistan, while opium growing and trading involves economic risk, neither the Taliban nor their opponents treat these as criminal activities, and there is consequently neither a high risk premium nor violent competition for markets. The opium trade in Afghanistan is by and large peaceful and competitive.[38] In eastern Afghanistan the market is more centralized, with higher markups between the farmgate and bazaar prices than in the south.

The UN Drug Control Program estimates that the 1999 bumper crop was worth $183 million at the farmgate at harvest prices.[39] In 1998, when prices were higher for a smaller crop, the markup from the farmgate to the border was in the vicinity of 50 percent.[40] Processing, of course, can be more profitable. It appears that opium from eastern Afghanistan is processed into heroin in border laboratories controlled by the Pakistan-based Afridi tribe, while there is less processing, and often only into morphine base, in the south.[41] There are also reports of heroin being flown out of the country on private aircraft, by Arabs to the Persian Gulf, or by the Russian mafia to Central Asia, but no information is available about the economic value of such transactions.

It is difficult to estimate how much revenue the Taliban derive from this trade. Growers pay the Islamic tithe (ushr) at the farmgate on opium and other produce, mostly in kind. Less consistent reports indicate that the Taliban also levy zakat (Islamic taxes often collected in mosques) of 20 percent on traders in opium and opium derivatives. Some evidence indicates that this zakat is collected only in the south, not in the east, where Taliban control is less stable.[42] A very rough estimate would be that ushr (which seems to be used for local expenses, not the war effort) might amount to up to $15 million in 1999, while zakat of 20 percent on remaining opium in the south (60 percent of the total) marked up by 50 percent (the border price) would total about $30 million. These rough calculations indicate that Taliban may raise less revenue from opium trade than the transit trade. How much they might derive from taxing trade in morphine base and heroin remains an open question, though most processing seems to occur outside Afghanistan, and the Taliban have destroyed some heroin laboratories.

The transit and drug trades are complemented by service industries, such as fuel stations, shops, and tea houses. Much of the fuel is smuggled from Iran, where its subsidized price is approximately $0.03 per liter, less than a soft drink. The official budget in Kabul (which does not include military expenses) seems to be paid for by direct foreign aid from Pakistan (Rs. 500 million or about $10 million in 1998), and a few taxes from Kabul itself. Until late 1998 the Taliban also received direct financial assistance from Saudi Arabia, which provided subsidized fuel, as well as cash grants. These were ended in protest over the Taliban's failure to expel or curb Usama Bin Laden. Bin Laden himself is reputed to have put some of his wealth at the Taliban's service, paying, reportedly, for the capture of Kabul in September 1996.

Though the Taliban control all major branches of Da Afghanistan Bank (the central bank), they have not printed their own money. The Taliban continue to recognize the notes delivered by Russian printers to the Massoud-Rabbani forces, despite their protest against this funding of their enemies and the resulting devaluation of their currency. Taliban banking officials say they recognize the Rabbani currency because they do not wish to undermine national unity by circulating two currencies.[43] In practice, the Taliban would probably have difficulty obtaining professionally printed notes.[44]

Northeast Afghanistan, controlled by Massoud, produces only 3 percent of Afghanistan's opium today. Commanders levy ushr on opium farmers, and at least some local authorities tax opium traders as well.[45] There are a number of heroin refineries, though authorities have destroyed some. Besides the aid he receives, mainly from Iran, and the continued delivery of new Afghan currency, Massoud's main income comes from the gem trade. Since the beginning of the war Massoud taxed trade in lapis lazuli and emeralds, collecting ushr from mine owners and zakat from traders. In 1997, however, Massoud established a monopoly in purchase of the gems and in 1999 signed an agreement with a Polish firm, Inter Commerce, to market them. His aides estimate that, although the trade now brings in $40–60 million per year, the new joint venture might make as much as $200 million in annual income.[46]

The Taliban, like their opponents, are thus not throwbacks to medieval times but actors in today's global economy and society. For the first time in history, ulama dominate political and military life in Afghanistan because of geopolitics and resources made available by globalization. Pakistan, Saudi Arabia, and the United States supplied massive quantities of weapons only to religious parties rather than to Afghan nationalists who might ally with India or challenge Pakistan, while turning a blind eye to the growth of drug trade and other forms of criminality. Meanwhile, factions of the elites educated in Afghanistan's state institutions and in the West and the USSR busied themselves killing, arresting, and exiling each other with the help of foreign powers.

As the educated elite was destroyed, private madrasas offered almost the only education available for Pashtun refugee and rural boys after 1978, since the West did little to provide them with modern education. The madrasa networks accumulated social capital while other institutions were destroyed. The mullahs lost, however, the ties to the landlord-dominated local economy and society that had circumscribed their power. Both the state and the rural economy that had sustained tribal leaders collapsed. The Deobandi ulama became more autonomous in exile and in warlord-dominated Afghanistan, resulting in their becoming more extremist and deracinated. In exile they also became linked to international networks, both political and economic, including Pakistani political parties and intelligence agencies and the Arab Islamists who aided the jihad. Foreign aid, commercial agriculture (opium), and long-distance contraband provides this newly armed elite with the opportunity to mobilize resources to exercise power directly, as it never did before.

The domination of the country by this previously marginalized group has reversed the pattern of social, political, and economic bifurcation developed under the royal regime and intensified under the communists. The capital city is now ruled by a force from the countryside, which has reversed the reforms of past decades. The Taliban attitude toward the state and reforms are not the continuation of some unchanging "tradition," but the result of their own uprooting and trauma of the past twenty years, during much of which a central state dominated by a foreign ideology destroyed the country in the name of progressive reform. The annihilation of the state and the development and reformist agenda it had pursued under several governments has spelled the end for now of the emancipation of urban women through decrees by modernizing male leaders.

Transnational Networks

The Afghan war economy has spread internationally through a variety of social networks. The Taliban themselves are a transnational movement led by Afghans but organizationally present in both Afghanistan and Pakistan through Deo-bandi madrasas and parties. The Taliban recruit from both sides of the border. During the 1999 summer offensive, as many as 25–30 percent of their troops were estimated to be Pakistani volunteers, mostly recruited from madrasas and political groups, not the military. These fighters are often organized in separate groups, as are groups of Arabs and other international supporters. Besides Usama Bin Laden, who still has followers in the Arab world, the Taliban host members of radical Islamist groups from Pakistan, Egypt, Uzbekistan, Algeria, and many other countries. Several groups engaged in sectarian violence in Pakistan have training camps in Afghanistan, and the Pakistani intelligence (ISI) has used these groups in its "covert" operations in Afghanistan and Kashmir. As a result, as Pakistan confronts a severe economic and political crisis, it faces thousands of madrasa students who have returned after fighting for the Taliban, eager to establish a similar regime in Pakistan.

The religious and political networks are supported by the transborder eco-nomic networks described above that link traders and Persian Gulf businesses to the Taliban. These in turn have close relations with the local administration in Pakistan, where the goods are sold in smugglers' markets.[47] Given that country's fiscal dependence on customs duties and sales taxes on luxury goods, the tolera-tion of such a large black market contributes significantly to Pakistan's financial crisis.[48] Soon after he took power on October 12, 1999, General Pervez Mu-sharraf halted unlicensed export of wheat to Afghanistan, suspended the opera-tion of the ATTA pending the negotiation of stricter controls, and announced a crackdown on smuggling from Afghanistan. It is unclear, however, if he will suc-ceed in implementing the economic reforms he has announced, as such mea-sures not only are opposed by Pakistani constituencies that benefit from smug-gling but also conflict with an unchanged policy of supporting the Taliban and using Taliban territory as a base for operations in Kashmir.

The economic networks involved extend beyond Afghanistan and Pakistan. Dubai now contains the third-largest urban population of Pashtuns (Karachi is the first and Peshawar the second), and most Afghan industrial and com-mercial capital seems to be invested in the Persian Gulf. These networks made Afghanistan the second-largest trading partner of the United Arab Emirates (along with Saudi Arabia and Pakistan, one of the only three states that recog-nize the Taliban regime). This reflects the purchase of duty-free goods in Dubai by Afghan and Pakistani traders shipping them onward for smuggling into Pakistan.

The drug and arms trade have brought international organized crime into the region. Though over 97 percent of the opium is grown in Taliban-controlled southern and eastern Afghanistan, increasing portions of it are smuggled north-ward in cooperation with the Russian mafia. Russian organized crime groups have sold arms to Massoud and reportedly purchased heroin from traders on all sides. Opium products cross from territory controlled by Massoud into Tajikistan, where some are transported by Russian troops and border guards to Osh, Kyrgyzstan, for transshipment. There are reports that the Russian mafia also flies heroin out of Kunduz, a Taliban-controlled town in northern Afghanistan. Arabs who for years have flown private planes to southwest Afghanistan for hunting expeditions are now also reported to be flying out opium products to the Persian Gulf. Iran has deployed troops and police along the border, where hundreds have lost their lives in clashes with drug smugglers. The money involved in the drug and arms trades is undermining state institutions throughout Central Asia and is also affecting Russia and the Persian Gulf.[49]

Micro Political Economy of Conflict

Socioeconomic conflicts related to the war have also developed at the local level. The collapse and partial revival of the state, the destruction of assets, and the mass displacement and partial return of the population have created a crisis in property relations. The old regime in Afghanistan had established private property in land and pasture and used these regulations in favor of Pashtun nomads and settlers in northern and central Afghanistan. State protection of property in land also made possible absentee landlordism around major cities. Some landlords were better able to afford emigration or were enticed into the regime's program of "national reconciliation," which promised state protection of property and exemption from land reform, while tenants and the landless stayed to fight in the jihad—and for the land of those who sided with the regime.

Nomadic sections of Pashtun tribes such as the Ahmadzai formerly shifted their flocks into the high pasture of Hazarajat in summer. The nomads, whose mobility gave them an additional vocation as traders, also had more access to cash and acted as bankers for the local peasantry, who were often heavily indebted. When the Shia Hazaras revolted against the communists in 1979, they also, in effect, declared autonomy from the Pashtun-dominated Sunni Muslim state. Since that time Pashtun nomads could not use pastures in Hazarajat or collect their debts. Hence a number of the tribes that formerly migrated there have supported the Taliban reconquest of the area. Armed young men from Pashtun nomadic tribes have returned to Hazarajat with the intention of collecting twenty-year-old debts.[50]

Similarly, the fertile steppes north of Hazarajat are inhabited by largely Tajik (therefore Sunni) populations who were also favored by the state against their Shia neighbors. These groups lost land and other assets to the Hazaras over the past twenty years and now form the base of Taliban support in these areas. As

Bamiyan, the center of the Hazara-controlled areas in central Afghanistan, changed hands in early 1999 from the Taliban back to the Shia parties and then back again, Hazaras and local Tajiks engaged in several rounds of burning homes, killing, and expelling populations. This was due as much to local conflicts as to the national one.

Pashtun nomads also lost pasture on the northern steppes, and Pashtun landlords lost control of their agricultural lands in these areas. Landlords around Herat and Kandahar lost control to their tenants. Wealthier landlords were better able to afford the journey abroad and therefore were more likely to become refugees. In such cases local ulama often allotted use of their land to the families of mujahidin or martyrs. As people return from exile, they demand their land back, sometimes taking disputes to Taliban courts. All of these transformations have created a rich field for property and monetary disputes, sometimes connected to ethnic, tribal, or clan conflicts, as well as class.

Political Economy of Peace Making

The war economy makes peace making much harder. Standard international plans for ending civil wars involve negotiating a cease-fire with international monitors; establishing interim power-sharing leading to elections; integrating rebels into government security forces; rebuilding the economy and society under international auspices; and instituting accountability for abuses of human rights. But belligerents negotiate when they are exhausted or reach a stalemate, while continued foreign assistance and the open war economy of Afghanistan assure both sides of resources to continue fighting. Some may in fact prefer continued war that allows them to profit.[51]

Pakistan and Iran both have clear interests in a stable Afghanistan but competing interests in how power should be distributed and exercised. Negotiations between them confront the fact that Pakistan's interest in Afghanistan derives from its quest for strategic depth against India, not from items than can be negotiated with Tehran.

The reestablishment of a weak state in most of the country by one party would in other circumstances favor peace, by establishing a structure into which others could be integrated. Generalized predation plus accountability can develop into taxation and state building. But in this case the two sides do not even agree on which is the government and which the insurgents. The ideology that is a key component of the Taliban's social capital has thus far precluded both genuine power sharing internally and international recognition externally. Their bans on female education and employment as well as their harboring of Usama Bin Laden have made them the target of condemnation and sanctions. Even their genuine accomplishments seem at risk. Accounts of corruption and indiscipline in the ranks grow. Shopkeepers charge that in January 2000 Taliban guards burglarized Kabul's money market, making off with over $200,000.[52]

Furthermore, ending war in Afghanistan might transform the criminalized war economy into an even-faster-expanding criminalized peace economy. Whoever rules Afghanistan, the incentives for misgovernment are nearly irresistible. Only the drug, transit, and gem trades are worth taxing. The rest of the economy is hardly productive enough to recover the cost of governing it. Such a political economy would leave the power holders as unaccountable to most Afghan people as they were under previous regimes. Most of the population would be left to fend for themselves, perhaps in conditions of greater security, but without a development agenda, public services, or reforms, notably in the status of women.[53]

A more challenging alternative would be to consider peace making in Afghanistan as part of a larger problem, of transforming the political economy of a region. It has finally dawned on Europe and the United States that nothing less will work in the Balkans. There is no reason to think that Central and Southwest Asia will be a simpler problem. Even in Europe the rhetoric has outstripped the financing.

The military coup of October 12, 1999, was only a symptom of the deep crisis of Pakistan, whose policies toward Afghanistan arguably threaten that state itself. Pakistan cannot resolve its economic and political crisis without reforms that would also promote peace in Afghanistan, and the country's heavy international indebtedness provides leverage. Pakistan's policy of aiding the Taliban and using Afghan territory to train groups for jihad in Kashmir empowers armed groups guilty of sectarian terrorism and of the hijacking of the Indian airliner in December 1999. It also underwrites smuggling that bankrupts the Pakistani state. If General Musharraf wants to promote public order, he will have to suppress armed groups and move toward law-bound, civic politics. To stabilize the economy, his regime will have to reform the ATTA not in isolation but as part of a general change away from the high duties of an import substitution regime toward the legal institutionalization of the greater openness that exists de facto outside the law. This would reduce the incentive for transit trade, the Taliban's main source of funds. Pakistani businesses could benefit from legitimate trade with Afghanistan and even more from its reconstruction under international auspices. Pakistan should not be offered a financial rescue package if it is not willing to reform its own policies that create and intensify the crisis.

No major institution has started planning for reconstruction of Afghanistan or involved Afghans in thinking about it.[54] Yet a major untapped resource today is the hidden exhaustion of a vast majority of Afghans with the war and a historically unprecedented demand—arising from the people, not the state—for education and development. Starting a serious international process involving Afghan intellectuals and community organizations in planning for a reconstruction that would be conditional on a cessation of hostilities and observance of minimal humanitarian and human rights principles (the right of both sexes to available education and health care) might affect the current dynamic of conflict. Local actors assume that major aid for reconstruction will not be forthcoming, however they behave. It is not surprising that they find it relatively easy to dismiss international professions of concern about Afghanistan and their own behavior.

Aid for reconstruction of Afghanistan should be decided upon and disbursed in such a way as to build reciprocity between state and society and make the former more accountable to the latter. For instance, programs aimed at replacing opium poppies would also have to find alternative sources for financing state activities. The existing economic actors would have to be drawn into alternative forms of activities from which they could realize reasonable profits.

The international private sector could also be involved as a source of funds. Today positions on the proposed pipeline and other potential international investments in Afghanistan are polarized around attitudes toward the Taliban, and the United States has imposed unilateral sanctions on such investment. A more creative solution might find ways to finance the investment while reducing the risk that it would fund war or oppression. Could financing be offered on the condition that the rental income go not to any armed group but to a fund for community development and reconstruction? Airlines crossing Afghan territory on long-distance flights pay fees into a Swiss account managed by the International Air Transport Authority (IATA), which holds them in trust for spending on civil aviation requirements.[55] Perhaps such a fund from pipeline incomes could be administered by an international organization with Afghan participation.

It is virtually impossible to sustain curbs on smuggling in a region with such wide disparities in trade policy. International institutions should work with the regional powers toward something approximating a customs union that would both make legitimate trade more attractive and reduce incentives to smuggling. Greater cross-border cooperation and confidence-building measures with Iran, also undergoing a struggle over reform, might help reduce regional tensions and create a common stake in rebuilding the country.

Opium production presents particularly difficult obstacles. UNDCP's research has begun to outline what would be needed to move away from opium production: crop substitution, the growth of off-farm income opportunities, and the spread of education. These will require massive foreign involvement and investment, and none will be possible without legitimate governance.

Most important is working with Afghans to change the image and role of the state, seen largely as a distant and indifferent if not hostile power. Local power structures that have largely grown up as defensive measures of self-rule to keep the state or power holders away have to be incorporated into official structures of planning and service provision. Afghanistan needs a decentralized governance structure in which provinces and localities receive authority to tax and plan in consultation with local shuras (councils). In the past local societies developed unofficial power structures to shield themselves from the state, rather than participate in it, and the centralizing mentality shared by the Taliban and much of their opposition reproduces that past pattern. Instead, modest local resources under local control could be directed into locally accountable planning processes. The central state will still be needed for provision of basic security and dispute resolution, but a clear division of labor among levels of governance will promote greater accountability over the reconstruction process.

The disintegration of the state paradoxically opens such possibilities, though the criminalized economy has created interests that will resist it. Peace making also has dangers: attempts to exercise economic pressure on Pakistan risk precipitating a worse crisis there. Attempts to weaken or replace the Taliban could easily lead to the return of anarchy and predation and a yet bloodier civil war. But unless peace making can transform powerful economic actors into agents of peace, it will be limited at best to halting fighting in one place before social and economic forces provoke it once again elsewhere in this dangerous region. Without such an effort, spread of both conflict and the regional war economy remains the most likely prospect.

Notes

1. M. Tullius Cicero, "The Fifth Philippic of M. Tullius Cicero Against M. Antonius," in *Cicero Philippics*, trans. Walter C. A. Kerr (Cambridge, MA: Harvard University Press, 1951), V. ii. 5, 260, 261.

2. P. Collier and A. Hoeffler, "Justice-seeking and Loot-seeking in Civil Wars," Washington, DC: World Bank (1999), http://www-wds.worldbank.org/external/default/WDSContentServer/WDSP/IB/2004/03/18/000265513_20040318171154/Rendered/PDF/28151.pdf; P. Collier, "Doing Well out of War," Washington, DC: World Bank (1999), http://siteresources.worldbank.org/INTKNOWLEDGEFORCHANGE/Resources/491519-1199818447826/28137.pdf; K. Holsti, *War and the State and the State of War* (Cambridge: Cambridge University Press, 1995); F. Jean and J. Rufin, *Économie des guerres civiles* (Paris: Hachette, 1996); M. Kaldor, *New and Old Wars: Organized Violence in a Global Era* (Cambridge: Polity Press, 1999); D. Keen, *The Economic Functions of Violence in Civil Wars*, Adelphi Paper 320 (London: Oxford University Press, 1998); W. Reno, *Warlord Politics and African States* (Boulder, CO: Lynne Rienner, 1998).

3. S. Nunn, N. Lubin, and Barnett R. Rubin, *Calming the Ferghana Valley: Development and Dialogue in the Heart of Central Asia*, Preventive Action Reports, vol. 4 (New York: Council on Foreign Relations, 1999).

4. Collier and Hoeffler, "Justice-seeking and Loot-seeking," 3.

5. M. Castells, *End of Millennium, The Information Age: Economy, Society, and Culture*, vol. 3 (Oxford: Blackwell, 1998), 166–65.

6. United Nations International Drug Control Program (UNDCP), *Afghanistan Program, Annual Opium Poppy Survey 1999* (Islamabad: UNDCP, 1999), 1.

7. Barnett R. Rubin, *The Fragmentation of Afghanistan: State Formation and Collapse in the International System* (New Haven, CT: Yale University Press, 1995), 62–75; M. Fry, *The Afghan Economy: Money, Finance, and the Critical Constraints to Economic Development* (Leiden: E. J. Brill, 1974), 135–62.

8. Rubin, *Fragmentation of Afghanistan*, 296–97.

9. N. Dupree, "Afghan Women Under the Taliban," in *Fundamentalism Reborn? Afghanistan and the Taliban*, edited by W. Maley (New York: St. Martins, 1998), 145–66.

10. Swedish Committee for Afghanistan (SCA), *The Agricultural Survey of Afghanistan: First Report* (Peshawar: Swedish Committee for Afghanistan, 1988), 37.

11. For a literary treatment of this process, see S. Majrooh, "End of a Sojourn in the Abode of Refugees: Gul andam [body like a flower], or, The Story of Laughing Lovers," trans. Ashraf Ghani in *Izhda-yi Khudi* (*The Ego Monster*), book 1, vol. 5. Peshawar: Unpublished manuscript, 1984.

12. O. Roy, *Islam and Resistance in Afghanistan* (Cambridge: Cambridge University Press, 1986); Rubin, *Fragmentation of Afghanistan*.

13. G. Dorronsoro, "Afghanistan: des réseaux de solidarité aux espaces régionaux," in *Économie des guerres civiles*, edited by F. Jean and J.-C. Rufin (Paris: Hachette, 1996), 147–88.

14. Rubin, *Fragmentation of Afghanistan*, 153–64.

15. United Nations International Drug Control Program (UNDCP), Afghanistan Program, *Annual Opium Poppy Survey 1998* (Islamabad, 1998), p. ii.

16. SCA, *Agricultural Survey*.

17. F. Chipaux, "Des mines d'émeraude pour financer la résistance du commandant Massoud," Le Monde (Paris), July 17, 1999.

18. United Nations International Drug Control Program (UNDCP), Afghanistan Program, *Strategic Study #1: Analysis of the Process of Expansion of Opium Poppy Cultivation to New Districts in Afghanistan, Preliminary Report*; and *Strategic Study #2: The Dynamics of the Farmgate Opium Trade and the Coping Strategies of Opium Traders, Final Report* (Islamabad, 1998); Annual Opium Poppy Survey 1999; *Strategic Study #3: The Role of Opium as a Source of Informal Credit, Preliminary Report*; *Strategic Study #4: Access to Labour: The Role of Opium in the Livelihood Strategies of Itinerant Harvesters Working in Helmand Province, Afghanistan, Final Report*; and *Strategic Study #5: An Analysis of the Process of Expansion of Opium Poppy to New Districts in Afghanistan, Second Report* (Islamabad, 1999).

19. Data collected by the World Food Program, supplied by Zareen F. Naqvi of the World Bank. In May 1999 the afghani was trading at 42,675/dollar in Kabul and at 94,250/dollar in Mazar.

20. Barnett R. Rubin, *The Search for Peace in Afghanistan: From Buffer State to Failed State* (New Haven, CT: Yale University Press, 1995); W. Maley, ed., *Fundamentalism Reborn? Afghanistan and the Taliban* (New York: St. Martins, 1998); A. Rashid, "Pakistan and the Taliban," in Maley ed., *Fundamentalism Reborn?*, 72–89.

21. Collier, "Doing Well out of War."

22. Rubin, *Fragmentation of Afghanistan*.

23. This movement, named after a town in northern India where conservative ulama established a madrasa in the nineteenth century, was founded to combat Islamic modernism, and in particular, reforms in Muslim education.

24. Rashid, "Pakistan and the Taliban."

25. UNDCP, *Strategic Study #2*.

26. Chipaux, "Des mines d'émeraude."

27. Collier, Hoeffler, and Söderbom, "On the Duration of Civil War."

28. Z. F. Naqvi, *Afghanistan-Pakistan Trade Relations* (Islamabad: World Bank, 1999).

29. UNDCP, *Annual Opium Poppy Survey 1999* and *Strategic Study #5*.

30. In protest against the murder of Iranian diplomats and a journalist by Taliban troops in Mazar-i Sharif, Iran closed the border between August 1998 and November 1999. During that period the goods took a detour via Turkmenistan.

31. Naqvi, *Trade Relations*.

32. Ibid.
33. UNDCP, *Strategic Study #5.*
34. UNDCP, *Strategic Study #1* and *Strategic Study #5.*
35. UNDCP, *Annual Opium Poppy Survey 1999.*
36. Castells, *End of Millennium,* 165–66.
37. UNDCP, *Strategic Study #2.*
38. Ibid.
39. Farmers who sold some of their crops through futures contracts (salaam) received less, while those able to hold the opium could benefit from higher prices during the winter.
40. UNDCP, *Annual Opium Poppy Survey 1999* and *Strategic Study #2.* In southern Afghanistan in 1998, the average farmgate price was about $60 per kilogram, with various qualities selling for as low as $44 and as high as $82, twice the price in eastern Afghanistan. The southern border price was $73–95, with the highest-quality dried opium selling for $126 per kilogram. In 1999 fresh opium prices ranged from $27 to $72 per kilogram throughout the country. See UNDCP, *Strategic Study #2* and *Annual Opium Poppy Survey 1999.*
41. UNDCP, *Strategic Study #2,* 4.
42. B. Torabi, "Entretien avec Mollah Mohammad Omar," *Politique internationale* 74 (1996–97): 141–42; UNDCP, *Strategic Study #2,* 13; and Rashid, "Pakistan and the Taliban." According to sharia, zakat is a tax on wealth levied at 2.5 percent, or one-fortieth. It is unclear on what legal basis the Taliban impose this tax at a much higher rate and on a flow of commerce rather than a stock of wealth. It is unclear if the zakat is assessed on gross income or on profit.
43. Interviews with director of Bank-i Milli Afghanistan, Kandahar and deputy director of Da Afghanistan Bank, June 1998. Both of these officials were graduates of Pakistani madrasas with no economic, commercial, or financial background or experience.
44. The international legal regime for currency printing is complex and decentralized. In controversial cases the few companies that do "security printing" (of currency, passports, and other official documents) look to their host governments, usually their major customers, for guidance. These governments generally use political criteria in giving opinions about such contracts. The major security printers are in the United States, Germany, and France, none of which looks favorably on the Taliban. I thank R. Scott Horton for clarifying these points for me.
45. Anthony Davis and Bernard Frahi, personal communications with author.
46. Chipaux, "Des mines d'émeraude."
47. Rashid, "Pakistan and the Taliban."
48. Naqvi, *Trade Relations.*
49. Nunn, Rubin and Lubin, *Calming the Ferghana Valley.*
50. Bernt Glatzer and Ashraf Ghani, personal communications with the author.
51. Collier, "Doing Well out of War."
52. Agence France-Presse, "Kabul's Money Market Burgled," January 13, 2000.
53. For an analysis of this phenomenon in Africa, see Reno, *Warlord Politics.*
54. The following ideas draw, to an extent that I can no longer identify, on discussions with Ashraf Ghani, taking place over seven years, though I alone am responsible for the specific proposals here.
55. Agence France-Presse, "Kabul's War-Battered Airport Beats the Millennium Bug," June 29, 1999.

3

Arab Islamists in Afghanistan

Political Islam: Revolution, Radicalism

When a group of Muslim Arab immigrants were arrested for bombing New York's World Trade Center on February 25, 1993, investigations into their background pointed to a common link: most had participated in the war in Afghanistan.[1] News organizations seized on tenuous leads to see whether another Pulitzer Prize–worthy scandal might be uncovered. Did the CIA, in its all-out effort to oust the Soviets from Afghanistan, secretly train fanatical Muslim Arab terrorists who had now turned their U.S.-supplied weapons and skills on their former masters? More specifically, in return for services rendered in Afghanistan, had the CIA arranged entry to the United States for the group's spiritual leader, Shaikh Umar Abd al-Rahman, wanted in Egypt for authorizing killings by members of a radical Islamist group called al-Jihad? So charged, among others, President Hosni Mubarak of Egypt.

Similarly, when Saudi Arabia announced that it would execute four young men found guilty of placing a car bomb that exploded at a U.S.-run Saudi National Guard training center in Riyadh in November 1995 (killing five Americans and two Indians), the authorities first produced them on television. There they confessed to the bombing, and three of the four recounted their history of fighting in the Afghan jihad, where they learned both the ideological fervor and military skills they brought home with them.

To the surprise of no one who had followed Afghanistan before six Americans were killed in New York and five in Riyadh, the trail led back to Gulbuddin Hikmatyar, leader of the Hizb-i Islami (Islamic Party) of Afghanistan. Not that Hikmatyar or any other Afghan was even remotely implicated in this or any other act of violence outside of Afghanistan and its neighborhood[2]; and not

---

First published in John L. Esposito, ed., *Political Islam: Revolution, Radicalism, or Reform?* (Boulder, CO: Lynne Reinner, 1997).

that it had not been common knowledge among those who cared that Hikmatyar as well as other Afghan leaders who had not achieved his international bugbear status had been assassinating and terrorizing other Afghans for years; but all of the bombing suspects who had been to Afghanistan seemed to have worked with Hikmatyar's group. As had also been no secret for years, this was the group that had received the largest share of the U.S. and Saudi aid distributed to the mujahidin groups by Pakistan's Directorate of Inter-Services Intelligence (ISI).

U.S. and Saudi support for Islamist organizations that opposed Western policies and that also turned against Saudi Arabia in the 1990–91 Gulf War grew out of the Cold War bipolar view of the world. This view affected all U.S. foreign policy thinking and was especially dominant in the security agencies, particularly the secret ones. Overt support for "right-wing authoritarians" against "left-wing totalitarians" was not so different from covert support for terrorists or Islamic extremists. The standard put-down of critics of this policy (worthy of inclusion in any updated edition of Gustave Flaubert's *Dictionnaire des Idées Reçues*) was, "of course, he is not a Jeffersonian Democrat," implying that anyone who argued against arming political killers was naïve and ethnocentric enough to think that in foreign policy one could collaborate only with eighteenth-century Americans (slave owners, by the way, so perhaps the remark is not as apt as it might be). Hikmatyar and his ilk were even helping us avenge Vietnam by carrying out the supreme Cold War goal: "Killing Russians."[3]

On the other side, some of those ignorant of the situation in Afghanistan who have rushed to condemn a policy they ignored for years have extended their criticism to the whole Afghan resistance movement and the effort to assist it. It is worth remembering that the Soviet occupiers and their Afghan clients employed at least as much terror and violence as their most ruthless opponents.[4] The Afghans, who have suffered from these extremists more than anyone, do not constitute a "terror nation," as a CNN Special Report called it. To the extent that terrorists have found refuge and training in Afghanistan, the blame must go to all those who destroyed that country's fragile institutions, starting with the Soviet Union. Nor does the experience of Afghanistan alone explain violence by some Islamists in Egypt, Algeria, Saudi Arabia, and elsewhere, despite the predictable attempts of ineffective, corrupt, or dictatorial governments to find external scapegoats for their problems.

In some quarters, the undifferentiated image of the "fundamentalist terrorist" seems to be replacing that of the "Soviet-inspired Communist" (or, in Moscow, "American imperialist") as the enemy image of our time. Then as now, wise policy will take into account the real grievances that lead people to follow extremist leaders and will avoid labeling whole groups or nations with catchy slogans. As in the Cold War, simplified bipolar thinking can lead one into dangerous alliances.

International Islamist Links of the Afghan Islamic Movement

The links to the Arab world that contributed to the development of Arab participation in the Afghan jihad were initiated by the Afghan state in its quest for Islamic legitimacy. Afghan rulers feared privately (or poorly) educated ulama attached to tribes as well as ulama educated in British India or subsequently Pakistan because of their penchant for preaching jihad against the government, as a result of either "ignorance" or British/Pakistani gold. Since at least the late nineteenth century, Afghan governments had denounced such movements as "wahhabi," linking them to the anti-Sufi Salafi movement of Muhammad ibn Abd al-Wahhab. They in turn linked "wahhabism" to Britain and Western imperialist interests. Afghanistan's communist president, Najibullah, used identical rhetoric against the mujahidin a century later.[5]

Nonetheless, the government required a corps of competent and loyal ulama to administer the judicial system, whose relation to Hanafi jurisprudence was essential to state legitimacy. It therefore established a faculty of theology at Kabul University in collaboration with Egypt's al-Azhar University.[6] In conjunction with the founding of various faculties, nearly all with foreign sponsorship, Afghans who were to become professors received scholarships to study at the sponsoring institutions. Thus, for example, in the early 1970s, half of the teachers in the theology faculty had degrees from al-Azhar.[7]

In turning to al-Azhar, the regime undoubtedly had in mind the Azhar of, among others, Muhammad Abduh, whose version of Islamic modernism legitimated the same type of rule by secular figures, seemingly Western reforms of customs, the pursuit of modern professions, and the combination of Western, traditional, and Islamic legal sources that the Afghan monarchy sought to promote. A number of prominent figures of the old regime indeed brought exactly such views back from Cairo. Sending students into the turbulent Islamic milieu of Cairo in the 1950s and 1960s, however, inevitably brought the young Afghan scholars into contact with the Muslim Brotherhood and the exciting new writings of the Brotherhood's most charismatic thinker, Sayyid Qutb.

The expansion of the state funded by foreign aid created new elites, who organized political groups. Some of these groups adopted revolutionary ideologies; they sought to seize control of the state in order to transform society. Like revolutionaries elsewhere, they also included many who had studied abroad, an experience that provided a firsthand encounter with foreign models of modernity and a perspective from which to criticize their own society.

Most studies of revolutionary "counterelites" during the Cold War adopted the same bipolar view as the policymakers, equating revolutionaries with communists or leftists, foreign education with "Western" education, and cosmopolitanism or modernization with Westernization. In Afghanistan, however, as in the rest of the Islamic world, Islamic revolutionary ideas (Islamism) competed with Marxism, creating two distinct and opposed tendencies among the disaffected, with different international ties as well.

The Islamic movement in Kabul had roots in the 1950s, when a group of students and teachers at the faculty of theology, including some who had contacts with the Muslim Brotherhood while studying in Egypt, began meeting to study how to refute the arguments put forward by the Marxists on campus.[8] After 1965, as the university expanded rapidly with provincial recruits, a newly invigorated Islamic movement gained influence among students under the name of the Muslim Youth Organization (Sazman-i Javanan-i Musulman).[9] Around the beginning of 1973, the movement began to register its members and formed a leadership shura (council). The first meeting of the shura took place in the home of Burhanuddin Rabbani,[10] then a junior professor of the sharia faculty, who was elected leader and chairman of the leadership council. Ghulam Rasul (later Abd al-Rabb al-Rasul) Sayyaf, also a lecturer at the sharia faculty, was elected deputy leader.[11] All three had studied at al-Azhar. Gulbuddin Hikmatyar, a former student of the engineering faculty, was in jail for having ordered the murder of a Maoist student and was not present at the meeting, but he was to be in charge of political activities together with another jailed activist (since killed). The council later selected the name Jamiat-i Islami (Islamic Society) for the movement.[12] Two-thirds of the members of the Islamic movement's shura and about two-fifths of all the early leaders had advanced Islamic educations.[13] The top three leaders and the official in charge of cultural affairs had all studied at al-Azhar or in Saudi Arabia.

The Islamists had been in contact with the Egyptian Muslim Brotherhood and had regular contact with the Pakistani Jamaat-i Islami, but at first they had no formal links with either.[14] Although their opponents called them "Ikhwanis" (and this was an accurate depiction of their ideology), according to Roy the Egyptian Ikhwan did not organize formal branches outside the central Arab world.[15] The writer who seems to have influenced them the most was Sayyid Qutb, who was executed by Nasser about the time that the Islamic movement began to grow on the Kabul campus. Both Rabbani and Khalis translated his work in the 1960s.[16]

In exile, the Islamists set about their search for foreign aid. In 1974, Rabbani spent six months in Saudi Arabia. The Saudis provided assistance for the first year of exile, probably through the Muslim World League (Rabitat al-Alam al-Islami), but after 1975 and Daoud's shift toward U.S. allies, the Shah's Iran and the Saudis, they stopped their aid.[17]

The programs of Hizb and Jamiat clearly show the influence of Qutb and Mawdudi, particularly in their use of the term *jahiliyyah* (pre-Islamic ignorance or barbarism) to describe Western or communist societies, but neither fully adopted the ideology of takfir, declaring as unbelievers people who are Muslims by customary criteria (Muslim father, profession of the faith, prayer, etc.).[18] Qutb was the first to use this term the way Stalin used the term "revisionist"—as a capital crime.[19] Qutb's views were never adopted by the mainstream of the Ikhwan.

The question for many Islamists in the Arab world, whether to concentrate on the seizure of power from above (à la Lenin) or the Islamization of society from below (à la Gramsci), had little resonance in Afghanistan in the 1980s. Faced with a military occupation by an atheist power, Muslims had to engage in jihad, which in itself Islamicized society. The Islamists were as a whole the least Westernized (or Sovietized) of the Afghan elites. Their education embodied the Islamist slogan "Neither East nor West." Not a single one of them had been educated in the Soviet bloc or in non-Islamic Third World institutions such as the American University of Beirut or Indian universities. Their only significant international ties were with the Islamic ummah.

International Networks: Saudi Salafis, Muslim Brotherhood, Jamaat-i Islami

By the time the Soviets invaded Afghanistan, the Afghan Islamists were already connected to an international network that included both radical Islamists in the Arab world and the U.S. security establishment. The key links at the center of this network were the Saudi monarchy and the Pakistani military regime of Zia ul-Haq, the pillars of U.S. security policy in the Gulf. The development of the Islamic networks in the Afghan war resulted largely from the policies of the United States and these two Muslim states.[20]

The Saudi monarchy's legitimacy rested on its alliance with possibly the most conservative religious establishment in the Islamic world. The rise of the dynasty of ibn Saud consisted of the classic combination of a tribal chief and a charismatic preacher, in this case Muhammad ibn Abd al-Wahhab. Ibn Abd al-Wahhab preached return to the early days of Islam, to the original, former (Salafi) practice of the faith—before Sufism, excessive tolerance for non-Muslims, and other foreign practices had polluted the ummah. The Saudi monarchy claimed that the Quran was their only constitution and based the judicial system on the Hanbali school of jurisprudence, known as the strictest of the four Sunni schools.

Nonetheless, the Saudi use of Islam in international relations was not a pure outgrowth of ideology. It was aimed at two rivals in the Muslim world: secular Arab nationalism, especially in its leftist, anti-imperialist, Soviet-leaning forms (as represented by Gamal Abdul Nasser); and later, the Iranian revolution, which was both revolutionary and Shia.

A principal organization used by the Saudis in this struggle was the Rabitat al-Alam al-Islami, founded in 1962.[21] This organization financed the printing of Qurans and other religious literature; it supported Islamic centers in various parts of the world, including the United States.

At the time the Rabita was founded, the Saudis were engaged in a direct military struggle with Nasser in Yemen, and it is reasonable to suppose that this organization was intended to strengthen their alliance with the Ikhwan there against their common enemy. Although the Brothers' revolutionary and anti-imperialist orientation was anathema to the Saudi monarchy, their opposition to "communism," of which Nasserism was for them only a local variant, made them allies. The evolution of the wing of the Brothers led by Hudaybi and then Talamasani, rejecting Qutb's teaching and favoring a strategy of Islamicizing society from below rather than seizing political power (what Olivier Roy calls "neo-fundamentalism," in distinction from Islamism) fit well with the Saudi strategy.[22] This strategy also made them amenable to Anwar al-Sadat in the 1970s, as he purged Nasserites from the state and attempted to use the Islamists against the leftists on the street and the university campuses. This strategy of Sadat enjoyed the support of Saudi Arabia and the United States.[23] Saudi Arabia, via the Rabita, is thought to have supported Muslim Brotherhood activity throughout the Arab world. In return, the Ikhwan never tried to organize a branch, even clandestinely, in Saudi Arabia.[24] In South Asia, the Saudis supported the Jamaat-i Islami of Pakistan, whose more conservative approach was already closer to their views.

After the Iranian revolution, the Saudis increased their activity as, for the first time, another state contested their position as the leading Muslim state. The jihad in Afghanistan arrived at the right time for this effort, and much of the Saudi effort there must be understood as directed at establishing a militant Sunni Islamist movement, anti-Shia and under their patronage.

In the 1970s, after the OPEC price rises and the division of Pakistan, Pakistan and Saudi Arabia became closer in foreign policy. At the same time, the Jamaat, though deprived of any direct access to the state under the regime of Zulfiqar Ali Bhutto, had been pursuing a policy of recruiting sympathizers in the military. The Pakistani officer corps had been undergoing a social change that replaced the more aristocratic officers recruited and trained by the British for their colonial army (the archetype of which was Ayub Khan) with more-middle-class Punjabis from rural or provincial families, a social group much more amenable to Islamist appeals.[25] One such officer, the chief of army staff, General Zia ul-Haq, seized power in a coup in July 1977. As he sought a way to legitimate his rule, he seized on "Islamization" in the fall of 1979, for which reason he enjoyed the support of the Jamaat. At the same time, the U.S. government (especially after the election of President Ronald Reagan a year later) was eager to build up his regime as a partner to Saudi Arabia both in the Gulf and in resisting the Soviets in Afghanistan.

Under the Nixon doctrine, the United States sought regional partners in the Third World. After the loss of the shah's Iran, a principal regional partner, Saudi Arabia and Pakistan replaced that partner in the region. The Saudi government supported Zia ul-Haq financially (as did the United States); the Saudis also

supported the Rabita, which funded various branches of the Muslim Brotherhood and the Jamaat-i Islami, which in turn supported Zia ul-Haq. These networks were reflected in the cooperation that later developed among the intelligence agencies of the three countries, with the Jamaat as principal local
implementing partner and activists from the Rabita, Muslim Brotherhood, and
other Arab Islamist organizations in supporting roles.

Besides these mainstream groups, the international Islamist movement
included a variety of splinter factions of more extreme orientation. Though they
differed on many counts, they generally accepted one version or another of Qutb's
teaching, including the idea that Muslims were obligated to wage armed jihad
against all regimes that did not fully implement Islam, and that many of those
commonly labeled Muslims were in fact unbelievers or, worse, apostates. There
were at least as many variations on these themes as on the Trotskyite idea of the
degenerate workers' state, and this account cannot do them justice.[26] These
groups' relation to the main Muslim Brotherhood organization varied from country to country; in some they were part of it, in others opposed. The Arab world,
especially the youth of Egypt, generated many such groups in the 1970s and
1980s. In Pakistan, the only kindred group seems to have been the well-established
Ahl-i Hadith, which was much more akin to extreme Salafi teachings (rejection of
the schools of fiqh in favor of direct reference to Quran, Sunna, and hadith, opposition to Sufism and the adornment of tombs rather than working for the seizure of state power). Ahl-i Hadith, which had also received the support of the
Saudi religious establishment for decades, established several madrasas in northwest Pakistan and one (ironically enough in a town called Panjpir, or five pirs) in
Kunar province of Afghanistan. The Afghan Ahl-i Hadith movement later brought
Salafi fighters and money from the Gulf to join the jihad there.[27]

The Arab Role in Aid to the Mujahidin

Once the communists seized power and, later, the Soviets invaded, a far broader
section of the Afghan population supported jihad, whereas under the old regime
the Islamists had been a tiny isolated group. Nonetheless, the more mainstream
nationalist and traditionalist groups failed to form equally effective groups in
the jihad, partly because of the opposition to them by Pakistan (Afghan nationalists had irredentist claims against Pakistan), and partly because aid to the resistance primarily mobilized the international networks described above with
which the Islamists were already articulated. All of these Islamic networks combined with U.S., Pakistani, and Saudi intelligence agencies to form the network
that supported the mujahidin. Arab Islamist volunteers played an important
role in this system; they were not merely incidental or members of a parallel
system.

Of course, just as support for the Afghan resistance crossed the political spectrum in the United States (as shown by the unanimous congressional votes approving aid to the mujahidin), so support for the jihad crossed the Islamic spectrum in the Middle East. Nonetheless, among U.S. personnel involved directly with the Afghan war effort as volunteers (rather than officials), one could note a disproportionate number of right-wingers, ranging from extreme conservatives to a few genuine nut cases. These were the people in the United States who responded most viscerally to an armed struggle against the Red Army. Similarly, among the Arabs and other Muslims who provided various forms of aid to the Afghans, a disproportionate number came from extreme groups who longed for armed jihad and found it in Afghanistan. Both President Anwar al-Sadat and Shaikh Umar Abd al-Rahman supported the mujahidin, but it was the latter who said, "When the Afghans rose and declared a jihad—and jihad had been dead for the longest time—I can't tell you how proud I was."[28]

The Soviet invasion of Afghanistan violated basic norms of international conduct and law, appeared (if deceptively) to pose a threat to the oil resources of the Gulf, and placed the first Muslim state to join the modern state system under the occupation of an avowedly atheist power. The West (led by the United States), the Islamic world (led by Saudi Arabia), and China gave substantial and growing support to the Pakistani effort to aid the mujahidin. Various agencies of the Iranian government also aided Shia mujahidin parties who followed the line of Khomeini.

The Pakistani ISI, which administered the distribution of the aid, insisted on controlling and directing the military operations of the mujahidin. The ISI tried to control military operations through a form of brokerage based on the distribution of weapons to parties and small groups of fighters. This means of control favored those commanders who conformed to Pakistan's military and political goals.[29]

To implement this system of brokerage, the ISI distributed weapons not only for use in operations but also (and in greater quantity) as the reward for carrying them out. For instance, for each plane confirmed downed by a Stinger, the commander responsible received two more missiles.[30] Hence, downing a Soviet plane took at least three missiles: one that was fired and two that were delivered as a reward. And Stingers were the most closely held and strictly controlled weapon. This tactic is the traditional one used in the "tribal" policies of governments; it both corresponded to and stimulated the tribal norm of competing for influence by obtaining resources from external patrons. Together with the equally profligate Soviet aid, this program made Afghanistan into probably the world's largest recipient of personal weapons during the late 1980s and left it by 1992 with more such weapons than India (the world's largest arms importer during the same period) and Pakistan combined.[31]

U.S. aid grew from $30 million in 1980 to more than $600 million per year by 1986–1989. Saudi and other Arab aid matched or slightly exceeded the U.S. share.[32] The Chinese mainly sold weapons to the CIA. The agencies that managed this immense flow of money and arms were the CIA, the ISI, and the Saudi General Intelligence Presidency (Riyasat al-Istakhbarah al-Ammah). The Afghan operation became the single largest program of each of these agencies.

In Saudi Arabia, besides the "official" aid overseen by Istakhbarah (headed by Prince Turki al-Faisal al-Saud), there were several other major aid sources. The Rabita funded many schools and madrasas for refugees, especially those of Hizb-i Islami, for which it supplied many of the educational materials. The Afghanistan support committee headed by Prince Salman bin Abd al-Aziz, governor of Riyadh, funded the Arab volunteers recruited by the Muslim Brotherhood who worked for Sayyaf's party and other groups and went to fight alongside the mujahidin in Afghanistan. Prince Salman's committee may well have funded the volunteers who later blew up the training center in the city he governed. The Islamic Salvation Foundation, created by Usama Bin Laden, who had made billions in construction in Saudi Arabia, provided aid to favored Afghan groups as well as to Arab volunteers. Until breaking with the Saudi royal family over its invitation to U.S. troops in the first Gulf War, Bin Laden worked closely with Prince Turki.[33]

Besides the Saudi sources, other Arabs also gave money. The Salafis in Kuwait were a particularly important source of contributions, either to Sayyaf or to various support committees. The Muslim Brotherhood in its various offices also collected funds, as did many other offices, such as the now notorious Al-Kifah Refugee Center in Brooklyn. The Arab volunteers and the Muslim Brotherhood workers coordinated their activities through several offices. The NGOs working with refugees and in cross-border civilian projects formed the Islamic Coordination Council in Peshawar, headed by Abdullah Azzam, a Palestinian who was assassinated with two of his sons by a car bomb in Peshawar on November 24, 1989. Abdullah Azzam was also described as a "guide to hundreds of Arab Mujahedeen in Afghanistan."[34]

After Abdullah Azzam's assassination, Hizb-i Islami published the following biography as part of his obituary:

> Born in a Palestinian village, Sella Haressiyya, in 1941, Abdullah Azzam completed his early education at his native village. He graduated in theology from Damascus University in 1966 and then joined Al-Azhar University in Cairo to get his M.A. and Ph.D. degrees. He joined the well-known Islamic movement operating throughout the Arab world, Al-Ikhwanul Muslimoon, took part in the struggle against Zionist hegemony, and participated in the 1967 Arab-Israeli war.

After the war he emigrated from the West Bank to Jordan. At the Jordanian University in Amman, he started his professional career as a lecturer of theology. Abdullah Azzam's difficulties increased with every passing day. He became disappointed in his profession, in the political setup of his country, in the Palestinian leadership for their secular attitudes, and in the narrowness of his platform for addressing the Muslim Ummah. In view of this, he may have been relieved rather than grieved when, after one of his usual fights with the authorities, he was dismissed from his University position. He knew it was useless to protest or to try to reverse the decision, as it enjoyed the blessings of higher circles. So he packed up his belongings and departed for Saudi Arabia where he hoped to fare better in his search for a suitable climate for his ideology.

In 1980 while in Saudi Arabia, Abdullah Azzam had the opportunity of meeting a delegation of Afghani Mujahideen who had come to perform Haj. He soon found himself attracted to their circles and wanted to know more about the Afghan Jihad. When the story of the Afghan Jihad was unfolded to Abdullah Azzam, he felt that it was this cause of the Afghan people for which he had been searching for so long. He arranged visits to Afghanistan where his impressions about the Afghan Mujahideen were confirmed beyond doubt. He shifted to Pakistan and started delivering lectures at the Islamic University, Islamabad [this university, where Ramzi Ahmad Yusuf, charged with planning the bombing of the World Trade Center, had a network of contacts, was run by Jamaat-i Islami and funded by Rabita]. He later decided to devote himself fully to the cause of the Afghan people, and settled in Peshawar. . . .

He has participated in Jihad and has helped others to participate with either their services or their financial contributions. He has established the Islamic Coordination Council which includes nearly 20 Islamic organizations working in support of the Afghan Jihad, offering services inside and outside Afghanistan in the fields of education, health, relief, social care, and the like, administered by efficient staff stationed in numerous places in the liberated areas and refugee camps. . . .

Dr. Azzam left behind . . . a Mujahida wife. . . . She has her own Jihad activities in the refugee camps in Pakistan—ten schools and a nursery and a sewing and training center for widows and sisters of Shaheed [martyrs].[35]

With his connections to the Ikhwan, Saudi Arabia, Rabita, and Jamaat-i Islami, Abdullah Azzam embodied the Islamist networks supporting the mujahidin.[36]

These networks were fully incorporated into the aid effort. In 1978, when the Saudis first wanted to resume aid to Afghan opponents of the new communist regime, they approached the Jamaat for guidance and used it as their channel. The military officers who ran the arms pipeline in the ISI and who dominated the Pakistan refugee administration at least in the early years of the war were largely (although not all) militants of Jamaat and supporters of Hizb-Hikmatyar. Throughout the war, Saudi government funds were vital to the purchase of weapons, and private Arab funds became vital for that purpose when the U.S. Congress began cutting back the U.S. contribution after the Soviet withdrawal. From the beginning, private Arab funds (like those from Bin Laden) and Arab volunteers were essential to keeping the system for transporting arms running.

The arms pipeline consisted of three parts.[37] First, the CIA (using Saudi and U.S. funds) bought weapons from China, Egypt, Israel, and elsewhere.[38] Second, once the weapons had arrived in Pakistan, the ISI took custody. They trucked the weapons to the depots controlled by the mujahidin groups in the border region. The CIA paid for these transport expenses through monthly deposits into special accounts in Pakistan.[39] In addition to weapons, the mujahidin needed food, clothing, and other supplies, also paid for from the CIA accounts.

These funds frequently ran short, and only "Arab money saved the system."[40] This money, however, benefited only the Islamist groups integrated into the international networks, not the more nationalist and traditionalist groups who arrived only after the communist coup in April 1978.

Third, it was the responsibility of the parties to distribute the weapons to commanders and oversee their transport into Afghanistan. Transport was left to the private sector.[41] Attempts to build up a centralized supply network would have interfered with the flourishing businesses of both Afghans and Pakistani Pashtuns from the tribal territories who had converted their previous smuggling and trucking operations into far more profitable ones related to the transport of weapons and drugs. The transport of weapons was extremely expensive; in 1986, it cost $15 to $20 per kilogram to move supplies from Pakistan to north Afghanistan, amounting to $1,100 for one mortar or $65 for one bomb. Total transport costs ran to $1.5 million per month.[42] To pay these costs, the Saudi Red Crescent maintained offices in the border regions funded by the Saudi Afghanistan Support Committee. These offices were staffed by Arab volunteers. They gave the Afghan Islamist parties 100 percent of estimated transport costs plus an extra 5 percent for contingencies, while they gave the traditionalist-nationalist parties only about 15 percent of total costs.[43]

The volunteers seemed to have considerable discretion over whom to fund. In the fall of 1986, when Rabbani took time out from leading a mujahidin delegation to the UN General Assembly to meet President Reagan (which Hikmatyar had refused to do the previous year), the volunteers cut off funding for Jamiat's transport for several weeks. They also tried to pressure Jamiat to expel female European medical personnel working in north Afghanistan.

The aid went disproportionately to those parties favored by the Islamist network, and these parties (in particular those of Hikmatyar and Sayyaf) provided training for Islamist militants. To guard against Pashtun nationalism, Pakistan insisted that only religiously oriented parties and leaders could operate on its soil. The Saudis largely treated Afghanistan as a religious issue and deferred to their own religious establishment, which preferred the Islamists, and particularly the Salafis among them. Aid to the Afghan jihad both helped to legitimate the Saudi regime at home and in the Islamic world, and it provided a diversion for activist Islamists who might otherwise have focused their energies on their own country, as, indeed, they later did.

In addition to weapons, the ISI also provided training. Brigadier Yousaf claims that eighty thousand mujahidin passed through courses between 1983, when the program was expanded, and 1987.[44] According to some reports, these training camps also included members of Jamaat and some of the Arab volunteers. Some of the mujahidin parties also set up their own training camps in the border area; both Hikmatyar and Sayyaf commanders appear to have trained Arab, Kashmiri, and other volunteers.

Once the Soviets were gone, many of the less ideological mujahidin considered that jihad was over; they became more concerned with their local rivals and with making money through smuggling, the drug trade, and other activities. They also began to reach accommodation with cotribals or coethnics in the government.[45] Especially after the failed attack on the city of Jalalabad in March–June 1989, they resisted efforts by the ISI and CIA to get them to attack targets in their area. The more "conventional" army of Hikmatyar raised in the refugee camps, especially from the Arab-funded Hizb schools, and the Arab volunteers whose only goal in Afghanistan was to perform jihad, had no such distractions. According to former Pakistan ambassador to the United States Abida Hussein, by the time of the November 1991 offensive against Gardez, Paktia, the vast majority of the "mujahidin" taking part were Arab and other non-Afghan volunteers.[46]

Early in the 1980s, Sayyaf's party was the main one favored by private Arab donors and volunteers. This organization was linked to virtually no social networks in Afghanistan, but its leader spoke excellent Arabic, supported Salafi Islam, and proved adept at raising millions of dollars in the Gulf. Sayyaf had too few commanders for them to figure significantly in any of the available datasets on commanders from the mid-1980s, but the head of the ISI's Afghanistan operation during 1983–1987 claimed that Sayyaf received 17–18 percent of the weapons distributed among the seven parties in 1987. Arabs affiliated with his party distributed large amounts of cash to commanders who would join them.[47] As an opponent of nationalism and supporter of pan-Islamic ideals, Sayyaf strongly supported the participation in the resistance of Arab and other Islamic volunteers, who swelled his ranks and created considerable friction with the Afghan mujahidin. Only the Arab-funded commanders of Sayyaf and, later, the Salafi organization Jamaat al-Dawa paid wages to the mujahidin.[48]

Arab Islamist money was also behind the role of Sayyaf and his party members in mujahidin "interim governments" supported by Pakistan and the United States. When under ISI and U.S. pressure the seven leaders agreed to an "interim government" in June 1988, the list showed considerable deference to Saudi sensitivities, as Saudi princes agreed to pay the "government" $1 million per month.[49] The prime minister was a "Wahhabi," a member of Sayyaf's party. Again, when a Pakistani-convened shura appointed by the seven parties met to choose the Islamic Interim Government of Afghanistan (IIGA) in February 1989, the government it chose resulted from ISI and Saudi manipulation of the shura's electoral process. On the first day of the shura, when the chairman tried to push through a resolution making Sayyaf's deputy the president, the body rose in protest, claiming they did not want a "Wahhabi" president.[50] According to U.S. diplomats, the Saudi intelligence service ultimately spent $26 million during the shura. Others claim that each of the 519 delegates received at least $25,000.[51] Sayyaf finally became prime minister in deference to the Saudis, who promised to fund a conventional "Islamic army" for the government if their sect were adequately represented.[52] For several years afterward, U.S. policy insisted on treating the IIGA as the "most representative group of Afghans," despite the well-known circumstances of its creation.[53]

In the summer of 1989, however, the global strategic situation was changing. As the Soviet threat receded, the U.S. State Department began to challenge the large share of aid that went to Hikmatyar and Sayyaf as well as the sole use of the Peshawar parties as conduits for assistance. In the fall of 1989, a new decision defined the goal of U.S. policy not only as "self-determination" for Afghanistan but as seeking a negotiated political settlement that would lead to the "sidelining of extremists," including Najibullah, Hikmatyar, and Sayyaf. The United States engaged in a two-track policy, beginning a diplomatic dialogue with the USSR on a UN-sponsored political settlement, while trying to improve the military performance of the mujahidin.[54] In an attempt to keep the two tracks from contradicting each other, the United States also decided that no weapons paid for by its funds would be given to Hikmatyar or Sayyaf, who opposed such a settlement. They would mainly go to regional or local military shuras inside Afghanistan.[55] Saudi and other Arab funds, however, took up the slack in aid to the mujahidin "extremists," so this policy made little if any difference on the ground. The operations wing of the CIA, which maintained close links with the ISI and the Saudi Istakhbarah, looked with skepticism if not hostility on the new policy. In practice, the continued U.S. maintenance of the arms pipeline continued to strengthen the Afghan groups that U.S. policy was allegedly aimed at weakening.

During this period, political "unity" of some sort among the mujahidin groups was a major goal of U.S.-Pakistani-Saudi policy. Arab supporters of jihad gained a new role as promoters of unity, especially between the feuding Islamists, Hizb and Jamiat. In July 1989, in the so-called Farkhar Valley or Takhar incident, a Hikmatyar commander captured and killed a group of Massoud's commanders as they were returning from a key strategy meeting. Massoud later captured the commander responsible and hanged him and his brother after a trial by ulama.

Abdullah Azzam traveled to the north after this incident in an attempt to make peace between the two: "He believed that one of the most serious designs of the enemies of Jihad was the conflict between the Hizbi-Islami and the Jamiat-i-Islami resulting in the Takhar incident." He brokered an agreement between Rabbani and Hikmatyar that "was concluded in the night before his assassination."[56] In 1990, after the assassination of Abdullah Azzam, Abd al-Rahman was invited to Peshawar, where his host was Khalid al-lslambouli, brother of one of the assassins of Sadat. Two of Abd al-Rahman's sons participated in a three-hundred-man detachment of the Egyptian al-Jamaat Islamiyyah that fought in eastern Afghanistan's Nangarhar province. On this trip, reportedly paid for by the CIA, Abd al-Rahman preached to the Afghans about the necessity of unity to overthrow the Kabul regime.[57]

Arab Volunteer Fighters

Before the Soviet withdrawal, even though the role of the Arab volunteers in humanitarian aid was common knowledge, and a little investigation revealed how key they were to the logistics svstem, one heard very little about their actual fighting. Usama Bin Laden in an interview said that the Afghans originally told him that they needed only financial assistance, not volunteers. He ascribed his decision to join the fighting to personal religious and political concerns, not the needs of the Afghan effort. He emphasized (as did many of the mujahidin) the personal obligation (fard al-'ain) of every Muslim to participate in jihad as well as the need to prepare himself to defend Mecca and Madina from the "Jews."[58]

By the late 1980s, however, hundreds, then thousands, of Arab youths, largely recruited from the extremist fringes of the Islamic movement, came to Afghanistan to perform jihad. The ISI used Saudi funds to construct a large base for one Sayyaf commander, Mawlawi Arsala Rahmani, near Urgun, Paktika.[59] Hundreds of Arab "mujahidin" trained there.

The Arab volunteers also set up their own training programs and camps in eastern Afghanistan. One, in Jaji, Paktia province, was named Maasadat al-Ansar. It was constructed with the help of Usama Bin Laden and hosted several hundred volunteers from Saudi Arabia, Egypt, Yemen, Syria, Algeria, Libya, and Morocco in 1988. The Arabs were described as working with Hikmatyar and Sayyaf.[60]

In 1989, after the Soviet withdrawal, as mujahidin forces in eastern Afghanistan concentrated in provincial centers and other towns abandoned by the Soviet and regime troops, both foreigners and Afghans became more aware of the presence of Arab fighters. Some stories came from Kunar province, where mullahs trained at the Saudi-funded Ahl-i Hadith madrasa at Panjpir controlled several districts. Northern Nuristan came under the control of Mawlawi Afzal, who founded the Dawlat-i Inqilabi-yi Islami-yi Nuristan (Islamic Revolutionary State of Nuristan), generally called the Dawlat (state). The Dawlat received direct financial support from some Salafi religious groups in Kuwait and Saudi Arabia. There had been no government presence in the area since 1978, however, so the opportunities for becoming either ghazi (a killer of unbelievers in jihad) or shahid (a martyr in jihad) were slim; few if any Arab fighters joined Mawlawi Afzal.

The first widely circulated reports of Arab fighters came from the Kunar River valley in the southern part of the province, which had been the scene of many heavy offensives as the Soviets tried to relieve the isolated garrisons along the Pakistan border, which were supplied by air. Jamil al-Rahman, another Panjpir-educated mullah, from the Safi tribe of Pashtuns, had originally joined Hikmatyar. He left Hizb-Hikmatyar in 1985 to form a strict Salafi party, the Jamaat al-Dawa ila al-Quran wa Ahl al-Hadith.[61] This group was hardly known outside of Kunar until the government evacuated several areas, including the provincial center (Asadabad, known as Chaghasarai in Pashto), which were then overrun by mujahidin in the fall of 1988.

These mujahidin included several hundred Arabs fighting with Jamaat al-Dawa, which Afghans generally referred to as "the Wahhabis." Jamaat al-Dawa set up its own shura, separate from the seven parties; in the summer of 1989, it allied with Hizb, when the latter suspended participation in the IIGA over the conflict with Massoud. JuD took over the principal mosque in the city, where worship was thenceforth conducted according to the rite of Ahl-i Hadith, which differed from the Hanafi traditions.[62] Most notoriously, mujahidin reported that Jamaat al-Dawa applied a version of the takfir doctrine: they treated Afghans living in government-controlled areas as unbelievers to whom Muslims should apply the laws of futuhat (conquest), including execution of adult males who resisted and enslavement of women and children.[63] Stories circulated of video-taped executions of captured members of tribal militia, of rapes, and of captured women being sold in Peshawar and sent to the Middle East. To some extent, Afghans may have been trying to blame offenses committed by a variety of groups on this deviant one, and particularly on the Arab foreigners. Jamaat al-Dawa also opposed accepting aid from non-Muslims[64]; its mujahidin attacked

Western journalists and relief workers, including some traveling under the protection of commanders of Hizb-i islami. Isolating the mujahidin and Afghanistan from any Western contact was a goal they shared with the Arab volunteers.

With extensive support from Saudi and Kuwaiti private sources, Jamaat al-Dawa grew to be even more powerful in the area than the seven parties. Increasing numbers of Arabs came to fight in its ranks. Nonetheless, it soon retreated into preaching orthodoxy rather than pursuing a political strategy—that is, it retreated from "Islamism" to "neofundamentalism."[65] Its militants spent their time knocking down flags and monuments erected over tombs and opposing other "non-Islamic" Afghan customs, often connected with Sufism.

The money supporting this group largely came from the Saudi Afghanistan support committee, but it seems that Prince Salman was not necessarily more aware of where the money was going than Dan Rather was of the tactics of some of his cameramen in Afghanistan. Some Saudis who were concerned that this group was detracting from jihad tried to convince Prince Salman to stop funding it and give the money he collected to Hikmatyar or Rabbani.

The more politically minded Arab mujahidin formed their own groups in eastern Afghanistan or fought with Hikmatyar or Sayyaf groups. Their number at the time of the fall of the Najibullah government in 1992 is usually given as about five thousand. Whereas the Arabs in the Salafi groups seemed largely to come from the Gulf countries, those with Hikmatyar came from the countries with more politicized Islamic movements, including Algerians, Palestinians, Sudanese, and Egyptians. Some came for long periods of time, others for short stints. Some travel agents organized two- or three-week jihad tours, and students could spend their school vacations participating in jihad in Afghanistan. Journalist Jamal Khashoggi reported in 1988:

> "Visiting" Mujahedeen include students and employees who arrive during their summer or annual vacations. More than 500 youths have so far come here as "visitors" from Saudi Arabia and they stayed for two or three weeks, during last mid-year school break. Military training programs are arranged for these visitors in camps like Sada along the Afghan border. After training they move to camps like Maasada and Meeran Shah and usually take part in the night watch and reconnaissance in the company of highly trained personnel.[66]

The conflict in the Islamic world over the approaching Gulf War in late 1990 and early 1991 temporarily weakened the financial support for the Arab volunteers and their sponsors. Open conflict broke out between those groups, such as Jamaat al-Dawa, who were close to Saudi and Kuwaiti Salafis, and those allied with the Muslim Brotherhood and the Islamist takfir groups. The Salafis supported Saudi Arabia, whose invitation to U.S. and other Western forces was opposed by the radical elements of the Afghan mujahidin, in particular Hikmatyar and Sayyaf, the Jamaat-i Islami of Pakistan, key mujahidin supporters in the Pakistani military and ISI, and the other Arab volunteers.[67] As is now widely known, this issue led Usama Bin Laden to turn against the Saudi royal family. The civilian government of Pakistan, along with the nationalists and moderates among the mujahidin, supported the U.S.-Saudi position. The Saudis had made arrangements to transport two thousand Afghan mujahidin to Saudi Arabia to offer symbolic support to the U.S.-led coalition, but the project was repeatedly held up by objections from radical mujahidin groups and Pakistani military officers, including the chief of army staff, General Mirza Aslam Beg. The Saudis at least temporarily cut off funding to Hikmatyar and some other groups, though they started funding them again a few months later. At the local level, the Gulf War broke the alliance in Kunar between Hikmatyar and Jamil al-Rahman. A battle in the summer of 1991 ended in August when an Egyptian gunman assassinated Jamil al-Rahman.

Bin Laden and other leaders of the Arab mujahidin left the region temporarily after the Soviet withdrawal, but some Arab fighters stayed. They came to international attention once again after the security belt around Kabul had been breached during the fall of Najibullah in April 1992. Massoud, Hikmatyar, and other mujahidin started to flow into Kabul, set up checkpoints, and engage in looting. These guerrillas included Arab Islamists. They made even more difficult the problem of negotiating over power sharing with the newly mobilized Shia population of Kabul. During the spring and summer of 1992, Shia mujahidin armed by Iran, who controlled about one-fourth of Kabul city, repeatedly clashed with Sayyaf and other Salafi mujahidin aided by Arab volunteers. By October, hundreds of civilian hostages taken in these clashes in June were still missing.[68]

Until Hikmatyar fled before the new movement of the Taliban (Islamic students) in February 1995, reports continued to circulate of Arabs fighting for him in the battle for Kabul. Sayyaf's group switched sides and allied with Rabbani in January 1993, when Hikmatyar signed an agreement with Hizb-i Wahdat, the unified Shia party sponsored by Iran. Massoud's forces in Kabul repeatedly captured Arabs and Pakistanis fighting for Hikmatyar. In 1993 Massoud circulated videotapes of two Algerian prisoners. In February 1995, his forces captured a nineteen-year-old Palestinian who said he had been recruited by Hizb-i Islami in Saudi Arabia. His original group of recruits included three men from Yemen and two from Saudi Arabia. They all received three months of military training.[69]

The support for these efforts seemed no longer to come from Saudi Arabia or Pakistan (not to mention the United States). Saudi Arabia ended official funding of these networks during the Gulf crisis. After the bombing of the World Trade Center, pressure on Pakistan to shut down the networks intensified. By some reports, the unwillingness of the government of Prime Minister Nawaz Sharif to arrest and deport some of the Arabs was one of the factors leading to his dismissal by President Ghulam Ishaq Khan in April 1993. (Nawaz Sharif was politically allied with the Jamaat at that time, and his director of ISI was a sympathizer of the Islamists.) In early 1994, Saudi Arabia confiscated the assets and revoked the citizenship of Usama Bin Laden, who had settled in Khartoum.

But the networks established under the aegis of these states during the war, now nourished by private donations and the drug trade, continue to function. Veterans of the war in Afghanistan appear to form the core of the Armed Islamic Group in Algeria (the group responsible for the most assassinations), as well as the armed groups of the most extreme Islamists in Jordan, Yemen, Egypt, Gaza, Saudi Arabia, and elsewhere. One of the units of the Palestinian Islamic Jihad Group is now named after Abdullah Azzam.

Besides fighting, Arab NGOs associated with the Islamic Coordination Council are active in relief and reconstruction efforts in many parts of Afghanistan, especially in Jalalabad and Kunduz, where activists are also providing military aid and training to refugees from the Tajik civil war. Their attempts to exclude Western organizations from Afghanistan have led to a number of clashes. Some charge that Arab Islamist extremists were responsible for the killing of two UN expatriates and two Afghan UN employees near Jalalabad and of two UN High Commissioner for Refugees (UNHCR) expatriate staff near Kunduz in February 1993.

Arab Islamists in North Afghanistan and the Tajikistan Conflict

The Arab activity in Kunduz is particularly important, though it does not seem to involve a large number of people. About half of the estimated sixty thousand refugees from Tajikistan who remained in northern Afghanistan by summer 1993 were in the Kunduz area.[70] The Islamic Renaissance Party (IRP) established its exile headquarters in Taluqan, the administrative center of neighboring Takhar province and of Ahmad Shah Massoud's Supervisory Council of the North.[71]

Kunduz has been nominally under the control of a shura dominated by Jamiat and Sayyaf commanders. The governor of Kunduz, Haji Rahmatullah, a member of Jamiat, exercises little real power. The administrative center of the province, Kunduz city, was controlled by Amir Chughai, a commander of Sayyaf's party until his death in fighting during the summer of 1995. Since November 1993, however, control of the city changed hands several times, as the former communist general turned Uzbek warlord, Abdul Rashid Dostum, repeatedly attacked it. Russia and Uzbekistan were anxious to wipe out this base of support for the Tajikistan Islamic resistance.

According to reports in early 1994, the most powerful people in Kunduz were a small group of Arabs who set up an office of the Islamic Coordination Council. They derived their power from the fact that they are the only source of aid for the Tajik refugees and the shura. Those whose nationalities could be identified (by their Arabic accent and dialect) seem to be Algerian, probably members of the Armed Islamic Group.[72] In early 1996, their influence seemed to have diminished, as they had far less money to distribute, apparently because of a crackdown on their fundraising in their homelands.

The Tajik refugees do not receive regular assistance from UNHCR, whose office in Kunduz is staffed only by local employees and occasional UN volunteers. UNHCR withdrew its international staff from Kunduz in early 1993, when guerrillas attacked a UNHCR convoy of refugees moving from Kunduz to rejoin family members in Camp Sakhi, and two staff members were killed. At around the same time, two UNHCR international contract employees and their Afghan driver and translator were assassinated near Jalalabad. UNHCR pulled virtually all international staff out of posts in Afghanistan at that time.

In March 1993, Kunduz shura leader Amir Chughai expelled the Afghan UNHCR team leader from Kunduz city. Thereafter the refugees received assistance only from representatives of Arab Islamist groups. They transported supplies to Kunduz from Peshawar. In early June 1993, one observer stated that the Arabs had not supplied food to the refugees in May, claiming that a new law in Saudi Arabia restricting donations to foreign organizations had dried up their resources. This law aimed at ending the donation of zakat to revolutionary Islamic groups not approved by the Saudi government and was adopted partly in response to the World Trade Center bombing.

Other reports from Kunduz, however, indicated that Arab donations for weapons and military trailing of IRP fighters continued. Perhaps three to five thousand members of the IRP were undergoing military training by Afghan mujahidin in different parts of Kunduz and Takhar. The Arab Islamists are still part of the same network as before, including some political forces in Pakistan. In March and April 1993, General (ret.) Hamid Gul, former chief of ISI, and Qazi Husain Ahmad, leader of the Jamaat-i Islami, visited the IRP headquarters in Taluqan. In 1994, the Russian-supported government of Tajikistan reported capturing a few Arab fighters participating in operations with the Tajik Islamic resistance movement.

The Arab Islamists and their Pakistani supporters also supplied the refugees with a hospital, medicines, housing, and food. They have resisted the intrusion of the UN and Western relief organizations into the area.

Nonetheless, subsequent incidents may hold out some lessons. In November 1993, Médecins Sans Frontières (MSF) returned to Kunduz with support from the Soros Foundation and the European Community Humanitarian Organization to aid Tajik refugees. The Afghan shura welcomed them, and the governor immediately authorized them to work. As soon as they arrived at the hospital, however, they were rudely expelled by an Arab NGO worker, apparently an Algerian from the Islamic Coordination Council. Repeated appeals to the shura were fruitless, as the Arabs were paying all the bills. The Tajik doctors, certainly no "fundamentalists" or Islamists, were also reluctant to work with the MSF staff, for fear that they would lose their Arab funding, which had proven much more dependable than the intermittent presence of Western organizations. After weeks of negotiations, however, Abbas, the Algerian head of the ICC office in Kunduz, agreed to allow MSF to work there after being assured that they would stay for six months and were sincerely trying to give aid, not undermine the Arabs politically. The new policies of the governments of Pakistan and Saudi Arabia restricting the activities of these groups had placed them in some financial difficulties. There were rumors that they were unable to pay some debts to the bazaar.[73] When I visited these same areas in 1996, Western visitors were more welcome, and the Tajik refugee leaders appealed for more external aid, from whatever source.

In this case, a combination of pressure, the offer of an alternative source of aid, and patient negotiation eventually led to an agreement on cooperation. Unfortunately, the main warring Islamist political groups in Afghanistan as well as the Taliban can still collect and use funds without obstacles, and the international community is not providing Afghans with any reliable alternative to the aid provided by the Arab Islamists. Under these circumstances, their influence will inevitably grow in Afghanistan, and perhaps beyond.

Do these groups constitute a threat of terrorism to the whole world? Of course, some of the returning "Afghanis" have been dissatisfied with the moderation of groups at home and have turned to violence.[74] A few who returned to New York bombed the World Trade Center in 1993 and planned other terrorist acts. Some of the returnees to Saudi Arabia bombed the training center in Riyadh and may be responsible for the attack on the U.S. barracks in Khobar in June 1996. The training these militants received in Afghanistan may have made them militarily more effective, though the car bombs used in the attacks were never used in Afghanistan, to the best of my knowledge. The violence in Egypt, Algeria, and elsewhere is due mainly to the political and social blockage experienced by the youths of those countries, not a handful of activists returning from Afghanistan. The principal victims of the extremists among the Afghan Islamists and their Arab supporters remain the people of Afghanistan themselves. Afghans yearn to recover their country for themselves and to end the day when its territory is merely a field for the battles of others.

Notes

1. Much of this chapter has appeared in another form in Barnett R. Rubin, *The Fragmentation of Afghanistan: State Formation and Collapse in the International System* (New Haven: Yale University Press, 1995).
2. Afghan volunteers (ethnic Tajiks) have apparently fought with some Islamic guerrillas in Tajikistan. Hikmatyar also rented one thousand of his fighters from the Jalalabad area to the government of Azerbaijan to help it resist ethnic Armenian forces covertly backed by the Armenian government. In late 1994, Hikmatyar withdrew the fighters in protest when Baku permitted the opening of an Israeli diplomatic mission. Some of the Afghans reportedly joined the fighting in Chechnya rather than return home.
3. I heard this view expressed by government officials myself. For quotations from the late director of the Central Intelligence Agency, William Casey, and U.S. Congressman Charles Wilson (D.-Tex.), see Mohammad Yousaf and Mark Adkins, *The Bear Trap: Afghanistan's Untold Story* (London: Mark Cooper, 1992), 63, 79.
4. Jeri Laber and Barnett R. Rubin, *A Nation Is Dying: Afghanistan Under the Soviets* (Evanston: Northwestern University Press, 1988).
5. The attempt to label Islamic movements "Wahhabi" has a history in late and post-Soviet Central Asia as well. The Tajikistan Islamic opposition is called Wahhabi by the same officials who accuse Iran of supporting it. In a May 13, 1993, interview, officials of the Tashkent municipal government regretted that they had accepted Russian scholars' classification of Islamic movements as Wahhabi. On May 17, 1993, the deputy mufti of Kyrgyzstan, a Naqshbandi from Daghestan, told a U.S. delegation that Wahhabism was started by a British intelligence agent. This is a common theme in Iranian writing on Wahhabism (see Olivier Roy, *L'Echec de L'Islam Politique*, Paris: Editions du Seuil, 1992, 158). The career of "Wahhabism," as a political label for international conspiracy deserves a study of its own. As the Afghan war shows, however, Western powers have indeed at times used militant Islam, including its Salafi varieties, against their opponents.
6. Louis Dupree, *Afghanistan*, 2nd ed. (Princeton: Princeton University Press, 1980), 598.
7. Marvin G. Weinbaum, "Legal Elites in Afghan Society," *International Journal of Middle East Studies* 12 (1980): 48.
8. Sayyed Musa Tawana, "Glimpses into the Historical Background of the Islamic Movement in Afghanistan: Memoirs of Dr. Tawana, Part 4," *AFGHANews* 5 (May 15, 1989): 5ff. Tawana's articles give the views of Jamiat-i Islami on the early years of the Islamic movement (though in a dispute with Rabbani he has since abandoned Jamiat and joined Abdul Rashid Dostum's organization). For a brief summary of its rival Hizb-i Islami's view, see Farshad Rastegar, "Education and Revolutionary Political Mobilization: Schooling Versus Uprootedness as Determinants of Islamic Political Activities Among Afghan Refugee Students in Pakistan" (Ph.D. diss., University of California, Los Angeles, 1991), 112.
9. For a participant's memoir of this period, also from the Jamiat viewpoint, see Mohammad Es'haq, "Evolution of Islamic Movement in Afghanistan, Part 1: Islamists Felt Need for a Party to Defend Islam," *AFGHANews* 5 (January 1, 1989), 5, 8.
10. Ibid., 8; Sayyed Musa Tawana, "Glimpses into the Historical Background of the Islamic Movement in Afghanistan: Memoirs of Dr. Tawana, Part 1," *AFGHANews* 5 (April 1, 1989), 6–7. This article contains a detailed account of the meeting.
11. "Ghulam Rasul," meaning slave or worshipper of the Prophet, was Sayyaf's given name, a common one in Afghanistan. In line with Salafi teachings, he later changed it to Abd al-Rabb al-Rasul, or "worshipper of the Master of the Prophet."
12. Tawana, "Glimpses, Part 4," 5, describes the choice of name. Hizb claims that "Jamiat" was the name only for the professors' association, not the whole movement.
13. For details on the dataset and statistical tables, see Barnett R. Rubin, "Political Elites in Afghanistan: Rentier State Building, Rentier State Wrecking," *International Journal of Middle East Studies* 24 (1992): 77–99; or Rubin, *Fragmentation of Afghanistan*, chap. 4.
14. According to Tawana (ibid.), they chose the name *Jamiyyat* (or Jamiat) for the movement "because it resembled the word 'Jamaat' in the name of 'Jamaat Ikhwan Muslemeen' of Egypt and 'Jamaat Islami' of Pakistan but was also distinct from both."

15. Roy, *L'Echec de l' Islam Politique*, 141–45.
16. Olivier Roy, *Islam and Resistance in Afghanistan* (Cambridge: Cambridge University Press, 1986), 70.
17. Mohammad Es'haq, "Evolution of the Islamic Movement in Afghanistan, Part 4: Life in Exile from 1975 to 1978," *AFGHANews* 5 (February 15, 1989), 6; Roy, *Islam and Resistance*, 76–77.
18. For this use of the term *jahiliyyah*, see *Fishurdah-yi hadaf va mariam-i Jamiyyat-i Islami-yi Afghanistan* [A Summary of the Aims and Program of the Islamic Society of Afghanistan] (Peshawar? n.p., 1978 or 1979?), 8; *Maram-i Hizbi Islami-yi Afghanistan* [Program of the Islamic Party of Afghanistan] (Peshawar? n.p., 1986–87), vi.
19. Hamied N. Ansari, "The Islamic Militants in Egyptian Politics," *International Journal of Middle East Studies* 16 (1984): 140. See also Roy, *Islam and Resistance*, 77–78.
20. As Roy argues more generally (*L'Echec de l'Islam Politique*, 138), "L'évolution de l'islamisme me relève pas seulement de facteurs idéologiques, mais s'inscrit aussi dans les jeux géostratégiques du monde musulman. Il est clair aujourd'hui que l'islamisme n'a pas modifié en profondeur ce contexte géostratégique, dominé par les strategies d'Etats et non par des mouvements idéologiques et transnationaux."
21. Ibid., 148.
22. On these developments, see Gilles Kepel, *Le Prophète et Pharaon: Aux Sources des Mouvements Islamistes*, 2nd ed. (Paris: Editions du Seuil, 1993).
23. Ibid.
24. Roy, *L'Echec de L'Islam Politique*, 142.
25. Stephen P. Cohen, *The Pakistan Army* (Berkeley: University of California Press, 1984), 55–74.
26. Kepel, *Le Prophète et Pharaon*, describes the Egyptian ones in some detail.
27. Roy, *L'Echec de L'Islam Politique*, 152.
28. "Talk of the Town," *New Yorker*, January 10, 1994 (interview by Marianne Weaver). For a similar statement by Shaikh Abdullah Azzam, see Jamal Khashoggi, "Arab Mujahedeen in Afghanistan-II: Masada Exemplifies the Unity of Islamic *Ummah*," *Arab News*, May 14, 1988, 9.
29. For a fuller description, see Rubin, *Fragmentation of Afghanistan*, 196–201.
30. Yousaf and Adkin, *Bear Trap*, 177.
31. Ian Anthony, Agnes Courades Ailebeck, Gerd Hagmeyer-Gaverns, Paolo Miggiano, and Herbert Wulf, "The Trade in Major Conventional Weapons," in *SIPRI Yearbook 1991: World Armaments and Disarmament* (Oxford: Oxford University Press, 1991), 199, 208; Patrice Piquard, "Pourquoi le Chaos Afghan Peut Faire Exploser L'Asie Centrale." *1'Evénement du Jeudi*, January 13, 1993, 7.
32. Yousaf and Adkin, *Bear Trap*, 77.
33. On Bin Laden, see Jamal Khashoggi, "Arab Youths Fight Shoulder to Shoulder with Mujahedeen," *Arab News*, May 4, 1988, 9; and "Arab Veterans of Afghanistan Lead New Islamic Holy War," Federal News Service, October 28, 1994. The former article includes a photograph of Bin Laden inside Afghanistan.
34. Khashoggi, "Arab Mujahedeen-II."
35. "Sheikh Abdullah Azzam Is Martyred," *Mujahideen Monthly* 4 (January 1990): 10–11. Azzam told Khashoggi ("Arab Mujahedeen-II") that it became too difficult to perform jihad in Palestine because of Israeli security measures: "I later searched for another place where I could perform this Ibadah (devotional service) of Jihad. I couldn't find a better place than Afghanistan where the battle is apparently between Islam and atheism. No doubt about it."
36. According to Roy (*L'Echec de L'lsiam Politique*, 150), Azzam considered Muhammad Abu al-Nasr, leader of the Egyptian Muslim Brothers, as his "spiritual guide."
37. Yousaf and Adkin, *Bear Trap*, 97–112.
38. Both China and Egypt manufactured versions of the Kalashnikov rifle and the SAKR ground-to-ground missile. Israel had captured many Soviet-manufactured weapons in Lebanon in 1982.
39. Many of these accounts were in the Bank of Credit and Commerce International.
40. Yousaf and Adkin, *Bear Trap*, 106.
41. Roy, *Islam and Resistance*, 163–64.

42. Yousaf and Adkin, *Bear Trap,* 106.
43. Interview with logistics officer of a traditionalist-nationalist party, Khyber Agency, Pakistan, February 1989. According to a National Islamic Front of Afghanistan (Gailani) commander of Pashtuns in Kunduz province, "In NIFA party there is no transportation cost for mujahedin. . . . Usually weapons of NIFA and Professor Mojaddedi are sold because of this transportation cost" (files of Cash for Food Program, Swedish Committee for Afghanistan, Peshawar).
44. Yousaf and Adkin, *Bear Trap,* 117.
45. For a detailed analysis, see Rubin, *Fragmentation of Afghanistan,* chap. 11.
46. Talk at Columbia University, December 1991.
47. In February 1989, in Nangarhar, I stayed one day with an Ahmadzai nomad commander of NIFA, who recounted how "Arabs" from Sayyaf's party had offered him huge amounts of money to join. "I spit on their shoes," he said. "They think jihad is a business." Later I heard he had taken their money and joined Sayyaf for a while. He subsequently went back to Gailani.
48. In the summer of 1989, when the Kandahar commanders' shura refused to carry out the ISI's plan to attack the city, the ISI brought two commanders from Wardak (an area populated by different Pashtun tribes than those in Kandahar) to carry out the attack. According to one Kandahari, "They paid each of their mujahidin Rs. 500 per day, plus Rs. 50,000 in case of death and Rs. 20,000 in case of injury [Rs. 20 then equaled about $1]. This created a terrible reaction. It was not jihad but a mercenary war. People began to ask themselves, is this still jihad?" (interview, Arlington, VA, May 1990).
49. *The Independent,* September 13, 1988.
50. Interview with several delegates at the shura.
51. Interview with U.S. diplomat in Riyadh, March 20, 1989; Richard Cronin, *Afghanistan After the Soviet Withdrawal: Contenders for Power* (Washington, DC: Congressional Research Service, May 1989), 7.
52. *The Independent,* February 2, 1989.
53. Assistant Secretary John Kelly, Testimony Before the Sub-Committees on Europe and the Middle East and Asia and the Pacific, Committee on Foreign Affairs, House of Representatives, March 7, 1990.
54. For details, see Barnett R. Rubin, *The Search for Peace in Afghanistan: From Buffer State to Failed State* (New Haven: Yale University Press, 1995); and Rubin, "Post-Cold-War State Disintegration: The Failure of International Conflict Resolution in Afghanistan," *Journal of International Affairs* 46 (Winter 1993): 469–92.
55. *Washington Post,* September 9, 1989; *New York Times,* November 19, 1989.
56. "Sheikh Abdullah Azzam Is Martyred," 11, 68
57. "Arab Veterans."
58. Khashoggi, "Arab Youths Fight."
59. Yousaf and Adkins, *Bear Trap,* 182.
60. Khashoggi, "Arab Youths Fight," 9.
61. The name means "Group for the Call to the Quran and People of the Hadith."
62. This created much bitterness among the local Afghan population, as if the Islam for which they had fought and died for more than a decade was not Islamic enough.
63. "Actions of the Pakistan Military with Respect to Afghanistan: Human Rights Concerns," News from Asia Watch, February 27, 1989; this was based on my own reporting from Peshawar and Nangarhar.
64. Hikmatyar has taken this position verbally at times, but in view of the massive aid he received from the United States, Afghans did not take his statements on this subject too seriously.
65. Roy, *L'Echec de l'Islam Politique.*
66. Khashoggi, "Arab Youths Fight."
67. Roy claims that Rabbani supported the Saudis (*L'Echec de l'Islam Politique*). This seems to have been the case when he talked to Saudis and Americans, but he also signed a document opposing the U.S.-led coalition that was issued by a Jamaat-convened international conference in Lahore. Rabbani explained to U.S. diplomats that he had to do so out of Islamic solidarity.

68. *Guardian,* October 14, 1992.
69. Reuters, Kabul, February 10, 1995.
70. The rest were near Mazar-i Sharif, in an area largely controlled by former communist Uzbek militia leader Abdul Rashid Dostum. On Tajikistan see Barnett R. Rubin, "The Fragmentation of Tajikistan," *Survival* 35 (Winter 1993/94): 71–91; and Olivier Roy, *The Civil War in Tajikistan: Causes and Implications: A Report of the Study Group on the Prospects for Conflict and Opportunities for Peacemaking in the Southern Tier of Former Soviet Republics* (Washington, DC: United States Institute of Peace, December 1993). I visited all of these camps (as well as one run by the Iranian Red Crescent Society) in North Afghanistan in January 1996.
71. *Washington Post,* April 29, 1993.
72. Khashoggi ("Arab Mujahedeen-II") reported in 1988 that Massoud had an Algerian assistant. [Massoud's assistant was Abdullah Anas, son-in-law of Abdullah Azam, who in 2013 was living in London and a prominent spokesman against al-Qaeda in Arab media. Abdullah Anas played a role in starting the Saudi Channel for dialogue with the Taliban in 2008.]
73. Interview with MSF doctor, February 28, 1994.
74. Roy, *L'Echec de l'Islam Politique,* 147.

PART TWO

NATION BUILDING LITE

Afghans Can Be Our Allies

As the United States plans an attack against Usama Bin Laden and the Taliban regime that continues to shelter him, we need to recognize that destroying Afghanistan will accomplish nothing. The Soviets, the Islamic militants we once armed, and the Taliban and their Pakistani backers have already done so. About a third of the capital, Kabul, is as ruined as the World Trade Center. Ordinary Afghans have already suffered for years from wartime devastation. Increasing the suffering could fuel more terrorism. A successful American operation against terrorism based in Afghanistan would have to help people there establish a legitimate government and rebuild their country.

Despite the Taliban decision yesterday not to hand over Mr. Bin Laden, the suggestion the day before by the Afghan clerics that he leave the country voluntarily may reveal dissension within the leadership.

After all, Afghans did not join that movement in order to wage war on the United States in defense of foreign terrorists. Rather, they were hoping to address the chaos in their country through the imposition of strict Islamic law. Over time, elements of the Taliban developed close ties to non-Afghan militants, but not all want to destroy Afghanistan on their behalf. A month after the Soviet collapse ended aid to Afghanistan's Communist government, its top military commanders mutinied. Some Taliban commanders may similarly now have their fingers to the wind.

The Taliban's chief sponsor, Pakistan, terrified by the consequences to itself of a possible American attack on Afghanistan, should be using all its resources to induce the Taliban leadership to deliver the wanted men. And we must ensure that our own need to respond to last week's horror does not lead us to take actions that stir up Afghan nationalism that will only bolster the Taliban leadership and the foreign extremists to whom it has given safe harbor.

The United States and its allies must also work with two other focal points of Afghan politics: the United Front, the armed resistance led by Ahmed Shah

---

Originally published in *New York Times*, September 22, 2001.

Massoud until his recent assassination; and exiles working with the former king, Zahir Shah, now in Rome, who are trying to convene a loya jirga, or a traditional Afghan assembly. Together, these two forces combine leaders of all the country's ethnic groups. And individuals within them are trying to work together on Afghanistan's political future.

The United Front's forces are in areas dominated by ethnic minorities, but some now involved with Zahir Shah, including former mujahidin, might also be able to raise troops, including recruits from the predominant Pashtun ethnic group in whose territory Mr. Bin Laden's followers are largely based.

This would require international support. The United States should ask Pakistan to guarantee full freedom of action to Afghan leaders who appear capable of establishing a stable government that will meet minimal international standards. In return, these Afghans should acknowledge Pakistan's concerns by, for instance, settling the two countries' long-standing border dispute. The United States could also accede to Pakistani requests for economic aid and debt relief in exchange for agreeing to these and other conditions, like those relating to American military access.

Simply overthrowing an objectionable government, as the Communists were overthrown in 1992, is not enough. The result then was the anarchy that gave rise to the Taliban and created opportunities for foreign terrorists. This time, the United States and other countries must push for a more stable outcome by planning now for the reconstruction of an Afghanistan governed by legitimate authorities, possibly with the assistance of the United Nations. This would give Afghans a stake they now lack in the global community. It would also allow the new government to secure the country and win the cooperation of local people in rooting out terrorists.

This will take time, but President Bush has said that he intends to win this war against terrorists and those who harbor them, not engage in halfway measures. To do this, he will need Afghan leaders with a sure knowledge of the country and popular support. Historically, those who have invaded Afghanistan have met ignominious ends. Mr. Bin Laden and his allies may hope that they can draw the United States into the same trap that devoured the Soviet Union. If we lash out militarily without a political plan for Afghanistan, they could achieve this. But we can frustrate their hopes if we recognize that the Afghan people can be our firmest allies in this fight.

4

A Blueprint for Afghanistan

For years, those concerned with the suffering and ordeals of the people of Afghanistan found it difficult to gain a hearing in the precincts of "high politics," where security dominated. Afghanistan was defined largely as a "humanitarian emergency" to be treated with charity. Leaders of some neighboring states, especially those from Central Asia, argued repeatedly that the failure to rebuild Afghanistan and provide its people with security and livelihoods threatened the region. Since 1998, an increase in what may, in retrospect, be called relatively small acts of terror traced to the al-Qaeda organization placed Afghanistan on the global security agenda. But the means chosen to address the threat—sanctions against the Taliban combined with humanitarian exceptions, with no reference to the country's reconstruction—showed that those setting the international security agenda had not drawn the connection between the terrorist threats to their own security and the threats to human security faced daily by the people of Afghanistan.

The Afghan people have for more than twenty years faced violence, lawlessness, torture, killing, rape, expulsion, displacement, looting, and every other element of the litany of suffering that characterizes today's transnational wars. Groups aided by foreign powers have, one after another, destroyed the irrigation systems, mined the pastures, leveled the cities, cratered the roads, blasted the schools, and arrested, tortured, killed, and expelled the educated. Statistics are few, but a 1988 study by demographer Marek Sliwinski estimated that "excess mortality," in his phrase, amounted to nearly one-tenth of Afghanistan's population between 1979 and 1987.

Some results of this destruction are summarized in Table 4.1. It shows that by whatever measure of human welfare or security one chooses—life expectancy, the mortality of women and children, health, literacy, access to clean water, nutrition—Afghanistan ranks near the bottom of the human family. But this table shows something else as well. The figures in it are all rough estimates compiled by international organizations. Afghanistan is no longer even listed in

Originally published in *Current History* (April 2002), pp. 153–57.

Table 4.1 **Measures of Human Security in Afghanistan**

Indicators	Afghanistan	South Asia	Developing Countries	Industrial Countries
Human Development Index Rank (out of 174)[a]	169	N/A	N/A	N/A
Pop. % with access to: Health Care (1985-93)[a]	29	65	79	100
Safe water (1990-95)[b]	12(rural 5, urban 39)	77	69	100
Daily calorie supply per capita (1992)[b]	1,523	2,356	2,546	3,108
Infant mortality per 1,000 live births (1993)[b]	165	85	70	N/A
Under five mortality per 1,000 live births (1993)[c]	257	122	101	N/A
Maternal mortality per 100,000 live births (1993)	1,700[d] or 640[e]	469	351	10
Life expectancy at birth in years (1993)[a]	44	60	62	76
Adult literacy rate (%, 1993)[a, b]	28 (men 45, women 14)	48	68	98

Note: All comparative data from other regions are from source (a) above. One indicator of humanitarian emergency in Afghanistan is the collapse of institutions able to produce such statistics. Hence, unlike such presumably better governed countries as Sierra Leone and Burundi, Afghanistan has not been listed in the standard source for such data. UNDP's *Human Development Report*, since 1996.

Sources:
a. UNOCHA, 1996, p. 4; citing UNDP, *Human Development Report 1996*.
b. UNOCHA, 1997, p. 4; citing UNDP, Human Development Report 1997.
c. Ibid.; citing UNICEF, *State of the World's Children Report 1996*.
d. Ibid.; citing Study by UNICEF/World Health Organization, 1996.
e. UNDP, 1997.

the tables of the World Development Report published yearly by the United Nations Development Program, because it has no national institutions capable of compiling such data.

In a widely reprinted 1981 lecture, Professor Amartya Sen compared the records of China and India in food security, particularly in the prevention of famine, and demonstrated a fundamental result: access to information is a chief guarantor of human security. Sen showed that the restrictions placed on freedom of expression by the Chinese government allowed famine to rage unchecked during the Great Leap Forward in the late 1950s, whereas India's freer system more easily halted such disasters.

Afghanistan also faces a challenge of information, but an even more fundamental one than 1950s China: it has no institutions capable even of generating information about the society that could be used to govern it. Over the past two decades Afghanistan has been ruled, in whole or in part, at times badly and at times atrociously, but it has not been governed. Above all, the crisis of human security in Afghanistan is due to the destruction of institutions of legitimate governance. It is as much an institutional emergency as a humanitarian one. Accountable institutions of governance that use information to design policies to build the human capital of their citizens and support their citizens' economic and social efforts and that allow others to monitor them through the free exchange of information are the keys to human security.

The insecurity due to the absence of such institutions and the effect on the population accounts for many threats that Afghanistan has posed. The rise and fall of one warlord or armed group after another is largely the result of the ease with which a leader can raise an army in such an impoverished, ungoverned society. One meal a day can recruit a soldier. No authorities impede arms trafficking, and no one with power has had enough stake in the international order to pay it heed.

The expansion of the cultivation and trafficking of opium poppy constituted a survival strategy for the peasantry in this high-risk environment. Opium cultivation supplied not only income and employment but cash for food security. Before 1978 Afghanistan was self-sufficient in food production, but it now produces less than two-thirds of its food needs. Futures contracts for poppy have constituted the only source of rural credit, and only the cash derived from these futures contracts enabled many rural families to buy food and other necessities through the winter. The ban on opium cultivation by the Taliban during their last year in power met one Western demand, but donors withdrew even the previously meager support for crop substitution, although pilot programs had shown some success. Cultivators and laborers suffered, while the regime continued to profit from unhindered trafficking at inflated prices of stocks remaining from two years of previous bumper opium crops.

The Fruits of Anarchy

The lack of border control, legitimate economic activity, and normal legal relations with neighbors, combined with disparities in trade policy between the free port of Dubai and the protectionist regimes elsewhere in the region, made Afghanistan a center of contraband in all kinds of goods. This smuggling economy provided livelihoods to a sector of the population while undermining institutions in Afghanistan's neighbors.

The lack of any transparency or accountability in monetary policy since the mid-1980s has both resulted from and intensified the crisis of institutions. Governments or factions posing as governments received containers of newly printed currency, which they transferred to militia leaders or other clients to buy their loyalty, bypassing the inconvenience of taxation or nurturing productive economic activity. Several currencies remain in circulation, none of them backed by significant reserves of a functioning bank. The resultant hyperinflation has driven wealth out of the country and contributed to the already bleak prospects for investment. It virtually wiped out the value of salaries paid to government workers, including teachers, undermining the last vestiges of administration and public service, except where international organizations paid incentives to keep people on the job. Since the inauguration of the Interim Administration of Afghanistan on December 22, 2001, government employees have received salaries monthly, thanks to foreign donors, although they have barely met the deadlines.

This is the context in which Afghanistan became a haven for international terrorism. The origins of the problem date to the creation of armed Islamic groups to fight the Soviet troops and the government they had installed. Islamist radicals, mainly from the Arab world, were recruited to join the ranks of the mujahidin. But the Afghans did not want these fighters to stay after the Soviet troops left in 1989. If the people of Afghanistan had been able to rebuild their country and establish institutions of governance, they would have expelled the terrorists, as they are doing today. But in the atmosphere of anarchy and lawlessness, the armed militants were useful to some Afghan groups and their foreign supporters.

The money that could be mobilized by Usama Bin Laden and his networks also played a role. As the Taliban, in particular, became increasingly alienated from the official international aid community, with their various strictures and demands concerning the status of women and other matters, they increasingly turned to this alternative unofficial international community. The financial and military support they received helped cement the ideological and personal ties that grew between the top leadership of the Taliban and al-Qaeda. In an impoverished, unpoliced, ungoverned state with no stake in international society, al-Qaeda could establish bases to strengthen and train its global networks.

That network's most spectacular act of terrorism, on September 11, revealed the dangers of allowing so-called humanitarian emergencies or failed states to fester—dangers not only to neighboring countries but to the world. An American administration that came to power denouncing efforts at "nation building" and criticizing reliance on international organizations and agreements has now proclaimed that it needs to ensure a "stable Afghanistan" to prevent that country from ever again becoming a haven for terrorists. The United States, along with every other major country, has committed itself to supporting the reconstruction of Afghanistan within a framework designed by the United Nations.

"Administration," Not "Government"

The Agreement on Provisional Arrangements in Afghanistan Pending the Reestablishment of Permanent Government Institutions—to give the December 5, 2001, Bonn agreement its full and accurate title—resulted directly from this new level of commitment by both Afghans and major powers. Most reports on this agreement treat it as a peace agreement, like those that have ended armed conflicts elsewhere. But in Bonn the UN did not bring together warring parties to make peace. The international community has defined one side of the ongoing war in Afghanistan—the alliance of al-Qaeda and the Taliban—as an outlaw formation that must be defeated. In Bonn the UN brought together Afghan groups opposed to the Taliban and al-Qaeda, some possessing power and other forms of legitimacy, notably through Muhammad Zahir Shah, the former king of Afghanistan. They set themselves the central task of protecting human security: starting the process of establishing—or, as the Afghans insisted, in recognition of their long history, reestablishing—permanent government institutions.

This agreement thus differs from many others that, as critics have noted, sometimes amounted to the codification of de facto power relations, no matter how illegitimate. This agreement does recognize power especially in the allocation of key ministries to the relatively small group that already controlled them in Kabul thanks to the U.S. military campaign. In most respects, however, the Bonn agreement attempts to lay a foundation for transcending the current rather fragile power relations through building institutions.

The Interim Administration of Afghanistan established by the agreement will include three elements: an administration, a supreme court, and a special independent commission to convene the Emergency Loya Jirga (national council) at the end of the six-month interim period. It also requested an international security assistance force, one of whose major purposes is to ensure the independence of the administration from military pressure by power-holding factions.

The Bonn agreement does not contain a supreme or leadership council composed of prominent persons. Such institutions in previous Afghan agreements gave legitimacy to de facto power holders, including those whom some call warlords, as well as leaders of organizations supported by foreign countries. Some of the discontent with the agreement derives from the fact that it does not give recognition to such leaders. Many Afghans seem to consider this a positive step.

Instead the agreement emphasizes the administration. The term "administration" rather than "government" indicates its temporary and limited nature, but it also emphasizes that the role of this institution is actually to administer—to restore services. The presence of the supreme court as well as measures defining an interim legal system require this administration to work according to law; the chair of this administration, Hamid Karzai, has also emphasized this. Some had hoped that this administration would be largely professional and technocratic in character, and that is certainly true at least of its women members. In Afghanistan as elsewhere, women can usually obtain high positions only by being qualified, whereas men have other options for advancement.

Some little-noticed elements in the agreement are designed to strengthen the ability of the administration to govern through laws and rules and provide for transitions to successively more institutionalized and representative arrangements. The international security assistance force should insulate the administration from pressure by factional armed forces. At the insistence of the participants, the judicial power is described as "independent." The Special Independent Commission for Convening the Emergency Loya Jirga has many features to protect it from pressure by the administration, including a prohibition on membership in both. The Special Representative of the Secretary-General (SRSG) for Afghanistan is also given special responsibility for ensuring its independence.

The agreement confronts the country's monetary crisis by authorizing the establishment of a new central bank and requiring transparent and accountable procedures for the issuance of currency. This measure is partly aimed at ensuring that the authorities will be able to pay meaningful salaries to officials throughout the country, thus reestablishing the administrative structure that has been overwhelmed by warlordism. Appointments to the administration are to be monitored by an independent Civil Service Commission. Although this body will face severe constraints, it is aimed at curtailing arbitrary appointments, whether for personal corruption or to assure factional power. The Civil Service Commission will be supplemented with a formal Code of Conduct, with sanctions against violators. For the first time, the Afghan authorities will establish a Human Rights Commission, which will not only monitor current practice but also become the focal point for the extremely sensitive discussion about accountability for past wrongs. The SRSG also has the right to investigate human rights violations and recommend corrective actions.

The agreement provides for the integration of all armed groups into official security forces. Although this is not what specialists refer to as a "self-executing provision," other measures will reinforce it. The international security force will assist in the formation of all-Afghan security forces. Monetary reforms and foreign assistance to the authorities may enable the latter to pay meaningful salaries to soldiers and police, providing an incentive for them to shift their loyalties from warlords. The latter may become generals, governors, politicians, or businesspeople, as institutions are built and the economy revives.

Whose Afghanistan?

Building these Afghan institutions will constitute the core task of protecting human security in Afghanistan. The agreement provides a framework. But implementation in such a war-torn and devastated society will largely depend on how the international donors and the UN system approach the task of reconstruction.

As donor agencies and nongovernmental organizations rush in, they risk losing sight of the central task: building Afghan institutions owned by and accountable to the people of Afghanistan. The Bonn agreement states that the SRSG "shall monitor and assist in the implementation" of the agreement, but it does not establish a UN transitional administration in Afghanistan. It vests sovereignty in the Interim Administration. The Afghan participants at the meeting scrutinized every provision that provided for international monitoring or involvement to ensure that the new authority would be fully sovereign. The lessons of the past two decades in Afghanistan and elsewhere are that only accountable and legitimate national institutions, although open to the outside world and subject to international standards, can protect human security.

There is a real risk that the actors in the reconstruction market, as they bid for locations in the bazaar that is opening in Afghanistan, may harm, hinder, or even destroy the effort to build Afghan institutions. Donors and agencies seeking to establish programs need to find clients, and it is often easier to do so by linking up directly with a de facto power on the ground. Such uncoordinated efforts have reinforced clientelism and warlordism in Afghanistan for years in the absence of a legitimate authority. Programs must now be coordinated to ensure that they work together to reinforce the capacities and priorities of Afghan institutions. At the January 2002 conference on reconstruction in Tokyo, Chairman Karzai asked the donors to coordinate, and the conference established an "Implementation Group" chaired by the Afghan administration in Kabul to monitor the effort. The group has yet to meet, but bilateral donors and NGOs are already racing to duplicate projects, and Afghan ministers spend so much time traveling abroad and meeting delegations that they have little time for their primary task: reestablishing governance.

The growing international presence, with high salaries and big houses, is already overwhelming the new administration and distorting the economy. Rents for large houses in central Kabul have risen from $100 to $10,000 per month; Afghan NGOs can no longer afford office space in the center of the capital.

When the mujahidin took power in Herat in 1992, the city had ten qualified Afghan engineers working in the municipality. Before long it had only one since the other nine went to work as drivers for UN agencies, where they earned much higher salaries. These are just some examples of how the normal operation of the international aid system can actually deprive countries of the capacities they need.

If the vast sums that seem to be flowing toward Afghanistan are to help reinforce rather than undermine the fragile institutions established in the Bonn agreement, international actors must establish new bodies to monitor and control the disbursements in partnership with the Afghan authorities. The expenditures must follow the priorities they set in consultation with the SRSG, not the multiple priorities set by the agendas of various countries or agencies. The international community may have to sacrifice some of its immediate interests, but as it has learned only too bitterly, it is worth paying a modest price to protect the self-determination and human security of the people of Afghanistan. The international community's own security depends on it.

5

The Politics of Center-Periphery Relations in Afghanistan

WITH HELENA MALIKYAR

The relationship of the central government of Afghanistan to the other units of government is in many ways a proxy for the relationship of state to society. It would not be so if the state were more institutionalized and in control of the territory and population of the country. But the current situation, where the direct administrative control of the government is largely limited to the capital city and environs, and in which the government relies on international support ("foreign" support to its opponents) to exercise that control, has precedents in other eras of Afghan history.

The Bonn agreement, which provides the legal framework for the current government, reinstated the administrative provisions of the Constitution of 1964. Under that constitution Afghanistan is a unitary state administered according to the "principle of centralization." Laws enacted by succeeding governments have divided that unitary state into thirty-two provinces (*wilayat*), three of which were established during the past twenty-five years of conflict. The number of districts (*wuluswalis*) into which these provinces are subdivided has been a matter of controversy, as local authorities claim to have established new districts in a number of locations that the ministry of internal affairs and other authorities do not recognize. Some wuluswalis were further divided into *alaqadaris* (subdistricts), but these became recognized as wuluswalis, apparently during the period of rule by President Rabbani. According to the Minister of Internal Affairs, Ali Ahmad Jalali, the country had 216 legally established wuluswalis before the start

Unpublished paper written for the World Bank (March 2003).
Note: Barnett R. Rubin wrote this paper, drawing extensively on the research and writings done previously by Helena Malikyar. Malikyar deserves credit for much of the research, but Rubin is responsible for all views expressed.

of the conflict; it now has 354. The Independent Commission for Convening the Emergency Loya Jirga identified 383 claimed wuluswalis in the country. The system also includes municipalities and rural municipalities.

The governors, district commissioners, and other officials of this structure are, legally speaking, representatives of the centralized unitary state in their areas, appointed directly by the minister of internal affairs and the president. The provincial and local representatives of other ministries (education, agriculture, water and power, etc.) report directly to their ministries in Kabul. The governor has only a loose coordinating role and does not have executive authority over the representatives of ministries other than interior. There is no provincial budget or system of block grants. Provisions of past constitutions providing for provincial or district councils to participate in decisions about the execution of policy were never implemented. The judicial system was similarly centralized, as the same law applied uniformly in all provinces, and all courts came under the direct authority of the Supreme Court in Kabul.

Even before the past quarter century of conflict, this highly centralized system had very limited reach. The lowest level of territorial administration at which the state was present was generally the district, or sometimes the subdistrict. The widely reported institutions of local self-government and dispute resolution (jirga, shura) had no legal existence; nor did the constitution or legal code mention or recognize the widely used systems of customary law. The villages, in which most people lived, appointed representatives (*malik, arbab*) who represented them in dealings with the *wuluswal* or governor. Government policing did not extend outside of the district center. The base of taxation was extremely small: the government's revenue remained under 10 percent of GDP and came almost entirely from taxes on foreign trade, state monopolies (petroleum, tobacco), sale of natural gas, and foreign aid. Hence the state apparatus barely penetrated the country's economy and in particular hardly taxed at all the predominant activities of agriculture and pasturage, with the exception of a small set of commercial export crops. Social norms dictated that disputes should be settled as much as possible outside official institutions. Even those dissatisfied with the outcome of a jirga or shura might not want to disrupt local social relations or risk the pressure for bribes that came with resort to the official system. Hence the system whose legal framework is now in effect was a highly centralized but weak state, with very limited penetration into the society and scope for policy making or implementation.

The reality of the exercise of power today is quite different. Although the legal administrative subnational unit is the province, of which there are thirty-two, the territorial unit over which powerful figures actually exercise subnational power is the region or zone (*hawza*), of which there are about seven in addition to Kabul. These zones correspond to the old provinces of Afghanistan, which in turn were related to tribal or ethnic identities that have reemerged as transformed units of political identity and mobilization as a result of the war. The monarchy and its successors developed the current framework of territorial administration precisely to divide, weaken, and overpower the tribal and regional forces of these ancient zones, and the reemergence of these units results from the breakdown and weakening of this always fragile superstructure of control.

Political Development of Afghanistan

In analyzing the politics of relations between the center and other levels of government in Afghanistan, it is important to bear in mind the distinction of state and administration. Elements of the administrative structure of Afghanistan have remained relatively stable for centuries. In his memoirs, the *Baburnama*, Zahiruddin Muhammad Babur, who became the first Mughal emperor of India, recounts his journey of conquest and plunder across much of the territory of today's Afghanistan. Throughout his travels he describes the districts through which he passes and characterizes the main sources of revenue in each one. Though Babur led one of a number of roving warrior bands seeking to build states on this territory and neighboring ones, the instability of the state structures contrasted with the stability of the administrative ones, which had been erected during previous centuries of imperial rule. The combination of these districts into provinces and of provinces into emirates, khanates, kingdoms, and empires varied, but the administrative substructure constituted a relatively stable reality for ruler and subject alike.

No one saw the construction of states as a means to express the identity or to protect the rights of those who lived in them. States were organizations through which conquerors exercised control over population and territories. States could create security that enabled merchants to increase wealth, in return for which they paid tribute to the state. The legitimacy of a state and its ruler depended on the degree of justice the ruler delivered, as defined by Islam, but the provision of justice was a duty of the ruler, not a right of the subjects, who were not citizens.

The concept that control of the state constitutes war booty belonging to the victor appears to remain embedded in much of the politics of the region. In today's Afghanistan it is expressed by those among the "mujahidin," especially the Panjshiris in Shura-yi Nazar, who say that they deserve to predominate in the government because they resisted the Soviets, the Communists, and the Taliban and finally prevailed. It explains why they regard sharing power, in however limited a way, as a significant concession. The prevalence of this view should serve to caution observers that those who protest Panjshiri domination may not be democrats, but contenders for capture of that same booty—the state—for other groups.

The term *Afghan* was originally an ethnonym for the people today known as Pashtuns. Ahmad Shah Durrani, the ruler who in 1747 founded the empire from which today's Afghanistan descends, held the title of "King (Padishah) of the Afghans," not "King of Afghanistan." Afghanistan at that time denoted not a state but a territory, the area now known as the tribal region shared by Afghanistan and Pakistan.

The state founded in 1747 was a tribal conquest empire. According to official accounts, the king was elected at a jirga of the tribes of Kandahar, primarily belonging to the Abdali confederation (*wulus*), which was then renamed "Durrani," after a royal epithet. This jirga should not be confused with the loya jirgas established by later rulers as a legitimation device. At that time, the tribes constituted the military force of the empire, and their agreement on a matter was self-enforcing. Led by Ahmad Shah, the tribes formed alliances with other groups and conquered richer revenue-producing areas such as Kabul, Herat, Punjab, Kashmir, and Turkistan (today's north Afghanistan). The state apparatus erected by Ahmad Shah and his successors was a mechanism by which the Pashtun tribes under his command ruled over other territories. It extracted revenues from conquered areas and remitted them to Kandahar (to Kabul, after 1775, when it became the capital). It did not tax the ruling tribes. The ruler constantly struggled to gain autonomy from the tribes by building an army directly dependent on him, often recruited from non-Pashtun groups, and paid for by royal revenues.

This history forms one level of the consciousness of the people of Afghanistan about the role of the state. As recently as 1959, Kandaharis rioted when the government tried to collect land tax from the province. Some Pashtuns, and particularly Kandaharis, view the Afghan state as a mechanism through which a Pashtun-dominated elite should rule over others. Many non-Pashtuns have viewed it the same way and therefore want to transform it. The calls for "federalism" from some quarters largely express this protest.

It would be mistaken to regard the Pashtun character of the state as a manifestation of ethnic politics in the modem sense. The state never attempted to incorporate all Pashtuns into the ruling group, even symbolically. Rulership always resided in a particular lineage: for the first decades after 1747 in the Saddozai lineage of the Popalzai tribe, and thereafter in the Muhammadzai lineage of the Barakzai tribe. These lineages competed, as did various family and clan groups within each lineage. In these battles ethnic considerations were largely irrelevant. Muhammadzais fought Muhammadzais allied with Uzbeks, Tajiks, Ghilzai Pashtuns, or anyone else whose allegiance could be won or bought. The state was never exclusively Pashtun in its composition or staffing, even at high levels, and the idea of ethnic purity would have seemed a nonsensical and useless limitation of the ruler's freedom of maneuver. The state did not attempt to legitimate itself in the name of Pashtun nationalism, culture, or language until the 1930s. Despite the narrow base of rulership, legitimation was expressed through the universal values of Islam, in particular by the role of the king as defender and supporter of the faith and by establishing courts of sharia at least in the major towns.

The major provinces corresponded to regional kingdoms, each consisting of a market center and its hinterlands: Herat, Kandahar, Kabul, and Turkistan (centered on Balkh, then Mazar-i Sharif). The king (amir during 1826–27) generally appointed his brothers or sons as governors to reduce the risk of revolt, but it nonetheless occurred, as tax farmers converted themselves into contenders for rule.

Amir Abd al-Rahman Khan (reigned 1880–1901) converted this military feudal state into one with centralizing absolutist aspirations. He could do so because of the financial and military subsidies he received from the British Empire, which enabled him to break the military power of the tribes and peoples of all regions of Afghanistan, collect taxes from them, and establish a centralized military, administrative, and judicial system. He brought nearly all the Muhammadzais to Kabul, separating them from their tribal base, and named them "Partners of the State" (Sharik al-Dawlat). The state provided them with subsidies and appointed them disproportionately to offices. They thus became a court nobility dependent on the patronage of the amir rather than an independent tribal military power.

Amir Abd al-Rahman Khan established the basic institutional framework of the Afghan state that has now been largely destroyed and that the current government of Afghanistan is trying to reestablish. He kept his family at court and appointed professional administrators and generals rather than family members. Using his coercive apparatus, he penetrated the economy more deeply than subsequent Afghan states did, collecting direct taxes on agricultural produce and land, in addition to the subsidies from British India. He legitimated his absolutist rule through Islam, claiming to be the imam of Afghanistan, who defended the realm of Islam through jihad and enforced sharia, to whom the people therefore owed obedience. He focused rule and legitimation on his person and dynasty, not, as before, on the entire Muhammadzai clan, whose elders agreed not to contest his dynasty's authority.

He conquered the autonomous regions of Hazarajat and Nuristan, converting the latter to Sunni Islam from paganism and enslaving many of the Shia Hazaras. He mobilized Ghilzai and Durrani Pashtuns against each other and exiled many of their khans and elders in an attempt to break down tribal power, but not before he used Pashtun tribal armies to conquer the Hazaras. By his own estimate he crushed forty rebellions and won eight civil wars. He erected piles of skulls on many roadsides and kept the executioners and torturers busy, but he died in his bed and passed his rule uncontested to his son, the first—and so far the last—time that rulership was transferred peacefully and legally in Afghanistan. He did so by suppressing the military-political organizations based in Afghanistan's regions and subjecting the population instead to a hierarchical, centralized, absolutist system of rule.

This version of the centralized system continued until 1928, when a revolt based in the Tajik peasantry north of Kabul ousted King Amanullah Khan, grandson of Amir Abd al-Rahman Khan. Amanullah, Afghanistan's autocratic reformer, had given the country its first constitution in 1923, its first budget, and its first development program. Amanullah Khan's government divided the four large provinces into ten smaller ones, but it also appointed military generals as governors-general (rais-i tanzimiyya) over regional groupings of provinces. [In 2011, with the appointment of presidential confidante Asadullah Khalid as "security coordinator" for the south after the assassination of Ahmad Wali Karzai, President Karzai appeared to be reviving that system.] Reduction of the size of provinces aimed to increase the leverage of the administration and break up the society into more manageable and smaller units, while the governors-general served as troubleshooters, assuring the governors' loyalty to Kabul and adherence to rules.

The constitution of 1923 mentioned "decentralization of power" (ghair-i markazi budan-i qudrat) as one of the principles of the administration, but this seemed to refer to devolution of power to the officer in the field, like the British Indian Civil Service, rather than to the people themselves. Amanullah's attempt to tax the peasantry and the border tribes to finance a program of Westernization and modernization provoked a revolt where opposition to state penetration invoked the symbols of Islam.

The Muhammadzai dynasty (that of Nadir Shah) that ousted the Tajik Amir Habibullah after nine months took a different tack. Again, the state and capital (which was looted) had been captured as booty by a coalition of Pashtun tribes, this time mostly from eastern Afghanistan, since Nadir Shah had entered Afghanistan from British India. These tribes received exemptions from conscription and taxation. They engaged in punitive raids against the Tajik areas north of Kabul, including Panjshir, kidnapping women among other forms of loot. The memories of these raids are alive today and affect perceptions of contemporary politics.

Nadir Shah and his brothers, who acted as regents for Nadir's son Zahir Shah after the former's assassination in 1933 by a partisan of Amanullah Khan, decided to encapsulate rather than penetrate and transform rural society. Until the mid-1950s, they tried to develop state-supported commercial agriculture on newly irrigated lands settled by Pashtuns in north Afghanistan. Cotton was the centerpiece of their strategy, as it was in Soviet Central Asia directly north of Afghanistan. The income from these new crops supported a very modest expansion of state institutions, while direct taxation of the peasantry declined. The administration continued to be centralized, as before, but it ceased its ambitious efforts to penetrate and control the society.

From the mid-1950s, the availability of foreign aid from the Cold War rivals enabled the Afghan government under Prime Minister Daoud Khan to pursue a variation on the strategy of encapsulation. It nationalized the Afghan development bank (Bank-i Milli) and built a new army, educational system, roads, dams, and other development projects with foreign aid. The state, the capital city, and the class of state-educated people who ran the state and lived in the capital greatly expanded as a result, but the direct tax base of the state continued to shrink. As the state expanded, its penetration into rural society under the level of the district actually contracted.

At the same time, a new urban, educated class emerged. New Democracy during 1963–1973 was designed to give them more of a voice in the state they served, but the failure to legalize parties drove many of them underground. The parliament was dominated by local notables and *ulama*, whose main legislative success was the further reduction of taxation of land and flocks. Hence the professional intelligentsia became increasingly frustrated by the power of rural elites who had been weakened but not defeated by the state. During this period the ten provinces of the 1950s were divided into twenty-nine.

The coup d'état by Daoud Khan in 1973 marked the first time that these elites effected a change in power, in their role as army officers and bureaucrats. The communist coup in 1978 was an even more direct seizure of power by one faction of the intelligentsia, since it did not have the cover of being led by a member of the royal family, as in 1973.

Breakdown and Reconfiguration of the State

The attempt by the communists to use the state to transform the society with Soviet backing quickly exposed the weakness of that apparatus. Revolt broke out quickly, but the pattern of revolt is quite significant. The first two regions to escape from state control almost completely were Hazarajat and Nuristan, the last two regions conquered by the Afghan state. Hazarajat became more or less united initially under a Council of Unity (Shura-yi Ittifaq), while Nuristan eventually split into two parts, the Islamic State of Nuristan under Mawlawi Afzal and a less consolidated area.

Although both of these units incorporated districts that remained more or less unchanged, their somewhat amorphous boundaries did not coincide with the provincial ones demarcated by the Afghan state. They corresponded instead to ethnic identities that were identified with geographical homelands. Neither of these units was stable (Hazarajat in particular was torn apart by conflict between Iranian-supported groups and more traditional ones), and neither of them sought independence from Afghanistan. The importance of Nuristanis to the Afghan state elite and of Hazaras in the cities of Kabul and Mazar-i Sharif precluded any such demands. Nonetheless, the establishment of de facto autonomous authorities spanning bureaucratically defined provincial borders created the base for challenging the relations between state and society in Afghanistan. However imperfectly, the administration in these territories represented the identity of those living there, not control by an elite in Kabul.

In 1991, the Republic of Afghanistan under Najibullah recognized the de facto autonomy of Nuristan by creating a new province of that name from districts of Kunar and Laghman. In 1990 Najibullah created the new province of Sar-i Pul from predominantly Hazara districts of Balkh, Samangan, and Jauzjan. In 2003, the Hazara leader (and minister of planning) Muhammad Muhaqqiq was developing plans to separate predominantly Hazara districts of Ghazni, Uruzgan, and Ghor, presumably preparatory to the creation of a predominantly Hazara Central Zone. He has taken these proposals to President Karzai, who initially refused, as such changes would be quite provocative to Pashtuns at this time. [Since this paper for the World Bank was written in 2003, the predominantly Hazara district of Daikundi has been separated from Uruzgan and made a province in its own right.]

Hazarajat and Nuristan are both mountainous areas with few roads or resources and of relatively little strategic value. Hence the communist regime and the Soviet military more or less left them alone. Other areas of the country, however, they managed to keep divided and separated, as long as the Soviet troops were present.

The administration began to collapse in 1979, before the arrival of Soviet troops. Starting with the mutiny of the Herat garrison in March 1979, led by captains Ismail Khan and Alauddin Khan, nearly every major military garrison and many others erupted in revolt, refusing to enforce the regime's programs and repression. Much of the army dispersed or defected to the growing mujahidin revolt, though that revolt proved unable to absorb professional military units or officers. The resultant growth of insecurity and of predation along the highways—a combination of criminal and political activities that were often difficult to distinguish—made the government unable to deliver salaries or operating funds to some provinces and many districts. Many governors and wuluswals lived in Kabul, unable to take up their posts. Local army units often reached accommodation with the local mujahidin: the former stayed in their garrison, while the mujahidin ran the locality, to the extent that anyone did. In addition to the Soviet bombing and indiscriminate offensives, the insecurity and factional fighting that resulted from the collapse of administration and growth of fragmented guerrilla forces also contributed to the refugee exodus.

During this period the Soviets and the Afghan military established a system of zones (hawza), each commanded by a general. Though these generals had no formal role in the civil administration, they developed roles similar to that of the governors-general. It is not clear at this point how this zonal division related to the emergence of regional militia formations, but both reflected a geographical reconfiguration of power.

As the Soviet troop withdrawal proceeded, and especially after it was completed, mujahidin and militia commanders began to develop regional political military formations like those in Hazarajat and Nuristan in different parts of the country. The government, unable to rely on the Soviet troop presence anymore, also used freshly printed money to pay off commanders, whose "tribal" (*qawmi*) militias also exercised regional influence and increasingly came to resemble "mujahidin" units. The major efforts were as follows:

- In 1986 Ahmad Shah Massoud founded the Supervisory Council of the North (Shura-yi Nazar-i Shamali), which originally functioned as a coordinating body for forces mainly affiliated with Jamiat-i Islami and mainly Tajik in northeast Afghanistan. SCN eventually exercised influence over parts of Kapisa, Parwan, Kabul, Kunduz, Baghlan, Balkh, Takhar, and Badakhshan provinces. After the Soviet withdrawal Massoud captured the town of Taluqan, capital of Takhar province, which served as the de facto capital of Shura-yi Nazar's administration in the northeast. This quasi-state included its own armed forces (the core of those now commanded by Defense Minister Muhammed Qasim Fahim) and departments of education, finance, interior, and others. It was mainly funded by foreign aid, the emerald trade, humanitarian assistance, and, perhaps, the drug trade.
- Ismail Khan emerged as the predominant commander of Western Afghanistan. In 1988 he called a meeting of internal commanders from all over Afghanistan, though most of those that came were from the West. Massoud did not attend, which became a point of contention. Through this and similar gatherings Ismail Khan consolidated his influence in the area, though he could not emerge openly as a regional commander until the fall of the Herat garrison in 1992.
- Abdul Rashid Dostum advanced from a security guard at the natural gas fields in his home province of Jauzjan to the commander of the most powerful of the militias of Najibullah's regime, recruiting largely from his own Uzbek ethnic group. This militia defended the security of the road from Hairatan on the Afghan-Soviet (now Uzbekistan) border to the Salang pass, where another militia, composed of Ismaili Hazaras, took over. This road constituted the regime's main supply route and this militia consequently received a high level of support.

- In Kandahar, the commanders were unable to form a common military front, but the ulama established an Islamic court of Baluchistan and Southwest Afghanistan that dealt with the affairs of Afghans in both Pakistan and Afghanistan. In many respects this court rather than the commanders became the most influential body in Southwest Afghanistan. Many of its judges later became officials of the Taliban.

Others had tried and failed to carry out such schemes. The late Abdul Haq, a commander from the prominent Arsala family of the Jabbarkhel clan of the Ahmadzai tribe in Nangarhar province, brother of the late Vice-President Hajji Abdul Qadir, and of the present governor of Nangarhar, Hajji Din Muhammad, tried to extend his influence from Nangarhar to Kabul and form a common front in Eastern Afghanistan. His refusal to destroy the country's essential infrastructure (electric pylons in particular), however, led Pakistan to cut off his assistance. The southeastern provinces of the Pashtun tribal zone remained largely fragmented, though Jalaluddin Haqqani of Paktia presided over a loose tribal shura. He later became an important Taliban commander.

In an attempt to consolidate some of these efforts, major commanders, with support from Pakistan and the United States, held a meeting of a "national commanders' shura" (NCS) in early 1990. In 1989, as the Soviets were leaving Afghanistan, the United States, Pakistan, and Saudi Arabia had supported a gathering in Rawalpindi that chose an Interim Islamic Government of Afghanistan. Commanders inside Afghanistan, though affiliated to the same parties as those that chose the IIGA, largely opposed the move and argued instead that those leading the fighting inside Afghanistan should build a new government. The NCS presented itself as no more than a means of military coordination, but it also embodied a potential state-building project. The shura opposed the attempt to establish the IIGA in Afghanistan through attacks by Pakistan-based Afghan militias, and instead called for the establishment of nine zones, each led by a prominent commander, that would capture provincial outposts and eventually move against Kabul.

The NCS thus proposed a decentralized strategy instead of the centralized, top-down one supported by Pakistan. The zones would each have included several provinces or portions thereof and would have been led by commanders originating in that region. The model of creating a new Afghan state from locally led and organized zones seemed to presage a federation. When one author (Rubin) called the NCS resolution a model for a federal state, however, he learned how sensitive Afghans were to this term. Rubin had used the term in a paper he wrote for the Carter Center in January 1992, and which he sent to Muhammad Eshaq, then editor of *AfghaNEWS*, a Peshawar weekly newspaper representing Ahmad Shah Massoud's views. Today Eshaq is the director of Radio

Television Afghanistan in the Ministry of Information and Culture. Eshaq faxed a lengthy refutation of the charge that this model represented federalism, which he said would be a formula for the division of the country. The NCS was solely an organizational model for military operations, he claimed.

When Najibullah's government split and fell, to be succeeded by the Islamic State of Afghanistan (ISA), the country attained the highest degree of fragmentation. Massoud emerged as the predominant leader in Kabul, but only through constant battles that destroyed the capital, first with Gulbuddin Hikmatyar's Hizb-i Islami and then with his former allies. He continued to rule much of northeast Afghanistan through SCN. Dostum formed an alliance with other regime militias and some mostly Uzbek mujahidin groups to form the National Islamic Movement of Afghanistan (Junbish, NIMA), which predominated in the north, though it fought with elements of SCN over control of Mazar-i Sharif and Kunduz, both of which controlled important bazaars and trade routes. Central Afghanistan was dominated by Hizb-i Wahdat. Ismail Khan dominated the west as "Amir of Herat," and collected the customs revenue from the burgeoning trade with Iran. A shura in Kandahar never pacified the area, and opium growing predominated in the southwest. The southeast was even more fragmented. A shura in Jalalabad exercised a kind of loose dominance over the country's second-largest opium-growing region. Hikmatyar continued to use the east and southeast as staging areas for his attacks on Massoud, though he controlled little territory himself. Thus the country was divided into about eight zones, including Kabul and environs, each reflecting a particular ethnic mix and leadership. Kabul's main income was printing money, as the zones now retained their own customs revenue. It sometimes paid the salaries of officials in some areas, but the continuous issuance of new money had reduced the value of these salaries to almost nothing. The lack of central control over the provinces was also instrumental to the increased freedom of action of the Arab militants in the country, mostly in the eastern and southeast regions. It also made it possible for Usama Bin Laden to return to Afghanistan when he was expelled from Sudan in May 1996.

Although power was fragmented, UN agencies and NGOs attempted to deliver services to people, largely in rural areas. To do so they had to develop a stable method of interaction with the counterparts. The Swedish Committee for Afghanistan, which had pioneered cross-border assistance, had always insisted that local commanders settle their differences before it would deliver aid to the locality. When USAID and the CIA began to deliver cross-border "humanitarian" assistance from Pakistan to Afghanistan, they tried to create a centralized bureaucracy from the staff of the jihadi parties in Pakistan. Most NGOs and agencies, however, developed the SCA model further by telling villages that, in order to receive aid programs, they had to "revive" their traditional "shuras." Several programs of UNDP and UN Habitat focused on both rural and urban community development through collaboration with local shuras. The humanitarian and development agencies viewed these direct links to communities as a way of bypassing a state that they saw as either ineffectual or illegitimate. This tendency grew even stronger under the Taliban. As it has elsewhere, the attempt to use aid as a substitute for politics and community development as a substitute for state building did not succeed. It did, however, strengthen the capacity of some communities to design and implement projects through some sort of participation. This capacity of community self-reliance, which one observes in other situations of state collapse, such as the Democratic Republic of Congo, can make eventual devolution of power more feasible. Such an outcome is probably preferable to a recentralization that once again deprives communities of participation in the country's development.

When these regional power centers emerged, many observers, and some Afghans, saw them as the development of more grassroots forms of political organization that might provide a more effective and accountable alternative to the overly centralized Afghan state. During the period of the ISA, however, when the power of these regional coalitions was at its height, they became identified instead with warlordism, predation, and corruption. Faced with an "infidel" central government supported by the Soviet Union, Afghans had turned to local, tribal, ethnic, and regional alliances for resistance and had attacked the symbols of the central state with weapons received from the United States, Pakistan, Saudi Arabia, Iran, and China. When the mujahidin and militia leaders became identified with the destruction of the capital and predatory rule, sentiment began to shift, it appears, back toward a more centralized form of government. "Strong central government" became the Afghan term for "rule of law," and this sentiment underpinned some of the initial support that the Taliban received.

The brief interim of Taliban rule, under the Islamic Emirate of Afghanistan, represented an attempt at recentralizing the state. Under the ISA the relatively impotent core of state power was held by SCN, that is, in most Afghans' views, by the qawm of Panjshiris. But this qawm never consolidated its hold over the country, as did the Muhammadzais and the dynasties of 'Abd al-Rahman Khan and Nadir Shah. The core of Taliban power was a group of Kandahari mullahs educated in Deobandi madrasas, most of them from rather low-ranking tribal backgrounds. Their link to the network of mullahs enabled them to expand around the country. The weakening by the war of competing elites facilitated their expansion.

Their social linkages, ability to deploy the legitimating discourse of Islam and to use sharia as a tool of rulership, together with the assistance they received from multiple sources in Pakistan (not solely the military) and eventually their Arab allies enabled the Taliban to recentralize power. They expelled the mujahidin and ex-communist warlords, abolished zones, and reconquered the country. Their ability actually to suppress opium cultivation illustrates the reach of their administration. Though they sailed through the Pashtun areas of the country with little fighting, and squeezed Massoud out of Kabul in a pincer movement, their conquest of northern and central Afghanistan was brutal, reprising the massacres of Hazaras carried out by Amir Abd al-Rahman Khan. They reestablished the practice of appointing governors and wuluswals from outside the areas they governed and were able to transfer them. The Taliban army broke up the smaller units based on solidarity groups led by commanders in favor of a more hierarchical system that, unlike any mujahidin or militia units, it could deploy anywhere in the country to concentrate forces against a threat. It also employed some turncoat qawmi units, but these were many fewer than among their opponents.

Initially, the Taliban's expulsion of warlords and imposition of some kind of law, even if a brutal and simple one, won them support, at least in the Pashtun areas. The security of travel that they provided helped reinvigorate commerce, which mostly consisted of transit trade, or smuggling. They collected the customs revenues and remitted them to central control, though they did not seem to practice a very systematic form of record keeping, except where the experienced bureaucrats continued doing what they had done under every regime. In an interview in Kandahar in June 1998, Wakil Ahmad Mutawakkil, who later became the foreign minister of the Islamic Emirate and is now a prisoner of the United States, reportedly near Kandahar, stated, much like Muhammad Eshaq, that federalism as practiced, for instance, in Pakistan was unsuited to Afghanistan, which required a strong, central government. [In 2013 Mutawakkil was living in Kabul as one of a small group of prominent "reconciled" Taliban.] The ideal system he outlined, a highly centralized administration based on Islamic law, resembled a great deal the goal of Amir Abd al-Rahman Khan.

Current Situation

The U.S. and coalition offensive destroyed the Taliban's centralized system. The United States made its first military alliance in Afghanistan with Fahim, who succeeded Massoud as military commander of Shura-yi Nazar after the latter's assassination. The United States also supported other former regional commanders whom Massoud had brought back, in particular Dostum and Ismail Khan. In the south and east, where no single leader stood out, the United States supported some of the same commanders as in the past, including Hajji Abdul Qadir, whose brother, Abdul Haq, was executed by the Taliban and whose family had led the Jalalabad shura during 1992–1996; and Gul Agha Shirzai, who had been governor of Kandahar for part of that period and whose father, Hajji Abdul Latif, had been a commander of the National Islamic Front of Afghanistan and the Barakzai tribe in Kandahar.

The resurrection of the same regional commanders and warlords defeated and expelled by the Taliban created a situation in the provinces similar to 1992–1996. The major difference was at the center. Massoud had decided not simply to treat the state as war booty if he ever retook it, but instead to seek broader alliances, in particular with the former king, Zahir Shah, and through him with Pashtuns. This strategy bore fruit to some extent in the Bonn agreement, which legitimated a government led by a Kandahari Pashtun associated with the former king, Hamid Karzai, with the security organs under Panjshiri control, and other factions given other ministries. As mentioned previously, the legal framework for this government was the 1964 constitution minus the monarchy, abrogating the Islamist enactments of both the Taliban and the Islamic State of Afghanistan.

The actual distribution of power resulted largely from U.S. decisions about how to conduct the war, mainly by funding allied ground forces rather than putting U.S. troops in harm's way. At the end of the initial campaign, U.S. Secretary of Defense Donald Rumsfeld reversed a previous decision by ordering Shura-yi Nazar into Kabul city. Previously, SCN had promised not to enter the city, and the Bonn agreement, signed after the city had fallen, requested an International Security Assistance Force to provide security there. The agreement provided for the withdrawal of all other military forces from Kabul, in order to remove the capital from factional control, but Fahim refused, and everyone else acquiesced. ISAF's presence has done a great deal to enhance the national and neutral status of the capital, but the constant presence of Panjshiri soldiers and of pictures of Massoud reinforces a message about who is in control. Massoud may have decided not to treat the state and the capital as war booty, but this message did not reach some of his followers.

The result today is a mix of the legally mandated centralization with a military pseudo-federalism based on armed groups built up over years of war and reinvigorated by the United States and its coalition partners as part of the war on terrorism. The leadership in Kabul wants to recentralize the government but is split between advocates of a direct assault on regional forces and proponents of gradualism. The technocrats returned from the West tend to be in the former camp and the former Northern Alliance commanders in the latter. A few leaders, mainly outside the central government, propose federalism or decentralization. The international community involved in assisting Afghanistan in such matters pays lip service to the agenda of strengthening the central government but works pragmatically with a variety of regional forces, reinforcing fragmentation. Global trends that see decentralization as conducive to democracy and grassroots development legitimate such decisions.

Most Afghans seem to identify warlordism (*jangsalari, tufangsalari*) as the source of the country's current problems. Ironically, some of the individuals whom others see as warlords advocate eradication of warlordism. Many people also agree on the creation of a national army and the emergence of a strong central government. Most people qualify their statements in favor of a strong central government and national army by adding that the current government in Kabul, seen as dominated by Shura-yi Nazar, does not enjoy sufficient national legitimacy to integrate the various regional forces.

The biggest change appears to be that most Afghans no longer accept the notion that the state is booty to be won by the strongest, provided that the ruling group deals justly with the people by enforcing sharia. Many Afghans today want to participate in their government as citizens of Afghanistan, even if they have widely different interpretations about what that means. If they reject control by unaccountable regional warlords in favor of what they call "strong, central government," it does not mean they would accept an unaccountable, strong, central government, even if the latter somehow eradicated the warlords. Given the geographic and ethnographic realities of Afghanistan, such participation will require significant devolution of power, though not to the current regional armed groups.

Most regions in Afghanistan today are under the predominant influence of figures who exercise extralegal power, such as governors-general, combining military and administrative functions over several provinces. They effectively replace the central government's authority, though they may have sworn allegiance to it. Whether they are officially provincial governors (Ismail Khan, Gul Agha Shirzai, Hajji Din Muhammad), military generals (Abdul Rashid Dostum, Ata Muhammad, Hazrat Ali), or incumbents of other offices (Vice-President Abdul Karim Khalili), they have gained their positions not by appointment from the center but because they command armed militia forces aided by the United States, in most cases affiliated with one or another faction of the former United Front (Northern Alliance). The remaining governors are also mostly former commanders from the provinces where they now exercise authority. Though all governors and generals have received letters of appointment from the president as required, they received these appointments because they have power, rather than the reverse.

The big so-called warlords have brought smaller armed groups of their province or region under their command or influence. Some poorer or weaker provinces acknowledge the suzerainty of a neighboring governor or regional commander, creating de facto zones. Ismail Khan in Herat and Gul Agha Shirzai in Kandahar are governors without official military positions, but they are simultaneously the de facto chiefs of the military forces not only of their own but also of their neighboring provinces. Abdul Rashid Dostum and Ata

Muhammad are military generals without official administrative positions, but they have divvied up, and occasionally fight over, the civil administration in the northern provinces. They have appointed governors and other high officials and set policy in the provinces under their influence. A more complex case is that of the eastern region, where Hajji Din Muhammad is the governor of Nangarhar, and Hazrat Ali is the military commander of the Jalalabad garrison. Theirs is an uneasy condominium, as they belong to different factions and ethnic groups. The relative balance of power between the two may be due to the fact that the governor of Nangarhar enjoys local tribal support and some influence in neighboring provinces, while the military commander has strong backing from the defense minister in Kabul.

Further divergence from the old system is visible in the intraprovincial appointments and chain of command. Most provincial strongmen—be they governor or military ruler—appoint wuluswals. The governor of Herat, for example, has appointed all wuluswals of his province. In districts close to the provincial capital or with larger Tajik population, the wuluswals have managed to exercise control. In some districts, where the inhabitants are predominantly Pashtun, the governor's Tajik appointees are accused of practicing gross ethnic discrimination. In Chisht, for example, there exists a power structure parallel to that of the official district government. In the district of Shindand, where Ismail Khan also attempted to appoint a wuluswal, the situation has escalated into open military confrontations between the governor's forces and those of the local Pashtuns, under the command of Amanullah Khan. The latter has received some support from Gul Agha Shirzai, governor of Kandahar.

The governor of Nangarhar also claims that in most cases he has appointed wuluswals and district security chiefs who are not natives of their districts of assignment. Kandahar is a somewhat atypical case in that the governor at first experimented with district-level elections but interfered later. First, he authorized shuras in each wuluswali to elect the wuluswals. Three months later, the governor shifted all the elected wuluswals from their original districts to other ones.

The district of Spin Boldak, which is inhabited predominantly by the Achakzai and the Nurzai tribes, seems to have presented a particular problem. According to Kandahar high officials, the two tribes "could not resolve their problems and nominate a wuluswal." The deputy governor explained, "Finally, the Governor sent a sayyid as their wuluswal." The sayyid, a member of a religious descent group outside the Pashtun tribal structure, is originally from the district of Panjwa'i and was brought to Spin Boldak with the help of the governor's armed forces.

The tribal chiefs in Spin Boldak, however, vehemently deny such a disagreement during the elections process and claim that the governor manipulated the process to serve his economic interests. According to a prominent Nurzai khan, "The governor does not have any particular tribal or ideological competition with us. The entire issue is over the control of commercial trucks." In Spin Boldak, the governor has directly appointed all government officials from among individuals who do not belong to any of the two strong tribes of the region and come from other districts or even provinces.

On occasion, strong commanders have even appointed governors in the provinces in their zones of influence. In the immediate aftermath of the fall of the Taliban, General Dostum appointed the governors of Jauzjan and Faryab, who in turn appointed the wuluswals. Soon after taking office in February 2003, Interior Minister Ali Ahmad Jalali named new governors to those posts after consulting with Dostum, who reportedly raised no objection. When the new governor of Jauzjan tried to take up his post, however, factional fighting broke out. In Ghor province, where the governor was named by the central government, the deputy governor was appointed by Ismail Khan. The governor, who is from a district in the south of the province, could not even enter the provincial capital, Chaghcharan, which is located in the district to which his Herat-appointed deputy belongs. The deputy governor therefore conducted the affairs of the province with financial support from Herat.

This power structure has affected all elements of the state. The military units stationed in garrisons around the country are entirely recruited from those regions and serve the regional commanders. The Kabul garrison is almost entirely composed of Tajiks from Panjshir and Shamali. In this sense there is a factional rather than national army. At times the different military units fight each other, especially in the north.

The judiciary formally reports, as previously, to the Supreme Court in Kabul. That court itself is currently operating contrary to the law in several ways (size of the bench, age of the judges, rules of standing for considering cases). The provincial judges, however, are subject to pressures and threats from the local commanders so that rendering justice is precluded in any case in which the regional commander has an interest.

The change in the operation of the revenue system is, of course, fundamental. The bureaucracy set up for tax collection by central governments in the past still exists, if in a weakened form, but it now generally functions not as part of a national state but under the control of regional commanders. Customs revenues have become a point of contention between Kabul and the provinces where major customs posts are located, as well as among rival commanders and provinces.

Since the mid-1990s Pakistan has banned twenty-some commercial items from passing through its borders into Afghanistan under the Afghan Transit Trade Agreement (ATTA), which provides for duty-free import into Pakistan of goods under seal for reexport to Afghanistan, which facilitates smuggling into Pakistan. After the ban, trucks carrying those contraband goods found new transport routes through Iran and Turkmenistan, into Afghanistan through

Herat. This shift in transport routes has decreased the customs revenues of Kandahar and Nangarhar, while it has placed Herat in a markedly advantageous position. According to a high official of the customs service interviewed in Jalalabad, 70 percent of Afghanistan's foreign trade was transiting through Iran in mid-2002. This will only increase with the new transit agreements negotiated with Iran by Afghan Minister of Commerce Sayyid Mustafa Kazemi in 2003. [Kazemi was assassinated by a suicide bomber in November 2007.]

Under so-called normal circumstances (which have not existed for decades), customs duties collected by the provincial customs office are deposited in the finance ministry's bank account at the provincial branch of Da Afghanistan Bank. Then, according to the expenditure allocation for the province determined by the various ministries in their budgets, the ministry of finance in Kabul authorizes the provincial *mustufiat* (finance office) to withdraw money from that account and disburse it to the provincial governmental offices. If there is a surplus, the excess is transferred to Kabul. In case of shortage, additional funds are transferred from Kabul to meet the province's budgetary requirements. According to Minister of Finance Ashraf Ghani Ahmadzai, Herat is the sole province that consistently enjoys a revenue surplus; all others rely on the central government's revenues to cover their shortfalls.

In the past, too, customs revenue was rarely enough to cover all the expenses of a province. As the *mustufis* (finance officers) of Herat and Kandahar emphasized, "Taxes collected at customs were never physically sent to Kabul." Therefore, officials of these two provinces believe, they are not violating existing laws and procedures by not sending the customs revenue to Kabul. In reality, the governors of these provinces commit a gross procedural violation when they assume the role of the finance ministry in deciding on the disbursement of these funds.

There are similar difficulties in northern Afghanistan, where the major commanders split the revenues from the Hairatan customs house. Though the shares have been a repeated subject of fighting and renegotiation, by early 2003 the division of spoils, according to UN officials, seems to have stabilized at 50 percent for General Atta Muhammad of Jamiat, 37 percent for Dostum, 12 percent for Muhaqqiq and Hizb-i Wahdat, and the remaining 1 percent perhaps used for the cost of transactions.

This system has aggravated conflict among regions, particularly between Herat and Kandahar. "Ismail Khan is collecting taxes that are our rights," said the deputy governor of Kandahar. The pre-1978 law says that a customs office can levy tax only on companies that are registered in that province. "Herat illegally taxes the companies that are registered elsewhere," complained the Kandahar mustufi. Consequently, when a company registered in Kandahar brings its goods in through Herat, it pays duties in Herat. When its trucks reach Kandahar, that province's customs office levies an additional tax on them because this is the province where the company is registered. If the final destination is Kabul, the company may pay import tax for the third time. Traders have staged protests to call attention to this problem on a number of occasions.

Federalism, Decentralization, Unitary State

Ismail Khan, General Dostum, and, previously, the leaders of Hizb-i Wahdat (Khalili and Muhaqqiq) have supported a federal system of government. Partly because of the unprecedented degree of participation in the central government by Shia in both the interim and transitional administrations, and partly because of their recognition of continued resistance to federalism by Pashtuns, Hizb-i Wahdat has moderated its program to calling for measures of devolution and nondiscrimination against Shia jurisprudence. Over dinner at his residence, Muhaqqiq joked about Hizb-i Wahdat's advocacy of federalism: "Dostum is with us with his four families [chahar khana], the Tajiks are reluctant, and the Pashtuns consider that federalism is *kufr* [unbelief] and that it is beyond the pale of the Islamic religion."

Among the specific issues at stake in the debate over "federalism" are the zonal system (whether provinces should be formally grouped into zones or regions for administrative, fiscal, and political purposes); whether the leadership of the administration of provinces or zones should be elected, appointed, or some combination of the two; and what powers these subnational units should have, especially in the fiscal area, raising taxes and determining their own expenditures.

More generally, the issue is whether the current diffusion of power among various centers constitutes a positive devolution that can make the Afghan state more responsive, if these power centers are integrated into a legally functioning system, or whether they constitute inherently disruptive warlordism that should be suppressed by a strong central government.

Among political elites, those exercising power in the provinces and representing regions and ethnic groups that have long felt themselves to be subjects of a Pashtun-dominated state in Kabul rather than equal citizens of Afghanistan tend to advocate federalism or decentralization. Those exercising power in Kabul and Pashtun elites who see Afghanistan primarily as a Pashtun-led state advocate a strong, centralized government.

Popular perceptions seem to have evolved with changing experience. At the beginning of jihad, in 1979–80, before most fighters were organized into parties or organizations, they often spontaneously attacked the physical presence of the central government. People affiliated themselves with leaders largely from their own group who could provide security or dispense patronage. Now, however, after years of "gunlordism" (tufangsalari) by local commanders, popular sentiment has largely shifted in favor of a "strong central government." The proceedings of the loya jirga in June 2002, which appeared to reflect popular sentiment quite closely, were notable for the absence of calls for decentralization or regional autonomy. The most popular theme was the need for the central government to subordinate or eliminate the "warlords" and provide security. One should not necessarily conclude therefore that government should be as centralized as in the past: confronted with an ineffective, corrupt, or oppressive central government, a possibility that one can hardly exclude, popular sentiment could shift once again.

President Karzai strongly opposes the zonal system and has insisted, for instance, that the consultations on the new constitution be organized in thirty-two provincial offices rather than in eight zonal offices, as the Emergency Loya Jirga elections were. Although he has compromised with the de facto decentralized power structure by confirming appointments of local officials from their own areas, in private discussions as early as Nawruz 1381 (2002) he confided his intention to return to the tradition of appointing governors and wuluswals from outside the areas they administer and said that this corresponded to popular demands.

Since his appointment as minister of finance at the 2002 Emergency Loya Jirga, Ashraf Ghani Ahmadzai, former senior social scientist of the World Bank, has emerged as one of the most forceful advocates of centralization. Since assuming office he has dedicated himself to trying to centralize finances and reform the customs service and treasury department of the ministry of finance. He has persuaded Ismail Khan to turn over new afs 100 million on several occasions and has held up payments to northern Afghanistan in order to pressure Dostum and the other northern commanders to turn the customs revenue over to central control. He has also held up payments to the defense ministry, insisting on a plan for reducing the size of the forces and clear identification of those whose salaries are being paid.

These demands have placed him in sharp conflict with Marshall Qasim Fahim, vice-president and minister of defense. Fahim does not challenge Ghani's agenda of centralization. In an interview he stated: "A strong central government is imperative. The central government must have total control over the entire country; otherwise, it can't be called a state." What Fahim challenges is whether the centralization process should be used gradually to incorporate the armed forces of the Northern Alliance or to marginalize them in favor of a state structure dominated by a technocratic, and largely Pashtun, elite.

The governors and governors-general in the Pashtun areas also state they favor centralization, even if not under the current power structure. Gul Agha Shirzai of Kandahar states that he supports the establishment of a strong central government as the only means to a return to the rule of law, stability, and equitable economic development. Similarly, Hajji Din Muhammad, governor of Nangarhar, said: "Federalism is not the right formula for Afghanistan. The federal systems that are in place in Pakistan or in Germany will not be successful in Afghanistan. They would only push the country towards disintegration."

The argument that federalism will lead to disintegration derives from the experience of the past decades, in which regionally based commanders developed independent patronage and supply relations with governments and other support networks in neighboring countries. These political and economic linkages provided the infrastructure for the proxy war that took place on Afghan territory, pulling the country apart. Of course, in genuine federalism, armed force and security would still be centralized.

Sometimes Afghan commanders and governors-general speak as if federalism were a system where each zone would have its own army. This is not federalism, but the association of the term with these facts on the ground colors how Afghans perceive it.

The differences over state structure are not only about the goals, but about the process. The conflict over the nature of the process is most intense between Ashraf Ghani and Marshall Fahim, but it expresses the difference in viewpoint between the returning technocrats and those associated with previous regimes, on the one hand, and those whose road to power was through the jihad and the struggle against the Taliban.

The former position advocates a kind of "shock therapy" centralization. Its advocates seek to use international financial assistance to the central government as leverage to subordinate the regional or zonal authorities, construct a centralized administration, and win the loyalty of the people and former fighters to the government. A Kabul-based elite with a heavy admixture of Western-trained and Western-returned technocrats would exercise most political power.

The gradualist group largely associated with the former Northern Alliance, however, seeks to incorporate the de facto decentralized military and administrative structures, headed by members of their own and allied organizations into a more centralized structure. An elite composed of former commanders and regional leaders (warlords) would share rulership with Western-trained and returned technocrats while retaining a predominant, though not exclusive, role in the security forces.

Two cabinet ministers in Kabul who participated in the Bonn Talks as members (in one case as leader) of different delegations offered intermediate solutions that accepted the need for a process of state building that would transform current realities gradually and keep evolving.

Muhammad Yunus Qanuni, minister of education and former minister of the interior, who led the United Front delegation in Rome, expresses the gradualist point of view: "The debate should not be on either an all-powerful central state or a federal system. Neither is realistic at the moment." Qanuni suggested that a series of authorities should go to the center, while the remaining one should be given to governors.

> For example, all level I and level II [rutba-yi awal wa rutba-yi du, the highest-ranking civil servants] officials should be appointed by the center—including governors and wuluswals, and the rest by the governors. Fifty percent of customs revenue should be sent to the center. Teachers should be appointed locally. All this, until a strong central state is established.

M. Amin Farhang, minister of reconstruction, who was a member of the Rome delegation, argued:

> A federal system cannot be established in the short-term. Currently escape from the center is a reality, but this will take Afghanistan towards gradual disintegration. The muqam-i sarkari [state authority] must be reinstated. Only after a strong central government is established can we slowly begin to move towards decentralization.

In this view, a central power must be established before it can be devolved. The illegitimate regional power centers must be dissolved or subordinated, before laws on new forms of devolution can take effect.

Conclusion

For now, centralization is popular as slogan or symbol among the common people throughout the country, but it is far from certain that the popularity of this idea would long survive its implementation. This view reflects people's strong distrust of the existing local and regional rulers, whose use of ethnic, regional, and tribal grievances to legitimate their power people seem largely to reject. Even after a quarter of a century of war and disintegration of the central government, state structures and procedures that were deeply engraved in the minds of the people and of the cadre of remaining bureaucrats were quickly revived in both the center and the provinces and districts. New leaders have changed the rules of politics, but administrative structures and bureaucratic procedures have stubbornly remained the same.

The popular views of government, however, may not be as simple as they appear. Decades of conflict, exile, and politicization have created an Afghan public quite different from that of several decades ago. Many Afghans want to be participating citizens, not passive subjects. One author (Rubin) asked an ad hoc assembly in a mosque in a village near Bamiyan how the relations of the center to the provinces and districts should be structured. One local man who was clearly a leader in the community responded that the people should elect the wuluswals, and that the central government should appoint the governor from a list of three candidates submitted by the local people, presumably by a provincial assembly. We are confident that others have such ideas as well, which would help the Afghan political debate move beyond the sterile polarization of "federalism" versus a "strong, central government."

The drafting of the new Afghan constitution should provide an occasion to debate these issues more fully, though merely adopting a plan for the structure of the government will not guarantee its implementation. Probably the best constitutional framework would be a unitary state structured in such a way as to provide for participation at all levels through elected councils and that is flexible enough to permit extensive devolution of power to provinces, districts, and localities. The desirable amount of devolution will vary with the sector and over time.

Popular sentiment clearly wants a more consolidated state right now, and particularly the demobilization of militias. To the extent that Afghanistan has an army, it must, of course, be centralized. Policing is an area ripe for new models, at least once a minimally professional national gendarmerie is reestablished. Tax collection will have to be largely nationalized, but provinces could be allowed certain revenue powers. More important, given the great disparity in resources among provinces, the government should consider establishing an institutional structure that will make it possible to give block grants to provinces, districts, and communities to budget as they see fit for certain purposes. Elected councils could be given jurisdiction over such allocations. The idea of appointing governors and wuluswals from the center is deeply ingrained but can at some point be reconsidered. Some form of zonal system may be necessary for economic and social planning, if not for political participation. It would be remarkably inefficient if every national program had to be administered through one office in Kabul and thirty-two provincial offices, rather than through eight or so regional offices.

All these topics can be the subject of rational debate, but the political issues are those that might plunge the country back into conflict. A weak and largely unaccountable state dependent on foreign aid and foreign advisors before 1978 nurtured a political elite that was concentrated in a few neighborhoods in Kabul and increasingly culturally and politically distant from the rest of the country, which it barely controlled through a highly centralized but ineffective administration. Today's rapid recentralizers and their foreign backers risk creating a similar situation. They also risk reigniting conflict if they too aggressively attack well-entrenched regional powers, before they have alternatives ready for the fighters and, even more important, their leaders. Already one hears that little aid leaves Kabul and is mainly used for international organizations, foreigners, and a small clique of Westernized Afghans who speak their language. Such a system will be even more unsustainable in the Afghanistan of the twenty-first century than in the previous one. Today's warlords could be tomorrow's champions of revolt against the foreign imposition of a small, unaccountable elite in Kabul. Afghans do not support the regional gunlords, but they will not accept rule by aid-lords either. The political task of reconstruction will be to help Afghans use the assistance they need to construct a state structure that is unitary enough to unite the country and decentralized enough to permit real participation to a population that is politicized as never before.

6

Transitional Justice and Human Rights in Afghanistan

Since the defeat of the Taliban and signing of the Bonn Agreement on December 5, 2001, Afghanistan has begun what many hope will turn out to be a transition from war to peace, from chaos to order, from an unjust order and unjust disorder to a new kind of order, where all may seek justice and live in security. During such a phase, nations and international actors confront the challenge of "transitional justice": measures by which a society accounts for past abuses as it moves from a condition of dictatorship or conflict, where the perpetrators of violence enjoy impunity, to one of civil peace, where the state seeks to provide justice and security to its citizens.

If posttransition justice is routine, transitional justice cannot be; it is exceptional. It cannot punish or even record all abuses according to the ordinary law of peacetime. This can be mathematically proved in respect of Rwanda, where the number of accused participants in genocide, the most serious crime known to humanity, exceeds the capacity of any known court system to try them. The people of Afghanistan have suffered a decades-long succession of crimes that constitute a virtual catalogue of all that is supposedly forbidden but remains prevalent in human affairs.

Originally published in *International Affairs* 79, no. 3 (2003), 567–81.

Note: This article is a revised version of the Anthony Hyman Memorial Lecture, delivered at the School of Oriental and African Studies, University College London, on February 3, 2003. Anthony Hyman, a writer and commentator, died in December 1999 at the age of fifty-three after a long illness. Hyman, author of *Afghanistan Under Soviet Domination* (first published by Macmillan in 1982), had a long-term commitment to the human rights and welfare of the people of Afghanistan, which he manifested in his scholarly writing, his journalistic commentary, and his participation in the Afghan Refugee Information Network. He also served on the editorial board of *Central Asian Survey* and wrote extensively on Central Asia and that region as well. The School of Oriental and African Studies, where Hyman studied and occasionally lectured, held a widely attended memorial meeting for Hyman in February 2000. Soon after that event, Hyman's friends and colleagues decided to establish a series of annual lectures in his memory and invited Barnett R. Rubin, a friend and colleague of Hyman, to deliver the first lecture in his memory.

We should not romanticize Afghanistan before the communist coup d'état of April 1978. Afghan prisons were punishing, and the interrogators might have been surprised to learn that all Afghan constitutions since 1923 had prohibited the use of torture. The police could be corrupt and brutal. But the revolution of 1978 brought about an intensity and scope of violence that had not been seen at least since the formation of the modern Afghan state in the closing years of the nineteenth century.

From April 1978 to December 1979, the Khalqi faction's communist regime attempted to eradicate its enemies through mass arrests and executions. The regime subsequently installed by the Soviet Union, dominated by the Parchami faction, published a list of about twelve thousand people said to have disappeared in Pul-i Charkhi prison under Khalqi rule. Others put the actual figure higher. Throughout the country, the Khalqi regime, at times with the apparent complicity of Soviet advisers, executed an unknown number—probably in the tens of thousands—of religious, tribal, and clan leaders. In a few cases, people were buried or burned alive. After a military mutiny led by Captains Ismail Khan and Alauddin Khan, the city of Herat was bombed indiscriminately, with thousands of casualties.

During the Soviet occupation, hundreds of thousands of civilians, possibly a million or more, lost their lives in the indiscriminate bombing and shelling of villages thought to be sheltering the resistance. Populated areas by roadsides were razed. Millions became refugees. Irrigation systems, orchards, and grain and seed storage were destroyed. Torture became part of an intelligence effort and hence more systematic, with the aid of Soviet and East German advisers. A diplomat of the regime once estimated to me that 150,000 people had been arrested in Kabul by his government, and virtually all prisoners were tortured. Gradually, especially after 1986, torture decreased, to be replaced by skilled interrogation. Indiscriminate bombing decreased, to be replaced by indiscriminate bribing. But debasement of the currency is not yet classified as a war crime.

As both the mujahidin resisting the regime and the loosely controlled tribal militias fighting for it gained in strength, so their abuses also increased. Since fleeing to Pakistan in the 1970s some mujahidin leaders, notably Gulbuddin Hikmatyar, had assassinated others. Their turf wars in Afghanistan also proved brutal for civilians. The treatment of prisoners by guerrilla irregulars has never been one of the bright spots in the history of warfare, and this conflict was no exception: one even heard of captured Soviet soldiers being skinned alive, though some were allowed visits by the International Committee of the Red Cross, after the regime agreed to give it access in 1986. With U.S. and Pakistani supplies and direction, mujahidin in the late 1980s began to rocket the city of Kabul indiscriminately, killing and mutilating many civilians. Arab extreme Islamists brought with them their own brutal doctrines of warfare, advocating the execution of "communist" civilian men and the capture or trafficking of their women.

When the Soviet-installed leader Najibullah fell in April 1992, the country entered a period of virtual statelessness, in which ethnic antagonisms increased. The Soviet war destroyed the countryside; the war among the mujahidin and militias destroyed the capital, killing tens of thousands of people. The destruction of entire neighborhoods and historic features of this great and ancient city constitutes a crime in itself, as does the looting and destruction of the precious relics of the Kabul Museum.

For the first time in the history of Afghanistan, as far as I know, rape became a regular feature of war. Factions killed captured enemies with a spike through the head or held them in the summer in sealed shipping containers, where they suffocated in the heat. Armed predators robbed civilians and subjected them to extortion. Outside Kabul, commanders often became lawless warlords, preying upon travelers and traders, abducting and raping young boys and girls, and profiting from smuggling and drug trafficking. Assassination became a regular means of settling disputes. Though the USSR had dissolved and the United States disengaged, virtually every faction found a regional foreign backer that kept the weapons and money coming. Arab fighters from what we now know as al-Qaeda became increasingly prominent.

This was the context in which the Taliban emerged as both an indigenous southern Pashtun response to warlordism and an instrument of Pakistani policy. The abuses of the previous period provided the justification for the Taliban's own harsh rule. They imposed the Quranically imposed *hudud* punishments of amputation and stoning in the areas under their rule, and suspected opponents were dealt with harshly. The damage they wrought to the already fragile and debased education and health of Afghans through their obscurantist restrictions on women may not constitute crimes against humanity, but they deserve their own mention in this chronicle. The destruction of the Bamiyan Buddhas and as yet uncounted other treasures by the most extremist wing, allied with al-Qaeda, helped obscure the vast cultural destruction presided over by their predecessors.

For all this, the principal war crimes and crimes against humanity during this period occurred during the battle between the Taliban and various components of the opposition Northern Alliance for control of northern and central Afghanistan. The Taliban and al-Qaeda turned the plain north of Kabul into a ruined wasteland, executing some of the inhabitants, destroying the orchards and vineyards, and expelling the people. In the battle for Mazar-i Sharif, ethnic Uzbek and Hazara commanders of various Northern Alliance factions murdered hundreds, maybe thousands, of Taliban prisoners in June 1997. The Taliban returned to kill many more thousands of civilians in August 1998, including Iranian diplomats. Pakistani groups were implicated in these killings. Similar killings, if on a smaller scale, occurred as Bamiyan and Yakaolang in Hazarajat changed hands several times.

Taliban rule ended with the military campaign of the United States and its allies after the attack of September 11, 2001—itself a crime against humanity, and the only one of these that I witnessed personally, but one in which no Afghans were directly involved. After the fall of Kunduz to several factions of the U.S.-aided Northern Alliance, including those recruited from the groups massacred by the Taliban in 1998, Northern Alliance commanders transported thousands of Afghan and Pakistani Taliban and al-Qaeda prisoners, who were told they would be released, toward Mazar-i Sharif. Some apparently suffocated in containers or were shot, to be buried in mass graves in the same area as the victims of 1997 and 1998. Others arrived at Qala-yi Jangi only to die in the suppression of an insurrection under disputed circumstances, including bombing of the prison by the United States and Britain.

Since that time hundreds, perhaps thousands, of civilians have died in U.S. bombing raids, without public investigations or payment of compensation. The only trial—of pilots who accidentally killed Canadian soldiers, not Afghan civilians—resulted in an acquittal. Underground groups opposing the U.S. presence have killed civilians in bombings in Kabul and elsewhere. The commanders of the Northern Alliance and others who returned with U.S. and coalition assistance have established themselves in their areas again and are engaging in the same brutality in some areas as in the early 1990s. Hazara and Uzbek militias have expelled Pashtun communities in northern Afghanistan, and violence and extortion prevail in much of the country. At least one prisoner has died under torture in government custody, and two members of the cabinet have been assassinated, in one case by members of the dominant faction, with no one charged or held accountable. Islamist extremists have asserted the right to execute Muslims for "blasphemy" or "apostasy" and have started to use such charges against their opponents.

Despite this history, or perhaps because of it, the voices calling for accountability for past abuses have been relatively weak and few. No one, to my knowledge, has proposed the establishment of a special court to try those responsible, though at least one commander, Abdullah Shah, has been tried in Afghanistan for his egregious abuses. Abdullah Shah was caught chasing one of his wives down the street, trying to kill her. After he was jailed other victims came forward.

In some postconflict situations the peace settlement itself includes an agreement on transitional justice. In the case of Afghanistan, however, there is no peace settlement, as usually understood. The Bonn Agreement of December 5, 2001, was not an agreement among the warring groups to lay down their arms and build a new society. The parties did not painstakingly negotiate over a period of years how to structure a government that would resolve the conflicts that had torn the society apart, create new armed forces and a new police service, and confront the painful legacy of the past to lay the groundwork for national reconciliation. Quite the contrary: one side of the armed conflict, the Taliban and al-Qaeda, was still in the process of being pulverized by U.S. bombs when representatives of four anti-Taliban groups convened in a hotel on a hilltop outside Bonn. They met there for ten days under extreme pressure, as a dentists' convention had reserved the same hotel after 5 December. These groups, together with the UN and major powers with a stake in the outcome, chose the ministers of what came to be called the Interim Administration of Afghanistan in the single night of 4–5 December, before the UN secretary-general's sleepless special representative, Lakhdar Brahimi, presided over a signing ceremony. Only one of the four Afghan groups participating, the Islamic United Front for the Salvation of Afghanistan (UF or Northern Alliance), had armed forces on the ground, and they were fighting the Taliban, not the other groups at Bonn. Hence the political dynamic in negotiations between combatants who agree to a legitimate process to lay to rest in some way the charges each leveled against the other, as in South Africa or El Salvador, was absent in this case.

Nonetheless, the prospect of some reckoning with the past was on the mind of some delegates at Bonn, as well as those of the UN team. One challenge that the latter faced was: Who would be appointed to various offices? As one of Brahimi's advisers, I participated in discussions, and at one time I suggested in a pre-Bonn discussion paper that no one guilty of war crimes, crimes against humanity, or gross violations of human rights should serve as a minister in the interim administration. In discussions of the need to form new security forces, we noted the desirability of screening recruits, especially to the officer corps, to prevent the appointment of those who had committed serious abuses. These discussions came to naught: first, because no judicial or similar process was in place to determine who was ineligible, and it would be impossible to obtain agreement on its mandate and establish a process with sufficient legitimacy in the time we had; and second, because the U.S.-led coalition's policy of arming these and other commanders as allies on the ground gave Afghanistan a de facto new set of armed forces without any such process. The creation of these armed forces based on the commanders still shadows all such efforts today and constitutes the major obstacle to forming a genuinely national army and police.

During the talks, the issue emerged again. The final text of the Bonn Agreement contains no reference to transitional justice, except for the establishment of the Human Rights Commission, whose mandate was understood, though not stated, to include coping with past as well as current abuses. Nonetheless, the issue did figure in the debates, as the UN drafters had included a paragraph stating that the interim administration should decree no amnesty for war crimes or crimes against humanity.

This paragraph forbidding an amnesty caused a furor within the meeting and an even greater one outside. The two members of the UF delegation from the party of Abd al-Rabb al-Rasul Sayyaf claimed that this measure was aimed at defaming the struggle of the mujahidin. We learned that the leaders of the UF were insisting to Muhammad Yunus Qanuni, the head of the delegation, that the paragraph be removed, and I overheard some rather heated discussions over Qanuni's British-supplied satellite telephone. In the drafting session, Mr. Brahimi recalled to the delegates the danger of an amnesty. As he did several times during the negotiations, he referred to his own background in the Algerian struggle for independence. He reminded the delegates that a retired French military officer had recently published a memoir in which he had confessed to, even boasted of, his role in the torture and killing of Algerian prisoners during the war there. Yet because the French government had declared a blanket amnesty, it was impossible to take any action against him.

The resistance to the paragraph forbidding an amnesty for war crimes formed part of a broader political struggle that helps define of the political context for today's decisions about transitional justice. Other items that caused conflict were:

- A paragraph drafted by the UN consisting of what we thought of as standard boilerplate for peace agreements, namely a call for demobilization, disarmament, and reintegration of unofficial armed groups. When some argued that it was dishonorable to call on mujahidin to abandon their arms, Brahimi once again referred to his past as a mujahid, noting that his decision to lay down arms and enter diplomacy was a good thing.
- Annex I on security, which called on the UN Security Council to authorize an international security assistance force for Kabul, and eventually other areas.
- The role of the former king, Muhammad Zahir Shah, in the Emergency Loya Jirga (Grand Council) and potentially the government, and the initial lack of any mention of or role for Burhanuddin Rabbani, president of the Islamic State of Afghanistan, which the Taliban had deposed but which still held the country's UN seat.

Rabbani and Sayyaf used these issues to mobilize support against the agreement. They told their followers that the purpose of the agreement was (1) to bring Western troops to Afghanistan through the invitation of the International Security Assistance Force, (2) to disarm and demobilize the mujahidin, and then (3) to try the mujahidin for "war crimes." International legal standards are not well known or understood in Afghanistan. The phrase "war crime" (*janayat-i jangi*) might be interpreted there to mean the crime of waging war, implying that all those who had taken up arms in the jihad could be tried.

Impending victory over the Taliban followed by a power-sharing agreement under U.S. and UN sponsorship was causing anxiety among the fighters. Most international concern has rightly been focused on the women of Afghanistan and the civilian victims of the conflict, but the fighters, too, are victims. The young men fighting in Afghanistan in 2001, twenty-three years after the Sawr revolution, had known nothing but war and conflict their whole lives. They had been raised on and lived an ideology of jihad; they had never known a united Afghanistan where competing groups did not resort to arms; they had little education and few skills; and in the economy they had known bearing arms, growing opium, and smuggling seemed the only relatively lucrative professions. They might long for peace, but they also feared it. Peace might seem, if anything, less secure than war. Their commanders, some of whom stood to be the greatest losers in any peaceful settlement, could play upon these fears.

This point was brought home to me during the hours I spent negotiating the draft of a paragraph that now appears in the preamble of the Bonn Agreement, praising the "mujahidin" for their sacrifices, and heralding their (as yet untested) determination to become heroes of peace and reconstruction. I remember the anxious face of my counterpart as he waited for us to finish the translation of the paragraph so he could fax it to Kabul. A top official of Afghanistan's National Security Directorate told me in Kabul in August 2002 that this paragraph was essential to winning the support of major armed groups for the agreement. Other concessions included the omission from the agreement of any explicit mention of disarmament or demobilization. Instead the agreement called for all armed groups to come under the command of the new administration and be integrated into national armed forces, which would be reorganized according to need.

Sometime during the all-night negotiations necessary to clear out the hotel for the dentists, the paragraph forbidding an amnesty for war crimes was also struck out. Still, a year and a half after its installation, neither the interim administration nor its successor, the Islamic Transitional State of Afghanistan, has declared any amnesty for past violations. The goal was achieved without being explicitly proclaimed as a demand, something to bear in mind when making future policy recommendations about sensitive issues. [In 2006, in response to a report by Human Rights Watch calling attention to violations committed in the 1990s by important figures in the post-2001 government, parliament passed a bill intended to provide general amnesty for participants in the various stages of war between 1978 and 2001. The bill, however, makes no reference to war crimes or crimes against humanity. The text appears to refer only to military activities.]

Similar political tensions were on display at the Emergency Loya Jirga in June 2002, when a coalition of various mujahidin leaders pushed through a resolution changing the name of the new government from the Transitional Administration of Afghanistan, the phrase used in the Bonn Agreement, to the Islamic Transitional State of Afghanistan. Denunciations of warlords and war-lordism, especially by women delegates, led Sayyaf to declare that criticizing mujahidin was equivalent to blasphemy, and hence deserving of death. President Hamid Karzai, despite his declared goal of eliminating warlordism, did not feel strong enough to abandon the policy of accommodation, and he included major regional commanders in his government.

During this same period, the discussion on transitional justice began, very slowly and tentatively. No major human rights organization, as far as I know, has called for the establishment of any special tribunal, international or mixed, to try war criminals in Afghanistan. All appear to accept that the situation is too complex and currently too fragile for such measures. The judicial system in Afghanistan is clearly incapable of exercising even the basic functions of legal order, let alone taking on a major task of historical accountability. The one trial of a commander that has taken place, that of Abdullah Shah, was based on ordinary criminal law. Although the victims and their relatives welcomed the condemnation of the accused, the trial clearly failed to meet not just international but historic Afghan standards of fairness. In fact, there was hardly any trial. Asma Jahangir, the UN Human Rights Commission's Special Rapporteur on Extra-Judicial Killings, while welcoming the conviction, called for the revocation of the death penalty imposed on the grounds that the trial was unfair.

The Bonn Agreement placed the responsibility for transitional justice implicitly on the Independent Human Rights Commission, and during the preparatory process for its establishment it convened a working group on accountability for past crimes. At the public meeting establishing the commission, President Karzai surprised those assembled by announcing that, though he did not know if it was within the powers of the interim administration to do so, perhaps the transitional administration that would follow it would establish a truth commission to investigate the past. At dinner at the palace on the New Year's festival, Nawruz, in March 2002, a minister suggested establishing a museum of the atrocities of the Taliban. Karzai rejected the idea, saying that the problem was not only the Taliban but all the crimes of the past twenty-three years of war. At times he indicated to visitors that he wanted to deal with this issue, and quickly; but by early 2003 he seemed to have settled on the message that peace is a necessity and justice a luxury that Afghanistan cannot afford right now. He now says that his administration has taken a firm decision to draw a line between the present and the past.

The Independent Commission for Convening the Emergency Loya Jirga required candidates to sign a statement swearing that they had not killed innocent people or engaged in drug trafficking or terrorism; but this proved a hollow gesture with no enforcement mechanism. Many known to have violated those conditions served without obstacle. The cabinet ratified Afghanistan's membership in the International Criminal Court, to which spokesmen such as Foreign Minister Abdullah Abdullah have pointed as a sign of Afghanistan's intention to fulfill its responsibilities under international humanitarian and human rights law. Once Afghanistan's accession takes place, on May 1, 2003, the ICC will have jurisdiction over war crimes and crimes against humanity committed in Afghanistan from that date onward.

A number of international human rights organizations have sent missions to sound out Afghans on the right approach to the past. Most have concluded that what Afghans need at present is the opportunity to reflect on and debate the issue in order to understand the variety of options that have been tried under different circumstances. The International Center for Transitional Justice, headed by Alexander Boraine, former vice-chairman of South Africa's Truth and Reconciliation Commission, has sent a small mission to work with the AIHRC to help it think through alternatives and learn from international experience.

The main issue that has attracted attention to transitional justice in Afghanistan in the last year has been the discovery, or at least publicizing, of mass graves in Dasht-i Leili district in northern Afghanistan, apparently containing the remains of Afghan and Pakistani Taliban prisoners, as well as perhaps some al-Qaeda militants, taken into custody by UF forces in the northeast Afghan city of Kunduz in November 2001. Their captors transported these prisoners in shipping containers, the ubiquitous sheet-metal boxes used for smuggling goods from Dubai and for building housing, shops, and makeshift jails throughout the country. At least some prisoners suffocated to death, and others may have been shot. The UF forces were then receiving assistance from U.S. Special Forces and CIA operatives.

Probably because of the charges of U.S. involvement, these graves have received far more attention than others in the same region containing the remains of people killed in previous rounds of massacres in 1997 and 1998. The local authorities, including General (now Deputy Defense Minister) Abdul Rashid Dostum, had promised to cooperate with investigations at that time, but the Office of the UN High Commissioner for Human Rights, despite repeated requests from Lakhdar Brahimi, then the special envoy of the secretary-general, failed to push through those investigations, leaving a heritage of suspicion.

The organization Physicians for Human Rights, which participated in the preliminary forensic examination of those older graves, has also visited these newer sites. In April 2002, in confidential letters to President Karzai and key members of the Security Council, it called for the sites to be preserved. Although many observers consider him a chief suspect, Dostum claims he is guarding the sites, and UN political officers visit them regularly. As of early 2003, they did not appear to have been disturbed. PHR, which has a track record of work on graves in this area and elsewhere, notably Bosnia, has undertaken a mission to the region on behalf of the UN High Commissioner for Human Rights and appears to have recommended caution, in view of the unsettled conditions and continuing conflict in the area. No major human rights organization has advocated making investigation into these sites the centerpiece of accountability in Afghanistan. Focusing solely on the recent past, and on particular cases with a political angle that contemporary politics makes attractive, risks defeating the purpose of transitional justice. For transitional justice must be not only just but also fair. Justly calling perpetrators to account for certain crimes while ignoring others undermines the process, by making it seem captive to a political agenda. It may then reinforce factionalism and polarization, rather than reconciliation and peace. Above all, it may discredit the idea of transitional justice, making it seem a political tool.

Another proposal has come from Asma Jahangir. In her forthcoming report on Afghanistan, the UN Human Rights Commissioner's special rapporteur on extrajudicial executions has called for an international commission of inquiry, which could "undertake . . . a stocktaking of grave human rights violations in the past that could constitute a catalogue of crimes against humanity." The commission would undertake a comprehensive catalogue of abuses since 1978, not seeking to list every event or attribute legal responsibility, but to establish a public, official record to be used as a benchmark in any effort that Afghans and the international community may undertake in the future. [Patricia Gossman and I later drafted this report, which has still not been made public.]

Why is there so much consensus on caution? Sometimes people explain this by saying that one should not "destabilize" the new order. Others respond that one should not stabilize an unjust order. The difficulty lies in the outcome of the activity; destabilizing the current order risks a return to the unjust disorder from which Afghanistan has barely emerged.

The injustices of the current order are clear, as is its fragility. Jahangir reports what others have also observed, that "there is a climate of fear, and those who leak information on violations of human rights are threatened." This climate of fear effectively prevents Afghans themselves, including the Independent Human Rights Commission, from seeking redress for current violations or pursuing transitional justice.

This problem of intimidation is merely one manifestation of a more pervasive problem, the one that nearly all Afghans identify now as their primary challenge: security. Security and human rights are often considered as separate problems: security as a problem for army and police, the "security forces"; human rights as a problem for the judiciary, NGOs, and, where they exist, official human rights commissions. In fact, security and human rights are the same problem. The main obstacle, or at least the immediate obstacle, to both in Afghanistan, as in other collapsed or failed states, is what Afghans call tufangsalari: rule by gunmen. In most of the country, regardless of the legal and constitutional structures established by the Bonn Agreement, effective power is in the hands of factional commanders who were armed by the coalition in 2001. For many Afghans, that characterization includes the current ministry of defense, under Marshal Mohammad Qasim Fahim. Most of these commanders were leaders in the jihad and the mujahidin government, but some, like Dostum, were former militia leaders of the communist regime. Some changed sides and also worked for the Taliban. Some of the commanders, and their followers, including both the major regional commanders often described as warlords, were those whose opposition threatened to derail the Bonn Agreement.

It would be wrong simply to blame these individuals and think that order and security would return to Afghanistan if the so-called warlords and past abusers were removed from power. The key to this sentence, which I have heard so often, is the passive voice, indicating a lack of certainty as to who would carry out the task. More fundamentally, however, what will bring more peace and more justice to Afghanistan is not the removal of offending individuals, but the creation of a system of institutions to control them and make government effective and law-bound. Ending impunity by punishing offenders is part of that process, but it is neither the sole part nor necessarily the first part.

The issue that will make or break virtually all others in Afghanistan—security, reconstruction, human rights—is the disarmament, demobilization, and reintegration of these former combatants, and the creation of a civilian administration and a system of law and justice. This in turn will require what has become known as the "reform" of the defense ministry, a euphemism for removing it from domination by Fahim and his followers from the Supervisory Council of the North (SCN), founded by the late Ahmad Shah Massoud. Some former fighters will be integrated into the new Afghan National Army (ANA) or the police. Most will need alternative employment, and probably training, loans or grants, and other forms of assistance. Even more challenging will be finding alternative roles for the commanders, many of whom have used their weapons and men to seize houses, businesses, and other assets. The war-disabled are already mobilizing in protest against the government, which has failed to carry out its modest promises of assistance. This is a mere foretaste of the problems that the demobilized could cause if they are disappointed.

The government has assigned responsibility for both demobilization and the creation of the new security forces to a National Defense Commission, including major political and military leaders, among them the major "warlords." The United States as the primary sponsor of the ANA and the UN as overseer of the entire process also play major roles, though the Pentagon has refused to allow U.S. forces to participate actively in demobilization by acting as monitors.

The process of arriving at a common plan has sparked bitter debates. The major issue was the same one as at Bonn: how to reassure the hundreds of thousands of barely controlled, largely unpaid armed men that they will still have a future. The ministry of defense, controlled by the SCN, proposed a plan under which the base of the future army would be the mujahidin, mostly UF fighters, whose numbers would be gradually winnowed down. Those who were closer to the former king, or independent, argued for demobilization and disarmament of nearly all existing forces in favor of new ones created from those untainted by past battles and the unprofessional habits of guerrilla war. Though the debate was not conducted in the language of human rights, among the concerns raised by the latter group was the fear that the new forces would turn into a more efficient but still predatory group, which would abuse rather than protect the population. After being appointed at the Emergency Loya Jirga in June 2002, Minister of Finance Ashraf Ghani tried to compel reduction in these forces by refusing to pay salaries for the two hundred thousand men Fahim claimed to have on his payroll, creating severe tensions in the government.

As one would expect, the process is marked by vast mistrust, delays, trickery, maneuvering for position, and insecurity on the part of those eventually called upon to disarm. No one wants to give up his only source of livelihood or to disarm before his rivals or enemies do. But if this process fails, there will be no justice, transitional or otherwise, and no peace either. Afghanistan will remain a chaotic, misruled, or unruled state, living, to the extent that it does, from narcotics and smuggling, and offering a free recruiting ground to all sorts of armed groups. But there is little intellectual challenge in spinning disaster scenarios for Afghanistan.

To argue that the success of demobilization, disarmament, and reintegration (DDR) is essential, and, to the extent that there is a contradiction, that it should take priority over immediate measures to bring past abusers to account, is not to argue that "peace" should take priority over "justice." Without successful DDR, Afghanistan will have neither peace nor justice. A state at peace is one where people have a reasonable expectation that justice may be done. Justice cannot be done in a state of war and collapse of institutions. Peace and justice are interdependent, not contradictory.

But in building institutions of governance after a conflict, it is important to carry out efforts in the right sequence. Elections before disarmament sparked renewed conflict in Angola and Cambodia in the absence of legal institutions strong and legitimate enough to enforce the outcome. Of course, a political and social process is not like a machine that one operates by pressing the right buttons in the right order. People's need for justice and recognition of their suffering, and their pain and fear at being ruled by those who violated and abused them in the past, may erupt, as they did at the trial of Abdullah Shah. Most Afghans, however, seem to hope for the maintenance of today's fragile peace and stability, and the government's caution reflects their concern.

One danger is a repetition of what happened during the Bonn negotiations: that poorly timed external pressure for measures of transitional justice may lead the fighters or their leaders to connect disarmament and transitional justice, and to conclude that, since the foreigners—the coalition and the UN—have come to Afghanistan to disarm the mujahidin and try them for war crimes, they need to keep their weapons for self-defense. Such fears did not ultimately manage to derail Bonn, thanks in part to intervention from the coalition, and similar intervention might keep spoilers in check in the future. But it could be all too easy for those who oppose the process to play upon such fears, especially in the charged political atmosphere of 2003–04, with the debate over the constitution under way and elections scheduled for June 2004.

Yet one cannot simply postpone work on justice. The risks I have outlined are not certainties. They show how to be careful; they do not argue for paralysis. The U.S. military states that it will carefully vet those recruited to the ranks of brigade commander and above in the ANA; those keeping records of who has done what in the past should watch over this process and ensure that the new security forces, at the very least, eliminate the Abdullah Shahs. The Independent Human Rights Commission, with the help of others, should prepare a set of proposals for public discussion, bearing in mind that this will coincide with another potentially divisive and difficult discussion, over the constitution. The panel of experts suggested by Asma Jahangir can be constituted and carry out its work in a low-key way. It need not interview victims in Afghanistan in a manner that would draw public attention to its work. So much has been documented, or alleged, in public documents over the past twenty-three years that it could perform a service merely by collecting those records together into a coherent account that could constitute a public reference point once it is completed.

The president should clarify his own position and at least give a consistent message to his various interlocutors. He could ease some fears by issuing a decree declaring amnesty for all who have taken up arms for or against any Afghan government or political group since 1978, with the exception of those who have perpetrated war crimes, crimes against humanity, and genocide. He could take the opportunity to explain to the cabinet and public what those exceptions mean, while leaving it to the AIHRC to propose how to deal with them.

I cannot say exactly what Afghans should or can do. If today's fragile peace holds and is further consolidated, the best option, in my view, would be a national documentation process that includes measures to clarify the fate of the disappeared and establish the truth about numerous massacres. No one will ever make answerable the numerous foreign actors for crimes of war, and this in turn will make it difficult if not impossible to pursue those Afghans responsible. Some, especially minor figures guilty of horrendous crimes, like Abdullah Shah, may eventually stand before the bar of common justice. If the process is comprehensive and fair enough, it may be possible to structure a process of recognition that allows those in positions of authority to admit their implication in serious crimes during the long decades of violence, in return for further participation and international legitimacy. If the coalition moves against some such figures, more will be possible, but at the risk of politicizing the process. It will never be possible to offer compensation to all the victims, or to punish all those responsible.

It may be unfortunate if abusers retain their positions, but a process of accountability need not focus primarily on retribution. Actions are the result not solely of people's character but also of their circumstances. Some past abusers may change. Najibullah, though certainly a notorious violator of human rights, presided over major reforms in his later period in power. Many in Afghanistan remember him, at least in private, as better than the rulers who succeeded him. Removing this abuser from power did little or nothing to protect the human rights or security of Afghans.

Nor should we forget the tragic fact that twenty-five years of violence have left many brutalized and disturbed. I remember sitting outside in the clear winter sun of Peshawar with the late Anthony Hyman and Dr. Muhammad Azam Dadfar in January 1989. Dr. Dadfar, an Afghan psychiatrist who later participated as an observer in the UN Talks on Afghanistan in Bonn and was elected a deputy chairman of the Emergency Loya Jirga, had set up the only psychiatric clinic for the three to four million Afghan refugees in Pakistan, a clinic he later had to close when it was attacked by extremists. I had helped Dr. Dadfar obtain initial funding for that clinic from Amnesty International, in order to provide some treatment to victims of torture suffering from posttraumatic stress syndrome.

On that visit I saw the lines of those applying for treatment winding through the lanes of the Nasir Bagh refugee camp. Dadfar spoke of the vast range of psychological disturbance he had found among the Afghan population: in addition to the numerous torture victims, not only did a population of several million people have a proportionate number of schizophrenics and other "normally" mentally ill people, but many refugees had persistent fantasies that their lost relatives would be found somewhere—in Russia, in prison, somewhere. Many suffered from intense suspicion, bordering on paranoia and sometimes crossing that line. Depression and sleeplessness were rampant, and increasingly angry and hostile fantasies prevailed, often acted out in violence against women or neighbors, or in war. The tensions between the sexes and generations over honor, pride, and marriage that contributed to the Taliban phenomenon were already evident. The cycles of violence in places like Mazar-i Sharif, Bamiyan, and Kabul were not merely political or ethnic in any simple sense. Many are enraged and disturbed by suffering, indifference, loss of honor, feelings of being wounded and of loss, which provide a pool of potential recruits for violent movements. I remember one of the wisest remarks I ever saw quoted from an official of the Taliban, Deputy Minister of Health Stanikzai. Protesting against the international isolation of his government, he asked a *New York Times* reporter, "If you think a family member has gone mad, shouldn't you try to give him help through treatment, through talking?"

Afghanistan is a wounded society, and its people need healing, both as individuals and as a nation. We know that individuals cannot heal the wounds of the past by denying or suppressing them. One way or another, they need to confront them, in their own way, in their own time, when they are strong enough to do so, with the help of skilled and empathetic outsiders, and in some cases institutions of justice. If we are lucky, in Afghanistan the basic foundations that will make this process possible are just being laid; if we are unlucky, I do not know how the Afghans will survive. As the late Dr. Muhammad Yousef, the first prime minister of Afghanistan's New Democracy in the 1960s, once said to me in support of a negotiated withdrawal of Soviet troops, the people of Afghanistan are not made of iron and steel. They are made of flesh and blood.

To those Afghans who are seeking that difficult way of reconciling their society with its past, we, the so-called international community, owe our support and, to the extent possible, our protection. We should provide that support in a way that advances the entire process of rebuilding order and justice in Afghanistan. It is too easy to make defiant statements from a distance and leave others to face the consequences.

It is also too easy to forgive offenses committed against others. As we say in America, "It ain't hard to get along with somebody else's troubles." Islam, like Judaism before it, teaches that there are two types of sin: against God and against one's fellow human being. For the former, repentance before God suffices, but God will not forgive a sin against another until we seek that person's forgiveness ourselves. Afghans will have to decide how to conduct the lengthy and difficult process. Their culture and religion are replete with customs and traditions for reconciling disputes and wrongs, including murder, though the tribal rites of reconciliation between feuding clans were never meant to atone for the massacre and torture of thousands, of hundreds of thousands, of millions.

Struggling with these ambiguities lacks the moral clarity that I had when documenting violations of human rights and humanitarian law during the Soviet occupation. But the longer I have studied and lived with those crimes, the less I have been able to perceive them with the simple moral clarity with which I began. The discourse of transitional justice often sorts people into categories such as abusers and victims, but many in Afghanistan are both. I know a man presiding over a branch of an intelligence service that arrests and intimidates people who lost many of his own family to torture and assassination. Foreign intervention confronted the commanders of poorly equipped and undisciplined militias with the alternatives of capitulation or brutal, indiscriminate resistance. The collapse of institutions that provide security sometimes made violence seem the only alternative to victimization. Competition for desperately scarce resources led some communities to ally with warlords to wage war against one another. Najibullah, who once presided over the largest torture machine Afghanistan has known, was himself tortured, mutilated, murdered, and exposed.

Caught up in the clash and fall of contending ideologies and empires, showered with weapons and money, prodded into and subjected to violence by vast forces beyond their control, and now, at least provisionally, sheltered by forces over which they have just as little control, Afghans have had few moments to consider how to remake their shattered and brutalized society. Despite our wishes, Afghanistan will not heal quickly from decades of violence. Let us help Afghans without pushing them, knowing that international support and protection are fickle and unreliable, and that Afghans will have to live with one another when recent arrivals have gone home.

The opening sura of the Holy Qur'an begins: "Bismillah al-rahman, al-rahim; al-hamdu lillah, rabb al-'alamin al-rahman, al-rahim; malik al-yawm al–din. llyaka na'budu wa iyaka nasta'in. Ihdina al-sirat al-mustaqim" (In the name of the Merciful, the Compassionate: praise be to God, the Ruler of the universe, the Merciful, the Compassionate, Master of the Day of Judgment. You do we worship, and on You do we rely; show us the right path).

One can interpret these words in several ways. The attribute of God's rulership is preceded and followed by two attributions of mercy, and the attribution of judgment comes only after those four attributions of mercy. On the other hand, even after four attributions of compassion, judgment still follows. And the invocation ends with a humble prayer for guidance. Whoever wishes to help the Afghans recover from their decades of violence might invoke these words at least five times a day.

7

Crafting a Constitution
for Afghanistan

On January 4, 2004, nearly all 502 members of the Constitutional Loya Jirga (Grand Council) meeting in Kabul silently stood to approve a new constitution for the "Islamic Republic of Afghanistan." President Hamid Karzai signed and officially promulgated the document on January 26, 2004, inaugurating Afghanistan's sixth constitution since Amir Amanullah Khan promulgated the first in 1923. Delegates hoped that this relatively liberal Islamic constitution would provide a framework for the long task of consolidating basic state structures, as the country struggled to emerge from decades of anti-Soviet jihad, interfactional and interethnic civil war, and wars of conquest and resistance by and against the radical Islamists of the Taliban movement. In his speech to the closing session of the Loya Jirga, President Karzai explained why he thought that the new constitution—which mandated a presidential system with a bicameral parliament, a highly centralized administration with unprecedented rights for minority languages, and an Islamic legal system safeguarded by a Supreme Court with powers of judicial review— would meet the needs of a desperately indigent but proud country searching for a period of stability in which to rebuild.

The constitution was the next-to-last step on the road map to "reestablishing permanent institutions of government" outlined in the Bonn Accords of December 5, 2001. Afghans signed that agreement under UN auspices as the United States was completing the job of routing the Taliban regime that had given refuge to Usama Bin Laden. The constitution provided a framework for the "free and fair elections" to choose a "fully representative government" that were to complete that process. But two and a half years—the time frame of the Bonn Agreement—could hardly suffice to turn a failed state into a stable democracy. Whether the constitution, and

Originally published in *Journal of Democracy* (July 2004) 15: pp. 5–19.

Note: This chapter benefited from the comments of Kawun Kakar and Donald L. Horowitz. I thank them, noting that they bear no responsibility for any statements in this chapter.

with it the international effort in Afghanistan, could achieve its stated goals still depended on efforts beyond its scope, such as demobilizing militias and eradicating the drug trade and other illicit activities that accounted for more than a third of the Afghan economy.

Unlike some postwar agreements, the Bonn Accords set out a process rather than a detailed settlement of major political issues. This reflected the time pressure under which the Accords were forged, which set a speed record as such things go. Afghanistan had been through twenty-three years of many-sided civil strife marked by the overt and covert involvement of regional and global powers, yet only nine days elapsed between the UN's opening of talks in the former West German capital and the affixing of signatures on December 5, 2001.

Once U.S. president George W. Bush announced on October 1, 2001, that the United States would support a political transition and a UN-coordinated reconstruction program in Afghanistan, the pressure was on to cobble together a successor regime to the ousted Taliban movement, whose rule had sheltered al-Qaeda while that organization made Afghanistan into its base for global terrorism.[1] Four Afghan groups participated in Bonn. The two most important were the Islamic United Front for the Salvation of Afghanistan, commonly known as the Northern Alliance (NA), which had received the bulk of U.S. military assistance leading up to and during the military operations that began on October 7; and the "Rome group," representing exiled King Muhammad Zahir Shah, a resident of the Italian capital since his overthrow by a 1973 military coup.

The NA represented force on the ground and a mixture of ethnic claims with those of politicized Islam, both Sunni and Shia. Figuring prominently in NA ranks were members of such northern and central ethnic groups as the Tajiks, the Uzbeks, and the Hazaras—all of which had armed and mobilized themselves during decades of warfare. Their Taliban foes represented a reassertion of the power of the historically dominant Pashtun ethnic group, this time in the guise of a harsh Islamic fundamentalist militia. Most of the NA groups had fought against the Soviets as mujahidin (holy warriors), though the main Uzbek group had begun as a tribal militia under the communist regime.

The Rome group, consisting of exiles mostly living in the West, brought with it the claim to legitimacy of the ex-king, whose forty-year reign (1933–1973) marked the last time that Afghanistan had enjoyed any substantial degree of peace or stability. Although long-suffering Afghans felt great sympathy for their former monarch, he had no political or military organization in the country and nothing resembling a concrete program. The ex-king seemed valuable to the United States and the UN as a possible source of historic continuity and a potential rallying point for Pashtuns, who had no non-Taliban armed organizations comparable to those of the NA. The Pashtun-led groups in the NA, including a radical Islamist formation under Abd al-Rabb al-Rasul Sayyaf, had no ethnic or tribal base of support in the southern heartland of the Pashtuns. The other two groups—known as "Peshawar" and "Cyprus" after places where they had met—included small, ad hoc groups based in Pakistan and Iran.

Despite this attempt at ethnic inclusiveness, the group assembled in Bonn did not represent the people of Afghanistan, either directly or indirectly. The UN veteran and former Algerian foreign minister Lakhdar Brahimi, who chaired the talks in his capacity as Secretary-General Kofi Annan's special representative, repeatedly stressed that no one would remember how unrepresentative the meeting had been if the participants managed to fashion a process that would lead to a legitimate and representative government.

The Path to Legitimacy

The process that the Bonn participants agreed upon aimed at forming such a government. The approval of a new constitution and the holding of the elections were to be the final steps. Given the insecurity and disarray besetting Afghanistan, immediate direct elections would clearly be impossible. To fill the resulting gap, the Bonn Accords drew on an institution that had figured in the crafting of all of Afghanistan's five previous constitutions (1923, 1931, 1964, 1977, and 1987), the loya jirga. Previous rulers had summoned such meetings to legitimate key decisions. Mostly these earlier jirgas had been appointed, docile bodies. A few, such as the Constitutional Loya Jirgas (CLJs) of 1923 and 1964, had actively debated issues. And one, in November 1928, had actually rejected reform proposals put forward by King Amanullah and set the stage for the revolt that would drive him from his throne two months later.

The loya jirga developed as a state institution, but it harked back to large jirgas that Pashtun tribes had held in earlier centuries, when these tribes constituted both the main military force and, in effect, the electors of the king. During periods of turmoil when Afghans recognized no legitimate ruler, such jirgas had taken key national decisions. Drawing on these precedents, Zahir Shah's followers had developed a proposal for an Emergency Loya Jirga (ELJ) as a first step to reconstituting state power. The NA, despite the misgivings of some members, agreed to a UN-monitored ELJ as the legitimating device for the process of building a more representative government. Like all former constitutions of Afghanistan, the one drafted as part of the Bonn process was also to be approved by a loya jirga.

As an interim measure, the agreement reached at Bonn reinstated much of Zahir Shah's 1964 basic law, which had turned Afghanistan into a constitutional monarchy. That constitution had provided guarantees of public liberty unprecedented in Afghan history, but it failed to establish a stable system of government. Over a mere ten years, the country had three elections and four governments, none of which succeeded in implementing needed reforms. Many Afghans greeted with relief the constitutional monarchy's overthrow in 1973 and the establishment of a more authoritarian republic by Zahir Shah's cousin, Daoud Khan.

The Bonn Accords did not reestablish the monarchy, of course, but instead vested both executive and legislative power in the cabinet, to be headed by a president who would be head of state as well as chief of government. The 1964 constitution had followed its predecessors in making Afghanistan an officially Sunni Muslim state. Religious rites performed by the state were carried out in accord with the Hanafi sect, one of the four main schools of jurisprudence followed by Sunni Muslims (Article 2). In cases where judges could find no provision in the constitution or written law to resolve a case, they were required to follow "the basic principles of the Hanafi jurisprudence of the sharia of Islam and, within the provisions set forth in this constitution, render a decision that in their opinion secures justice in the best possible way" (Article 102). Hence, as in most "moderate" Sunni constitutions, the 1964 constitution was supreme over a judge's interpretation of Islam. No law could be contrary to the "basic principles of the sacred religion of Islam" (Article 64), but the king, not the judiciary or the ulama (Islamic scholars), was the ultimate arbiter of this provision. The 1964 constitution also declared Afghanistan a unitary state organized according to the "principle of centralization" (Article 108). As of late 2001, however, power was in fact anything but centralized, pointing to a disjunction between legal and ground-level realities that would soon become a focus of much political and constitutional controversy.

The participants in Bonn chose the personnel of an interim administration to serve under these provisions. Though the Accords claimed that considerations of "professional competence and personal integrity" had guided the choice of interim officials, no one should be too surprised that they were mostly selected to offer patronage to different factions and to recognize the distribution of armed might on the ground. The interim administration's chairman, Hamid Karzai, was a Pashtun, originally from Kandahar but more recently residing in exile, who had ties to the king and who had come back to Afghanistan with U.S. assistance to raise forces against the Taliban in its own southern bastion of Kandahar Province. The "power ministries"—defense, interior, and foreign affairs—all went to the leading faction within the NA, which also controlled the powerful intelligence service, developed in the 1980s on the model of the Soviet KGB. This faction, the Supervisory Council of the North (Shura-yi Nazar, or SN), was based in the Tajik areas in and around the Panjshir Valley just north of Kabul. The SN's founder, military leader Ahmed Shah Massoud, was murdered on September 9, 2001, by al-Qaeda suicide bombers posing as journalists. When Taliban and al-Qaeda forces fled Kabul under U.S. bombing on November 17, the SN moved in and began placing its own candidates in key posts.

Most Afghans probably saw the government chosen at Bonn as tilted in favor of the heavily Panjshiri SN. The Bonn process was designed to make the government gradually more representative. The first step was to be the holding of an ELJ by June 2002, with the mission of electing a head of state and approving what the Accords called the "structure and key personnel" of a transitional administration. With UN and other international help, the government held the ELJ on time. The indirectly elected body of about fifteen hundred representatives voted to keep Hamid Karzai as Afghanistan's chief executive for another two years. After lengthy negotiations, Karzai named a government on June 19, 2002, the last day of the nine-day meeting. Many delegates objected that the ELJ had not in fact enabled them to vote on the "structure and key personnel" of the transitional administration and that the new administration (named the Islamic Transitional State of Afghanistan) was not significantly more representative than its predecessor.

Show of Hands or Show of Force?

The same factors that limited the accomplishments of the ELJ bedeviled the constitutional process that followed. Afghanistan was and is not a place where a show of hands at a meeting can decide who will hold power. The U.S.-led coalition gave commanders weapons and cash to fight the Taliban. The commanders used those resources to remobilize patronage networks into armed groups. These groups were then able to seize control of assets such as land, customs posts, and businesses as well as smuggling routes for drugs, lumber, or gems. The mutually reinforcing personal control of armed groups and economic assets meant warlordism. The warlords occupied the power vacuum left by the collapse of the state over decades and the destruction of the Taliban administration. Though international aid and troops ensured that the Karzai government would hang on in Kabul, the first post-Taliban year saw little in the way of effective efforts to widen the reach of President Karzai's writ or boost state building. Even within Kabul, Karzai had only limited control over his own government, many of whose top officials led militias that had fought or were still fighting against the Taliban with U.S. support. It was little wonder that he hesitated to dislodge such leaders.

The Karzai government's inability to guarantee the security of voters during the stages of voting for the ELJ, or of the delegates once elected, hampered the entire ELJ. In some districts, armed commanders occupied the polling places, and the UN canceled or invalidated the elections. More commonly, intimidation was harder to prove but just as clear to its objects. Agents of the security services worked inside the loya jirga tent. One Islamist leader (Abd al-Rabb al-Rasul Sayyaf) claimed that anyone criticizing "mujahidin" deserved the death penalty for blasphemy. Fear of the intimidation tactics used by Islamists at the ELJ made the UN and the Karzai government cautious about opening the constitutional process to the public too early. Previous Afghan constitutions had been drafted in secret by governments that controlled the outcome. This was the first Afghan constitutional process where the outcome was open to political debate, and the UN insisted on introducing a measure of public consultation into the process. Brahimi also saw the UN's role as ensuring that the constitution would create a "workable" form of government and conform to basic international standards. Ultimately, the commission consulted Afghans in every province, in the refugee communities of Pakistan and Iran, and through tens of thousands of written questionnaires. Nonetheless, the government and UN thought it best to keep the content of deliberations confidential until the commission could make public a thoroughly vetted text.

The president first appointed a drafting commission of nine members, which completed a text based heavily on the constitution of 1964. A larger commission of thirty-five members reviewed the text, which was also shown to a few international experts and the government's National Security Council (NSC).[2] The government did not publish the text even during the public-consultation sessions. It published the commission's final draft, with changes incorporated at all these stages, on November 3, only thirty-seven days before the scheduled opening of the CLJ, which finally convened a few days late on December 14, 2003.

The CLJ went better than many had dared to hope it would. The UN had more time and experience in making the meeting secure, and the president and his supporters were better organized. Hence warlords and jihadi leaders had lost some of the capacity to intimidate that they had exercised at the ELJ. The result was a constitution that reflected to a considerable extent the agenda shared by Karzai and those cabinet members who considered themselves "reformers." The constitution, nonetheless, is a product of the fluid situation that is postconflict Afghanistan. It remains to be seen whether measures crafted with an eye to the immediate demands of state building will serve equally well the needs of long-term governance. We can explore this question by examining what the new Afghan constitution has to say on such key issues as the form of government, the place of Islam, the structure of the state, language and ethnic identity, and the judiciary.

Debate over these issues reflected historical realities as well as current dilemmas. Afghanistan began as a Pashtun empire ruled by tribal dynasts from Kandahar, and even today the ethnic question in its plainest form asks whether the state is to be the instrument of a mostly Pashtun elite, or a mechanism through which all citizens may equally take part in self-government. Both loya jirgas showed the strength of a supra-ethnic "Afghan" national identity, but this national identity coexisted with strong ethnic identities, and ethnic politicians from different groups advocated their own views of how to constitute the

Afghan nation. Pashtuns have tended to want a strong and Pashtun-run central state. Tajiks have focused on power sharing in the central state, while Uzbeks and Hazaras have desired recognition of their identities and mechanisms of local self-government. Strengthening the central government was also a goal of those CLJ delegates who saw the regional warlords as illegitimate and who supported state-initiated reforms. Among the strongest advocates of centralizing reforms were Westernized Pashtuns. Their opponents, including non-Pashtun Islamist commanders, charged that an ostensibly "nonethnic" position actually served the interests of the largest group. All agree that Pashtuns are the largest group, but by how much and whether they are a majority are hotly contested issues.

Debate over basic institutions reflected assumptions about ethnic politics. Everyone took it for granted that the first elected president would be a Pashtun, and furthermore, one who enjoyed U.S. approval—that is, Hamid Karzai. In a departure from the electoral system developed on the basis of the 1964 constitution, which gave more weight to Pashtun areas, the new constitution provides that the new bicameral parliament's popularly elected lower house, the Wolesi Jirga, will be filled by deputies elected "in proportion to population." This reflects the contention by opponents of Pashtun domination that Pashtuns are not a majority. These opponents therefore expect that the Wolesi Jirga, now scheduled to be elected concurrently with the president in September 2004, will be a mostly non-Pashtun body in which local and regional power holders will exert great influence. [Ultimately the Wolesi Jirga elections took place a year after the presidential election, in September 2005. No ethnic group or bloc gained control over it. Yunis Qanuni, who had led the United Front/Northern Alliance delegation to Bonn and had been a key aide to Ahmad Shah Massoud, was elected speaker.]

The Debate over Presidentialism

The draft constitution had called for a semipresidential system until the NSC-review stage (the last phase before the CLJ met). Drafting commission members had hoped that the probable combination of a directly elected Pashtun president and a non-Pashtun prime minister (chosen by the Wolesi Jirga, and possibly a Panjshiri) would provide ethnic balance. Hence the commission members resisted making the prime minister fully subordinate to the president, an essential element of stable semipresidential systems.

For a long time, in keeping with the power-sharing model, the commission insisted that the prime minister, after being named by the president, would need to pass a confidence vote in the Wolesi Jirga before taking office. The argument that this would breed instability in a highly factionalized and armed society by creating two executives with competing bases of power—the popular vote versus the support of parliament—led in September 2003 to the adoption of a more workable system in which the president's appointed PM would not need a vote of confidence to serve, but could be removed by a no-confidence vote.

Late in the joint review by the NSC and the drafting commission came a shift to full presidentialism. The office of prime minister was eliminated and the president received full power to appoint a cabinet (whose members could not be serving legislators) subject to parliamentary approval. Splits within the NA bloc and among the SN leaders in the cabinet had set the stage for this move, long resisted by the drafting commission. Major SN figures such as Education Minister Yunous Qanooni and Defense Minister Mohammed Qasim Fahim had taken different positions—the former had his eyes on a prospective premiership, while the latter aspired to become sole vice-president under Karzai—and the broader NA bloc had split as well. Qanooni found himself the cabinet's only supporter of the soon-to-be-rejected premiership option, while Fahim failed to deliver the support of any of his faction's CLJ delegates to the presidential system. The ethnic-Hazara vice-president, Abdul Karim Khalili, however, delivered some support for the proposal, and Karzai then backed the idea of two vice-presidents, one of whom would presumably be Khalili.

The issue of governmental systems came into sharp relief at the CLJ as calls rang out for an up-or-down vote on presidentialism versus parliamentarism. Nearly all Pashtun delegates, joined by some members from other ethnic groups, came out for presidentialism. A bloc of non-Pashtun delegates, however, strongly supported a parliamentary system. Both sides made cases that mixed genuine public considerations with ethnopolitical ambitions. For Pashtuns and reformers, presidentialism provided a way for one of their own—everyone knew that the first incumbent would be Karzai—to emerge from the Bonn compromise with non-Pashtun armed factions as the popularly elected head of state. There would be no uncertainty about who held legitimate executive power in Kabul, and Washington would retain the benefit of having a clearly identifiable Afghan partner whom it would know well and indeed preferred. The largely non-Pashtun delegates who opposed presidentialism saw in it a risk of personal and ethnic dictatorship. A parliamentary system, they argued, would likely result in coalition governments that would be more representative and inclusive, safer from potential abuses of executive power, and hence stabler.

To some extent, the debate rehearsed standard arguments about the relative merits of presidential versus cabinet government, but with a twist: Afghanistan has been struggling to leave behind years of failed statehood. The challenge for any new government there is not to enact this or that policy so much as it is to found the basic institutions that must exist and function if the very idea of "policy making" is to mean anything at all. Afghanistan, in other words, needs to build a state. Decades of internal warfare have left standing only the weakest of security institutions. The rule of law still does not extend over much of the country, and political parties are feeble and embryonic. Some believe that a parliamentary system could better serve such a multiethnic country, though ethnic factions have also captured parliamentary systems. The presidentialists' argument persuaded those who worry that a parliament chosen under these arduous conditions is too likely to be a fragmented body dominated by warlords, local factions, and even drug traffickers. In his speech to the CLJ's closing session, President Karzai cited post-1945 Italy and India since the Congress Party's decline as negative examples. Afghanistan's most urgent need is a functioning government. Presidentialism's advocates—who are not all Pashtuns—say that such a system, with its greater potential for what Alexander Hamilton called "energy and dispatch," is more likely to bring such a government about.

Another bruising issue concerned qualifications for office. This revolved around the difficult relations between the elites who had remained in Afghanistan and those who were returning after decades of exile, in many cases having become citizens of developed countries where they found refuge, most often the United States. Two key cabinet members, Finance Minister Ashraf Ghani and Interior Minister Ali Ahmad Jalali whom Karzai had appointed in 2003 as part of the process of broadening and professionalizing the composition of the cabinet, belong to the latter group. By virtue of their roles, they have been on the front lines of building a state and opposing warlordism. Both are U.S. citizens and lived in the Washington, D.C., area as officials of the World Bank and the Voice of America, respectively. During public consultations on the constitution, a powerful nativism surfaced, with people from all over the country calling for a ban on ministers' holding dual citizenship. This feeling also crossed ethnic and partisan lines at the CLJ, but the president and international actors voiced strong opposition to such a ban. The compromise that was reached seems to keep the ban but then provides that if the president nominates a minister with dual citizenship, the Wolesi Jirga will vote on it. Since the Wolesi Jirga has to confirm all ministerial appointments anyway, nothing new is added. The struggle over this issue, however, divided the cabinet and left more bruised feelings than any other question.

The Constitutional Status of Islam

The debate on the role of Islam involved numerous elements of the constitution, and the final result is a package deal that contains potential contradictions to spark future conflicts. More than almost any other issue, this one involved balancing outside actors' demands for the acceptance of international standards with the demands of domestic actors, notably Islamist politicians and the ulama, for a constitution that conforms to their understandings of Islam and empowers Islamic elites.

From the start of the drafting, international actors made it clear that, although they accepted that the new constitution would declare Afghanistan an Islamic state, they did not want any explicit reference to sharia in the text. In addition, the rising political influence of Shia Afghans, mostly ethnic Hazaras, as well as the insistence of neighboring Iran required that the constitution for the first time make Islam alone, rather than the Hanafi sect, the state religion. Shia jurisprudence enjoys near-parity in the current constitution, a milestone of sorts in national inclusiveness.

The final text passed at the loya jirga resulted from hard, late-stage bargaining among Islamists, President Karzai, and international representatives, along with some adroit tactical moves.[3] In quiet negotiations diplomats made clear to Islamist leaders what the international community's red lines were, and the final result reflected negotiation among many Afghan and international parties. The commission's draft named the state the "Islamic Republic of Afghanistan," a move pushed through the commission by the chair, Vice-President Nematullah Shahrani, despite opposition from many members. At the CLJ, the Islamists did not oppose a presidential suggestion to change Article 2's sweeping statement that "the religion of Afghanistan is the sacred religion of Islam" to the more qualified "the religion of the state of the Islamic Republic of Afghanistan is the sacred religion of Islam." The Islamists also accepted a presidential proposal to expand the constitutional scope accorded the religious activities of non-Muslims. Whereas Article 3 had previously declared non-Muslims "free to perform their religious ceremonies," it would after the president's suggestion give non-Muslims the broader-sounding freedom "to exercise their faith."

As part of the negotiated deal, Islamists also dropped their attempts to have the constitution cite Islam or sharia as limits on Afghanistan's international human rights obligations. Article 7 unqualifiedly requires that the state observe the Universal Declaration of Human Rights and all covenants to which the government is a party, which include the major human rights covenants. Nor did Islamists ultimately oppose Article 22, which declares the legal equality of men and women without any of the qualifications found in sharia, stating that "the citizens of Afghanistan—whether women or men—have equal rights and duties before the law." The women delegates to the CLJ—about 20 percent of the total—made this passage their core demand.

In return, Islamists advanced their position on other important parts of the constitution. Article 3 contains a provision—which in some form is standard in the constitutions of predominantly Muslim countries—that bans laws contrary to Islam. Earlier drafts had reiterated the 1964 constitution's decree that no Afghan law could be against the "basic principles of the sacred religion of Islam and the values of this constitution." At one point this clause had been whittled down simply to "Islam." The final draft goes farther than did the 1964 document toward enshrining sharia by specifying that laws cannot contradict any of Islam's "beliefs and provisions" and by omitting the 1964 reference to other "values of this constitution."

This article promises to be more central to political life than in the past, as the constitution for the first time grants the Supreme Court the power to review the constitutionality of legislation, presidential decrees, and international treaties. The president's team rejected the commission's proposal for a separate constitutional court, expressing the fear that it would resemble the Council of Guardians in Iran, but by granting the same power to the Supreme Court, a body that has always been dominated by ulama trained in islamic jurisprudence rather than constitutional law, the president's advisors may have worsened their future predicament. For it is almost inevitable that conflicts will arise between the constitution's acceptance of international human rights standards and embrace of male-female legal equality, on the one hand, and the requirement that no law may contradict the "beliefs and provisions" of Islam, on the other. When that happens, one may safely predict that political rather than purely interpretive considerations will shape the outcome.

The Islamists tried and failed to push a measure requiring that the president be male, but they made no objection to the constitution's requirement that at least a quarter of lower-house seats and 16 percent of upper-house seats be filled by female legislators. Behind these numbers lay a notable victory for female CLJ delegates, who had successfully campaigned to double the lower-house quota to 25 percent by insisting on two female deputies from each province.

Even though non-Pashtun delegates from northern Afghanistan failed to win any decentralization measures, the CLJ debates marked a milestone in the recognition of cultural pluralism. Afghanistan's origin as an empire can be seen in its de jure unitary state: the administration was meant to enable the center to control the periphery, not to help local communities exercise self-government. Provincial governors and district commissioners are appointed by the center, and there was a long-standing practice of naming administrators who are not natives of the places they govern, which the current government is trying to revive. The new constitution retains this "principle of centralization." The constitution also provides for elected councils at all levels, elected mayors of municipalities, and potential devolution of some powers to councils through legislation.

Whatever the law may say, however, the fact is that under the interim and transitional administrations many governors and military commanders received their posts because they already had power, rather than having power because of their official positions. A few, the major warlords, exercised power over several provinces. Uzbeks from northern Afghanistan, as well as Hazaras, though less insistently, wanted institutionalization of aspects of this less centralized administration. They had retreated from earlier demands for federalism, but at the CLJ

Uzbek delegates proposed that governors be elected rather than appointed. As a weaker alternative, they proposed that the center appoint governors from among a pool of candidates proposed by provincial councils. Uzbek delegates explained that these proposals were designed to prevent the center from imposing Pashtun governors on them. In the past such governors allocated land and assets to Pashtun settlers and engaged in other kinds of abuses.

The government, which had an active lobbying team on the floor of the CLJ, rejected all of these proposals. Some Pashtuns insist on centralism for ethnic reasons; many people of all ethnic groups genuinely fear the disintegration of the country. During the decades of war, regional commanders developed close ties to patrons in neighboring countries. Kabul has less influence over parts of Afghanistan than do Iran, Pakistan, or Uzbekistan. These commanders remain so potent that strengthening local government could simply mean strengthening them or other criminalized elements. Many serious Afghans argue that centralization is needed now to help overcome the obstacle posed by extralegal local power holders— perhaps by persuading them that it is time to incorporate themselves into the state-building process that Kabul hopes to direct. Decentralization or devolution can come later.

Acknowledging Afghan Diversity

Despite its rejection of administrative decentralization, the constitution takes major steps forward in recognizing Afghanistan's cultural diversity. During the drafting phase, a major issue was the relation of the two state languages, Pashto and Dari (Afghan Persian). In the past, Pashto was the language of the dominant ethnic group and Dari was the language of urban life, high culture, and the bureaucracy. The rulers were Pashtuns, but many could not speak Pashto, and Dari was the de facto language of government. The 1964 constitution gave official status to both tongues, while mandating the state to "implement an effective program for the development and strengthening of the national language, Pashto" (Article 35).

In 2003, the draft constitution recognized more linguistic pluralism than ever before: Pashto and Dari remained the official languages but five others received mention, along with a guarantee of the freedom to broadcast or publish in any of them. For the first time, the draft also encouraged the development and teaching of all languages in areas where they were spoken. The relationship between Dari and Pashto became the biggest topic of controversy at the CLJ. A proposal to require the state to train employees to work in both languages fell before objections voiced by Tajiks, who feared that the provision was a threat to fire all functionaries not conversant in Pashto. They did agree, if reluctantly, that the national anthem should be in Pashto.

In the CLJ, the northern bloc that had called for parliamentarism also demanded recognition of the multiethnic character of Afghanistan, including official recognition of Turkic tongues (Uzbek and Turkmen) as national languages. Some leaders of this group even raised the issue of the meaning of "Afghan," a noun that originally referred to Pashtuns but that this constitution, like the one of 1964, defines as applicable to any and every citizen. For instance, they demanded that citizens be called "Afghanistanis" and that the name of the currency be changed from the afghani to the paisa. These demands aroused a backlash from Pashtun delegates, who then sought to make Pashto the sole official "national" language again.

It would take a novel to do full justice to the manner in which this Gordian tangle of issues was at last resolved, but here I can sketch the results. After negotiations at the CLJ, the constitution recognizes for the first time both the ethnic pluralism and the political unity of Afghanistan. As Article 4 states:

> The nation of Afghanistan is comprised of Pashtun, Tajik, Hazara, Uzbek, Turkmen, Baluch, Pashai, Nuristani, Aymaq, Arab, Kyrgyz, Qizilbash, Gujar, Brahui, and other ethnic groups.
> The word Afghan applies to every citizen of Afghanistan.

The constitution makes Pashto and Dari official languages. The national anthem is in Pashto, but its lyrics must mention all the ethnic groups listed in Article 4, and the chorus must contain the Islamic phrase "Allahu akbar" (Arabic for "God is great," which also appears in the Dari lyrics of the anthem used from 1992 to 1996). Pashtun delegates long resisted making the Turkic languages official, partly out of a desire not to hand a victory to the ex-communist Uzbek warlord Abdul Rashid Dostum. In the end, the CLJ settled on making Turkmen and Uzbek, along with Pashai, Baluch, Nuristani, and Pamiri, additional official languages in areas where a majority speaks one of them rather than Pashto or Dari as its first language. In addition to keeping the national anthem in Pashto, the constitutional provision on language (Article 16) also states that Pashto nomenclature for certain institutions and titles must be retained in Dari and other languages as well. This article, however, was added without public discussion after the CLJ had already voted on the text.

One area about which there was unfortunately no controversy was the judiciary. This was a shame since in Afghanistan the judges have become a self-perpetuating caste. The Supreme Court is not only the ultimate appellate forum, now with the power of judicial review, but also the chief administrative organ of the judiciary. It controls judicial budgets and appoints, pays, promotes, and disciplines the lower-court judges. Judicial nominees must win presidential confirmation, but Karzai has never refused a candidate whom the Supreme Court has put forward. During the public consultations on the constitution, judicial corruption was an oft-heard complaint. The constitutional commission's leaders privately admitted that the current system creates corrupt networks of judges. Yet the new constitution retains this system: judgeships form the main source of employment for the ulama, and neither the president nor the commission wanted to confront them. Given the expanded powers of the Supreme Court and the interest of the ulama in keeping a monopoly of the power to interpret Islam, the failure to create more constitutional space for judicial reform could prove a serious barrier against needed change in the future.

A Good Start?

Given its difficult circumstances, Afghanistan is fortunate to have arrived at a result this positive. And yet the new constitution contains many obstacles to stable and effective governance. The pressure of time and inhibitions on public discussion due both to intimidation and self-censorship on sensitive issues prevented full discussion of many important questions. In some respects, Afghanistan has lost a one-time opportunity to rethink its social compact in depth. The elderly leadership of the constitutional commission sometimes seemed more intent on recovering lost traditions than on figuring out how to meet the demands of radically new conditions.

But perhaps the biggest challenge is the central paradox of postconflict constitution making. Societies emerging from civil conflict need to agree on rules for national decisions that seem reasonably fair to all or most parts of the society. A constitution is most often written—and the Afghan constitution is no exception—to be difficult to amend and to last for a long time. Yet this historical moment when societies most need a constitution is also the one when they are least prepared to adopt it. Not only are their national capacities depleted by war and emigration, but it is uniquely difficult to draft for the ages when even the fairly immediate future is so uncertain.

As noted earlier, the type of institutional or political structure needed for state building may not be the same political structure that will later provide the best governance. One powerful minister, considered a stalwart supporter of presidentialism and centralization, confided in private that he thought a more decentralized parliamentary system would ultimately be better for a stable and inclusive Afghanistan, but that adopting such options in the short run would delay or even prevent the building of urgently needed institutions.

Right now, the main challenge is to create a stable locus of authority. Yet broader inclusion and participation remain important goals, even if this is not the time to stress them above all else. So parliamentarism might someday be the better choice, and it may not be wise to lock decisions dictated by a temporary situation (decisions such as the option for presidentialism) into a hard-to-change constitution. Perhaps the Bonn Accords should have furnished an interim constitutional arrangement of more than two years. Perhaps the new constitution should also have been equipped with a "sunset clause" or other mechanism to guarantee popular review after a certain period. Some postconflict constitutions, such as that of East Timor, contain such provisions. Afghans to whom international advisors suggested such options, however, were wary of doing anything that could undermine a document already so beset with threats to its realization and enforcement. In his final speech to the CLJ, President Karzai stated:

> [T]he constitution is not the Koran. If five or ten years down the line we find that stability improves, proper political parties emerge, and we judge that a parliamentary system can function better, then a Loya Jirga can at a time of our choosing be convened to adopt a different system of government.[4]

It seems likely that such a revision will indeed be necessary in five to ten years, if this document can last that long. This will depend on many things, some of which of course lie far outside the scope of the constitution itself. Yet among them will be the question as to whether Afghans can evade the pitfalls and contradictions that their new constitution contains.

Notes

1. See Larry P. Goodson, "Afghanistan's Long Road to Reconstruction," *Journal of Democracy* 14 (January 2003): 82–99.
2. Whereas many international experts offered advice of one sort or another to the commission, the author was one of three who worked with it closely. The other two were Yash Pal Ghai of Kenya and Guy Carcassonne of France. The author recruited other experts to draft papers on issues identified by the commission.
3. The commission drafted the text in Dari and translated the working text into Pashto as needed. The UN provided unofficial English translations of the drafts for its own use and that of the international experts permitted to see the text. At the CLJ, the text was distributed in a bilingual edition in Dari and Pashto.
4. Hamid Karzai, "Address to the Closing Session of the Constitutional Loya Jirga," January 4, 2004. See http://www.kabul-reconstructions.net/images/KarzaiCLJClosingAddress.pdf

8

The Political Context of Public Administration Reform in Afghanistan

Over the course of the twentieth century, Afghanistan developed a civil service and pubic administration that became increasingly professional and skilled, while exhibiting many of the same weaknesses as the administration in other poor, developing countries. Unlike most developing countries, Afghanistan never experienced direct colonial rule. Its public administration developed from the indigenous model of the region, based on the appointment of *munshis*, or secretaries, for various civil functions. The administration of justice was largely the province of the Islamic learned clergy, or ulama. Both the administration of justice and civil administration came under the influence of continental European models, often by way of adaptations made by other Sunni Muslim states such as Egypt or the Ottoman Empire. These reforms, which introduced to Afghanistan the model of merit-based recruitment and promotion for public service, always competed with other models of state service and recruitment, conceived of as service to the ruler rather than the public, and based on tribal and family relations. The exchange of obligations and service among different clans, tribes, and families followed a set of norms loosely known as *wasita*, a system of exchange of favors.

The Afghan state has a history as, first, a tribal conquest empire, and then a subsidized buffer state. In the tribal conquest empire, a charismatic leader led armed Pashtun tribes in the conquest of wealthier territories (Punjab, Kashmir, Turkestan) and redistributed the wealth extracted therefrom. He established an administration

Originally unpublished, World Bank (2006)

Note: This chapter was prepared for the World Bank to provide background information on the political context for public administration reform in Afghanistan as well as analysis, and an assessment of the political context for public administration reform in Afghanistan. Although various bank staff members reviewed and commented on the paper, the views expressed are those of the author and do not necessarily reflect the position of the World Bank on the topics and issues discussed.

to govern the urban areas and the conquests under his control for the benefit of the ruling tribes. The ruler tried to establish an autonomous state apparatus in order to provide himself with a basis of power independent of the tribes.

The advent of Western colonialism destroyed the possibility of external conquest. The attempt by the British to incorporate a pacified Afghanistan into India's border defenses led to the payment of subsidies directly to the ruler, who obtained a source of income independent of the military power of the tribes. The creation of Afghanistan as a centralized buffer state thus tipped the balance of power away from the tribes and toward the ruler, leading to the creation of an absolutist state that gradually developed a professional army and bureaucracy.

Outside of the cities and towns, the administration did not penetrate the society much, and the activities of governance mainly consisted of negotiation with local power holders through intermediaries. The conquest of the country was carried out in the same way. After some combination of negotiation and military conquest, the king or amir would form a hierarchical alliance with a local ruler. This alliance would be cemented through kinship: the king would marry a woman from the local ruler or tribal leader's family, and the king would take the son of the local ruler or chief to court as a kind of privileged hostage. These *ghulam bachas* (slave sons) were trained as officials to serve the ruler. Together with the Muhammadzai ruling clan, they formed the core of the state elite of the old regime in Afghanistan.

Such a court created a politics based on kinship and intrigue, with family ties to the wives of the ruler and other officials, marriages among members of the elite, and other forms of alliance playing the principal role. Members of the elite used these ties to appoint relatives and clients to positions of power, in return for which they were supposed to favor the interests of their patron. This system created durable relations of trust and confidence among members of the elite, while dividing them into fluid competing factions.

The factionalized elite presided over a small, weak, and highly centralized administration, the main task of which was to impose stable control over the territory by the rulers in the interest of the foreign powers that were funding them. Such a centralized administration ensured control by the center over the very limited functions that the administrators were called upon to perform. This structure was ill suited to provide services to the population or implement major investments, but the population relied on its own resources for most services, which were provided by informal local governance structures. Petty corruption was pervasive, and nepotism was more the predominant system of elite recruitment than a form of corruption. The lack of major revenue streams and sources of wealth limited the scope of corruption.

During the Cold War, Afghanistan's state expanded its functions to meet the new demands of development. In response to the Pashtunistan dispute with

Pakistan and the need to establish state authority somewhat more firmly, Kabul expanded the military with aid from the USSR. It expanded the system of education with aid from the United States and European countries. Foreign aid funded road building, the construction of dams and power stations, and the extraction of natural gas, which was exported to the USSR. These limited tasks required the formation of a new educated class of military officers, engineers, teachers, and doctors. The state needed a corps of people with a degree of competence in literacy and numeracy as well as foreign languages and professional skills to acquire and use the new knowledge and to manage the new state functions. The state recruited the new elite from all parts of the population, largely through newly established provincial high schools. These high schools, as well as Kabul University, recruited individuals of diverse backgrounds largely on merit, leading to a channel of upward mobility. Highly desired scholarships to study abroad, however, which were the pathway to the highest and most coveted positions, continued to be distributed among elites largely according to patronage. For instance, one woman who is now an academic in the West and who has served as a deputy minister was enabled to take up a scholarship to study in Germany in the 1960s only because her father, a prominent elder of the Popalzai tribe (the same tribe as the Karzais and of the founder of the Afghan state, Ahmad Shah Durrani), intervened with the Ministry of Higher Education to get them to waive the rule that a woman studying abroad had to be accompanied by a mahram, or male family member acting as guardian. A woman from a humbler background would not have been able to take up such a scholarship. Hence modernization (including the higher education of women) and acquisition of foreign training became a privilege of an elite based on patronage.

For those who obtained senior positions in the administration, the salary and perks of office were such as to provide a dignified if not wealthy life, and officials enjoyed considerable social prestige. It became the ambition of many families to educate a son and place him in the civil service, where he could provide a valuable point of contact and financial support for the entire extended family. Hence success in a merit-based system was seen as a means to obtain benefits through wasita.

The newly educated faced a situation common in developing countries. First, even though entry to the civil service was largely based on merit, assignment and promotion still depended heavily on patronage and connections, leaving a feeling of frustration and injustice. Second, the public sector could not absorb all of the new graduates; nor did the private sector expand to offer them opportunities. Finally, the highest level of political decision making remained opaque and unaccountable, based on intrigues among elites around the various factions of the royal family. The resulting politics of frustrated counterelites generated a variety of radical movements, including pro-Soviet and pro-Chinese Marxism, radical nationalism, ethnic separatism, and radical Islamism, both Sunni and Shia. Such a weak state situated on a fault line of the Cold War and in proximity to the oil supplies of the Persian Gulf could not withstand these tensions, leading to the wars, invasions, and state collapse of the past nearly thirty years.

During the various historical periods since 1978, Afghanistan has been ruled by several communist factions, mujahidin and militia groups, the Taliban, and now an internationally sponsored government drawing largely on returned exiles. Regardless of the ideological and political differences among these regimes, one policy they all had in common was transforming control of the government into an employment creation scheme for the ruling group's political adherents and family/clan/tribal/ethnic group.

The Interim Afghanistan National Development Strategy (I-ANDS) summarized the effect of these years on the legitimacy and capacity of the state as follows:

> The series of coups, attempts at social change through violent coercion in the name of an alien ideology, and the capture of state administration by armed commanders damaged the legitimacy of the state. During the communist regime, hiring and promotion in the civil service, as well as entry to institutions of higher education, largely depended on membership in and loyalty to factions and sub-factions of the ruling party, undermining whatever weak commitment to merit-based recruitment had previously existed. During the mujahidin years of 1371–75 (1992–96), each region and ministry was controlled by a different faction which awarded positions and resources to its supporters. Under the Taliban, only clergy of the ruling movement could typically hold leadership positions. Some skilled and dedicated officials remained in the government through all these changes, but personnel decisions were based on neither technical nor professional merit.
>
> Government ceased to be an instrument for providing even modest services to people. Though loyal civil servants tried to perform their duties, government either became an instrument of control through fear and violence, or simply disintegrated. The state lost the capacity to collect even basic information about the society it supposedly governed. The outbreak of war in 1357 (1978–79) halted the country's first attempt to carry out a population census, which remained incomplete. Decades of war led to chronic political instability, fragmentation of society, militarization of public life and competition among power structures across the country. The repeated failure of successive governments led to the emergence of informal governance structures and to domination of political life by unstable, but interconnected criminalized political, economic and social networks.

We may add that, upon taking power, the first and most consistent policy of the Khalqi faction of communists was the arrest, torture, and large-scale liquidation of competing elites, including a large number of government officials whose political allegiance was suspect. Arrest and exile, though not execution, of such elites continued during the succeeding rule dominated by the Parchami communist faction. During the communist period, though no figures are available, it appears that most of Afghanistan's Western-trained elites were executed or fled the country, usually for exile in the countries where they had been educated. As no new elites were trained in the West during that period, and as the quality of professional education and training in Afghanistan declined, the result was a twenty-year hiatus in the production of professional elites and the physical, social, and political separation of such elites from their rapidly changing society of origin. As the I-ANDS noted, "To replace the skilled elites who were imprisoned, killed, or driven into exile, the communist regime and its foreign sponsors trained a young generation of technocrats in Soviet-inspired management and governance, including a commitment to expanding the role of the state in the economy."

As the USSR planned its withdrawal, the regime shifted from the direct use of coercion to large-scale bribery and subsidy of militias, financed mainly through the printing of money. The I-ANDS noted the effect of the resulting hyperinflation on public service:

> Hyperinflation made salaries of government employees that had once provided a dignified if modest standard of living utterly insufficient to survive. The result was a further decline in the commitment and performance of public servants, including teachers, police, and the judiciary, and further incentive for corruption, which had also spread widely due to the politicization and factionalization of the administration. For lack of any alternative employment, however, functionaries remained at their posts even when earning less than US$20 per month, often seeking to supplement these earnings through corruption, trading, or other jobs.

The erosion of state resources by hyperinflation also resulted in a decline in the quality of physical facilities and working conditions. The government made no new investments in supplies or methods of operation. During the period that the world was rapidly developing an information-based economy using multiple forms of telecommunications, Afghanistan lacked a functioning telephone system. Documents were produced on manual typewriters, for which new ribbons could only rarely be found. Accounting and payment methods similarly stagnated or regressed. As money around the world became increasingly electronic, the Afghan banking system collapsed, leaving cash (devalued bills) as the only form of payment and handwritten entries recorded in account books with hard-to-obtain pens as the only form of record keeping. In 1998, when I visited Kabul as a UN consultant, I defied UN rules against capacity building of the Taliban administration by supplying a pen to the protocol department of the foreign ministry in order to expedite the issuing of my exit visa. By thus doubling the number of functioning pens in the department, I enabled an official to work on my forms, while another worked on those of a Sikh trader going on a business trip.

As the state lost capacity, however, it expanded. The number of ministries, departments, provinces, and districts continued to increase, driven by the logic of creating positions to accommodate interests, rather than the delivery of public services.

Mujahidin rule was characterized by a culture of predation. Officials from that time tell of ministers bringing their families from the provinces in order to distribute the furniture of the ministry among them. Positions became personal property, and the idea of public service seemed lost. In Herat and Mazar-i Sharif, where strong leaders imposed a greater degree of order than in fragmented Kabul, the administration seems to have survived in somewhat better condition. Many remaining officials fled Kabul for Mazar, Pakistan, or Central Asia.

The Taliban did not recognize technical qualifications except for religious (and medical) training and appointed mullahs to all significant positions. Their advent in Kabul led to a further migration of families marginalized by their strictures on women and their takeover of the administration.

The I-ANDS described the legacy of these events as follows:

> The state inherited by the Interim Authority of Afghanistan in 1380 (December 2001) . . . was responsible for a large range of functions, all of which it performed very poorly or not at all. It was disconnected from the people at every level and accountable to virtually no one, including the government. The state was highly centralized in principle but in fact non-functional or operating under the control of different authorities. For years, demoralized government staff had received neither genuine salaries, training to meet new challenges, nor the leadership and equipment they needed to do their jobs. Virtually all institutions were penetrated by networks of corruption.

Some members of the UN team that convened the Bonn negotiations tried to address these issues. They envisaged the interim regime as a small technocratic administration and proposed reducing the large number of ministries to fifteen departments, each headed by a technical expert from Afghanistan or the Afghan diaspora who would be forbidden from running for office in the future. Another proposal was to establish a trust fund to finance government expenditure, in part to remove discretionary power over spending from these new officials and insulate them from the pressure of wasita. (This proposal evolved into the Afghanistan Reconstruction Trust Fund.) The original draft of the Bonn Agreement proposed a powerful civil service commission, which would vet all appointments down to the district and subdistrict level for probity and technical competence. The draft also proposed a strict code of conduct to prevent the emergence of corruption.

The Afghan delegates, however, rejected most of these measures. Those that nonetheless slipped through into the agreement were not implemented. When the UN proposed reducing the number of ministries, delegates stated that there were twenty-nine ministries, and that the Bonn meeting could not eliminate any of them. Instead, it added one more, a ministry for women's affairs. When it came time to fill the positions, Lakhdar Brahimi, the UN SRSG who was chairing the meeting, asked each of the four delegations to submit candidates for each position on the basis of technical competence alone, not political affiliation. The main delegations instead proposed their own members for ministries. It was clear to everyone that ministerial positions were allocated according to factional loyalty, as spoils of victory, not in order to provide public services with greatest efficiency.

The discussion of the civil service commission was long and painful. All groups concurred that the agreement should in no way limit their ability to appoint whomever they wanted to government posts. In the end, the agreement stated that the civil service commission would "provide the Interim Authority and the future Transitional Authority with shortlists of candidates for key posts in the administrative departments [ministries], as well as those of governors and uluswals [district administrators], in order to ensure their competence and integrity." The agreement did not impose on the government any obligation actually to appoint officials from among the candidates on these short lists. In practice, the civil service commission never compiled or submitted such lists. Instead it defined its purpose as "reform" of the system.

The UN draft required adoption of a strict code against corruption and sanctions for members of the administration who violated it. This also aroused near-universal opposition, on the grounds that it was not necessary beause an anti-corruption law from the 1970s was still in effect, among others. The agreement finally stipulated somewhat vaguely:

7. The members of the Interim Administration shall abide by a Code of Conduct elaborated in accordance with international standards.
8. Failure by a member of the Interim Administration to abide by the provisions of the Code of Conduct shall lead to his/her suspension from that body. The decision to suspend a member shall be taken by a two-thirds majority of the membership of the Interim Administration on the proposal of its Chairman or any of its Vice Chairmen.

Neither of these measures has been implemented to date.

When the interim administration took over in Kabul, it faced a chaotic situation. It announced that all those dismissed for political reasons by previous regimes, or who had fled the country as refugees and now returned, would be reinstated in their posts. This included both all the women dismissed by the Taliban and any men hired to replace them. When I visited the Ministry of Education in March 2002, the entire ministry was packed with returning teachers bearing a variety of certificates and other documents, asking to be rehired. There were no common standards or any method of testing for competence. The result was the swelling of the ranks of the bureaucracy without rationalization of tasks.

Because offices were allocated as spoils of victory, and because ministers and other high officials were political figures who had been marginalized for years, their followers and kinsmen flocked around them asking for jobs. Afghans said that the men came to the front door at dawn and the women came to the back door at night. One minister was once late for a breakfast meeting with Brahimi because—so he claimed—he was besieged by two hundred petitioners and job seekers he had to see before he could leave his home. My own informal observations were consistent with the general belief that most ministers hired primarily from their own factional, ethnic, regional, or tribal group.

The scramble for jobs was greatly aggravated by lack of employment and the increase in the cost of living. The war had generated its own expanding cash economy, in which warlords, commanders, opium traffickers, and other smugglers moved large amounts of cash through both domestic and international transactions, driving up domestic prices, while the productive assets of the country depreciated or were destroyed with no investment or upkeep.

The rapid expansion of the military and civilian international presence in Afghanistan after the inauguration of the interim administration created a second parallel economy, which placed the public sector under more pressure. The arrival of international staff, with their demand for first-world-standard housing, imported food and household goods, curios, restaurants, bars, prostitutes, vehicles, drivers, security, clerical staff, local administrators, translators, fixers, and others, rapidly drove up the cost of living in urban areas. The international agencies competed for the scarce supply of Afghan skilled labor. The result was to remove capacity from the government at the time that it most needed it, as the most skilled officials were hired by embassies, UN offices, and military forces.

The attempt to increase the capacity of the Afghan administration by attracting professionals back from the Afghan diaspora created further complexities. Roughly speaking, the diaspora could be divided into two groups: those living in the region (mainly Pakistan and Iran) and those living in developed countries (the United States and Europe). Programs operated by UNDP, the International

Organization for Migration (IOM), the Open Society Institute, and probably others created parallel higher salary scales for these returnees, so that although an Afghan who had never left would be paid up to $50 per month, a returnee from the neighboring countries might be paid up to $500 per month, and one from the developed countries up to $3,000 per month.

The situation was further complicated by the presence of returned Afghan refugees and exiles who had become citizens of developed countries. Their foreign passports, degrees, and professional experience entitled them to full salaries and consulting fees as international expatriates; but their Afghan dual citizenship also entitled them to serve in the Afghan government. Sometimes they did so while continuing to receive the salary of an international or developed-country official through secondment or while receiving international consulting contracts rumored to amount to $20,000 per month or more. Resentment of Afghans who returned with dual citizenship to serve as ministers and other high officials turned out to be a very emotional issue during the drafting of the 2004 constitution. This issue led to an angry division between cabinet members from the Northern Alliance and returnees from the West. The delegates to the Constitutional Loya Jirga, like most of those who responded to requests for public consultations, largely opposed allowing Afghans with dual citizenship to serve in the government. Only a last-minute compromise, requiring special parliamentary approval for such appointees, made it possible.

It was in this highly charged political atmosphere that the Independent Administrative Reform and Civil Service Commission (IARCSC) began its work. President Karzai appointed Vice-President Hedayat Amin-Arsala as chair of the IARCSC. Arsala, a former official of the World Bank, had been foreign minister in one of the exiled mujahidin governments and was a member of the Rome group's delegation at Bonn. He is a descendant of one of the most important Pashtun tribal families in Afghanistan, which dominates the city of Jalalabad and the areas of Nangarhar province south of the Kabul River.

Forming the civil service commission was not a high priority for the interim administration, in which Arsala served as minister of finance. Most of its energy was devoted to its primary task, convening the Emergency Loya Jirga, and trying to restart the functioning of a moribund apparatus of government. After the still-unsolved assassination of his cousin, First Vice-President Hajji Abdul Qadir, in July 2002, Arsala became first vice-president in the position de facto reserved for Ghilzai Pashtuns from Eastern Afghanistan. In that capacity he became chair of the Civil Service Commission, which defined its mission as reforming the civil service rather than vetting appointments.

Since 2005 and the inauguration of President Karzai after his election, the IARCSC has come under the direction of First Vice-President Ahmad Zia Massoud, brother of the late commander Massoud. Inclusion of Massoud on his ticket was President Karzai's gesture toward the core Panjsheri group of the Northern Alliance after his decision not to run with Defense Minister Fahim. Under the administrative system of the Afghan government, the two vice-presidents chair various cabinet committees, and the first vice-president chairs the economic committee, in which capacity he also oversees the work of the IARCSC. The new head of the IARCSC is a Northern Alliance appointee. It seems to have declined in influence relative to Arsala's tenure.

The major reform introduced by the commission was the program of Priority Reform and Restructuring, which was supposed to establish centers of excellence within ministries. The most effective officials would be transferred to PRR units, which were exempted from the usual salary scales, so that they could be rewarded according to merit. Eventually the idea was to reduce the size of the ministry establishments and retain the best officials, who would go through the PRR process. Both the president and the ministers, however, resisted aspects of such a process. The president did not want to dismiss people from government employment when alternative employment was not available, and ministers, though welcoming the opportunity to pay some of their officials more, did not want to fire anyone, especially those whom they had hired through patronage. There are no doubt cases where PRR has functioned as planned, but its general reputation is as a program for raising salaries largely at the discretion of ministers, without increasing competence or streamlining ministries.

Those ministries with the greatest success in delivering services thus far have done so not by reforming the existing administration but by bypassing it altogether. The Ministries of Rural Rehabilitation and Development and of Public Health have implemented the National Solidarity Program and the Basic Package of Health Services largely by contracting with NGOs and international organizations for the delivery of services. The activities of these contractors are supervised by small groups of expatriates and Western-returned Afghans within the minister's office. Similarly, the Ministry of Defense presides over an entirely new Afghan National Army, the creation and management of which is largely controlled by the U.S. Department of Defense. No more than 2 percent of its recruits came from the militias that constituted the former Ministry of Defense.

Two important ministries that currently have ministers from the former Northern Alliance—Interior along with Energy, Power, and Water—illustrate some of the obstacles to reform. The Ministry of the Interior has extraordinary importance in a highly centralized unitary state. All governors and police chiefs are employees of the MOI, with governors holding the rank of deputy minister and serving at the pleasure of the president.

Afghanistan suffers from a severe lack of energy, and the lack of electrical power in Kabul is a politically explosive issue. According to the Afghanistan

Compact, donors and the Afghan government will meet targets for increasing power supply by the end of 2010, and the government of Afghanistan will engage in reforms to ensure cost recovery for power supply. [By that time Kabul received a significantly increased electricity supply through transmission lines from Uzbekistan, but the Kajaki Dam project in Helmand, which was to provide power for southern Afghanistan, has still not been completed in 2012. No measures for cost recovery have been implemented successfully.] The agreement makes no provision for how power is to be supplied before 2010; only emergency provision of diesel fuel for generators can make up the gap. Donors demand that rather than only wait for them to pay for expensive and inefficient power supplies, the government should immediately start measures to recover more costs. The obstacle, however, is more complex than a public unaccustomed, unwilling, or unable to pay. In fact, many people do pay exorbitant amounts for power. Some pay for private provision through generators (this is what all foreigners do). Many others, however, have unofficial connections to the grid. It is common knowledge in Kabul that one has to pay bribes to the workers at the local power relay station in order to get a newly rented house hooked up or to ensure continuity of power supplies to an existing hookup. Many of the connections concluded through this parallel system are never recorded, like the power connections in a Brazilian favela.

The bribery does not stop there. The workers' superiors know that this is going on and expect that the workers will kick a percentage upward, and so on toward the top. This is only fair, since the employees owe their jobs to favors that their superiors did to their families, and wasita dictates that they must reciprocate. "Corruption" is an inadequate word to describe a pattern of behavior that constitutes not so much deviance from an existing system as a parallel system that is more real than the de jure one. The minister himself, Ismail Khan, is not generally thought to be involved in this system, as his political and patronage base is not in the ministry but in his native province of Herat, where he was the major leader of the anti-Soviet and anti-Taliban resistance for decades.

Indeed most institutions in Afghanistan work this way. The Ministry of the Interior largely consists of various predatory factions, increasingly engaged in protection and organization of the narcotics trade. As documented in a recent report from the World Bank and the United Nations Organization on Drugs and Crime (UNODC), appointments of police chiefs and sometimes governors require the payment of huge bribes, which can be recovered (as expected) only through the "taxing" of narcotics trafficking, extracting bribes in the course of crop "eradication," and confiscation of drugs seized in the course of "law enforcement." This tribute flows upward into the highest levels of the government, where the drug trade's political protectors are to be found.

Views on Subnational Administration

As noted above, the Afghan state is highly centralized. It was created in this form to enable a ruler supported by foreign powers to control the territory through officials whose mandate was to serve the ruler, not the public. In this sense, "public administration" is a misnomer; a more accurate term would be "state administration." The state, however, legitimated its power variously by agendas of Pashtun ethnic nationalism, modernization, or Islam. Therefore Pashtun ethnic nationalists, modernizers, and radical Islamists (especially when they are Pashtun) have tended to support centralization.

The reality of power in Afghanistan is a complex combination of a de jure centralized administration and a de facto decentralized (and, most importantly, deinstitutionalized) exercise of power, often through networks that reach far across the country's border to governments and private organizations in neighboring countries and beyond. Hence an agenda of decentralization or federalism also conjures for many the fear of disintegration of the country and its division among the neighbors.

During the drafting of the constitution, the non-Pashtun groups took different positions on how to balance the power of a presumably Pashtun president. Tajiks, who could compete for power at the center, favored a dual executive system with a president and prime minister to check each other. Uzbeks asked for the election of governors or at least the right of provincial councils to provide the president with shortlists from whom he would have to choose, to prevent the imposition of Pashtun governors who would seize land and engage in other abuses as in the past. They eventually compromised on obtaining recognition of their language. Hazaras retreated from the demand for federalism in return for recognition of Shia jurisprudence for personal law among Shia and the establishment of Afghanistan as an Islamic state rather than a Hanafi Muslim state.

The Pashtun modernizers around the president argued that, under the current conditions of the Afghan state, localities would be captured by armed commanders, and that the central state would be powerless. They saw the central state as the agency of reform and service delivery, especially through the creation of direct links to the villages, as in the National Solidarity Program (NSP), with international organizations and NGOs acting as intermediaries using foreign aid. Most people in the country of all ethnic groups echoed the demand for a strong central government, which they seemed to define as a government that would eliminate the gangs of armed men that were abusing them, seizing land, and generating insecurity.

As noted below, however, in the current security environment and with the growth of drug trafficking and administrative corruption, fewer people see the central government as a consistent agent of reform. Given the reality of a government that is largely dysfunctional and corrupt, the idea of devolving service delivery to local authorities with little or no capacity (or even buildings) has little appeal.

The one arena where some devolution has taken place is through the provincial reconstruction teams (PRTs), and it has happened by accident. Each PRT has a budget for the province where it is stationed. These are the first provincial budgets in the history of Afghanistan. Within the Afghan government itself, there is no provincial budgeting process, as the center never wanted to allow any alternative centers of power to develop. For similar reasons President Karzai rejected the original proposal by the U.S.-led coalition for Joint Regional Teams in eight or nine regions, as these JRTs would have tended to interact with the major regional leaders that emerged from the 2001–02 war with their own U.S.-funded armies. Instead he insisted that these teams be organized at the provincial level, so that their interlocutors would be governors, appointed by him. To the extent that the PRTs work closely with governors and do not insist on flying their own flags over what they do, the governor has in effect a provincial development budget for the first time, which he can use not only to deliver benefits to the province but to build a political coalition of support for the government. The management of the provincial budget by the PRT provides a check on the creation of autonomous provincial power, which reassures the center.

The PRTs' partnerships with governors could become focal points in some cases for the creation of processes of budgeting and public inspection (through provincial development shuras and provincial councils) at the provincial level. So far this is not reflected at all in the formal rules of the state administration or in legislation.

At the same time, much service provision takes place at the village level through funds administered by the mosque or local tribal or clan leaders. The mosque is the most important institution in most villages. The mosques collect some Islamic taxes, such as zakat and ushr, for public purposes. These include taxes on local incomes from opium production and trade. Villagers have greater confidence in services provided by these means precisely because they are provided outside the state, which remains a distrusted and foreign body. To some extent the indigenous village councils meeting in the mosque are competing with the new elected Community Development Councils established by NSP. The latter have much more money, but villagers also know that the money comes from foreign donors through incomprehensible and opaque processes and can stop at any moment, whereas the mosque is eternal.

Both the NSP and some independent Afghan and international researchers are now trying to understand better these locally rooted and trusted methods of service provision. These institutions, if they are articulated at all with the state, answer to the Ministry of Hajj, Awqaf and Irshad (often called Religions Affairs) through the Department of Mosque Management, not to the MoI like the administration down to the uluswali (district) level or to the Ministry of Rural Rehabilitation and Development (MRRD) like the CDCs. Some are considering whether it might be possible to unite the separate channels of administration and service provision and incorporate these village institutions more productively into the state and its development models. UNICEF has successfully made use of mosques and religious leaders in its vaccination programs. In order to carry out its programs, NSP often has to make unofficial use of the same institution and elite. Mosques provided a basic social safety net, or perhaps more accurately were used by villagers to provide one to themselves. Now, however, mosques are much more integrated into national and even international Islamic political movements, so that making use of mosques for service provision could also strengthen those forces. In any case, using mosques for service provision would confront obstacles in the differing perceptions of opium income and foreign aid on the part of villagers on the one hand and foreign donors on the other. For now Afghan state elites and Afghan villagers retain a high level of mistrust for each other, which poses a nearly insuperable obstacle to integrating the two systems.

Political and Security Environment

The high point of reform in Afghanistan was probably the period from the Berlin conference of March–April 2004, which constituted the major triumph of Finance Minister Ashraf Ghani, and the appointment of a new cabinet without Ghani by President Karzai after his inauguration as elected president in December 2004.

Since that time, the weakening of reformist leadership, perceptions of increased corruption, and the decline in security—and in particular the remobilization of the Taliban—have had additional negative effects on prospects for reform. The insurgency confronts the government with an immediate security threat. Reforms based on professionalism and merit will take years to create effective security agencies and ministries for service delivery. In the meantime there are only two alternatives to fill the gap: international provision of security and services, or reliance on the mechanisms of patronage that became strengthened and took on new forms during the decades of war. The international community now presses President Karzai to rely on it and the reform programs it now sponsors, rather than warlords that the United States formerly sponsored, but Karzai and many other Afghans have progressively lost faith in international support, which has seemed too little and too late and utterly ineffective in coping with the sanctuary that the Taliban enjoy in Pakistan. The president points to weak support for the police, in particular, for the first five years, and asks what alternatives he has.

The nature of the struggle was revealed by the 2006 tug-of-war over the governorship of Helmand. For several years the governor of Helmand was Sher Muhammad Akundzada, a commander and big landlord of the Alizai tribe. He was reputed (like virtually every power holder in Helmand) to be involved in the drug trade and also of creating problems by favoring his clansmen in northern Helmand. His family was a prominent one. His uncle, Mullah Nasim Akhundzada, had become one of the largest commanders and drug barons in southwest Afghanistan in the 1980s, as well as the deputy defense minister of the exiled mujahidin government in 1988. That year he struck a deal with U.S. Ambassador to Pakistan Robert Oakley to stop opium poppy cultivation in Helmand in return for a mere $1 million in development projects. As a result Akhundzada was assassinated, probably by other factions to whom he had promised to deliver the raw material. When the U.S. Congress intervened and banned such negotiations with drug dealers, his successor reinstituted cultivation.

According to press reports, under pressure from the British, who were preparing to deploy several thousand troops to Helmand, Karzai moved Akhundzada to the upper house of Parliament and replaced him with Engineer Daud, a respected technocrat, while leaving Akhundzada's brother as deputy governor. Over the summer of 2006, the battle in Helmand became very intense. Governor Daud was instrumental in negotiating a controversial truce between ISAF and the Taliban through elders in Musa Qala district. Daud complained, however, that Akhundzada's brother made it impossible for him to work properly and came to Kabul to demand his removal. President Karzai, under pressure from supporters of Akhundzada ostensibly over the security situation in Helmand, from the United States over the Musa Qala deal, and from the British over drugs and other issues, finally dismissed Daud. The president claimed he was ineffective, while Daud attributed the decision to insistent pressure from the drug mafia.

The relevant consequence for public administration reform is that the immediate security emergency plus the strengthening and consolidation of political control over drug trafficking have weakened efforts at professionalizing the administration. In accord with the Afghanistan Compact, in October 2006 the government established a vetting mechanism for senior appointments similar to the one originally proposed at Bonn. Despite the adoption of this formal institution, however, the security crisis is aggravating ethnic tensions, driving many Afghans to seek refuge in the patronage relationships that actually function, if imperfectly and unjustly, rather than trusting new institutions that would be preferable if—a big if—they could actually be established and would then function as advertised. The continued involvement of some officials of the government and their close relatives as patrons and protectors of the drug trade and the creation of pyramids of narco-trade protection payments similar to those described above for electricity supply discredits counternarcotics efforts and leads some people to conclude that reform is just a charade to legitimize a Western counterterrorism agenda from which they are unlikely to benefit. Though there are many appointments at issue other than the high-profile ones of governors and police chiefs mentioned here, these set the tone for the entire public sector. In the big political game that is now going on over the control of the state and assets of Afghanistan, the IARCSC is not a very important player and cannot do much if anything to change the political atmosphere. At most it can present plans that may be adopted and that eventually might be implemented at least partially if the atmosphere changes.

9

Peace Building, State Building

Constructing Sovereignty for Security

In the aftermath of war, international actors often fret about the incoherence, tribalism, and division of war-torn countries. Those living in those countries, however, recognize that the divisions, rivalries, and fragmentation of authority of the "international community" constitute just as big an obstacle to what the UN calls "peace building."

Such operations have the paradoxical mission of helping others build sovereign states. They constitute the contemporary version of a long-standing security task: the stabilization of the periphery by great powers, which now must be carried out in a world governed by a regime of universal juridical sovereignty of the national state. Even the administration of U.S. President George W. Bush, which adopted a doctrine of preventive war on the basis of unilateral judgment that governments might threaten U.S. security, was constrained to act within the same regime. Its inability to motivate Iraqis or international partners to collaborate with an occupation regime forced the administration to call on the UN to assist in the transfer of sovereignty to Iraqis.

This recourse to the UN, despite political differences between proponents of multilateral peace building and prosecutors of unilateral preventive war, shows that these projects respond to a common security environment. The central fact of the environment in the past half century has been the replacement of global juridical imperialism by global juridical national sovereignty. The UN incorporates this organizing principle into its charter. This structure has altered the options available to great powers for coping with security threats or challenges to their interests.

Originally published in *Survival* 47, no. 4 (Winter 2005–06), 93–106.

From Imperialism to Peace Building: Doctrines in Historical Context

The use by various states and organizations of *sui generis* terms such as "peace building," "postconflict reconstruction," "nation building," or "stabilization" displaces these operations from their historical context. The use of such terms and the different types and degrees of political conflict over the interventions in Afghanistan, Iraq, or Darfur shows that not all such actions are manifestations of a common project. The U.S. pursuit of security from both terrorism and challenges to its strategic dominance has different implications from the pursuit of human security through processes of global governance. These doctrines, however, constitute different responses to a common problem: maintaining order and security, however defined, in an increasingly integrated global system juridically and politically organized around universal state sovereignty.

For centuries stronger powers have intervened along their peripheries to establish politically acceptable forms of order. Initially unlinked regional empires (China, Rome, Mayans) tried to stabilize relations with unruly peoples on their frontiers. With the construction of a more tightly linked system of mutually recognized and demarcated states in post-Westphalia Europe, the quest for security and profit on the periphery became an imperial—and ultimately global—extension of interstate competition among a single system of core states. European states tried to ensure their interests by integrating new territories through conquest or royal marriages, imposing direct or indirect colonial rule, supporting subordinate buffer states, settling occupied territories with immigrants from Europe, and waging one kind of war against rebellious natives and another kind of war against each other. They tried to regulate their competition and make it more predictable through meetings such as the Berlin Conference, which tried to establish a stable division of colonial rule in Africa. For the first time, states cooperated to impose a common juridical framework over the entire globe, if one that institutionalized unequal political and legal status for diverse territories and peoples.

Creating such a common global framework was a precondition for transforming it. The contemporary global framework for security developed with the foundation of the United Nations system after World War II. That war not only defeated fascism but also ended imperialism as a legitimate legal doctrine. The UN's first task was overseeing decolonization, extending the international regime of national sovereignty enshrined in the charter to the entire globe, a process that continued through the UN-supervised transition to independence of Timor Leste.

During the Cold War, the struggle over building postcolonial states largely took the form of competing foreign aid projects by the alliance systems led by the United States and USSR. Postcolonial states positioned themselves within the strategic relations of the Cold War. To extract aid, they sometimes adopted, or pretended to adopt, structures based on models supported by one or the other global contenders.

The end of the Cold War freed the UN and some regional organizations to replace unilateral clientelism with multilateral state-building efforts, especially in the aftermath of conflict. Agreement by the Security Council to entrust such operations to the UN reflected both the end of zero-sum strategic competition and the lowering of the stakes in who controlled these states. Major powers had less interest in either undermining or supporting such efforts.

The attack of September 11 showed that the United States could now be attacked from even the weakest state and hence reignited strategic interest of U.S. nationalists in the periphery. The regime of universal sovereignty, however, requires more powerful states and international organizations to work through the institutions of national states. Postwar operations attempt to *transform* states, rather than *absorbing* them into other, more powerful, units.[1]

Peace Building and Stabilization as State Building

At the most schematic analysis, state formation consists of the interdependent mobilization by a sovereign of three types of resources: coercion, capital, and legitimacy.[2] The sovereign wields coercion, in the form of what we hopefully call security institutions, to exercise a monopoly of (legitimate) force over a territory. He needs the accumulation of capital to produce income that can be extracted as revenues to fund state functions and services. Symbolic and cultural resources consecrate the use of force and public revenues as legitimate and link them into a meaningful whole to induce people to comply voluntarily as citizens. The state claims to exercise its power as the delegate of an imagined community: the nation.

These three types of resources have been mobilized in numerous combinations and contexts to build, destroy, or undermine states. Contrary to nationalist historiography, states do not form in isolation but in relation to each other, as part of an interstate system. Interstate borders need states on both sides. The Great Wall defending the Chinese empire was not a border in the modern sense, as the Middle Kingdom did not recognize any equivalent entity on the other side. States' locations in the international strategic and market systems have largely determined how they have formed. Some developed as trading (capital-intensive) states and others as more militarized (coercion-intensive) ones. Some extracted resources from foreign conquests or investments and others from domestic economic development or external relations of dependence or exchange.

The generalization of the sovereign national state and the consecration of the territorial integrity of existing states by the UN system has altered the environment for latter-day state builders. Epigrammatically, during the formation of national states in Europe, rulers struggled and negotiated with subjects who became citizens to extract resources to wage war against external threats. In the postcolonial world, rulers struggled and negotiated with external powers to gain aid or capital to protect themselves from domestic threats. Citizens often became disenfranchised, as rulers looked to foreign patrons rather than citizens for power resources. External powers were motivated not by concern for apolitical "stability" but by the strategic competition of the Cold War, and now the Global War on Terror, as well as by economic interests.

This process of extroverted state formation underlies many changes in the international system, including the shift from interstate to intrastate warfare and the crises of legitimacy and capacity of postcolonial states, leading to the violent contestation and collapse of many. Some states have collapsed from a lack of strategic importance combined with access to resources that funded armed oppositions (Sierra Leone, Liberia), and others from competing political projects on the part of global or regional powers that undermined weak states (Afghanistan, Democratic Republic of Congo). These crises have thus generated many of the apparently domestic armed conflicts that have confronted international actors in the past several decades.

Participants in peace building or stabilization operations attempt to use foreign resources of the same types to build acceptable states in areas that pose a perceived threat to powerful actors. The threat may derive from the control of a state by an anti-status-quo leader (rogue states—the main concern of the United States) or the breakdown of control under the impact of strategic or economic competition (failed or collapsing states—of greater concern to globalist humanitarians). These operations aim at building states, sometimes after a transitional stage of international administration or occupation. They aim to make such states more effective agents of control over their own territories and population. To what extent states exercise this control as sovereigns, in service of nationally determined goals, and to what extent as agents of externally defined interests, whether hegemonic powers or international standards, constitutes what Ghassan Salamé calls the "dual legitimacy" problem of global state formation.[3]

Internationalized State Building

The doctrines of the states and organizations engaged in this effort often contradict the goal of state building. Building a national state means creating a sovereign center of political accountability, which is not necessarily the same as building an ally in the War on Terror. Multilateral operations often consist of juxtaposing existing capacities—humanitarian aid, war fighting, peacekeeping, economic guidance and assistance, civil society support, democracy assistance—without a coherent strategy. A strategic decision maker would require command and budgetary authority over the entire operation, which was the rationale for the Brahimi report's proposal for "integrated missions," but the main instruments of strategic planning often remain endless "coordination" meetings among rival organizations and the stapler, which serves to assemble those organizations' programs into a single "plan."[4]

Such operations make use of the same types of resources as other processes of state building: coercion, capital, and legitimacy. The core tasks of security provision are peacekeeping or other forms of international transitional security provision; dismantling irregular militias that compete with the state's monopoly of coercion (demobilization, disarmament, and reintegration, or DDR); and building new security forces, called Security Sector Reform (SSR), which enables the state to exercise that monopoly of coercion. Completion of DDR and SSR allows the international security force to depart. These tasks are essential for developing legitimate rule, as they permit what Anthony Giddens describes as the "extrusion" of violence from politics and administration. This is the process through which military and police functions are distinguished, separating the inside of the state, regulated by rule of law, administration, and policing, from external relations, regulated by diplomacy, military violence, and the balance of power.[5]

Coercion and Security

The initial distribution of the means of violence in these operations varies. In cases of civil war or failed states, the lack of effective, legitimate monopoly of force constitutes the problem. The foreign military defeat of incumbent regimes destroys a preexisting monopoly of violence, claimed by the invader to be illegitimate. Generally such interventions provoke an insurgency, which a new regime must co-opt or destroy, or which must succeed itself to implement its own state-building agenda.

One can characterize the pre-operation security situation as Tilly characterizes challenges to state building, namely the degree of accumulation and of concentration of violence. "Accumulation" refers to the amount of means of violence available, and "concentration" to how widely control over them is distributed. Afghanistan, for instance, had a high degree of accumulation and a low degree of concentration (many armed groups with a lot of weapons), while East Timor had a low degree of accumulation and a high degree of concentration (few armed groups with few weapons). Low accumulation and high concentration of weapons combined with a high degree of legitimacy or consent constitutes the most favorable environment for peacekeeping. Higher accumulation, lower concentration, and less consent require more international forces with a stronger mandate.

Peacekeeping mandates in the early part of the 1990s presumed full agreement among warring parties and full legitimacy of the operation among all parties. This is the case of "warlord democratization" under which armed groups voluntarily demobilize in order to resolve a security dilemma, requiring confidence-building measures and transparency enforced by peacekeepers.[6]

When the agreement enjoys less consent, where some armed groups are outside the agreement, or where there is no agreement, the intervener's role cannot be one solely of resolving a security dilemma. The military intervention to defeat the Taliban and al-Qaeda enjoyed broad legitimacy both internationally and domestically in Afghanistan, but the consent of the Northern Alliance factions to the power sharing in the Bonn agreement was obtained under pressure. The deposed groups (al-Qaeda and Taliban) were not parties to the Bonn Agreement, and successful state building requires eliminating or co-opting them. The Iraq invasion was far less legitimate, as the Security Council did not endorse it, significant portions of the Iraqi population continue to fight it, and even parts of the population who initially consented to the invasion's political results appeared to want the invaders to leave.

State-building operations following internal armed conflict must include measures for DDR of combatants and for the changes in government security agencies (SSR). In cases of repressive, ethnicized, or racialized states, the security forces must be depoliticized and constrained to operate within the rule of law (El Salvador, South Africa, Burundi); in cases of state collapse, security forces must be created, trained, and empowered to act within the rule of law (Afghanistan).

All of these processes are intensely political. The provision of security to some means making those who threaten it insecure. In Afghanistan, the actors have had their own security missions. The coalition came to ensure the security of Americans from al-Qaeda and then the Afghan government from the Taliban, initially with the assistance of local commanders and warlords. The International Security Assistance Force (ISAF) was supposed to provide the Afghan administration with security from warlord pressure, while helping the government to create new security agencies and administer a political transition to fully representative government. The UN, aid agencies, and NGOs define *security* as safe access to areas by civilian aid workers. Afghan civilians expected a "security assistance force" to provide them with security of their person and property, but no international force has had a mandate to provide such protection to Afghans.

Demobilizing militias and building security agencies are intimately related to the development of new political institutions. Where states and political institutions are weak, armed groups are simultaneously political, military, and economic actors, the latter by necessity if they are to survive. In a model of implementation of a peace agreement, groups agree to disarm in return for guarantees of nonviolent political participation. Often, however, they cannot exercise as much power in the civilian realm and must be compensated. Senior leaders can receive state positions or become political leaders. Rank-and-file fighters may enter the new security forces, but that is a highly fraught political decision, as they are likely to politicize or corrupt the new forces, and it is difficult to retrain guerrillas as lawful security agents.

Training and reforming security agencies is equally political. The intense, quasi-religious esprit de corps of military organizations derives from the human need to believe intensely in something for which one risks one's life. Forming effective armies and police requires formation of a national authority that can command such loyalty, not just technical training. The formation of an officer corps depends on forming its coherence and spirit in service to a mission. Hence, though effective security is necessary to carry out credible elections and other political processes, political processes that build credible, legitimate national leadership are essential to building effective security forces. It is no wonder that first elections almost invariably require international security forces.

If the state cannot sustain the recurrent cost of its security forces, its stability will always be at risk. Nor can any state long survive the funding of its army and police by foreign powers. The "Afghan National Army," fully paid for by the United States and deployed with embedded U.S. "trainers," can be only a transitional measure. States must eventually develop an economic and fiscal capacity to pay for their security forces. Economic development, capital accumulation, collection of revenue, and suppression of illegal, untaxable parallel economies (such as trafficking in drags and other forms of smuggling) all require effective security forces. Hence among the tasks of transitional international security providers should be some they are often reluctant to assume, in particular strengthening the government's fiscal capacity and providing security for property rights.

Public Finance, Assistance, and Capital Accumulation

When peace-building or stabilization operations begin, local economies and the capacity of the state to deliver services are typically damaged by war. Many people need humanitarian assistance to return to their homes and survive. Basic assets such as roads, schools, power supplies, and financial institutions have to be built or rebuilt for economic recovery to start. To varying degrees, war-torn societies need massive building of human capital through education, training, and health care. States have often lost the capacity—to the extent that they had it—to mobilize even modest amounts of resources and to supply even the most basic services. Much of the economy may be informal or illegal, producing incomes for mafias or patronage networks that capture parts of the state but do not contribute to it. These economic actors use illicit force and official corruption to seize assets and exclude competitors, stifling investment.

Just as the provision of security requires transitional international security provision, so the development of state capacity to deliver public services and foster economic development requires transitional international assistance. But just as various international and local actors define security differently, so they also define economic strategy according to their own models.

In the language of donors, aid must start with humanitarian assistance, make a transition to reconstruction, and then move on to development. The dominant modes of assistance delivery, however, ignore and indeed often undermine the fundamental strategic goal of economic assistance to state building: strengthening sustainable state capacity to mobilize resources to deliver services, which requires the growth of licit economic activity, which in turn requires public services such as security, rule of law, fiscal and monetary management, and education. The mobilization of resources requires that the state develop both legitimacy (partly through service delivery) and capacity.

The central state institution that coordinates mobilization of resources, provision of services, and legitimation of state power is the budget. And it is the process of mobilizing those resources domestically, and particularly the struggle over the budget, that is at the center of the process of state formation and legitimation.

In postconflict situations, however, international donors provide most of the resources for public services. These donors are reluctant to support recurrent expenditures and usually fund other expenditures directly, through their own implementing agencies. Rather than disbursing money from a common account under the control of a political authority that can be held accountable to the nation receiving the aid, each donor country or agency maintains its separate spending mechanisms and procedures, which are accountable to its own political authority. In the 2005 budget presented by the Afghan authorities, for instance, less than a quarter of all expenditures were channeled through the Afghan government's budget.[7] The creation of what Ashraf Ghani has called the "dual public sector" constitutes the problem of dual legitimacy in the fiscal realm. The internationally sponsored public sector operates according to its own rules. Its salary scales tend to suck capacity out of the national government by drawing most qualified nationals into the service of international organizations. Its inflationary effect on price levels may further depress the real value of state salaries.

Accountability also suffers. As far as donor states are concerned, aid money is "spent" when it is disbursed to an agency, not when the agency implements a program. Hence multilateral "state-building" operations keep few accounts of what has been spent before projects are completed. Since citizens of the recipient countries, who hear reports of huge figures unmatched by what they think of as proportionate results, have no way to demand accountability for the funds, the frequent result is populist politics such as the campaign against NGOs in Afghanistan.

This method of giving "aid" fails to build the legitimacy and capacity of the recipient government. The government cannot make decisions about what services are to be provided, track expenditures, or gain experience in providing public goods. Multilateral operations risk creating elected governments fragmented among clienteles of several aid agencies, with no political authority to pursue a coherent strategy for building sovereignty. Elected governments without budgetary authority or control over security provision hardly merit the term "democracies."

Of course, the governments of countries emerging from war or violence are often incapable of exercising such responsibilities. International organizations have created a number of mechanisms to enable governments to increase their responsibility and build capacity. The most common such mechanism is a trust fund for categories of expenditure. Donors deposit unearmarked funds in return for a voice in the management of the fund. The recipient government must provide full documentation of expenditure for approval by the fund's governors. The joint governance of the fund institutionalizes dual legitimacy transparently by providing both aid donors and the recipient government with a voice in accounting for expenditure, while empowering the government to make decisions and learn by doing. This method does not, however, enable donors to plant flags on projects or impose agendas.

The problem of dual legitimacy can also occur in the area of economic policy. War economies lead to hyperinflation, parallel economic activities as both survival strategies and funding mechanisms for militias, and the capture of productive assets (including land), state enterprises, and regulatory bodies by "mafias" linked to armed groups. The standard international response is development of the rule of law, shrinking the state to core functions, and privatization. Some criticize the international imposition of this liberal development model in ways that preclude societies' formulating their own economic policies through political processes. International development institutions (and some recipient governments, such as Afghanistan) support these measures on the grounds that they are dismantling the institutions not of a welfare state but of corrupt networks. Just as the alternative to a corrupt state based on patronage, cronyism, and corruption is a democratic state based on transparency and the rule of law, so the alternative to the criminalized economy that supports the corrupt state and armed groups is a market system based on transparency and the rule of law.

The problem in implementing such policies is that they contrast an actually existing economy (what Duffield calls "actually existing development") with an idealized model of a market economy, including government-sponsored social safety nets and markets devoid of "illicit" power.[8] The "actually existing economy," criminalized as it may be, is providing livelihoods for many people, and those who are benefiting the most from that economy are liable either to control the process of marketization or to see it (possibly correctly) as a political plot by their opponents. The criminalized economy is at least nationally owned and operated.

Legitimacy, Transitional Governance, and Democracy

Almost by definition, international state-building operations begin under conditions where states lack not only the capacity to provide security and services but also legitimacy. Legitimacy begins with that of the international operation. At one extreme, few contest the legitimacy of UN operations requested by all parties to a conflict to assist in implementation of a peace agreement approved by the Security Council. At the other extreme lies the war in Iraq, conducted with neither the consent of parties nor approval by the Security Council. International legitimacy of such operations appears to increase domestic legitimacy. Involvement by the UN provides a more neutral and credible interlocutor for political groups than an occupying power, as the Bush administration found to its apparent surprise in Iraq. International approval also communicates to opponents of the operation (called "spoilers" by those who support it) that they are less likely to gain external support.

The next stage is the establishment of a transitional administration. Besides a UN transitional administration or a foreign occupation regime, this may take the form of a coalition among national forces pursuant to an agreement or a monitored government consisting of previous incumbents. The main purpose of the transitional government is to preside over a process that establishes a legitimate legal framework for political contestation and rule (generally, a constitution) and to administer the first stages of the implementation of this framework.

Though the UN, unlike some regional organizations, has no clear standards for the type of government legitimate for its members, its operational doctrine requires that the transition lead to adoption of a constitution providing for at least an appearance of liberal democracy, with elections constituting the principal benchmark. The United States even more explicitly has made "democracy" (defined as a government elected by universal adult suffrage) the goal of such operations. International actors also require that any constitution or basic law profess adherence to international standards of human rights. Diplomats note that their parliaments at home may refuse to allocate aid funds without such adherence. This insistence may cause conflict with local elites, whether because of their belief in competing standards such as some interpretations of sharia or preference for more authoritarian limits on rights.

Elected governments presiding over a society that visibly supports them, however, will be better able to mount campaigns for empowerment by international actors than interim governments of dubious legitimacy. Hence the first election of a legitimate government, though a key step in the state-building process, is far from its termination point and may mark its true beginning. After his election, Afghan president Hamid Karzai openly opposed U.S. plans for aerial eradication of opium poppy, showing greater independence than previously.

Politics of State Building

Studies of state-building operations often try to identify "best practices" without asking whom they are best for. Actors can learn how better to achieve their goals, but every step of the process of internationally sponsored state building generates political conflict.

Nonetheless, in a strategic environment where the goals of actors are interdependent, negotiation may lead to convergence among actors with differing motivations. The Bush administration entered Afghanistan committed not to engage in "nation building." Eventually, though, it needed an "exit strategy," which would be sustainable only if the United States and other international actors helped Afghans build institutions that would serve the common interests of Afghanistan and the international community.

Hence even though there is no purely technical solution to the political debate over the conditions for legitimacy of operations, the nationalist concept of "exit strategy" and the globalist concept of "sustainability" may at times converge on a mission of building a legitimate and capable state. Doing so effectively requires transitional governance institutions that incorporate the inescapable need for dual legitimacy transparently, as does governance of a trust fund, rather than in a fragmented and secretive way through ad hoc pressures.

This organizing principle of the contemporary global system requires that state building, and particularly multilateral state building, be placed at the center of the global security agenda. To do so will require negotiated delegation of some sovereign functions, not only of the reconstructed country but also of the donor countries. They will better serve their own needs by giving aid in ways that are more accountable to the reconstructed country's citizens, not just their own.

Notes

1. Robert Jackson and Carl G. Rosberg, "Why Africa's Weak States Persist: The Empirical and the Juridical in Statehood," *World Politics* 35(1), 1982, 1–24. For a more recent interpretation, see Michael Barnett, "The New United Nations Politics of Peace: From Juridical Sovereignty to Empirical Sovereignty," *Global Governance* 1(1), Winter 1995, 79–97.
2. Charles Tilly, *Coercion, Capital, and European States: AD 990–1992*, Studies in Social Discontinuity (Cambridge: Blackwell, 1992).
3. Ghassan Salamé, *Appels d'empire: Ingérences et résistances à l'âge de la mondialisation* (Paris: Fayard), 1996.
4. *Report of the Panel on United Nations Peace Operations* (the Brahimi Report); UN Doc. A/55/305-S/2000/809 (2000).
5. Anthony Giddens, *The Nation State and Violence* (Berkeley: University of California Press, 1987).
6. Barbara F. Walter and Jack Snyder, eds., *Civil Wars, Insecurity, and Intervention* (New York: Columbia University Press, 1999). See also Leonard Wantchekon, "The Paradox of 'Warlord' Democracy: A Theoretical Investigation," *American Political Science Review* 98(1), 2004, 17–33.
7. From a presentation given by Abdullah Abdullah, minister of foreign affairs of Afghanistan, at the presentation at the Afghanistan Development Forum, April 2005.
8. Mark Duffield, "Reprising Durable Disorder: Network War and the Securitisation of Aid," in Bjorn Hettne and Bertil Oden, eds., *Global Governance in the 21st Century: Alternative Perspectives on World Order*, Expert Group on Development Initiatives (EGDI), Swedish Ministry for Foreign Affairs (Stockholm, Sweden: Almqvist, 2002).

10

The Politics of Security in Postconflict State Building

The appropriate mandate for peace-keeping or security forces in postconflict or peace-building operations has been one of the most difficult and contentious issues since the end game of the Cold War led to the increasing involvement of the UN in multifunctional operations. The controversy over the enforcement of provisions on demobilization and human rights in Cambodia and, especially, the disasters that overtook UN forces in Rwanda and Bosnia-Herzegovina led to evaluations of what went wrong.[1] In one influential analysis, Steve Stedman argued against the assumption that international forces were always present to overcome security dilemmas and monitor compliance with an agreement; instead he argued there are often actors, labeled "spoilers," who use violence to prevent implementation and that mandates needed to change accordingly. The 2000 Brahimi report on UN peace operations adopted the category of "spoilers" and argued that troop deployments, mandates, and resources must correspond to a realistic threat assessment, rather than to existing doctrine or the degree of interest of the Security Council or troop contributors.[2]

The insurgencies and civil conflicts in Afghanistan and Iraq have similarly drawn attention to the primacy of security in state-building operations that take place without a comprehensive peace agreement (as in Afghanistan, where the Bonn Agreement did not include the apparently defeated Taliban) or with no agreement or international mandate whatever (as in Iraq). Many observers have argued that more security forces, better coordination, and other changes of strategy are needed for "success."[3] Yet sending even more troops into Iraq has been even less successful in providing security than in Afghanistan.

All such operations aim at political objectives, not just building "states," let alone "peace," and their success is crucially linked to the international and domestic

Originally published in Charles T. Call, ed., with Vanessa T. Wyeth, *Building States to Build Peace* (Boulder, CO: Lynne Rienner, 2008).

legitimacy of those objectives and the ability of leaders to mobilize people to defend them. The challenge of legitimacy is doubly difficult in such operations because even though state building always requires a struggle for legitimation among citizens, internationalized operations must also meet a high standard of international legitimation, including appropriate authorization and political support in each of the states that provide financial or military aid. These various sources of legitimacy may contradict as well as complement each other. Understanding the challenge of providing security in internationalized state-building or peace-building operations requires situating both the operations and the accompanying efforts to provide security in their political context. This chapter first examines the concept of security in internationalized state-building operations and analyzes its relation to other components of the state-building process.

Using this conceptual framework, the paper then examines several political issues relating to security in such operations. These include the legitimacy of the international security deployment with both the citizens of the affected state and the international community; whether international deployments support or displace the creation of national capacity; the relation of security sector reforms to both interim power-sharing arrangements and the transition to permanent institutions; priorities among different types of security and security institutions; the need for legitimation, among the general population but particularly within the security forces; and sustainable finance for the security sector. Throughout these sections, I draw extensively on the case of Afghanistan, partly because I have followed the country for more than two decades and advised the United Nations during the postwar transition period, but also because the case exemplifies many of the key claims of this chapter. Finally, the paper draws on this analysis to discuss some major questions over the sequencing and interrelationships of various components of peace-building and state-building operations, in particular the relationships among security, democratization, and reconstruction or development. The interdependence of security, legitimacy, and economic development in the state-building process provides a framework for a comprehensive analysis that transcends the usual stovepiped discussions of peace keeping, security sector reform, reconstruction, and governance.

The Context: Internationalized State-Building Operations

Operations known as "postconflict," "reconstruction," "peace building," or "stabilization" do not form a homogeneous group. Despite the recent emergence of some of these terms, such operations have a long history.

The use of international coercive forces as part of an operation aiming to build national capacity (rather than absorb a territory as an imperial or colonial possession) represents the latest historical iteration of interaction between powerful states' self-interest and the prevailing juridical forms of power, especially state sovereignty.[4] Internationalized state building responds to the problem of maintaining security, however defined, in a global system juridically and politically organized around universal state sovereignty. With the construction of more tightly linked systems of mutually recognized and demarcated states in post-Westphalian Europe, the quest for security and profit on the periphery became an imperial—and ultimately global—extension of interstate competition among core states. The contemporary global framework for security developed with the foundation of the United Nations system after World War II. That system extended the international regime of national sovereignty enshrined in the charter, both by legitimizing recognized states as actors on the international stage (the UN's "member states") and by delegitimizing colonialism and imperialism as legal doctrines.

During the Cold War, the struggle over building postcolonial states largely took the form of competing foreign aid projects by the alliance systems led by the United States and USSR. The end of the Cold War freed the UN and some regional organizations to replace unilateral clientelism with multilateral state-building efforts, especially in countries emerging from internal wars. Agreement by the Security Council to entrust most such operations to the UN reflected both the end of zero-sum strategic competition and the lowering of the stakes in who controlled these states.

The attack of September 11 showed that the United States could now be attacked from even the weakest state and hence reignited strategic interest of U.S. nationalists in the periphery. Because the regime of universal sovereignty prevents such peripheral territories from being absorbed into more powerful units, however, international security after September 11 requires the transformation or strengthening of existing national states. Consequently, current internationalized state-building operations, even those labeled "peace building" or "stabilization," reflect the impulse of Western powers to exercise influence.[5] The terminology deployed, the very endeavor to "build" states, and the process by which international mandates are defined and undertaken all reflect an inherent political dimension, one that is not benign and selfless, but self-interested and instrumental.

International Peace-Building Resources: Complements or Substitutes for National Capacity?

International participants in peace-building or stabilization operations attempt to build states in accord with their interest in areas that pose a perceived threat to them. Such operations make use of the same types of resources as other processes of state building: coercion, capital, and legitimacy. This section elaborates on the international tools, and the positive or negative effects of these state-building resources. When the intervention occurs in a country where state power is weak or contested, preventing relapse to war requires the interveners to jump-start the mutually reinforcing process of security provision, legitimation of power, and economic development by providing international resources or capacities to cover initial gaps in all three. *Coercion* includes transitional international security provision or intervention (peacekeeping, peace enforcement, security assistance, or occupation); the demobilization, disarmament, and reintegration (DDR) of at least some combatants; and the building of new security agencies or reform of existing ones (security sector reform, SSR). *Capital* takes the form of both international financial assistance for recovery, reconstruction, and development and of efforts to invigorate the national economy and the fiscal capacity of the government. The *legitimacy* of the operations derives from both the legitimacy of the international operation or intervention and that of the system of rule that this operation tries to institutionalize. The outcome depends on initial conditions and the combination of national and international capacities in these areas.[6]

In the best case, such transitional assistance will help launch a new self-sustaining dynamic, but there is a danger, to borrow terms from public finance, of "crowding out" as well as "crowding in."[7] Crowding out occurs when international efforts or structures displace existing or potential new domestic-level state institutions that might carry out similar functions—i.e., hindering state building. Crowding in occurs when international efforts or institutions provide the space, resources, or training and mentoring for domestic-level actors or institutions in ways that enhance their capacity and potential sustainability—i.e., promoting state building. These possible interactions and their effects are illustrated in Table 10.1.

International security provision may provide a sheltered environment for building national security forces, or it may give contending factions the space to continue to feud without confronting the consequences. External financial aid may fund the creation of national capacities, the building of institutions, and development, but it can also create parallel systems that suck capacity out of national institutions and create unsustainable white elephants: roads that cannot be maintained, overpasses to nowhere, schools with no teachers, or "security" forces with no salaries. International support may strengthen the legitimacy of interim or transitional arrangements through authorization by the Security Council and guarantees of respect for human rights and secure political participation for all; but it may also undermine legitimacy by weakening incentives for leaders to be accountable to citizens or exposing conflicts between local and international standards, as in the case of the apostate Abdul Rahman in Afghanistan. To what extent states built in this manner exercise power as sovereigns, in the service of nationally determined goals, and to what extent they act as agents of

Table 10.1 **Resources for Internationalized State Building and Their Interactions**

Resource	National	International	Promotes State Building When:	Hinders State Building When:
Coercion	Existing Security Forces; DDR; SSR	Peacekeeping, security assistance, or occupation forces	Supplying security and monitoring for DDR; training and equipping new forces (SSR); providing security for political process	Contradictory security goals; reduce incentives to cooperate by externalizing costs of conflict; unsustainable security forces established with foreign aid
Capital	Domestic capital formation, resource mobilization, taxation	International assistance for recovery, reconstruction, and development	Building capacity, support through budget, building sustainable physical and human capital	Creating parallel systems that monopolize capacity; technical assistance without capacity development; unsustainable projects that eat up funds for recurrent expenditures
Legitimacy	Historically and socially embedded claims of nation, religion, ethnicity, values	UNSC authorization of intervention; conformity of interveners to international law and norms; assistance to political transition and elections, legal and judicial reform; human rights standards and monitoring	Enabling state to develop inclusive, fully representative, and capable government; protecting rights of broad participation; shielding vulnerable from threats	Coercive imposition of international norms at odds with local values and culture; rushed timetables for foreign political goals

externally defined interests, constitutes the "dual legitimacy" problem of global state formation.[8]

In the 1990s, UN peacekeeping mandates underwent a shift that would prove crucial for understanding "security" in postconflict operations. In the early 1990s they presumed full agreement among warring parties and full legitimacy of the operation among all parties. This produced what some have called "warlord democratization," where armed groups voluntarily demobilize in order to resolve a security dilemma, requiring confidence-building measures enforced by peacekeepers.[9] Here the main task is protecting the security of the former combatants. The disastrous UN operations in Rwanda and Bosnia along this model led to interventions with stronger mandates.[10] Hereafter the UN would not act only with consent but also authorize the use of force against "spoilers" seeking to block implementation of agreements or fight their way into a better deal.[11] But the change in the situations in which intervention occurs has required more than a change in security mandates. Security mandates are always closely tied to legitimacy.

In 1985, UN special envoy Diego Cordovez told me that "the UN is not in the business of changing the governments of member states." Only two years later, however, as the talks that led to the Geneva Accords on Afghanistan reached their end game, Cordovez himself became involved in just such an activity. Since then, internationalized "postconflict" operations have usually taken place after internal war, though some parties may continue fighting after the so-called postconflict operation starts. The stake is precisely the nature of the government and who controls it.

What Is Security?

The term *security*, like *peace building*, contains an embedded political claim. Consistent with the use of technocratic language that obscures political issues, debates over security often neglect to define whose security is at stake and for what purpose. Conventional means of providing security through the use or threat of force and violence rely on the paradox of security provision: making some people and institutions secure by making those who would threaten them insecure. In its conventional use to denote the goal of military and police operations, "security" means the use or threat of legitimate force to prevent illegitimate violence. The claim that any specific use of force creates "security" is a political claim that the force is legitimate and that those against whom it is directed are outlaws or "spoilers." The transformation of coercion into security through the rule of law, as much as the transformation of predation into taxation through accountability and service provision, are essential to building legitimacy as part of the process of state building.

The transformation from civil war to "peace," whether the latter is defined negatively as the absence of war or positively in terms of sustainable human security, requires transformation in the organization and control of the means of violence. Given a state of civil war, at least some armed groups are outside state control. In the course of such wars, both states and nonstate armed groups often create multiple, unaccountable, politicized armed forces. Other parts of the security sector, such as police, public prosecutors, and the judiciary, are likely to be weak, corrupt, or subordinate to the political demands of civil warfare. Armed groups rather than civilian political parties or institutions are likely to have become the principal means used for political contestation or gaining control of assets. The interrelated establishment and stabilization of control of the means of legitimate violence and authority, combined with mobilizing the resources to sustain these institutions, constitutes the process of state building.

Parties to a civil conflict resolved by means other than partition have to be integrated into a common state.[12] In the usual cliché, they must substitute "ballots for bullets," that is, settle differences through a civilian political system, in which violence is regulated by law for public purposes (security), not used as the premier tool of political competition. The process of building security institutions after a civil war is not only a technical task of building capacity but also central to the distribution of political power that makes a settlement possible. It requires both political legitimacy and a fiscal basis that makes the institutions sustainable. Given the weakness of civilian institutions, the very process of empowering the latter is political, independently of the explicit struggle over who controls those institutions. As argued in the previous chapter, DDR and SSR are technical terms for historical processes essential for state building. This in turn requires building states with sufficient legitimacy and capacity to allocate resources and resolve disputes without overt violence. In the rare event that international actors assist in establishing a new state (East Timor, potentially Kosovo), the previously subordinate territory needs support and aid to develop the capacity to exercise self-government.[13] [Kosovo was recognized by the United States and members of the European Union (among others) as the independent "Republic of Kosovo" in 2008.]

International Transitional Security Provision

The outcome of peace-building processes depends both on the degree of difficulty and the amount and effectiveness of international resources deployed. Doyle and Sambanis analyze what they call the "Peacebuilding Triangle," the dimensions of which are determined by three factors: the severity of the conflict (measured by numbers of casualties and refugees, whether or not the conflict is ethnic, the degrees of ethnic and political fragmentation, and the outcome of the war before the operation); national capacities for peace (measured by levels and type of economic activity and human development); and international capacities (measured by type of mandate, and size of the international intervention).[14]

The first two dimensions define the initial conditions. One can characterize the initial security conditions, as noted in the previous chapter, as the degree of accumulation and of concentration of violence. These are roughly equivalent to Doyle and Sambanis's measures of conflict intensity and political fragmentation.

Since both initial conditions (including severity of conflict and national capacities) and international capacities shape the outcome, there is in effect a trade-off between them, as Doyle and Sambanis argue there is among the three dimensions of peace building: the greater the initial challenges (hostility and lack of national capacities), the more international resources would be required to attain an equivalent outcome. The trade-off is not necessarily linear, however. The provision of international resources may affect the provision of national capacities, either positively or negatively. The most effective level and type of international force depends on the extent to which international security forces and their claims of legitimacy crowd in or crowd out—promote or hinder—national security capacity and legitimacy.

These resources include the nature of the mandate and the number of troops, but also the overall legitimacy of the effort and financial resources. In cases where the state has kept paramount control of the means of violence over most of the territory (Guatemala) or where a guerrilla movement wins and captures the state (Uganda, Eritrea), international security provision is unlikely. Opposition or minority groups may want it, but the state can block it, and the state can protect international aid providers. In cases where the control of violence is more divided or fragmented, an international security mandate is likely to be necessary, as argued in the previous chapter. The *supply* of international security provision, however, depends not only or even primarily on the need but on the degree and nature of interest among those states with the capacity to supply it. Given the limited supply of deployable troops and the limited commitment to many operations, powerful states accept a higher risk of failure in cases of low strategic interest (often in Africa) by providing or paying for fewer troops than needed and insisting on weaker mandates in order to ensure availability of high-quality troops for cases they consider more important to their interests (the Balkans for Europe, Iraq for the United States).

Reluctant troop contributors may argue for lower levels of force on the grounds that international deployments crowd out local capacity. U.S. Secretary of Defense Donald Rumsfeld originally argued against expansion of the deployment of the International Security Assistance Force (ISAF) in Afghanistan on the grounds that it might displace efforts to build the Afghan National Army.[15]

Others argued that broader deployment of an international force with a mandate to demilitarize key political centers (the original mandate of ISAF in the Bonn Agreement) would have supported DDR and created a more favorable environment for creating professional security forces free of factional control. Whereas the latter argument eventually prevailed, with some limits, it appears to remain true that too large a deployment can be counterproductive. SRSG Lakhdar Brahimi's argument for a "light footprint" in Afghanistan, though directed mainly toward civilian rather than military deployments, was based on opposition to crowding out. Too large a military deployment that appeared to be an invasion or occupation could provoke a backlash that increases insecurity and undermines efforts to create national forces.

Whether international deployments provide security as a public good that strengthens national security capacity depends largely on the domestic legitimacy of the deployment. This legitimacy affects the likelihood that the political actors these forces protect will enjoy sufficient trust and access to build security institutions and the rule of law, if that is their goal. International approval both provides legitimacy, as argued in the previous chapter, and also communicates to opponents of the operation (called "spoilers" by those who support it) that they are less likely to gain external support.

A process endorsed by the UN supposedly enjoys the support of humanity's global political body and hence should enjoy full legitimacy. Although no body or court has the power to overturn a decision of the UN Security Council, that body is nonetheless political and its structure reflects the undemocratic reality of international power politics. The Bush administration is not alone in believing that its own definition of interest and legitimacy trumps decisions of the Security Council, though the United States is uniquely positioned to implement its defiant views. The United States was able to have the Security Council approve a UN "peace-building" operation in Iraq based on an invasion that most members considered illegal. Some cases also involved armed actors who rejected the legitimacy of the intervention or the proposed (or imposed) political settlement, and others (notably Kosovo) also began with interventions not sanctioned by the Security Council. This point is more than a mere footnote: the effectiveness of all security operations and efforts to build security institutions depend on their local and international legitimacy as well as the volume of resources put at their disposal, as a comparison of the effectiveness of the operations in Iraq and Afghanistan illustrates. Because of conflicting goals and values, attempts to legitimate deployments with the national publics of troop-deploying states may conflict with attempts to legitimate those deployments where they take place. In Afghanistan the issue of narcotics exemplifies this problem: the British government has largely legitimated its deployment to southern Afghanistan by telling the British public that the troops are needed there because this region is where the opium poppy that is the source for heroin sold in the UK is grown; but the more these troops engage in direct counternarcotics action, especially crop eradication, the less Afghans will believe that the troops are present to provide for their welfare and security. The case of the Afghan who converted to Christianity posed an even harsher conflict of basic values, as most Afghans appeared to insist that apostasy was a capital crime, while the countries supplying troops and assistance insisted on the basic human right to hold or change religious beliefs.

Security Sector Reform, Power Sharing, and Legitimacy

As the previous chapter notes, international state-building operations begin under conditions where states lack not only the capacity to provide security and services but also legitimacy. Building national capacity for security and legitimate governance is essential to the sustainability of peace.[16] The doctrines and organizational practices of these two tasks are usually isolated from each other in different organizations working in parallel but without coordination, although in practice they are closely linked. Building legitimate institutions requires sufficient security for unarmed citizens and nonmilitary officials to participate. Building security institutions requires sufficient legitimacy to motivate participation, risk, and sacrifice. The interim power-sharing agreements that are often needed to start a transition process are just as likely, if not more so, to involve participation in and control over the security forces as participation in and control over the ostensibly authoritative civilian positions.

The standard model for legitimizing international state-building operations is known as "democratic peace building."[17] The predominant view of such operations links this political model to a legal model based on liberal human rights and an economic model based on the market. Therefore the entire package delivered to countries constitutes a "liberal" model of peace building. Elections are the preferred path to establish such legitimacy, but elections can fulfill that function only if certain demanding conditions are met. They require a constitutional process (whether or not the process eventuates in a formal constitution) to establish a broad consensus on the institutions of government and structure of the state to which officials will be elected, as well as on the electoral system and administration. Elections require security against both those who wish to disrupt and discredit them and those who wish to use violence and intimidation to win them. They require both adequate administrative capacity (domestic or international) to ensure that the system is workable, and sufficient agreement on the rules and the mode of enforcement to ensure that losers accept the outcome and winners do not overstep their authority. It is no wonder that first postconflict elections therefore require international security forces and international civilian assistance, except where the incumbents' legitimacy is established through decisive military victory.

The liberal model, however, has no explicit linkage to the process of state building needed to make the political, legal, and economic institutions meaningful. It also includes no basis of local or national legitimacy other than pure legal and electoral claims, which are generally insufficient to motivate people to sacrifice their lives. The success of SSR requires growing legitimacy of the state and creation of what the previous chapter described as the "esprit de corps" of military officers. Sacrifice usually requires strong religious, nationalist, or group loyalties, which may be more or less compatible with the liberal model but are not contained within or generated by it.[18] This model also separates the recognized political process—elections, legislation—from the process of disarming militias and creating or reforming security institutions, as if the latter were an administrative or technical process. A fuller understanding of these operations, however, requires analyzing the politics of interim power sharing and restructuring the forces of violence, which often has greater political consequences than the ostensibly political institutions.

The first stage toward national legitimacy in an internationalized state-building operation is the establishment of an interim administration and agreement on a transition process. Besides a UN transitional administration or a foreign occupation regime, this may take the form of a coalition among national forces pursuant to an agreement or a monitored government consisting of previous incumbents. The main purpose of the transitional government is to preside over a process that establishes a legitimate legal framework for political contestation and rule (generally, a constitution) and to administer the first stages of the implementation of this framework. The transitional government normally must accommodate the claims for inclusion of a variety of parties to the conflict, though in some cases either monitoring of the incumbents or imposition of a UN transitional administration constitutes an alternative.

Establishing a transitional government and implementing a political process often requires protection of international security providers, whether to ensure against defection, to defend the process from its enemies ("spoilers"), or to provide the logistical support needed for the demanding task of holding national elections. Such a protected transitional government can then benefit from international assistance to build its legitimacy and capacity, including the legitimacy and capacity of the national security agencies. International security provision is particularly important in operations that provide for the dismantling or demobilization (DDR) of some forces, as this is likely to generate a security vacuum and heighten tensions. Research indicates that the provision of international security assistance is most needed at the start of the process, while financial aid needs to expand for a considerable period afterward, as national capacity grows.[19]

Without the separation of politics from violence and the regulation of the latter by law, however, civilian politics and politicians are impotent and the usual power-sharing agreements of limited value. One of the most common complaints from citizens of postconflict societies against international actors is that despite the latter's rhetoric of peace and democracy they speak mainly with warlords who are the enemies of both, instead of with "civil society." Depending on the weakness of civilian institutions, it may be more or less possible for international mediators or interveners to engage meaningfully with unarmed political forces. But as long as armed force constitutes the main currency of power, engagement with armed actors, backed up by sufficient international leverage, constitutes the only means to transform their roles. Only the demilitarization of politics makes engagement with nonmilitarized political forces meaningful. The nature of the process for the demilitarization of politics (concentration of the means of violence in the state and the separation of unmediated violence from politics in favor of law enforcement) determines what forces can be engaged. An invasion force can choose its interlocutors, until insurgents blast their way into the political arena. To the extent that DDR and SSR are negotiated with combatants, these combatants become the main interlocutors. The demilitarization of politics is at least as important to the political transition as the holding of elections; the latter are meaningless without the former.

Some states, such as Afghanistan or the Democratic Republic of Congo, have weak civilian institutions and strong armed groups that benefit from foreign aid and/or predation on global markets (narcotics, gold, diamonds, coltan). In such cases, the security forces themselves, not the civilian institutions, constitute the chief arena of competition for power. On several occasions when the interim Afghan government wanted to neutralize the power of regional warlords without openly confronting them, President Karzai appointed them to senior government posts in the capital. By placing these individuals at the head of a largely powerless administration, while separating them from their regionally based armed groups, the government deprived them of power rather than sharing it with them. In doing so it gambled on legitimacy at the expense of capacity.

Building the capacity of security agencies can become technical only to the extent that the agencies are politically neutral and serve a legitimate state and its laws, not political leaders, factions, parties, or ethnic groups. Even in fully consolidated democracies, political struggles continue over the mission, role, financing, and recruitment of the security forces. In a country barely emerging from civil war, the transformation of the institutions of violence and coercion constitutes the main arena for power struggles. Actors devise and evaluate such proposals not on the basis of their technical effectiveness—though they will use such arguments when they seem useful—but on the degree to which they maintain their power and their own security, not necessarily that of a politically neutral, inclusive—and elusive—"public."

Foreign professionals who specialize in one or the other function may see these tasks as separate, but armed groups, which are the most powerful form of association in post–civil war situations, pursue political, military, and economic objectives simultaneously. By proposing the separation of these functions into different organizations, the liberal peace-building model threatens to undermine the society's most powerful individuals and threatens the welfare of their followers, unless local capacities for liberal development grow sufficiently to offer employment and new roles for exercising power and accumulating wealth to the elites that emerged during the war. Such elites may lose from open warfare, but they also stand to lose from consolidated peace, if it means undermining personalistic power. Hence they have a strong interest if not in reversing peace agreements then in resisting their full implementation.

The negotiations over power sharing in the Bonn Agreement, DDR, and SSR in Afghanistan illustrate the centrality of the security sector to politics in post-war state building. At the UN Talks on Afghanistan in Bonn, international actors negotiated a government power-sharing deal with Shura-yi Nazar (the Supervisory Council of the North, the core of the Northern Alliance). The international actors accepted for the time being that faction's control of all "security" agencies (Ministries of Defense and Interior and the intelligence agency), in return for its agreeing to measures of civilian power sharing. These included accepting a chair of the interim administration (Hamid Karzai) who was not from the Northern Alliance and was not a military commander; sharing civilian ministerial posts with other groups; promising to adhere to a process of gradual broadening of the base of the government, though without specific commitments to give up control of the security agencies; and accepting international monitoring of all these.

Afghanistan's experience after the Bonn agreement illustrates several political features common to countries experiencing internationalized efforts to build state security forces. Despite frequently agreeing to succumb to civilian political authorities, armed factions (including government armed forces) often fortify parallel or preexisting command or authority structures to weaken the actual power of nominal civilian control. The Northern Alliance, for instance, accepted civilian power sharing but resisted measures to dilute its control of the security organs or to disempower armed commanders.

Similarly, armed factions whose commanders are reluctant to relinquish control over their soldiers commonly employ such tactics as formal delays, foot dragging, efforts to interpret or rewrite agreed-on depoliticization of security forces, and outright duplicity. Consider the negotiations over the composition and powers of the new Afghan National Army. These largely secret negotiations, which occurred in Kabul in 2002–03, mainly involved UNAMA [the United Nations Assistance Mission in Afghanistan], the United States, a few members of the Afghan government, and the Shura-yi Nazar leadership of MoD. The latter, led by Marshall Fahim, demanded full pay for the clearly exaggerated figure of two hundred thousand militia members (even after settling on one hundred thousand, many turned out to be phantoms). It also asked for a permanent army of the same size and insisted that the officer corps and rank and file of the new army come mainly from former members of mujahidin units. These demands would have ensured domination of the state by these armed groups, whatever civilian "power-sharing" measures were introduced. In the end, the Karzai administration and international allies were able to overcome most of these early efforts to undermine security sector reforms.[20] They did so not through simply formal or technocratic responses but via the deployment of capital and limited coercion, as well as the legitimacy that internal and external recognition offered warlords.

Reform of the leadership of the main security institutions in Afghanistan illustrates how these politically sensitive appointments respond to a political context more than to technical needs of SSR, and that such political criteria are not necessarily misplaced. Changing the Afghan ministers of defense and interior and the chief of intelligence, as well as key staff in each ministry, required difficult political decisions, which threatened violent fallout in every case. These changes were closely associated with key political events: the minister of the interior was changed at the Emergency Loya Jirga, the chief of intelligence was changed after the Constitutional Loya Jirga, and the minister of defense was changed as a result of the first presidential election.

The warlords accepted these appointments in Kabul in large part because of pressure from the U.S.-led coalition, whose support they needed to protect them from the Taliban and other enemies. In this case the judicious application of internationally supplied coercive resources provided the government with the opportunity to build the state by ending the capture of administration by informal power holders. The same changes had the potential to increase the legitimacy of the government, if it could deliver better than the warlords, and to increase the government's fiscal base, as it took direct control of major customs points. The removal of Fahim as minister of defense encouraged many commanders to demobilize and increased the supply of recruits to the ANA. These are examples of the political use of international forces in support of state building.

Differing Security Priorities

Political interest affects the definition of security objectives and hence priorities among the security tasks. International interests focus on challenges to international security, and international action therefore concentrates on military institutions, often equating building a large army with building "security." Often, interveners continue to treat the aftermath of a civil war as largely a military security problem, whereas the end of warfare often creates new security problems, such as crime and economic predation.[21]

In Afghanistan there was from the start a contradiction between the security objectives of the United States and the security imperatives of state building and the political process. The United States and its coalition partners intervened in Afghanistan to protect their own security from al-Qaeda, not to protect Afghans from al-Qaeda, Taliban, the Northern Alliance, militias, drought, poverty, and debt bondage to drug traffickers. The military strategy for accomplishing the former objective was to dislodge the Taliban and al-Qaeda with air strikes while using the CIA and Special Forces to equip, fund, and deploy the Northern Alliance and other commanders to take and hold ground, including cities. Although the United States halfheartedly tried to prevent the Northern Alliance from seizing the capital, it inevitably did so, as the United States was not prepared to occupy Kabul itself any more than it was later prepared to provide security in Baghdad.

The Bonn Talks therefore had to deal with the task of preventing the victorious militias from looting, fighting with each other, and seizing power. The International Security Assistance Force emerged as a coping mechanism, if not quite a solution. Through an act of diplomatic ventriloquism by the UN team, the parties to the Bonn Agreement asked the Security Council to authorize deployment of a "United Nations mandated force to assist in the maintenance of security for Kabul and its surrounding areas." The agreement went on to note, "Such a force could, as appropriate, be progressively expanded to other urban centres and other areas." The participants in the talks also agreed "to withdraw all military units from Kabul and other urban centers or other areas in which the UN mandated force is deployed." This UN-mandated force became known as the ISAF. Since August 2003 it has been under the command of NATO. Neither the withdrawal of militias from Kabul city nor the expansion of ISAF to provinces began until then, largely because of opposition from the U.S. Department of Defense, which wanted to ensure priority for its war-fighting goals over the internal security goals of ISAF.

The same hierarchy of priorities among security goals led to the establishment of the "lead-donor" system for SSR, which delayed progress and blocked coordination. As the United States initially wanted to devote resources solely to the "counterterrorist" operation, it took on responsibility for building the new Afghan National Army, while asking other Group of Eight (G8) countries to take on DDR, police, justice, and counternarcotics. The Afghanistan Compact finally jettisoned this system after the United States and others realized, in the words of the compact, that "Security cannot be provided by military means alone. It requires good governance, justice and the rule of law, reinforced by reconstruction and development."

The specific circumstances of the intervention in Afghanistan, in particular the presence of a direct threat to the United States, intensified the contradiction between different security goals and means, but similar problems exist elsewhere. Nationals of the postconflict country often oppose the focus on armies and elections and ask for more efforts to be devoted to rule of law, human rights, justice, police, parties, and civil society.[22] These institutions would provide ordinary citizens with more security and genuine representation. They would make elections more meaningful in a way that building an army cannot. Charles Taylor was able to win a presidential election in Liberia in 1997 largely because of his control of extralegal "security" institutions, which enabled him to intimidate the electorate. Former Liberian President Amos Sawyer has argued that the international community's focus on building an army for Liberia did little to improve the security of Liberians, who associate an army with insecurity rather than security. They were in much greater need of police and a justice system.[23]

Partly this results from international actors doing what they know how to do rather than what needs to be done. Military institutions are easier to build with external aid than police, justice, and legal institutions, because military violence depends less on local knowledge and legal and social norms.[24] Previous analyses, however, have demonstrated the close interrelationship within the security sector of military and police reform, and the need for police reform to be coordinated with legal, judicial, and penal reform.[25]

State Building and Security: Sequencing and Interdependence

If building security institutions, separating military from civilian roles, and strengthening civilian institutions and the rule of law are necessary conditions for electoral politics to meaningfully arbitrate among contenders for power, does state building, or building basic local capacities for security or economic development, have to take primacy over holding elections or building other democratic institutions? Analyses of past operations suggest that holding elections before DDR, at least, can reignite conflict and be more likely to lead to destabilization, since the elections can be viewed as winner take all.[26]

Some have posed the question in terms of sequencing or priorities. International operations are too short and lack the long-term commitment (in time, mandate, or resources) needed to implement sustainable transformation of political structures and state building. One study found that the single variable that best explained success in "nation-building" operations was the length of international engagement.[27] Providing security—including the demobilization of nonstate armed groups, the disempowering of abusive groups that came to power through violence, the reform of official coercive capacities so that they enforce the rule of law rather than factional or personal interest or political agendas, and the building of new security agencies and administrative capacity—must precede elections and the broad political mobilization over conflictual issues that elections stimulate.

Marina Ottaway, challenging the viability of the democratic peace-building model in the Democratic Republic of Congo, Afghanistan, and other fragile states, has advocated initial focus on core issues of security and state control, going so far as to oppose international pressure even to form a central state in Afghanistan, let alone a democratic one. A number of other analysts have argued that the emphasis on democracy is premature or misplaced. Jack Snyder and Edward Mansfield argue that elections often generate more conflict. Francis Fukuyama and Fareed Zakaria, in works on state building and illiberal democracy, argue that rule of law and basic institutions of governance must precede the development of institutions for contestation of power.[28]

Some practitioners echo these cautions. In a series of speeches, Lakhdar Brahimi has argued that UN operations are expected to accomplish a complete agenda of political, social, and economic transformation in some of the world's poorest and most violent countries on a tight schedule and with few resources.[29] Pressure for elections, transitional justice, accountability for human rights violations, and social reforms (notably in the status for women) builds early, as a result of the commitments of donor governments and NGOs, as well as the high expectations of the beneficiary population. UN political officers often find that these pressures fail to take into account the time needed for basic social transformation, the difficulty (not to say impossibility) of social engineering according to a timetable, the unforeseeable consequences of or backlash from such engineering in divided societies, and the amount of resources needed to build the institutional capacity to implement such changes.

The burst of effort at the start of an operation and the mobilization of international actors with short-term time horizons fail to build local capacity or the basic institutions needed for sustainable peace, while focusing efforts on visible benchmarks such as elections. Elections may accentuate differences and stimulate conflict before the society and state have the capacity to manage them. These capacities include both the institutional strength of rule-of-law institutions and the social capital of trust, built through postconflict reconciliation and cooperation in economic recovery.

Brahimi, in a "nonpaper" that he circulated to the diplomatic community before leaving Afghanistan at the beginning of 2004, noted that provision of security, economic reconstruction, and national reconciliation had not kept pace with the political timetable. As the international community prepared to help Afghanistan hold elections, there was still no rule of law, the means of violence were still under the control of numerous armed groups, and there was still a gulf of mistrust among various groups. Nor had economic development and service delivery taken off enough to build the capacity of the state, bind people's loyalties to it, or provide alternative livelihoods to those involved in armed groups or the drug economy.

But even though not everything can be done at once with inadequate resources, sequencing alone is too simple a model to capture the relationship between security and political reform or democratization. There is often a mutually interdependent relationship between security and political legitimacy that makes it difficult to separate these functions in a temporal sequence. The international operation must be sufficiently legitimate that its protection helps to legitimate rather than delegitimate the transitional administration. This internationally provided transitional security is necessary for building the legitimacy of government institutions through participation and increasing the government's capacity to mobilize resources and deliver services through the state. Only governments enjoying a significant degree of legitimacy can build sustainable national capacity to deliver security.

Both commanders and ordinary combatants (including part-time combatants) also need an economy that can sustain them without recourse to armed predation. Security provision and the rule of law are also necessary for building state capacity and enabling the state to provide the needed environment for economic growth. International security provision may be necessary to protect and support the initial processes of state fiscal reform. The Ministry of Finance in Afghanistan was able to operate with some autonomy from the armed groups in the Ministry of Defense only because of the presence of ISAF and the coalition, which provided its personnel with a margin of security.[30] This security was essential to enable it to bargain from a position of confidence with the Ministry of Defense over the integrity of the payroll. These negotiations permitted DDR to proceed. The international protection extended to the central government by ISAF also made it possible to maintain the integrity of the Da Afghanistan Bank (the central bank) and enabled the Ministry of Finance to overcome strong resistance and centralize revenue in a single treasury account. Without these measures, the Ministry of Defense and other factionally controlled armed forces could have intimidated, threatened, or even attacked the officials leading the reform, ensuring that systems that facilitated the capture of state revenues and payments by factions remained in place.

Once it had reformed its internal operations, the Ministry of Finance sought further assistance from the international security forces to help it gain control of customs points and provincial branches of state banks. Such control is essential if the national government put in place by the Bonn Agreement and now functioning under an elected president is to gain control of payments in the provinces and receive the revenues from import duties. The international forces, however, failed to see these as part of their mission, which left major obstacles to state building in place. Such control of state revenues and payment systems is necessary to enable the state to establish and operate police, courts, and other institutions of the rule of law that can create the security of contract and operations that according to the liberal model will encourage investment, marketing, and economic development.

This analysis indicates that even though there is no simple formula for sequencing, there is a hierarchy of priorities. An international peace-building or stabilization operation must take as its first priority providing whatever transitional security assistance is needed to enable a transitional government to start the process of legitimizing state power. To do so, that operation must itself be legitimate. The negotiation of the security transition is as important to the success of the operation as (if not more important than) the negotiation of what is usually called the "political" transition, which bears mainly on civilian authorities. The successful and mutually reinforcing action of international security provision and national legitimacy may then make it possible to build national capacity for domestic provision of security. Both international and domestic security provision can assist a legitimate government to build its capacity to provide other services, needed for the welfare and security of the people and the growth of the economy.

Notes

1. United Nations, *Report of the Independent Inquiry into the Actions of the United Nations During the 1994 Genocide in Rwanda,* UN Doc. S/1999/1257 (1999); United Nations, *Statement by the Secretary-General on Report of the Independent Inquiry into the Actions of the United Nations During the 1994 Genocide in Rwanda,* UN Doc. SG/SM/7263 (1999); United Nations, *Report of the Secretary-General Pursuant to General Assembly Resolution 53/35: The Fall of Srebrenica,* UN Doc. A/54/549 (1999).
2. Stephen John Stedman, "Spoiler Problems in Peace Processes," *International Security* 22, no. 2 (Autumn 1997): 5–53; United Nations, *Report of the Panel on United Nations Peace Operations* (Brahimi Report), UN Doc. A/55/305-S/2000/809 (2000).
3. On Afghanistan, see Michael Bhatia, Kevin Lanigan, and Philip Wilkinson, "Minimal Investments, Minimal Results: The Failure of Security Policy in Afghanistan," Afghanistan Research and Evaluation Unit (AREU) Briefing Paper, June 2004; James Dobbins et al., *America's Role in Nation-Building: From Germany to Iraq* (Santa Monica: RAND, 2003); Seth G. Jones, "Averting Failure in Afghanistan," *Survival* 48, no. 1 (Spring 2006): 111–28.
4. Robert H. Jackson and Carl G. Rosberg, "Why Africa's Weak States Persist: The Empirical and the Juridical in Statehood," *World Politics* 35, no. 1 (October 1982): 1–24. See also Michael Barnett, "The New United Nations Politics of Peace: From Juridical Sovereignty to Empirical Sovereignty," *Global Governance* 1, no. 1 (Winter 1995): 79–97.
5. Classifying operations in one or another category can itself be a political claim. A term such as "peace building" contains an implicit claim of legitimacy, since the goal is defined as "peace," a pure public good, rather than as reducing the level of violent contestation against a particular (and perhaps unjust) distribution of power and wealth. Different but related claims pertain to "postconflict" and "stabilization," for example.

6. Doyle and Sambanis analyze the success of UN peace operations (defined as nonreversion to collective violence plus minimal democratization) using indicators of conflict intensity, national capacities, and international capacities (see Michael W. Doyle and Nicholas Sambanis, "International Peacebuilding: A Theoretical and Quantitative Analysis," *American Political Science Review* 94, no. 4, Dec. 2000, 779–801). This chapter suggests a theoretical basis for further conceptualizing and measuring those capacities, both national and international, and their interaction.

7. James Boyce, introduction to James K. Boyce and Madalene O'Donnell, eds., *Peace and the Public Purse: Economic Policies for Postwar Statebuilding* (Boulder, CO: Lynne Rienner, 2007).

8. Ghassan Salamé, *Appels d'Empire. Ingérences et Résistances à l'âge de la mondialisation* (Paris: Fayard, 1996).

9. Barbara F. Walter and Jack Snyder, eds., *Civil Wars, Insecurity, and Intervention* (New York: Columbia University Press, 1999). See also Leonard Wantchekon, "The Paradox of 'Warlord' Democracy: A Theoretical Investigation," *American Political Science Review* 98, no. 1 (2004): 17–33.

10. See note 1.

11. See *Supplement to an Agenda for Peace: Position Paper of the Secretary-General on the Occasion of the Fiftieth Anniversary of the United Nations*, Report of the Secretary-General on the Work of the Organization, UN Doc. A/50/60-S/1995/1, January 3, 1995; and United Nations, *Report of the Panel on United Nations Peace Operations* (Brahimi Report).

12. Anthony Giddens, *The Nation-State and Violence*, vol. 2, *A Contemporary Critique of Historical Materialism* (Berkeley: University of California Press, 1987).

13. Of course these cases are most similar to decolonization, in which the UN played a major role, though not in exercising trusteeships or international transitional administrations as in these cases. The challenge of transforming colonies into sovereign states has proved to be a difficult one.

14. Doyle and Sambanis, "International Peacebuilding."

15. Henry L. Stimson Center, "Views on Security in Afghanistan: Selected Quotes and Statements by U.S. and International Leaders," Peace Operations Factsheet Series, June 2002.

16. Doyle and Sambanis, "International Peacebuilding."

17. Marina Ottaway and Anatol Lieven, "Rebuilding Afghanistan: Fantasy Versus Reality," *Carnegie Endowment for International Peace: Policy Brief* 12 (2002): 1–7; Ottaway, "One Country, Two Plans," *Foreign Policy* 137 (2003): 55–59; Ottaway, "Nation Building," *Foreign Policy* 132 (Sep.–Oct. 2002): 16–24; Roland Paris, *At War's End: Building Peace After Civil Conflict* (Cambridge: Cambridge University Press, 2004).

18. Benedict Anderson, *Imagined Communities: Reflections on the Origin and Spread of Nationalism* (London: Verso, 2006).

19. Paul Collier, with V. L. Elliott, Havard Hegre, Anke Hoeffler, Marta Reynal-Querol, and Nicholas Sambanis, *Breaking the Conflict Trap: Civil War and Development Policy* (New York: Oxford University Press, 2003).

20. Instead, the total to be demobilized turned out to be closer to sixty thousand; the ultimate strength of the armed forces is now planned to be forty to seventy thousand, which some think is still larger than the country needs or can afford; and fewer than 2 percent of the Afghan National Army's recruits are former mujahidin. The latter have been largely accommodated in the police, where their continuing ties of group solidarity undermine attempts at reform.

21. Charles T. Call, "Conclusion," in *Constructing Justice and Security After War* (Washington, DC: United States Institute of Peace Press, 2007), 25–27.

22. Amos Sawyer, comment during Center on International Cooperation and International Peace Academy Conference on Post-Conflict Transitions: National Experience and International Reform, New York, March 28, 2005.

23. Ibid.

24. Francis Fukuyama, *State-Building* (Ithaca, NY: Cornell University Press, 2004). In his book, Fukuyama argues that some institutions are easier to transfer to new environments because the requirements for them to be successful are more general, since they function in more or

less the same way everywhere. The central bank and the military are cited as examples of this, whereas other institutions, such as a judicial system, are more dependent on local norms and embedded practical knowledge.

25. The Brahimi Report, for instance, suggested measures to ensure that UN transitional administrations are able to adopt an off-the-shelf legal system devised for such situations. See United Nations, *Report of the Panel on United Nations Peace Operations* (Brahimi Report).

26. Chester A. Crocker, "Peacemaking and Mediation: Dynamics of a Changing Field," *Coping with Crisis: Working Paper Series*, International Peace Academy (March 2007); Simon Chesterman, Michael Ignatieff, and Ramesh Thakur, "Making States Work: From State Failure to State-Building," International Peace Academy/United Nations University (July 2004); International Peace Academy/Center on International Cooperation, "Post-Conflict Transitions: National Experience and International Reform," Meeting Summary, Century Association, New York, March 28, 2005.

27. Dobbins et al., *America's Role in Nation-Building*.

28. Fukuyama, *State-Building* (Ithaca, NY: Cornell University Press, 2004); Edward D. Mansfield and Jack Snyder, "Democratic Transitions and War: From Napoleon to the Millenium's End," in *Turbulent Peace: The Challenges of Managing International Conflict*, ed. Chester A. Crocker, Fen Osler Hampson, and Pamela R. Aall (Washington, DC: United States Institute of Peace Press, 2001), 113–26; Fareed Zakaria, *The Future of Freedom: Illiberal Democracy at Home and Abroad* (New York: Norton, 2003).

29. See United Nations, *Report of the Panel on United Nations Peace Operations* (Brahimi Report).

30. Ashraf Ghani, Clare Lockhart, Nargis Nehan, and Baqer Massoud, "The Budget as the Linchpin of the State: Lessons from Afghanistan," in *Peace and the Public Purse: Economic Policies for Postwar Statebuilding*, ed. James K. Boyce and Madalene O'Donnell (Boulder: Lynne Rienner, 2007), 153–83.

11

Regional Issues in the Reconstruction of Afghanistan

WITH ANDREA ARMSTRONG

For much of the modern era, Afghanistan might credibly be defined as a large body of rocky land surrounded by neighbors who export their own conflicts onto its territory. Several networks have linked Afghanistan to a wider arc of conflict, or a regional conflict formation, stretching from Moscow to Dubai.[1] Networks of armed groups, often covertly aided by neighboring states, link the conflict within Afghanistan to violence in Kashmir, Chechnya, Tajikistan, Kyrgyzstan, and Uzbekistan. Networks of narcotics traffickers collaborating with armed groups link Afghan poppy fields to global markets via Pakistan, Iran, and Central Asia. Networks of traders, more benignly, seek access to buy and sell their goods, even when profit requires avoidance of customs regulations. Cross-border social ties among the region's various ethnic and religious groups underpin all of these networks.[2]

The conflict that gripped Afghanistan over the past twenty-five years was much more than a local or national power struggle and must be seen in its regional context if the project of reconstructing the country is to succeed. Recent reports indicate that covert state support for armed groups is on the rise, undermining not only the new government in Kabul but peace in the region. Unless regional actors see that they have a stake in the reconstruction of Afghanistan, this picture is likely to become bleaker. Seen from a broader perspective, therefore, incorporating trade and energy issues and narcotics interdiction into a reconstruction strategy may lay the basis for regional cooperation rather than continued regional conflict.

Originally published as "Regional Issues in the Reconstruction of Afghanistan," *World Policy Journal* 20 (spring 2003), 1: 37–48.

The collapse of the Afghan state as a result of the Soviet invasion in 1979 and the factional fighting among the mujahidin that followed the withdrawal of the Soviet army in 1989 led to a political vacuum, creating an opportunity for other states in the region such as Pakistan and Iran to carve out spheres of influence. By supporting various armed Afghan groups, including the Taliban, Pakistan tried to redress its insecurity relative to India, curb Pashtun nationalism, and create a corridor for trade with Central Asia.

Surrounding states, including Iran, Russia, and Tajikistan, tried to balance Pakistan's involvement in Afghanistan by supporting competing Afghan groups. Iran and Russia, in collaboration with Tajikistan, supplied the anti-Taliban United Front (Northern Alliance). The Uzbekistan government supported a militia of Uzbeks from Tajikistan and Afghanistan that had bases and operations in both countries.

The proliferation of armed groups in the region has contributed to a violent "Kalashnikov culture," as militias in the region accumulate arms beyond the control of institutionalized armed forces. Moreover, the states themselves continue to import weapons and ammunition, despite the redistribution of weapons from the Afghan conflicts throughout the region. Russia, in a bid to gain political influence and promote its military industries, is providing weapons to Uzbekistan at below cost. The United States, Great Britain, India, Turkey, and China have all concluded agreements on arms sales or military training with states in the region since September 11, 2001.

In addition to covert state support, armed groups have relied on a combination of cross-border ethnic ties, the parallel economy, and the drug trade. In the late 1990s, Afghanistan became the world's largest producer of the opium poppy and the source of 70 percent of global illicit opium production in 2000.[3] (The Taliban banned poppy cultivation the following year.) The income from this crop helped sustain the Taliban, al-Qaeda, and the Islamic Movement of Uzbekistan (IMU), as well as some components of the Northern Alliance, and it promoted the corruption of military and law enforcement officials throughout the region. In addition to existing trafficking routes through Pakistan and Iran to the Persian Gulf or Turkey, corrupt government officials and Russian border guards helped open new routes through Central Asia. As a result, the number of addicts in the region skyrocketed. A UN report that examines the regional impact of the opium economy of Afghanistan notes that the number of government-registered drug addicts grew by 16 to 28 percent annually in Central Asia between 1992 and 2000, resulting in a sum total of approximately 400,000 opium and heroin abusers in the five Central Asian states. Pakistan is home to approximately 800,000 chronic heroin and opium users. Iran may have as many as 2 million opiate consumers, of whom 800,000 to 1.2 million are chronic users.[4] Associated social ills such as prostitution and HIV/AIDS have also increased dramatically, outpacing the worst-case scenarios of the early 1990s.[5] Some of the same criminal networks involved in the drug trade are also involved in the trafficking of women between Central and South Asia and the Persian Gulf.

In developing countries, economic activity accepted as legitimate by most of the population often occurs in a "gray market" outside formal legal structures. Such patterns of exchange, along with the drug trade and trafficking of women, support a network of organized crime around the littoral of the Indian Ocean and inland, exploiting the weakness of the states in the region. The trade in emeralds from Afghanistan's Panjshir Valley (much of it marketed through Dubai) and the transit trade in goods purchased duty-free in Dubai and smuggled, largely through Afghanistan, into Pakistan, India, and beyond deny import duties to the state and strengthen armed groups in the region.

Taxing such trade now provides one of the major sources of income to the regional strongmen ("warlords") who control most of Afghanistan. Official restrictions on trade items also divert India-Pakistan trade through Dubai and Pakistan-Iran trade through Afghanistan. Such black or gray markets are a strong incentive for both government employees and regional strongmen to maintain weak states. Both are partners in the parallel economy through various forms of corruption. Shifts in trade can affect the balance of forces in Afghanistan. The shift from transit via the Pakistan-Kandahar route to the Iran-Herat route, for instance, has strengthened Herat and contributed to tension between the two regional/ethnic centers.

Nearly all the major ethnic groups in the region, including Pashtuns, Tajiks, and Uzbeks, are found in more than one state. For example, Pashtuns live in both Pakistan and Afghanistan, and Tajiks live in both Afghanistan and Tajikistan. Whereas these ethnic diasporas have not become incubators for active ethnic territorial claims, they have facilitated recruitment to militant groups and the parallel economy. Growing refugee communities and cross-border ethnic ties supported the growth of armed groups in Tajikistan (now reconciled in a fragile peace agreement) and the militant Islamic Movement of Uzbekistan. Ethnic diasporas also facilitated covert operations by states that manipulate ethnicity, as Pakistan did by using Pashtuns to manage its relations with the Taliban. The persistent poverty of Pashtuns on both sides of the Durand Line, which forms the Afghanistan-Pakistan border, has fostered emigration, smuggling, drug trafficking, and recruitment to militant groups in territories where the Pakistani and Afghan states have been either unwilling or unable to maintain firm control. Instability in Afghanistan has led to refugee flight and economic emigration, expanding transnational communities of Afghan origin in Pakistan (beyond the

Pashtun areas), Iran, Central Asia, and the Persian Gulf. These communities have become important links in a variety of political and economic transnational networks.

All of the governments in the region are performing far short of their populations' expectations. Afghanistan has lost decades of investment due to war, but the Central Asian states have also regressed economically. Pakistan has at best stagnated, and Iran faces high and rising unemployment. Key resources are in short supply and are the source of conflict between and within states. Shortages of water and land are the cause of strife in the volatile Ferghana Valley (which forms part of Kyrgyzstan, Tajikistan, and Uzbekistan) and in the Pashtun tribal territories (in the cross-border region between Afghanistan and Pakistan). The distribution of energy resources, both hydroelectric and hydrocarbon, is also a source of contention but could form the basis for future regional cooperation.

Where Things Stand

The presence of U.S. military forces and the establishment of the internationally supported interim and transitional administrations in Afghanistan have temporarily curbed the regional competition that fed the upheavals of the 1990s. Despite repeated assurances by American officials, however, few in the region feel confident that either the U.S. commitment to rebuild Afghanistan or the internationally sponsored government and reconstruction effort will last. The possibility of a new war in Iraq only served to reinforce those doubts. Thus, although states and other regional actors are seeking to benefit from the U.S.-led war on terrorism as well as the Afghan relief and reconstruction efforts, they are quietly maintaining ties to their former allies and provincial warlords, which could lead to the return of regional proxy competition on Afghan soil.

In the fall of 2001, it appeared that in response to U.S. pressure Gen. Pervez Musharraf, Pakistan's president, was beginning to focus on development while making strides in curbing militant groups, enforcing order, and reforming the madrasas that had incubated the Taliban and other extremist groups. As the Musharraf regime, which came to power following a military takeover in 1999, elaborated on its plans for a "controlled democracy," where the military retains the right to veto key policies, it became evident that it meant to use its collaboration with the United States in Afghanistan to attain international legitimacy and consolidate domestic power. Its approach to militant groups and madrasas has been circumspect, though it has cooperated with the United States to arrest some prominent al-Qaeda leaders. Many experts suspect that the Inter-Services Intelligence Directorate has resumed interfering in Afghanistan's affairs by supporting elements of the Taliban as well as Gulbuddin Hikmatyar, former mujahidin commander and leader of Hizb-i Islami. Hizb-i Islami, the extremist party that received the largest share of U.S. aid to the Afghan resistance in the 1980s, has now declared jihad against U.S. forces and has claimed responsibility for bomb and rocket attacks in Kabul, Jalalabad, and elsewhere in Afghanistan. Islamabad also hopes that its closer relations with Washington will translate into leverage over India in Kashmir and has apparently resumed infiltrating largely non-Kashmiri Islamic militants into the disputed province.

The destruction of the Taliban regime and al-Qaeda bases in Afghanistan disrupted the operation of some militant organizations in the region. The mainly Arab groups affiliated with al-Qaeda, Pakistani militant groups associated with the Taliban, and the IMU lost their bases in Afghanistan. Some of the militant units dispersed, with individual members making their way to surrounding states. A number of these units appear to have regrouped in Pakistan, where they have been attempting to destabilize the Musharraf regime by targeting Westerners and Pakistani Christians.

States in the region have also resumed interfering in Afghanistan's affairs, perhaps anticipating the shift in Washington's attention from Afghanistan to Iraq. They are undermining the Karzai government by strengthening the militias of various warlords who control most of Afghanistan outside Kabul. The United States, Kabul's main supporter, stopped arming independent commanders who were temporary allies in the fight against al-Qaeda only belatedly and inconsistently. Russia is sending military equipment directly to Afghanistan's minister of defense, Mohammad Qasim Fahim, instead of supplying the newly constituted Afghan National Army. Iran, in addition to resuming its funding of Ismail Khan of Herat, has been accused of giving refuge to members of al-Qaeda fleeing U.S. troops in Afghanistan. The ethnic Uzbek deputy minister of defense, Gen. Abdul Rashid Dostum, a former Communist militia commander who joined the Northern Alliance, is seeking aid from Uzbekistan and Turkey to either maintain or increase his control of much of northern Afghanistan. Thus the change of government in Afghanistan has not yet led to an improved security environment.

Among other problems facing Afghanistan is the resumption of drug trafficking. Kabul made a belated attempt to suppress poppy cultivation in spring 2002 after most of the harvest was in, but trafficking, with prices for opium nearly 50 percent above their previous highs, is a lucrative business. The trade in goods transiting Afghanistan from Dubai to be smuggled into Pakistan, though disrupted to some extent by the war and lack of security along some routes, has been a major source of revenue for warlords in control of Afghanistan's border regions, in particular Ismail Khan in Herat and Abdul Rashid Dostum in Mazar-i Sharif. According to a customs official we spoke with last May, approximately 70 percent of Afghanistan's foreign trade was coming by way of Iran and was subject to duties in Herat, rather than in Kandahar or Kabul. In addition to these drains on the Afghan economy, the return of refugees has outpaced all expectations, with more than two million returning in 2002 alone, well over the eight hundred thousand returnees projected by United Nations High Commissioner for Refugees. Ironically, the exodus of Afghan refugees from Pakistan is weakening the Pakistani economy, which previously benefited from foreign exchange earned from the export of carpets made by Afghans.

The problem of internally displaced persons within Afghanistan, especially of Pashtuns driven out of the north by Tajik and Uzbek militias, contributes to instability. The drought that began in the winter of 1999 continued into the fall of 2002, at least in southern Afghanistan and in the neighboring regions of Pakistan and Iran. Reconstruction assistance to Afghanistan has not yet led to significant improvement in the lives of the people of Afghanistan or of the neighboring countries. Hence, even though some causes of regional conflict are at least suppressed, many remain.

Afghanistan illustrates both the transnational and regional character of contemporary armed conflict and the difficulties in achieving regional cooperation in postconflict reconstruction. Influential figures in the Afghan government, and indeed most Afghans, attribute their country's misfortune to interference by their neighbors—especially Pakistan, but also Iran, Russia, and the Central Asian states—and are wary of engaging these same neighbors, at least without adequate security guarantees from third parties.

The Need for Regional Cooperation

Despite these problems, regional cooperation involving governments, the private sector, and other nonstate actors is essential to the sustainable reconstruction of Afghanistan, because however prolonged the involvement of the international community may be, the country will eventually be on its own. The changed political circumstances in the region in the aftermath of the U.S.-led invasion provide an opportunity to improve regional relations by expanding legitimate trade and initiating other forms of positive cooperation. Such regional cooperation could be based on participation in the reconstruction of Afghanistan; the surrounding states would, in turn, profit from a stabler and more just Afghanistan.

In the past year, the Afghan government focused on engaging with the United States, the United Nations, major aid donors, and other global actors in order to insulate itself from its neighbors. The government's draft National Development Framework (NDF) did not mention regional cooperation; its trade strategy focused on markets in developed countries.[6] In May 2002, one of the principal authors of the NDF described Afghanistan's relationship with its neighbors as a "cold peace" and said that, although regional cooperation might be necessary, the country was not ready to embrace it in the absence of political progress and security guarantees. However, in February of this year Foreign Minister Abdullah Abdullah announced that regional cooperation was to be a major focus of Afghanistan's foreign policy.[7]

The reconstruction of Afghanistan will require not only the repair and expansion of infrastructure and the revitalization of the economy but also the reconstruction of national institutions, beginning with the state itself. The political tasks of reconstruction mean that the Afghan authorities are leery of forms of cooperation that may serve to reinforce direct ties between regions of Afghanistan (which are controlled by competing warlords) and their immediate neighbors, as between Kandahar and Pakistan or between Herat and Iran. While Afghans are still debating how centralized their future government should be, the vast majority oppose a pattern of reconstruction that would reinforce local control based on armed force and alliances with neighboring countries. And whereas the Central Asian states would like to benefit from both relief operations and reconstruction, they are still wary of opening their borders to the south, which they fear may leave them even more vulnerable to drug and arms trafficking, and to the spread of ideologies they cannot control.

The prospects for regional cooperation will thus be strongly influenced by the actions of the United States. If it were to make the reconstruction of Afghanistan the keystone of regional cooperation, Washington would provide a sustainable basis for maintaining peace when the international community moves on. Until then, a strong U.S. commitment to preventing regional interference in Afghanistan will reassure the Afghan authorities, lessen their fears of being overwhelmed by outside interference, and give them the confidence to cooperate more closely with their neighbors.

Regional cooperation is more likely in some areas than in others. Cooperation on security issues, except for specific antiterrorist operations, is likely to be the last area to be broached. Precisely because of their history with respect to Afghanistan, neighboring states have been excluded from participation in both the International Security Assistance Force and U.S. and European efforts to build Afghan national security forces. Broad international security guarantees will be required for regional cooperation in other areas. Some have even advocated formal neutrality for Afghanistan, as for Austria. If all its neighbors agreed to respect Afghan neutrality, none would have to intervene to preempt actions by rivals.

If the region, with international assistance, does manage to attain a level of stability and security, governments and the private sector can begin to cooperate in a number of areas. Governments can cooperate bilaterally with Afghanistan and with each other, if necessary through Kabul, in reconstruction efforts and to redress their common development deficits. Indeed the two are linked, as a more cooperative region could provide larger markets for Afghanistan's trade and production, which could fund improvements in infrastructure.

Cooperation among law enforcement agencies will be necessary to control drug trafficking, although it is possible that such collaboration would provide greater opportunities for corruption, as the police forces and militaries of several regional states are already involved with drug mafias. In order to control opium production, crop substitution will be necessary, and here shared regional agricultural expertise can come into play. Farmers will probably want to plant alternative cash crops for export, rather than revert to subsistence farming, and nearby countries could provide important markets for fruits, vegetables, and cut flowers.

Promoting trade within the region and beyond is the sector where cooperation is most necessary and will be most beneficial.[8] An increase in regional trade will create a powerful lobby for peaceful relations within the region. According to the Afghan minister of commerce, Sayed Mustafa Kazemi, Pakistani businessmen have expressed strong interest in trade with Afghanistan but have encountered political obstacles from their own government. Islamabad's intransigence with respect to negotiating new trade agreements with Kabul despite pressure from its own business community has led the Afghan administration to concentrate on preferential trade agreements with Iran and India.

The Afghan administration has named road construction and repair as a top priority. The United States has started to rebuild the Kabul-Kandahar highway from Kabul, and Japan is slated to start rebuilding it from the Kandahar end as soon as Tokyo is satisfied with security conditions. The construction and repair of bridges and tunnels, better repair facilities for trucks, and insurance that is recognized across borders are vital to the economic health of this mountainous region. Kabul has signed trilateral trade agreements with Iran and India, which, among other things, commit them to upgrading road and rail lines connecting the three countries.[9] Iran and Afghanistan recently reopened a customs post in Milak in southwest Afghanistan, and Iran is planning to upgrade the road system connecting that transit point to the port of Chahar Bahar, which would decrease the cost and time of transit for goods. This new crossing point would also make it easier for the Afghan government to collect customs because the post is in a relatively deserted area, away from the control of any local power holder.

The great variety of national trade regimes and customs requirements in the region makes trade difficult. The World Bank has organized joint training for customs officials of a number of countries from the region. The Asian Development Bank (ADB) has initiated discussions with Central Asian and Chinese leaders with the aim of setting up a regional customs coordination committee. During an August 2002 visit to Islamabad by Afghanistan's finance and foreign ministers, Pakistan and Afghanistan established a joint economic commission chaired by the two countries' finance ministers to work on customs coordination, among other things. The ADB has also promised to help Afghanistan gain better access to regional markets: Iran, for instance, has a centralized state body for the purchase of grain, which makes it difficult for Afghan producers to market their wheat there. And the Central Asian states still by and large maintain cumbersome Soviet-style trade practices.

Measures to facilitate and promote trade would make it easier for the large number of existing traders, some of whom now operate in gray areas or through bribing customs officials, to legalize their activity. Instead of reinforcing the weakness of state institutions, trade activity could contribute to regional stability and development.

The region has both hydroelectric and hydrocarbon resources, but Afghanistan is relatively deficient in both. It does, however, have some hydroelectric plants and irrigation systems that are in need of repair, gas reserves in the north that have not been tapped since 1989, and potential oil reserves in the south. Stability and security in Afghanistan would also open up possibilities for energy transport through the country, including by way of a proposed gas pipeline from Turkmenistan to Pakistan via western Afghanistan. The presidents of the three countries signed a memorandum of understanding on that project in May 2002, and the ADB has allocated $1.5 million for a feasibility study. This project could be made profitable by building a gas liquefaction plant at the Pakistani port of Gwadar in Baluchistan to export liquefied gas by sea, but it would be even more economical to pipe gas directly to western India, a fast-growing industrial zone with an increasing demand for energy. Such a project would depend on peaceful relations between India and Pakistan. Some have speculated that Iran would oppose such a pipeline as competing with its own plans; Iranian officials from the reformist camp claim that Iran would support any economically feasible pipeline project, though it would oppose any that were implemented solely to bypass Iran. Tehran recognizes that an unstable Afghanistan is more costly to itself in terms of refugee flows and the narcotics trade than the loss of potential pipeline revenues. Tajikistan and Uzbekistan are currently providing electricity to Kunduz and Mazar-i Sharif, respectively.

The lack of water is one of the major constraints on growth and development in the region, never more so than now, with much of the area recovering from a four-year drought. Afghanistan shares river basins with all the neighboring countries: the Amu Darya and the Panj with the Central Asian states; the Kabul River, which flows into the Indus, with Pakistan, which in turn links it to the Indus-Punjab system shared by Pakistan and India; and the Helmand River with Iran. The Central Asian states share not only the Amu Darya but also the Syr Darya, the overuse of both of which is responsible for the desiccation of the Aral Sea and pollution in the region. International agreements regulate the sharing of water in all these river basins, but the recent drought has led to conflict between Afghanistan and Iran. Tehran claims that it has not been receiving its full allocation under the Helmand River agreement. Afghanistan, on the other hand, now uses less than a quarter of the water of the Panj-Amu Darya to which it is entitled. If it were to use its full allocation, it could find itself at odds with its Central Asian neighbors, who are already uneasy about Afghanistan's future water demands. Afghan officials, in turn, charge that Soviet-era artificial embankments on the Central Asian side of the Amu Darya and the Panj are causing the erosion of the natural Afghan shoreline. Rational planning for the use of scarce water resources will require regional cooperation and the sharing of expertise.

Afghans share languages and a common culture with all of their neighbors. Whereas in the past this has facilitated foreign interference, it could also be a source of positive interchanges. Afghan refugees and indigenous educated professionals in Central Asia feel that they have been overlooked in the reconstruction planning, though they could contribute a great deal as teachers, doctors, and engineers. Iran and Pakistan could also provide personnel who speak Afghan languages, as well as textbooks and training materials, but sensitivities are still quite high, especially regarding Pakistan, since these countries were a major source of foreign interference. Professionals from neighboring countries with expertise in agriculture, irrigation, and other areas where knowledge of local conditions is important could also contribute to the rehabilitation of the Afghan economy.

It will also be necessary to take a regional approach in dealing with the problems in border provinces, which have or may become incubators of conflict or violence because of their entrenched poverty and indigenous power structures. In 2001, the World Bank identified several such problem areas, including the Pashtun tribal territories in Pakistan and Afghanistan, the Ferghana Valley, and Sistan-Balochistan in Iran, together with the neighboring desert areas of Afghanistan and Pakistan. One Afghan scholar, highlighting the importance of the Pashtun areas, has remarked that they "have become a source of headaches for the whole region." A large proportion of the population (40 percent by one estimate) has no livelihood except for smuggling. Schools and hospitals are so few and the status of women so low that the human development indicators in this part of Pakistan are as low as, if not lower than, those in Afghanistan. Literacy in the tribal territories, for instance, is estimated at 11 percent for men and less than 1 percent for women.[10]

Some of these regional problems, particularly those having to do with infrastructure or public policy, are inherently the responsibility of governments and intergovernmental organizations. The Afghan administration's development framework, however, emphasizes that economic growth and reconstruction should be led by the private sector. When the finance ministers of Iran, Afghanistan, and Pakistan, together with the administrator of the United Nations Development Program (UNDP), signed a joint communique on economic cooperation in Tehran on May 18, 2002, they also emphasized the role of the private sector.

Private business interests are organized differently and have their own roles in relation to government in various countries. In Central Asia, the Soviet heritage has left the private sector relatively weak and dependent on government, while private businesses in Turkey, Iran, and Pakistan are actively looking for opportunities and contracts in the Afghanistan reconstruction project. Turkish businessmen have already organized a trade council for Turkish businesses working in Afghanistan. Relations between the Iranian government and private business are particularly close and supportive, and Iranian companies appear to be far ahead of others in the region in doing business in Afghanistan. The first private air service to Kabul airport, for instance, is being provided by the privately owned Mahan Airlines, based in Tehran. The Pakistani private sector, in contrast, is hampered by a license-permit raj that requires endless paperwork. Regularizing business practices and permissions should be a subject for the economic cooperation commission established at the meeting in Tehran last May.

What Can Be Done

Regional cooperation is likely only when states value the opportunities that openness can create more than the need for control. The latter, among other concerns, defeated a UNDP proposal for a joint development authority for the three states of the Ferghana Valley and limited the scope of the South Asia Association for Regional Cooperation (SAARC). The makeup of the states in the region makes cooperation more difficult. All have various weaknesses, with Afghanistan being an extreme case, where state structures have barely existed for much of the past twenty-three years. Agreements on cooperation do not in themselves create the management capacity to benefit from cooperation. Cooperation is also more difficult when states' administrative systems and trade regimes are incommensurate.

This region is unlikely to become organized under a single, multifunctional umbrella organization like the European Union, the Organization of American States, or the African Union. Rather, various efforts at cooperation for specific purposes among different parts of the region, possibly linked to neighboring regions, could potentially evolve into a thicker network of cooperation, even in the absence of an overarching organization. Such cooperation does not have to begin with states. Traders from Turkey, United Arab Emirates, Iran, Afghanistan,

Pakistan, and India are already organized and accustomed to working together. Traders from Iran, Pakistan, and Afghanistan, including many based in Dubai, attended the meeting on economic cooperation in Tehran in significant numbers. The Civil Society Forum supported by the Swiss Peace Foundation in Kabul is helping Afghan traders organize and communicate their needs to the authorities.

Official cooperation can evolve gradually from technical work. Along these lines, the Asian Development Bank launched a project in Central Asia in 1997, starting with technical studies of transport, trade, energy, and water. The Central Asia Regional Economic Cooperation program (CAREC) includes Azerbaijan, Kazakhstan, Kyrgyzstan, Tajikistan, Uzbekistan, and Xinjiang province of China, and Turkmenistan is expected to become active soon. There is still considerable resistance to regional cooperation in Central Asia, and the state leaderships tend to focus on their national economies and links to developed countries, rather than links to their neighbors. However, when Afghanistan's finance minister participated in a CAREC meeting in Shanghai in May 2003, he suggested that Afghanistan, Iran, and Pakistan might join the organization in the future. Clearly, there is growing political will in the region with respect to economic cooperation, despite the legacy of suspicion and mistrust from years of regional strife.

The widespread discussion of a hoped-for Marshall Plan for Afghanistan implicitly evokes a wish for U.S. leadership and support for reconstruction of the entire region. But the United States has clearly stated that although it will lead the military efforts in Afghanistan, it will play only a supporting role in reconstruction. A more modest approach for funding regional initiatives in support of Afghan reconstruction would be for donors to support a World Bank proposal for the establishment of a trust fund for that purpose separate from the Afghanistan Reconstruction Trust Fund.

Such initiatives would most likely have to come from the region and most certainly could be sustained only if regional participants felt themselves to be in charge. Since political considerations are of such importance in determining attitudes toward regional cooperation, the establishment of an informal regional forum might be useful for discussing potential areas of cooperation. The present circumstances provide an occasion for the creation of such a forum, with leadership coming from Afghanistan itself now that the country's government is internationally recognized. The Karzai government has taken the first step in this process by asking the six neighboring states to sign the Kabul Declaration on Good-Neighborly Relations in December 2002. The declaration affirms "their commitment to constructive and supportive bilateral relationships based on the principles of territorial integrity, mutual respect, friendly relations, cooperation and non-interference in each other's internal affairs." This is a good starting point.

Just as regional cooperation may be essential for Afghanistan's sustainable recovery, Afghanistan's sustainable recovery may be essential for regional cooperation. If the economic benefits of reconstruction are accompanied by increasingly just and legitimate states, the reconstruction of Afghanistan could even contribute to genuine regional peace building. Such peace building will be possible and effective only if the international community supports the construction of a more stable Afghan national state and actively supports regional cooperation. Earmarking funds for regional cooperation and investing now in the transport, energy, and communications infrastructure needed to connect the countries of the region to each other and to the world will make any other investments in reconstruction more fruitful and sustainable.

Notes

1. Regional conflict formations are transnational conflicts that form mutually reinforcing linkages with each other throughout a region, making for more protracted and obdurate discord. In South Central Asia, the regional conflict comprises state and nonstate actors in Afghanistan, Kyrgyzstan, Iran, Pakistan, Tajikistan, Turkmenistan, Uzbekistan, and Kashmir.
2. See Stephen Blank, "The Arming of Central Asia," *Asia Times Online,* August 23, 2002, http://www.atimes.com/atimes/South_Asia/DH24Df02.html.
3. United Nations Office for Drug Control and Crime Prevention, *Global Illicit Drug Trends* (New York: United Nations, 2002).
4. United Nations Office for Drug Control and Crime Prevention, *The Opium Economy in Afghanistan: An International Problem* (New York: United Nations, 2003).
5. United Nations Integrated Regional Information Networks, "Central Asia: HIV/AIDS Growing Rapidly," October 2, 2002.
6. The National Development Framework is available on the website of the Afghan Assistance Coordination Authority, www.afghanaca.com.
7. See Peter Tomsen, "Untying the Afghan Knot," *Fletcher Forum on World Affairs,* vol. 25 (winter 2001), p. 17.
8. See Frederick S. Starr, "Afghanistan: Free Trade and Regional Transformation" (New York: Asia Society, February 2002).
9. See Ahmed Rashid, "Afghanistan Develops New Trade Routes Beyond Pakistan," *Nation* (Pakistan), January 23, 2003. India is committed to building the Zaranj-Delaram road in southwestern Afghanistan and to working with Iran to rebuild the railroad from the port of Chabahar on the Gulf of Oman, linking it with the Iranian railway network. Iran is committed to building the Milak Bridge over the Helmand River into Afghanistan and upgrading the Chabahar-Milak road to international standards.
10. World Bank, "Afghanistan Border States Development Framework Approach Paper: Discussion Draft," November 12, 2001.

12

Afghanistan's Uncertain Transition from Turmoil to Normalcy

Introduction: The Afghanistan Compact

Before the terrorist attacks of September 11, 2001, and all that followed, Afghans and the handful of internationals working on Afghanistan could hardly have imagined being fortunate enough to confront today's problems. The Bonn Agreement of December 2001 providing for the "reestablishment of permanent government institutions" in Afghanistan was fully completed with the adoption of a constitution in January 2004, the election of President Hamid Karzai in October 2004, and the formation of the National Assembly in December 2005.

From January 31 to February 1, 2006, President Karzai, UN Secretary-General Kofi Annan, and British Prime Minister Tony Blair presided over a conference in London of about sixty states and international organizations that issued the Afghanistan Compact, setting forth both the international community's commitment to Afghanistan and Afghanistan's commitment to state building and reform over the next five years. The compact supports the Afghan National Development Strategy (ANDS), an interim version of which (I-ANDS) the Afghan government presented at the conference.[1] The compact provides a strategy for building an effective, accountable state in Afghanistan, with targets for improvements in security, governance, and development, including measures for reducing the narcotics economy and promoting regional cooperation.[2] The compact also prescribes ways for the Afghan government and donors to make aid more effective and establishes a mechanism to monitor adherence to the timelines and benchmarks. The compact places responsibility for meeting these goals on the government of Afghanistan, which can easily be held accountable, and the "international community," which cannot be. The United States, United Kingdom, and other donors strongly opposed language

Originally published as Council on Foreign Relations Special Report, April 10, 2006, http://cfr.org/publication/10273/.

in the compact that would have held those present at the London conference (listed in a compact annex), rather than an abstract entity, responsible for implementation.

During his visit to Afghanistan, India, and Pakistan from March 1 to March 5, 2006, President George W. Bush praised Afghan successes, telling President Karzai, "You are inspiring others, and the inspiration will cause others to demand their freedom." He did so the day after the administration's own intelligence chiefs reported that the antigovernment insurgency in Afghanistan is growing and presents a greater threat "than at any point since late 2001."[3] Some Afghan officials say the world thus far has put Afghanistan on life support, rather than investing in a cure. The following conditions make it clear that Afghanistan has the potential to be a disastrous situation if intelligent, measured steps are not taken:

- An ever-more-deadly insurgency with sanctuaries in neighboring Pakistan, where leaders of al-Qaeda and the Taliban have found refuge;
- A corrupt and ineffective administration without resources and a potentially dysfunctional parliament;
- Levels of poverty, hunger, ill health, illiteracy, and gender inequality that put Afghanistan near the bottom of every global ranking;
- Levels of aid that have only recently expanded above a fraction of that accorded to other postconflict countries;
- An economy and administration heavily influenced by drug traffickers;
- Massive arms stocks despite the demobilization of many militias;
- A potential denial of the Islamic legitimacy of the Afghan government by a clergy that feels marginalized;
- Ethnic tensions exacerbated by competition for resources and power;
- Interference by neighboring states, all of which oppose a long-term U.S. presence in the region;
- Well-trained and well-equipped security forces that the government may not be able to pay once aid declines in a few years;
- Constitutional requirements to hold more national elections (at least six per decade) than the government may be able to afford or conduct;
- An exchange rate inflated by aid and drug money that subsidizes cheap imports and hinders economic growth; and
- Future generations of unemployed, frustrated graduates and dropouts from the rapidly expanding school system.

The compact addresses these challenges insofar as is possible in an international declaration. Its principal recommendation is that all stakeholders should fully fund and implement the Afghanistan Compact and the I-ANDS. This Council Special Report makes some additional recommendations, organized to the three pillars of the compact and I-ANDS: security; governance, rule of law, and human rights; and economic and social development. As in those documents, counter-narcotics and regional cooperation are treated as crosscutting issues.

Recommendations elaborate on the following themes:

- Afghanistan has received inadequate resources in terms of both troops and funds; this is not the time to draw down the military presence or to reduce aid.
- Afghanistan can be stable and secure only if it is well integrated into its region, both economically and politically. Achieving this goal will require sustained efforts to deescalate and eventually resolve the country's long-standing conflicts with Pakistan over relations with India, the border, ethnic issues, and transit trade, and to insulate Afghanistan from conflict relating to Iran.
- None of the problems of this destitute, devastated country can be addressed effectively without sustained, equitable economic growth. In addition to security, this requires extensive investments in infrastructure, governance, and the justice system.
- Economic growth also requires a policy of eliminating narcotics that does not impoverish people. There should be no short-term conditionality of aid on eliminating narcotics. Elimination of narcotics will take well over a decade, and crop eradication is a counterproductive way to start such a program. Foreign donors should support the Afghan government's long-term plan and not impose their own programs.
- A stable and secure Afghanistan requires a legitimate and capable state. To ensure that international aid fulfills this objective, the United States and other major aid donors that have not done so already, notably Germany and Japan, should provide multiyear aid commitments and channel increasing amounts of aid through the government budget by mechanisms such as the Afghanistan Reconstruction Trust Fund, the Law and Order Trust Fund for Afghanistan, and the Counter Narcotics Trust Fund for Afghanistan.

Security

There are two international military commands in Afghanistan: the U.S.-led coalition and the International Security Assistance Force (ISAF). The coalition, whose primary mission is defined as counterterrorism and counterinsurgency, and which enjoys freedom of action under the United States's right of self-defense, came to Afghanistan to ensure first the security of Americans from al-Qaeda and then of the Afghan government from the insurgency.[4] ISAF's mission is to help the Afghan authorities provide security according to the Bonn Agreement, relevant UN Security Council resolutions, and a bilateral agreement with the Afghan government.

The avowed goal of both commands is to provide security directly until Afghan security forces are prepared to do so themselves. Building Afghan national capacity to provide security requires the policies known as security sector reform (SSR), including both the dissolution of irregular armed groups through demobilization, disarmament, and reintegration and the creation or transformation of previous forces into professional units.

Both the coalition and ISAF have operated with a light footprint that has been inadequate to deliver security.[5] Achieving this goal has also been hampered by lack of coordination between the two commands' differing definitions of security priorities. The coalition armed and funded Afghan commanders to seize and hold ground after the Taliban and al-Qaeda fled the U.S. air offensive. Some of these commanders used the money and arms they received to invest in drug production and engage in land grabs, predation, political intimidation, and ethnic cleansing—a major source of insecurity for Afghans. Meanwhile, ISAF first deployed to Kabul, and then elsewhere, to provide security from the commanders allied with the coalition, as well as from Taliban and al-Qaeda. The militias allied with the coalition were supposed to withdraw from areas occupied by ISAF; they did not, and the United States declined to press them to do so. Although ISAF has helped prevent factional clashes in Kabul, the militias' continued presence in Kabul, regional cities, and border posts provided them with political leverage and the ability to engage in predation and trafficking.

By mid-2002, U.S. commanders on the ground understood the need to provide Afghans with reconstruction and governance to consolidate military gains, despite the administration's original opposition to "nation building" and "peace keeping." Although the Pentagon continued to oppose ISAF expansion until late 2003 (and other countries were not exactly lining up to volunteer), ground commanders won approval for coalition-led Provincial Reconstruction Teams (PRTs). PRTs are small, joint civilian-military organizations. These deployments of dozens of people—predominantly from the military, with a few embedded civilian aid providers—are intended to create an "ISAF effect without ISAF." In the summer and fall of 2003, when the Pentagon relaxed its opposition, the North Atlantic Treaty Organization (NATO) took command of ISAF and started extending it outside of Kabul. Germany, Spain, Canada, and other NATO members who wanted to find a way to affirm their alliance with the United States, despite opposition to the invasion of Iraq, now stepped forward to contribute, although sometimes with restrictive national caveats on their operations. NATO took on PRTs as the template for expansion. NATO and the coalition have since worked out a plan for nationwide coverage by PRTs in four stages. The United States, whose forces are overextended due to the war in Iraq, would like to withdraw forces as ISAF expansion continues, leading to the unification of command with a common mission. Because the U.S. coalition has presided over a strengthening rather than defeat of the insurgency, however, NATO troops would have to engage in active combat, which most alliance members are not prepared to do.

The compact calls on both the coalition and ISAF to continue support of the Afghan government's efforts to establish security and stability, including commitments to carry out "counterterrorism" operations in close coordination with the government, expand coverage by PRTs, help disband illegal armed groups, and build fiscally sustainable military and police forces bound by the rule of law.

Insurgency

After years of claiming that greater American and Afghan casualties are either signs of "desperation" on the part of foundering terrorists or the result of more aggressive U.S. tactics that are pushing opposition fighters out of their safe havens, the U.S. government has now admitted that the insurgency is growing and becoming more effective. U.S. and Afghan government casualties caused by the insurgency are higher in 2005 than in any previous year (see Figure 12.1). Insurgent activities have increased in lethality, with increased use of tactics seen in Iraq, including suicide bombings, which the Defense Intelligence Agency (DIA) estimates have quadrupled in the past year, and improvised explosive devices, whose use has doubled. According to Ahmed Rashid, a Pakistani journalist based in Lahore, "In the past few months, at least thirty attacks have killed nearly one hundred people in Afghanistan, including NATO peacekeepers and a Canadian diplomat."[6] Afghanistan and the Arab world have now switched places:

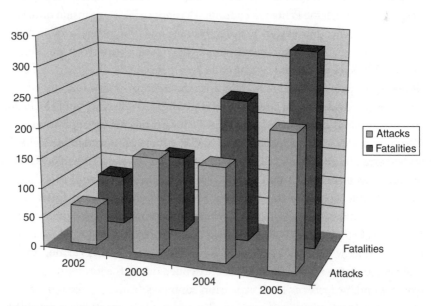

Figure 12.1 Growth in Insurgency: Attacks on and Fatalities of Coalition and Government Forces in Afghanistan, 2002–2005. Source: Data from RAND-MIPT Terrorism Incident Database, courtesy of Seth Jones.

whereas before September 11, 2001, Arab jihadists created a base for terrorism in Afghanistan, the war in Iraq now provides a training and testing ground for new jihadi tactics, which have spread to Afghanistan.

The coalition and the Afghan government have disagreed over the diagnosis of the insurgency and the strategy against it. The United States is largely relying on cooperation with Pakistan for action against al-Qaeda and Taliban sanctuaries in that country, although President Bush has noted that more needs to be done.[7] The coalition is also waging aggressive campaigns against insurgency sanctuaries in Afghanistan and trying to increase development and governance efforts in areas of Taliban activity through PRTs and civil affairs projects. Although during his March 2006 visit President Bush praised both President Karzai and President Pervez Musharraf as staunch allies in the war on terror, the two presidents were waging an active war of words against each other in the media both before and after his visit. Relations deteriorated rapidly, with little apparent action by the United States to address this conflict.

The Afghan government wants Washington to reduce unpopular actions inside Afghanistan, reduce its unilateral actions, and instead focus pressure on Pakistan. Karzai has stated that "No coalition forces should go to Afghan homes without the authorization of the Afghan government. . . . The use of air power is something that may not be very effective now."[8]

Yet more than four years after the initial offensive and the establishment of what is supposed to be a fully sovereign Afghan government, U.S. forces and their contractors still enjoy full "freedom of action" without any status-of-forces agreement. The Bush administration's insistence on independence for U.S. forces and impunity for contractors is undermining support for coalition presence, damaging its sustainability.

The government of Afghanistan also has discreetly joined the global chorus of protest over the mistreatment of detainees by the Bush administration. During his Washington visit in May 2005, President Karzai asked for the transfer of Afghan detainees to his government's custody and for more control by Afghanistan over coalition operations. The United States has since signed an agreement for the gradual transfer of Afghan detainees, although the Afghan government protested the failure to adequately punish U.S. soldiers for the torture and murder of two detainees in Bagram air base and the sacrilegious burning of the bodies of Taliban who had died in battle.[9]

The Joint Declaration of Strategic Partnership of May 17, 2005, providing for "freedom of action" by U.S. forces, must give way to a status-of-forces agreement between Afghanistan and the United States that affirms Afghan sovereignty, commits both sides to respect international humanitarian law, and limits threats to neighboring states from U.S. bases. Such an agreement should regulate the legal status of detainees and U.S. contractors on the basis of international law. It also should make clear that the U.S. presence in Afghanistan is directed solely at combating terrorism and insurgency and that Afghanistan will not become a permanent U.S. base.[10]

Such an agreement alone, however, would not constitute a counterinsurgency strategy. The strategy also has to emphasize an end to foreign sanctuaries and the strengthening of the Afghan government and economy in affected areas. More aggressive military action by the coalition in the past year has led to successful adaptation by the insurgents. The Pentagon's plan to reduce U.S. coalition forces from twenty thousand to sixteen thousand represents only a return to the levels of 2004 and is supposed to be compensated for by deployment of British, Canadian, and Dutch forces to southern Afghanistan, but it is causing anxiety in Kabul as a sign of decreasing U.S. commitment. This anxiety may not be justified on military grounds. The UK and Canada, in particular, have extensive experience in ISAF. The chief of staff of the Canadian armed forces, General Rick J. Hillier, is a former ISAF commander who is well regarded for his innovations and strategic thinking. These units, experienced in peace support and counterinsurgency activities, may be at least as effective as the U.S. forces, despite the latter's superior firepower. Nonetheless, the decision by the United States to reduce forces at the same time that its intelligence agencies have reached a consensus that the insurgent threat is greater than ever has sent the wrong message about U.S. commitment. Reversal of this relatively small reduction would reassure Afghans and send a clear message to the entire region.

Strategy Toward Pakistan and the Rest of the Region

Studies of insurgency indicate that logistical and support networks are critical to their survival. The U.S. and Afghan governments agree that, despite Pakistan's denial, the Taliban enjoy "safe havens" there, but they differ in their analysis of the role of official policy.[11] Success is not possible without a coherent U.S. strategy not only toward Pakistan and Afghanistan but also toward the Pakistan-Afghanistan relationship. This relationship, which has been tense for most of the last sixty years, has been the source of much of the region's instability and is today the key factor ensuring continued sanctuary for the Taliban, foreign jihadists, and other extremists. The current antagonistic relations between the two countries mimic previous relations between the two states during most of the period since 1947, when Pakistan gained independence in its current borders over the objections of Afghanistan, which challenged the incorporation of the Pashtun areas. The Bush administration has treated both governments as allies in the "War on Terror" and has seemed tone-deaf to the historically troubled relations between them, which continue to pose obstacles to the cooperation needed for success. The March 2006 presidential visit to the region, which also featured unprecedented concessions to India on the development of nuclear power that underscored Pakistan's insecurity, exacerbated the antagonism between Kabul and Islamabad.

Many Afghans, apparently including President Karzai, believe that the Taliban could not operate from Pakistan without official support. President Karzai has urged the coalition to "concentrate on where terrorists are trained, on their bases, on the supply to them, [and] on the money coming to them."[12] Many members of the current Afghan government, including the president and minister of defense, worked for mujahidin groups in Pakistan during the 1980s and are intimately familiar with Pakistan's intelligence agencies and covert action structure. President Karzai also has revived the relations between the Afghan state and Pashtun tribal and political leaders in Pakistan. He met some of them, including outspoken opponents of President Musharraf, during his February 15, 2006, visit to Pakistan. In this Afghan view, the continued insurgency signals that stability in Afghanistan cannot be achieved at the expense of Pakistan's interests, particularly regarding an Indian presence in Afghanistan. Afghanistan has never recognized the British-drawn Durand Line dividing the Pashtun areas as an international border; the cross-border insurgency pressures Afghanistan to accept the border as the price for stabilizing it. Additionally, Pakistan may wish to keep its options open against the day that the United States withdraws.

President Musharraf, however, characterized Karzai's charges that Pakistan is harboring Taliban leaders, terrorists, and suicide bombers as "humbug and nonsense" on the eve of President Bush's arrival.[13] After the president's visit, Musharraf charged that the insurgency was due to the internal weaknesses of Afghanistan, that Karzai was "totally oblivious of what is happening in his country," and that there was a "conspiracy going on against Pakistan in [Karzai's] Ministry of Defense and his intelligence setup."[14] Musharraf claimed that India was feeding anti-Pakistan intelligence to Kabul. During President Karzai's visit to Islamabad, while Karzai and his intelligence chief presented (and leaked to the press) evidence of Taliban and al-Qaeda activities in Pakistan, the Pakistan intelligence agency made a presentation charging that intelligence agents in the Indian consulates in Jalalabad and Kandahar were funneling weapons and funds to opposition groups in Pakistan, in particular the insurgency in Baluchistan.

President Bush endorsed Musharraf's commitment to the War on Terror, even as the latter admitted there had been some "slippage" in Pakistan's performance, perhaps alluding to the terrorist killing of a U.S. diplomat and four others in Karachi the day before Bush's arrival and the virtual occupation of the Waziristan Tribal Agencies by Taliban and foreign jihadists, who declared an Islamic state there. Pakistan launched a three-day offensive against these groups the day before Bush arrived, taking the town of Miran Shah and killing more than one hundred guerrillas as ten thousand civilians fled the area. The magnitude of the engagement indicated the Taliban and foreign jihadists had a greater presence and more control of territory in Pakistan than in Afghanistan. American officials privately acknowledge that parts of the Pakistani state may not be fully on board. They argue that, given Musharraf's vulnerability (he has barely escaped assassination four times), Washington should stick to a policy of "public support and private pressure," so as to not destabilize the regime. This approach rests on the belief that stability in Pakistan depends solely on the military, a self-serving view promoted by the latter to their American counterparts for decades, and one that has survived the Bush administration's claim to move from a commitment to stability to a commitment to "freedom." President Bush did raise the issue of "democracy" during his visit, by which he apparently meant the holding of elections, but there is no indication that he discussed the fundamental issue of military dominance of the most important state institutions, including the judiciary.

Stabilizing this region requires a comprehensive policy toward the Afghanistan-Pakistan relationship, whose interaction with the India-Pakistan conflict has been the source of the region's troubles for nearly sixty years and now threatens global security. Although the most immediate issue is the bases and support networks for jihadi extremists in Pakistan, the use of these networks by the Pakistani military for several decades derives from that state's reliance on asymmetric warfare to compensate for its fundamental insecurity, which cannot be relieved solely by increasing pressure. Afghanistan and Pakistan will be unable to extricate themselves from this conflict without active engagement and assistance by the United States and other international actors to help them restructure their relationship in a more cooperative direction, including recognition of an international border and cooperative development of the tribal areas on either side. Any measure that lessens tension between India and Pakistan will also contribute to stability in the area, although how to bring that about is beyond the scope of this report.

Recommendations:

• The administration should insist on the Pakistani government's full cooperation in isolating and ending the neo-Taliban insurgency as part of a larger strategy that offers Pakistan benefits other than military equipment. In this component of the strategy, Washington must push for the Pakistani government to arrest Taliban leaders whose locations are provided by U.S. and Afghan intelligence agencies; take aggressive measures to close down the networks supporting suicide bombers that have been identified by those agencies; end public recruitment campaigns for the Taliban and pro-Taliban speeches at government institutions, including those by former leaders of Pakistan's Inter-Services Intelligence Directorate; close training camps (e.g., in Mansehra, Miran Shah, and Shamshattu) for Taliban, including those for Kashmiri guerrillas where Taliban are trained; and cut off housing and pension benefits to retired military and government personnel engaged in supporting the Taliban. Until now the administration has conveyed mixed messages: when spokesmen praise Musharraf's cooperation against al-Qaeda, they have given the impression that ending sanctuary for the Taliban is a lower priority. Both public and private statements must place those engaged in violence in Afghanistan as equally threatening to U.S. interests and therefore of equal importance to the United States.

- The U.S. government must recognize that security in Afghanistan hinges on democratizing Pakistan. Military domination of the Pakistani state is the problem, not the solution. Elections will not democratize Pakistan as long as the military continues to control state institutions. The United States needs to signal at a high level that it wants to see the withdrawal of military control from Pakistan's civilian institutions and genuine freedom for political parties. It should support Pakistan's development by lifting restrictions on Pakistani textile imports into the United States, as Pakistani business has a strong economic interest in the stabilization of Afghanistan. This measure should not be held out as a reward for good behavior but should be enacted immediately to show commitment to cooperation with Pakistan on new terms.

- In response, Afghanistan will have to respect legitimate Pakistani concerns about the border and an Indian presence. Currently Afghanistan is following the historical pattern of turning to India to balance the threat from Pakistan, particularly in the context of the drawdown of U.S. forces and doubts about future U.S. commitment. The United States should strengthen its presence on the Afghan side of the border, and encourage India and Afghanistan not to engage in any provocative activity there. India has legitimate consular interests in Jalalabad and Kandahar involving Indian businesses and Afghan Sikhs and Hindus with family ties in India, but Afghanistan should encourage confidence-building measures with Pakistan in the area. Afghanistan also should refrain from relations with Pashtun leaders in Pakistan that give the impression that the government represents Pashtuns, which aggravates both relations with Pakistan and ethnic relations in Afghanistan.

- The United States should help Afghans realize that Islamabad will not respect a border that Kabul does not recognize. This is a very sensitive ethnic and political issue domestically, and it will be necessary to show that the border issue is not a zero-sum conflict and that recognizing the border need not isolate Pashtuns from each other, though they live in different states. Current efforts to promote development along the Durand Line, bringing benefits to those on both sides, should be expanded, and both transit rights and access to Pakistani ports in Karachi and Gwadar should be guaranteed.

- Settling the border issue will require transforming the status of the tribal areas in Pakistan. Currently, these areas have lost their autonomy: they have experienced offensives by the Pakistani army but have not enjoyed social and law enforcement services. The inhabitants of these areas must have the opportunity to participate in decisions about their future through genuine elections, which they have never had. Stabilizing the border also will require coordinated investments in the underdeveloped areas on both sides, although such coordination can be scaled up only as agreement on the political status of the border develops, and security threats no longer override other considerations.

- In order to launch a long-term program to stabilize and develop the Afghanistan-Pakistan border region, the United States and the UK should sponsor both official and second-track discussions involving all stakeholders in the border region. These discussions should ultimately aim to create a context in which Afghanistan can recognize an open border, the tribal territories of Pakistan can be integrated into and receive a full range of services from the Pakistani state, and the border area can become a region for cooperative development rather than insecurity, extremism, and antagonism.

Other Regional Dilemmas

Afghanistan's regional dilemmas go beyond Pakistan. Afghanistan's weakness has always posed a strategic dilemma for its rulers. Because the country has never produced enough wealth to pay the cost of governing or defending itself, Afghanistan has been stable only when its neighbors or imperial powers agreed to strengthen it as a buffer or nonaligned state to serve external security interests. The resulting lack of domestic legitimacy, however, has created opportunities for other foreign powers to interfere. Afghanistan's experience of interference after the Soviet withdrawal has intensified the country's mistrust of its neighbors and made many skeptical that nonalignment without effective deterrence of interference would suffice to guarantee the country's independence. Hence, Afghans tolerate the international presence, including that of the U.S. military, as the needed deterrence to its neighbors' interference. Concerns that the United States might reduce its presence led President Karzai to seek long-term guarantees in the form of the Declaration of Strategic Partnership, which gave the United States rights to military bases in Afghanistan and "freedom of action" for its forces.

Although Afghans largely accept the need for the U.S. presence, neither they nor the country's neighbors have accepted the overt nullification of the country's nonalignment that many saw in the Strategic Partnership. Soon after President Karzai announced his intention to seek such an agreement with the United States, demonstrations broke out around the country, in part against granting permanent bases to the United States. An underground leaflet ("Night Letter") circulating in Kabul during the rioting called Karzai a "U.S.A. servant" who put the interests of his "evil master" ahead of Afghanistan.[15]

Iran then drafted a proposed treaty with Afghanistan, including a provision that neither party would permit intelligence operations by third countries against the other. The United States opposed this treaty, which Afghanistan could not have enforced. When President Karzai wanted to visit Tehran for the inauguration of President Mahmoud Ahmadinejad on August 3, 2005, Iran told him he was not welcome if he would not sign the agreement. A call from U.S. Secretary of State Condoleezza Rice forced President Karzai to cancel a trip to Iran aimed at reaching economic agreements in January 2006. Afghanistan was caught between Tehran, which tried to use Afghanistan's need for transit to break out of its isolation over its nuclear program, and Washington, which deprived Kabul of the opportunity to exploit Tehran's discomfiture for its own benefit.

China and Russia issued veiled protests of Washington's actions in public and sharp rebukes in private. On July 5, 2005, the heads of state of the members of the Shanghai Cooperation Organization, which includes Russia, China, Kazakhstan, the Kyrgyz Republic, Tajikistan, and Uzbekistan, asked the United States to set a date for closing its military bases in Central Asia. These countries believe that the United States is exploiting their cooperation on counterterrorism to pursue long-term strategic objectives inimical to their interest. Subsequently, China and Russia conducted joint military operations on each other's territory for the first time, in part over these concerns.

Yet having good regional relations is extremely important to Afghanistan. Landlocked and arid, it can develop economically only through regional cooperation to manage its water resources, connect to the international market, and obtain energy. Because none of Afghanistan's neighbors welcomes a long-term U.S. military presence, they may resist such cooperation. Although the potential economic cooperation described in this report may help build confidence, regional cooperation will be limited in the absence of a U.S. understanding of Afghanistan's geopolitical and regional identity.

Recommendation:

- The United States and its coalition partners, especially its principal NATO allies, should seek to promote a regional consensus on the geostrategic role of Afghanistan as a state not aligned against any neighbor. This requires developing understandings of how to insulate Afghanistan from conflicts in and over surrounding areas, including Iran, as was done for the first three decades of the Cold War and in the early part of the twentieth century, despite sharp political antagonisms in the region. Longer-term stability in the region will develop only as the Afghan state becomes stronger and able to articulate and implement relations with its neighbors. The United States should not undermine this eventual process by insisting that Afghanistan's foreign and security policy conform to U.S. strategic objectives. For instance, the United States has the means to confront the threat posed by Iran's nuclear program without forcing landlocked Afghanistan to forgo economic agreements with one of its most important partners for trade and transit, where more than a million Afghans live.

Stabilization Operations

The Bonn Agreement defined the international stabilization mission in Afghanistan as helping Afghans to provide security until they were able to do so themselves. ISAF was confined to Kabul for nearly two years, and the coalition did not initially define the domestic security of Afghanistan as part of its mission. Hence, militias and drug traffickers easily consolidated control of much of the country in 2002. Since late 2002, the coalition has been devoting more resources to stabilization by means of the PRTs. Since ISAF expansion in 2003, NATO has been trying to field more troops and equipment, but it took NATO more than a year, from 2003 to 2004, to deploy a few transport helicopters.[16]

Some European NATO members are resisting unification of command with the coalition that might lead to their troops' participation in counterinsurgency operations and lead them to turn over detainees to the U.S. government, in whose custody they risk treatment in violation of international humanitarian law.[17] They have now decided to turn prisoners over to the Afghan government on the condition that prisoners will neither be executed nor transferred to U.S. custody. Several troop contributors also have adopted national caveats for other reasons, even against proactive patrolling and measures to press for demobilization of militias. Success in Afghanistan, however, requires NATO contributors to find a way to carry out the mission while respecting international law, despite obstacles posed by the U.S. administration.

Recommendation:

- Troop contributors should adopt a common mission and rules of engagement, rather than insist on national caveats, even if this requires bilateral agreement with the Afghan government on treatment of prisoners or constructing separate detention facilities, to assure respect of Common Article 3 of the Geneva Conventions.

Provincial Reconstruction Teams

The PRT terms of reference now state that they will "assist the Islamic Republic of Afghanistan to extend its authority, to facilitate the development of a stable and secure environment in the identified area of operations, and enable SSR and reconstruction efforts."[18] In response to Afghan concerns that PRTs were building projects that the government had no budget to operate, the coalition now reviews projects to align them with Afghan government priorities. But the coalition's development activities are still not integrated into the coordination procedures of the civilian aid donors; nor are military officers the best development partners for local administration.

Recommendation:

- PRTs should be reconfigured to support governance and development more effectively, by including more political officers and development specialists from NATO member countries, a possible role for the European Union. The development funds disbursed by PRTs should be subject to the same criteria for effectiveness as other assistance; those funds would be more effective if disbursements were accountable to provincial administration and elected councils, as through a trust fund.

Power-Holder Impunity

Stabilization of the country will eventually require an end to the impunity of power holders. Despite several homicides by U.S. officials and contractors, and crimes by Afghan power holders including land grabbing, forced marriages, human trafficking, drug trafficking, and other abuses, none of the guilty have received significant sanctions.

Recommendations:

- The United States must impose meaningful punishment on its personnel and contractors for homicides and torture of detainees.
- The Afghan government, with the support as needed of the coalition and NATO, should begin a process to arrest powerful Afghan criminals (not just apolitical or pro-Taliban drug traffickers, as in the past year) and either punish or extradite them.

Security Sector Reform

The Group of Eight (G8) adopted the current system of "lead donors" for SSR at the January 2002 Tokyo donor conference. The United States, with its focus on counterterrorism and reluctance to engage in "nation building," took on building the Afghan National Army (ANA), while other donors took on other parts of the security sector. The fewer resources and lesser commitment by other actors in the lead-donor system have meant that development of the army is far ahead of that of the police, and both of these areas are more advanced than the justice system. A U.S.-led overhaul of the Ministry of the Interior and police began in late 2005. The Afghanistan Compact has brought this lead-donor system to a close, and SSR, like all other parts of the international effort, will be coordinated and monitored by a joint board cochaired by the Afghan government and the UN.

The irregular units initially absorbed into the Afghan Ministry of Defense (about sixty-two thousand men) have been demobilized. The government and UN with Japanese funding have now launched programs for disbanding illegal armed groups (DIAG), of which there are an estimated eighteen hundred, most of them quite small. Some leaders of these groups occupy seats in the National Assembly and posts in local administration. Strengthened vetting and enforcement could provide sanctions and incentives to disarm these groups, but DIAG will require much more coalition and ISAF pressure on commanders and political leaders. As former Minister of the Interior Ali Jalali has observed:

> The United States has long hesitated to support the removal of defiant warlords. . . . While the PRTs are mandated to help extend the authority of the central government and facilitate stability, in certain cases they have discouraged government action against spoilers because of concerns about their own security. . . . However, failure to hold [militia leaders] accountable . . . continues to undermine the establishment of the rule of law.[19]

Using pressure to hold such leaders accountable and disarm them does not mean warfare but rather local negotiations backed up with pressure and threats when needed. Leaders and members of armed groups were supposed to be banned from running for parliament or the provincial councils, and the coalition offered to help cope with resistance from potential candidates during the vetting process, indicating the military's estimate that such actions would not lead to warfare.

Recommendation:

- The Coalition and ISAF should increase pressure, in cooperation with the Afghan government, on commanders and political leaders to disarm and demobilize illegal armed groups. NATO and the U.S. Department of Defense should issue clear guidance authorizing PRTs to engage in this process. What is needed is a capacity for local coercive diplomacy. Coalition forces have occasionally taken such actions, by briefly firing on a group that refused to disarm or buzzing the house of a leading warlord with fighter aircraft. These incidents always ended peacefully soon after, as these groups are opportunistic rather than ideological in motivation.

The United States, with aid from France and the United Kingdom, has been training a new national army, which has now reached about twenty-six thousand troops. The ANA was designed by the Department of Defense, and it deploys troops with embedded U.S. trainers. The U.S. model of an army, however, has a high price tag. According to the World Bank, the ANA cost 13 percent of gross domestic product (GDP) in fiscal year 2004–05, and total security sector spending topped 17 percent.[20] Currently, the ANA depends on U.S. trainers for air support, logistics, and medical evacuation. Transferring the ownership of these functions to the ANA will cost even more.

The coalition has slowed ANA growth. Defense Secretary Donald Rumsfeld informed the Afghan government that the United States will expect it to pay the military's salaries from its budget in 2006–07. According to Afghan sources, he also told Kabul that the ceiling for the ANA would be forty-five thousand men, compared to the seventy thousand that the Afghan Ministry of Defense thinks it needs.

Although the belated concern for fiscal sustainability is welcome, this unilateral decision has placed the Afghans in a difficult position. The United States, not Afghanistan, determined the salary levels of the ANA, and now the United States is insisting that this impoverished, insecure country, just embarking on a major development strategy, take on this fiscal burden. Secretary Rumsfeld has reportedly assured the Afghans that the United States will ensure Afghanistan's external security, but the failure of the United States to neutralize the Taliban and al-Qaeda sanctuaries in Pakistan has made the Afghans skeptical of such guarantees.

Because Afghanistan cannot have a foreign-supported army for long, some adjustment of the quantity or quality of the force is inevitable. Besides simply making the ANA smaller, the Afghan government could move away from the U.S.-inspired structure toward a more cost-effective, if less professional, army, such as one based on conscription and compensation in kind (housing and other facilities) rather than cash. Similar adjustments must be made for the Afghan National Police (ANP). Current plans to raise police salaries to a level comparable to that of the ANA will further inflate the budget beyond the country's means. Because of the insufficiency of both international and national security forces, the Afghan government continues to raise informal militias, mostly in Pashtun areas, where the Taliban are active. This has created some anxiety among non-Pashtuns, who have seen their much larger militias disbanded. The need for regional and ethnic equity must be taken into account in the structure of the security forces.

Recommendations:

- The Afghan government and its partners in SSR should reexamine the structure and mission of the army and police as the Afghan security sector must be fiscally sustainable. To enable the ANA to become more self-sufficient, the force may need to be smaller than initially planned and more cost-effective. This may require a change from the U.S.-inspired model of a highly paid, all-volunteer army.

- The central police force also must be relatively small to be effective and affordable. Rather than trying to deploy a centralized security force throughout the country, the government should police the cities, main roads, border points, and national installations, while organizing, disciplining, and lightly subsidizing locally based forces in much of the country.

- Coalition forces should reduce intrusive foreign presence in the security forces. The coalition must begin planning a reduction of the pervasive role the United States plays in the ANA. Embedded advisers planned for the ANP should not patrol.

Governance, Rule of Law, and Human Rights

The compact provides benchmarks for strengthening democratic institutions, in particular the National Assembly and other elected bodies, and for building the capacity and accountability of the administration. It emphasizes reforming the judiciary and strengthening the rule of law, including the protection of human rights. It provides for implementation of a transitional justice action plan to confront the past abuses.

Judicial Reform

Police cannot provide security without courts. The judiciary is the sole part of the state still dominated by the ulama, the learned clergy, who play a central role in determining—and undermining—the legitimacy of governments. Hence, judicial reform involves sensitive issues. By now, however, the lack of judicial reform has become a bottleneck for security, governance, and economic development.

The judiciary has been headed by Chief Justice Fazl Hadi Shinwari, who is also head of the official Council of Ulama. Shinwari is widely reported to be corrupt, his legal scholarship appears deficient, and he has offended many with his conservative views against gender equality. Nonetheless, President Karzai has found him useful in maintaining the consent of religious leaders to the system of government and the international presence. Shinwari has also used his Islamic credentials to negotiate with Taliban who wish to surrender to the government.

Because the Afghan Supreme Court is the administrative as well as judicial head of the court system, President Karzai's appointment of a new supreme court, as required by the constitution, is critical to reform. If the new judicial appointments simply appease the most conservative elements, reform will stall again. But if the new supreme court includes more progressive Islamic scholars, it can transform many of the ulama into allies in the process.

Afghans also have shown that they want and need some reckoning with their immense suffering over the past several decades. At the same time, many of those now in positions of power or influence are widely held to be responsible for past crimes. The Afghan government has adopted the Action Plan on Transitional Justice, and the compact requires it to implement this plan by 2008. The groups that formed the Northern Alliance fear that this process will be used against them, as they are political competitors with the president, and will spare both the communists, who now claim to support democracy, and the Taliban, who are being wooed to put down their arms. The implementation of this program should remove any such suspicion.

Recommendations:

- President Karzai should replace Shinwari as chief justice and form a court composed of judges of top legal, scholarly, and personal credentials, trained in Islamic, civil, and constitutional law, including Shia and women.
- Donors should support efforts to engage rather than confront or appease the ulama by reviving engagement of Afghan Islamic scholars with the main centers of learning in the Islamic world, as existed decades ago.
- Donor countries and the UN should support implementation of the Action Plan on Transitional Justice without politicizing it. Ensure that this process examines abuses by communists, mujahidin, other militias, Taliban, and foreign forces (Soviet, Pakistani, al-Qaeda, American) impartially with a view to establishing truth, reconciliation, and justice.

Government Institutions

The convening of the National Assembly on December 19, 2005, following the September 18, 2005, elections to the lower house and provincial councils, effectively completed the Bonn process, which aimed at reestablishing permanent institutions of government. The election of representatives, however, is a means to accountable provision of public services by the state. If the state is incapable of providing those public services, elections can lead to kleptocracy rather than democracy, and many Afghans fear that this process is already under way.

Resources

Afghanistan has one of the weakest governments in the world. The International Monetary Fund (IMF) estimates that government revenue will total 5.4 percent of nondrug GDP in 2005–06, less than any country with data. Furthermore, the administration has difficulty disbursing the funds it has: the ten poorest provinces receive the smallest budgetary allocations, leading to nonexistent government presence and rampant security problems.[21]

Attempts to raise domestic revenue are stymied by the lack of control over the country's borders, the small portion of the economy in the formal legal sector, and the weakness and corruption of the administration, particularly in tax collection. Currently, would-be tax payers are discouraged by collectors, who suggest they pay bribes instead.

The Afghanistan Compact requires the government to raise domestic revenue to more than 8 percent of GDP by fiscal year 2011 and to be able to cover 58 percent of the recurrent budget with its own resources, compared to 28 percent in fiscal year 2005. Nonetheless, escalating costs of security and civil service reform will make these targets difficult to achieve.

Recommendations:

- The coalition and Afghan government should support continuing fiscal reform, including ISAF and coalition military deployments in support of control of borders (for revenue collection) and state banks (for expenditure). The government should rationalize the procedures for business taxation, abolish nuisance taxes, and find other ways to tax the expenditures of the international presence, as it has done through rent taxes. For instance, the government could tax nonwork-related imports.
- Aid programs should assist the Ministry of Finance in establishing electronic tax payment, revenue tracking, and expenditure systems, compatible with the treasury system already in place. Developing and funding of programs, including those sponsored by PRTs, through the Afghan budgetary process, rather than through independent donor mechanisms, is essential to developing a fiscally sustainable state.

Administration and Service Provision

The government has started reforms at the national level, but many ministries are still nonfunctional or corrupt. The provincial and district administrations, the face of government for most Afghans, are largely controlled by illicit or violent power holders.

In Afghanistan's centralized unitary state, the president appoints all ministers, deputy ministers, governors, and provincial security chiefs. The character of these appointees is one of the important political issues in the country. The Afghanistan Compact requires the government to establish formal vetting procedures by an independent board for senior appointments. This board would vet potential appointees for qualifications and involvement with drug trafficking, corruption, armed groups, or past human rights violations.

Recommendation:

- In addition to confidential vetting, the Afghan appointments board should introduce more transparency into the appointments process. Candidates should be required to make public their assets, as is required for the most senior figures by article 154 of the constitution, and extend this requirement to their families. Appointments of deputy ministers, governors, district officers, and provincial and district police chiefs should also be announced for public comment thirty days before taking effect.

Corruption

- Afghanistan's weak administration has few if any effective controls over corruption, which has undermined support for the government. Some systems have been instituted to prevent the most important types of corruption, notably a system requiring transparent public bidding for procurement. Increasingly, however, ministries are sidestepping this procedure and signing single-source contracts, many of which are then approved by the president in the interest of not delaying important projects. The compact obliges the government to fight corruption without saying how.

Recommendation:

- The Afghan president should tell his cabinet that he will no longer sign single-source contracts without exceptional circumstances and that all ministers found proffering such contracts will be sacked. International donors should invest in building the capacity of the Afghan government to draft proposals and process contracts so that transparent procedures do not lead to intolerable delays.

Self-Governance

At the local level, Afghans' self-governance institutions have enabled people to survive even when the central government collapsed. This capacity for self-government could bode well for the country's future, except that these institutions function largely outside the constitutional system. The framers of the country's 2004 constitution followed historical precedent in mandating a highly centralized administrative system. Although elected provincial councils have been formed, these have only advisory and watchdog roles. The budgets of the village-level Community Development Councils (CDCs) created by the

National Solidarity Program (NSP) are limited to block grants for specific projects approved by the ministry of rural rehabilitation and development.

Even within a unitary system, however, the delivery of services and accountability for public expenditure can be devolved to lower levels of government, creating potential for integrating local governance into the state. Unintentionally, the PRTs have for the first time in the history of Afghanistan introduced provincial development budgets. Currently, these are controlled by foreign officials of the PRTs, who disburse the funds with varying degrees of consultation with local authorities and society. From the bottom up, in a number of cases village CDCs have banded together to formulate district-level or larger projects for funding by the NSP. These show the potential for devolution.

Recommendation:

- The Afghan government should introduce measures to devolve service provision in Afghanistan's unitary state. As the provincial councils elected in September 2005 start to work, both they and the provincial administration should gradually gain greater oversight over provincial expenditures, including those by PRTs. The government and donors also should do more to encourage grassroots development cooperation by empowering provincial councils and administration to coordinate local development activities.

Integration of Religious Institutions

Afghanistan is an Islamic Republic, and Islamic institutions form part of the governance structure. The ulama are organized through the judiciary, the Council of Ulama, and the Ministry of Irshad (Instruction), Hajj (Pilgrimage), and Awqaf (Islamic foundations), which pays the salaries of official mullahs. Many "unofficial" mullahs are paid directly by the faithful through what are considered to be Islamic taxes, rather than voluntary donations. Mosques are centers not only for prayer and instruction but for community self-governance and service provision. The ministry and the ulama council can distribute weekly talking points for the Friday sermon to virtually every village.

This sermon, or *khutba*, is the main means through which the ulama communicate their views to the people. Khutbas now often highlight moral corruption, the increasing gap between rich and poor, and misdeeds by the coalition. These sermons reflect debate among the ulama over whether the new government is Islamic and whether the presence of non-Muslim forces in Afghanistan is legitimate. The government, short of budgetary resources, has been removing mullahs from the payroll. Many laid-off mullahs continue to be paid, by either local power holders (sometimes involved in the drug trade) or international Islamic sources.

The government and donors should proactively prevent the growth of religiously oriented opposition. Mosque management and the Council of Ulama need reform. Dropping mullahs from the payroll simply for lack of resources, or building mosques to show that the United States is not anti-Islamic (as some PRTs have done) without a strategy or policy is dangerous. The social capital that village mosques embody should be mobilized on behalf of the reconstruction of the country and the strengthening of its constitutional institutions.

Recommendation:

- The Afghan government should bring the mosque-based traditional village administration and dispute settlement procedures gradually into the ambit of state institutions. Donors should support this sensitive aspect of building an Islamic state.

Economic and Social Development

Basic indicators of human welfare place Afghans among a handful of the world's hungriest and most destitute, illiterate, and short-lived people. The country ranks approximately 173rd out of 178 countries in the basic index of human development, effectively putting it in a tie for last place with a few African countries.[22] Afghan women face the highest rate of illiteracy and the lowest standard of health in the world. Afghanistan has the youngest population in the world (an estimated 57 percent under eighteen years old), with few employment prospects in the offing.[23]

The livelihoods of the people of this impoverished, devastated country are more dependent on illegal narcotics than any other country in the world. According to estimates by the UN and IMF, the total export value of opiates produced in Afghanistan in 2005–06 equaled about 38 percent of nondrug GDP, down from 47 percent the previous year due to growth of the nondrug economy. Much of the trafficking profits do not enter the Afghan economy, but even if only one-third of trafficking income stayed in the country, the direct contribution to the domestic economy would amount to 15 percent of the total, with more attributable to the multiplier effect of drug-financed spending. The UN estimates that in recent years nearly 80 percent of the income from narcotics went not to farmers but to traffickers and heroin processors, some of whose profits corrupt the government and support armed groups.[24] The distribution of the proceeds of narcotics trafficking, not elections, largely determines who wields power in much of Afghanistan.

Economic Growth and Counternarcotics

Against this somber background, Afghanistan has experienced an economic recovery. The IMF estimates that real, nondrug GDP has averaged annual growth of nearly 17 percent from 2001–02 through 2005–06. The government has sought to set its development agenda, rather than ceding it to aid organizations. At the London conference it presented its I-ANDS, which international financial institutions hailed as one of the best they have received from any developing country.

Nevertheless, the postwar economic boom is coming to an end. The IMF warns that the sources of the rebound "will be insufficient over the long term to sustain growth and alleviate poverty." Additionally, counternarcotics policies, if implemented wrongly, risk reversing the economic recovery that has helped stabilize the country. An as-yet-unpublished macroeconomic simulation by an international financial institution demonstrates that different types of counternarcotics policies have different macroeconomic impacts and that a strategy including eradication at early stages can lead to a contraction of total GDP by nearly 6 percent. [Later published as Edouard Martin and Steven Symansky, "Macroeconomic Impact of the Drug Economy and Counter-Narcotics Efforts," in Doris Buddenberg and William Byrd. eds., *Afghanistan's Drug Industry: Structure, Functioning, Dynamics, and Implications for Counter-Narcotics Policy* (UNODC and World Bank, 2006).] A change from recent rapid GDP growth of nearly 20 percent per year to a significant contraction is likely to provoke instability and violence. The provision of "alternative livelihoods" to farmers alone would not fully compensate for the effect of such an economic contraction on poverty, nutrition, health, employment, investment, the balance of payments, the exchange rate, and the price level. Donor countries are threatening to limit their aid if narcotics production is not curbed quickly, regardless of its economic effects. The U.S. Congress "fenced" part of this year's aid disbursement, pending certification by President Bush that Afghanistan was cooperating with U.S. counternarcotics policies.

Recommendations:

- The main counternarcotics goal should be reducing the absolute and relative economic size of the opium economy while maintaining positive growth that favors the poor in the overall economy.[25]
- Counternarcotics development strategies must be comprehensive, not make-work programs. "Alternative livelihoods" need to include comprehensive rural development, including electric power, water, roads, credit, debt relief, agricultural extension, and nonfarm employment, particularly in rural industries. Counternarcotics policy must also address the macroeconomic measures needed to minimize the negative effect of this sector's contraction on the whole economy. Such policies need more than a decade to become fully effective.

This goal focuses on reducing the harm to the stability of Afghanistan, rather than following the illusory course of trying to solve the problem of drug consumption—which developed countries have not been able to solve with all the resources available to them—in the world's weakest state. Hence, the I-ANDS and the Afghan government's new Drugs Control Policy propose a "pro-poor" counternarcotics policy that focuses initially on interdiction, law enforcement, institution building, and building licit livelihoods, while investing in infrastructure, protection of rights, and an enabling framework for private sector growth that will make it possible to raise welfare while phasing out dependence on criminal activity. Crop eradication, which the U.S. Congress in particular views as critical, despite massive evidence to the contrary, raises the farm price of opium, creates incentives for production in remote high-cost areas, and raises the value of traffickers' inventories. Eradication in Afghanistan has led to abuses such as the sale of daughters by opium farmers to pay debts owed to traffickers.[26] Recommendations:

- To ensure that counternarcotics and economic development both contribute to stabilizing Afghanistan, the United States and other donors must support the integrated approach of the I-ANDS.
- The U.S. government should support the Afghan government's National Drugs Control Policy. Congress should not undermine these efforts by insisting on U.S. contracting; earmarking for particular projects or causes, such as aerial eradication (which the Afghan government opposes); or conditioning support on quick results.
- The preferred method for supporting counternarcotics is by contributing to the Counternarcotics Trust Fund managed by the UNDP. NATO and the coalition should support Afghan-led interdiction operations, especially those directed against heroin processing and narcotics inventories, and adopt a common mission and rules of engagement on counternarcotics. In much of the country, narcotics interdiction of high-level trafficking has proceeded without generating massive resistance. An exception is Helmand, where the British PRT is working with the governor to devise a strategy to address the strong links in that area between traffickers and the Taliban and other armed groups. Thus far, however, crop eradication has generated more violent resistance than interdiction. The Afghan drug market has so far not generated violent cartels; rather, it has remained more fragmented and competitive.

Financing Pro-Poor Growth

All efforts to stabilize Afghanistan will fail if the licit economy does not expand fast enough to provide enough employment, income, and investment to more than balance the loss of income from opiates and provide a fiscal basis for expanding public services. In 2004, the Afghan government estimated it would cost $27.6 billion to achieve stabilization goals over seven years with disbursements over twelve years starting in 2004–05; the I-ANDS tentatively revised this estimate upward. Initially, the resources devoted to Afghanistan hardly corresponded to the Marshall Plan to which President Bush compared the reconstruction of Afghanistan in April 2002.[27] Figure 12.2 compares troop presence and per capita aid to Afghanistan during the first two years of the transitional period with other stabilization operations. These figures do not include the military operations of the coalition or ISAF, both of which cost far more than the assistance budget. During 2002–03, Afghanistan was far below all Balkan operations, East Timor, and Iraq, and even below Namibia and Haiti. After this slow start, especially by the United States, funding for reconstruction is increasing toward the rate needed to meet the target of $27.6 billion. The cost of delivery of assistance, however, has been higher than expected, so that the money expended has produced less on the ground than planned, and much of the increase in aid has gone to the security sector, which has cost far more than projected.

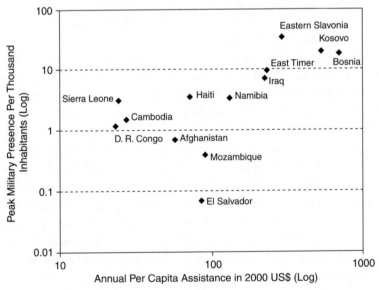

*Shows peak security presence and average yearly per capita economic assistance for the first two years of each operation, including Afghanistan in 2002–2003.

Figure 12.2 Security and Economic Assistance in Peace Building Operations. Source: James Dobbins, Keith Crane, Seth G. Jones, Andrew Rathmell, Brett Steele, and Richard Teltschik, "The UN's Role in Nation-Building: From the Congo to Iraq," RAND, 2005.

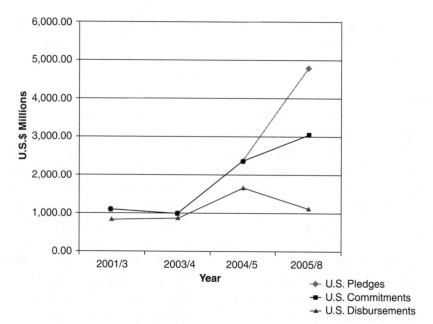

Figure 12.3   U.S. Assistance to Afghanistan. Source: Ministry of Finance, Afghanistan.

As shown in Figure 12.3, U.S. pledges of assistance rose dramatically in 2004–05, as Presidential Special Envoy and Ambassador Zalmay Khalilzad presided over a program called "Accelerate Success," intended to build support for President Karzai during his election campaign. Figure 12.3 also shows, however, that the United States was not able to match disbursements to its pledges and commitments.[28] Instead, the pressure for politically motivated quick results led to waste and failure to deliver on Afghans' expectations.[29] Other donors have experienced similar problems, but they are particularly severe for the United States.[30]

The Afghanistan Compact includes an annex on aid effectiveness. The Afghan government commits itself to transparency and accountability, to raising more domestic resources, and to improving its capacity to manage expenditure and implement programs. In return, the donors agree to allocate their assistance according to ANDS priorities; provide "multiyear funding commitments or indications of multiyear support"; increase untied aid channeled through the government budget; build Afghan capacity; and report on aid in a way that enables the Afghan government to integrate aid into its national budget and reports on its use to the National Assembly.[31]

More than 75 percent of all aid to Afghanistan funds projects directly implemented or contracted by donors. This mode of delivery, although initially inevitable, is ultimately self-defeating. If prolonged, it undermines, not builds, the state. Enabling the state to provide services directly promotes legitimacy and responsibility; integrating aid projects into the budgetary process promotes sustainability. A government that cannot report to its parliament about public expenditure can hardly be called democratic, no matter how many elections it holds.

Three of the largest donors, however—the United States, Japan, and Germany—insisted on weakening these provisions. U.S. officials claim that the U.S. government's fiduciary responsibility to taxpayers makes it difficult to channel money through the Afghan government's budget. Like other donors, the United States cites the prevalence of corruption and lack of capacity in Afghanistan, which are valid concerns, though they do not prevent the UK from channeling aid through the budget. The argument of fiduciary responsibility, however, collapses under the weight of evidence of what the U.S. government actually does with much of taxpayers' money in Afghanistan. It disburses it to U.S.-based contractors who spend a significant (and unreported) part of the funds setting up office. In one case, their services were of such poor quality that the Afghan ministry they were supposed to help expelled them. Security regulations sometimes prevent U.S. contractors from implementing projects in the field and impose significant additional costs. Both the fiduciary responsibility to the U.S. taxpayer and the policy goals of the U.S. government would often be accomplished better by direct budgetary support to the Afghan government, combined with programs for capacity building.

Recommendation:

- International donors, and the United States in particular, should give aid in accord with the priorities of the ANDS. They should overcome legal and political obstacles to funding through the government budget by setting specific criteria for doing so. Congress should not undermine these efforts by insisting on U.S. contracting or earmarking. The best mechanisms for such direct budgetary support are the Afghanistan Reconstruction Trust Fund, managed by the World Bank, and the two funds managed by UNDP, the Law and Order Trust Fund for Afghanistan and the Counternarcotics Trust Fund. These trust funds provide strong incentives, benchmarking, and monitoring for the Afghan government to build its capacity and improve its accountability and performance.

Regional Dimensions of Reconstruction

Afghanistan's development requires the cooperation of this landlocked country with its neighbors, especially Pakistan and Iran, which provide outlets to the sea.[32] Without confidence in regional security arrangements, neighboring countries may resist the economic and infrastructural integration that is indispensable for Afghanistan's future.

Recommendations:

- The United States and other donors should support regional economic cooperation, in (among other areas) infrastructure, trade and transit, water use, energy, migration and manpower, and development of border regions, by establishing dedicated funding frameworks for regional economic cooperation in this region. This will require both national budget lines for regional cooperation and funding mechanisms, such as a trust fund for development of regional cooperation in support of the development and stabilization of Afghanistan.
- The United States and its allies, perhaps through NATO, should initiate high-level discussions to insulate Afghan economic development from conflict with Iran or concerns over the coalition military presence.

Conclusion

The sketch of Afghanistan's problems in this report is meant to be realistic; these are the challenges facing Afghanistan. We already know that the cost of failing is virtually incalculable. The Afghanistan Compact provides many elements of a plan for sustainable security, governance, and development. This report has tried to supplement that by suggesting additional measures for implementation. If the international community is unable or unwilling to meet the cost of success, or if Afghan authorities are unable or unwilling to make the decisions needed to use assistance effectively, they must answer the question: What risks are they willing to accept? Afghans are determined not to revert to a past they abhor; will their leaders and international actors enable them to succeed?

Notes

1. The Afghanistan Compact and the I-ANDS are available respectively at http://www.nato.int/isaf/docu/epub/pdf/afghanistan_compact.pdf and http://www.nps.edu/programs/ccs/Docs/Pubs/unands_Jan.pdf.
2. For this conceptual framework for peace building, see Barnett R. Rubin, "Constructing Sovereignty for Security," *Survival*, Vol. 47, No. 4 (Winter 2005), pp. 93–106.
3. Walter Pincus, "Growing Threat Seen in Afghan Insurgency: Defense Intelligence Agency Chief Cites Surging Violence in Homeland," *Washington Post*, March 1, 2006.
4. The United States began building a "coalition of the willing" against terrorism on September 12, 2001; there are currently [2006] seventy nations supporting the global war on terrorism. To date, twenty-one nations have deployed more than sixteen thousand troops to the U.S. Central Command's region of responsibility. In Afghanistan, coalition partners are contributing

approximately eight thousand troops to Operation Enduring Freedom and to the ISAF in Kabul.

5. Michael Bhatia et al., "Minimal Investments, Minimal Results: The Failure of Security Policy in Afghanistan," Afghanistan Research and Evaluation Unit, June 2004; James Dobbins et al., *America's Role in Nation-Building: From Germany to Iraq* (Santa Monica: RAND, 2003); Seth G. Jones, "Averting Failure in Afghanistan," *Survival*, Vol. 48, No. 1 (Spring 2006).

6. Ahmed Rashid, "He's Welcome in Pakistan," *Washington Post*, February 26, 2006.

7. "Bush Praises Pakistan Terror Role," BBC News, March 4, 2006.

8. Daniel Cooney, "Karzai Wants End to U.S.-Led Operations," Associated Press Online (Kabul), September 20, 2005.

9. Tim Golden, "Years After Two Afghans Died, Abuse Case Falters," *New York Times*, February 13, 2006.

10. White House, "Press Release: Joint Declaration of the United States-Afghanistan Strategic Partnership," May 23, 2005, http://georgewbush-whitehouse.archives.gov/news/releases/2005/05/20050523-2.html.

11. For a critical view from a former Pakistani insider, see Husain Haqqani, "Pakistan Is Playing a Cat and Mouse Game," Gulf News, October 19, 2005, http://gulfnews.com/news/gulf/uae/general/pakistan-is-playing-a-cat-and-mouse-game-1.304796. [Former Pakistani insider Husain Haqqani became an insider again in 2008, when newly elected Pakistan President Asif Ali Zardari appointed him as ambassador to the United States. He reverted to his former status after being forced to resign and implicated in a case, largely regarded as dubious, in the 2012 "Memogate" affair.]

12. Cooney, "Karzai Wants End to U.S.-Led Operations"; Jones, "Averting Failure in Afghanistan."

13. "Martha Raddatz Interview with President Musharraf," ABC News, February 27, 2006. Full transcript supplied by ABC News.

14. "Pakistan President Blasts Afghan Leader," CNN.com, March 6, 2006.

15. John Lee Anderson, "The Man in the Palace," *New Yorker*, June 6, 2005.

16. During his October 2005 trip to Kabul, NATO Secretary-General Jaap de Hoop Scheffer announced that NATO would increase its force in Afghanistan to as many as fifteen thousand soldiers and will take on counterinsurgency operations as it expands its mission into southern Afghanistan in the coming months. See Carlotta Gall, "NATO to Expand Force and Task in Afghanistan," *New York Times*, October 7, 2005.

17. Eric Schmitt and David S. Cloud, "United States May Start Pulling Out of Afghanistan Next Spring," *New York Times*, September 14, 2005; James Travers, "Smart Move to Sidestep Afghanistan Prison Controversy," *Hamilton Spectator* (Ontario, Canada), March 4, 2006.

18. Islamic Government of Afghanistan, "Terms of Reference for the Combined Forced Command and ISAF PRTs in Afghanistan," January 27, 2005.

19. Ali A. Jalali, "The Future of Afghanistan," *Parameters* (Spring 2006), p. 6.

20. World Bank, *Afghanistan: Managing Public Finances for Development, Main Report*, vol. 1 (Washington, DC: World Bank, November 27, 2005), p. 24.

21. Ashraf Ghani, Clare Lockhart, Nargis Nehan, and Baqer Massoud, "The Budget as the Linchpin of the State: Lessons from Afghanistan." In *Peace and the Public Purse: Economic Policies for Postwar Statebuilding*, ed. James K. Boyce and Madalene O'Donnell. Boulder, Colo.: Lynne Rienner, 2007.

22. Along with Somalia, Afghanistan is one of two countries in the world unable to produce accurate enough data to be ranked in UN Development Program's annual Human Development Report. Using available data, however, Afghanistan's *National Human Development Report 2004* estimated that Afghanistan would have ranked 173rd out of 178, barely ahead of the African states of Chad, Mali Burkina Faso, Sierra Leone, and Niger. UNDP, *Afghanistan: National Human Development Report 2004*, http://hdr.undp.org/docs/reports/national/AFG_Afghanistan/afghanistan_2004_en.pdf.

23. For population statistics on Afghanistan, see Afghanistan's Millennium Development Goal report: http://www.undp.org/content/dam/undp/library/MDG/english/MDG%20Country%20Reports/Afghanistan/MDG-2010-Report-Final-Draft-25Nov2010.pdf.

24. UN Office on Drugs and Crime and Government of Afghanistan Counter Narcotics Directorate, *Afghanistan: Opium Survey 2005*, p. 9, http://www.unodc.org/pdf/afg/afg_survey_2005_exsum.pdf.

25. The "poor" in Afghanistan are defined as either (1) those without enough food to meet basic caloric needs consistently (about 40 percent of the rural population) or (2) those living on less than one U.S. dollar per day (for which data are not yet available). Pro-poor growth is important because the few rich will otherwise monopolize most of the benefits on investment.
26. Farah Stockman, "Afghan Women Pay the Price for War on Drugs," *Boston Globe*, September 29, 2005.
27. President George W. Bush, "Remarks on War Effort Delivered to the George C. Marshall ROTC Award Seminar on National Security at Cameron Hall," Virginia Military Institute, Lexington, Virginia, April 17, 2002, available at http://georgewbush-whitehouse.archives. gov/news/releases/2002/04/20020417-1.html.
28. A pledge is a promise of an amount; a commitment is a signed contract for a specific use of funds. Commitments lead to disbursements, which are deposits into the accounts of trust funds or implementing agencies. Disbursed funds are turned into expenditures as projects are implemented, which can take years in some cases. Donors report on disbursement, which constitutes expenditure by the donor government, but not on final expenditure on development, which is of greatest interest to the aid recipient.
29. See Carlotta Gall and Somini Sengupta, "Afghan Electorate's Message: The Provinces Need Public Works and Restoration of Order," *New York Times*, September 20, 2005.
30. Data from the Ministry of Finance for aid through the end of calendar year 2005 show that the United States had disbursed 36 percent of commitments for that year, compared to 58 percent for other donors.
31. The World Bank–administered Afghanistan Reconstruction Trust Fund supports the government's recurrent and development expenditures. Trust funds managed by the UNDP provided support for SSR and counternarcotics.
32. See Barnett R. Rubin with Andrea Armstrong, "Regional Issues in the Reconstruction of Afghanistan," *World Policy Journal*, Vol. 20, No. 1 (Spring 2003), pp. 37–48; and S. Frederick Starr, "A Partnership for Central Asia," *Foreign Affairs* (July/August 2005).

13

Afghanistan 2005 and Beyond

Prospects for Improved Stability Reference Document

WITH HUMAYUN HAMIDZADA AND ABBY STODDARD

Introduction

Since the overthrow of the Taliban by the U.S.-led coalition and the inauguration of the Interim Authority based on the UN-mediated Bonn Agreement of December 5, 2001, Afghanistan has progressed substantially toward stability. Not all trends are positive, however. Afghanistan has become more dependent on narcotics production and trafficking than any country in the world. It remains one of the world's most impoverished and conflict-prone states, where only a substantial international presence prevents a return to war. The modest results reflect the modest resources that donor and troop-contributing states have invested in it. Afghans and those supporting their efforts have many achievements to their credit, but declarations of success are premature. The establishment of the major institutions required by the Constitution of 2004 will constitute the end of the implementation of the Bonn Agreement. That agreement on transitional governmental institutions, pending the reestablishment of permanent constitutional governance, was drafted and signed at the UN Talks on Afghanistan in Germany in November–December 2001. The election of the lower house of parliament (Wolesi Jirga) and provincial councils, now set for September 18, 2005, will mark the end of that transitional process, though only with a bit of constitutional stretching. Elections to district councils, needed to elect part of the Meshrano Jirga (upper house of the National Assembly), cannot be held in 2005, and the government will therefore establish a truncated upper house. [The parliamentary and provincial council elections were held as scheduled. At date of publication, district council elections have not been held.]

Originally published by Netherlands Institute of International Relations "Clingendael" Conflict Research Unit, April 2005.

The establishment of elected institutions hardly constitutes the end of Afghanistan's transition toward stability. The long-term strategic objective of the joint international-Afghan project is the building of a legitimate, effective, and accountable state. State building requires balanced and mutually reinforcing efforts to establish legitimacy, security, and an economic base for both. Thus far internationally funded efforts to establish legitimacy through a political process (the only mandatory part of the Bonn Agreement) have outpaced efforts to establish security and a sustainable economic base. The next strategic objective must be to accelerate the growth of government capacity and the legitimate economy to provide Afghans with superior alternatives to relying on patronage from commanders, the opium economy, and the international presence for security, livelihoods, and services.

Afghanistan will not be able to sustain the current configuration of institutions built with foreign assistance in the foreseeable future. Given current salary levels and future staffing plans, maintaining the Afghan National Army will eventually impose a recurrent cost estimated at about $1 billion per year on the Afghan government. This is equivalent to about 40 percent of the estimated revenue from narcotics in 2004. In order for Afghanistan to cover the cost of the ANA with 4 percent of legal GDP (near the upper limit of the global range of defense spending), it would have to more than quintuple its legal economy. The constitution requires Afghanistan to hold presidential elections every five years, Wolesi Jirga elections every five years, provincial council elections every four years, and district council elections every three years. This works out to between eight and ten nationwide elections every decade, depending on whether presidential and WJ elections are concurrent. Currently each election (including voter registration) costs international donors more than $100 million, which is equivalent to 40 percent of the government's current yearly domestic revenue. Hence the current efforts risk leaving Afghanistan with elections it cannot afford and a well-trained and well-equipped army that it cannot pay. Projecting the results of such a situation does not require sophisticated analytic techniques.

The end of the implementation of the Bonn accord should thus constitute a benchmark for the renewal of international commitment, rather than the declaration of success and the start of disengagement. The entire range of international actors in Afghanistan needs to publicly recommit themselves to support an Afghan-owned and -led process. The UN Security Council has extended the mandate of the United Nations Assistance Mission in Afghanistan (UNAMA) until March 24, 2006. The resolution identified the main future tasks in Afghanistan as holding free and fair parliamentary elections; combating narcotics; completing the demobilization, disarmament, and reintegration of armed groups; continuing to build Afghan security forces; continuing to combat terrorism; strengthening the justice system; protecting human rights; accelerating economic growth to ensure that reforms are sustainable; and fostering regional cooperation.[1]

The coalition has moved from a war-fighting mandate toward one of stabilization through the establishment of Provincial Reconstruction Teams (PRTs) and an "allegiance program" to reintegrate returning Taliban. The North Atlantic Treaty Organization (NATO), having assumed command of the International Security Assistance Force (ISAF), has also established PRTs in a growing number of provinces and is considering a U.S. proposal for unification of CFC-A and ISAF under a joint NATO command with a common mission focused on stabilization. International financial institutions, the United States, the European Union, and other donor governments have responded with growing rather than shrinking commitments to reconstruction, largely in response to the coherent and farsighted plan proposed by the Afghan government in its report *Securing Afghanistan's Future,*[2] presented to the Berlin Conference on March 31–April 1, 2004. Some have suggested reaffirming commitment to all of these goals through a "Kabul process," culminating in an international conference hosted by Afghanistan to establish the framework for political, military, and economic support beyond the Bonn Agreement.

This document reaches these conclusions by using the Stability Assessment Framework methodology developed by the Clingendael institute (The Hague) to help governments and other institutions plan assistance to countries at risk of conflict.[3] The document first presents qualitative assessments of the trends and levels of key indicators since the establishment of the Interim Authority. These indicators, which comparative research has shown to provide early warning of violent conflict, include political, economic, and social factors.

Understanding these indicators requires what F. Scott Fitzgerald called "the test of a first-rate intelligence": "the ability to hold two opposed ideas in the mind at the same time, and still retain the ability to function." One must evaluate both indicators' *level* and their *trend* or *direction of change.* The *levels* of indicators in Afghanistan place it among the world's most unstable, destitute, and conflict-prone countries, while many *trends* are positive. Trends that are not clearly positive, such as the size of income and assets derived from narcotics trafficking, the security of Afghan civilians and property rights, corruption, and the quality of local governance, require focused attention.

After presenting the indicators, the analysis assesses the capacity and legitimacy of institutions necessary to provide stable governance. These include the key institutions of government, especially those for security and the rule of law, as well as those that finance its operations. These institutions are constituted by actors, whose orientations, strategies, and resources the paper examines next. It starts with national actors and continues with the international actors present in Afghanistan. Long experience of violence and instability makes Afghan and regional actors reluctant to invest their assets fully in strategies on the basis of expectations of stability, but the longer change for the better persists, the more actors will gradually adjust their strategies toward stabilization. Any change in expectations remains fragile.

Finally, the paper presents policy recommendations to redress the gaps revealed by the foregoing analysis.

Indicators

Until the shock of September 11, 2001, and the international response it provoked, the situation in Afghanistan, as in many states undergoing crises of governance, could be characterized as what the World Bank has called an "informal equilibrium" at low levels of development and security. (See Figure 13.1.) Insecurity and lack of infrastructure, due to both lack of investment and wartime destruction of assets, combined with pressure on scarce economic and natural resources, favored the development of criminalized economic activities, especially those fueled by demand in the developed countries. These activities funded, as they still do, illicit organized violence (warlordism and terrorism),

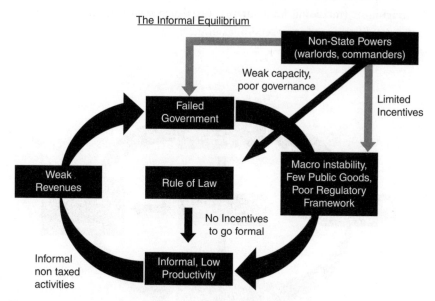

Figure 13.1 The Informal Equilibrium. Source: World Bank, *Afghanistan—State Building, Sustaining Growth, and Reducing Poverty: A Country Economic Report*, 2005, p. xi.

which also derive their resources, especially weapons, from more developed countries. This dark side of globalization hinders attempts to constitute accountable, lawful governance. The consequent lack of security discourages licit investment, reinforcing the vicious circle of poverty, integration into global organized crime, and violence.

Moving from this harmful equilibrium to a virtuous circle where security and legitimate development reinforce each other to promote both the rule of law and the growth of productive global economic opportunities requires balanced efforts to transform the political, economic, and social factors, as well as the international environment, in a positive direction. Although such efforts are under way, Afghanistan is still far from the "formal equilibrium" that characterizes stabler, more economically developed societies (Figure 13.2).[4]

This section evaluates the key elements of Afghanistan's vicious circle to estimate how far the country has moved away from that equilibrium in the past three years. Figure 13.3 lists the twelve indicators. This report groups the indicators in four categories: governance, economy, social pressures, and international environment. Indicators of the state of governance include (1) the legitimacy of the state, (2) the delivery of public services, (3) the rule of law and human rights, (4) the coherence of the political elite, and (5) the performance of the security apparatus. Indicators of economic performance include (6) the general state of the economy and (7) the relative economic positions of groups. Indicators of social pressures include (8) demographic and environmental pressures, (9) migration (including brain drain), (10) displacement, and (11) group-based hostilities. Finally this section examines (12) Afghanistan's international environment.

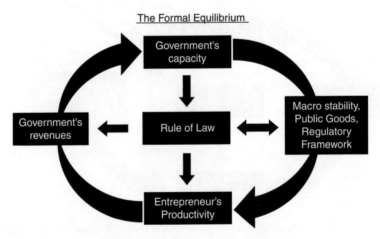

Figure 13.2 The Formal Equilibrium. Source: World Bank, *Afghanistan—State Building, Sustaining Growth, and Reducing Poverty: A Country Economic Report*, 2005, p. xi.

Box 4.1 Twelve Top Indicators

Nr.	Indicators of (In)stability	Trend Assessment
	Governance Indicators	
1	Legitimacy of the State	Is the state viewed primarily as illegitimate or criminal, or as a legitimate actor representative of the people as a whole?
2	Public Service Delivery	Is public service delivery progressively deteriorating or improving?
3	Rule of Law and Human Rights	Are human rights violated and the rule of law arbitrarily applied or suspended, or is a basic rule of law established and are violations ceasing?
4	Leadership	Are elites increasingly factionalized, or do they have national perspectives? Are leaders capable of winning loyalties across group lines in society?
	Security Indicators	
5	Security Apparatus	Does the security apparatus operate as a "state within a state," or is a professional military established that is answerable to legitimate civilian control?
6	Regional Setting	Are destabilizing regional cross-border interventions increasing or reducing?
	Socio-Economic Development Indicators	
7	Demographic Pressures	Are pressures mounting or easing?
8	Refugee and Internally Displaced Persons (IDPs) Situation	Is there massive movement of refugees and IDPs, creating humanitarian emergencies, or are these resettled and resolved?
9	Group-based Hostilities	Is there a legacy of vengeance-seeking group grievance and paranoia, or is there reconciliation and a reduction of hostilities?
10	Emigration and Human Flight	Is there chronic and sustained human flight or a reduction in the rate of emigration?
11	Economic Opportunities of Groups	Is there uneven economic development along group lines, or are such disparities lessening?
12	State of the Economy	Is there sharp or severe economic decline, or is the economy growing?

Figure 13.3 List of Indicators for Stability Assessment Framework.

Governance Indicators

Legitimacy of the State

During the past quarter century, the legitimacy of the state in Afghanistan fell to an all-time low. Since the installation of the Interim Authority of Afghanistan on December 22, 2001, however, it has gained a diffuse legitimacy, based on its stated goals, increasing representativeness, adoption of a constitution, and holding of the first presidential election in Afghan history. This diffuse legitimacy is not yet supported by legitimacy based on performance, as the delivery of public services falls far short of popular demands and expectations.

Reinforcing the state's legitimacy faces a daunting contradiction and is interrelated with all other aspects of state building. Without steps to eliminate the narcotics trade, which the UN estimates equaled 60 percent of the legal and hence 40 percent of the total economy in 2004–05, the government cannot implement the rule of law, diminish corruption, gain control over its local appointees, and curb illicit power holders. Yet the state cannot increase its legitimacy while destroying nearly half of the country's economy with foreign military assistance.[5] *Securing Afghanistan's Future* estimated that growth in the legal economy would have to average 9 percent per year for more than a decade in order to draw people out of the drug economy while supporting the institutions needed for the rule of law. The IMF projects growth for 2004–05 as falling below that level.

The Bonn Agreement outlined a process to build the legitimacy of an initially unrepresentative government. The Afghan authorities have met the benchmarks of that process. The Emergency Loya Jirga of June 2002 inaugurated a broadening of power beyond the armed groups aided by the United States and the coalition to fight the Taliban and al-Qaeda. The subsequent constitutional process led to the loya jirga that convened in December 2003 and approved a new constitution on January 4, 2004. The electoral registration and subsequent election of the president, on October 9, 2004, showed the strong desire of Afghans to participate in the new system of government.

Currently, Afghans appear to support the idea of a strong, central state, mainly to protect them from decentralized armed groups. Surveys show that an overwhelming majority (88 percent) of Afghans of all regions and ethnic groups call for the central government to end the rule of gunmen.[6] Nonetheless consensus on how to organize that order remains fragile. The Constitutional Loya Jirga exposed a significant ethnic divide, as did the results of the presidential election. One opponent of state centralization describes the circles of power as "the handpicked Karzai and his small circle of Western-educated Pashtun technocrats."[7] The "Pashtun technocrats" deny that their ethnic background determines their state-building strategy and ask to be judged on their performance for the whole nation. The country's history of mistrust, personalized politics, and political exclusion places a heavy burden on officials to prove that they are acting as legitimate state leaders rather than dispensers of ethnic or political patronage. Given the weakness of institutions and the lack of trust within the political elite, demands for inclusion are often posed in ethnic rather than political or merit-based terms.

The state does not yet have the capacity to sustain itself without foreign military and financial support, though, as shown below, that small capacity is growing. The forces that might undermine the state are less ideological opposition than factors fueled by the population's pervasive insecurity and destitution, as well as Afghanistan's continuing vulnerability to international destabilization. Most leaders accept that the current process of stabilization is better than a return to civil war, but the state could not yet mitigate the security dilemma that militias and their supporters in neighboring countries would face in the absence of the international presence, or if that presence turned destabilizing.

The government has started to improve the delivery of public services, but it has a long way to go before meeting minimal standards or people's expectations

Security

Some Afghans say that their security has improved, but they overwhelmingly cite it as their principal problem.[8] The peaceful conduct of the presidential elections was a milestone in the reestablishment of security, but that resulted in 2004 from uniquely intense, temporary international efforts.

Different actors define security differently. The coalition measures it as security from attacks by insurgents. Coalition spokesmen claim that as a result of military campaigns, changes in Pakistan's behavior, and the offer to reintegrate Taliban, this threat has decreased, though it continues.[9]

The UN and aid community focus on attacks on aid workers, which have increased. Preliminary data collected by the Center on International Cooperation show that the number of "major incidents" (killings, kidnappings, ambushes, land mines, and other injuries due to violence) affecting humanitarian workers in Afghanistan increased from none under the Taliban in 2001 to four, ten, and then sixteen in the three following years. Data collected by the Afghan NGO Security Office (ANSO) on killings of all NGO staff shows thirteen killed in 2003 and twenty-one killed in January–August 2004, many of them in connection with election preparation rather than humanitarian work.

Afghans cite the general state of impunity exploited by commanders, not the Taliban or al-Qaeda, as the main source of insecurity, and they see establishment of the rule of law and disarmament as the solution. Many militias have been disbanded, but some claim that DDR has increased insecurity, especially in northern Afghanistan, as the former fighters have retained their personal weapons and are not reintegrated, and the new security institutions are not yet effective. Afghans also cite violent crime in the south and southeast as having increased since the defeat of the Taliban.[10]

The differing definitions of security on the part of the Afghans and internationals in Afghanistan result in very different perceptions of which parts of the country are more secure. Figure 13.4 compares the map of security incidents

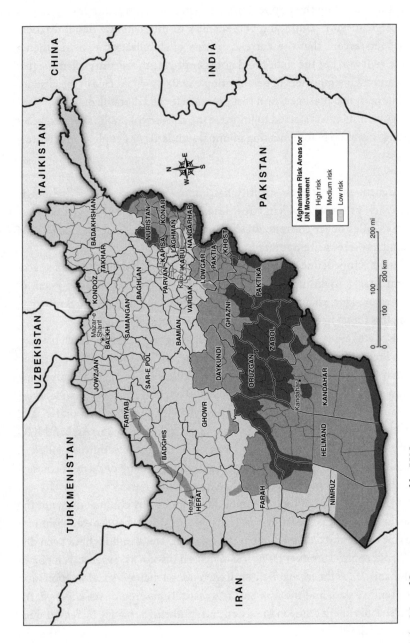

Figure 13.4a Map of Security as reported by U.N.

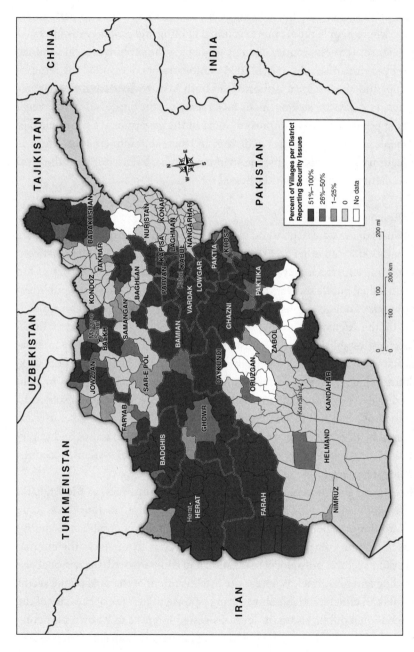

Figure 13.4b Map of Security as Perceived by Rural Afghans.

distributed by the UN with a map based on a survey of Afghan perceptions. It shows that international actors consider the Pashtun areas, where Taliban are active, as the main source of insecurity, while Afghans living in those areas actually feel more secure than those living in the northern and western parts of the country, where people report more factional fighting and property disputes.[11]

A major source of insecurity cited by Afghans is the capture of local administration by commanders. In March 2005 demonstrators demanded the removal of corrupt and abusive local authorities in both Mazar-i Sharif and Kandahar.[12] Although hard data are lacking, many observers have the impression that, even if cabinet appointments have improved, most of the government's provincial appointments and a larger number of district and local appointments constitute de facto legitimation of control by commanders. Afghans have not seen the clear improvement in security that they hoped for.

Public Revenue and Budget

The abilities of the state to plan and manage expenditure and to raise revenue are a precondition for all other areas of public services. The Afghan state must contend not only with the legacy of a historically weak state and decades of war but also with a dual public sector. Most international aid and hence most public expenditure does not go through the government budget or any mechanism controlled by the Afghan authorities, but rather through a separate international public sector established in Afghanistan by donors and contracting by international actors on the ground, especially the coalition. Unlike national public expenditure, which is accounted for by the budget process and, after reform, paid from a single treasury account, international public expenditure is not subject to any comparable control by an authority that can be held accountable. It is administered by dozens of donors, international agencies, contractors, and implementing organizations, all of which have their own financial systems, accounts, and reporting procedures.

The Afghan government has introduced mechanisms, such as the Afghanistan Development Forum and the Consultative Groups, to introduce some order into donor expenditure, but these rely on voluntary compliance and reporting. Coalition contracting is not subject to even this oversight. The international public sector is not subject to taxation and competes with the national one for funding and personnel. Whereas the establishment of the dual public sector constitutes an understandable short-term response to the lack of capacity of the Afghan national public sector, it develops vested interests in its own perpetuation that threaten the development of the Afghan national capacity that is essential for stability and political accountability.

The difference between positive trends and a very low level of indicators is evident in the fiscal development of the national public sector. Former Minister of Finance Ashraf Ghani instituted a budgetary process as the main instrument of policy, centralized revenue in a single treasury account, reformed and simplified customs, and gained increasing control of revenues captured by commanders. His successor is continuing the process of reform. Afghanistan has adhered to an IMF staff-monitored program (SMP) since 2002. It has exceeded all of the IMF revenue targets, though the government's internal targets were higher. *Securing Afghanistan's Future* laid out a scenario for raising government domestic revenue to $1.5 billion per year in five years, though this required a level of interim budgetary support that donors have not supplied. The government did not meet the SMP expenditure targets in 2004–05 because of a decision to curtail excessive expenditure before the presidential elections. The delay in appointing the cabinet extended what was intended as a short-term measure.

Despite resource mobilization efforts, Afghanistan's ability to raise revenue is still far less than that even of a poor neighbor such as Pakistan, as shown in Figure 13.5. The annual domestic revenue of the Afghan state currently stands at 4.5 percent of GDP, while both Pakistan and Thailand (low-income and lower-middle-income Asian states) are able to mobilize 16–17 percent of their GDP. Hence the domestic revenue of the Afghan state, the cost of services it can provide from its own resources without foreign aid, amounts to less than $11 per capita per year.[13] Furthermore, as long as the cash economy depends on tax-free international aid and illegal narcotics, the government will be able to tax most of the cash economy only indirectly. The government has tried to capture some of the income generated through import duties and by levying a new tax on high housing rents in Kabul.

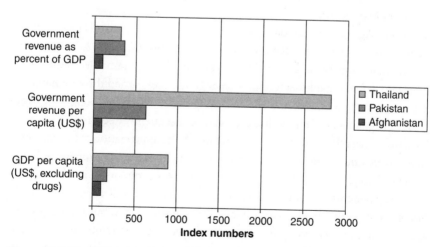

Figure 13.5 Fiscal Capacity of the Afghan State in Indexed Comparison (Afghanistan = 100) to an Asian Low-Income Country (Pakistan) and an Asian Low-Middle-Income Country (Thailand).

These figures do not reflect the ability of Afghans to pay taxes, however. These figures include only the funds that are deposited into the single treasury account. Afghans pay substantially more taxes. Some are "legal" taxes that are retained by local power holders. Some power holders have also imposed their own taxes and fees. General Dostum, for instance, collects a capitation fee (head tax) through local mosques in the provinces under his control, though there is no basis for this tax in national law. Hence the government could substantially raise revenue while actually decreasing the current tax burden on the people by coordinating security and revenue policies.

The government has developed one mechanism to deliver public goods to communities while bypassing the public expenditure system: the National Solidarity Program (NSP). This program offers up to $20,000 in block grants to villages. The villages must elect representative councils, including women, and agree on a development project to be financed with NSP funds and implemented by the village. The government has contracted with NGOs and international agencies to assist the councils in planning and to deliver and monitor the expenditure. Government officials claim that this program has been successful in making villagers feel like citizens of the country again by establishing direct links to the central government. In addition, by encouraging the villagers to achieve consensus and implement projects, it builds social capital for development, rather than fragmenting society to ensure state predominance, as in the past. Government critics claim that NSP has established a patronage network to build political support for the government, which it is not always easy to distinguish from the legitimacy of the state.

Monetary Management

The Bonn Agreement mandated a reform of the central bank (Da Afghanistan Bank, DAB), which introduced a new currency at the end of 2002. The new currency, redenominated after decades of hyperinflation, has remained stable or appreciated, largely thanks to foreign exchange reserves earned through narcotics exports, remittances, aid, and the operating expenditures of foreign organizations in Afghanistan. Transaction costs have consequently decreased, and prices have stabilized relative to past hyperinflation.[14] The appreciation of the exchange rate may be due to the "Dutch disease" resulting from foreign expenditures and a single-crop (opium) economy, pricing other exports out of the market.

Most payments, including within the government, are still carried out in cash. Some international banks have opened branches in Kabul, but their high fees and minimum balance requirements, combined with the continuing nonconsumer orientation of DAB, means that modern banking services are not available to the public, which relies on the hawala system for payments, transfers, and remittances. Reform of the state banking system is also lagging.

Education

Under the Taliban in 2000, only 32 percent of Afghan school-aged children and only 3 percent of Afghan girls were reported to be enrolled in school.[15] Reported school registration in Afghanistan is now at record highs for both boys and girls, passing four million children, one-third of them girls, in 2003. UNICEF now estimates school attendance at 56 percent.

These trends are positive, but Afghanistan's National Human Development Report, released in February 2005, stated that Afghanistan still has "the worst educational system in the world."[16] Buildings and equipment are still lacking, the quality of teaching is low, and fewer than 15 percent of teachers have professional credentials.[17] Afghanistan's literacy rate of 36 percent is one of the world's lowest, and at 19.6 percent it probably has the lowest female literacy rate in the world.[18] Figure 13.6 compares Afghanistan's literacy and enrollment rates with Pakistan and Thailand. With a tremendous youth bulge in the population and a transformation of attitudes toward education, the demand for education is growing rapidly, while expansion is constrained by the lack of schools, teachers, texts, and equipment. International assistance has concentrated on elementary education, and secondary and higher education are still limited, especially outside of major cities.[19] Donors are also more likely to fund school buildings than teacher training, potentially leaving future governments with infrastructure they cannot use or maintain.[20] Overcrowding and poor facilities at Kabul University led to demonstrations in November 2002. Inept police repression turned these demonstrations into riots in which six students were killed.

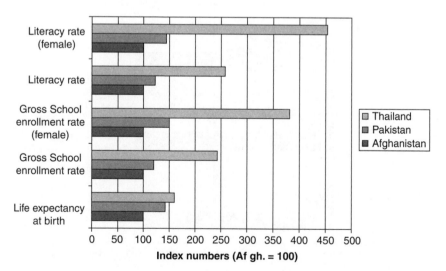

Figure 13.6 Human Capital Goods: Education and Life Expectancy (Indexed Comparison, Afghanistan = 100).

Health

The government has responded to the country's exceedingly poor state of health with a plan for a Basic Package of Health Services (BPHS), developed by the Ministry of Health with the World Health Organization. In view of its lack of capacity, the government is offering contracts to NGOs and international organizations to deliver these services in various locales.[21] It will take time, however, to improve Afghanistan's disastrous mortality and morbidity rates, which more resemble the most deprived, war-torn countries of sub-Saharan Africa than any country in Asia. As the comparison in Figure 13.7 illustrates, Afghanistan has some of the lowest health indicators ever seen, especially for women. UNICEF and the Centers for Disease Control and Prevention found in 2002 that the maternal mortality rate in Afghanistan was the highest in the world, estimated at 1,600 deaths per 100,000 live births, with pregnancy and childbirth complications accounting for nearly half the female deaths between ages fifteen and forty-nine.[22] Afghanistan also ranks among the lowest in the world for infant and child health, with an infant mortality rate of 165 per 1,000 live births, an under-five child mortality rate of 257 per 1,000 (the fourth highest in the world), and 48 percent of children underweight for age.[23]

Efforts to lower infant, child, and maternal mortality have started.[24] In 2002 UNICEF and the government reached 80 percent measles immunization, but UNICEF estimates that thirty-five thousand Afghan children still die of measles every year.[25] Afghanistan recently recorded its first deaths from AIDS. Drug use and road construction will inevitably spread HIV unless preventive measures are undertaken.[26]

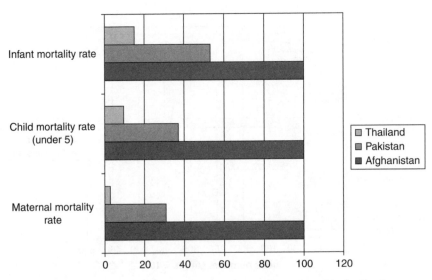

Figure 13.7 Human Capital Bads: Indicators of Mortality and Health. (Indexed, Afghanistan = 100).

Mental health has been neglected. Some surveys indicate that Afghans are among the world's most traumatized populations, and that posttraumatic stress disorder, depression, sleep disturbance, substance abuse, domestic violence, and other syndromes are widespread.[27] The current government includes a psychiatrist, Dr. Mohammad Azam Dadfar (minister of refugees), who has studied and tried to treat these disorders, but thus far Afghans have virtually no access to mental health services.

Transport

The government envisions transforming Afghanistan from a landlocked country to a land-bridge country, but investments have not kept pace with this vision. In fall 2002 President Karzai convinced President Bush that the United States should sponsor reconstruction of the Kabul-Kandahar highway. With great trouble, and with some Japanese assistance, a single layer of asphalt was laid down in a year. Reports claim that the road is already deteriorating after a difficult winter. Some other road improvement projects have begun, but Afghanistan still had only 0.15 km of paved road per 1,000 people and 16 percent of roads paved in early 2004.[28] Pakistan, in comparison, has 0.72 km of paved roads per 1,000 people (see comparison in Figure 13.8). Road building has been delayed by donor procedures and security concerns.

Municipal buses supplied by India and Japan have improved public transportation in Kabul, Herat, and Mazar-i Sharif. Kabul airport, controlled by ISAF, has improved in every respect since 2002, though it was so bad to begin with that it still does not meet the most basic international standards. The national air carrier, Ariana, and a few other carriers (UN, Azerbaijan Airlines, and private charters) have increased service to major cities and selected international destinations, but

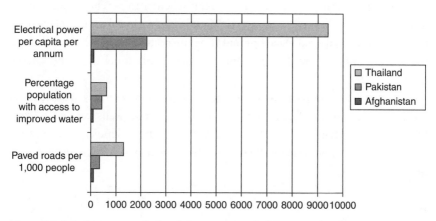

Figure 13.8 Infrastructure: Indexed Comparison of Afghanistan (100), Pakistan, and Thailand.

safety and quality are poor, as indicated by the February 4, 2004, crash of a KAM Air flight from Herat to Kabul. Corruption is high, and drug smuggling is reported as part of some operations. Ariana, a state monopoly, has blocked the expansion of service by others (e.g., Qatar Airways). High officials of the government claim that air transport is controlled by powerful "mafias."

A transport issue of great symbolic and political importance has been the repeated scandals surrounding the travel of Afghan pilgrims to Mecca. The minister of aviation was murdered at the airport during the Hajj in 2002 and no one has been arrested, although (or because) evidence indicated that a high official of the Ministry of the Interior from the Shura-yi Nazar faction was responsible. In 2005, thirty thousand Afghan hajjis registered to travel, but only around ten thousand were transported until the last days, while the rest suffered in unheated waiting facilities during the winter. The new minister of aviation, Enayatullah Qasimi, succeeded in transporting all by exceptionally operating the airport around the clock for several days with lighting borrowed from ISAF. The country has no railroads.

Electricity and Energy

The availability of electricity was curtailed by both the war and the lengthy drought, and it has hardly improved. Foreigners, the powerful, and the wealthy rely on private generators, lessening pressure to improve public electrical supply. At the beginning of 2004, only 6 percent of Afghans had access to power, one of the lowest rates in the world (see Figure 13.8). A third of 234,000 energy consumers connected to the public grid were in Kabul.[29] Yet Kabul receives electricity only intermittently even in the better-off neighborhoods. Some cities (Herat, Mazar-i Sharif) purchase electricity from neighboring countries, but there is a shortage of transmission lines, and supply is sometimes cut for failure to pay arrears. The government is considering several schemes to purchase more power from neighboring countries. There is no significant provincial or rural electrification. Among all National Development Program sectors, donors have disbursed the smallest proportion (11 percent) of their commitments to the energy sector.[30]

Fuel is available in part due to smuggling from Iran, which is subject to no quality control. North Afghanistan has natural gas, but the wells, capped in 1989, have not been rehabilitated. Other reported oil and gas deposits have not yet been explored. No efforts have been made thus far to exploit Afghanistan's geothermal reserves.[31]

Water

Water scarcity is worsening, as a result of drought, population growth, and opium poppy cultivation. Organization of government for water management is poor, as it involves at least ministries for energy and water, mines and industry, public works, urban development and housing, rural development, and agriculture. Under the first phase of the cabinet reform, several ministries were merged to form the Ministry of Energy and Water. Afghans have less access to improved (let alone clean) water than any of their neighbors (Figure 13.8).

Public Employment

There has been little improvement in excessive but underpaid public employment. Generally public sector employment is in accord with the allotted amounts (*tashkils*), but the salaries are so low and the training of employees so poor (as are the systems they work with) that the public sector is nonetheless full of unneeded workers. The president has been understandably reluctant to authorize dismissals in the absence of alternative employment. Public sector overemployment is less of an issue than quality of service and corruption.[32] Though hard to quantify, public sentiment feels that the influx of foreign aid, foreign contracting, and narcotics money has significantly worsened corruption.[33] Afghans see foreign involvement more as the source of corruption than as its solution.

Agricultural Extension and Investment Support

With international aid, the Ministry of Commerce has opened the Afghanistan Investment Support Agency, which provides one-window service for granting investment licenses. It is now possible to register a company in one day, but Afghan businessmen still complain that the government hinders their legitimate activities.[34] Banking and payment services have slightly improved with the currency reform and the opening of some banks, but land titles and legal services essential for legitimate business remain rudimentary to nonexistent.

Agricultural extension is being increased largely as part of the counternarcotics alternative livelihoods program, which means it is concentrated in a few poppy-producing provinces. The best functioning agricultural extension program in Afghanistan is still the one operated by opium traffickers.

Rule of Law and Human Rights

Afghans characterize the situation of the past few decades and even today in most localities as "tufangsalari," or rule by the gun, indicating the lack of rule of law or respect for human rights.[35] In contrast to other Afghan governments since 1978, the current government does not carry out mass killings, mass arrests, or systematic torture of political opponents. Most abuse results from the weakness of national government compared to armed commanders, who often took power in localities in 2001–02 and have seen their positions legitimized by official appointments, including to the police. One detainee held for investigation during the recent UN hostage crisis died in custody, apparently as a result of torture, despite police reform. There are occasional charges of blasphemy levied against liberal or secular writers or newspapers, which have caused a few people to flee the country. Rights are also violated by the coalition, including homicides of detainees, arbitrary detention, and torture and mistreatment of detainees. There is no legal recourse for these violations, at least within Afghanistan.[36] Taliban and elements linked to al-Qaeda conduct regular attacks on the government (especially police) and terrorist acts.

Protection of property rights, essential for economic development, seems to have deteriorated rather than improved. Afghans sometimes remark that protection of property rights has become worse since the overthrow of the Taliban, whose courts were more impartial and effective, and whose commanders were less corrupt, though at times very brutal. A Sikh businessman who said his property had been seized illegally under several governments made such a claim to one of the authors. Thirty-one percent of complaints received by the Afghanistan Independent Human Rights Commission (AIHRC) in the first half of 2004 were related to land grabbing by government officials.[37]

Land grabbing set off a major political scandal in 2003, involving an attempt by Defense Minister Muhammad Qasim Fahim to distribute land belonging to the ministry on which people had been living for decades to members of the cabinet and presidential administration. This incident was the subject of reports by both the UN Special Rapporteur on the Right to Housing and a special commission of inquiry.[38] The latter report charged that a large majority of cabinet members were to have received land. Gul Agha Shirzai, governor of Kandahar, has openly allocated public land to his family members and followers. According to an email from a government official whose identity must be withheld to protect him:

> Ismail Khan in Herat destroyed some houses and grabbed part of the people's land to expand the land for the shrine of his son. In Takhar militiamen loyal to Daud grabbed land belonging to a weaker sub-tribe, which led to a relatively tense situation unresolved till now in Farkhar district. In Badakhshan, Commander Nazir Mohammed has started his own township and is creating a Yaftali settlement to consolidate his power in Faizabad. Iranians are secretly helping Shia to buy more land in Farah, Herat, and Mazar-i Sharif as well as west of Kabul. In the Shamali plains [north of Kabul, Commanders] Almas and Amanullah Guzar are distributing government-owned land to their relatives and followers. Governors of Paktia, Nangarhar, Helmand, Uruzgan, and Khost have also been in one way or another involved in land grab.

Coherence of the Political Elite

The formation of a national leadership or political elite that agrees on the rules of legal, peaceful political competition is essential to stability. After years of violent intra-elite conflict and disruption of the social fabric, during which a number of elites were killed, arrested, persecuted, expelled, and dispersed to various parts of the world, Afghanistan's leaders and skilled people are once again returning to Kabul and interacting with each other in a national framework. This process requires time to build both institutions and the trust to make them work. The reluctance of the losing candidates to accept the outcome of the presidential election shows how the lack of trust undermines adherence to rules.

The Bonn Agreement established an uneasy coalition government including commanders and officials of the United Front (Northern Alliance) and other Coalition-supported militias, former officials of the royal government, and some Western-trained Afghans without political affiliation. The new cabinet is largely composed of educated individuals without personal followings or armed groups. Except for Ismail Khan and Abdul Karim Brahui, they are not former commanders or warlords. A number of other NA officials have remained at their posts or even been promoted. One test of elite integration will be whether these leaders can perform well under the new conditions and be integrated into the new elite. Besides Ismail Khan, these include Foreign Minister Dr. Abdullah Abdullah, Army Chief of Staff Bismillah Khan, NDS Chief Amrullah Saleh, and Deputy Minister of Internal Affairs for Counternarcotics General Muhammad Daud. The next stage of elite integration will be development of a consensus over the election and conduct of the National Assembly and broadening the national leadership to include parliamentarians.

Security Apparatus

The security apparatus has made the first steps away from factional control and toward professionalism based on legal authority, but the newly trained portions of the security forces are still pilot programs confronted with the power of militia groups and drug traffickers. All security forces are now commanded by members of the "reformist" camp: Minister of Defense Abdul Rahim Wardak, Minister of Interior Ali Ahmad Jalali, and NDS head Amrullah Saleh. The UN secretary-general reports that reform of the Ministry of Defense is "now in its fourth and last phase."[39] NDS reform, though a late starter, has also progressed. The Ministry of the Interior, which has the larger and more complex job of managing both the police and the territorial administration, is still largely captured by commanders in some departments and at the middle and lower levels.

The trend of demobilization of militias and establishment of new security forces is positive, if mixed and slow. A contrary trend is the formation of unofficial armed groups by drug traffickers (also often commanders) and others. In early 2005 the Afghanistan's New Beginnings Program (ANBP) of the UN began to survey such "illegal armed groups" (IAGs) with a view to demobilizing and disarming them before the Wolesi Jirga and provincial council elections.

Economic Indicators

General State of the Economy

Growth of the non-opium economy has slowed, just as the counternarcotics program has been launched. A counternarcotics policy with an inadequate program of alternative livelihoods and macroeconomic support and a premature emphasis on eradication is the most likely immediate source of economic retrogression and of consequent political and social conflict.

In 2002–03 and 2003–04 the legal Afghan economy was estimated to have grown by 29 and 16 percent per year respectively. In January 2005 the IMF downgraded its growth projection for 2004–05 to only 8 percent (see Figure 13.9), though a month later it projected slightly stronger performance (10 percent growth) for 2005–06.[40] The growth in the first two years resulted in part from a rebound in agricultural production due to good rains after three years of severe drought and an influx of foreign aid, including the pump-priming effect of the hundreds of millions of dollars in cash supplied to commanders by the United States.[41] Afghanistan estimated that a growth rate of 9 percent per year in the non-opium economy was the

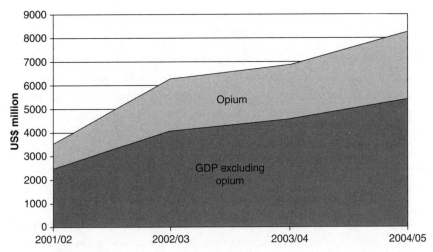

Figure 13.9 Growth of Opium-Related and Non-Opium-Related GDP, 2001–2004.

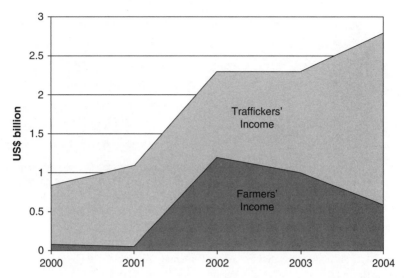

Figure 13.10 Distribution of Opium-Related Income, 2001–2004 (UNODC Estimates).

minimum needed for recovery. Thanks to government monetary and fiscal policy and an influx of foreign exchange, hyperinflation has abated.

The narcotics economy has been the most dynamic sector, though the gains appear to have gone mainly to traffickers and commanders and only secondarily to farmers, many of whom are heavily indebted (Figure 13.10).[42] UNODC administrator Antonio Maria Costa has observed, "Just like people can be addicted to drugs, countries can be addicted to a drug economy. That's what I am seeing in Afghanistan."[43] Afghanistan is now more dependent on narcotics income than any country in the world (Figure 13.11).

Relative Economic Position of Groups

The economic opportunities of identity groups do not differ systematically at the national level. Leaders of all groups complain of discrimination in the pattern of public expenditure and distribution of aid. The lack of transparency in aid distribution, which depends largely on donors' priorities and responses to perceived security threats, contributes to suspicions. Objectively, deprivation is shared, but the sense of injustice and need is so intense that even small perceived differences could incite strong resentments. Within families, women bear the brunt of the worst deprivation, including the sale of daughters for survival.

Otherwise, the major dividing line regarding economic opportunities is between the cities and the countryside and, within the cities, between those who can work in English and those who cannot. Most expenditure and aid goes to Kabul, though the expenditure in Kabul largely consists of salaries paid to the

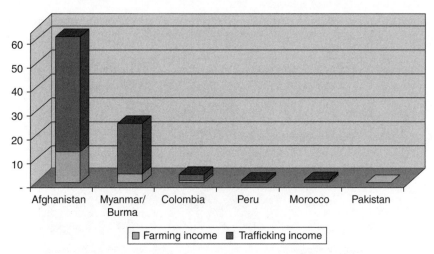

Figure 13.11 Narcotics-Related Income as Percentage of Legal GDP (Based on Estimates from UNODC and INCB, Various Dates, 2001–2004).

central government rather than public services to the city. This results not from discrimination but from lack of capacity to deliver services. The standard of living of many people in Kabul and other cities has actually deteriorated since the defeat of the Taliban. The opportunities for those with access to the aid economy, together with the spread of Western liberal social practices among both expatriates and the Afghans who work for them, has given rise to a nativist reaction. Imams preach on Fridays against foreigners, alcohol consumption, and cable television, which have provoked several *fatwas* from the chief justice. These are symbols of resentment and desperation over skyrocketing costs of housing and fuel, disruption of transport mainly by the huge U.S. presence, and neglect of urban services despite a visible influx of money.[44]

The poorest people in the country are probably tribal Pashtuns along the Afghan-Pakistan border, Pashtun nomads devastated by the drought, and the Hazaras in the Central Highlands. Emigration and remittances from family members working in the Persian Gulf Arab states or Iran have mitigated poverty among these groups since the 1970s. Moves to expel Afghans from Iran and other Persian Gulf countries would have an impact on them.

The legal status of women has greatly improved since the defeat of the Taliban. The new constitution guarantees legal equality and a presence in legislative bodies beyond what they enjoy in most developed countries. Women participated in both loya jirgas, where they were the most outspoken and controversial speakers. The school enrollment of girls is at an all-time high, though girls' schools have been attacked in Pashtun tribal areas. These attacks do not appear to reflect community sentiment, which increasingly favors universal education.

Nonetheless, the deficits in education, health, social status, and economic opportunity of Afghan women are so deeply embedded in family and social structure that it will take generations to change them. Families still sell daughters to settle debts, forced marriage is common, and women are denied even the half share of inheritance to which Islam entitles them. Domestic violence against women is endemic, partly as a cultural phenomenon and partly as a result of the society's unacknowledged trauma after a quarter-century of pervasive violence.

Social Indicators

Demographic and Environmental Pressures

Demographic and environmental pressures are associated with demands for services that outstrip state capacity. In particular, a "youth bulge" in the population is statistically associated with outbreak of violent conflict, as uneducated, unemployed, and frustrated young men can be recruited to armed groups or organized crime. Afghanistan has such a youth bulge, with 45 percent of the population under the age of fifteen, more than any of its neighbors (Figure 13.12).[45] A few simple improvements in health care that lower infant and child mortality (immunization, treatment for diarrhea) may soon make the population even younger, before demographic transition sets in. The expansion of education and employment is not able to keep up with the growth of the youthful population.

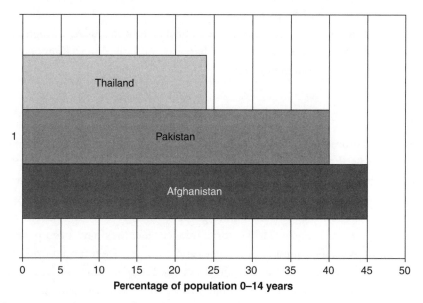

Figure 13.12 Percentage of Population Under Fifteen Years of Age.

Population pressure is particularly visible in the degradation of cities and the shortage of water. Several cities, most of all Kabul, are overrun with returning migrants, who have undergone forced urbanization as a result of displacement. Kabul, which was estimated to have a population of eight hundred thousand before the war, now contains more than three million people, on the same land and with less water. The consequences include traffic congestion and transport delays, crowded housing at skyrocketing prices, air pollution, and lack of sanitation. There are many illegal settlements on land without services. Shantytowns could become incubators for protest movements.

Availability of water has always been the main constraint on human settlement and agriculture in Afghanistan. During 1999–2001, Afghanistan suffered from one of the worst droughts in decades, lowering the water table as much as 15 feet (5 meters) in many areas.[46] Several areas to which refugees and IDPs are returning (e.g., the Shamali plain north of Kabul) have had insufficient water to support them. Water shortage is also a constraint on food production needed to feed the growing population and an incentive for cultivating opium poppy, a drought-tolerant cash crop. Only tube wells can now reach the water table in some areas, and only poppy cultivation can produce the income to finance the operation of diesel-powered tube wells. These wells are mining the underground aquifers that constitute the country's water reserves.[47] One study reported the water table dropping by one meter per year in tube well areas.[48]

Other parts of Afghanistan's environment have also become severely degraded. Both the hardwood forests of the east and the pistachio groves of the north have been rapidly depleted by peasants seeking firewood and timber merchants seeking construction materials. Soil quality has been eroded through lack of care and leeching by repeated poppy harvests. Air pollution in Kabul city is now among the worst in the world.[49]

Migration and Brain Drain

Since 1978 more than a third of Afghans became refugees, and many were displaced within the country. Persecution killed and drove into exile many of the most skilled and educated Afghans. According to UNHCR, since the inauguration of the Interim Authority 3.5 million refugees have returned to Afghanistan, including all regions and ethnic groups.[50] Refugees from Pakistan are pulled back to Afghanistan, while some refugees feel they have been pushed out of Iran. A smaller number of refugees and émigrés have returned from developed countries, sometimes to high positions. President Karzai asked eight members of the current cabinet to renounce citizenship in the United States, Germany, Switzerland, and Sweden. A few individuals have fled the country, sometimes temporarily, because of politically motivated threats, but such cases are rare.

A less visible brain drain, however, is depriving the country of much-needed capacity. Most Afghans with modern skills, especially those who can work in English, are now employed by international organizations in the dual public sector. Many working for the government are paid high salaries by donors, outside of the official framework. Efforts to build the capacity of Afghans in government stumble, as those trained leave to work for international organizations at far higher salaries, even if the new job is less skilled. In addition, as young Afghans receive more scholarships to study abroad, more decide to stay there. Whenever the international presence in Afghanistan diminishes, many Afghans now working for international organizations in Afghanistan will seek to emigrate, if current conditions persist.

Displacement

During the consolidation of the power of Northern Alliance commanders in North Afghanistan in 2001–02, incidents of ethnic cleansing of Pashtun communities in northern Afghanistan displaced tens of thousands of people, now mostly sheltered in IDP camps around Kandahar.[51] This violence, including some killings and rapes, was the latest round in disputes over control of land dating back to the settlement of Pashtuns in that area by the Afghan monarchy in the late nineteenth century. Some of the earlier rounds in which Pashtuns dispossessed non-Pashtuns were equally violent.

The government and UN established a security commission to help the IDPs return. IDPs in the Kandahar area also include nomads whose herds and pastures have been destroyed by drought. Both they and the victims of ethnic cleansing have now requested to be resettled on the barren land where they have been temporarily housed, for lack of any alternative.[52]

Security and survival are still so precarious in many areas that small disturbances can lead to forced migration. The residents of one border district with Pakistan belonging to the Mohmand tribe have reportedly decided to return to Pakistan [in 2005] because they will not be able to survive if the government prevents them from growing opium. Reduction or eradication of opium poppy production without sufficient alternative livelihoods may provoke more emigration.

The return of refugees and IDPs has generated numerous land and water disputes, as land titles and water rights, not always recorded in rural areas, have become clouded over decades in which successive occupants fled, sold, or leased land.[53] According to a government official: "Land-related disputes have led to tribal clashes in Khost, Jalalabad, Takhar, Badakhshan, Kabul, Ghazni, Herat and

Kapisa. . . . In Ghazni, Kuchis [Pashtun nomads] and Hazaras fought last year over pastures. In Nangarhar, two big tribes are at each other's throat over the land grab issue."

Many returnees to Kabul from the West found their former houses occupied by commanders. Returnees to rural land also find that their homes, land, and wells are occupied by others. Except for the expulsions of Pashtuns from the north, also related to land disputes, none of these has yet escalated to the political level, but the existing dispute resolution and legal institutions cannot resolve them satisfactorily.[54]

Group-Based Hostilities

This land conflict in the north is one example of intergroup hostility, including mass killing and ethnic cleansing. Other instances of mass intergroup conflict or killing from the decades of conflict include:

- Killings and looting in Paghman (Kabul province) and in Kandahar by Jawzjani militias of the Najibullah regime in 1988–1996.
- The massacres of all communities that accompanied the battle for control of Kabul city among former mujahidin and former communist regime militias during 1992 and 1993.
- The scorched-earth policy of the Taliban and al-Qaeda in the Shamali plain north of Kabul, leading to the expulsion of many of the inhabitants, accompanied by extrajudicial executions and the destruction of land, crops, and property.
- The massacre of probably over a thousand Taliban prisoners by some Northern Alliance militias in Mazar-i Sharif in May–June 1997.
- The revenge massacre of probably several thousand Hazara and Uzbek civilians by Taliban in and near Mazar-i Sharif and at the Kunduz airport in August 2001.
- The executions of dozens or hundreds of Hazara civilians by Taliban in Hazarajat in summer–fall 1998, which was accompanied by a struggle over control of valuable pasture between Pashtun nomads and local Hazaras.

This is only a short list of better-known incidents. Especially because these events occurred during a civil conflict that included many instances of political or opportunistic killing and persecution with no ethnic overtones, Afghans disagree over whether it is legitimate to interpret these incidents as cases of ethnic conflict. In the absence of any political or judicial process of fact finding, accountability, or restitution, however, resentments that ethnopolitical entrepreneurs can exploit may grow.

International Environment

Compared to the global neglect and regional interference of the 1990s, Afghanistan has benefited from the international attention it has received in the past few years. The country's role as a front-line state in the U.S. Global War on Terror (GWOT) motivates continuing U.S. engagement but also risks embroiling the country in a conflict between the United States and Iran. Such conflict could threaten the formation of a regional consensus on the stabilization and sovereignty of Afghanistan, which is essential to peace and development there.

Afghanistan borders three regions: Central Asia, South Asia, and Iran and the Persian Gulf. All of these regions have exported and imported instability to and from Afghanistan. All neighboring governments officially support the current Afghan government and do not oppose the coalition presence there, though Iran protested the increased U.S. presence in western Afghanistan at the end of 2004, which was connected to the removal of Ismail Khan. All neighbors seek transit and trade agreements and compete for shares of trade with Afghanistan. Hence all have both growing stakes in Afghan stability and residual doubts about how long it will endure.

The India-Pakistan conflict has led Pakistan to try to impose a pro-Pakistani government on Afghanistan to create "strategic depth." Competition with Pakistan has led India both to support anti-Pakistan forces in Afghanistan and to seek to use Afghan territory for intelligence operations aimed at its neighbor's rear. U.S. pressure after September 11 forced Islamabad to reverse its open support for the Taliban and toleration of al-Qaeda activities. Pakistan has collaborated in the search for al-Qaeda, but until recently the Taliban acted against Afghanistan from Pakistani territory with impunity. Some claim that the Pakistani intelligence agency, the Directorate of Inter-Services Intelligence (IS1), supported a low level of Taliban activity to exert pressure over the presence of Indian consulates in Jalalabad and Kandahar and to maintain a pro-Pakistani force in readiness for the day the United States leaves Afghanistan.

On the other hand, the burgeoning trade between Afghanistan and Pakistan, consisting largely of Pakistani exports to Afghanistan, has shown Pakistani elites that a stable Afghanistan can benefit Pakistan even if its government is not subservient to Islamabad. Current political trends have also alleviated some Pakistani concerns. The relative marginalization of the Northern Alliance, which Pakistan perceives as pro-Indian, is a source of satisfaction to Pakistan. Pakistan's open advocacy of a Pashtun-ruled Afghanistan aggravates ethnic competition.

Russia and Central Asian governments have not been pleased with the change of fortune of the Northern Alliance, and they too aggravate ethnic conflict. The Russian minister of defense, Sergei Ivanov, recently provoked a harsh incident when he stated at a press conference with his counterpart in New Delhi that "attempts to Pashtunize Afghanistan" could lead to "a new war."[55]

Iran collaborated with the United States in overthrowing the Taliban and establishing the Interim Authority. Only a few months later, President Bush labeled Iran a member of the "Axis of Evil." Given the Bush administration's inflexible hard line on Iran, Iran has treated the U.S. presence in Western Afghanistan as a security threat. The Pentagon has not denied the report by Seymour M. Hersh in the *New Yorker* that special intelligence units of the DoD have used western Afghanistan as a base for covert operations in Iran, though officials of the coalition in Afghanistan have also tried to reassure Tehran.[56] The U.S. decision to offer conditional support to the European negotiations with Iran may calm tensions temporarily, but the potential for disruption remains.

At the same time, Iran, in collaboration with India, has invested heavily in transportation infrastructure linking Afghanistan to Persian Gulf ports and has signed very favorable trade and transit agreements with Afghanistan. A stable Afghanistan with political space for Shia and some recognition of Shia jurisprudence is in Iran's interest, but a U.S. military and intelligence presence on its border is not.

Landlocked Afghanistan desperately needs stable, secure relations with all its neighbors for transit to international markets. The same routes that Afghanistan needs for its international trade could also link the three bordering regions to each other and to the global market. Both hydroelectric and hydrocarbon energy sources could be transported from Central Asia to South Asia via Afghanistan. The best-known example of such transit projects is the proposed Trans-Afghan Pipeline (TAP), carrying natural gas from Turkmenistan to Pakistan. The three countries have signed protocols, and the ADB recently completed a feasibility study.[57] Afghanistan has signed a protocol with Uzbekistan to provide transit to the Pakistani ports of Gwadar and Karachi, but this, like other transit projects, is held up by the slow pace of road construction and the lack of railroads. Regional markets in electricity, water, and labor can also be expanded.

Criminal and corrupt official elements in the surrounding regions are involved in the trade in opiates originating in Afghanistan, as well as other forms of trafficking (timber, persons). Figure 13.13 shows the main trafficking routes for opium according to UNODC. This map shows the path of opiates from Afghanistan to the retail markets. The direction of the arrows could be reversed, showing the path of demand, money, and precursor chemicals from markets and organized-crime groups into Afghanistan. These organized-crime groups have links to all security and intelligence services in the region and can also supply weapons and other contraband.

Coalition presence currently deters open regional competition, but the international community has not invested sufficiently in regional cooperation. The growing drug trade carries the potential for regional destabilization. Growing regional legitimate trade has the opposite impact, but the fear of drugs and other threats from Afghanistan makes neighboring countries reluctant to allow free passage of people or cargo.

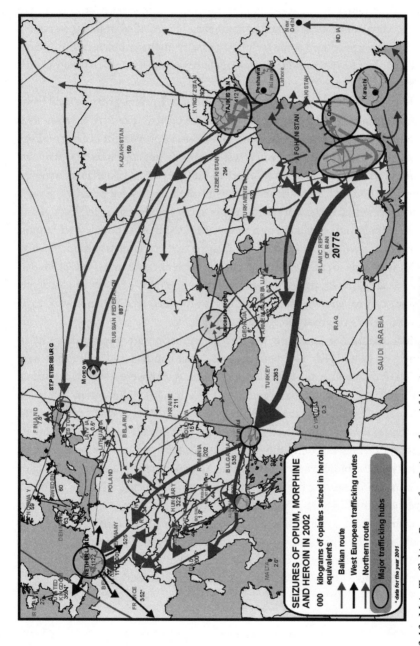

Figure 13.13 Main Trafficking Routes for Opiates from Afghanistan. Source: UNODC.

Institutions

At the start of the Bonn process all major Afghan state institutions either did not exist (parliament) or exercised limited functions under the control of armed groups. Many if not most trained personnel had been killed or fled the country. Soviet training produced some technical capacity in, for instance, health and engineering, but Soviet management models have added another level of resistance to reforms.

Efforts are under way to create new institutions. In some areas (central bank, Afghan National Army), the efforts have produced visible results. In other areas (judicial reform, civil service reform), almost no improvement is evident. Even in the most successful areas, the new institutions do not appear to be sustainable under current projections. In an effort to compensate for Afghanistan's enormous gaps, donors have launched new institutions that quick calculations such as those presented at the start of this paper show could be financed by Afghanistan only if its GDP expanded by a factor of at least five. Although international commitments will certainly continue, an army that is completely funded by foreign powers will sooner or later (probably sooner) cease to behave or be perceived as a "national" army. Paying for all the operations of a security force one does not control will also pose dilemmas for funders, who may not want to be responsible for everything an Afghan army will do.

Most institutions and processes of transformation are perceived rightly or wrongly as politicized: Northern Alliance commanders and politicians have seen DDR as aimed against non-Pashtun militias, who were much better armed than Pashtuns. Some Afghans continue to complain, without clear evidence, that the ANA is predominantly Tajik or Panjshiri. Northern Alliance leaders suspect the minister of the interior of imposing a Pashtun agenda, while others accuse him of having done too little to break the hold of Panjshiris over his ministry. "Mujahidin" have accused the Afghan Independent Human Rights Commission of serving the political agenda of its director, who has a past involvement with "Maoist" groups. Liberal or pro-democratic forces believe that the court system is controlled by followers of hard-line Islamist Abdul Rabb Rasul Sayyaf. Except for the president himself, there are no institutions that all sectors of the political elite consider reasonably impartial. That fact is a measure of both Hamid Karzai's achievement and that achievement's fragility.

Executive (Presidency and Cabinet)

Hamid Karzai became chairman of the Interim Administration without leading any powerful group, which enhanced his legitimacy by placing him above factionalism but deprived him of direct levers of power. The government consisted of a coalition of commanders with individuals either affiliated to the former king or with international technical skill or backing. Most ministers had no expertise in their ministries or administrative experience. The government executive has improved, but it is still lacking in political clout, policy expertise, and management skills.

The president's style of leadership has been consensual and therefore sometimes appeared indecisive. Since being popularly elected, he has shown greater strength by, for instance, removing Abdul Rashid Dostum from the north and stopping U.S. plans for aerial spraying of opium poppy fields. He has projected a vision that commands considerable consensus both within the country and internationally. He has not shown comparable skills in ensuring implementation of the policies he articulates.

Many Afghans have seen President Karzai as dependent on the United States, and specifically on U.S. Ambassador Zalmay Khalilzad. Though the president resisted U.S. pressure for aerial poppy eradication, Ambassador Khalilzad seems to have discreetly supported him against other actors in the U.S. government. The fact that the president is guarded by a U.S. private security company and sometimes relies on the United States and other foreign militaries for his transport damages his legitimacy, though many Afghans accept the need for such arrangements.

The cabinet has progressed as a decision-making body. It has passed four budgets, a process with which most cabinet members were not familiar. Despite being composed mostly of newcomers to government, it has far more responsibilities than other national cabinets, as it is both the executive and legislative body until the formation of the National Assembly. This dual responsibility has placed a heavy burden on the cabinet, leaving a backlog of unenacted legislation and insufficient attention to governmental management.

Professional support for the executive remains weak. The presidency and cabinet are only starting to constitute expert bodies of advisors on economic or strategic analysis or on policy making. The National Security Council has developed limited expertise in its own field. The presidency inherited a large bureaucracy (Idara-yi Umur, the Department of Administration) of about fifteen hundred employees, which has sometimes proved more of an obstacle than help. The lack of discipline in the president's office has resulted in meetings with too many attendees and lack of note taking and follow-up, though discipline has improved since the president's direct election.

The problem of succession remains. Under the constitution, should Hamid Karzai die or be incapacitated, the presidency would pass for three months to his first vice president, Ahmad Zia Massoud, who does not command a strong following in either his own group or the country at large. The country would be constitutionally obliged to hold new elections within three months; given the difficulty and expense of the last election, it seems unlikely that it could do so.

Security Sector

The professional army collapsed in 1992, leaving a vacuum of state power that was filled by various armed groups. After the fall of the Taliban, the military consisted of recently uniformed armed factions of common ethnic or tribal origin under the personal control of commanders, originating as anti-Soviet mujahidin or tribal militia of the Soviet-installed regime. The police served various factions, were corrupt, and routinely beat those they arrested. The courts and attorneys-general had no legal texts; hence they tended to apply a rudimentary conservative interpretation of the Islamic sharia.

Annex 1 of the Bonn Agreement called upon the Security Council to deploy an international security force to Kabul and eventually other urban areas, for the militias to withdraw from Kabul and eventually those other areas to which the force would deploy, and for the international community to help Afghans establish new security forces. Those new security services have made the first steps away from factional control and toward professionalism based on legal authority, and the power of warlords and commanders at the national and regional levels has diminished. Many if not most localities, however, are still under their sway, as the central government initially appointed commanders to official positions, often in the police, in the areas where they seized power. The government is now trying to transfer some of them away from their places of origin, and hence their power bases.

The Afghan National Army (ANA) could defeat any warlord militia, but the security strategy of the government, UN, and coalition is based almost entirely on negotiation and incentives, not confrontation. The structure, size, and mission of the new security forces have not been the subject of any Afghan political deliberation and have resulted more from the decisions of the major donors and troop contributors.

The security services consist of the army and air force under the Ministry of Defense; the police forces, including national, border, highway, and counternarcotics under the Ministry of the Interior; and the intelligence service, the National Directorate of Security (NDS). All consist of a combination of low- to midlevel personnel who have served all governments, commanders, and others from the militias that took power at the end of 2001, and new units trained by donor and troop-contributing countries.

The former militias now within the Ministry of Defense are referred to as the Afghan Militia Forces or AMF, while the new army trained by the United States with help from the UK and France, and deployed with embedded U.S. trainers, is the ANA. Within the Ministry of the Interior, the newly trained forces are called the Afghan National Police (ANP), while the border, highway, and counternarcotics police are new units. Demobilized militia fighters constitute fewer than 2 percent of the ANA, with the rest being fresh recruits, while the ANP consists largely of retrained militia and former MoI personnel. The NDS leadership was changed after the Constitutional Loya Jirga, and the new director is gradually introducing new personnel and structures.

In addition to this formal security sector, there is also an "informal" security sector, composed of numerous militias and private security agencies employing both Afghans and foreigners for a variety of tasks. The coalition has funded, armed, and deployed militias for fighting the insurgency. The United States and UN have hired private military and security contractors (Global Risk, Dyn-Corp) to provide security for President Karzai, elections, road construction, poppy eradication, and other tasks. International actors often respond to the inadequacy of Afghan security forces by creating ad hoc armed groups for specific purposes without any clear legal framework. The result has often been confusion on the ground. The authors of a study of security for the Afghanistan Research and Evaluation Unit depicted the security "architecture" of Afghanistan in early 2004 in the diagram reproduced in Figure 13.14.[58]

Military

The establishment of a lawful military consists of (1) disarmament, demobilization, and reintegration (DDR) of the militia forces; (2) reform of the ministry of defense; and (3) the training of the new army. These processes were linked. Many commanders refused to demobilize so long as the MoD was under factional control. MoD reform met with considerable resistance under Defense Minister Fahim. Rahim Wardak, a U.S.-trained professional soldier from the royal regime, who also served as a military official of the anti-Soviet mujahidin, enjoys the confidence of the UK and United States. Chief of Staff Bismillah Khan, former deputy of Ahmad Shah Massoud, is a respected former mujahid who, unlike Fahim, has inherited Massoud's honorific "Amir sahib" (chief commander). He may help integrate new and old elements in the ministry.

According to some reports, however, the diversification of the ministry's personnel is occurring through negotiation among diverse patronage networks, rather than through a unified merit-based system. One security official claimed:

> The candidates who fill these positions will naturally have their first loyalty to their ethnic group not to the system, because it was not the system in the first place that gave them a position, but their ethnic

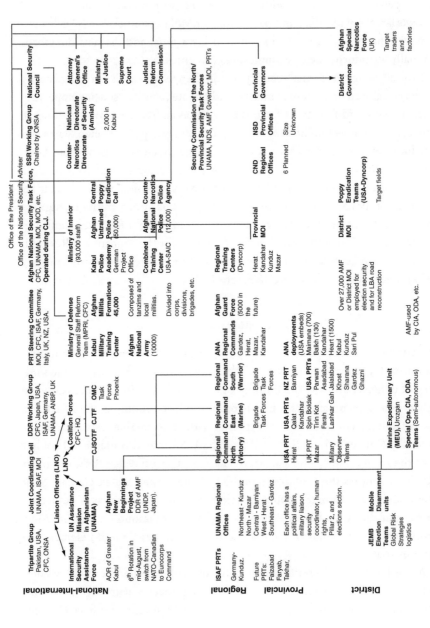

Figure 13.14 Security Architecture of Afghanistan, Early 2004. Source: Courtesy of Bhatia, Lanigan, and Wilkinson (2004).

group, and their loyalty is to a guy, not to the government. This will work fine as long as CFC-A [the coalition] is there but will disintegrate into factions and ethnic division immediately after cessation of US funding.

This is precisely what happened to the Soviet-trained Afghan national army after the withdrawal of Soviet troops, which had kept a lid on factional fighting. Thirteen months after the Soviet withdrawal, Khalqi sections of the armed forces launched a failed coup against President Najibullah and the sectors of the security forces controlled by their factional rivals, the Parchamis.

ANBP reported that as of February 2005 the DDR process had cantoned 8,630 heavy weapons, with seven regions considered free of unsecured heavy weapons.[59] Despite initial resistance, by March 2005 all known heavy weapons had been cantoned in the Panjshir Valley, the last untouched major weapons cache. UNAMA has announced the completion of DDR in northern Afghanistan. ANBP is expected to conclude the demobilization of the AMF by June 2005.[60]

DDR has thus far dealt only with the AMF, those militias previously integrated into the Ministry of Defense. A new program of disbanding of Illegal Armed Groups (IAGs) is expected to start in April 2005, in coordination with the counternarcotics program, since many IAGs are involved with trafficking. Unlike the AMF, the IAGs will receive no incentives, and more resistance may occur.

Disarmament has referred only to the cantonment of heavy weapons. No effort has been made to collect all automatic rifles and other weapons possessed by households. Hence many policies, such as counternarcotics, must take into account that much of the population is still armed for guerrilla warfare. Reintegration is less successful, as the economy is not expanding quickly enough. Anecdotal evidence from northern Afghanistan suggests that demobilized fighters who kept their weapons may be preying on the population. One security official described the creation of "insecurity in vast areas of Afghanistan from Khairkhana to Wakhan and to Murghab River in Badghis," effectively in most of Afghanistan north of Kabul.

The ANA was reported to have twenty-one thousand men on duty as of February 2005 and is continuing to grow.[61] It appears to have overcome to some extent the problems of ethnic imbalance and high turnover that plagued it at the start. Growth has been slow, due to a valid emphasis on quality of recruits and training.

The ANA was originally deployed full-time only to the Central Garrison in Kabul, with mobile units occasionally going to the provinces. In 2005 the ANA is scheduled to be permanently deployed to the four major regional military garrisons. The ANA has performed well in the limited tasks it has been assigned, mainly involving stabilization operations where warlords have been weakened. It has not been consistently deployed on the front lines in the war against the Taliban.

The plan for the ANA calls for a force of seventy thousand men, a number that appears to have been chosen by the United States through negotiation with Marshall Fahim. Currently the ANA is entirely funded by international donors, mainly the United States, and also relies on the direct participation of embedded U.S. trainers. The troops are currently paid several times more than civil servants. Some analysts believe that the use of full cash payment rather than the provision of in-kind services for soldiers and their families weakens the attachment of soldiers to the institution. Soldiers must often go on leave to deliver pay to their families, some of whom live in Pakistan, where housing is cheaper than in areas of Afghanistan where land prices are inflated by drug trafficking and the international presence. The Afghan national government is unlikely to be able to sustain a force of this size, salary level, and technical sophistication using its own resources.

Police

Police in Afghanistan have always been concerned more with the security of the state than that of the public. They included only a national gendarmerie, whose paramilitary units expanded during the Soviet period. There was no local or community policing. Villages, where most of the population lived, provided their own security. By the start of 2002, Afghan police could have been the subject of Walter Mosley's novel *Always Outnumbered, Always Outgunned.*

Reform started with the appointment of Ali Ahmad Jalali as minister in November 2002. Jalali, then head of the Persian Service of the Voice of America, had been a military officer and professor of military history at the Kabul Military Academy before 1978. In exile in the United States, he had published several well-regarded books and articles on the military history of Afghanistan.

Germany has refurbished the police academy. Training centers have also been established in eight regions. A joint effort of Germany, the United States, and others has reportedly trained forty thousand Afghan National Police. The salaries of ANP officers increase from less than $20 to $70 per month upon graduation. The ANP has been deployed, sometimes with the ANA, in stabilization operations in provinces where warlords have been in conflict with each other or the central government (Balkh, Herat).

The number of police trained overstates the thoroughness of reform. When the UN sought to deploy for election security the thirty thousand police reportedly trained by October 2004, it found that only five thousand were actually available. Many police are rehatted militia fighters still loyal to their command-ers, rather than the national government. Without embedded monitoring, the reform may not last. The trained police return to an environment with enormous pressures from drug traffickers and corrupt officials. The police failed a major test at the end of 2004: when three UN international staff members were kid-napped in broad daylight in the center of Kabul, the police failed to turn up a single useful lead, arrested a number of innocent people, and tortured one de-tainee to death, all after two years of "reform." Indeed, Afghan government sources claim that the torture was carried out by personnel hired under the "reform" program.

The border police, as yet in poor condition, are expected to deploy by the end of 2006, if they receive sufficient funding. The highway police have acquired some basic equipment but require much development. The counternarcotics police are the most difficult to establish. They are subject to a unique mix of bribes and threats ("take this $1,000, or I'll kill you") and may require a similarly unique high pay level and intensive monitoring.

Another program involving the ministry of the interior is the reestablishment of territorial administration through the Afghanistan Stabilization Program (ASP). This program, implemented with the ministries of finance and commu-nications and the help of PRTs, aims to build physical and communications in-frastructure for administration in all provinces and district centers. In early 2005 there were six model district compounds constructed, while 110 others were contracted to be built. Some observers claim that a program that was supposed to build administrative capacity has become solely a construction program. Most district and many provincial administrations are either still controlled by or powerless against local commanders.

Judicial System

The Afghan judicial system is in a deep crisis of public confidence. During the public consultations over the constitution, people frequently cited judicial cor-ruption as a concern. The courts have shown less improvement than other secu-rity sectors. Because of the role of Islam and ulama in the judiciary, it is the most difficult sector for a largely non-Muslim international community to help reform.

Most Afghans rely on customary procedures for dispute settlement. These procedures treat criminal offenses as disputes, a practice that undermines the authority of the state, but they should be a valuable resource for the country if their functions are limited to genuine civil disputes. Developed countries are trying to develop alternative dispute resolution (ADR) to reduce the burden on courts, but Afghan legal elites reject them as reactionary, given that ex-change of girls between families in dispute is one of their features. Foreign experts, including Afghans from the Diaspora, have suggested regulating rather than replacing these traditions.[62]

At the Tokyo donor conference in January 2002, Italy was appointed lead donor in the judicial area. Italy developed some projects, but the Judicial Reform Commission and the government did not develop a strategy for judicial reform. The constitution of 2004 does not incorporate any judicial reforms. The judicial system consists of:

- The judiciary, controlled by the Supreme Court. Under the constitution, the president will appoint members of the Supreme Court, subject to approval by the Wolesi Jirga. The Supreme Court nominates all other judges; when they are first appointed, the president must make the actual appointment.[63] Thereafter the Supreme Court controls their careers, salary, and discipline, while also hearing their cases. This system creates what members of the constitutional commission privately called "corrupt networks among judges." Though this is not a constitutional or legal requirement, the current chief justice simultaneously heads the Council of Ulama, and he has not clearly distinguished between the court's role in issuing judgments on cases brought before it based on written law and the role of the ulama in issuing Islamic legal opinions (fatwas) based on fiqh (Islamic jurisprudence).
- The Attorney-General (Loy Saranwal), a general procurator, originally on a French-Turkish model but modified to conform to Soviet practice. The Saranwali is reported to be riddled with corruption, as it can use its power to initiate investigations to extract bribes. Under the 1964 constitution, the Saranwali is an executive organ of the state. It became independent during the 1980s and guards that prerogative today.
- The Ministry of Justice, which is responsible for drafting laws for the government, providing the government with legal advice, and overseeing the legal functioning of the administration.

All of these organs found themselves at the start of the interim and transitional periods without legal texts or clear guidance on what the law was. All were widely considered to be incompetent and corrupt, though including some qualified and honest officers. They lacked buildings and basic equipment.

The Judicial Reform Commission surveyed the physical infrastructure of the justice system, but it failed to get the government or constitutional commission to enact or even propose any major reforms, such as restricting the duties of judges to judicial ones or clarifying the role of the AG. Programs have begun to train judges, provide access to legal materials (the International Development Law Organization put all Afghan laws on CD-ROM), and construct new court buildings, but these measures are no substitute for institutional reform.

In the new constitution the judiciary remains a self-perpetuating caste managing its own funds and career paths, while the power of the Supreme Court has been augmented to include judicial review for conformity to the constitution and hence to the "beliefs and provisions of the sacred religion of Islam" (article 3). Since the provision for judicial review is not clearly limited to cases referred or appealed to the Supreme Court, the system of self-referral and conflation of Islamic fatwas with judicial decisions continues.

The United States is now sponsoring a drugs-only justice system—including a package of police, prosecutors, and judges as part of a fast-tracked counternarcotics policy. This is part of the general pattern in the security policy area described above of creating parallel institutions when the core institutions do not function. The limits of the judicial system are illustrated by the agreement of all Afghan and foreign officials that any major trafficker arrested in Afghanistan will have to be extradited abroad immediately. The police and courts are unable to deal effectively with daylight armed robberies within walking distance of the Ministry of the Interior in Kabul.[64]

The Bonn Agreement established the Afghan Independent Human Rights Commission, which was enshrined in the constitution, though with a weak mandate and without standing in court. With international assistance, the AIHRC has carried out a survey of attitudes toward past crimes, which found an extensive public demand for some form of accountability, at least in the form of exclusion of violators from public office.[65] The presidency is studying whether it can institute confidential vetting of executive appointments, many of which have institutionalized the power of commanders with records of abuse, but no institutions can carry out such a task publicly with the credibility required.

Public Finance and Administration

Fiscal and Monetary Institutions

The degree of improvement of these institutions has perhaps been more remarkable than any other sector, though central banks are relatively easier to reform than most other institutions.[66] After the fall of the Taliban, revenue was captured by whatever armed group controlled a customs post or bazaar. The currency was hyperinflated, with several competing versions and the largest denomination (afs 10,000) worth less than US $0.20. Since banks did not function, all payments, including within the government, were made in the hyperinflated banknotes. Accounting procedures were entirely done by paper and pen, when pens were available.

Since 1929, when rebels overthrew the last dynasty that relied on the direct taxation of agriculture, the domestic revenue of the government of Afghanistan has never exceeded 7 percent of GDP. Since the Soviet withdrawal, money creation increasingly financed spending, leading to hyperinflation. Under the mujahidin government of the early 1990s, the ministry of finance lost control of the major revenue source, customs revenues collected at the border.

After Ashraf Ghani became minister of finance in June 2002, he undertook reform of the internal procedures of the ministry and of the revenue capacity of the state. Against considerable resistance, he computerized the treasury in Kabul to track funds and was trying to extend this measure to regional offices. He demanded from ministers, notably of defense, that they provide lists of those to be paid. He used the new currency and no-overdraft rule as leverage to insist on accountability, telling ministers he could not simply print money to pay whatever they asked.

Ghani started a reform of the customs. Afghanistan abolished export duties and introduced a unified exchange rate and simplified import duties, abolishing an antiquated system that had imposed high nominal rates on deflated prices calculated with an overvalued exchange rate. Through a series of regional visits backed up by pressure from other sources, Ghani gradually gained leverage over customs houses controlled by governors and other regional power holders. The government is installing an integrated information system for all customs houses and is planning to rebuild all of the installations to comply with contemporary standards.

During the first three quarters of 2004–05, Afghanistan slightly exceeded the IMF's target for domestic revenue.[67] To put this effort in perspective, that target aims at a domestic revenue of afs 12 billion, or US $260 million, or $11 per capita, about 4.5 percent of GDP.[68]

The Bonn Agreement required the interim administration to establish a central bank to emit currency in a transparent and accountable fashion. The Afghan government successfully carried out this major reform in less than a year. Between October 2002 and January 2003 the Afghan government and Da Afghanistan Bank exchanged existing banknotes throughout the country for a new afghani at a rate of one thousand to one. The new currency was printed in Germany with the newest counterfeit-resistant technology (similar to the Euro) and has maintained a stable or appreciating exchange rate.[69] The DAB has met the IMF SMP targets for monetary growth. Reform of the state banks, however, is lagging, which partly explains the government's difficulty in making payments.

Civil Service

The lack of capacity of the civil service has become a major bottleneck in reconstruction. Even the most technical ministries are unable to prepare the projects or feasibility studies required by donor agencies, especially since each agency has its own requirements.[70] The deterioration of the public service has resulted from decades of politicization, purges, and neglect. Fifteen years of war-induced hyperinflation had reduced the value of the highest salary to less than $30 per month—when it was paid, as it often was not. Hence many if not most bureaucrats were often absent to earn money in other ways, and corruption was endemic. The civil service had advanced beyond the socialist stage ("they pretend to pay us, and we pretend to work") to the withering away of the state, as envisaged by Marx ("they don't even pretend to pay us, and we don't even pretend to work"). Provincial and district administration had little contact with Kabul, and, given the lack of any reliable form of communication or electronic data management, ministries worked poorly even in Kabul.

The Bonn Agreement required the government to establish a Civil Service Commission to vet appointments. This commission's purpose was to ensure competence and prevent nepotism and patronage. It was consequently resisted by both principal delegations to the UN Talks on Afghanistan. The interim administration delayed forming it and diminished its authority, in particular by exempting security agencies from its jurisdiction. The new constitution contains no guarantees for the independence of the civil service from political interference.

The Civil Service Commission was also authorized to recommend reforms in the civil service. Headed by Vice-President Hedayat Amin-Arsala, it worked extremely slowly. In conjunction with the ministry of finance, it developed the program of Priority Reform and Restructuring (PRR) to create "centers of excellence" outside the regular pay and promotions structure in each ministry, but these have been implemented in only a few ministries. The CSC also proposed a system of chief secretaries and chief financial officers for each ministry, leaving the minister and his deputies with mainly policy-making responsibility. According to the CSC, ministers of the transitional administration resisted this change, as it stripped them of most of their executive powers. The president has also used offers of official jobs as bargaining chips without clearing his offers with the CSC. In addition, he was reluctant to approve measures to dismiss public employees before the 2004 presidential election.

Recent Afghanistan Research and Evaluation Unit (AREU) research on administration in Kandahar, Herat, Faryab, and Bamyan found only a few minor improvements since 2002:

- Provincial financial management seems to have improved, with better internal reporting of money transfers, and better accounting and audit procedures.
- Serious issues have not been addressed, such as low pay, low tashkil (personnel allotment), cash authorization system, late arrival of personnel and fiscal

budgets, delayed payment, lack of sufficient training manuals, and lack of guidance to staff.

- Recruitment and staff appointment has seen little change, as many see CSC-guided appointment of senior staff as politically and ethnically motivated. The PRR has largely been used to raise salaries of a few while leaving those unaffected resentful.
- Province-level coordination among directorates of a number of ministries and civil-military relations has improved.

Parliament

Afghanistan has not had a functioning parliament since 1973. The Bonn Agreement vested legislative authority in the cabinet. The constitution of 2004 continues this arrangement, stating that until the formation of the National Assembly in accord with the constitution, all powers of the National Assembly are vested in the council of ministers chaired by the president.

The constitution provides for a bicameral National Assembly. The lower house (Wolesi Jirga, people's assembly) is directly elected "in proportion to population" with seats reserved for women to ensure them an average of two seats per province. The upper house (Meshrano Jirga, elders' assembly) consists of one member elected by each provincial council, one member elected by the district councils of each province, and one-third members appointed by the president, half of which must be women. Hence the National Assembly cannot be fully constituted according to the constitution until after elections to provincial and district councils. Both UN and Afghan officials are increasingly coming to the conclusion that holding district council elections poses nearly insuperable obstacles for the foreseeable future.

Currently Afghanistan has no parliament building, parliamentarians with legislative experience, or parliamentary staff. France, which has agreed to be lead donor for parliamentary development, has trained eight Afghans to become the core of the staff. During the decade of New Democracy (1963–1973), the parliament passed almost no laws, and the king generally ruled by decree. The legislative process in the constitution, regarded by experts as dysfunctional, will reinforce this tendency. Twenty percent of the members of the WJ may summon a minister to answer questions, and half of the members may dismiss an individual minister on a vote of no confidence. This could become a powerful tool to blackmail ministers (with the collusion of their rivals in the cabinet) in order to pursue the interests of members of the WJ. The government's decision to adopt the electoral system of the Single Non-Transferable Vote (SNTV) will accentuate the tendency of WJ members to seek individual benefit by blackmailing ministers.[71]

Despite allegations that the constitution creates a powerful president, it grants the executive few tools to advance the legislative process, and the results of the SNTV system will make its task even harder. But formation of the parliament is a political necessity, not only because it is required by the constitution but because it is the only institution that will provide political voice and inclusion for the leaders who opposed Hamid Karzai in the election and their constituents, who include 45 percent of the electorate. Parliamentary and local elections will also provide a mechanism to include Taliban members and sympathizers in the institutional life of the country.

Political Actors

Collective political actors in Afghanistan are not clearly defined. Politics is highly personalized, tending to crystallize around powerful men and their patronage networks.

One clear dividing line is between those waging war against the current political arrangement and those competing within it. At present the Taliban and their supporters and allies can still carry out acts of violence but are not effective spoilers of the political process. There are three main groups among what the United States calls "ACF" or anticoalition forces: al-Qaeda, the Taliban, and the part of Hizb-i Islami that still follows Gulbuddin Hikmatyar. Al-Qaeda is not predominantly concerned with Afghanistan, but rather with waging a global war against the United States. The top leaders of al-Qaeda (Usama Bin Laden and Ayman al-Zawahiri) are probably close to the Pakistan-Afghanistan border, but fighting in Afghanistan is not their top priority. Hikmatyar is active in the northeast corner of the Pashtun belt, but he is not a strategic threat. Most of his former party members around the country have accepted the government, and some serve as governors, police chiefs, and other officials.

The Taliban are still mounting an insurgency in the east and south of the country, with bases and recruitment areas in Pakistan. Until recently the insurgency appeared to be growing, in part due to counterproductive efforts to defeat it. Anyone associated with the Taliban felt threatened with indefinite detention and possibly torture by the United States without judicial review. Aggressive counterinsurgency tactics, especially house searches and bombings of villages, also generated vendettas against the United States.

The peaceful conduct of the election, including in areas considered to be Taliban strongholds, may have marked a turning point, however. Pashtuns no longer feel excluded from power. Although President Karzai has rejected the term "national reconciliation," which Najibullah used for a program of co-opting mujahidin commanders, the president is now proposing such a process to reintegrate the Taliban, called "Strengthening Peace." In some postconflict situations, "national reconciliation" is a public process to create a sustainable base for peace after conclusion of a peace agreement among elites. In Afghanistan, however, there is no peace agreement with the Taliban. The Strengthening Peace program seeks a kind of piecemeal peace agreement with Taliban rank and file rather than a comprehensive agreement with the leadership. It is administered by a commission chaired by Sebghatullah Mojaddedi, an Islamic scholar, former mujahidin leader (Hamid Karzai served as his foreign affairs advisor), and chair of the Constitutional Loya Jirga. Resistance by elements of the former Northern Alliance has prevented approval of this program by the cabinet. The coalition is implementing its own version, the "allegiance program."[72]

Within the coalition that supports or accepts the government, politics remains inchoate. Political parties are virtually nonexistent. The Interim Administration of Afghanistan (the government formed at Bonn) was dominated by the Shura-yi Nazar-i Shamali (Supervisory Council of the North), founded by Ahmad Shah Massoud of the Panjshir Valley, and originally affiliated with the Jamiat-i Islami party, a predominantly Tajik group led by Burhanuddin Rabbani. Shura-yi Nazar broke with Rabbani at Bonn in order to form a coalition with the former king's supporters and others, rather than return to Kabul without an agreement, as Rabbani wished. Rabbani apparently wanted to reestablish himself as president at that time. Shura-yi Nazar gained control of the ministries of interior, defense, and foreign affairs, as well as the intelligence service. This reflected the situation on the ground and generated considerable resentment among groups that felt excluded, notably Pashtuns.

The Bonn process aimed gradually to "broaden" the government and make it more representative. This process, of building the government's legitimacy, formed part of a broader process of state building, which has dominated the political agenda. As this process required the displacement of factions based on patronage within identity groups, the struggle to control, define, or resist state building has become ethnicized. One can understand this struggle neither by attributing motives to leaders solely on the basis of their ethnic identities nor by ignoring the power of ethnic identity as an interpretive and mobilizing discourse.

The government has increasingly pursued an agenda of centralization, which, depending on how it is implemented, can be perceived as either a Pashtun ethnic or a non-ethnic national goal. A Pashtun ethnic agenda seeks asymmetric centralization of the government in order to gain control of the superior resources of northern Afghanistan and regain military power after two decades of the arming of non-Pashtun regional militias, while treating Pashtuns more as a ruling group than as citizens. Such asymmetrical centralization characterized the Afghan state through much of its history, as the tribes resisted efforts even of Pashtun dynasties to impose more uniform centralization.

Centralization can also serve a non-ethnic national agenda that seeks to replace loyalty to commanders based on patronage with loyalty to a uniform administration and rule of law based on citizenship rights and service delivery. Such an agenda confronts resistance from warlords and commanders of all ethnic groups, but in the past few years the non-Pashtun militias of northern and western Afghanistan, which took over major parts of the state security agencies, have put up the strongest resistance to rule-based centralization. The commanders of these areas had formed the largest political-military units for reasons going back to the conduct of the anti-Soviet war in the 1980s, and their military advantage was reinforced by the U.S. decision to arm and fund the Northern Alliance against the Taliban in 2001.

In this highly ethnicized and insecure context, the pursuit of even a non-ethnic centralization agenda by Pashtun office holders triggers ethnic reactions. Non-Pashtun commanders claim to be defending the welfare of their group rather than the predatory power of their followers. The lack of an organized political base has led President Karzai—a committed non-ethnic nationalist—to rely on a Pashtun base of support against the resistance from the non-Pashtun warlords. One of his political strategists, arguing that an ethnic base can support a non-ethnic strategy, said that "[Pashtuns who oppose the reform agenda] have nowhere else to go," and Karzai's refusal to organize a party leaves no alternative. Karzai may be right in thinking that under present circumstances any party will degenerate into one of the ethnicized factions that Afghans despise. His current strategy at least does not freeze the current alignment in an organization that will have vested interests in maintaining it.

In this context of weakening influence, the Northern Alliance essentially disappeared. Little had held it together other than opposition to the Taliban. Professor Rabbani and the part of Jamiat loyal to him resented how Shura-yi Nazar had cast him aside at Bonn. Within Shura-yi Nazar, Fahim and Qanooni split, with the former losing support in Panjshir as he pursued personal wealth and unsuccessfully tried to assure himself of a strong vice-presidency as successor to Karzai. The Uzbek and Hazara components of the NA went their own ways, each with splits in its ranks.

Ethnic, factional, and political tensions came to a head at the Constitutional Loya Jirga over several issues, especially over whether ministers could hold dual citizenship. The pattern of using an alliance of a Pashtun ethnic base with a smaller group of multiethnic reformers to support the program of President Karzai largely succeeded there. The president's political effort at the CLJ, led by Minister of Rural Rehabilitation and Development Haneef Atmar, united the Pashtun bloc of delegates (about half) with various other groups consistently enough to win on nearly every major issue. Tensions over the issue of whether to permit dual citizenship for ministers, a symbol of competition between elites returning from exile and those who had stayed, nearly led to the resignation of Foreign Minister Abdullah, a former close aide to Ahmad Shah Massoud.

Despite the aggravation of ethnicized factionalism within the elite, the open—and nonviolent—discussions of highly charged issues at the Constitutional Loya Jirga led to peacefully negotiated, groundbreaking measures of inclusion. These included the recognition for the first time in history of the multiethnic composition of Afghanistan (fourteen groups mentioned in article four); the recognition of two official and, for the first time, six locally official languages in article 16; the requirement that the national anthem be only in Pashto, but, also for the first time, that it mention all the country's ethnic groups (article 20); and the recognition, also for the first time, of Shia jurisprudence as a source of law for cases involving only Shia (article 131). A paragraph of article 16 providing for the maintenance of "national" (i.e., Pashto) terminology for certain offices and institutions was omitted from the text distributed to delegates for a vote, leading to protests by some non-Pashtun politicians when it was included in the promulgated text. Balanced implementation of all of these measures could foster the development of a stable coexistence between an Afghan national identity and multiple ethnic identities.

The results of the presidential elections illustrate the combination of ethnicized factionalism and national identity (Figure 13.15 compares ethnic and electoral maps). The four leading presidential candidates, who collectively won 93.4 percent of valid votes, consisted of President Karzai and three leaders of ethnically different factions of the former Northern Alliance. Each major candidate came from one of the four major ethnic groups: Karzai-Pashtun, Qanooni-Tajik, Dostum-Uzbek, and Muhaqqiq-Hazara. Of these, each losing candidate had a mono-ethnic base of support. Karzai, a nonfactional, nonmilitary leader, carried more than 90 percent of Pashtun voters, but he also received support from non-Pashtun urban voters.

Ethnicities remain discursive coordination mechanisms, not ideologically charged blocs. All major candidates had multiethnic tickets, and none ran an explicitly ethnic campaign. Despite the ethnicization of elite politics, 63 percent of the population does not attribute the conflicts of the past thirty years to ethnic factors.[73] Surveys show that most Afghans claim to give higher priority to religious and national rather than ethnic identification, that avowed interethnic hatred is low, and that ethnic politics is not considered legitimate.[74]

Islam fosters allegiance across ethnic groups. Ethnic conflict results from competitive political or military mobilization for national power, and this conflict can turn to hatred when the competition is conducted through violence. The grievances left by the past have not yet been resolved through any process of transitional justice or national reconciliation. Formation of a National Assembly with weak parties is likely to heighten the political salience of

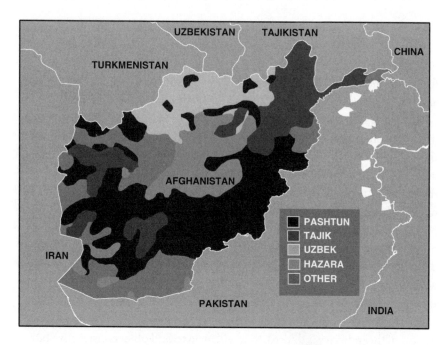

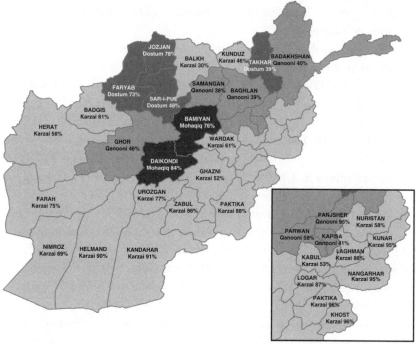

Figure 13.15 Simplified Ethnic Map [CNN] and Official Electoral Map (October 2004 Presidential Elections).

ethnicity. Furthermore, the Islamist forces feel besieged and the non-Pashtun faction leaders doubly so. They are being pressured to disarm and being promised that in return they can run for election to the WJ. The launch of programs for counternarcotics and transitional justice leads them to believe that the West and the returned exiles will use these to disqualify them as candidates.

The ulama and other Islamic figures have remained rather quiet. Friday preaching often attacks the un-Islamic behavior of the government and elites in the cities, but on the whole ulama are following rather than leading the main tendencies. The political role of Chief Justice Shinwari in ensuring the consent of the ulama to the new regime is not always appreciated by Westerners who see him as a bastion of reaction, but he has led the ulama in support for the Bonn process, acceptance of the foreign presence, including the coalition, and employment and voting by women. In return, reformers have had to tolerate the delay of judicial reform and some fatwas against television programs. Few ulama were elected as delegates to either the Emergency or the Constitutional Loya Jirga, indicating that they are returning to their historical roles after decades of occupying much of the country's political space. Especially if the ulama's monopoly of the judiciary is diluted, they will need to find other constructive rather than purely critical roles in the society if they are not to turn into a destabilizing opposition constituency.

Political parties, all of them small factions at this point, are trying to organize in anticipation of Wolesi Jirga elections. The party system that results from these elections will be determined as much by the electoral system as by the distribution of political opinion in Afghanistan. Thirty-five of forty parties that participated in a conference organized by the National Democratic Institute (NDI) in Kabul on January 17, 2005, issued a declaration in favor of a proportional representation list system, which would strengthen parties. Antipathy to political parties, often identified in Afghanistan with foreign supported armed factions, led the cabinet to support adoption of the SNTV system for the WJ elections, which marginalizes parties. This system, currently used in Jordan, Vanuatu, and the Pitcairn Islands, favors victory by well-organized minorities. It creates unmanageable parliaments of individuals who all compete against each other. It also favors the use of bribery and intimidation, as small shifts in votes can alter the outcome.[75]

Especially given the SNTV system, regional and local power brokers will exercise great influence over the WJ elections, as they seek to place those loyal to or dependent on them close to the seat of power. Given the universal importance of money in electoral politics, and given the relatively few sources of money in contemporary Afghanistan, drug traffickers and allied commanders are likely to play a major role, possibly generating violence over local rivalries, a tendency that SNTV will reinforce. Hence drug money is likely to infiltrate the political process, as it has the administration and security services.

Much of Afghan politics remains localized and outside of official political institutions, except insofar as these are instrumentalized to allocate control of resources, often in alliance with one or another power holder at the center. The warlords and commanders, though still strong, are declining in influence and are turning their attention either to money making or future elections (or both). None are intent on overturning the system, though they may resist its consolidation to protect their interests. No political program, such as federalism, ethnic nationalism, Islamism, or liberalism, has emerged as a coherent alternative to the rather inchoate dominant tendency. Karzai's leading opponent, Yunus Qanooni, articulates almost exactly the same vision as Hamid Karzai, though he claims that his management style would be different, and he has his own ethnic base of support. Thus far the difference of ethnic base of support has not translated into ethnically divergent political programs.

As long as the Taliban and their allies are kept at bay, the main threats to political stability derive from drug-fueled corruption and the fragmentation of the political scene by a large uncoordinated group of local interests. These local interests are liable to form shifting, unstable coalitions in the parliament or other national bodies in order to seek rents from the state, a process that will prove an obstacle to governance. Militarized regional-ethnic coalitions will reemerge as political actors only if international aid is withdrawn, and the state collapses again.

Afghans who have lived through the past decades are united in their anxiety over the fragility of the current trends of stabilization. Several leaders of political trends have stated in private that they are reluctant to form an opposition movement, because the government is simply too weak to tolerate it. Afghans have seen what unbridled division can inflict on their society, and one of their most important resources is the determination to resist the forces that may drive them back to violence.

Policy Interventions

Several overt policy interventions have taken place in Afghanistan since September 11, 2001. Each has distinct though related goals. They are:

- Operation Enduring Freedom, the military action in Afghanistan commanded by the U.S.-led coalition, the first front in the "global war on terrorism."
- The implementation of the Bonn Agreement of December 5, 2001, led by UNAMA.
- The ISAF, now under NATO command, which assists the Afghan authorities in providing security.

- The recovery, reconstruction, and development effort, initially led by the UN, international financial institutions, and donor agencies, now by the Afghanistan Development Forum and Consultative Groups, chaired by the Afghan government.

In comparative terms, the overall level of resources devoted to Afghanistan by the "international community" is at best modest. Figure 12.2, in the preceding chapter, compares Afghanistan to other postconflict and stabilization operations across two dimensions, maximum international troop presence and average yearly assistance during the first two years, in per capita terms. The degree of effort places Afghanistan far below all Balkan operations, East Timor, and Iraq, and even below Namibia and Haiti in the 1990s. The diagram suggests that Afghanistan may be seriously underresourced, or, as Ashraf Ghani has stated, that international actors are pursuing "state building on the cheap" in Afghanistan.

We first consider three actors particular to Afghanistan and their tasks, namely CFC-A, UNAMA, and ISAF. We then discuss the interventions by the missions of security, governance, reconstruction, and regional cooperation.

Actors

CFC-A

The coalition is a military operation whose primary goal has been to destroy the forces that committed the attacks on September 11 (al-Qaeda), the remnants of the Taliban regime that sheltered them, and the insurgency against the regime that replaced the Taliban.[76] CFC-A is under the command of the U.S. Department of Defense Central Command (CentCom). It includes covert activities undertaken by intelligence agencies, mainly the CIA and MI-6. This intervention is legitimated by the right of UN member states to self-defense and has been supported by the UN Security Council, though the United States and its coalition partners did not seek Security Council authorization as a condition for the intervention. Coalition actions are not subject to bilateral agreements with the Afghan government.[77]

The counterterrorist goal of CFC-A has at times conflicted with the governance goals of other parts of the operation, especially due to CFC-A's reliance on Afghan commanders ("warlords") as military partners, whom it has aided and armed, regardless of their records of human rights violation or drug trafficking. Forming armed groups outside of Afghan government control has contradicted the provision of the Bonn Agreement calling for the incorporation of all armed forces under the authority of the government.[78] Since 2003, the U.S. government has progressively tried to reduce or eliminate this contradiction.

UNAMA

The UN Assistance Mission for Afghanistan, under the leadership of the Special Representative of the Secretary-General for Afghanistan, has the primary goal to "monitor and assist in the implementation" of the political agreement that led to the formation of the interim and transitional administrations, the adoption of the constitution of 2004, and the election of President Karzai.[79] The Bonn Agreement was concluded hastily by Afghan groups convened by the UN. The agreement's purpose was to establish institutions of government to fill the vacuum created by the U.S. destruction of the Taliban regime and outline a process to increase that government's legitimacy and capacity. The United States put intense pressure on the UN to form an Afghan government quickly, insisting that political efforts be timed to harmonize with U.S.-led military efforts, not the reverse. The Bonn Agreement is not a peace agreement among warring parties and did not settle the previous civil war. It relies for its implementation on coalition victory, though the latter is not mentioned in the Bonn Agreement.

Besides the political processes mentioned above (two loya jirgas, constitution, elections), implementation of Bonn also includes a variety of reform and state-building processes. The agreement indirectly mentions DDR, but because of the objections voiced by mujahidin commanders at Bonn it refers only to the incorporation of mujahidin and other armed forces under the authority of the Interim Authority and their subsequent reorganization.[80] Annex 1 also calls for assistance by the "international community" in the formation of new security forces.

Besides DDR and building new security forces, the Bonn Agreement also calls for other state-building processes mentioned previously, including reform of the judiciary through a judicial commission, establishment of a Civil Service Commission, establishment of a reformed central bank, and establishment of an independent Human Rights Commission to monitor violations and promote human rights education. The agreement also required UNAMA to monitor human rights. The AIHRC and international human rights organizations charge that UNAMA has not been active enough in monitoring human rights violations.

A UN-drafted provision forbidding the interim authority from declaring an amnesty for war crimes or crimes against humanity ultimately could not overcome resistance from the most Islamist groups in the Northern Alliance, but no such amnesty has been declared. The UN Office of the High Commissioner for Human Rights has worked on transitional justice in collaboration with the AIHRC.

The Bonn Agreement imposed certain obligations on Afghan authorities, the implementation of which UNAMA monitors and assists, but it did not impose any obligations on the UN member states without whose assistance and support the Bonn Agreement cannot be implemented. Hence the UN and the Afghan government are in the curious but usual position of relying on voluntary financial and troop contributions from member states to implement binding obligations.

ISAF

The deployment of the force that became known as ISAF was requested in Annex 1 of the Bonn Agreement and subsequently authorized by the Security Council.[81] ISAF operates under a bilateral agreement with the Afghan government. Its mission is to provide assistance to the Afghan authorities in providing security until such time as their security forces can do so unaided. ISAF has operated as a "coalition of the willing" with a new command every six months. Since ISAF IV, the mission has been under the command of NATO, though without the participation of the United States. Command nations so far have been the UK, Turkey, Germany, the Netherlands, NATO-Germany and Canada, NATO-Canada, NATO-EuroCorps, and NATO-Turkey.

The principal mission of ISAF as envisioned by the drafters of the Bonn Agreement was the demilitarization of Kabul city and, subsequently, provincial urban centers, to enable the state apparatus to function free of pressure by warlords and their militias. This is why Annex 1 provides for the withdrawal of all other military forces from areas to which ISAF is deployed.

In practice, the militias did not withdraw, and ISAF collaborated with them, in effect legitimating them as Afghanistan's army. ISAF's presence in Kabul was essential to the national political developments of the past three years by preventing any coup d'état, but only in the fall of 2003 did it start to fulfill its mission of demilitarizing Kabul, by starting to canton heavy weapons. The AMF has only partly withdrawn, though that is likely to be completed under the new minister of defense as the final (rather than initial) phase of DDR. ISAF failed to expand to major provincial centers, partly because of U.S. opposition and partly because of the reluctance of other nations to provide troops. Instead of ISAF leading the expansion of security provision in the provinces, the coalition developed the model of PRTs and exported the model to ISAF, which now uses it as the template for a belated expansion. ISAF commanders have repeatedly expressed frustration that NATO and their capitals have not given them the mandate or resources to accomplish their mission.

Missions

Security

Annex 1 of the Bonn Agreement defines two components of international security policy in Afghanistan: direct international provision of security as a transitional measure, and the training of new Afghan security forces (Security Sector Reform, or SSR). A report by international specialists found that the security issue area was ill-defined, uncoordinated, and underresourced.[82]

International Provision of Security

As noted, definitions of the word *security* vary. The United States intervened in Afghanistan to safeguard Americans from terrorist attack. In pursuing victory over the ACF, the coalition has used Afghan allies whom others see as sources of insecurity and has also used tactics that threaten the security of Afghan civilians. As the coalition's goals evolve from war fighting to stabilization, its definition of security has also evolved. Work in PRTs and the increased salience of consolidation of the government and rule of law highlighted the role of commanders, warlords, and drug traffickers in undermining security.

The principal role of ISAF, as envisaged by the drafters of Bonn, was to protect Afghan government officials and other political actors from insecurity caused by commanders who captured urban areas, especially Kabul, by overseeing their withdrawal from population centers and maintaining security thereafter until professional, politically impartial Afghan security forces could do so. ISAF, however, initially focused on providing generalized security in Kabul, in conjunction with, rather than substituting for, the AMF.

No international organization has a mandate to protect Afghans from the commanders and warlords whom they identify as the main threat to their security.[83] The partial exception is UNAMA, whose mandate is restricted to monitoring and investigating human rights violations.

The international provision of security has been bedeviled by the persistence of the Taliban insurgency.[84] The Bonn Agreement was drafted as if the war against the Taliban and their allies had concluded with the unconditional defeat of the latter, and it contains no provision for reconciling the various efforts against numerous security threats. The continuation of war fighting led the U.S. Department of Defense to oppose the expansion of ISAF for the first eighteen months, as it did not want a force with a "peacekeeping" mandate in the same area of operation as CFC-A. This situation also intensified the reluctance of some European countries to support the expansion of ISAF and to contribute troops to it, as they did not wish to be drawn into U.S.-led war fighting. ISAF's first expansion outside of Kabul came when NATO took over the German PRT established in Kunduz in the fall of 2003.

Provincial Reconstruction Teams

Late in 2002, the coalition began to develop a plan to create what its leaders called the "ISAF effect" without ISAF. This was the effort that developed into the PRTs, first deployed in November 2002. The initial purpose of PRTs was to overcome the vicious circle in which the lack of security and the lack of reconstruction reinforced each other. As described by CFC-A commanders, the goal was to insert a joint civil-military team to jump-start reconstruction and thus increase security by bringing people to the side of the government. This model was based on analysis of the security threat as coming from the ACF and also created friction with the aid community.

PRTs were devised by the coalition to bridge the gap between security and reconstruction. Their mission has evolved so that they are now supposed to do so by supporting governance. Here is the mission statement for PRTs as accepted by both CFC-A and ISAF: "Provincial Reconstruction Teams (PRTs) will assist the Islamic Republic of Afghanistan to extend its authority, in order to facilitate the development of a stable and secure environment in the identified area of operations, and enable SSR and reconstruction efforts."[85]

Some international NGOs continue to reject PRTs as a violation of "humanitarian space," but the military has tried to meet some of their objections.[86] The model is currently used by CFC-A, ISAF, UNAMA, the Afghan government, and donors. A PRT Executive Steering Committee chaired by the Ministry of the Interior oversees the PRTs, while a PRT working group convenes weekly.

The original coalition concept of PRTs was based on CFC-A's experience in its main areas of operation combating the Taliban insurgency and was not clearly distinguished from civil affairs operations designed to "win hearts and minds" in a combat zone. A mixed team of military, diplomatic, and assistance professionals would provide for its own security and build quick-impact projects that would win over the local population (from the Taliban), producing intelligence and then greater security, which would enable other reconstruction actors to enter.

Besides ignoring that there are many greater obstacles to the reconstruction of Afghanistan than violence from the Taliban, this model also distorted the security threat in Afghanistan. Since PRTs would operate with consent, they would need to negotiate their presence with local power holders, often the same commanders whom Afghans identify as the main threat to security. Cooperation with governors and district administrators strengthens the national government only if the officials have actually been appointed by and are loyal to the national government. If they are instead commanders whose de facto power has simply been ratified by an impotent or factionalized government, a PRT that collaborates with them will reinforce abusive power holders. When military teams without political analysts entered Paktia in late 2002, this is what happened initially. Hence to many these PRTs appeared to be an extension of the coalition strategy of cooperating with warlords to fight the Taliban. After some time on the ground, the PRT in Paktia apparently gained a better understanding of the political dynamics and was instrumental in helping the central government replace commanders appointed by the minister of defense (Fahim) with more professional and legitimate officials.

In addition, the funds available in the first year came from the Department of Defense's ODHACA program: Overseas Disaster, Humanitarian, and Civic Aid. These funds could be used only for small-scale projects (wells, schools, clinics) that NGOs were already building, and that were useless or even harmful unless integrated into a development plan.

An alternative model of PRT was pioneered by the UK in Balkh and New Zealand in Bamiyan. In both of these areas the main security threat was "green on green" (local factional) fighting rather than anticoalition forces. This model focused on "peace support" such as aggressive patrolling, supporting DDR and other parts of SSR (excluding counternarcotics, which no PRT will touch), and separation of local forces. This model proved more acceptable to the aid community and popular with Afghans.

Once ISAF under NATO belatedly began to expand, it took the PRT as the model for doing so. The coalition and ISAF divided up the country in the run-up to the elections, with the coalition assuming responsibility for establishing PRTs in the mainly Pashtun areas, where ACF were a threat, and ISAF deploying across northern and western Afghanistan, taking over the UK-led coalition PRT in Mazar-i Sharif. It has continued to be a struggle to find the troops and equipment for ISAF expansion. It took several years to find a few transport helicopters, a very basic piece of equipment for peace support operations in a large, mountainous country with few roads.

The expansion across the country forced a debate to generate a common mission for PRTs more than two years after their first deployment. The PRT terms of reference now put the first emphasis on provision of security and mention reconstruction only later. The reconstruction efforts of PRTs may include initial quick-impact projects to win consent but then are supposed to be limited to actions to protect civilian activities and in sectors (such as major infrastructure) where military organizations may possess unique expertise.

The performance of PRTs in meeting these goals and abiding by these guidelines appears to vary widely, depending on the nature of the PRT leadership (both national and individual), the nature of the local Afghan authorities, and whether the Afghan national government has a viable political strategy for the province. The short rotations of both ISAF and coalition troops (generally six months) have impeded institutional learning and memory.

Security Sector Reform

The original framework for SSR was set at a side meeting of the Tokyo donor conference in January 2002. The Bush administration initially did not want to be involved in "nation-building" activities. Hence at Tokyo in January 2002 it convened a sidebar meeting of the G8 for SSR. Rather than lead an integrated multilateral effort, it proposed a system of "lead donors." The United States took responsibility for building the Afghan National Army (seen as its ally in fighting the war on terror), with help from France in training the officer corps. Otherwise, it wanted allies to take charge of other areas of SSR. The resultant division of labor was Germany for police training, Britain for counternarcotics, Japan for DDR, and Italy for judicial reform. This structure did not include reform of the Ministry of Defense, which ultimately turned out to be the key to both disarmament efforts and the formation of the ANA, or reform of the NDS, which has mainly been the responsibility of the CIA and MI-6.

This attempt to keep the United States away from nonmilitary "nation-building" activities stovepiped the several security sectors, failed to take into account their close interrelationship, and failed to coordinate SSR with the implementation of the Bonn Agreement. Because of the interrelationships of the various sectors and the inadequate capacity of other donors, the United States has been drawn into each sector in an ad hoc and uncoordinated manner.

For instance, the U.S. Department of Defense originally insisted that although the coalition would build the ANA, it would not be involved with DDR, which was the responsibility of Japan. UNAMA eventually convinced the United States that this made no sense, as a central issue in DDR was how many demobilized AMF could join the ANA. Hence at the end of 2002 the United States joined the DDR working group, though without operational involvement. Washington's commitment to elections led to another wake-up call. At the start of 2004 the United States realized that DDR was lagging so badly that it would be difficult to hold credible elections. Ambassador Khalilzad therefore announced in February a target of demobilizing 40 percent of the AMF by June (when elections were then scheduled), and DOD drafted a plan to meet this goal. We suggest below how the SSR area might be reorganized.

There is a particularly grave lag in police training and institution building. "National Police, Law Enforcement and Stabilisation" remains the second most underresourced sector of the National Development Program. By March 2005, of $545 million in commitments to this sector, only $267 million had been disbursed by donors, and only $169 million had been activated for implementing programs.[87] Unlike the ANA, there are no embedded monitors with the police.

A more lasting approach to security will also require ending the impunity of armed commanders and establishing the rule of law. Though the Bonn Agreement could not mention transitional justice, this topic was included in the Terms of Reference of the AIHRC. Thus far it has proved impossible to address past crimes, as many of those responsible are in positions of power, and no international security force has the mandate or aim of providing security for those who raise the issue.

How to proceed with exposure of past crimes has provoked a debate. One side argues for immediate public reporting on past human rights violations to put pressure on violators and remove them from power. The other argues that releasing such reports now would have the opposite of the intended effect. As the UN is embarking on the final most difficult stage of DDR (disarming Panjshir, militias in Kabul, and informal militia forces), at the same time that counternarcotics policy is also creating anxiety, releasing such a report could generate more resistance, thus blocking DDR, the most important measure for human rights protection.

Governance

The government has met, if sometimes tardily, the benchmarks in the Bonn Agreement for broadening the government and making it more legitimate, from the Emergency Loya Jirga to the election of President Karzai. Completing the implementation of the Bonn Agreement and continuing the implementation of the constitution will still require many further activities, including:

- Elections to the Wolesi Jirga in 2005. These require new voter registration to establish in what province voters may cast their ballots, the registration and vetting of thousands of candidates, a more challenging security effort, and a reasonably accurate count of the population in order to allocate seats among constituencies (provinces) in proportion to population. The Central Statistical Organization with aid from UNFPA has been working on a census since 2002, but questions about its objectivity have led the cabinet to choose use of 1979 preliminary census figures instead of current pre-census results.
- Elections to provincial, district, and municipal councils as well as of mayors, which will be yet more demanding technically and in their security requirements, legislation outlining the functions of these councils in local governance, and indirect elections from provincial and district councils to form two-thirds of the Meshrano Jirga, followed by presidential appointments to the MJ. In the absence of district councils, the provincial councils will elect their members of the MJ, and the president will appoint half of the total allotted to him, to maintain the balance among indirectly elected and appointed members.
- Training and technical assistance to both houses of parliament and local councils to enable a country with no experienced legislators to operate a bicameral National Assembly and three or more tiers of local councils.
- Appointment of a new Supreme Court, approved by the WJ, and enactment of a new law on the operation of the judiciary.

These are just a few of the constitutionally mandated tasks required for the government to function. Even if the basic institutions of government are formed according to the constitution and law, many state and administrative organs are still not functional. At present there is no agreed international framework for assisting with these tasks.

A general problem in the area of international assistance to governance is that international actors consider the political process the core of the task in Afghanistan. The Bonn Agreement, like most postconflict peace or transitional agreements, contains specific benchmarks and timetables for political processes. The processes of state building, however, that can make these political processes meaningful receive no comparable high-level attention. There are no deadlines or benchmarks for state building. Because of the direct interest of the United States in certain aspects of security in Afghanistan, building the army received attention and support, but civil service reform, public finance, public administration, legal reform, and service delivery are lumped in with long-term economic development. The World Bank, rather than any political actor, generally takes the lead in assistance in these areas, as if the structure of the state were not a political issue. The elevation of state-building tasks to equal importance with purely political ones is an issue not for Afghanistan alone, but for all attempts to build stability after war.

Recovery, Reconstruction, Development

Without addressing the country's pervasive poverty, no other goals can be accomplished. Afghanistan is one of the poorest countries in the world, with a per capita (legal) domestic product of less than US $200. According to UNDP, Afghanistan's human development indicators place it in a tie for last place in the world with sub-Saharan African countries such as Sierra Leone, Burundi, and Niger. Combined with the lack of security and of governance capacity, this makes "reconstruction" of the country—actually construction, from almost nothing, of a functioning economy—a daunting task.

Architecture of the Reconstruction Effort

This effort is requested in the Bonn Agreement, Annex 2. After an initial launch by international donors, the effort has come under the coordination of the Afghan government as chair of the biannual Afghanistan Development Forum and the convener of the Consultative Groups. There have been two major donor conferences, in January 2002 in Tokyo and in March 2004 in Berlin. Both of these were co-chaired and convened by the UN and donors. At the Tokyo conference, the only documentation was a "needs assessment" that was basically a desk study prepared with few data and no Afghan guidance by UNDP, the World Bank, and the Asian Development Bank.[88] The Berlin conference was organized

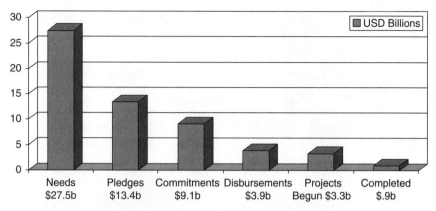

Figure 13.16 Reconstruction Assistance: Bottlenecks in Implementation (in US$ billions). Source: Afghanistan Donor Assistance Database, February 16, 2005. Needs: Over seven years, based on "Securing Afghanistan's Future." Pledges: Total pledged at the International Conference for Reconstruction Assistance to Afghanistan in Tokyo, January 2002, for first five years of reconstruction ($5.2 billion), plus pledges made at the Berlin pledging conference in March–April 2004 for the years 2004–2006 ($8.2 billion). Commitments: Total committed as of February 2005 ($9.1 billion). Disbursements: Total disbursed as of February 2005 ($3.9 billion). Projects Begun: Total disbursements for ongoing or completed ($3.3 billion). Projects Completed: Total expenditure on completed projects ($.9 billion).

around a massive report (*Securing Afghanistan's Future*) prepared jointly under the supervision of the Afghan government (primarily Ashraf Ghani) and the World Bank with the same partners, plus UNAMA.[89]

Although Afghan ownership and the level of financial commitment were major issues for the first several years, implementation of reconstruction has now become the major issue. By the end of 2004, only 7 percent of the funds committed at Berlin for that fiscal year (ending March 20, 2005) had been disbursed, mainly because of the inability of the Afghan government to prepare projects and feasibility studies for dozens of donors with multiple requirements.[90] Figure 13.16 shows the size of the bottleneck in implementation. Of more than $9 billion committed, less than $4 billion has been disbursed. "Disbursed" means only that money has been transferred to the account of an implementing agency; $3.3 billion has been disbursed for projects that have begun, and less than a billion dollars' worth of projects have been completed. The total international aid disbursed since the start of the operation for projects that are ongoing or completed ($3.3 billion) is less than half of the estimated income from the drug economy ($6.8 billion) during the same period (Figure 13.17).[91]

Former Minister of Finance Ashraf Ghani, from his arrival in Kabul with the UN mission in January 2002, tried to establish an Afghan-led framework for

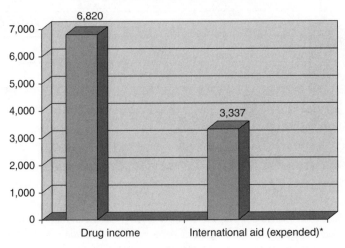

Figure 13.17 Income from Opium Compared to International Aid to Afghanistan (2002–2004, US$).

reconstruction, starting with his critical review of the initial needs assessments, establishment of the Afghan Assistance Coordination Agency (AACA), setting up payments and procurement systems through the consulting firms Crown Agents and Bearing Point, drafting of a National Development Framework, and the preparation of a budgetary process. The AACA, with the help of UNAMA, UNDP, and the World Bank, developed the Afghan Donor Assistance Database to track donor commitments and activities, as well as procedures for project support. As AACA became a political football, its name was changed to the Afghanistan Reconstruction and Development Services (ARDS), which provide project services.

During his thirty-month tenure, Ghani put in place the basic institutional structure of the reconstruction program.[92] It is divided into three pillars—social assistance and human capital, physical infrastructure, and private sector development of which a large part is governance and rule of law. Under these are fifteen sectors, three of which are in the security area. Each sector is coordinated by a consultative group chaired by the relevant Afghan ministry with the involvement of donors in that sector.

The Afghan government expressed a preference for increased aid through direct budgetary support, which it will need for several years simply to pay its operating expenses, but which it would also like to use for program rather than project support in order to build government capacity. There are three trust funds for this purpose: the Afghanistan Reconstruction Trust Fund (ARTF), administered by the World Bank; the Law and Order Trust Fund for Afghanistan (LOTFA), administered by UNDP, for expenditures related to police and security; and a new Counter-Narcotics Trust Fund, administered by UNDP. A few donors have responded, notably the Netherlands, Norway, the UK (partly), and the EU (for LOTFA). For a while, the ARTF could initially reimburse only a small portion of the nonwage expenses submitted, owing to inadequate documentation.[93] The government of the UK has scheduled a pre-G8 meeting in London in support of greater funding of the Afghan government's budget through the trust funds.

For off-budget expenditures by donors who prefer to use the dual public sector, the consultative groups and Afghanistan Development Forum serve as coordination mechanisms to ensure that the projects undertaken by donors are consistent with the programs and priorities of the Afghan government, especially as listed in the National Priority Programs (NPPs).

For the first two years, the commitment of donors was far less than the need, and a large portion of the aid was spent on emergency response rather than on reconstruction. In response, Ghani envisioned a full study of what was needed to achieve the goals of Afghanistan and the international community in that country. The result was the report *Securing Afghanistan's Future*, probably the most comprehensive and well-researched plan ever presented to the international community by an impoverished country recovering from war. Many donors resisted releasing the report because it implied that Afghanistan needed more than they were willing to give. In addition, donors were concerned that announcement of the cost of a seven-year program, which could not be met at even the best possible meeting, would lead the press to call the meeting a failure. The government persisted, and the result was one of the most successful peace-building conferences ever, in Berlin, March 31–April 1, 2004. Donors pledged to the full goal of the program for the first year ($4.5 billion) and committed two-thirds of the goal for year two and a third for year three. Many donors (notably the United States) did not pledge beyond their own budgetary year, and these figures have risen, as indicated by the Bush administration's request in the FY 2006 supplemental appropriations act.[94]

This apparent success, however, has revealed how weak the foundation for reconstruction is. Currently the time elapsed between commitment to a project and start of work is at least two years. The ARDS is trying to shorten the lead time of project preparation by creating a special fund to hire consultants to prepare feasibility studies and project proposals, but growth of the legal economy has slowed, little investment is arriving, even Kabul has no reliable electric power or water supply, and bureaucrats paid less than $50 a month in a capital where the housing market caters to internationals prepared to pay $10,000 a month for a house resist reforms that they fear might throw them out on the street. The main political reaction has been a demagogic campaign against NGOs, accused by the former planning minister and much of the press of wasting money destined for reconstruction.

Counternarcotics Policy

Narcotics constitute the largest sector of the Afghan economy. No country can establish a sustainable, accountable government and security structure while nearly half of its economy—the most dynamic half—is based on illegal production. Hence the opium economy constitutes a major strategic threat. But trying to eliminate nearly half the economy of an impoverished, well-armed country through law enforcement is also a sure recipe for destabilization.[95] Hence it is no wonder that Ashraf Ghani wrote in the New York Times that "Today, many Afghans believe that it is not drugs, but an ill-conceived war on drugs that threatens their economy and nascent democracy."[96]

It is a measure of the misunderstanding of this issue that donors have classified it as part of "security sector reform" rather than reconstruction. Most of the funding to combat it is going for eradication, law enforcement, and interdiction, rather than into expanding the nonnarcotics economy and dealing with the crisis of rural livelihoods in a comprehensive way.

After ignoring the drug issue for three years, the United States has now focused on it. President Karzai, who had for some time proclaimed narcotics a bigger threat than the Taliban or al-Qaeda, convened a national conference on the subject two days after his inauguration in December 2004. The United States initially announced an allocation of $778 million to the effort for U.S. FY 2005. The Afghan government, which had been unable to get U.S. attention on the issue, now came under severe pressure to conform to made-in-Washington prescriptions. Washington's initial program allocated only $120 million to alternative livelihoods and $313 million to eradication, including $152 million for aerial eradication by spraying. The rest was for interdiction, Afghan law enforcement, and public information. Resistance by the Afghan government, and specifically by President Karzai, with apparent support from the U.S. embassy in Kabul, has led to a withdrawal of plans for aerial spraying this year and reallocation of funds to alternative livelihoods. This constitutes an improvement, though the strategy still errs in introducing crop eradication too early in the process, before either alternative livelihoods or interdiction have a chance to change the decision-making environment of the peasantry.[97]

Counternarcotics policy in Afghanistan suffers from a confusion of goals. Its purpose cannot be to end or even reduce drug consumption outside Afghanistan, as supply-focused policies cannot succeed in reducing demand for an addictive product. The goal of counternarcotics in Afghanistan is building stability and the rule of law in Afghanistan. Hence the measure of success is not reducing the amount of opium poppy grown by peasants, but curtailing the flow of income to and accumulation of wealth by traffickers and commanders, while maintaining adequate growth in the legal economy (9 percent per year, according to

Securing Afghanistan's Future). Reducing production in a way that drives up prices and hence the value of traffickers' stocks may look like success but constitutes failure.

The U.S. standard policy on counternarcotics, the "War on Drugs," focuses on crop eradication, including by aerial spraying. Modeled on Plan Colombia, it treats drug-producing areas as if they were bases of antigovernment insurgency, rather than strongholds of support for a U.S.-supported president and government, as in Afghanistan. It fails to take into account the economic importance of the opium sector in Afghanistan. As noted above, UNODC estimates that the Afghan narcotics sector contributed $2.8 billion to an economy otherwise producing about $4.6 billion of goods and services in 2004 (see Figures 13.10, 13.11, and 13.12).[98] The total funding for the U.S. packages of "alternative livelihoods" to poppy-growing provinces for FY 2005 initially amounted to about 4 percent of the estimated value of the opium economy in 2004. Even if this amount doubles as eradication funding is reprogrammed, it is still too little and will not have an impact for some time. Given the macroeconomic importance of drugs, which is not comparable in magnitude to that of any other drug-producing country (Figure 13.11), the country needs to develop an alternative economy, not just alternative livelihoods for farmers.

In December 2004, drug traffickers in Nangarhar were reported to be supporting crop eradication, because they anticipated it would increase the value of their accumulated opium stocks.[99] Prices rose from about $90 to $400 a kilo in Nangarhar after announcement of the counternarcotics program. By March 2005 the price of dry opium in Nangarhar fell to about $220, perhaps because of interdiction efforts.[100] Farmers, however, may be anticipating greater benefits from alternative livelihood programs than can be delivered in one year. CARE reports that farmers are already saying they will plant more opium next year if they are not satisfied with the aid they receive. One said, "If we do not receive the assistance we were promised, we will grow poppy next year."[101] Hence there may be pressures for a rebound in production next year, especially for the sizable number of cultivators who are landless, land-poor, or seriously indebted. For these farmers, opium cultivation is the only means to obtain credit, cash income, access to land, and, in many cases, access to water from tube wells. Crop eradication will aggravate these conditions, and the current program of alternative livelihoods has no solution for most of these problems.

Regional Cooperation

One of the obstacles to Afghanistan's participation in regional cooperation is the country's lack of membership in an institutionalized "region." Many governments and organizations have treated Afghanistan as on the margins of the Middle East

(Iran and the Persian Gulf), South Asia (India and Pakistan), and Central Asia (formerly the Soviet Union). Afghanistan shares culture, populations, and trade networks with all of these regions, yet it is entirely a member of none of them.

Afghanistan is a member of or affiliated with several regional organizations. The Economic Cooperation Organization, headquartered in Tehran, groups most of the countries of immediate economic interest to Afghanistan, including all of its neighbors but China, as well as Turkey, Azerbaijan, Kazakhstan, and Kyrgyzstan. The Asian Development Bank, headquartered in Manila, includes Afghanistan and its neighbors, and it has been one of the most active supporters of regional infrastructure projects. Afghanistan is a member of the Organization of the Islamic Conference and may soon join the South Asia Association for Regional Cooperation. It is a Partner for Cooperation of the Organization for Security and Cooperation in Europe.

During the latter years of the decades of conflict, the UN convened Afghanistan's immediate neighbors, plus the United States and Russia, as a sort of "friends of Afghanistan" group under the name "six plus two." This same group of countries, now together with Afghanistan itself, signed the Kabul Declaration of good neighborly relations in December 2002. They issued a joint declaration in Dubai in September 2003 on building economic cooperation on the basis of open economies. At the Berlin conference in April 2004, they issued a joint declaration on cooperation on counternarcotics. Certainly the core of any regional process would involve Afghanistan and its immediate neighbors, and it would also require the support of the United States, Europe, and the big economies of East Asia.

In addition to these multilateral declarations involving Afghanistan and all its neighbors, Afghanistan has reached numerous bilateral and multilateral agreements with neighboring countries. The United Nations Development Program cosponsored a conference in Bishkek in April 2004 that brought together Central Asian countries, Afghanistan, Iran, and Pakistan.[102] The World Bank and Asian Development Bank have held several conferences on regional coordination of customs and border procedures.

Meetings have also dealt with security. A meeting in Doha, Qatar, in late 2004 discussed regional police cooperation. A meeting in Riyadh earlier in 2005 dealt with cooperation on counterterrorism. The U.S. Department of Defense Central Command convened a conference in January 2005 on regional security in Germany involving diplomatic, police, and military personnel from Afghanistan, Pakistan, and all Central Asian states.

Afghanistan and its neighbors do not constitute a relatively self-contained "security community," in which most security concerns derive from, and therefore can be handled within, a grouping of those states. Pakistan's main security concerns derive from its conflict with India, which has outlasted the Cold War that intensified it for several decades and even developed into the world's only confrontation between two nuclear-weapons states. Iran's main security concerns since the end of its war with Saddam Hussein's Iraq have derived from its conflict with the United States. The competition of regional powers in Afghanistan developed from the interaction in the post–Cold War period of Pakistan's concern with India, whose influence it wished to eliminate from Afghanistan, and Iran's concern with the United States, which it saw as Pakistan's supporter and sponsor. This competition could therefore not be resolved solely in the region immediately around Afghanistan.

These conflicting regional security interests have blocked some efforts at regional cooperation. A pipeline transporting natural gas from Turkmenistan through Afghanistan to Pakistan would be far more feasible if it could also bring the gas to the growing industrial regions of western India, but India is unwilling to depend on energy transit through Pakistan. The U.S. goal of maintaining economic sanctions on Iran leads it to prefer access routes through Pakistan, regardless of the economic advantages. Currently Pakistan is competing with India and Iran for shares of the transit trade to Afghanistan.

Policy Recommendations

The analysis suggests that the principal strategic obstacle to success is no longer either the Taliban insurgency or the entrenched power of warlords. Neither has disappeared, but both are in decline. *The main obstacle to stability at this point is the slow growth of government capacity and the legitimate economy to provide Afghans with superior alternatives to relying on patronage from commanders, the opium economy, and the international presence for security, livelihoods, and services.* Achieving these goals will require some adjustments and some more significant changes in how international actors provide assistance to enhance security, governance, and reconstruction. All require shifting from a solely national focus on Afghanistan to a regional approach.

These goals will require sustained engagement with Afghanistan and the region. Hence in addition to making specific recommendations we discuss a proposal for a comprehensive renewal of international commitment to Afghanistan beyond the implementation of the Bonn Agreement through what some have called a "Kabul process." [This proposed "Kabul process" developed into the Afghanistan Compact.]

Security

The security area is badly in need of greater coherence and clarity about goals to focus on a common mission of international provision of security to support state building, governance, and reconstruction, including security sector reform. Hence we suggest three basic pillars of change in this area: accelerating a political solution to the insurgency, unifying the command of international forces in the country with a common mission, and reconfiguration of SSR under Afghan leadership.

Ending Insurgency

Military actions against the Taliban, the construction of political legitimacy, and gradual changes in Pakistan's policy have now advanced to the point that the insurgency can be dealt with increasingly through political means. The Afghan government's Strengthening Peace program and the coalition's "allegiance programs" are good steps in that direction. The opposition to these programs from groups that fought or were especially persecuted by the Taliban, however, shows the need for this program to be combined with more general efforts to repair the country's social fabric.

Further reforms are needed to introduce more legality into U.S. detention policy, such as respect for common article 3 of the Geneva Conventions for captured Taliban fighters and punishment of U.S. officials guilty of abuse, including those guilty through command responsibility. Rank-and-file Taliban need assurance that they will not be detained arbitrarily and indefinitely and possibly tortured. Their families need to know the status of current detainees, as many as possible of whom should be released.

Though it appears that the coalition and Afghan government have decided against issuing a specific blacklist, Taliban leaders charged directly with harboring al-Qaeda or ordering war crimes or crimes against humanity, such as the massacre of civilians or prisoners, would not be eligible for reintegration. But reintegrating Taliban and even offering local positions of authority to some of them has already aroused anxiety and resentment among those groups who suffered most at their hands, while punishing only Taliban for past crimes will appear to be ethnically and politically biased. Hence ending the insurgency in a way that does not threaten another round of resentment requires a balanced program of national reconciliation and transitional justice, which we discuss below under governance.

Unification of Command and Mission

NATO has accepted in principle the unification of CFC-A and ISAF with continued U.S. participation under the organization's command. This move provides an opportunity to rethink the structure of transitional international security provision in Afghanistan, including the role of PRTs.

In a letter to the secretary-general of NATO, Canadian Major-General Rick Hillier proposed a reorganization of ISAF, which will apply equally to the new unified command. He suggested a combination of lightly armed Provincial Stabilization Teams (as PRTs should be renamed), responsible for peace support thorough programs such as the Afghanistan Stabilization Program and support to SSR, and regionally or nationally organized, highly mobile, quick-response teams for crisis situations. Such changes should be jointly considered by ISAF and CFC-A during the transition to a unified command. Some of these changes are already being introduced.

The role of CFC-A and ISAF in counternarcotics has continued to be controversial, as military professionals resist pressures to become involved in law enforcement. Given the militarized character of trafficking organizations, some international military support to counternarcotics operations is desirable. But the issue of appropriate military roles cannot be separated from the design of an appropriate counternarcotics strategy. A counternarcotics strategy that focuses disproportionately on coercion rather than the generation of economic alternatives will both fail on its own terms and detract from the overall military mission. The problem, however, as discussed below, derives from a counterproductive strategy, not from the involvement of the military per se.

Security Sector Reform

The structure of assistance to SSR needs revision. Instead of the stovepiped lead-donor system, SSR should be placed under a joint steering committee chaired by the Afghan government, with UNAMA, ISAF, the coalition, and participating donors. The DDR subarea already functions this way: Japan, the United States, UNAMA, and the Afghan government jointly oversee it. The existing lead donors can still maintain a special responsibility, given their experience. One positive aspect of the lead-donor system is that it encourages G8 donors other than the United States to take responsibility for specific areas.

The mission of an SSR steering committee would overlap to some extent with that of the steering bodies for the PRTs and the ASP. All of these bodies could be merged into a single one chaired by the Afghan National Security Council to oversee interrelated areas of security and governance. This structure could address the close relationship among the different SSR areas, as well as their interdependence with governance and reconstruction.

The international community needs to help Afghans accelerate all aspects of building of the police and justice system and needs to consider embedded monitoring of both police and courts. Judicial mentoring would presumably require Muslim judges, given the nature of the Afghan legal system. The EU managed to get two thousand police monitors embedded in Bosnia. CFC-A is now developing a system of embedded police monitoring based on its experience with the ANA, but it would be useful if this program could become multinational, including participation by ISAF and the UN.

Constitutional Implementation and Governance

The international community needs to establish a framework of cooperation with Afghanistan to support the implementation of the constitution beyond this year's elections. The G8 informally designated France as lead donor for support to the National Assembly, but the experience of SSR does not really justify the readoption of the lead-donor system. Both donor coordination and the need for Afghan leadership and a single point of contact might be simplified by the long-term assumption by UNAMA of a mandate to monitor and assist constitutional implementation beyond the Bonn timetable and creation of an Afghan-chaired multinational and multiagency task force to support that work.

Such a governance consultative group could take on other activities as well. Improving provincial and local government will be central to integrating Afghanistan's disparate groups into a common polity. The proliferation of local councils for various purposes will have to end—with all ad hoc councils giving way to the three-tiered structure mandated by the constitution.[103] These councils should have the power to examine local administration's finances. Whether they should also administer block grants, as villages do in the NSP, also remains to be examined.

Such a working group could as well help bring greater transparency to provincial and local appointments. All appointments must be published in the *Official Gazette* (*Rasmi Jarida*), but this publication provides no background details on appointees and is not widely available. Currently the Ministry of the Interior is developing a database with background information on all appointees. This information should be opened to public examination and made available through radio, internet, and other means in all national languages and English.

Since reintegration of most Taliban will entail exclusion of Taliban war criminals, this must eventually be integrated with a more comprehensive program of transitional justice. Currently, the AIHRC and the OHCHR are preparing the ground for this work, which many Afghans interpret in a highly politicized way. A successful approach to this sensitive issue will require both careful and time-consuming political work and establishment of transparent procedures and criteria to show that it is not biased. It is unlikely that many people will be tried and punished for the crimes of the past quarter-century, especially as a number of those most responsible are not Afghans, but the constitution reflects common sentiment in requiring that no one convicted (*mahkum*) of war crimes can hold high office. The original draft stated that no one "accused" (*mutahham*) of war crimes could hold office, and an appropriate solution might be exclusion from office on the basis of a criterion stronger than mere accusation but falling short of criminal conviction. Debate in the national assembly and other forums is likely to suggest further measures of accountability and restitution, if not punishment. It could be years before intergroup trust becomes strong enough to make it possible to establish an institution with such a function whose impartiality would be respected. International actors should let Afghans set the pace of this process.

International support is needed to implement some of the important agreements on ethnic identity and language reached at the Constitutional Loya Jirga, in particular the measures for official use of multiple languages in some localities. In addition, the scattering of millions of Afghans to neighboring countries has damaged a long tradition of bilingualism that is essential to Afghan national identity. Afghans raised in Pakistan may know Pashto and Urdu but not Persian, while those who have lived in Iran know Persian but not Pashto. A program to restore bilingualism would do much to repair the national fabric.

Reconstruction

At this point the major bottleneck to the quantity of reconstruction is the absorption capacity of the Afghan government rather than the commitment of donors, reversing the situation of the first three years. Major donors, in particular the United States and Japan, continue to resist financing the government even through trust funds. The ARDS has been developing a plan for a special fund for project development and feasibility studies to bypass the ministries until their capacity develops. Relevant ministries have to be trained in the course of this development. Funding should be unblocked as soon as possible for major infrastructure projects, such as road building (begun but going slowly) and power generation. In addition to these areas, this analysis suggests a number of sectors as particularly strategic:

- *Public finance.* Creating a self-sustaining and effective public sector is a key part of any long-term disengagement strategy. The World Bank's public expenditure review should provide a focal point for a comprehensive international meeting on this issue to chart a path to fiscal self-reliance for the Afghan government. In addition, the public consultations planned by the government for launching a National Development Strategy could be the occasion to initiate drafting of an Interim Poverty Reduction Strategy Paper (I-PRSP) in order to develop a strategy for relief of pervasive destitution.
- *Strengthening the national portion of the dual public sector.* Donors may be reluctant to increase funding through ARTF and LOTFA so long as ministries and

other Afghan government bodies lack capacity in fiscal accountability, the building of which will take years. Hence donors should support the purchase of capacity by the Afghan government as an interim measure. The government could, for instance, hire accountants from neighboring countries as part of the development of regional labor markets (see Regional Cooperation).

- *Teacher training.* This is the major bottleneck in the expansion of education, especially secondary and vocational education.
- *Expanded aid to higher education.* The need for management capacity argues against an education system that focuses solely on basic skills. Donors should support efforts to establish high-quality training in the analytic and management skills needed for reconstruction.
- *Water management, soil conservation, and forestry.* These issues are reaching crisis proportions, and there is hardly any policy or institutional framework to address them.
- *Urban development.* Kabul in particular has virtually no functioning urban management or planning structure. Overcrowded and sprawling cities such as Karachi are breeding grounds for extremism and violence.
- *Market opportunities for Afghan exports.* The country will not abandon opium only to revert to subsistence farming. Sustainable growth of the legal economy will require the identification and protection of international markets for Afghanistan, especially high-value agriculture. Possibilities that have already started include fashion garments with handiwork, natural flavors and fragrances, home furnishings, and horticulture. A special body responsible for finding markets for Afghan products is needed to compete with the sophisticated marketing skills of the opium industry.

A carefully designed counternarcotics policy is essential to reconstruction. The Afghan drug economy is large relative to a very small economy, not in absolute size. Given that the population engaged in poppy cultivation is a key constituency of the internationally supported government, the strategy for reducing it must be gradual and based on proper sequencing of development and law enforcement. The initial priority should go to increasing the size of the rest of the economy, not reducing the least harmful part of the drug economy, the income of farmers.[104] Establishing a credible and visible rural development strategy including development, education, employment credit, debt relief, and security in both opium-growing and other areas is fundamental. But narcotics are not only a rural issue. The income and foreign exchange earned by drug exports finance construction and imports. Therefore a counternarcotics policy must incorporate macroeconomic support, considering the effect on effective demand, the balance of payments, money supply, price level, and government revenue, which depends on customs duties levied on imports partly financed by narcotics exports.

Law enforcement should take a long-term approach, building the capacity of the Afghan counternarcotics police, including both embedded monitoring and tactical backup from international forces, to curtail the power of commanders involved with traffickers. Immediate enforcement tactics should be aimed at the top end of the value chain in Afghanistan, not farmers. International military forces can play a role in supporting such efforts. After an initial focus on farm production, it appears in April 2005 that more effort is now going, as it should, to the destruction of laboratories and stocks. High-level criminal figures and chemists involved in heroin production should be arrested and, if possible, extradited. U.S. officials claim that efforts are under way to move against "high-level targets," but the evidentiary and legal obstacles are formidable. The credibility of the program will ultimately rest on showing that it will attack the powerful, not just the powerless.

The Afghan government is considering an amnesty for those willing to bring illicit profits into the public domain and forswear future trafficking. As it is no more possible to arrest everyone who has been involved in drugs than it is to eliminate from government everyone who has violated human rights, some extraordinary measure—call it transitional counternarcotics, like transitional justice—is called for. In either case, however, unconditional amnesty creates perverse incentives. Hence amnesty should be conditional on measures of restitution, such as contribution of a portion of illicit profits to public purposes. The ulama should be solicited for suggestions on an Islamic solution to the problem of illicit profits.

Regional Cooperation

Afghanistan needs access to markets through Pakistan and Iran. The Central Asian states need access to Pakistani and Iranian seaports, at least partly through Afghanistan. Pakistan and Iran stand to gain from transit fees. The current high cost of transit is one of the region's greatest obstacles to economic growth. Afghanistan has received significant concessions for exports to the United States, Europe, and Japan, but high transport costs inhibit taking advantage of these agreements. Lowering transportation costs would be one of the greatest contributions to economic development of Afghanistan and its neighbors.

Most of the attention in this area has gone to physical infrastructure improvements, which are politically easier and doubtless necessary. Sometimes, however, "software" changes can have a greater impact on reducing transit times at a much lower cost. A World Bank official, for instance, estimated that total Tashkent-Karachi transit time could be reduced by about eight to ten days with a moderate investment in computerized customs clearing procedures, while a much larger investment in road repair and construction would reduce the transit time by two to four days.

Harmonizing customs policies and procedures as well as border security arrangements is not only, or perhaps primarily, a technical exercise. Pakistan, Iran, Afghanistan, and the states that have emerged from the USSR all have very different economic and administrative policies and institutions. Harmonizing them so as to create a more open economic environment would confront entrenched interests in many countries. Hence external donor funding to pay the costs of transition and ease the burden of adjustment will be necessary.

Besides trade in goods, trade in energy and management of water are also key, interrelated issues for regional arrangements. The pattern of distribution of these resources, in particular of water and hydropower resources and of hydrocarbon resources, creates possibilities for trade within the region as well as for transit trade in energy to outside the region. The Trans-Afghanistan Pipeline (TAP), subject of a recent feasibility study by ADB, is the best-known such initiative. There are several other project ideas, involving the sale of hydropower from Tajikistan to Pakistan and the increased purchase of electricity by Afghanistan from neighboring states.

Water management is central to reviving agriculture. To the north, Afghanistan claims that the 1947 border agreement with the USSR entitles it to a much larger share of water from the Amu Darya-Panj river system, while the Central Asian states argue that the agreement must be revised. In the southwest, control of the waters of the Helmand has been a source of conflict with Iran for decades. In the east, Afghan plans for use of the Kabul River could affect one of the main sources of the Indus Valley system.

Labor and human capital could also be subjects of regional cooperation. An administrative regime for refugees is no longer the most relevant approach to population movements in the region. Jalalabad-Peshawar, Quetta-Kandahar, and Herat-Mashhad are all integrated transborder labor markets. Unskilled Afghan labor migrates from Afghanistan, while skilled Iranian and Pakistani labor (as in the building trades) migrates to Afghanistan. Yet there are few regional or even bilateral agreements on such labor movements. Afghanistan, for instance, badly needs financial professionals such as accountants to strengthen the capacity of both government and the private sector to manage the funds available for reconstruction. Especially if Afghanistan introduced the use of uniform systems of best practice in accounting, it would be relatively easy to find qualified professionals from the neighboring countries to help build up the needed capacity until Afghans attain it.

The movement of people in the region is also connected to the growth of disease vectors. There is evidence that drug-resistant malaria, which has done so much damage to economic development in Africa, is becoming more prevalent in the region. Tuberculosis is endemic in Afghanistan and parts of Central Asia. India is the site of the world's largest caseload of new HIV-AIDS infections. The epidemic is growing rapidly in Central Asia, as drug use (including more frequent injection) is becoming rampant in Pakistan and Iran. An unintended but foreseeable consequence of building the regional transport infrastructure advocated above will be the spread of HIV/AIDS along trucking and drug trafficking routes. Hence regional prevention strategies will have to be implemented quickly to avoid major human costs.

Since the purpose of such investments would be to facilitate private-sector-led growth, ways should be sought to associate the private sector itself with regional cooperation. Business associations of several countries, including Afghanistan, participated in the May 2004 Bishkek conference. Any interstate committees that are formed to oversee or monitor projects should also include representatives of the private sector, and the latter's organizations should be supported as well.

Besides such support for macroeconomic growth, there are particular subregions along the borders of states in this region that have particularly low levels of development, which escape from control by state security forces, and where narcotics and other forms of trafficking are concentrated. These include the Badakhshan area on both sides of the Afghanistan-Tajikistan border, the area on either side of the Durand Line between Afghanistan and Pakistan, including the Pashtun tribal areas of Afghanistan and the Federally Administered Tribal Areas of Pakistan, and the Sistan-Baluchistan border area where Pakistan, Afghanistan, and Iran meet. A conceptual framework for such work developed in a November 2001 World Bank discussion paper advocated starting with small projects and gradually scaling up.[105]

These programs would pay dividends in security, as the border regions are disproportionate sources of threats. Direct regional cooperation on security is also under way. A broader range of police cooperation, beyond just counternarcotics and counterterrorism, could create a more secure environment for legitimate cross-border activities.

The political structure of the region, as well as its unbounded character, probably precludes the formation of rigid or permanent regional structures. But there are a number of steps that could be taken, notably:

- Afghanistan, its neighbors, the ADB, the World Bank, and UNDP could form a working group on regional issues at an appropriate level. Initially, this working group could take an inventory of regional initiatives, agreements, and projects related to the reconstruction or economic development of Afghanistan as well as the building of trust and confidence within the region among both states and societies. It could examine them for compatibility, try to eliminate overlap, and facilitate funding and planning through informal regular meetings. It could, for instance, constitute an executive committee or steering committee on regional issues that would meet regularly in Kabul, as does, for instance, the working group on PRTs.

- This group, as well as the development banks, could study the establishment of a special trust fund for regional initiatives.[106] The fund could be managed along the lines of the Afghanistan Reconstruction Trust Fund, but it should be reserved for funding programs that involve Afghanistan and at least one other country, preferably several, or that involve investments that promote regional cooperation and integration in ways favorable to the reconstruction of Afghanistan. This trust fund could be funded from budget lines for aid to several countries or from newly created budget lines. It would serve as a focal point for a regional planning and budgetary process, as well as for oversight.

Finally, we should not lose sight of the larger strategic picture in the region. Even though support from the United States is needed, especially to reassure Afghanistan, escalating conflict between the United States and Iran could also endanger Afghanistan. The UN, Europe, and Afghanistan should do all they can to ensure that these two countries do not revive the Great Game, in which the countries of the region were, in Lord Curzon's words, "pieces on a chessboard upon which is being played out a great game for the domination of the world."

A Kabul Process?

Some of those engaged in discussing the future of international involvement in Afghanistan have suggested that a public recommitment of all stakeholders to the goals of the next stages of the stabilization process would itself reinforce the objectives. It would both demonstrate international staying power and strengthen coordination among the many strands of activity required. Some have dubbed this the "Kabul process," in contrast with the "Bonn Agreement," to indicate both that it would take place in Afghanistan, under Afghan sponsorship, and that it would include a number of stages, not just a one-time resolution, agreement, or conference.

This term leaves open the question of the form the process might take. Comprehensive international conferences are more often the end point than the start of a process. They ratify agreements that have already been reached in other forums. Moving such a process forward might be one of the future tasks of UNAMA and the SRSG for Afghanistan, in collaboration with the government of Afghanistan.

Whatever forms such a process might take, the assessment presented here shows that Afghanistan still requires comprehensive, coordinated international support to enable it to take its place as a full member of the international community of states. The events of September 11, 2001, showed that interdependence of security is a fact of life, not an abstract idea. A spokesman of the Ministry of Defense echoed this recognition when announcing Afghanistan's modest contribution of medical personnel to relief for victims of the Asian tsunami: "We have our own problems, but we are part of the family of nations." Others have it in their power to help them fully rejoin that family.

Notes

1. United Nations "Security Council Extends UN Mission in Afghanistan for Additional 12 Months, Unanimously Adopting Resolution 1589" (2005), UN Press Release SC/8341, (March 24, 2005), http://www.un.org/News/Press/docs/2005/sc8341.doc.htm.

2. *Securing Afghanistan's Future: Accomplishments Aid the Strategic Path Forward*, a report prepared by the government of Afghanistan in collaboration with the ADB, IMF, United Nations Development Program, and the World Bank (March 2004).

3. Suzanne Verstegen, Luc van de Goor, and Jeroen de Zeeuw, *The Stability Assessment Framework: Designing Integrated Responses for Security, Governance and Development* (The Hague, Clingendael Institute, 2005).

4. This "formal equilibrium" constitutes the "liberal" model for democratic development in a market economy. A substantial critique of the liberal model has developed, arguing that it is not feasible in conflict-prone developing countries. Jolyon Leslie and Chris Johnson offer a critique of the application to this model to Afghanistan in *Afghanistan: The Mirage of Peace* (London: Zed Books, 2004). The Constitutional Loya Jirga affirmed Afghanistan's commitment to a liberal political model, within an Islamic framework. There is as yet no comparable public consensus on an economic development model.

5. *Take the Guns Away: Afghan Voices on Security and Elections (June–July 2004)*, survey undertaken by the Human Rights Research and Advocacy Consortium (HRRAC), a group of twelve Afghan and international NGOs, including CARE, Mercy Corps, Oxfam, and Save the Children.

6. Ibid.

7. M. Nazif Shahrani, "Afghanistan's Presidential Elections: Spreading Democracy or a Sham?" *MERIP Reports*, October 7, 2004. Shahrani opposes state centralization in favor of decentralized democracy based on community self-government. Many Afghans believe that this option is not possible given the current security situation. The idea does, however, have some common points with government initiatives such as the National Solidarity Program (NSP).

8. "Speaking Out: Afghan Opinions on Rights and Responsibilities" (November 2003), HHRAC; "Afghans Most Concerned About Security" (March–April 2004), national poll conducted by IRI and Williams & Associates; and *Take the Guns Away*.

9. Maj. Gen. Eric Olson, second in command of U.S. forces in Afghanistan, warned that the insurgent threat remained grave, and a premature drawdown of troops combined with increased militant activity in Pakistan would constitute "an incredibly volatile combination" (February 25, 2005). http://www.cbsnews.com/stories/2005/02/25/world/main676660.shtml?tag=mncol;lst;3.

10. CIC researcher Kate Clark reported that Afghans in Khost stated that there was less crime under the Taliban because of the enforcement of sharia. See also N. C. Aizenman, "Afghan Crime Wave Breeds Nostalgia for Taliban," *Washington Post*, March 18, 2005.

11. "Human Security and Livelihoods of Rural Afghans, 2002–2003," a report for the United States Agency for International Development (Feinstein International Famine Center, Medford, MA: Tufts University, June 2004), pp. 38–46.

12. Amin Tarzi, "Afghan Demonstrations Test Warlords-Turned-Administrators," Radio Free Afghanistan, March 9, 2005.

13. *Islamic State of Afghanistan—Second Quarterly Review Under the Staff-Monitored Program and the 2004 Article IV Consultation Concluding Statement* (November 3, 2004), http://www.imf.org/external/np/ms/2004/110304.htm.

14. Ibid.
15. Basic Education Coalition, "Education in Emergencies: Afghanistan and Other Hot Spots" (figures quoted from UNICEF and USAID), March 2004.
16. UNDP, *Afghanistan National Human Development Report 2004: Security with a Human Face* (February 2004), 66.
17. UNICEF, "Afghanistan Education Fact Sheet" (September 2004); IRIN Afghanistan, "New School Year Opens on Optimistic Note" (March 22, 2004).
18. UNDP, "Human Development Index for Afghanistan."
19. Asian Development Bank, "Afghanistan: Comprehensive Needs Assessment in Education," Final Draft Report, July 2002.
20. The Afghan Government's Donor Assistance Database (DAD) lists 101 separate projects funded by international donors for "educational infrastructure" (buildings, repairs, etc.) totaling $198 million, but only 20 projects totaling $25 million under "curriculum, materials, and teacher development." http://dadafghanistan.gov.af/dad/.
21. Transitional Islamic Government of Afghanistan Ministry of Health, "A Basic Package of Health Services for Afghanistan" (March 2003).
22. UNICEF, "Afghanistan Is Among Worst Places on Globe for Women's Health, Say UNICEF and CDC," Joint press release (November 6, 2002), http://www.unicef.org/newsline/02pr59afghanmm.htm.
23. Figures from UNICEF and UNDP Human Development Index, http://hdr.undp.org/en/reports/global/hdr2005/.
24. USAID, "Afghanistan Health Program," presentation (2004), www.afghanchild.org/uploads/USAID_Health_program.ppt.
25. UNICEF, "At a Glance: Afghanistan," http://www.unicef.org/infobycountry/afghanistan.html.
26. The Afghan Ministry of Health reports thirty-one clinically proven cases of HIV/AIDS but estimates the true total to be between six and seven hundred cases nationwide. IRIN, "Afghanistan: Struggle to Raise HIV Awareness as First Official AIDS-related Deaths Reported," (December 1, 2004), http://www.irinnews.org/printreport.aspx?reportid=26515.
27. Barbara Lopes Cardozo et al., "Mental Health, Social Functioning, and Disability in Postwar Afghanistan," *Journal of the American Medical Association* (2004): 292:575–84.
28. *Securing Afghanistan's Future: Accomplishments Aid the Strategic Path Forward,* a report prepared by the government of Afghanistan in collaboration with the ADB, IMF, United Nations Development Program, and the World Bank (March 2004).
29. Power Sector Technical Annex (January 2004), *Securing Afghanistan's Future.*
30. Out of $798,522,475 in committed funds, only $86,892,995 has been disbursed and $83,352,995 activated in programs. Figures are from the Donor Assistance Database (DAD, http://dadafghanistan.gov.af/dad/).
31. Daud Saba, M. E. Najaf, A. M. Musazai, and S. A. Taraki, "Geothermal Energy in Afghanistan: Prospects and Potential," http://www.mindfully.org/Energy/2004/Afghanistan-Geothermal-Energy1feb04.htm.
32. AREU, "Subnational Administration Update, Initial Findings and Conclusions from the Provincial Visits," AREU (Kabul, 2004).
33. IRIN, "Bittersweet Harvest: Afghanistan's New War," IRIN web special on the threat of opium to Afghanistan and the region, July 2004, http://www.irinnews.org/Report/60994/AFGHANISTAN-Bittersweet-Harvest-Afghanistan-s-New-War.
34. Don Ritter and Saad Mohseni, "Privatizing Afghanistan," *Washington Times,* March 17, 2005.
35. UN General Assembly, "Report of the Independent Expert of the Commission on Human Rights on the Situation of Human Rights in Afghanistan," September 21, 2004.
36. Human Rights Watch, "Killing You Is a Very Easy Thing for Us," Open letter to Secretary Rumsfeld, December 13, 2004, http://hrw.org/reports/2003/afghanistan0703/. The Afghan Independent Human Rights Commission also reported complaints of human rights violations by international coalition forces. These consisted of bombings of civilians, beatings, detention of innocent people, damage to houses, injuries to people, and a lack of respect for Afghan culture during coalition raids.
37. Afghan Independent Human Rights Commission, *2003–2004 Annual Report,* http://www.aihrc.org.af/.

38. Relief Web, "Special Rapporteur on Adequate Housing Expresses Concern over Forced Evictions in Kabul," Relief Web, September 10, 2003, http://reliefweb.int/report/afghanistan/special-rapporteur-adequate-housing-expresses-concern-over-forced-evictions-kabul. See also AIHRC's *Annual Report 2003–04*, 28.

39. United Nations Security Council, "The Situation in Afghanistan and Its Implications for Peace and Security: Report of the Secretary-General," United Nations Security Council (S/2005/183), (March 18, 2005), para. 19.

40. IMF, "IMF Executive Board Concludes 2004 Article IV Consultation with the Islamic State of Afghanistan" (January 27, 2005), http://www.imf.org/external/np/sec/pn/2005/pn0509.htm. See also IMF, "Islamic State of Afghanistan, Third Review Under the Staff Monitored Program—Concluding Statement" (February 3, 2005), http://www.imf.org/external/np/ms/2005/020305.htm.

41. World Bank, *Afghanistan: State Building, Sustaining Growth and Reducing Poverty*, World Bank, September 2004, http://siteresources.worldbank.org/INTAFGHANISTAN/News%20and%20Events/20261395/AfghanistanEconomicReportfinalversion909.pdf.

42. William Byrd and Christopher Ward, "Drugs and Development in Afghanistan," World Bank *Social Development Papers, Conflict Prevention and Reconstruction*, Paper No. 18. World Bank: December 2004, http://siteresources.worldbank.org/INTCPR/214578-1111996036679/20482462/WP18_Web.pdf.

43. Quoted in Anne Barnard and Farah Stockman, "US Weighs Role in Heroin War in Afghanistan," *Boston Globe*, October 20, 2004.

44. Miloon Kothari, UN Commission on Human Rights, "Adequate Housing as a Component of the Right to an Adequate Standard of Living," Report by the Special Rapporteur, Miloon Kothari (UN Commission on Human Rights, E/CN.4/2004/48/Add.2), March 4, 2004.

45. CIA, *The World Fact Book: Afghanistan* (July 2004 est.), https://www.cia.gov/library/publications/the-world-factbook/geos/af.html.

46. Marta Colburn, "Water Conservation and Scarcity in Afghanistan," in *Mercy Corps International, The Many Faces of Afghanistan Curriculum Guide*, Mercy Corps International.

47. International Center for Agricultural Research in Dry Areas (ICARDA), "Seed and Crop Improvement Situation in Afghanistan," http://www.icarda.org/seed_unit/pdf1/FINAL-DRAFT.pdf.

48. "FAO/WFP Crop and Food Supply Assessment Mission to Afghanistan," Special Alert No. 309 (September 8, 2004), ftp://ftp.fao.org/docrep/fao/007/j2971e/j2971e00.pdf.

49. Daud Saba, "Environment and Human Development in Afghanistan," background paper for UNDP, *Afghanistan National Human Development Report 2004: Security with a Human Face*, February 2004.

50. IRIN, "Pakistan: Afghan Refugee Returns Top 100,000 in 2004" (May 10, 2004); UNHCR OCM Afghanistan, "Return Information Updates" http://www.unhcr.org.uk/afghanistan/; UNHCR, "Return to Afghanistan" (January, 2005), http://www.unhcr.org/refworld/pdfid/47c3f3ca0.pdf.

51. Human Rights Watch, "Paying for the Taliban's Crimes: Abuses Against Ethnic Pashtuns in Northern Afghanistan" (April 2002), http://hrw.org/reports/2002/afghan2/; "Afghanistan: IDPs Willing to Settle in South," IRIN, December 27, 2004, www.irinnews.org.

52. Ibid.

53. Afghanistan Research and Evaluation Unit (AREU) published three case studies on land-use rights in 2003–04: L. Alden Wily, *Land Relations in Bamyan: Findings from a 15 Village Case Study* (Kabul: AREU, 2004); Wily, *Land Relations in Faryab Province: Findings from a Field Study in 11 Villages* (Kabul: AREU, 2004); and M. Patterson, *The Shiwa Pastures, 1978–2003: Land Tenure Changes and Conflict in Northeastern Afghanistan* (Kabul: AREU, 2004).

54. Ibid.

55. Russian Minister of Defense Sergei Ivanov, RIA Novosti, http://en.rian.ru/onlinenews/20041201/39774641.html.

56. Seymour M. Hersh, "The Coming Wars," *New Yorker*, January 24 and January 31, 2005. Stephen Graham, "General in Afghanistan Urges Care on Iran," Associated Press (Bagram), January 24, 2005.

57. U.S. Department of Energy, "Afghanistan Fact Sheet" (June 2004), http://www.eia.gov/countries/country-data.cfm?fips=AF.

58. Michael Bhatia, Kevin Lanigan, and Philip Wilkinson, *Minimum Investments, Minimum Results: The Failure of Security Policy in Afghanistan* (Kabul: AREU, 2004).

59. The regions are Kabul, Jalalabad, Kandahar, Gardez, Mazar-i Sharif, Bamyan, and Panjshir. UNDP, Afghanistan's New Beginnings Program (ANBP), http://www.anbp.af.undp.org/homepage/index.php?option=com_content&view=article&id=2:afghanistans-new-beginnings-programme&Itemid=2.

60. Ibid.

61. Kevin Dougherty, "Building an Army for Afghanistan," *Stars and Stripes*, European ed., February 3, 2005.

62. Ali Wardak, "Building Post-War Justice System in Afghanistan," Crime, Law & Social Change 41: 319–41, 2004, http://www.usip.org/files/file/wardak_article.pdf.

63. The constitution follows sharia, according to which only the ruler of the Islamic community can appoint a nonjudge to become a judge. Hence the Supreme Court nominates and the president appoints. After initial appointment, the Supreme Court determines all further appointment, transfer, and promotion of judges.

64. The Afghanistan Research and Evaluation Unit (http://www.areu.org.af, a highly respected, internationally sponsored research institution with offices on a major thoroughfare of central Kabul, Shahr-i Naw), where the authors presented a draft of this paper on February 26, 2005, was robbed by armed gunmen on January 1, 2005. Despite police appearance at the crime scene and the temporary detention of some of AREU's staff, no arrests have been made.

65. AIHRC, "A Call for Justice: A National Consultation on Past Human Rights Violations in Afghanistan" (Kabul: AIHRC, January 28, 2005), http://www.aihrc.org.af/media/files/Reports/Thematic%20reports/rep29_1_05call4justice.pdf.

66. Francis Fukuyama, *State-Building: Governance and World Order in the 21st Century* (Ithaca, NY: Cornell University Press, 2004).

67. IMF, "Islamic State of Afghanistan, Third Review Under the Staff Monitored Program—Concluding Statement" (February 3, 2005), http://www.imf.org/external/np/ms/2005/020305.htm.

68. Ibid.

69. Ibid.

70. Ibid.

71. Barnett R. Rubin, "The Wrong Voting System," *International Herald Tribune*, March 16, 2005.

72. Carlotta Gall, "Taliban Trek Rocky Road Back to Afghanistan," *New York Times*, March 20, 2005.

73. United Nations Assistance Mission in Afghanistan (UNAMA) and Afghan Independent Human Rights Commission (AIHRC), "Joint Verification of Political Rights," Third Report, 24 August–September 30, 2004, http://www.unhcr.org/refworld/publisher,AIHRC,,,47fdfad10,0.html.

74. See HHRAC surveys, op cit.

75. Rubin, "The Wrong Voting System."

76. General John Abizaid, "Update on the Global War on Terrorism in the U.S. Central Command Area of Responsibility," testimony before the U.S. House of Representatives Armed Services Committee (March 3, 2004), http://www.globalsecurity.org/military/library/congress/2004_hr/040304-abizaid.pdf.

77. United Nations Security Council Resolutions 1368 of September 12, 2001; and 1373 of September 28, 2001.

78. Bonn Agreement, V: 1.

79. Bonn Agreement, Annex II.

80. Bonn Agreement, V: 1.

81. United Nations Security Council Resolution 1386 (December 20, 2001).

82. Bhatia, Lanigan, and Wilkinson, *Minimum Investments, Minimum Results*.

83. "Speaking Out: Afghan Opinions on Rights and Responsibilities" (November 2003), survey undertaken by the Human Rights Research and Advocacy Consortium (HRRAC), (November 2003); "Afghans Most Concerned About Security" (March–April 2004),

national poll conducted by IRI and Williams & Associates, funded by USAID (March–April 2004); Human Rights Research and Advocacy Consortium (HRRAC), *Take the Guns Away: Afghan Voices on Security and Elections* (June–July 2004), survey.

84. Vice Admiral Lowell E. Jacoby, U.S. Navy, director, Defense Intelligence Agency, "Current and Projected National Security Threats to the United States," Statement for the Record, Senate Select Committee on Intelligence (February 24, 2004).

85. "Terms of Reference for CFC and ISAF PRTs in Afghanistan" (January 27, 2005).

86. See, for instance, Médecins Sans Frontières, "After 24 Years of Independent Aid to the Afghan People MSF Withdraws from Afghanistan Following Killing, Threats and Insecurity," transcript of press conference (Kabul, July 28, 2004).

87. Government of Afghanistan, Donor Assistance Database, as of March 22, 2005.

88. World Bank, Asian Development Bank, United Nations Development Program, *Afghanistan: Preliminary Needs Assessment for Recovery and Reconstruction* (January 2002).

89. Government of Afghanistan, *Securing Afghanistan's Future.*

90. Disbursement figures provided by the government of Afghanistan's Donor Assistance Database, http://dadafghanistan.gov.af/dad/.

91. On the aid effort, see Barnett R. Rubin, Abby Stoddard, Humayun Hamidzada, and Adib Farhadi, "Building a New Afghanistan: The Value of Success, the Cost of Failure," Center on International Cooperation, New York University, in cooperation with CARE, 2004.

92. Government of Afghanistan, "National Development Framework, Revised Draft, 2002," http:www.af./resources/itsafig-april/NDF_revised_Draft.pdf.

93. IMF, "Islamic State of Afghanistan: First Review Under the Staff-Monitored Program," November 2004, http://www.imf.org/external/pubs/ft/scr/2004/cr04364.pdf.

94. White House, Office of Management and Budget, "Request to Congress for Fiscal Year 2005 Supplemental Appropriations" (February 14, 2005).

95. For a more detailed treatment, see Barnett R. Rubin, "Road to Ruin: Afghanistan's Opium Economy" (Center for American Progress and Center on International Cooperation, New York University, 2004).

96. Ashraf Ghani, "Where Democracy's Greatest Enemy Is a Flower," *New York Times*, December 11, 2004.

97. Arnaud Aubron, "L'éradication précipitée du pavot peut avoir un coût humain catastrophique," interview with Pierre Arnaud Chouvy, *Libération*, March 12, 2005.

98. UN Office on Drugs and Crime, *Afghanistan Opium Survey 2004*, UNODC (November 2004).

99. Barnett R. Rubin and Omar Zakhilwal, "War on Drugs or War on Farmers?" *Wall Street Journal*, January 11, 2005.

100. UN Office on Drugs and Crime, *Afghanistan: Opium Rapid Assessment Survey. March 2005* (Vienna, 2005).

101. CARE and Center on International Cooperation. "Too Early to Declare Success: Counter-Narcotics in Afghanistan," Afghanistan Policy Brief (March 2005).

102. "Afghanistan's Regional Economic Cooperation: Central Asia, Iran and Pakistan," report of a conference in Bishkek, May 10, 2004 (Kabul: UNDP, 2004), http://www.undp.org.af/Publications/KeyDocuments/2004_bishkek_conference_report.pdf.

103. Sarah Lister, "Caught in Confusion: Local Government Structures in Afghanistan" (Kabul: AREU, 2005), http://www.areu.org.af/EditionDetails.aspx?EditionId=53&ContentId=7&ParentId=7.

104. Aubron, "L'éradication précipitée du pavot."

105. World Bank "Afghanistan Border States Development Framework" (discussion draft), November 12, 2001.

106. Ibid.

PART THREE

BACK TO WAR

The Death of an Afghan Optimist

Hakim Taniwal [handwritten annotation]

Hekmat Karzai, director of a Centre for Peace and Conflict Studies, called me from Kabul last Sunday. "Barney," he said. "We lost a friend today." A suicide bomber had blown up the car of Hakim Taniwal, the governor of Paktia province on Afghanistan's frontier with Pakistan, killing him and two aides. The attack took place outside Taniwal's office, where I had gotten into the same car with him five weeks earlier, and where we had our final conversation.

I first met Taniwal in Peshawar, Pakistan, in 1985, where he had joined other intellectuals fleeing the Soviet occupation of his homeland. When the scholar and poet Said Bahauddin Majrooh was gunned down in his Peshawar home in February 1988 by radical Islamists favored by Pakistan and the CIA, these scholars started to disperse. Taniwal left for Australia, and would return to his native Afghanistan only after the Karzai government came to power.

As his name indicated, this bearded sociologist was part of the Tanai tribe, one of Afghanistan's border groups so often depicted as fierce and warlike. But Taniwal, educated in Europe, exemplified another side of tribal life: the soft-spoken elder who leads and reconciles by wisdom and eloquence.

Hekmat Karzai, who has documented how tactics such as suicide bombing have migrated to Afghanistan from the new terrorist haven of Iraq, told me that after learning of Taniwal's death, he walked with President Karzai in the garden of Afghanistan's presidential palace. How, they wondered, could they still ask Afghanistan's professionals to help govern the country? Yet without them, the government could not possibly meet popular expectations, could not begin to restore hope to a nation nearly bereft of that emotion. The last time we spoke, Taniwal repeatedly emphasized that stability was possible only with the support of ordinary Afghans. "We should invest in peace," he said, "not in fighting." He backed military operations based on precise intelligence, but such operations, he believed—even if they killed, captured, or routed some Taliban—would have little long-lasting effect without popular support and economic development. Elders from ten provinces,

military operations based on intelligence [handwritten annotation]

Originally published in *Washington Post Outlook*, September 17, 2006.

whom I met the day before my visit with Taniwal, had agreed, denouncing corrupt state officials. "The people have totally lost trust in the government," they told me.

The Taliban "are slowly neutralizing the people," Taniwal said. "The government can't protect them, so they will go to the other side. They will not help the government to keep security." An elder from the neighboring province of Paktika had offered a similar conclusion: "If the people were not distressed with the current government, the Taliban could not do anything. If the government starts negotiation with the elders and recognizes them, then we will be the police for the government." A minister in Kabul estimated the annual cost of putting elders in each district on the government payroll at $5 million—a small price to pay for greater stability in a country where violence such as the suicide bomb that killed Taniwal is increasingly resembling that of Iraq in intensity, if not yet in scope.

Taniwal and I did not debate whether Pakistan was supporting the Taliban. As we sat a few miles from the frontier between the two countries—the Pakistani tribal district of North Waziristan was a two-hour drive away on a dangerous road—the answer was too obvious. "All the Taliban were once in Afghanistan," Taniwal said. "Now they are in Pakistan. The Taliban are helped by the [Pakistani] government." As we ate lunch at his home, a call from the police told of a suicide attack against a convoy on that very road to Pakistan.

Taniwal opposed big offensives by the U.S.-led coalition. "They roll over and flatten the whole area," he said. "But the enemy just goes from our side to the other side." The other side was Pakistan, where Taniwal, like so many other Afghans, had found a combination of refuge and persecution. Pakistan was then negotiating a truce with Taliban who had gained control of most of North Waziristan. The final agreement, announced four days before Taniwal's killing, ceded control of the area to the militants in return for expelling "foreigners" (Arabs, Chechens, Uzbeks, and others) and ending infiltration into Afghanistan. According to reports from the region, however, the suicide bomber who killed Taniwal four days later may have been sent on his mission from Waziristan.

Taniwal wanted the coalition to "pressure Pakistan more and more to keep the people there and also arrest and send them to Afghanistan." But for him, pressuring Pakistan was aimed not at destroying the Taliban but reintegrating them. He wanted them, and all Afghans, "not to solve problems with the Kalashnikov. The Taliban should join with the government, the society, and have their own party," like the Taliban's sympathizers in Pakistan, who run in elections.

Though he asked me to keep this confidential, his death allows me—indeed, it obligates me—to reveal that he also advocated settling Afghanistan's historic conflict with Pakistan over the Pashtun territories across the frontier known as the Durand Line, which Afghanistan has never recognized as a border, even under the Taliban. "All the troubles up until now have been because of this problem," Taniwal said. Afghanistan built its army with Soviet aid to counter Pakistan, a U.S. ally. As a result, he said, "we did not gain Pashtunistan, but we almost lost Afghanistan." If international mediators can help resolve this conflict, "then there will be peace, development, business," Taniwal said. "Then Pakistan will be secure, and Afghanistan will be secure."

Taniwal feared that the United States and the current Afghan government would make the same errors as the Soviets and the governments they supported, but he recognized the difference between the two eras. "This is not an occupation," he said. "Afghanistan was a base for terrorists. These bases have been destroyed. Now they are trying again, and we have to fight back. But we should not make mistakes. Afghanistan is slowly going to be like the problem in Iraq if we don't solve these problems."

He put on his turban. We left his office, accompanied by a few lightly armed guards, and walked toward his car.

14

Saving Afghanistan

Taliban Resurgent

Afghanistan has stepped back from a tipping point. At the cost of taking and inflicting more casualties than in any year since the start of Operation Enduring Freedom in 2001 (and four times as many as in 2005), NATO troops turned back a frontal offensive by the Taliban last summer (2006). The insurgents aimed to capture a district west of Kandahar, hoping to take that key city and precipitate a crisis in Kabul, the capital. Despite this setback, however, the Taliban-led insurgency is still active on both sides of the Afghan-Pakistani border, and the frontier region has once again become a refuge for what President George W. Bush once called the main threat to the United States: "terrorist groups of global reach." Insurgents in both Afghanistan and Pakistan have imported suicide bombing, improvised-explosive technology, and global communications strategies from Iraq; in the south, attacks have closed 35 percent of the schools. Even with opium production at record levels, slowing economic growth is failing to satisfy the population's most basic needs, and many community leaders accuse the government itself of being the main source of abuse and insecurity. Unless the shaky Afghan government receives both the resources and the leadership required to deliver tangible benefits in areas cleared of insurgents, the international presence in Afghanistan will come to resemble a foreign occupation that Afghans will ultimately reject.

For decades—not only since 2001—U.S. policymakers have underestimated the stakes in Afghanistan. They continue to do so today. A mere course correction will not be enough to prevent the country from sliding into chaos. Washington and its international partners must rethink their strategy and significantly increase both the resources they devote to Afghanistan and the effectiveness of their use. Only dramatic action can reverse the perception, common among both Afghans and their neighbors, that Afghanistan is not a high priority for the United States—and that the Taliban are winning as a result. Washington's appeasement

Originally published in *Foreign Affairs* 86: 1 (January–February 2007): 57–78.

of Pakistan, diversion of resources to Iraq, and perpetual underinvestment in Afghanistan—which gets less aid per capita than any other state with a recent postconflict rebuilding effort—have fueled that suspicion.

Contrary to the claims of the Bush administration, whose attention after the September 11 attacks quickly wandered off to Iraq and grand visions of transforming the Middle East, the main center of terrorism "of global reach" is in Pakistan. Al-Qaeda has succeeded in reestablishing its base by skillfully exploiting the weakness of the state in the Pashtun tribal belt, along the Afghan-Pakistani frontier. In the words of one Western military commander in Afghanistan, "Until we transform the tribal belt, the U.S. is at risk."

Far from achieving that objective in the 2001 Afghan war, the U.S.-led coalition merely pushed the core leadership of al-Qaeda and the Taliban out of Afghanistan and into Pakistan, with no strategy for consolidating this apparent tactical advance. The Bush administration failed to provide those Taliban fighters who did not want to defend al-Qaeda with a way to return to Afghanistan peacefully, and its policy of illegal detention at Guantánamo Bay and Bagram Air Base, in Afghanistan, made refuge in Pakistan, often with al-Qaeda, a more attractive option.

The Taliban, meanwhile, have drawn on fugitives from Afghanistan, newly minted recruits from undisrupted training camps and militant madrasas, and tribesmen alienated by civilian casualties and government and coalition abuse to reconstitute their command structure, recruitment and funding networks, and logistical bases in Pakistan. On September 19, 2001, Pakistani President Pervez Musharraf told his nation that he had to cooperate with Washington in order to "save Afghanistan and Taliban from being harmed"; accordingly, he has been all too happy to follow the Bush administration's instructions to focus on al-Qaeda's top leadership while ignoring the Taliban. Intelligence collected during Western military offensives in mid-2006 confirmed that Pakistan's Inter-Services Intelligence (ISI) was continuing to actively support the Taliban leadership, which is now working out of Quetta, the capital of Balochistan Province, in western Pakistan. As a result, a cross-border insurgency has effectively exploited Afghanistan's impoverished society and feeble government.

In May 2006, Amrullah Saleh, the director of Afghanistan's national intelligence agency, completed an assessment of the threat posed by the insurgency. Saleh, who acted as the Northern Alliance's liaison with the CIA during Operation Enduring Freedom, concluded that political progress in Afghanistan had not been matched by an effective strategy of consolidation. "The pyramid of Afghanistan government's legitimacy," he wrote, "should not be brought down due to our inefficiency in knowing the enemy, knowing ourselves and applying resources effectively." U.S. commanders and intelligence officials circulated Saleh's warning to their field commanders and agents in Afghanistan and their superiors in Washington. Sustaining the achievements of the past five years depends on how well they heed that warning.

"Still Ours to Lose"

In the past year [2006], a number of events have raised the stakes in Afghanistan and highlighted the threat to the international effort there. The future of NATO depends on its success in this first deployment outside of Europe. Although it suffered a setback in the south, the Pakistan-based, Taliban-led insurgency has become ever more daring and deadlier in the southern and eastern parts of the country, while extending its presence all the way to the outskirts of Kabul. NATO deployed to areas neglected by the coalition, most notably to the southern province of Helmand—and the Taliban responded with increased strength and maneuverability. On September 8, a particularly bold attack on a coalition convoy in the city killed 16 people, including two U.S. soldiers, near the U.S. embassy, the most heavily fortified section of Kabul. Even as NATO has deployed its forces across the country—particularly in the province of Helmand, a Taliban stronghold that produces some 40 percent of the world's opium—the Taliban have shown increasing power and agility.

Meanwhile, the effectiveness of the Taliban's limited institutions and the ruthlessness of their retribution against "collaborators" neutralized much of the Afghan population; only successful political consolidation of NATO and coalition military victories can start to build confidence that it is safe to support the government. In some areas, there is now a parallel Taliban state, and locals are increasingly turning to Taliban-run courts, which are seen as more effective and fairer than the corrupt official system. Suicide bombings, unknown in Afghanistan before their successful use by insurgents in Iraq, have recently sown terror in Kabul and other areas. They have also spread to Pakistan.

On the four trips I made to Afghanistan in 2006 (in January, March–April, July–August, and November), the growing frustration was palpable. In July, one Western diplomat who had been in Afghanistan for three years opened our meeting with an outburst. "I have never been so depressed," he said. "The insurgency is triumphant." An elder from Kunar Province, in eastern Afghanistan, said that government efforts against the insurgency were weak because "the people don't trust any of the people in government offices." An elder from the northern province of Baghlan echoed that sentiment: "The people have no hope for this government now." A UN official added, "So many people have left the country recently that the government has run out of passports."

"The conditions in Afghanistan are ripe for fundamentalism," a former minister who is now a prominent member of parliament told me. "Our situation was not resolved before Iraq started. Iraq has not been resolved, and now there is fighting in Palestine and Lebanon. Then maybe Iran. . . . We pay the price for all of it." An elder who sheltered President Hamid Karzai when Karzai was working underground against the Taliban described to me how he was arrested by U.S.

soldiers: they placed a hood on his head, whisked him away, and then released him with no explanation. "What we have realized," he concluded, "is that the foreigners are not really helping us. We think that the foreigners do not want Afghanistan to be rebuilt."

Yet no one I spoke to advocated giving up. One of the same elders who expressed frustration with the corruption of the government and its distance from the people also said, "We have been with the Taliban and have seen their cruelty. People don't want them back." A fruit trader from Kandahar complained: "The Taliban beat us and ask for food, and then the government beats us for helping the Taliban." But he and his colleagues still called Karzai the country's best leader in thirty years—a modest endorsement, given the competition, but significant nonetheless. "My working assumption," said one Western military leader, "is that the international community needs to double its resources. We can't do it on the margins. We have no hedge against domestic and regional counterforces." After all, he noted, the battle for Afghanistan "is still ours to lose."

The Thirty-Year War

The recent upsurge in violence is only the latest chapter in Afghanistan's thirty-year war. That war started as a Cold War ideological battle, morphed into a regional clash of ethnic factionalism, and then became the center of the broader conflict between the West and a transnational Islamist terrorist network.

It is no surprise that a terrorist network found a base in Afghanistan: just as Lenin might have recommended, it picked the weakest link in the modern state system's rusty chain. Today's Afghanistan formed as a buffer state within the sphere of influence of British India. Because the government, then as now, was unable to extract enough revenue from this barren territory to rule it, its function had more to do with enabling an elite subsidized by aid to control the territory as part of the defense of foreign empires than with providing security and governance to the people of Afghanistan. Hence, the oft-noted paradox of modern Afghanistan: a country that needs decentralized governance to provide services to its scattered and ethnically diverse population has one of the world's most centralized governments. That paradox has left the basic needs of Afghanistan's citizens largely unfulfilled—and thus left them vulnerable to the foreign forces that have long brought their own struggles to the Afghan battleground.

In the eighteenth century, as neighboring empires collapsed, Afghan tribal leaders seized opportunities to build states by conquering richer areas in the region. In 1715, Mirwais Khan Hotak (of the same Kandahari Pashtun tribe as the Taliban leader Mullah Muhammad Omar), overthrew the Shia governor of Kandahar, then a province of the Iranian Safavid empire; seven years later, his son sacked Isfahan, the Iranian capital at the time. Subsequently, a Turkmen leader, Nader Shah, captured Isfahan and went on to conquer Kabul and Delhi. When Nader Shah was assassinated in 1747, the commander of his bodyguard, Ahmad Khan Abdali (a member of the same Kandahari Pashtun tribe as President Karzai), retreated back to Kandahar, where, according to official histories, he was made king of the Afghans at a tribal jirga. He led the tribes who constituted his army on raids and in the conquest of Kashmir and Punjab.

The expansion of the British and Russian empires cut off the opportunity for conquest and external predation—undermining the fiscal base of the ruler's power and throwing Afghanistan into turmoil for much of the nineteenth century. As the British Empire expanded northwest from the Indian subcontinent toward Central Asia, it first tried to conquer Afghanistan and then, after two Anglo-Afghan wars, settled for making it a buffer against the Russian empire to the north.

The British established a three-tiered border to separate their empire from Russia through a series of treaties with Kabul and Moscow. The first frontier separated the areas of the Indian subcontinent under direct British administration from those areas under Pashtun tribal control (today this line divides those areas administered by the Pakistani state from the Federally Administered Tribal Agencies). The second frontier, the Durand Line, divided the Pashtun tribal areas from the territories under the administration of the Amir of Afghanistan (Pakistan and the rest of the international community consider this line to be the international border between Afghanistan and Pakistan, although Afghanistan has never accepted it). The outer frontier, the borders of Afghanistan with Russia, Iran, and China, demarcated the British sphere of influence; the British enabled the Amir to subdue and control Afghanistan with subsidies of money and weapons.

In the twentieth century, however, the dissolution of these empires eroded this security arrangement. The Third Anglo-Afghan War, in 1919, concluded with the recognition of Afghanistan's full sovereignty. The country's first sovereign, King Amanullah, tried to build a strong nationalist state. His use of scarce resources for development rather than an army left him vulnerable to revolt, and his effort collapsed after a decade. The British helped another contender, Nadir Shah, consolidate a weaker form of rule. Then, in the late 1940s, came the independence and partition of India, which even more dramatically altered the strategic stakes in the region.

Immediately tensions flared between Afghanistan and Pakistan. Afghanistan claimed that Pakistan was a new state, not a successor to British India, and that all past border treaties had lapsed. A loya jirga in Kabul denied that the Durand Line was an international border and called for self-determination of the tribal territories as Pashtunistan. Skirmishes across the Durand Line began with the covert support of both governments. At the same time, Islamabad was aligning itself with the United States in order to balance India—which led Afghanistan, in turn, to rely on aid from Moscow to train and supply its army. Pakistan, as a result, came to regard Afghanistan as part of a New Delhi–Kabul–Moscow axis that fundamentally challenged its security. With U.S. assistance, Pakistan developed a capacity for covert asymmetric jihadi warfare, which it eventually used in both Afghanistan and Kashmir.

For the first decades of the Cold War, Afghanistan pursued a policy of nonalignment. The two superpowers developed informal rules of coexistence, each supporting different institutions and parts of the country; one Afghan leader famously claimed to light his American cigarettes with Soviet matches. But this arrangement ultimately proved hazardous to Afghanistan's health. An April 1978 coup by communist military officers brought to power a radical faction whose harsh policies provoked an insurgency. In December 1979, the Soviet Union sent in its military to bring an alternative communist faction to power, turning an insurgency into a jihad against the invaders. The United States, Pakistan, Saudi Arabia, and others began spending billions of dollars to back the anticommunist Afghan mujahidin and their Arab auxiliaries—laying the foundations for an infrastructure of regional and global jihad.

The civil war seemed to come to an end with the 1988 Geneva accords, which provided for the withdrawal of Soviet troops (while allowing continued Soviet aid to the communist government in Kabul) and the end of foreign military assistance to the mujahidin. But the United States and Pakistan, intent on wiping out Soviet influence in Afghanistan entirely, ignored the stipulation that they stop arming the resistance. The result was a continuation of the conflict and, eventually, state failure.

In the early 1990s, as the Soviet Union dissolved and the United States disengaged, ethnic militias went to war. Drug trafficking boomed, and Arab and other non-Afghan Islamist radicals strengthened their bases. Pakistan, still heavily involved in Afghanistan's internal battles, backed the Taliban, a radical group of mostly Pashtun clerics (the name means "students"). With Islamabad's help, the Taliban established control over most of Afghanistan by 1998, and the anti-Taliban resistance, organized in a "Northern Alliance" of feuding former mujahidin and Soviet-backed militias, most of them from non-Pashtun ethnic groups, was pushed back to a few pockets of territory in the northeast. As their grip over Afghanistan tightened, the Taliban instituted harsh Islamic law and increasingly allied themselves with Usama Bin Laden, who came to Afghanistan after being expelled from Sudan in 1996.

After the fall of the Soviet Union, Washington assumed that the collapse of Afghanistan into warring chiefdoms—many of them allied with neighboring states or other external forces—was not worth worrying much about. The

Clinton administration began to recognize the growing threat in Afghanistan after the al-Qaeda bombings of two U.S. embassies in Africa in 1998. But it never took decisive action, and when the Bush administration took office it gave priority to other concerns. It took September 11 to force Washington to recognize that a global terrorist opposition was gathering strength—using human and physical capital that the United States and its allies (especially Saudi Arabia) had supplied, through Pakistan's intelligence services, in pursuit of a Cold War strategic agenda.

Opportunities Lost

When the Bush administration overthrew the Taliban after the September 11 attacks, it did so with a "light footprint": using CIA operatives and the Special Forces to coordinate Northern Alliance and other Afghan commanders on the ground and supporting them with U.S. airpower. After a quick military campaign, it backed the UN effort to form a new government and manage the political transition. It also reluctantly agreed to the formation of the International Security Assistance Force (ISAF) to help the new Afghan government provide security and build new military and police forces. In 2003, ISAF came under NATO command—the first-ever NATO military operation outside of Europe—and gradually expanded its operations from just Kabul to most of Afghanistan's thirty-four provinces. About thirty-two thousand U.S. and allied forces are currently engaged in security assistance and counterinsurgency under NATO command, while another eight thousand coalition troops are involved in counterterrorist operations. The UN Assistance Mission in Afghanistan coordinates the international community's support for political and economic reconstruction.

In the immediate aftermath of the Taliban's overthrow, the presence of coalition troops served as a deterrent against both overt external subversion and open warfare among the various forces that had been rearmed by Washington. This deterrent created an opportunity to build a functioning state; that state, however, now at the center, rather than the margins, of global and regional conflict, would have had to connect rather than separate its neighboring regions—a much more demanding goal. Accomplishing that goal would have required forming a government with sufficient resources and legitimacy to secure and develop its own territory, and with a geopolitical identity unthreatening to its neighbors—especially Pakistan, whose deep penetration of Afghan society and politics enables it to play the role of spoiler whenever it chooses. Such a project would have meant additional troop deployments by the United States and its partners, especially in the border region, and rapid investment in reconstruction. It also would have required political reform and economic development in the tribal areas of Pakistan.

Too little of this happened, and both Afghanistan and its international partners are paying the consequences. Rearming warlords empowered leaders the Afghan people had rejected; enabling the Northern Alliance to seize Kabul put those whom Pakistan most mistrusted in charge of the security forces. And the White House's opposition to "nation building" led to major delays in Afghanistan's reconstruction.

Effective economic aid is vital to addressing the pervasive poverty that debilitates the government and facilitates the recruitment of unemployed youths into militias or the insurgency. Economically and socially, Afghanistan remains far behind its neighbors: it is the poorest country in the world outside of sub-Saharan Africa, and its government remains weak and ineffective. Last year, it raised domestic revenue of about $13 per capita—hardly enough to buy each of its citizens one case of Coca-Cola from the recently opened bottling plant near Kabul, let alone take on all of the important tasks at hand.

Because Afghanistan has been so poor for so long, real nondrug growth averaged more than 15 percent from 2002 until this year, thanks in large part to the expenditures of foreign forces and aid organizations and the end of a drought. But growth fell to 9 percent last year, and the UN and the Afghan government reported in November that growth "is still not sufficient to generate in a relatively short time the large numbers of new jobs necessary to substantially reduce poverty or overcome widespread popular disaffection. The reality," the report intoned, "is that only limited progress has been achieved in increasing availability of energy, revitalizing agriculture and the rural economy, and attracting new investment."

High unemployment is fueling conflict. As a fruit trader in Kandahar put it to me, "Those Afghans who are fighting, it is all because of unemployment." This will only get worse now that the postwar economic bubble has been punctured. Real estate prices and rents are dropping in Kabul, and occupancy rates are down. Fruit and vegetable sellers report a decline in demand of about 20 percent, and construction companies in Kabul report a significant fall in both employment and wages. A drought in some parts of the country has also led to displacement and a decline in agricultural employment, for which the record opium poppy crop has only partially compensated.

Moreover, the lack of electricity continues to be a major problem. No new major power projects have been completed, and Kabulis today have less electricity than they did five years ago. While foreigners and wealthy Afghans power air conditioners, hot-water heaters, computers, and satellite televisions with private generators, average Kabulis suffered a summer without fans and face a winter without heaters. Kabul got through the past two winters with generators powered by diesel fuel purchased by the United States; this year the United States made no such allocation.

Rising crime, especially the kidnapping of businessmen for ransom, is also leading to capital flight. Although no reliable statistics are available, people throughout the country, including in Kabul, report that crime is increasing—and complain that the police are the main criminals. Many report that kidnappers and robbers wear police uniforms. On August 24, men driving a new vehicle with tinted windows and police license plates robbed a bank van of $360,000 just blocks away from the Ministry of the Interior.

The corruption and incompetence of the police force (which lacks real training and basic equipment) were highlighted after riots in May 2006, set off by the crash of a U.S. military vehicle. Rioters chanted slogans against the United States and President Karzai and attacked the parliament building, the offices of media outlets and nongovernmental organizations, diplomatic residences, brothels, and hotels and restaurants that purportedly served alcohol. The police, many of whom disappeared, proved incompetent, and the vulnerability of the government to mass violence became clear. Meanwhile, in a sign of growing ethno-factional tensions within the governing elite, Karzai, a Pashtun (the Pashtun are the largest ethnic group in Afghanistan), suspected opposition leaders of fomenting violence by demonstrators, who were largely from Panjshir, the home base of the main Northern Alliance group. (Panjshiri leaders deny the charge.) Karzai responded not by strengthening support for police reform but by appointing commanders of a rival Northern Alliance group to positions in the police force. Karzai argued that he was forced into such an unpalatable balancing act because of the international community's long-standing failure to respond to his requests for adequate resources for the police.

The formation of the Afghan National Army, which now has more than thirty thousand troops, has been one of the relative success stories of the past five years, but one reason for its success is that it uses mostly fresh recruits; the sixty thousand experienced fighters demobilized from militias have, instead of joining the army, joined the police, private security firms, or organized-crime networks—and sometimes all three. One former mujahidin commander, Din Muhammad Jurat, became a general in the Ministry of the Interior and is widely believed (including by his former mujahidin colleagues) to be a major figure in organized crime and responsible for the murder of a cabinet minister in February 2002. (He also works with U.S. Protection and Investigations, a Texas-based firm that provides international agencies and construction projects with security guards, many of whom are former fighters from Jurat's militia and current employees at the Ministry of the Interior.)

Meanwhile, the drug economy is booming. The weakness of the state and the lack of security for licit economic activity has encouraged this boom, and according to the UN Office on Drugs and Crime opium poppy production in the country reached a record 6,100 metric tons last year, surpassing the 2005 total by 49 percent. This increase belies past claims of progress, made on the basis of a 5 percent cultivation decrease in 2005. Although the decrease was due almost entirely to the political persuasion of farmers by the government, the United States failed to deliver the alternative livelihoods the farmers expected and continued to pressure the Afghan government to engage in counterproductive crop eradication. The Taliban exploited the eradication policy to gain the support of poppy growers.

Counternarcotics efforts provide leverage for corrupt officials to extract enormous bribes from traffickers. Such corruption has attracted former militia commanders who joined the Ministry of the Interior after being demobilized. Police chief posts in poppy-growing districts are sold to the highest bidder: as much as $100,000 is paid for a six-month appointment to a position with a monthly salary of $60. And while the Taliban have protected small farmers against eradication efforts, not a single high-ranking government official has been prosecuted for drug-related corruption.

Drugs are only part of a massive cross-border smuggling network that has long provided a significant part of the livelihoods of the major ethnic groups on the border, the Pashtun and the Baluch. Al-Qaeda, the Taliban, warlords, and corrupt officials of all ethnic groups profit by protecting and preying on this network. The massive illicit economy, which constitutes the tax base for insecurity, is booming, while the licit economy slows.

Sanctuary in Pakistan

Pakistan's military establishment has always approached the various wars in and around Afghanistan as a function of its main institutional and national security interests: first and foremost, balancing India, a country with vastly more people and resources, whose elites, at least in Pakistani eyes, do not fully accept the legitimacy of Pakistan's existence. To defend Pakistan from ethnic fragmentation, Pakistan's governments have tried to neutralize Pashtun and Baluch nationalism, in part by supporting Islamist militias among the Pashtun. Such militias wage asymmetrical warfare on Afghanistan and Kashmir and counter the electoral majorities of opponents of military rule with their street power and violence.

The rushed negotiations between the United States and Pakistan in the immediate aftermath of September 11 changed Pakistan's behavior, but not its interests. Supporting the Taliban was so important to Pakistan that Musharraf even considered going to war with the United States rather than abandon his allies in Afghanistan. Instead, he tried to persuade Washington to allow him to install a "moderate Taliban" government, or failing that, at least to prevent the

Northern Alliance, which Pakistanis see as allied with India, from entering Kabul and forming a government. The agreement by Washington to dilute Northern Alliance control with remnants of Afghanistan's royal regime did little to mollify the generals in Islamabad, to say nothing of the majors and colonels who had spent years supporting the Taliban in the border areas. Nonetheless, in order to prevent the United States from allying with India, Islamabad acquiesced in reining in its use of asymmetrical warfare, in return for the safe evacuation of hundreds of Pakistani officers and intelligence agents from Afghanistan, where they had overseen the Taliban's military operations.

The United States tolerated the quiet reconstitution of the Taliban in Pakistan as long as Islamabad granted basing rights to U.S. troops, pursued the hunt for al-Qaeda leaders, and shut down A. Q. Khan's nuclear-technology proliferation network. But five years later, the safe haven Pakistan has provided, along with continued support from donors in the Persian Gulf, has allowed the Taliban to broaden and deepen their presence both in the Pakistani border regions and in Afghanistan. Even as Afghan and international forces have defeated insurgents in engagement after engagement, the weakness of the government and the reconstruction effort—and the continued sanctuary provided to Taliban leaders in Pakistan—has prevented real victory.

In his September 21, 2006, testimony before the Senate Foreign Relations Committee, James Jones, a Marine Corps general and the supreme allied commander, Europe, for NATO, confirmed that the main Taliban headquarters remains in Quetta. According to Western military officials in Afghanistan, intelligence provides strong circumstantial evidence that Pakistan's ISI is providing aid to the Taliban leadership shura (council) there.

Another commanders' shura, directing operations in eastern Afghanistan, is based in the Pakistani tribal agencies of North and South Waziristan. It has consolidated its alliance with Pakistani Taliban fighters, as well as with foreign jihadi fighters. In September, Pakistani authorities signed a peace deal with "tribal elders of North Waziristan and local mujahidin, Taliban, and ulama [Islamic clergy]," an implicit endorsement of the notion that the fight against the U.S. and NATO presence in Kabul is a jihad. (During his visit to the United States in September 2006, Musharraf mischaracterized this agreement as only with "an assembly of tribal elders.") According to the agreement, the Taliban agreed not to cross over into Afghanistan and to refrain from the "target killing" of tribal leaders who oppose the group, and the foreign militants are expected to either live peacefully or leave the region. But only two days after the agreement was signed, two anti-Taliban tribal elders were assassinated; U.S. military spokespeople claim that cross-border attacks increased threefold after the deal.

Farther north, the veteran Islamist leader Gulbuddin Hikmatyar, a favorite of the ISI since 1973, operates from the northwestern Pakistani city of Peshawar and from the Bajaur and Mohmand tribal agencies, on the border with northeast Afghanistan. This is where a U.S. Predator missile strike killed between seventy and eighty people in a militant madrasa on October 30, 2006, and where Bin Laden and Ayman al-Zawahiri, al-Qaeda's number two leader, are most likely to be found.

The strength and persistence of the insurgency cannot be explained solely by the sanctuary the Taliban enjoy in Pakistan. But few insurgencies with safe havens abroad have ever been defeated. The argument that poverty and under-development, rather than Pakistani support, are responsible for the insurgency does not stand up to scrutiny: northern and western Afghanistan are also plagued by crime and insecurity, and yet there is no coordinated antigovernment vio-lence in those regions.

The Center Can Hold

For several years, Washington has responded to the repeated warnings from Karzai about the Taliban's sanctuary in Pakistan by assuring him that Islamabad is cooperating, that public protests are counterproductive, and that the United States will take care of the problem. But assurances that U.S. forces would soon mop up the "remnants" of the Taliban and al-Qaeda have proved false. Nor did the United States offer adequate resources to Karzai to allow him to strengthen the Afghan state and thereby bolster resistance to the Taliban. Karzai's short-term strategy of allying himself with corrupt and abusive power holders at home—a necessary response, he says, to inadequate resources—has further un-dermined the state-building effort.

Western and Afghan officials differ over the extent to which Pakistan's aid to the Taliban is ordered by or tolerated at the highest levels of the Pakistani military, but they have reached a consensus, in the words of one senior West-ern military leader, that Pakistani leaders "could disrupt the senior levels of [Taliban] command and control" but have chosen not to. Disrupting com-mand and control—not preventing "infiltration," a tactical challenge to which Pakistan often tries to divert discussion—is the key to an overall victory. That will require serious pressure on Pakistan.

So far, the United States and its allies have failed even to convey a consistent message to Islamabad. U.S. officials should at least stop issuing denials on behalf of Islamabad, as General John Abizaid, the commander of U.S. forces in the Middle East, did in Kabul on August 27 when he claimed that he "absolutely does not believe" that Pakistan is helping the Taliban. NATO and the coalition members have similarly failed to devise a common course of action, in part out of the fear that doing so could cause Pakistan to reduce its cooperation on counterterrorism. But failing to address Pakistan's support of the Taliban amounts to an acceptance of NATO'S failure. The allies must send a strong message to Pakistan: that a lack of forceful action against the Taliban command in Baluchistan constitutes a threat to international peace and security as defined in the UN Charter. Pakistan's leaders, who are eager to show that their government is a full participant in the international community (partly in order to establish parity with India), will seek to avoid such a designation. Washington must also take a stand. Pakistan should not continue to benefit from U.S. military assistance and international aid as long as it fails even to try to dismantle the Taliban's command structure.

On this issue, as on others, Washington should reverse the Bush administration's policy of linking as many local conflicts as possible to the global "war on terror" and instead address each on its own terms. A realistic assessment of Pakistan's role requires not moving Pakistan from the "with us" column to the "against us" in the "war on terror" account books but recognizing that Pakistan's policy derives from the perceptions, interests, and capabilities of its leaders, not from those of the U.S. government. The haven and support the Taliban receive in Pakistan are partly a response to claims Afghanistan has made against Pakistan and are also due to Islamabad's concern about both Indian influence in Afghanistan and Afghan backing for Pashtun and Baluch nationalists operating across the Durand Line.

Accordingly, unified pressure on Pakistan should be accompanied by efforts to address Islamabad's core concerns. The United States and its allies should encourage the Afghan government to open a domestic debate on the sensitive issue of recognition of the Durand Line in return for guarantees of stability and access to secure trade and transport corridors to Pakistani ports. Transforming the border region into an area of cooperation rather than conflict will require reform and development in the tribal territories. And Washington should ask India and Afghanistan to take measures to reassure Pakistan that their bilateral relations will not threaten Islamabad. If, as some sources claim, the Taliban are preparing to drop their maximalist demands and give guarantees against the reestablishment of al-Qaeda bases, the Afghan government could discuss their entry into the political system.

Such a shift in U.S. policy toward Pakistan requires a change from supporting President Musharraf to supporting democracy. Pakistan's people have shown in all national elections that support for extremist parties is marginal. The reassertion of the civilian political center, as well as of Pakistan's business class, which is profiting from the reconstruction of Afghanistan, has provided an opportunity to move beyond the history of the United States relying on military rulers. Washington must forge a stabler relationship with a Pakistan that is at peace with its neighbors and with itself.

Back from the Brink

Creating a reasonably effective state in Afghanistan is a long-term project that will require an end to major armed conflict, the promotion of economic development, and the gradual replacement of opium production by other economic activities. Recent crises, however, have exposed internal weaknesses that underscore the need for not only long-term endeavors but short-term transitional measures as well.

The two fatal weak points in Afghanistan's government today are the Ministry of the Interior and the judiciary. Both are deeply corrupt and plagued by a lack of basic skills, equipment, and resources. Without effective and honest administrators, police, and judges, the state can do little to provide internal security—and if the government does not provide security, people will not recognize it as a government.

In 2005, coalition military forces devised a plan for thoroughgoing reform of the Ministry of the Interior. The president and the minister of the interior appoint administrative and police officials throughout the country. Reform cannot succeed unless President Karzai overhauls the ministry's ineffective and corrupt leadership and fully backs the reform. In any case, this plan, already three years behind that of the Ministry of Defense, will show Afghans no results until mid-2007. In September, the government established a mechanism to vet appointees for competence and integrity. Finding competent people willing to risk their lives in a rural district for $60–70 a month will remain difficult, but if implemented well this vetting process could help avoid appointments such as those hastily made after the riots last spring.

Government officials have identified the biggest problems in civil administration at the district level. In interviews, elders from more than ten provinces agreed, complaining that the government never consults them. Some ministers have proposed paying elders and ulama in each district to act as the eyes and ears of the government, meet with governors and the president, administer small projects, and influence what is preached in the mosques. They estimate the cost of such a program at about $5 million per year. These leaders could also help recruit the two hundred young men from each district who are supposed to serve as auxiliary police. They are to receive basic police training and equipment and serve under a trained police commander. Unlike militias, the auxiliary police are to be paid individually, with professional commanders from outside the district. Elders could be answerable for the behavior of the auxiliary forces.

Courts, too, may require some temporary supplementary measures. Community leaders complain forcefully about judicial corruption, which has led many to demand the implementation of Islamic law, or sharia—which they contrast not to secular law but to corruption. One elder from the province of Paktia said:

Islam says that if you find a thief, he has to be punished. If a murderer is arrested, he has to be tried and executed. In our country, if a murderer is put in prison, after six months he bribes the judge and escapes. If a member of parliament is killed ... his murderer is released after three to four months in prison because of bribery.

Enforcement by the government of the decisions of Islamic courts has always constituted a basic pillar of the state's legitimacy in Afghanistan, and the failure to do so is turning religious leaders, who still wield great influence over public opinion, against the government.

The August 5, 2006, swearing in of a new Supreme Court, which administers the judicial system, makes judicial reform possible, but training prosecutors, judges, and defense lawyers will take years. In the meantime, the only capacities for dispute resolution and law enforcement in much of the country consist of village or tribal councils and mullahs who administer a crude interpretation of sharia. During the years required for reform, the only actual alternatives before much of Afghan society are enforcement of such customary or Islamic law or no law at all. The Afghan government and its international supporters should find ways to incorporate such procedures into the legal system and subject them to judicial or administrative review. Such a program would also put more Islamic leaders—more than twelve hundred of whom have been dropped from the government payroll this year—back under government supervision.

Attempts to inject aid into the government have hit a major bottleneck: in 2005 and 2006, the government spent only 44 percent of the money it received for development projects. Meanwhile, according to the Ministry of Finance, donor countries spent about $500 million on poorly designed and uncoordinated technical assistance. The World Bank is devising a program that will enable the government to hire the technical advisers it needs, rather than trying to coordinate advisers sent by donors in accord with their own priorities and domestic constituencies. The United States should support this initiative, along with a major crash program to increase the implementation capacity of the ministries.

As numerous studies have documented over the years, Afghanistan has not received the resources needed to stabilize it. International military commanders, who confront the results of this poverty every day, estimate that Washington must double the resources it devotes to Afghanistan. Major needs include accelerated road building, the purchase of diesel for immediate power production, the expansion of cross-border electricity purchases, investment in water projects to improve the productivity of agriculture, the development of infrastructure for mineral exploitation, and a massive program of skill building for the public and private sectors.

Afghanistan also needs to confront the threat from its drug economy in a way that does not undermine its overall struggle for security and stability. At first, U.S. policy after the fall of the Taliban consisted of aiding all commanders who had fought on the U.S. side, regardless of their involvement in drug trafficking. Then, when the "war on drugs" lobby raised the issue, Washington began pressuring the Afghan government to engage in crop eradication. To Afghans, this policy has looked like a way of rewarding rich drug dealers while punishing poor farmers.

The international drug-control regime does not reduce drug use, but it does, by criminalizing narcotics, produce huge profits for criminals and the armed groups and corrupt officials who protect them. In Afghanistan, this drug policy provides, in effect, huge subsidies to the enemies of the United States. As long as the ideological commitment to such a counterproductive policy continues—as it will for the foreseeable future—the second-best option in Afghanistan is to treat narcotics as a security and development issue. The total export value of Afghan opium has been estimated to be 30–50 percent of the legal economy. Such an industry cannot be abolished by law enforcement. But certain measures would help: rural development in both poppy-growing and non-poppy-growing areas, including the construction of roads and cold-storage facilities to make other products marketable; employment creation through the development of new rural industries; and reform of the Ministry of the Interior and other government bodies to root out major figures involved with narcotics, regardless of political or family connections.

This year's record opium poppy crop has increased the pressure from the United States for crop eradication, including through aerial spraying. Crop eradication puts more money in the hands of traffickers and corrupt officials by raising prices and drives farmers toward insurgents and warlords. If Washington wants to succeed in Afghanistan, it must invest in creating livelihoods for the rural poor—the vast majority of Afghans—while attacking the main drug traffickers and the corrupt officials who protect them.

Know Thine Enemy, Know Thyself

Contemptuous of nation building and wary of mission creep, the Bush administration entered Afghanistan determined to strike al-Qaeda, unseat the Taliban, and then move on, providing only basic humanitarian aid and support for a new Afghan army. Just as it had in the 1980s, the United States picked Afghan allies exclusively on the basis of their willingness to fight U.S. enemies, rather than on their capacity to bring stability and security to the state. The UN-mediated political transition and underfunded reconstruction effort have only partially mitigated the negative consequences of such a shortsighted U.S. policy.

Some in Washington have accused critics of the effort in Afghanistan of expecting too much too soon and focusing on setbacks while ignoring achievements. The glass, they say, is half-full, not half-empty. But the glass is much less than half-full—and it is resting on a wobbly table that growing threats, if unaddressed, may soon overturn.

U.S. policymakers have misjudged Afghanistan, misjudged Pakistan, and, most of all, misjudged their own capacity to carry out major strategic change on the cheap. The Bush administration has sown disorder and strengthened Iran while claiming to create a "new Middle East," but it has failed to transform the region where the global terrorist threat began—and where the global terrorist threat persists. If the United States wants to succeed in the war on terrorism, it must focus its resources and its attention on securing and stabilizing Afghanistan.

15

Resolving the Pakistan-Afghanistan Stalemate

WITH ABUBAKAR SIDDIQUE

On January 13, 2006, the sleepy village of Damadola in the Bajaur tribal district of Pakistan on the Afghan frontier became the focus of global attention. With the American news networks in the lead, global media broadcast coverage of the Central Intelligence Agency's attempt to kill al-Qaeda's number two, Ayman al-Zawahiri, who had reportedly attended a dinner in the village to commemorate the Muslim holiday Eid-ul-Adha. Pictures of tribal members digging dead bodies from the debris of their bombed-out mud houses were beamed around the globe. Pakistan's Islamist political parties called for severing all ties with the United States for this attack on the country's sovereignty.[1] President Pervez Musharraf, who initially minimized the attack's importance, later announced that at least five top al-Qaeda figures had been killed, although Zawahiri himself had escaped.[2]

Three days later, in what appeared to be a reprisal, a suicide bomber riding a motorcycle blew himself up among spectators of a wrestling match in the southern Afghan town of Spin Boldak, across from the Pakistani border town of Chaman. It was Afghanistan's worst suicide attack, killing twenty-two civilians and leaving dozens more injured.[3]

This was the largest in a rash of suicide attacks in Afghanistan, some of which have taken place even in the relatively secure northern and western provinces.[4] With fifteen hundred violent deaths, more members of the Afghan security forces and the U.S.-led international coalition were killed in combat in 2005 than in any year since the overthrow of the Taliban regime in late 2001. In the first six months of 2006, Afghanistan faced thirty-two suicide attacks, unprecedented in the country's three decades of violence.[5] Since May 2006 violence has reached

---

Originally published as a United States Institute of Peace Special Report (October 2006).

new levels. Some eight hundred insurgents, civilians, and soldiers died in the four southwestern provinces. The reorganized Taliban, operating in Afghanistan from bases in Pakistan, form the bulk of the insurgency, which also includes elements led by the Afghan Islamist Gulbuddin Hikmatyar's Hizb-i-Islami and foreign jihadi forces, including the leadership of al-Qaeda.

The violence, which has spread to both sides of the frontier, escalated in the run-up to President Bush's mid-March 2006 visit to South Asia—especially in Waziristan, a craggy region of 5,000 square miles divided into the South and North Agencies, or tribal districts. Some three hundred Islamist militants, civilians, and Pakistani soldiers died in the fighting, which forced tens of thousands of people to flee the Pakistani town of Miran Shah, administrative headquarters of the North Waziristan tribal district. In neighboring South Waziristan, skirmishes, rocketing, assassinations, and land mine blasts continue.[6] Since al-Qaeda's retreat from Afghanistan in winter 2001, some tribal areas have become a small-scale copy of Taliban-controlled Afghanistan, where Islamist militants can recover and plan fresh operations while gradually imposing their will on the secluded region. Violence also has spread into the adjacent districts of the Northwest Frontier Province (NWFP).[7]

Hot Wars on the Borders

Despite the presence of some eighty thousand Pakistani soldiers, Islamist militias have grown along the border. Before the fighting in Miran Shah in spring 2006, the violence in Waziristan had claimed the lives of some 250 members of the security forces and three hundred civilians. Unofficial casualty counts place the figure much higher.

The Pakistan military also claimed to have killed 194 foreign militants and 552 of their local supporters in periodic operations since mid-2002. The majority of these fighters were Uzbeks, Chechens, and Arabs led by Qari Tahir Yuldashev, erstwhile leader of the Islamic Movement of Uzbekistan, who survived American bombing in the northern Afghan town of Kunduz in 2001. Two senior al-Qaeda figures, Haitham al-Yamani and Abu Hamza Rabia, were killed in North Waziristan in 2005. International media attributed their deaths to Hellfire missiles fired from CIA drones.[8] In April 2006 Pakistani forces killed Muhsin Matwalli Atwah, an Egyptian known as Abdul Rahman, in an air raid north of Miran Shah. Charged with being a bomb maker who had participated in the 1998 bombing of the U.S. embassies in Kenya and Tanzania, Rahman had a $5 million price on his head.[9] A week later a Saudi national, Abu Marwan al-Suri, was killed at a checkpoint in Khar, the administrative headquarters of the Bajaur tribal district. Known for his expertise with explosives, he had been one of the targets of the January 13 strike in Damadola.[10]

Another insurgency along the border, in resource-rich southwestern Baluchistan province, also remains a major headache for Islamabad. Desolate but rich in mineral resources and hydrocarbons, Baluchistan is important to Pakistan's future development. This province provides Pakistan with most of its gas. With $150 million in Chinese assistance, Pakistan is building a major deepwater seaport in the small fishing town of Gwadar. Elsewhere it wants to dig oil and gas wells and excavate gold and other minerals. Today's Baluch nationalist rebels view these projects as exploitation of their province's wealth for the exclusive benefit of the Pakistani state, dominated by military officers and bureaucrats from Punjab and Urdu-speaking migrants from India who often call themselves *muhajirin* (immigrants). The Baluch nationalists call for maximum provincial autonomy and control over their resources before they will agree to mega-development projects such as the Gwadar port.

Since the 1947 creation of Pakistan, autonomy-minded Baluch nationalists have carried out five insurgencies, in 1948, 1958–59, 1962–63, 1973–1977, and 2004–2006. The military suppressed all of these revolts. During the 1970s insurgency six thousand Baluch tribesmen and three thousand Pakistani soldiers died. Some thirty thousand Baluch tribesmen went into exile in southern Afghanistan for more than a decade.[11]

A dormant insurgency in the region escalated in December 2005, when Baluch nationalist guerillas fired rockets at a gathering presided over by Musharraf while he was visiting Baluchistan. By June 2006, hundreds of Baluch militants, civilians, paramilitary fighters, and soldiers had died in the skirmishes and as a result of insurgent sabotage. The killing of Nawab Akbar Bugti, a respected politician and former governor of Baluchistan, made the insurgency both a major national crisis and a critical factor in Pakistan's relations with Afghanistan and India, where governments, parliamentarians, and the press condemned the killing.

The Islamist militancy and ethnic revolt on both sides of the Durand Line, the 2,400-kilometer frontier between Afghanistan and Pakistan, are linked to many complex global and regional problems. Policymakers and journalists say Usama Bin Laden and his deputy Zawahiri are hiding somewhere in the northeastern part of this rugged region. In December 2001, under intense U.S. pressure, Pakistan deployed regular military units in the Kurram and Khyber agencies to block al-Qaeda's exodus from Tora Bora, but a delay in their arrival and the U.S. decision not to deploy available U.S. Marines to the area allowed Bin Laden and his followers to escape. The number of Pakistani troops steadily grew to eighty thousand and drastically changed the region, which had been under "indirect rule" for more than a century.

Afghanistan never has recognized the Durand Line as an international border. The administration of President Hamid Karzai, charging Pakistan with supporting the Taliban, has leaned toward India. Further antagonized, Pakistan blames rising Indian influence in Afghanistan for the violent nationalist insurgency in Baluchistan. This dispute presents a problem for the United States, which has been trying to dislodge al-Qaeda and the Taliban from the region since early 2002. U.S. policies, however, have not addressed the long-standing conflicts over the frontier region.

Pakistan and Afghanistan inherited their multilayered border and its complex governance mechanisms from the British Empire. In the late nineteenth century the British tried to make Afghanistan an isolated buffer state between their empire and Russia, but nineteenth-century border arrangements on the margins of an empire do not work in an area at the heart of twenty-first-century global strategy.

The neighbors now need to resolve the myriad problems of the border region. They have to overcome past differences and circumvent the violence unleashed by nonstate actors, sometimes with official support, to reach a comprehensive settlement. The international community in general and the United States in particular have to facilitate such a process through diplomacy and help pay for the long-overdue reforms and economic development on the rugged frontier. They also may have to press reluctant actors to explore alternatives to deeply entrenched policies. Kabul and Islamabad must formulate policies to promote a peaceful and prosperous future rather than remaining hostages to the bitter disputes of the past.

Old Conflict and New Bitterness

The Durand Line is named after the British foreign secretary, Sir Henry Mortimer Durand, who in 1893 demarcated the boundary with agents of the Afghan Amir Abdul Rahman Khan. The Pakistan side of the border area includes the provinces of Baluchistan, NWFP, and the adjacent FATA. On the Afghan side the frontier stretches from Nuristan province in the northeast to Nimruz in the southwest. The border region is predominantly inhabited by ethnic Pashtuns, who were divided by the Durand Line. The thirty to thirty-five million Pashtuns in Pakistan represent 15–20 percent of the country's population. In Afghanistan they are the largest ethnic group, making up about half its estimated thirty million people. The Baluch also live on both sides of the Durand Line in the southwest border region, as well as in neighboring Iran.

This region's passes and trading routes have connected South Asia to Central and West Asia for millennia. The political and legal structure of the region is a product of centuries of empire building and resistance, but it started to assume its contemporary form in the early nineteenth century, when the British East

India Company was expanding toward northwest India. About twenty-five years after taking Delhi in 1804, the British became concerned about czarist expansion toward Central Asia. During the first Anglo-Afghan war (1840–1842), the British invaded Afghanistan but were defeated by an uprising in Kabul that turned into a rout.

By 1876 Russian advances in Central Asia reached the Amu Darya, the river that now constitutes Afghanistan's northern border. The Afghan amir's efforts to establish friendly relations with his northern neighbor led the British to launch the second Anglo-Afghan war in 1879, deposing the amir and occupying Kabul. This was the peak of the "Great Game," when the European powers vied for control of Central Asia, with Afghanistan as the central arena.

The British forced Amir Yaqub Khan to sign the Treaty of Gandamak in 1879, while their army was occupying Kabul. Successive Afghan governments have repudiated this treaty, claiming it was signed under duress. Afghanistan agreed to let the British open an embassy and gave up control of several frontier districts, including most of today's FATA and parts of Baluchistan. The treaty guaranteed British support to Kabul against external aggression and provided an annual subsidy of money and arms with which the Afghan ruler was to subdue his own territory. Anglo-Russian commissions demarcated Afghanistan's northern and western borders with Central Asia, Iran, and China between 1870 and 1896.

Following the second Anglo-Afghan war, the British set about developing what they hoped would be a durable border regime, involving separate statuses and mechanisms for Afghanistan, the border tribes, and the Pashtun and Baluch territories under the administration of British India. They invited Abdul Rahman Khan, a nephew of Amir Sher Ali Khan living in exile in Russian Turkistan, to assume the throne in 1880. During a brutal twenty-year reign, the "Iron Amir" laid the foundation of modern Afghanistan. He gave the country its administrative institutions and agreed to the formal demarcation of its borders, including the Durand Line. The amir always contended that excluding the tribal territories from Afghanistan was a mistake, as he could control the tribes better than the British could.

The demarcation of the Durand Line required the British to establish a regime to deal with the tribal borderlands. Five tribal regions were placed under the direct control of the central government in Delhi. After the creation of Pakistan in 1947, three new agencies were carved out of other tribal districts. The British devised a special legal structure called the Frontier Crimes Regulations (FCR). Evolving through the late nineteenth century, the regulations were finally promulgated as statutory law under Viceroy Lord Curzon in 1901 and are still the legal regime in FATA.

After the failure of the British "forward policy" in the first Anglo-Afghan war, Delhi settled on a "close border" policy to make the frontier into a buffer. To

British administrators, frontier meant a "wide tract of border country, hinterland or a buffer state." The most important feature of this arrangement was its trans-formation into a "frontier of separation," in contrast to a "frontier of contact." The result was the "threefold frontier." The first frontier was the outer edge of the directly administered territory (the river Indus in the nineteenth century and the settled districts of NWFP in the mid–twentieth century); the second was the Pashtun tribal area between Afghanistan and the settled districts of NWFP, which was placed under indirect rule; and the third comprised the protectorates of Nepal and Afghanistan on the outer edge of the sphere of influence.

In recent times Pakistan has used its support for the anti-Soviet mujahidin and then the Taliban to ensure that in the event of conflict with India, Afghanistan would provide Pakistan with support and use of its land and airspace if needed. Pakistani military planners referred to this as the quest for "strategic depth." The similarity of the threefold frontier to this quest in Afghanistan illustrates the continuity of strategic policy in this region.

The 1907 Anglo-Russian convention formally ended the Great Game. It divided Persia into zones of influence of the two great powers, protecting Afghanistan's western borders from Russian penetration. Both powers agreed to recognize Chinese control over Tibet. Russia conceded Afghanistan to the Brit-ish sphere of influence, but Britain was not to occupy or annex any part of the country or interfere in its internal affairs. Amir Habibullah of Afghanistan de-clared the convention illegal because Afghanistan was not a party to the agreement, but his protest went unheeded.

Popular resistance movements throughout the century of British rule also shaped the border region. At times these were local affairs, as when a clan or a tribe resisted the British; but on other occasions the tribes launched wider movements, sometimes coordinating with the larger Afghan and Indian strug-gles against European colonialism. Charismatic tribal leaders or clerics led many such rebellions. These leaders fought small-scale battles and larger wars, such as the one in Waziristan, where the British kept fifty thousand soldiers, more troops than on the rest of the subcontinent, as late as the 1930s. On other occasions the British used more indirect counterinsurgency methods. Seventy thousand tribal members serving as scouts under British officers suppressed the Great Tribal Uprising of 1897, in which most Pashtun tribes east of the Durand Line joined in an uncoordinated war against the British.

As Afghanistan lacked a modern army, the rulers of Kabul often mobilized the tribes to fight in the early twentieth century. The modernist and nationalist King Amanullah declared jihad for full independence from the British in 1919. Pashtun tribal *lashkars*, or posses, from both sides of the Durand Line fought the monthlong war. Afghanistan subsequently obtained full sovereignty from a weakened British Empire in the 1919 Treaty of Rawalpindi.

In 1929, King Amanullah lost his throne in a revolt led by a Tajik guerrilla leader, Habibullah Kalakani, who was supported by conservative clergy. A tribal posse headed by the king's distant cousin, Nadir Khan, and composed of Pashtuns from both sides of the Durand Line, put an end to the rule of Amir Habibullah II, commonly known as Bacha-yi Saqao (son of the water carrier) in admiration or mockery of his humble origins.

In return for their military services, Nadir Shah gave the tribes of the Loya, or Greater Paktia region of southeastern Afghanistan, maximum tribal autonomy. He exempted them from taxation and conscription on the assumption that they could mobilize lashkars if needed. Throughout the twentieth century Afghanistan also maintained a sizable number of tribal sympathizers east of the Durand Line through honorary and material rewards, including recruitment into the officer corps.[12] Members of the tribes that had fought for Nadir Shah from both sides of the Durand Line predominated among the military officers trained in the Soviet Union, who joined or sympathized with the Afghan communist groups.

Modern Pashtun nationalism emerged in NWFP in 1930, when British troops killed unarmed protesters in Peshawar. Khan Abdul Ghaffar Khan headed the Afghan jirga, which was later called the Khudai Khidmatgars (servants of God). Ghaffar Khan allied with the Indian National Congress to win the 1937 and 1946 elections in NWFP, after which his movement formed the provincial governments. The Khudai Khidmatgars parted ways with Congress in 1946, when the latter accepted the British partition plan providing for a plebiscite in the province on joining India or the new state of Pakistan. This movement demanded inclusion of an option to establish an independent state of Pashtunistan.

In August 1947 two states, India and Pakistan, emerged from the British Indian empire. The Afghan government voted against Pakistan's admission to the United Nations in 1947, arguing that Pakistan should not be recognized as long as the "Pashtunistan" problem remained unresolved. Afghanistan withdrew this objection after only a month, however, and in February 1948 it became one of the first nations to establish diplomatic relations with Pakistan. The Pashtun nationalist Khudai Khidmatgars moderated their stand soon after partition and declared their loyalty to the new country. Some tribal leaders in FATA maintained militias in the name of Pashtunistan. Successive governments in Pakistan tried to handle the Pashtun nationalist claims by suppressing their advocates.

Pakistan then ended the British policy of military control of tribal areas by withdrawing army units from the agencies. Soon Pakistan was able to mobilize a sizable Pashtun tribal posse from both sides of the Durand Line to fight for control of Kashmir, a Muslim majority state, when its maharaja declared accession to India in 1947. Although the tribal members made a spectacular march, they failed to capture Srinagar, the capital of Kashmir. Since 1947 Pakistan and

India each have occupied parts of Kashmir, divided by the line of control. Today Kashmir remains divided between India and Pakistan. India claims that the state of Jammu and Kashmir is now an integral part of the Republic of India, while Pakistan still demands implementation of UN Security Council resolutions calling for a plebiscite on whether Kashmir should join India or Pakistan. Some Kashmiri movements have demanded independence.

The Durand Line border dispute soon brought the Cold War to the Khyber Pass. In July 1949, after a Pakistani bombing raid on an Afghan border village, the Afghan government convened a loya jirga, or grand tribal assembly, in Kabul. This supreme national decision-making body declared support for the Pashtunistan demand. The jirga affirmed the Afghan government's position that Pakistan was a new state rather than a successor state to British India, and all past treaties with the British pertaining to the status of the border were therefore null and void. Such agreements included the 1893 Durand Agreement, the Anglo-Afghan Pact of 1905, the Treaty of Rawalpindi of 1919, and the Anglo-Afghan Treaty of 1921. It reaffirmed Afghanistan's rejection of the 1879 Treaty of Gandamak. Afghanistan eventually turned to the Soviet Union for military aid, because its position on Pashtunistan made it impossible to receive aid from the United States, which was allied with Pakistan.

For Pashtun nationalists in Pakistan and Afghanistan, Pashtunistan meant different things, ranging from an independent country to an autonomous province of Pakistan to an integral part of Afghanistan. The Soviet Union and India paid lip service to Pashtunistan for decades. The Soviets wanted to prevent Afghanistan from joining any Western military alliance and to pressure Pakistan; India wanted to divert Pakistan's military resources by cultivating the fear of an unstable western border.

The Pashtunistan demand served domestic Afghan political purposes as well. In the twentieth century successive Afghan rulers used the issue to strengthen Pashtun ethnic support for the state. By harnessing the state to the Pashtun ethnic cause, however, the government intensified ethno-linguistic rivalry between Pashtuns and non-Pashtuns.

In 1961 relations between the neighbors hit rock bottom when Pakistan closed the border and the countries broke off diplomatic relations. With Afghanistan's principal trade route cut off, the Afghan economy was pressed to the breaking point. Differences within the royal family led to the resignation of Prime Minister Daud Khan in 1963. In 1973, after ten years of constitutional monarchy with a contentious but ineffective parliament that dissolved the government three times, Daud launched a bloodless coup against his cousin, Zahir Shah. He justified it in part by claiming that Zahir's government had neglected Pashtunistan to improve relations with the United States and Pakistan.

Zahir's government was accused of not responding forcefully to the firing of the National Awami Party provincial governments in NWFP and Baluchistan by Pakistani Premier Zulfiqar Ali Bhutto in 1973. These governments were composed mainly of Pashtun and Baluch nationalists. After the dismissals, Nawab Bugti was appointed governor of Baluchistan. Eventually he became the political leader of the 2005–06 Baluch insurgency and was killed by the Pakistan military on August 26, 2006.

After the creation of Bangladesh in 1971, the Pashtun and Baluch nationalist movements along the western borders posed the most active secessionist threats to the remainder of Pakistan. Thus the 1972–1977 government of Zulfiqar Ali Bhutto both cracked down on nationalists and sought to extend Pakistani state authority by bringing economic development to the border region and FATA. It built some roads and hospitals and a few factories.

This meager development effort, however, was not matched by any political reforms. On the contrary, Bhutto's administration strengthened the colonial system by incorporating the border regime into the 1973 constitution. Pakistan also started supporting Afghan Islamists who opposed Daud's secular ethno-nationalism. The Islamists had publicly opposed the partition of Pakistan to create Bangladesh in 1971 and protested against foreign influence in Afghanistan by both the Soviet Union and the West.

The long history of each state offering sanctuary to the other's opponents has built bitterness and mistrust between the two neighbors. This intensified in the 1970s, when Kabul extended shelter to some thirty thousand Marri Baluch tribesmen who had escaped a Pakistani military crackdown after the nationalist insurgency in Baluchistan. Islamabad then extended refuge and military training to Afghan Islamists such as Ahmed Shah Massoud and Gulbuddin Hikmatyar, who staged an abortive uprising with Pakistani support in 1975. Pakistan hosted the Afghan mujahidin in the 1980s, while Afghanistan's pro-Soviet regime provided safe haven to al-Zulfiqar, a militant offshoot of the Pakistan Peoples Party. Headed by Murtaza Bhutto, the group intended to destabilize Gen. Muhammad Zia-ul-Haq's military regime, which had overthrown and hanged Murtaza's father, Zulfiqar Ali Bhutto. The current claims and counterclaims of sheltering each other's opponents indicate that the same strategies may be continuing.

Globalization of the Conflict Around the Borderlands

The final collapse of the Afghan Durrani ruling dynasty with the overthrow of President Daud by communist factions in April 1978 shattered cooperative relations in the borderlands, precipitating the rounds of war that continue. The

Christmas Eve 1979 Soviet invasion was the first major step toward globalizing the conflict in the border region.

The Soviet invasion made Pakistan a frontline ally of the United States. The country's ruling military virtually had a free hand to shape the Afghan resistance based in the refugee camps along the Durand Line. Pakistan wanted to prevent the establishment of Afghan nationalist guerrillas on its soil and thus refused to recognize parties and exiles associated with the old regime. It guided the supplies from the United States, Saudi Arabia, Western Europe, and China toward the Islamists, who were also generously funded by wealthy private donors in the Gulf. The regime of Gen. Muhammad Zia-ul-Haq promoted the jihad in neighboring Afghanistan as part of its overriding priority: using the "Islamization" of Pakistan to legitimize military rule. In the process it militarized and radicalized the border region.

From the funding of thousands of Islamic madrasas, or seminaries, to the arming of domestic Islamist organizations, Pakistan experienced a major transformation. Pakistan engaged in the successive wars in and around Afghanistan—the Cold War struggle, the post–Cold War civil conflict, and the war on terror—as a way of dealing with its basic national security threat: India, a country with more than eight times its population and economic resources. India's elites, at least in Pakistani perceptions, do not fully accept the legitimacy of Pakistan's existence. Pakistan's support for Islamist parties (especially for the Islamic Party of Gulbuddin Hikmatyar) and then for the Taliban-constituted attempts to impose on Afghanistan a government that would never allow an Indian presence on its territory, giving the Pakistani military a secure border and strategic depth. In other words, Pakistan sought to support a client regime in Afghanistan that was supposed to provide a space for the retreat and recuperation of the Pakistani military in case of a confrontation with India. This policy was a continuation under different conditions of the British policy of treating Afghanistan as part of the security buffer zone of South Asia.

After the Soviet withdrawal under the Geneva Accords of April 14, 1988, completed on February 15, 1989, a U.S.-Soviet dialogue tried to prepare the ground for a transitional government to preside over elections. Had they been implemented, the Geneva Accords would have resulted in a weak Afghan government, still close to the Soviet Union but without a Soviet troop deployment. In effect, Afghanistan would have become a de facto buffer within the Soviet sphere of influence. The war continued, however, in the absence of great-power agreement over the political settlement in the borderlands, eventually resulting in state collapse in Afghanistan. The United States and Pakistan pursued an anti-Soviet "rollback" policy (equivalent to the British "forward policy") to wipe out Soviet influence in Afghanistan by continuing to aid and arm the anti-Soviet Afghan guerrillas, the mujahidin. During this period, when many Afghans considered the jihad ended with the departure of Soviet troops, the rollback policy increasingly relied on Salafi Arab fighters, who joined the jihad for very different reasons than Afghans had.

Representative rule in Pakistan was restored following Zia-ul-Haq's death in an air crash in August 1988. The Pashtun nationalist political parties with seats in the Pakistani national and provincial legislatures moderated their demands, replacing the name Pashtunistan with "Pakhtunkhwa," denoting a province for all Pashtuns living east of the Durand Line. Such a province would include NWFP, some districts of Baluchistan, and the tribal agencies. The change to superficially civilian government between 1988 and 1999 hardly affected Pakistan's Afghan policy, which remained in the hands of the military.

In October 1994, the Taliban, a previously unknown group of clerics from the puritanical Sunni Deobandi sect, initiated a military movement to overpower the mujahidin factions. The Taliban originated in Kandahar province of Afghanistan and the neighboring Baluchistan province of Pakistan. They showed to what extent the mass violence, migrations, and ideological mobilization of the past three decades had transformed the border region. They are a phenomenon of the borderland, a joint Afghan-Pakistan network and organization. Afghan refugees, their children, and their grandchildren have coped with and interpreted their experiences in the refugee camps, tribal territories, and urban slums of Pakistan through the lens of the Islamist education that Pakistan's military regime and its Saudi and U.S. patrons offered them alongside their classmates from Pakistan, including FATA.

The unmonitored border and the ungoverned frontier between the two countries provided the space in which Pakistan could use the resulting social networks for asymmetrical warfare that served its strategic purpose on the Afghan and Kashmiri fronts, while sheltering itself through nuclear deterrence from conventional reprisal. The instability of this arrangement twice has precipitated the threat of nuclear escalation, once over the 1999 Pakistani intrusion in Kargil, in Indian-occupied Kashmir, and then over the 2002 attack on the Indian parliament by a Pakistan-based terrorist group.[13]

Pakistan's attempt to stabilize Afghanistan and gain strategic depth through control by the Taliban constituted a reprise with variations on the theme of a forward policy composed by the British Empire. This policy was to place Afghanistan under a nonhostile regime, harsh enough to control opposition with some military and financial assistance, and guarantee that hostile forces (mainly India, but also Russia and Iran) would not gain a foothold in the adjacent territory. Under the British, however, the Afghan ruler was an autocrat who used Islam to strengthen the central state while bringing the clergy under control. Founded as a state for Indian Muslims and basing its power on an alliance of the military and the mosque, Pakistan used Afghan clerics. Their Islamic allegiances would ensure their cooperation against secular "Hindu" India, Pashtun nationalists, and tribal leaders on both sides of the Durand Line.

The Taliban captured Kabul in September 1996. They moved north of the capital in a failed offensive in May–June 1997 but captured most of the north and center of Afghanistan by August 1998, only a few days after the bombing of U.S. embassies in Kenya and Tanzania. These bombings revealed to high-level policymakers and the general public a new dimension of globalization of the Afghan conflict: the consolidation of Usama Bin Laden's international network of anti-Western Islamist militants now known as al-Qaeda.

In the 1980s thousands of Islamist radicals from the Arab world and a lesser number from Southeast Asia flocked to Pakistan to fight and assist the anti-Soviet jihad in Afghanistan. They established support networks in NWFP and bases along the Afghan side of the Durand Line in areas such as the Jaji district of Khost (the al-Masada or "lion's den" camp) and Khugiani district of Nangarhar (Tora Bora). The concept of al-Qaeda formed in Peshawar, Pakistan, in the late 1980s. A decade later it had a somewhat formal organizational structure whose aims and objectives Bin Laden and Zawahiri announced to the world from Khost, Afghanistan, in 1998.

Al-Qaeda was founded in the borderlands, but none of its leaders was Pakistani or Afghan. The war in the borderlands produced the leaders and ideologues of modern global jihad such as Bin Laden, Zawahiri, and the Palestinian scholar Abdullah Azzam, who was killed in Peshawar in November 1989. After the Soviet withdrawal in 1989, many Arabs remained, and a second wave of jihadis gathered in the borderlands. During the 1990s additional waves of Islamists from Chechnya, Central Asia, Chinese Turkistan, Southeast Asia, and Europe joined the Arabs to form a truly global conglomerate.

This globalization of the Afghan conflict also introduced structural changes to Pashtun society and politics on both sides of the Durand Line. The fragmented tribal nature of this polity provided fertile ground for ideological penetration. Pashtun nationalism was modernist and secular, associated with the royalist elite, tribal leaders, and intellectuals. The Islamic conservatives joined the nationalists to oppose foreign domination during British colonialism, but they opposed the adoption of Western or liberal social or political institutions or values. The radical Islamists who began to organize in the 1960s opposed liberal institutions with at least equal fervor, but they tried to Islamize rather than reject institutions or concepts such as the nation-state, political ideology, political party, revolution, and development.

Pashtuns are no more or less prone to extremism than members of any other ethnic group in the region, but intelligence agencies and radical movements have used their cross-border ties and strategic location to spread extremism. The war in Afghanistan provided Pakistan with a golden opportunity to act on its long-standing desire to weaken Pashtun nationalism. It actively supported pan-Islamism among the Afghan refugees while bankrolling Pakistani Islamist parties in the border region. This resulted in a newer brand of Pashtun Islamism, some of whose characteristics were manifested and reinforced during the Taliban's ascent to power in Afghanistan, where pan-Islamist solidarity surpassed tribalism and ethnic cohesion.

Although decades of Pakistani investment in Pashtun Islamism turned it into a formidable political force and reduced the nationalist threat, it also created its own transborder ethnic realities, which are backfiring against its original sponsors, whose primary allegiance is to the state of Pakistan. The operational and strategic vision of a Pakistani nation-state directly clashes with the pan-Islamism of Talibanization, which demands a complete overhaul of the state and society in Pakistan, Afghanistan, and beyond. This new reality, however, corresponds to the goals of some in Pakistan who envisage a broader Islamist union of Pakistan, Afghanistan, and Central Asia.

During the early 1990s, Afghanistan became an international pariah as the United States walked away from the Cold War's last battleground. Successive U.S. administrations did not consider the collapse of Afghanistan as a threat to the United States or a global strategic issue. Not until the attacks of September 11, 2001, did they heed warnings that in the absence of legitimate order in the borderlands, a global terrorist opposition was consolidating its links and building its skills, using the human and physical capital they had supplied to these networks through Pakistan in pursuit of the Cold War strategic agenda.

As described in the previous chapter, the hurried negotiations between the United States and Pakistan immediately after September 11 changed Pakistan's behavior, but not its interests, which the generals in Rwalpindi believed were threatened by the distribution of power codified in the Bonn agreement. Nonetheless, to save its nuclear deterrent and military supply relationship with the United States, Islamabad acquiesced in reining in its support for the Taliban, while keeping the capacity in reserve.

The presence of the United States, the UN, and the International Security Assistance Force (ISAF, the UN-mandated, multinational force in Afghanistan, under NATO command since August 2003) initially acted as a deterrent to both overt external subversion and open warfare among the power holders the United States had rearmed in the war to oust the Taliban. This deterrent created an opportunity to build an Afghan state that could be reintegrated into the regions it borders. Given the cross-border movements of capital, trade, population, arms, ideologies, and identities, however, it was no longer possible for Afghanistan to play the role of a buffer or insulator state separating South Asia, Central Asia, and the Gulf. Instead, Afghanistan would have to become what its government calls a "land bridge" linking these areas.

The prerequisite for the stabilization of Afghanistan under these conditions has been the formation of an Afghan state with sufficient resources and legitimacy to control and develop its territory while posing no threat to any of its neighbors, especially Pakistan. Its deep interpenetration of Afghan society and politics enables Pakistan to play the role of spoiler whenever it chooses. For the United States, such a project would have required additional troops, whether from the coalition or ISAF, especially in border provinces; rapid investment in the infrastructure and development of the country; and an active program of diplomacy and regional cooperation. The Bush administration's opposition to U.S. investment in "nation building," which it did not relax until 2003, led to delays in all such projects. Nor did the United States or others address the long-standing conflicts over the frontier.

In this context, especially given the new U.S. doctrine of preventive war, Pakistan and other neighbors of Afghanistan see the consolidation of a state dependent on the United States as a long-term threat. Pakistan sees the United States increasingly favoring India, particularly in the area of nuclear cooperation, and faces an Afghan government whose rhetoric has become more confrontational. As a result, Pakistan sees no strategic advantage in eliminating the Taliban, who have established themselves in parts of southwestern and southeastern Afghanistan, control parts of FATA, and have their main headquarters and support networks in Baluchistan. The ability of this Pakistan-based group to destabilize Afghanistan sends a message that Islamabad, not Delhi or Kabul, is the key to stability in the region.

These transborder political and military networks are reinforced by the economic components of "network war," which relies on transnational links of communications, funding, recruitment, and armament, rather than a territorial base. Trafficking in drugs, arms, and other items—including people—is an important element of network war, and smuggling is the classic livelihood of the borderlands; both of the major frontier ethnic groups (Pashtuns and Baluch) gain much of their income from it. The borderlands already have become a land bridge for the criminal (drugs) and criminalized (transit trade) economies of the region. The transnational economic actors exploit the weakness and illegitimacy of statehood in the region to pursue profit, part of which pays for protection provided by transnational and parallel military and political forces. The fight to protect these transnational economic activities is increasingly inseparable from the armed conflicts around the borderlands.

The Anomaly of FATA

With an area of 27,000 square kilometers, slightly larger than Luxembourg, and a 600-kilometer border with Afghanistan, FATA is the real administrative, political, and economic anomaly in the border region. FATA is divided into seven agencies, or administrative units, which from north to south are Bajaur, Mohmand, Khyber, Orakzai, Kurram, and North and South Waziristan. A few more frontier regions adjacent to the settled districts of Peshawar, Kohat, Dera Ismail Khan, Bannu, and Tank are also part of FATA. The area had a population of some 3.1 million people at the time of the 1998 census, and current unofficial estimates range up to 7 million, mostly ethnic Pashtuns whose tribes straddle the Durand Line.[14]

Pakistan's 1973 constitution gives the president executive authority over the region. But he does not exercise this authority in Islamabad, where the people of FATA have representatives in the national assembly. The area is largely ruled from Peshawar, where the governor of NWFP, a presidential appointee, exercises enormous authority with no legislative check. The provincial government controls all the agencies that deliver services such as health care, education, support for agriculture, and communications in the tribal areas, but the people of FATA have no representation in the NWFP provincial assembly to which the government is accountable.

The real authority in a tribal agency is the political agent. He combines legislative, law enforcement, and economic management functions. Apart from being the top civilian official in the territory, the political agent is the judge, jury, police chief, jail warden, district magistrate, and public prosecutor. He collects and disburses revenue with virtually no accountability. He also oversees all development schemes and public service departments.

The political agent governs through the Frontier Crimes Regulations (FCR). For more than a century these regulations have been used as a whip to control the border tribes. Under them a political agent may impose an economic blockade or siege of "hostile" or "unfriendly" tribes or inflict fines on whole communities where certain "crimes" have been committed. He can prohibit the construction of houses and raze houses of tribal members as punishment for not meeting the agent's demands. Some of the harshest clauses establish collective responsibility, under which an entire tribe can be held responsible for crimes committed by a single member or occurring anywhere within that tribe's territory. The law empowers the political agent to deliver multiyear jail sentences without due process or right of appeal to any superior court. The political agent also can appoint and refer civil and criminal cases to a handpicked jirga, or tribal council. During the 2003–2006 crises in Waziristan, political agents invoked all of these clauses.

The administration also manipulates local politics through its exploitation of the *lungi* or *malaki* system of appointed tribal leadership. Handpicked tribal leaders are showered with government allowances and other economic incentives in return for loyalty. Every tribal administrator controls millions of dollars in secret funds to buy loyalty, leading to widespread corruption in the administration.

The British and their Pakistani successors have claimed that the FCR are rooted in tribal customs and traditions, but they contradict the egalitarian Pashtun ethos. The regulations also contradict the Pakistani constitution, which guarantees fundamental rights for all its citizens and respect for international human rights conventions. The administrative arrangements of FATA deprive tribal members of political participation and economic development. All political parties, aid agencies, and civil society organizations are banned from working in the tribal areas, although radical extremist clerics are free to preach and campaign. Such clerics consequently won most of the elections held on a nonparty basis after adult franchise was introduced in 1996.[15]

The economic situation in the borderlands is equally dire. The wars in and over Afghanistan during the past three decades have transformed the economy of these tribal territories from one based on subsistence agriculture and nomadic pastoralism to dependence on the unregulated, cross-border trade of goods, including contraband such as drugs and arms. The area depends on smuggling routes that exploit the Afghan Transit Trade Agreement, under which goods may be imported duty-free into Pakistan for reexport to Afghanistan; many are illegally reexported to or simply sold in Pakistan. In 2001 the World Bank estimated the value of such trade, as well as other transit trade through Afghanistan, at nearly $1 billion per year.

The deployment of military forces along Pakistan's western border, however, has threatened this cross-border trade. Pakistan and Afghanistan have set some of their respective tariff levels at par, eliminating most of the profit for smugglers. As both countries approach admission to the World Trade Organization, the cross-border trade may dry up. The unavailability of alternative livelihoods for FATA is likely to add a new dimension of economic resistance to the struggles in the region, as does the lack of alternative livelihoods for opium poppy farmers and opiate traders in Afghanistan.

Human development indicators in FATA are no better than in neighboring Afghanistan. The poverty level is as high as 60 percent, twice those in the rest of Pakistan.[16] Official statistics estimate the literacy rate in the tribal territories at 17.4 percent: 29.5 percent for men and less than 3 percent for women. The primary school enrollment rate is 68 percent for boys and 19 percent for girls. Only 102 colleges (equivalent to Western high schools) exist in the tribal areas, and only two or three of them are for women. On the other hand, madrasas have mushroomed, and today up to 300 operate in the region. Only 524 medical doctors practice in FATA, one for every 6,307 people, and there is no health care infrastructure in some remote regions. Only two or three hospitals in all of FATA have rudimentary facilities for complex surgical procedures.[17]

With 2.4 percent of the national population, FATA receives only about 1 percent of the national budget. The per capita development allocation is one-third of the national average. No aid agencies or NGOs can work in the tribal belt, while in the other regions of the country they run substantial development projects. The per capita income in FATA is half that of Pakistan's national average. The region had the country's highest emigration ratio even before the advent of Islamist militancy, which, along with army offensives, has further displaced tens of thousands of people. The unemployment rate is 60–80 percent, or even close to 100 percent seasonally, if remittances and migrant labor are not counted.[18]

Toward a Border Settlement

Pakistan enunciated its position on the border in 1947:

> [The] Durand Line delineated in the 1893 treaty is a valid international boundary subsequently recognized and confirmed by Afghanistan on several occasions. The drawing of this international border terminated any Afghan sovereignty over the territory or influence over the people east of [the] Durand Line. Pakistan as a successor state to British India derived full sovereignty over this region and its people and has all the rights and obligation of a successor state. In addition, the question of self-determination for Pashtuns was foreclosed by the British supervised plebiscite held in 1947 in NWFP in which 99 percent of votes cast were in favor of joining Pakistan. The Tribal Areas too expressed their assent through special Jirgas.[19]

No Afghan government has accepted these claims. Despite Afghanistan's formal position, however, no government has made any serious effort to advance territorial claims either bilaterally or in international forums. Instead, its governments have used these claims as bargaining chips or to address domestic political concerns.

In practice, Pakistan has done more than Afghanistan to undermine the status of the Durand Line as an international border. Successive governments in Islamabad have exploited the porosity of the threefold frontier to use covert asymmetrical warfare as a tool of national security policy. Even though the Pakistani military's deliberate fashioning of the Afghan resistance on an Islamist model gave Pakistan strategic depth and neutralized Afghan nationalism, it also relied on transnational networks that ignored the Durand Line as consistently as any border tribe. Pakistan is now paying the price for this policy by losing control of much of the frontier area to groups it has supported, groups that exploit their ties in Afghanistan just as the Taliban exploit their ties in Pakistan.

The Pakistan military's relationship with cross-border Islamist groups also affected the domestic situation in Pakistan. It strengthened and spread beyond an alliance vis-à-vis Afghanistan and Kashmir to cooperation in domestic politics, including elections. In the words of Husain Haqqani, a Pakistani author and former adviser to the country's government [and later Pakistan's ambassador to Washington, forced to resign over the "Memogate" affair], "[The] Islamists staunchly adopted the Pakistani state's national security agenda and, in return, an increasing number of officers accepted the Islamist view of a more religious state."[20] Increasingly, however, Islamist transnational goals have triumphed over the state's strategic objectives, as the Islamists have established a strategic presence in Pakistani state institutions, military, civil society, and campuses.

Since September 11, a clear tension has developed between these visions. Pakistan's stated position as a frontline ally in the "war on terrorism" has led to tensions within the Islamist-military alliance over arresting al-Qaeda leaders, cooperating with the United States, and cracking down on the Taliban and local militants. Islamist militancy, however, remains Pakistan's most successful strategic weapon against Indian regional hegemony, including its penetration into Afghanistan. However, by providing $650 million in economic and military assistance to the Karzai government, India is consolidating its position in Afghanistan. The semi-military Indian Border Roads Organization is building a major highway on the Pakistan border in the southwestern province of Nimruz, bordering on Baluchistan.

Pakistan is increasingly wary of this growing Indian influence and also accuses Indian consulates in the border cities of Jalalabad and Kandahar of fueling the Baluch nationalist insurgency. Pakistan sees the Indian presence as a major strategic defeat and a loss of years of investments that established an Islamist regime that kept all things Indian away from Pakistan's western borders.

Pakistani Pashtun nationalists, now organized in two major political parties, the Awami National Party and the Pakhtunkhwa Milli Awami Party, view their relations with the Pakistani state and Afghanistan differently than do Pakistan's civil and military establishment and the Islamist political parties. Since 1947, the Pashtuns have been integrated to varying degrees into Pakistan's economy and state institutions such as the army and bureaucracy, weakening separatist sentiments. They have relied mostly on parliamentary politics to demand democratization, provincial autonomy, and friendly relations with Afghanistan.

Although it still lacks internal communications, the remote border region has been linked more closely to the rest of Pakistan through the extension of roads and communication networks. The lack of economic development in the borderlands has motivated Pashtuns to use this transport infrastructure to migrate for employment to Punjab and Sindh, particularly the southern seaport city of

Karachi, which after Peshawar contains the largest urban concentration of Pashtuns, some 12 percent of its estimated population of twelve million.

Pashtun nationalists now propose restructuring the Pakistani state to unite all Pashtun regions in FATA, NWFP, and northern Baluchistan into a new province of Pakhtunkhwa. This new province would form part of a revitalized federal structure in which provinces would enjoy enhanced powers within a genuinely democratic Pakistan. Once such restructuring occurred, the Awami National Party would support the recognition of the Durand Line as an international border between Pakistan and Afghanistan and encourage Afghanistan to move in that direction. As long as Pashtun nationalists conclude that Pakistan is still essentially a centralized military dictatorship, however, they say they will maintain their present position.

In the interim, Pashtun nationalists are calling for fast-paced economic development and reforms in FATA. They maintain that the border between Pakistan and Afghanistan can be pacified only if Pashtuns in both countries have unhindered, cross-border movement through formal recognition of open borders. As Pashtuns dominate regional trade and transport, regional peace and open borders will bring major improvements to the economy of the borderlands.

Unlike the Pashtuns, the Baluch are divided among three states: Pakistan, Afghanistan, and Iran. The Baluch nationalists hold that the colonial boundaries weakened them economically and culturally, resulting in their impoverished life as minorities in all three states. They have viewed Afghanistan in a relatively favorable light, however, because Afghanistan's demand for Pashtunistan led Kabul to extend moral and material support to the Baluch nationalists as well.

As the fifth Baluch nationalist insurgency rages and expands into a nationwide political crisis with the killing of Bugti, many members of the ethnic group feel marginalized in the Pakistani state. With a population of nearly five million, Baluch nationalists feel extremely vulnerable to demographic extinction if mega-development projects such as Gwadar port are implemented in their province without guarantees of provincial autonomy within a federal Pakistan. Thus the Durand Line is not the foremost concern of the Baluch. But like Pashtun nationalists, they demand federal arrangements in Pakistan with enhanced provincial autonomy as a precursor to the settlement of the border and abandonment of secessionism. In contrast to Pashtun nationalists, the Baluch have used military means to protest and bargain politically with Islamabad.

Afghanistan's current government has not issued a formal policy on the Durand Line. In April 2006, however, Afghanistan's minister for border and tribal affairs, Abdul Karim Brahui, told the lower house of the Afghan parliament that Afghanistan does not recognize the Durand Line as an international border. Brahui, a member of a small ethnic group closely linked to the Baluch, stated that his government does not have the mandate to negotiate this old dispute. Only a loya jirga could settle the issue permanently, he claimed, just as a loya jirga first ratified Afghanistan's policies on the postpartition frontier.

Since 2002, Kabul has feared a regrouping of the Taliban and al-Qaeda in the border region. Although the Pakistani military buildup in the tribal areas is ostensibly to support the U.S.-led coalition's effort to eliminate the Taliban and al-Qaeda, Kabul has charged that these forces have occupied territory on the Afghan side of the Durand Line. It suspects that the deployment might provide a platform for further interference. Such fears, coupled with uncertainty over Western commitment, have pushed Karzai to align with India, seen as a more dependable, long-term, regional ally.

As post-Taliban Afghanistan has grappled with a plethora of domestic issues, Pashtunistan and the border region have not figured prominently in the national political discourse. Although some Pashtun publications play up the issue from time to time, the Afghan Mellat political party and other Pashtun nationalists are concentrating on domestic issues. Some non-Pashtun intellectuals and political activists, on the other hand, advocate agreement on a final border settlement in return for access to the sea and assurances of noninterference from Pakistan. Some argued for the inclusion of such an agreement in the 2004 constitution.

Afghan politicians of all ethnic groups, including nationalists, Islamists, and former communists, oppose reviving the conflict and heightening tensions with Pakistan. This is an issue of such political sensitivity that every Afghan leader we interviewed on the subject reemphasized that all comments were off the record before proceeding. Many call for confidence-building measures, such as open borders, enhanced bilateral trade, and more people-to-people contact, including direct interaction between the two countries' parliaments. Some argue that the time is ripe to seek a settlement. "If we cannot solve this now, with the support of the entire international community, we will never resolve it," said a leader of the parliamentary opposition.

Paktia Governor Hakim Taniwal, assassinated September 10, 2006, by a suicide bomber, noted how much this dispute had cost Afghanistan:

> The reason that Afghanistan adopted friendship with the Soviets was for Pashtunistan . . . and the result was, we did not gain Pashtunistan, but we almost lost Afghanistan. It would be good if we recognized the Durand Line—good for FATA, NWFP, Pakistan-Afghanistan relations. But we have to get something in return, such as a corridor to Karachi or Gwadar.

Others echo the traditional view that Pakistan, an "artificial state," is destined to dissolve, and that Afghanistan should not make any concessions while it is weak. Local leaders are discussing the issue as well. At a meeting of elders from eastern

Afghanistan, one volunteered that this unresolved issue gave the neighbors an opportunity to meddle in internal Afghan affairs. Just as Afghanistan no longer claimed territory it once ruled in today's Iran or Uzbekistan, "we should accept this border as a border." This proposal, however, prompted loud protests from others, who insisted that the Durand Line Treaty under which Afghanistan ceded control of the areas across the Durand Line, expired after one hundred years (in 1993), and Pakistan was obligated to return the territory. Among the leaders we interviewed, the myth of the expiration of the Durand Line Treaty was almost universally accepted.

Given the political sensitivity of the issue and opposition to Pakistan's Afghan policy, which people across all factions and ethnic groups see as a major threat to Afghanistan, no major leader has publicly supported rapid settlement of the border issue. Although the Karzai government has not aggressively raised the Pashtunistan issue, it has begun to follow the path of previous Afghan governments in using border issues and Pashtun cross-border ethnic solidarity as political tools. It has revived relations with Pashtun nationalists in Pakistan and fallen back on Afghan nationalism to wage a war of words with the neighbor.

Recommendations and Conclusion

Afghanistan, Pakistan, and the neighboring regions would all benefit from a recognized open border between the two countries. Such a border would clarify that all Pashtuns have rights as citizens of one or another state and would enable them to communicate, trade, and develop both their economy and their culture in cooperation with one another. Such a settlement would strengthen democracy in both states and facilitate both Pakistan's access to Central Asia and Afghanistan's access to the sea. It would lessen domestic ethnic tensions and strengthen national unity in both states. It would, however, require difficult internal changes in both countries, a reversal of the hostility that has predominated in relations between the two governments for sixty years, and credible international guarantees.

A major challenge to such objectives is the Islamist insurgency on both sides of the border. In 2005 Musharraf responded to charges that the Taliban were engaging in cross-border activity by proposing to fence and mine the Durand Line, a solution reminiscent of the policies of Israel and Uzbekistan. As in Central Asia and the Middle East, such a solution will not work for many reasons. International political and military officials in Afghanistan, as well as counterinsurgency experts, agree that the key to strategic success is disrupting the Taliban's command and control, mainly in Quetta and Waziristan, not wasting resources on the impossible task of blocking infiltration by easily replaceable foot soldiers across snowcapped mountains and trackless deserts. Fencing would further isolate the border region and create an additional obstacle to its economic development.

Crafting a twenty-first-century border settlement will require ending the nineteenth-century regime in FATA. Since September 11, Pakistan has ended FATA's autonomy by deploying eighty thousand troops in the mountainous region, but these operations have not been matched by political and economic reforms. Stabilizing the border region must include the political integration of FATA into Pakistan. Almost all Pakistani political parties have urged reform packages. The extension to FATA of the Political Parties Act of 2002 would allow mainstream political parties to organize there and counter extremist propaganda. These parties would provide an opportunity for tribal members to campaign for their rights in national institutions.

The Awami National Party, one of the most vocal proponents of reforms in FATA, wants to overhaul the administrative and judicial system. It supports tribal representation in the legislature of an NWFP that would include FATA. The Awami National Party emphasizes the fact that in the 1960s and early 1970s FATA was represented in the provincial assembly of a united West Pakistan. Over the past decades, many tribal members have acquired farmland and businesses in the settled areas. They also obtain health care and education in NWFP's urban centers.[21]

The Frontier Crimes Regulations have remained virtually unchanged since Lord Curzon promulgated their final version in 1901. Today human rights advocates and tribal intellectuals call for an overhaul of the law. They demand:

- Conformity of the law to contemporary human rights standards.
- Transfer to parliament of all legislative and administrative powers over FATA now resting with the president.
- Extension of the jurisdiction of higher Pakistani courts to FATA and separation of the region's judiciary from the executive.
- Abolition of collective punishment and territorial responsibility.
- Extension of political and civic freedoms to FATA.
- Implementation of a comprehensive disarmament and demobilization program in the region.[22]

No reform program would be successful without a complementary strategy for economic development. It is crucial to reinforce reconstruction in Afghanistan with a compatible model across the border in FATA. The Awami National Party has asked for a detailed baseline survey by the World Bank or another international agency to assess the economic situation and help Pakistan and the people of FATA devise a comprehensive strategy. Linking FATA to Afghan reconstruction and creating special opportunity zones along the Durand Line will be first steps in this direction. Work is under way to establish such zones on the Afghan side. In May 2006 Musharraf hinted at establishing them with the help of the U.S. government. Such development would also open U.S. markets to products produced in FATA.[23]

FATA's isolation can be broken only by improving its infrastructure. A major highway spanning FATA, from Bajaur in the north to Waziristan and Zhob in the south, is needed to encourage contact. Pakistan's bilateral trade with Afghanistan now surpasses $2 billion a year (with Pakistani exports to Afghanistan totaling $1.2 billion, and Afghanistan's exports to Pakistan totaling $700 million). But so far there are only two official border crossings, Torkham in the north and Chaman in the south. At least a dozen more border crossings could be opened to facilitate trade.

More than seventy FM radio stations broadcast illegally in FATA, often inciting sectarian violence and hatred, but the region has not joined the telecommunication revolution in the rest of Pakistan. The area needs mobile telephony and internet access. Trade and commerce also should be modernized by establishing tribal chambers of commerce and accounting and financial information systems. Since most of the land in the region is communal, there is a need for a baseline study of land rights and a strategy for reform. To accomplish this, the government should extend the municipal laws of land settlement to FATA. Proper utilization of several known mineral deposits in FATA will result in the growth of labor-intensive mining and manufacturing industries in marble and precious stones. Agriculture in general, and fruit in particular, can be made profitable by introducing new techniques to tribal farmers and helping them gain access to markets.[24]

Such a transformation requires complementary measures by Afghanistan, the United States, the UN, and NATO. The persistence of a safe haven for the Taliban insurgency in Pakistan threatens the objectives of the international community in Afghanistan. Success in Afghanistan is fundamental to the U.S. "war on terror," the UN's credibility, and NATO's viability. Forces whose command and control and networks of recruitment, funding, training, and equipment are located in Pakistan are killing Afghan, American, British, and Canadian troops and civilians. The United States, the UN, and NATO must agree quickly to send a message to Islamabad that the persistence of Taliban havens in Pakistan is, in the words of the UN Charter, a threat to international peace and security that Pakistan must address immediately.

The United States, UN, and NATO also must agree on sending a message to Afghanistan and India that they must do all in their power to encourage Pakistan to make such difficult decisions by addressing sources of Pakistani insecurity, including issues related to the border region and Kashmir. The international community must offer generous aid and support to Pakistan if it undertakes needed reforms in the governance of FATA and creates a development area along the border in coordination with the reconstruction effort in Afghanistan.

The United States should use its influence to impress on Pakistan the gravity of the risks it is taking by not disrupting the Taliban command and to persuade all governments in the region to lower the tone of confrontation. Only the United States is likely to be able to persuade Pakistan and Afghanistan to keep India out of their bilateral relationship by agreeing to a set of ground rules and to press India to abide by them. India's contribution to Afghanistan is welcome and mostly constructive, but it should reduce its staff and activities in the border regions for the sake of regional stability. The size of the Indian consulates should be limited and their roles strictly defined.

U.S. diplomacy prevented nuclear confrontations between India and Pakistan in 1999 and 2002 and helped these archrivals begin talking. It also should facilitate a political process between Pakistan and Afghanistan. The United States helped set up the tripartite commission composed of senior Afghan, Pakistani, and U.S. military officials in 2003; it now includes NATO but still deals only with military coordination. Until now, Pakistan has delayed responding to a proposal to expand the consultations to the political level. As part of their joint initiative, the United States and NATO need to press Pakistan for a positive response.

Afghanistan has more international backing and support than ever. A growing segment of opinion privately holds that now is the time to address these issues; but only leadership can encourage those harboring such ideas to propose them in public. The Karzai administration should take advantage of this situation to begin a national dialogue to develop a consensus on resolving the conflicts with Pakistan that have caused so much damage to both countries. Afghanistan needs to show goodwill to Pakistan regarding the border issue and make a historic compromise.

Both countries should facilitate and encourage people-to-people contact as well as contact between officials at all levels across the border. If the wars in Afghanistan had any positive impact, it was to expose Afghans to the outside world. Nearly half of today's Afghan population has visited Pakistan at some point, making it the country that Afghans are most familiar with outside their homeland. About sixty thousand Pakistanis currently work in Afghanistan, and ten thousand of them cross the border daily. Pakistan's exports to Afghanistan grew from $221 million in 2001 to $1.2 billion in 2006, but the economy in the border region faces a sharp decline. Despite the intimate contact of the two peoples, however, the governments remain isolated from each other. The governors and chief ministers of NWFP and Baluchistan should meet with counterparts in the Afghan border provinces regularly, as should police chiefs, customs officers, and other officials.

In 2006, no secessionist nationalist movement operates among the Pashtuns in Pakistan, and Afghanistan has not revived its irredentist claims. Tribes on both sides of the border are clamoring for development. Economic pressures have forced Pashtuns to migrate to Karachi and the Gulf region in huge numbers. Only policy changes in both Kabul and Islamabad can involve their Pashtun populations in mutual confidence building, which could lead to an amicable resolution of the border issue.

Three contending visions of relations between Pakistan and Afghanistan emerged in spring 2006. One was the launch of the friendship bus service between the eastern Afghan city of Jalalabad and the western Pakistani city of Peshawar. People in both countries celebrated the occasion and greeted the arriving delegations by showering them with rose petals, playing music, and dancing in joy.[25] Another vision of cross-border relations was expressed in the rather implausible proposal of fencing the Durand Line.[26] A third and worrying trend is Talibanization and escalating violence in the areas around the Durand Line. People in both countries have chosen the peaceful alternative; now their governments and leaders should follow suit.

Notes

1. "Pakistan Opposition Barred from U.S. Air-Strike Village," Reuters, January 23, 2006.
2. Fulzar Ahmed Khan, "Bajaur Raid Killed Five Foreigners: Musharraf," Dawn, February 12, 2006.
3. Ron Synovitz, "Afghanistan: Are Militants Copying Iraqi Insurgents' Suicide Tactics?" Radio Free Europe/Radio Liberty, January 17, 2006, accessed September 23, 2011, http://www.rferl.org/content/article/1064791.html.
4. Ahmad Qureshi and Ihsan Sarwaryar, "Suicide Attack at Herat PRT Kills Two, Injures Nine," Pajhwok Afghan News, April 8, 2006, accessed September 23, 2011, http://www.pajhwok.com/en/2006/04/08/suicide-attack-herat-prt-kills-two-injures-nine.
5. Hekmat Karzai and Seth Jones, "How to Curb Suicide Terrorism in Afghanistan," Christian Science Monitor, July 18, 2006.
6. "The Other Taliban," Economist, March 16, 2006.
7. Zahid Hussain, "Musharraf's Other War," Newsline Magazine (Karachi), January 2006.
8. "Senior al-Qaida Operative Struck by Predator Missile," ABC News, May 13, 2005.
9. Carlotta Gall and Muhammad Khan, "Qaida Bomber Is Reported Killed," New York Times, April 13, 2006.
10. "Wanted Al-Qaida Militant Killed," Dawn, April 21, 2006.
11. Zahid Hussain, "Terror in Miran Shah," Newsline Magazine, April 2006.
12. Sebastien Trives, "Afghanistan: Tackling the Insurgency, the Case of the Southeast," Politique étrangère, January 2006.
13. Steve Coll, "The Stand-off," New Yorker, February 13, 2006.
14. Abubakar Siddique and Iqbal Khattak, "War on Terror Highlights Development Needs in FATA," Friday Times (Lahore), January 23, 2004.
15. Human Rights Commission of Pakistan, "FCR—a Bad Law Nobody Can Defend," 2005.
16. "Development Backlog in FATA," Dawn, November 22, 2005.
17. Siddique and Khattak, "War on Terror."

18. "Federally Administered Tribal Area, A Development Framework," unpublished paper, Awami National Party, April, 2006.

19. Ainslie Embree, ed., *Pakistan's Western Borderlands: The Transformation of a Political Order* (Karachi: Royal, 1979), 134.

20. Husain Haqqani, *Pakistan: Between Mosque and Military* (Washington, DC: Carnegie Endowment for International Peace, 2005), 197.

21. "Federally Administered Development of Tribal Areas."

22. Human Rights Commission of Pakistan, "FCR—a Bad Law Nobody Can Defend."

23. Raza Shahzad, "Civil, Military Men to Be Political Agents," *Daily Times* (Lahore), May 10, 2006.

24. "Federally Administered Tribal Area."

25. "First Pakistan-Afghanistan Bus Service Runs," Agence France-Presse, March 15, 2006.

26. Qureshi and Sarwaryar, "Suicide Attack at Herat PRT Kills Two, Injures Nine."

16

Counternarcotics to Stabilize Afghanistan

The False Promise of Crop Eradication

WITH JAKE SHERMAN

In the past year (2007–08), opium production in Afghanistan reached a record level, estimated at 8,200 tons of raw opium. Traffickers also refined much of the opium into heroin before exporting it. The Taliban-led insurgency supported by al-Qaeda spread to new areas in both Afghanistan and Pakistan. The level of terrorism, especially suicide bombings, set a record in both countries, hitting high-profile targets such as Pakistan's most popular politician, Benazir Bhutto, and the Serena Hotel in Kabul. After six years of assistance to the Afghan government by the UN, NATO, the world's major military powers, the world's largest aid donors, and international specialists on all subjects, the expansion of both the illicit industry and the insurgency constitutes a powerful indictment of international policy and capacity.

In response, the U.S. government and other major actors decided to make counternarcotics in Afghanistan a priority in 2007 and 2008 and link it to counterinsurgency. To ensure coherence and coordination of this complex policy area, the government of Afghanistan and the United Nations agreed that the February 6, 2008, meeting of the Joint Coordination and Monitoring Board, a multilateral body that oversees implementation of the Afghanistan Compact and that they cochair, should focus on counternarcotics.[1] This meeting could reach agreement on effective measures to cope with the opiate industry and insurgency in Afghanistan, but it could also confirm international commitment to escalating eradication of the poppy crop in 2008, a policy that will invigorate both the opiate industry and the insurgency.

The UN Office on Drugs and Crime (UNODC) led off its *Afghanistan Opium Survey 2007* with findings linking the opium economy to the insurgency. It first summarized trends in opium cultivation[2]:

Originally published as *Report of the Center on International Cooperation*, February 2008.

First, the area under opium cultivation rose to 193,000 hectares from 165,000 in 2006. The total opium harvest will be 8,200 tons, up from 6,100 tons last year. . . .

Second, in the centre and north of Afghanistan, where the government has increased its authority and presence, opium cultivation is diminishing. The number of opium-free provinces more than doubled from six to thirteen, while in the province of Balkh opium cultivation collapsed from 7,200 hectares last year to zero. However, the opposite trend was seen in southern Afghanistan. Some 80 percent of opium poppies were grown in a handful of provinces along the border with Pakistan, where instability is greatest. In the volatile province of Helmand, where the Taliban insurgency is concentrated, opium cultivation rose 48 percent to 102,770 hectares.[3]

UNODC then "highlight[ed] three new circumstances" that linked the increase in opium poppy cultivation to the insurgency:

First, opium cultivation in Afghanistan is no longer associated with poverty—quite the opposite. Helmand, Kandahar and three other opium-producing provinces in the south are the richest and most fertile, in the past the breadbasket of the nation and a main source of earnings. They have now opted for illicit opium on an unprecedented scale (5,744 tons), while the much poorer northern region is abandoning the poppy crops.

Second, opium cultivation in Afghanistan is now closely linked to insurgency. The Taliban today control vast swathes of land in Helmand, Kandahar and along the Pakistani border. By preventing national authorities and international agencies from working, insurgents have allowed greed and corruption to turn orchards, wheat and vegetable fields into poppy fields.

Third, the Taliban are again using opium to suit their interests. Between 1996 and 2000, in Taliban-controlled areas 15,000 tons of opium were produced and exported—the regime's sole source of foreign exchange at that time. In July 2000, the Taliban leader, Mullah Omar, argued that opium was against Islam and banned its cultivation (but not its export). In recent months, the Taliban have reversed their position once again and started to extract from the drug economy resources for arms, logistics and militia pay.

These assertions are misleading and partly false. They have been cited in support of a plan to escalate poppy eradication, especially in the South, to deprive the

Taliban of funding and starve the insurgency. The proponents of this plan have also justified it on the grounds that it will not harm the "poor," who are in the north, but only the "rich and greedy" in the south. These arguments consist of a series of fallacies:

- First, the difference between the "rich" southern province of Helmand and the "poor" northern province of Balkh, according to UNODC's own survey of household income, is the difference between an average daily income of $1 per person in Helmand and $0.70 per person in Balkh.[4] Household studies of poppy cultivation in Afghanistan indicate that poor households are most dependent on poppy cultivation for their livelihoods. Poppy eradication in Helmand, especially in insecure areas not reached by development projects, may primarily harm the livelihoods of those earning less than $1 per day. The first UN Millennium Development Goal aims to reduce by half the number of people living on less than $1 per day. If these desperately poor people have easier access to armed resistance than alternative livelihoods, they may well choose the former.
- Second, poppy (or coca, or cannabis) cultivation migrates to the most insecure areas capable of producing it. Hence poppy cultivation migrated to Afghanistan and within Afghanistan to the areas most affected by the insurgency. Political and military conflict created the conditions for the drug industry, not vice versa, just as political and military conflict previously created conditions for cultivation of narcotics raw materials in Colombia and Burma. Field research on poppy cultivation has identified insecurity exploited by drug traffickers, not the greed and corruption of Afghan cultivators, as the primary driver of opium poppy cultivation.
- Third, the Taliban were not solely dependent on narcotics financing in 1996–2000; nor are they now. Research by the World Bank and others, including UNODC, indicated that the Taliban derived more income and foreign exchange in the 1990s from taxing the transit trade in licit goods smuggled through Afghanistan from Dubai to Pakistan than from the drug trade.[5] Today, too, the Taliban have other sources of income.

The advocates of responding to the drug problem by escalating eradication compound these errors with a further fallacy: the claim that poppy eradication reduces the amount of drug money available to fund insurgency, terrorism, and corruption. In 2000–01, when the Taliban prohibited poppy cultivation with almost complete success in the areas they controlled, they suffered no financial problems. Drug traders are not florists. Trafficking continued from stockpiles of opiates, and the loss in quantity was compensated by a tenfold increase in price. Eradication raises the price of opium and causes its cultivation to migrate to more remote areas. It does not provide for a sustainable reduction in the drug economy; nor does sustainable reduction of the drug economy start with eradication.

Focusing on poppy cultivation when economic alternatives are not secure conflicts with the broadly accepted view in Afghanistan that poppy cultivation is undesirable, but that it is inevitable in situations of dire poverty and insecurity. Hence pursuing eradication under these circumstances provides evidence that the international operation and the government that it supports derive their legitimacy not from Afghan people but from external powers.

According to a 2007 poll conducted by Charney Research, 36 percent of the national sample in Afghanistan (in both poppy-growing and non-poppy-growing provinces) believed that poppy cultivation was acceptable either unconditionally or if there was no other way to make a living. In poppy-producing provinces, a third of respondents believed that elimination or reduction of poppy was a bad thing. In Helmand, the main province targeted for eradication, this figure climbed to about one-half. More than 60 percent in all poppy-growing provinces and 80 percent in Helmand agreed that the farmers whose opium crops are eradicated are usually poor or don't pay bribes. Table 16.1 illustrates the perception of hardship imposed by poppy eradication in poppy-growing provinces (figures for Helmand in parentheses).[6]

Note that one out of seven respondents in poppy-growing provinces and one in four in Helmand said they knew of farming families who had sold their children (most likely girls) in payment of opium debts as a result of eradication. This might help explain why 38 percent of the Helmand respondents said they knew of someone who became more sympathetic to the Taliban as a result of eradication.

The Afghanistan Compact requires a different approach to counternarcotics. That agreement outlines a strategy to achieve two overriding goals: "to improve

Table 16.1 **Perceptions of Hardship as a Result of Poppy Eradication (Results from Helmand in Parentheses)**

Q-107. Are you personally aware of farming families in this province who have had opium crops eradicated who:	Yes	No	Don't Know
a. Suffered hunger or hardship as a result?	40% (73%)	52%	8%
b. Had to give up children to creditors because they could not pay debts?	14% (25%)	77%	9%
c. Ran away from this province because they could not pay their debts?	26% (52%)	65%	9%
d. Became more sympathetic to the Taliban as a result?	16% (38%)	74%	11%

the lives of Afghan people and to contribute to national, regional, and global peace and security." To accomplish these goals, the compact prescribes three pillars of activity: security; governance, human rights, and justice; and economic and social development.

The compact defines *counternarcotics* as a "cross-cutting" theme across these three pillars. It integrates counternarcotics with the other pillars both because achieving counternarcotics goals requires policies and programs under all pillars, and to emphasize that counternarcotics is not separate from or parallel to the overall goal of the compact and its three pillars. Achieving the compact's counternarcotics goal, "a sustained and significant reduction in the production and trafficking of narcotics with a view to complete elimination," is part of an overall strategy to build security, governance, and development to improve the lives of Afghans and provide security to Afghans, their neighbors, and the entire international community.

The threat to the compact's objectives comes not from drugs per se but, as stated in the *U.S. Counternarcotics Strategy for Afghanistan,* from "drug money" that "weakens key institutions and strengthens the Taliban."[7] According to estimates by UNODC, the "drug money" to which the *Strategy* refers comes mainly from the 70–80 percent of the gross profits of narcotics earned by traffickers, processors, and protectors, including Taliban, Afghan government officials, and other illegal armed groups, not from the 20–30 percent that goes to poppy farmers and laborers.[8]

Counternarcotics policy in service of the Afghanistan Compact's goals requires reducing the amount of illicit value created by the drug economy and should focus on the part of the drug economy that "weakens key institutions and strengthens the Taliban." This distinction has implications for how to define and measure success in counternarcotics and how to achieve it. The most commonly used measure of both the problem and the progress of counternarcotics—the extent of cultivation of opium poppy—biases policy in the wrong direction. It focuses attention on the quantity of narcotics rather than the value and toward the smallest and least harmful part of the drug economy: the raw material that produces income for rural communities. A better indicator of success is the one included in the benchmarks for economic and social development of the Afghanistan Compact: "a decrease in the absolute and relative size of the drug economy."

The Afghan narcotics industry, the annual gross profit of which is equal to approximately half of the country's licit GDP, makes a significant proportion of the Afghan population dependent for their livelihood on drug traffickers and those who protect them, whether corrupt officials or insurgents.[9] This includes not only the one in seven Afghans who are involved directly in poppy cultivation, according to UNODC—a figure that excludes sharecroppers and laborers from outside the village where the question was asked—but also all those involved in trafficking as well as the commerce, construction, and other economic activities that narcotics revenue finances. The political goal of counternarcotics in Afghanistan is to break those links of dependence and instead integrate the Afghan population into the licit economy and polity, which are in turn integrated with the international community's institutions and norms. This effort is the equivalent of the counterinsurgency goal of "winning hearts and minds" and the postconflict reconstruction goal of strengthening legitimate government and reconstruction.

Both globally and within Afghanistan, the location of narcotics cultivation is the result—not the cause—of insecurity. The essential condition for implementing counternarcotics policy is "a state that works."[10] Counternarcotics can succeed only if political efforts establish the basis for policing, law enforcement, and support for development. Unlike military action, policing and law enforcement require the consent of the population. State building includes military action to defeat armed opponents of the project, but in a weak state such as Afghanistan it succeeds only by limiting the scope of state activity and gaining sufficient legitimacy and capacity so that the population consents to the state's authority over those areas in which it acts. Winning consent for counternarcotics requires providing greater licit economy opportunities, and providing security for people to benefit from those opportunities. Scarce resources for coercion should be reserved for targeting political opponents at the high end of the value chain, rather than farmers and flowers. Winning a counterinsurgency while engaging in counternarcotics also requires acknowledging that the transition from a predominantly narcotics-based economy to a licit one will take years. It is not possible to win the consent of communities to state authority while treating their livelihoods as criminal, even where alternatives are not yet reliable.

Proponents of escalating forced eradication argue that the government and its international supporters do not have years; if the drug economy continues to expand, the whole effort will fail. Escalating forced eradication, however, will only make the effort fail more quickly.[11] Escalating forced eradication does not integrate counternarcotics with counterinsurgency; it makes counternarcotics a *recruiter* for the insurgency. What drives rural communities to align themselves with the Taliban is not illicit drugs but a program to deprive those communities of their livelihoods before alternatives are available. An internationally supported effort to help Afghan communities gradually to move out of dependence on the drug trade without being stigmatized as criminals during the transition will integrate counternarcotics with counterinsurgency and peace building. Many of the "substitute" crops being suggested by the USAID Alternative

Livelihoods Program (ALP) and others, such as saffron, pomegranates, apricots, and roses, have maturation periods of several years during which they will not provide income.[12]

In areas where the government and its international supporters have access to the population (including both poppy-growing and non-poppy-growing areas), a gradual policy should focus first on development of licit livelihoods; improving governance, including reduction of narcotics-related corruption; and interdiction, targeted especially against heroin production. The international community must contribute by ensuring markets for licit Afghan products, cooperating in interdiction with intelligence and force protection, preventing the import of precursors for heroin production into Afghanistan, and ensuring that its operations in Afghanistan do not enrich or empower traffickers. Many international organizations in Afghanistan employ private security companies linked to figures involved in drug trafficking or rent properties from such men. At least two organizations funded by USAID for the ALP rent their premises from men reputed to be major drug traffickers.

In areas where the insurgency prevents regular access by government, the first priority should be to gain access and establish state presence with consent of the local population. Introducing forced eradication whether by air or on the ground before the government is able to provide security or help communities develop alternative sources of livelihood undermines this effort.

The recovery of control over Musa Qala district of northern Helmand followed the pattern of putting access and security first, followed by interdiction and alternative livelihoods. The Afghan government and international forces carried out a joint political-military operation, gaining the support of a major Taliban commander (Mullah Abdul Salaam) and then defeating the remaining insurgents. Once in occupation of the district, government and international forces seized about $25 million worth of narcotics[13] and destroyed more than sixty heroin laboratories.

Confiscating products from the upper end of the value chain depended on regaining control of the territory. Had the government and international community engaged in forced eradication in Musa Qala before launching the operation, Mullah Abdul Salaam might not have changed sides, the local people might not have supported the government or remained neutral, and the district might have remained under Taliban control. If eradication had destroyed locally produced raw opium, the Taliban-supported heroin laboratories could have purchased opium from other sources. Having first undertaken political and military measures to establish security in Musa Qala, however, Afghan and international forces were able to interdict high-value illicit products without harming rural communities. They now can help communities break their dependence on the drug trade. This is how to integrate counternarcotics and counterinsurgency.

For both political and economic reasons, crop eradication should be implemented, as stated in Afghanistan's National Drug Control Policy, "where access to alternative livelihoods exists." Where communities are confident in alternative livelihoods, they will consent to the eradication of illicit crops.

From an economic point of view, crop eradication does not meaningfully increase the opportunity cost of illicit cultivation unless the cultivators are able to engage in other cash-earning activities.[14] Afghan farmers do not cultivate poppy out of greed for the highest possible return. They cultivate it because for many it is the only way to supplement their subsistence farming with a cash income for food and social security, which has become essential over the past few decades of war-induced inflation and destruction of the rural economy. The drug economy provides the only access to land, credit, water, and employment. There are many potential cash crops and sources of monetary income other than poppy cultivation, but additional investments and more security are required to make these economic opportunities available to most Afghan communities, especially those more distant from markets and in areas with less government presence.

From a political point of view, where these opportunities are available, eradication is hardly necessary, except to discipline some deviants, which communities can do themselves. Where these opportunities are not available, eradication promotes corruption and insurgency rather than alternative economic activities. Implementation of "forced eradication" in the absence of such conditions will neither reduce the size of the narcotics economy nor weaken the insurgency. Rather, it will strengthen insurgency while weakening and corrupting the Afghan government. Afghans will conclude that foreigners are in Afghanistan only to pursue their own interests, not to help Afghanistan.

Relation of the Narcotics Industry to Security, Governance, and Development in Afghanistan

The narcotics industry's profit derives from illegality. Producing a banned substance imposes two kinds of costs: (1) costs of production and marketing (capital, labor, land, transport), and (2) costs of illegality, including bribes, formation of illegal military organizations, and direct violence and deprivation of liberty and income resulting from law enforcement. The risk premium increases up the value chain from farmgate to retail distributor. Afghanistan's principal comparative advantage is not in poppy cultivation but in the production of illegality and insecurity.

The volume of production of illicit raw materials is mainly determined by demand from the richer consuming countries, but the location of production of raw materials responds mainly to shifts in security. Narcotics raw material production is often preceded by political destabilization, which the drug industry exploits. The migration of drug production to insecure areas in turn attracts investment of criminal capital to the destabilization of trafficking routes.

In Afghanistan, the state collapsed as a result of the 1978 communist coup d'état, the growth of the mujahidin movement, and the consolidation of international and transnational economic, military, and political support for both. Afghan political-military leaders allied with businessmen engaged in licit trade, arms dealing, smuggling, gem mining, timber trafficking, transit trade (smuggling to neighboring countries), antiquities smuggling, and drug trafficking. The businessmen depended on the strongmen for protection and patronage and in turn supported them financially. Such alliances often took the form of a division of labor among members of a family, with some brothers or cousins specializing in political-military activity and others in business.

At the same time, intensified counternarcotics efforts outside of Afghanistan raised the risk premium in several areas where poppy had been produced. The international drug industry seized the opportunity to move production from Turkey, Iran, and Pakistan to Afghanistan. It did so through links established in the late 1980s and early 1990s with strongmen in Afghanistan. They controlled access to (1) agricultural land where poppy could be grown, (2) markets and roads through which opium could be traded, (3) locations where heroin refineries could be established, and (4) with their international partners, the physical, administrative, and virtual borders of Afghanistan, the crossing of which was necessary for the export of opiates, the import of precursors for heroin manufacturing, and the transfer of money to pay for these transactions.

The initial links came through traffickers in Pakistan. After 1992, as the Eurasian "mafia" developed in the former Soviet Union, it entered the drug industry, establishing new routes to Western Europe. The civil war in Tajikistan, lasting from 1992 to 1997, facilitated the extension of the Eurasian drug trafficking mafia into Afghanistan. The Islamic Movement of Uzbekistan (IMU) established bases in areas of Tajikistan between the Ferghana Valley and opium-producing areas of north Afghanistan. The IMU's military efforts in the late 1990s appeared partly motivated by attempts to secure these trafficking routes.

The drug trade expanded further under the Taliban, because the Islamic Emirate was a peculiar type of state: internally it strictly enforced its own law and brought security to trade routes and rural areas, but the government was not recognized internationally and did not recognize international law, including the international counternarcotics regime. The Taliban issued several religious decrees (fatwas) stating that although narcotics consumption was strictly forbidden, production and trade of narcotics was merely inadvisable and could be undertaken in case of necessity. The latter provision essentially "legitimated" the opium economy within Afghanistan until the Taliban ban on cultivation in 2000–01. As the trade was taxed rather than banned, it remained a relatively competitive industry that produced only modest revenues and little corruption inside Afghanistan, compared to today.

As the Taliban took control of southern and eastern Afghanistan, increased security facilitated trade and hence the growth of poppy production in the two main areas with good natural endowments under their control, the irrigated areas in Helmand-Kandahar and Nangarhar. The other main production area, in Badakhshan, was mainly linked to the Eurasian route and was controlled by Northern Alliance commanders.

After 1998, as the Taliban consolidated control over most of northern and western Afghanistan, the trafficking markets became more integrated. Trafficking routes linking the north and south developed. Today, profits from drug trafficking persist in the "poppy-free" north, as raw materials are shipped over the Hindu Kush through various trade routes (via Chaghcharan in Ghor or the Shibar Pass linking Bamyan and Balkh).

In 2000, responding to pressure from both the international community and major traffickers, the Taliban used their authority to reduce the quantity of land cultivated in poppy by 95 percent. This was one of several instances when power holders with strong links to the drug trade sought recognition or support from the international community by using their influence and power to reduce poppy cultivation. Other instances include Helmand (1988 and 2002–03), Nangarhar (2004–05), and Balkh (2006–07).

At that time, as has also happened since, the accumulation of inventories (a form of risk management in an illicit business) created a tactical convergence of interest in reducing production of the raw material between drug traffickers and counternarcotics officials. The Taliban hoped both to win international recognition and aid, and to enjoy a fiscal bonus from taxes levied on trade inflated by the huge rise in price. Counternarcotics officials got to improve their "metrics of success." The farmgate prices of raw opium increased tenfold. This increase was transmitted up the value chain to traffickers in Afghanistan and then largely absorbed in the profit margins of the supply chain outside Afghanistan. Prices have declined since the Taliban were ousted from power, but they have not returned to the competitive levels of the previous period when the drug economy was not subject to sanction inside Afghanistan.

Military action by the U.S.-led coalition after the September 11, 2001, terrorist attacks on the United States led to a collapse of opium prices as traffickers engaged in panic selling of their stocks, anticipating attempts at seizure by the international forces. It soon turned out they had nothing to fear. The coalition regarded counternarcotics as mission creep, a distraction from the core task of killing and capturing terrorists. Nonetheless, the gradual adoption of *de jure* counternarcotics policies after conclusion of the first round of major military operations increased the cost of illicit business.

The United States and Iran jointly drafted an article included in the Bonn Agreement that provided the framework for the transition to the current government, requiring the new authorities in Afghanistan to "cooperate with the international community in the fight against terrorism, drugs and organized crime."[15] The current government is committed to (in the words of the preamble to the Constitution of 2004/1382) "restoring Afghanistan to its rightful place in the international community."[16] Hence, the constitution provides: "The state shall prevent all types of terrorist activities, the production and consumption of intoxicants (*musakkirat*), and the production and smuggling of narcotics."

The drug industry consequently has had to conceal some of its trafficking operations. This has required corrupting the administration, especially the police and the justice system. The rise in the cost of corruption has led to the consolidation of the industry, as only larger traders can afford the increased bribes and protection from political authorities.[17] Counternarcotics efforts (as well as counterinsurgency efforts) have supported the consolidation of market share by strongmen allied to power holders, just as production restraint under the Taliban served the interests of traffickers.

During the early years of the Bonn process, drug trafficking had only a marginal relationship to the Taliban and al-Qaeda. The drug trade was associated with the power holders, not with those contesting them. Just as drug production and trafficking exploit insecurity created by political factors, the insurgency began for political reasons but then maintained and created insecurity advantageous for narcotics production and trafficking. As a result, the most visible part of the industry (poppy cultivation) has become concentrated in the most insecure and insurgent-ridden regions of the country.

Participants in the narcotics economy—which comprises about a third of the total Afghan economy and at least half of the cash economy—must govern it through illegal activities. Afghan police and administrators, political leaders, and the antigovernment insurgents all offer protection services to poppy growers and drug traffickers. Competition for this lucrative role motivates much of the violence in the country and funds official corruption, such as the sale and purchase of offices in poppy-growing areas and along trafficking routes.

Hence, even though the illegality of the narcotics economy corrupts and weakens the government, undermines stable economic development, and funds terrorism and insurgency, the rents from that illegality fund security to the drug economy.[18] From the point of view of Afghan poppy cultivators, it is *eradicators* who provide insecurity, while leaders (whether in the government or the Taliban) who keep out or corrupt eradicators provide security.

Opiate Production, Governance, and Security: The Value Chain, the Corruption Chain

Opium is a gum harvested from the mature flower of the opium poppy, *Papaver somniferum,* by scraping the bulb with a specially designed knife. Opium has medicinal uses, but it can also be ingested orally or smoked as an addictive narcotic.

Relatively simple chemical reactions transform the active ingredient in opium gum into stronger narcotics: morphine, codeine, or heroin. These reactions require precursor chemicals that act as reagents in the manufacture of organic compounds. The principal precursor for opium processing is acetic anhydride, which is also used in the manufacture of aspirin and photographic film.

The value chain includes transactions at ascending prices. Cultivators sell raw opium at the farmgate, often as repayment of a debt under a futures contract. In recent years, as more processing has taken place in Afghanistan and the risk premium of trafficking has increased, cultivators have received at most 20–30 percent of the gross profits. The rest goes to traffickers, processors, and protectors.

The primary traffickers sell raw opium to larger ones or processors at opium bazaars. Specialized workshops (the term "laboratory" may conjure a deceptive image of white coats and stainless steel) refine the opium into heroin using precursor chemicals and scientific expertise. Traders consign shipments of the opiates either to individual smugglers, whose families are held accountable for the value in case the smuggler fails to return with the money, or to illegal armed groups, whether political or purely criminal, which transport it across the border. Prices increase exponentially as one ascends the value chain, accounting in part for the increasing share of opiate profits going to traffickers.[19]

At each stage of the value chain, power holders take shares of the profit. In villages, farmers often contribute a share of their profit to the mosque (sometimes couched as the Islamic tax, ushr, which is paid on all agricultural produce), which is used to pay the mullah and for local public expenditures, such as teachers' salaries, medical care, and irrigation. When eradicators come to the village, either the village may decide collectively which land is to be eradicated and compensate the cultivators, or the richer or better-connected villagers may make individual payments to have their land exempted.

The small traders who come to the village have to pay the police (or bandits) whom they pass on the road, who pass a share up to their superiors. The police chief of the district may have paid a large bribe to the Ministry of the Interior in Kabul to be appointed to a poppy-producing district; he may also have paid a member of parliament or another influential person to introduce him to the right official in Kabul. These officials may also have paid bribes ("political contributions") to obtain a position where they can make so much money.[20]

Running a heroin laboratory requires payments to whoever controls the territory—in most cases a local strongman, a government official, or the Taliban. Importing precursors requires bribing border guards (perhaps on both sides of the border) or paying an armed group for a covert escort. Smuggling the opium, morphine, or heroin out of Afghanistan requires access to an airfield or border crossing (controlled by the border police and Ariana Airlines, both of whose employees are reported to make significant income from drug trafficking),[21] the escort of armed groups (Taliban, tribes, commanders), or specialists in packaging such as those who seal heroin inside licit commodities for export. The bureaucratic, military, political, or social superiors of those directly involved in facilitating trafficking claim a right to shares of the resulting tribute, though the higher the money moves, the less evident is its connection to the flowers whence it originated.

Counternarcotics Regime

Opium and its derivatives are controlled substances under the Single Convention on Narcotic Drugs, 1961, an international agreement administered by the International Narcotics Control Board (INBC) in Vienna. The INCB delegates its day-to-day work of monitoring and supporting compliance to UNODC. The convention was later supplemented by the 1988 United Nations Convention Against Illicit Traffic in Narcotic Drugs and Psychotropic Substances. The convention supports controlled use of narcotics for scientific and medical purposes. Each state party to the convention is obligated to enact national legislation to outlaw "Cultivation, production, manufacture, extraction, preparation, possession, offering, offering for sale, distribution, purchase, sale, delivery on any terms whatsoever, brokerage, dispatch, dispatch in transit, transport, importation and exportation of drugs contrary to the provisions of this Convention."[22]

Conspiracy, preparation, or financial operations in connection with these acts must also be made criminal offenses. There is no provision in the convention for derogation from any of its provisions in times of armed conflict or emergency.

Counternarcotics Policy Tools

This regime mandates "counternarcotics" policies to prevent and punish the prohibited acts. But even though the enforcers use policy instruments in order to stop illicit use and transactions in narcotics, the effects of the instruments depend on how they structure incentives in the illegal narcotics market. Counternarcotics policy instruments intervene at various points of the value chain and thus affect prices, quantity, and the distribution of remaining profits differently. The strategy (combination and sequencing of tools) that lowers the physical supply of drugs the most is not necessarily the strategy that most effectively stops drug money from funding corruption and insurgency. Nor is it necessarily the strategy that improves security or creates stabilizing political alliances.

Eradication destroys some raw material produced by cultivators. Interdiction includes all interventions higher up in the value chain, such as arrests of traffickers, confiscation and destruction of drug contraband, interdiction of imports of precursor chemicals, destruction of heroin/morphine laboratories, removal from office or prosecution of officials corrupted by the trade, Security Council sanctions against travel and assets of traffickers under Resolution 1735, and measures to detect, prevent, and punish money laundering. "Alternative livelihoods" provide incentives to engage in licit activities rather than the narcotics industry. This includes incentive payments (such as the Good Performance Initiative) in return for reduction in or abstention from poppy cultivation. As discussed below, "alternative livelihoods" is a misnomer, as it implies a direct replacement of drug production by another activity, whereas a much more comprehensive development approach is needed. Afghanistan's National Drug Control Strategy also includes pillars for institution building, law enforcement, public information, and regional cooperation, but these are all in support of the primary tools, eradication, interdiction, and alternative livelihoods.

Reduction of Supply of Raw Material

Crop Eradication

Eradication is the destruction of the poppy crop in the field before harvest. It can be carried out manually, by knocking over the poppy stalks; mechanically, by crushing the crop under machinery; or with herbicides sprayed from either the ground or the air.[23] Nearly all eradication in Afghanistan is done manually by Afghan security forces, sometimes supervised by U.S. private contractors. The Afghan government has rejected proposals by the United States to use herbicides, including aerial spraying, as has been done in Colombia, partly on the grounds that it will recall the alleged use of aerially delivered chemical weapons by the USSR in the early 1980s. Seventy-one percent of Afghans interviewed in a 2007 survey opposed or were uncertain about aerial spraying.[24] Nonetheless, the U.S. Congress has for several years appropriated funds for the aerial eradication of opium poppy in Afghanistan. The *U.S. Counternarcotics Strategy* revives that proposal in careful language that nonetheless pressures the Afghan government to agree.

What effect does eradication have on the goals of counternarcotics? Eradication of the poppy crop has "forward" effects on the opiate value chain and "backward" effects on the rural population. The forward aim of eradication is to reduce drug money by reducing the amount of drugs, and the backward aim is to introduce more risk into the lives of the excessively secure Afghan cultivators so that they will plant other, less profitable crops. According to the National Drug Control Strategy of Afghanistan, the government will implement "targeted and verified eradication where alternative livelihoods are available," but there is no definition of what this means or a mechanism to implement it; in practice it is largely ignored.

Even if eradication did sustainably decrease the amount of opium supplied by farmers to traffickers, the effect on total revenue would depend on how elastically the price shifts in response to changes in the quantity supplied. Does the price change so slowly that revenue decreases, or does the relatively inelastic demand for an addictive substance and the high risk premium that makes the cost of production irrelevant higher in the value chain mean that incremental eradication actually raises traders' revenues? That no attempt has been made even to test this causal relationship indicates the intellectual bankruptcy of counternarcotics policy.

Both theoretical reasoning and empirical evidence indicate that any attainable amount of eradication (the current goal is 25 percent of the crop) is likely to increase drug revenue. Other things being equal, we would expect to see an increase in drug money, a rise in the cost of bribing eradicators, and a shift of income against those who cannot afford to bribe.[25]

Evidence from both the Taliban ban on cultivation in 2000–01 and from some localized decreases since then (especially Nangarhar in 2004–05) is consistent with this model. In 2001, when traders had little new product to resell or refine, their existing stocks increased in value, and sales continued. According to Omar Zakhilwal, president of the Afghanistan Investment Support Agency (who is both a Canadian-trained economist and a native of the poppy-producing Mohand area of Nangarhar province and in 2013 is minister of finance), opium traffickers were the main lobbyists for the ban with the Taliban leadership, as they wanted to increase the value of their inventories. Seizures of trafficked opiates across the border from Afghanistan in 2001 dropped by only 40 percent compared to the previous year, implying that trafficking continued from stocks at 60 percent of the previous volume but at a price several multiples larger, so that the higher prices led to an increase in revenue to the traders. There was no sign that the cultivation ban hurt the finances of the Taliban, who, like other power holders, benefited from the opium economy mainly by taxing traders, not farmers.

This example shows the effect of suppression of cultivation without interdiction of trafficking or alternative livelihoods efforts. An analysis that takes all of these into account is necessary to estimate the likely effect on narcotics revenue of different mixes of counternarcotics tools.

Pre-Planting Campaigns

Eradication is one way to reduce the quantity of opium supplied to traders. Another method is a pre-planting campaign that successfully convinces, coerces, or encourages (bribes) cultivators not to plant opium poppy. The latter method has "succeeded" to various extents on at least five occasions: Helmand in 1988 and in 2002–03, the Taliban in 2000–01, Nangarhar in 2004–05, and Balkh in 2006–07. In several of these cases prices were also falling as a result of large stockpiles, and it is difficult to separate the effect of the price change from that of the policy.

In 1988, Mullah Nasim Akhundzada stopped poppy cultivation in Helmand in return for aid projects promised by the U.S. Embassy in Islamabad.[26] Akhundzada was the most powerful mujahidin commander in Helmand. Because of objections by the U.S. Congress to negotiation with drug traffickers, the aid was not delivered. Mullah Nasim was assassinated, probably by traffickers to whom he had failed to deliver opium. Under his brother's command, opium poppy cultivation resumed the next year.

In the fall of 2000, the Islamic Emirate of Afghanistan issued a decree forbidding the cultivation of opium poppy throughout the territory under its control. Village headmen (maliks) were held responsible, and mullahs served as monitors. Cultivation was reduced by 95 percent. The price of raw opium rose tenfold, from $40–$60 per kilogram to $400–$600. The Taliban would probably not have been able to continue the cultivation ban at the higher prices, which meant that many cultivators' debts denominated in opium quantities went up 1,000 percent. The escalating indebtedness created unstoppable pressure for more planting, which indeed occurred in the fall of 2001, even before the fall of the Taliban. Making a virtue of necessity, Mullah Umar rescinded the ban.

In 2002, the governor of Helmand, Sher Muhammad Akhundzada, nephew of Mullah Nasim, succeeded in decreasing cultivation by almost 50 percent.[27] In the absence of security and development, production rebounded the following year and has now surpassed all records.

In 2004, Hajji Din Muhammad, a former mujahidin leader, used his tribal influence and the promise of massive U.S. aid (backed up by visits from U.S. Ambassador Zalmay Khalilzad) to obtain a 95 percent reduction in cultivation in Nangarhar. Cultivators largely sustained this reduction in areas close to Jalalabad, where they could market other horticultural crops with the help of alternative livelihood programs, but in the absence of effective aid delivery elsewhere, cultivation rebounded in the more isolated areas of the province. This year [2007–08] production appears to have decreased again, but it is impossible to tell at this point to what extent this is due to counternarcotics efforts and to what extent to the drop in opium prices caused by last year's record crop in Helmand.

In 2006, Muhammad Atta, governor of Balkh and a former mujahidin commander allied with Ahmad Shah Massoud, used his considerable influence and power to persuade the rural communities of Balkh not to plant opium. A year later, Governor Atta complained that the international community had not fulfilled its promises of aid and said he could not repeat the effort. If poppy cultivation in Balkh does not rebound in 2007–08, it will be because the summer marijuana crop may have offset the losses in income due to the poppy ban.[28] Nonetheless, the low prices may prevent a full-scale rebound.

Effect of Reduction of Supply of Raw Material

Eradication promotes the geographic spread of cultivation. Farmers in the remote province of Ghor for the first time found poppy farming profitable after the Taliban ban raised the price.[29] In 2004–05, the traffickers based in Nangarhar sent financial and extension agents to other areas (including Balkh) to ensure an adequate supply of raw material from other areas. Hence the 2005 harvest had the largest geographical distribution of any year.

Eradication or coerced reductions do not sustainably reduce cultivation, because Afghan peasants do not plant opium poppy out of greed. They do so out of insecurity. In these insecure conditions the opium industry is the only entity supplying the public goods needed for agriculture such as credit, marketing, extension services, and guaranteed access to land. Rural communities (not just farmers) need the capacity to invest and work in other activities (not just to plant other crops) to earn incomes.

Many farmers finance cultivation (with its high labor and other costs) and food consumption during the winter by selling opium to traders before planting on futures contracts, called salaam. For most of the past decade, traders advanced to farmers about half of the price at harvesttime of the amount contracted. For example, a farmer who made a salaam contract for 10 kilograms in the fall planting season of 2000, when opium was selling at about \$40/kg, would have been paid \$200. If he produced more than 10 kilos, he could sell the rest at the harvest price or keep it as inventory. If he produced less, he would owe the balance in cash at the harvest price, which he might pay, if he could, or roll over as debt to be paid off with opium from the next growing season.

Thus in the spring of 2001, the farmer who had contracted for 10 kilograms— which he was unable to produce because of the Taliban ban—would still owe the 10 kilos of opium, but now at the new price of nearly \$400/kg. So the farmer would owe $4,000 to pay back a $200 loan. Given these debt burdens, it is no surprise that farmers rushed to plant opium in the fall of 2001.

The salaam system shifts the risk of eradication to the farmers, especially the poor, and makes it more difficult for them to adjust to eradication by planting crops with which they cannot pay off their opium debt. According to David Mansfield, the world's leading researcher on the opium economy in Afghanistan, in response to the risk of eradication traders and moneylenders were advancing only about 30 rather than 50 percent of the market value at planting time in 2006 for salaam contracts, further shifting risk to the cultivator. Even when poppy is eradicated on land belonging to a large landowner, it is likely that the landowner has rented the land to sharecroppers to whom he has advanced salaam contracts. The sharecroppers' debts stand even if the crop is eradicated, and they stand to lose more than the landowner, who retains his claim on their assets. U.S. officials who claim that aerial spraying or other methods of forced eradication would enable them to be more evenhanded by eradicating crops of large landowners are ignoring how Afghan rural society actually works.

Afghan poppy-farming communities try to manage or reduce the risk posed to their livelihood by crop eradication. Thus far they have done so by adopting alternative crops only in those few areas, such as the districts around Jalalabad, where the market is developed enough that they can sell other products, mainly fruits and vegetables, to traders on futures contracts. Since these conditions exist in only a few areas, the main tools used to manage the risk are (1) bribery or political influence to halt eradication or divert it elsewhere, (2) emigration to Pakistan (the only available tactic during the Taliban ban in 2000–01), and (3) armed resistance.

Afghan farmers in most areas will choose legal livelihoods without eradication once they are confident that the alternatives will work. As long as they lack that confidence, they will respond to eradication with evasion or resistance. The more forcible the eradication, the more likely they are to turn to resistance. According to UNODC, "In 2007," there was "much more resistance to eradication than in 2006," with nineteen deaths (fifteen police and four farmers) and thirty-one people injured.[30]

Rural communities themselves must be consulted about whether they are in a position to meet their basic needs without recourse to poppy cultivation. The risk-averse Afghan farmer and the foreign official under pressure from the U.S. Congress or a parliament to show quick results have different definitions of when viable alternatives to poppy cultivation are available. Introducing eradication when foreigners claim alternatives are available, but before farmers feel secure in the alternatives, has led farmers in some areas to call upon the Taliban to protect them and to take up arms to prevent eradication teams from entering their areas. Teams from the U.S.-funded Alternative Livelihood Program, seen (rightly) as part of the same counternarcotics package, also cannot obtain access to many communities. Road-building teams are also attacked for fear that they will improve access for crop eradication.

More forcible eradication at this time, when both interdiction and "alternative livelihoods" are barely beginning, will increase the economic value of the opium economy, spread cultivation back to areas of the country that have eliminated or reduced it, and drive more communities into the arms of the Taliban.[31]

Alternative Livelihoods or Development?

The basic idea of "alternative livelihoods" is sound: participation in the narcotics industry fulfills economic and social needs, the legitimate satisfaction of which is difficult under current circumstances, and those engaging in these activities need legitimate alternatives. Designers of "alternative livelihood" programs, however, often misunderstand and underestimate the functions of the narcotics industry. Many confuse alternative livelihoods with "crop substitution," as expressed in the common question, "What other crop can they grow?" This question wrongly assumes that the sole noncriminal beneficiaries of the opium economy are "farmers" (who are presumed to cultivate their own land with mostly family labor), that the main reason "farmers" grow poppy is to increase their income, that there are no economic functions of the drug economy outside of cultivation, and that the only substitute for these functions is another "crop."[32]

All of these assumptions are wrong. Opium is not a crop but an industry. The statement made by UNODC and echoed by the U.S. that "only" 14 percent—one-seventh—of the Afghan population is directly involved in opium cultivation ignores the fact, also documented by UNODC, that "cultivation" generates only 20–30% of the export value of the opiates produced in Afghanistan. It also disregards the fact that a very large number of people are directly involved in sectors of the opium economy other than cultivation and that many people gain their livelihoods from activities generated indirectly from demand created by the opium economy in, for instance, construction and trade.

The reduction in poppy cultivation in Nangarhar province in 2004–05 provided a test of the substantial macroeconomic impact of the drug economy. The ban had an impact on a variety of socioeconomic groups beyond opium farmers. Rural laborers who owned no land but were hired during the weeding and harvesting season are estimated to have lost as much as U.S. $1,000 in off-farm income as a result of the ban. The contraction of income among the rural population significantly reduced their purchasing power, halving the turnover of businessmen and shopkeepers in provincial and district markets. Unskilled daily wage laborers in the provincial capital of Jalalabad experienced both a reduction in daily wages and the number of days they were hired.[33]

The greatest impact of the ban was felt by opium poppy-cultivating households, but those in areas with better access to resources fared better. Because of the ban, households with larger and well-irrigated landholdings encountered greater loss of on-farm income, but access to the agricultural commodity markets in Jalalabad enabled them to compensate for some of these losses by increasing cultivation of other high-value crops. Where possible, households also increased the number of family members engaged in daily wage labor. Thus, although the macroeconomic impact on comparatively resource-rich households was substantial, requiring reduced expenditure on basic food items, this group was generally able to avoid selling off both longer-term productive assets such as livestock and land, and investments generating licit income.

"In contrast," observes Mansfield:

> Those households most dependent on opium poppy and who typically cultivated it most intensively were found to adopt coping strategies in response to the ban that not only highlighted their growing vulnerability but threatened their long-term capacity to move out of illicit drug crop cultivation. *The loss in on-farm income that this group experienced was not offset even in part by an increase in cultivation of high-value licit crops.* This was due to constraints on irrigated land, the distance to markets, and the increasing control "local officials" had gained over the trade in licit goods. Instead, these households replaced opium poppy with wheat. However, due to land shortages and the density of population, wheat production was typically insufficient even to meet the household's basic food requirements. The loss in off-farm income during the opium poppy weeding and harvesting seasons (up to five months' employment) could not be replaced by intermittent wage labour opportunities paid at less than half the daily rate offered during the opium poppy harvest the previous year.[34]

Among members of the resource-poor group, the inability to pay existing debts threatened access to new loans. With no alternative income streams, households were forced to reduce expenditures on basic food items, withdraw children from higher education, and sell off livestock, household items, and investments in the licit economy. The resource-poor were also more likely than their better-off counterparts to send family members to Pakistan in search of employment. According to Mansfield, in some households the ban was felt so severely that even sole male members of working age were forced to leave in search of wage labor.[35] Moreover, it was the relatively poor households that vehemently opposed both the Afghan government and foreign countries assumed to be responsible for the ban.[36]

This real-life experiment underscores the significant economic damage to the poorest of Afghan poppy farmers—and the resulting loss of support for the government—when cultivation was suppressed. The development component of counternarcotics policy should help communities and households participate in alternative activities that meet the needs identified in this study. To be effective among the poor who are most dependent on opium poppy cultivation, investments in rural livelihoods must precede coerced reduction in cultivation or eradication. Otherwise poor farmers will not be able to benefit from the programs.

Alternative livelihood programs should be guided by the following findings. First, poppy cultivation is not a choice of crop that requires another crop to substitute for lost income; it is a component of livelihood strategies of extended families. These strategies include labor migration, education, wage labor, and serving in armed groups. This multidimensional function of poppy cultivation is the reason for the use of the term alternative "livelihood" rather than "crop."

The multiple functions of poppy cultivation in livelihood strategies refute the claims of advocates of eradication: that since no other crop produces the same gross income, eradication is necessary to force farmers to adopt other crops. Poppy cultivation fills needs that can be met by nonfarm activity. Furthermore, even cultivators who want to shift out of narcotics cannot do so without assistance. Eliminating cultivation before investing in assets needed for production actually deprives poor farmers of the capacity to adopt other crops and economic activities. Rural families do not need just another "crop." They need access to opportunities and assets that enable them to support themselves without poppy cultivation. These opportunities can come in forms other than "crops."

Secure employment is the most reliable "alternative livelihood." This is supported by the Charney survey data, which found that of ten proposed means for convincing farmers not to grow opium next season, eradication was the least likely to work. The most effective means for reducing opium cultivation were identified as financial (income support to farmers, access to low-interest credit, and cash advances) and agricultural (seeds and water) rather than coercion.[37]

Second, poppy does not provide access only to income but also to credit, land, water, food security, extension service, and insurance. As the Afghan public sector, both national and local, was destroyed by the past decades of war, private and sometimes criminal groups undertook the provision of public goods. This included collective violence for "security," in order to create conditions for their activities. Of course, when public goods are provided by private for-profit organizations without legal oversight, the provision is flawed (as the example of private security contractors in Afghanistan and Iraq shows). The opium industry privatized the provision of essential support services to the agricultural sector, as its rate of profit and global size made it the only industry with the resources and incentives to supply such public goods.

Third, the direct involvement of an estimated one-seventh of the Afghan population in opium poppy cultivation demonstrates that it is not a marginal activity. On the contrary, it signals a social revolution. For the first time in history, a substantial portion of the Afghan rural population is involved in the production of a cash crop for the global market. Never having come under direct colonial rule, and being distant and isolated from global markets over the past several centuries, Afghanistan's people never experienced the commercial penetration of their society as seen in colonized countries. The country never produced tea, coffee, sugar, indigo, rubber, copper, diamonds, gold, oil, jute, or any of the other commodities whose cultivation on plantations or extraction from mines led to new forms of labor control and migration, followed by social and political upheavals. Only Afghanistan's recent comparative advantage in the production of illegality and insecurity enabled it to join the global market by producing illicit crops. Hence, the economic alternatives to the opium economy must include, as the World Bank's William Byrd stated, the creation of "labor intensive agriculture exports of high-value added," not a return to subsistence farming.[38] This is what the Interim Afghanistan National Development Strategy calls for: "The ideal type of agricultural activity for Afghanistan is labor-intensive production of high-value horticultural crops that can be processed and packaged into durable high-value, low-volume commodities whose quality and cost would be adequate for sale in Afghan cities or export to regional or world markets."[39]

When USAID started the Alternative Livelihood Program in 2004, however, the initial package consisted of donations of wheat seed and fertilizer, much of which the farmers immediately sold to pay off their opium debts.

Fourth, the public goods and effective demand created by the opium industry in this predominantly rural and agricultural country have become central to macroeconomic stability. This is not the case in drug-producing countries where cultivation involves a negligible part of the economy and a marginalized part of the population located in border areas. Even in Colombia, the value of narcotics production is estimated at only 3–4 percent of the GDP. In Afghanistan, nearly a third of the economy and probably an equal percentage of the population depends economically on the opium economy. Drug production affects not just farm income. It affects the balance of payments, tax revenues (through imports), the rate of exchange, employment, retail turnover, and construction.

The broad scope of the effects of the drug economy in Afghanistan led the current U.S. *Strategy* to refer to "alternative development," rather than "alternative livelihoods." As with other improvements in analysis and terminology in this report, however, the *Strategy* fails to draw the logical conclusions: that counternarcotics in Afghanistan requires a macroeconomic and political strategy over a period of decades, not a quick fix based on accelerated eradication.

Fifth, since drugs are not marginal in Afghanistan, and changes in production and trafficking have significant macroeconomic impact, counternarcotics policy has national political impact. "Alternative livelihood" programs directed to regions in proportion to their volume of opium production generate perverse results: they become incentives to production of opium elsewhere. Just as eradication spreads poppy cultivation to new insecure areas with lower yields or a higher cost of eradication by raising the price, alternative livelihoods directed at opium-cultivating areas spread cultivation by acting as an incentive, raising the expected returns to poppy cultivation. In the fall of 2004, an elder of the Mohmand tribe from Nangarhar told one of the authors that the people in his area were saying that they had to grow poppy in order to get assistance from the government. When this author told a U.S. senior official that livelihood programs should therefore be targeted at areas that were not growing poppy, he was told that he was "not living in the real world." The current strategy responds to this with a program of incentives for "good performers." Recognizing the problem is a positive step, one that demonstrates a shift in thinking since 2004 but is insufficient by itself, as discussed later.

Alternative development for counternarcotics must start from macroeconomic plans to create employment by linking Afghanistan to licit international markets, especially through rural industries based on agricultural products. Since elimination of the narcotics sector risks causing a significant economic contraction of one of the poorest and most-armed countries in the world, planning for elimination of narcotics must start from a political and macroeconomic plan to ensure stability and overall growth; it must integrate counterinsurgency, peace building, and development with counternarcotics as part of a national strategy, precisely as called for in the Afghanistan Compact.

Securing Afghanistan's Future (SAF), the 2004 study prepared under the direction of Finance Minister Ashraf Ghani, proposed such a basic framework, though much more work was required, and those estimates are now out of date.[40] *SAF* estimated that to eliminate the narcotics economy in fifteen years without compromising a modest rise in standards of living would require a minimum real growth rate of 9 percent per year in the licit economy. The growth rate alone would not cushion the shock sufficiently, as the losses from eliminating narcotics might not occur in the same locations and social groups as the new growth; therefore, sectoral and redistributive policies would also be needed. The I-ANDS also referred to this target, but there has been no further work on the integration of counternarcotics into macroeconomic planning. Instead the development component has been limited to small-scale rural development.

Sectoral policies might have to address particular commodities. As Ghani has noted, cotton (the original cash crop produced in the irrigated areas of Helmand) is not competitive with opium poppy as long as U.S. and European Union producers drive down the price by dumping subsidized cotton on the international market. Estimates of the price impact of these subsidies vary.[41] Total U.S. cotton subsidies total more than $3 billion yearly, more than total U.S. development aid to Afghanistan.[42]

If the U.S. and EU subsidies cannot be eliminated due to pressure from domestic political constituencies, subsidies could still be provided in Afghanistan.[43] In meetings with counternarcotics officials, Helmand farmers have asked for government cotton subsidies as an incentive to shift from poppy to cotton, which used to be grown on irrigated land there, but so far Helmand farmers do not qualify for exemptions from the discipline of the "free" market. Even if cotton alone is not competitive, Ghani has suggested that textile and garment production would be competitive. Establishing textile quotas for Afghanistan in major markets and investing in simple garment factories in Afghan cotton-producing areas could increase employment. The appeal of a certified "Made in Afghanistan" (or "Made in Afghanistan by Afghan women") label could offset the increased costs of production and transport. This is just one example: creating markets for Afghan products and providing marketing assistance is key to alternative development. Should subsidies prove impractical under Afghan conditions, another approach is to expand local procurement by the international community in Afghanistan combined with attempts to encourage contract growing of high-value horticulture.[44]

Moving rural Afghanistan into the licit economy requires investment in many kinds of public goods: roads, security, credit, marketing, storage, extension service, and the creation of rural industries as well. All of this depends in turn on linking Afghanistan to regional and global markets and ensuring access to those markets. This requires political and business initiatives at the policy level. The U.S. State Department is soliciting proposals under their new Economic Empowerment in Strategic Regions (EESR) program to provide alternative income generation for farmers in southwestern Afghanistan through production and processing of agricultural fibers, oilseeds, and feed products. But USAID reportedly refuses to fund such initiatives on the grounds that they conflict with the Bumpers Amendment.[45] Until there is an official declaration of administration policy regarding the amendment, those qualified to submit proposals will be reluctant to do so.

Avoiding the perverse incentives generated by Alternative Livelihood Programs targeted at poppy-growing areas requires more than the Good Performance Fund, which rewards provinces that refrain from or reduce opium poppy cultivation by providing development funds to the governors. The concept of rewarding areas and communities for efforts against poppy is a good one, as it creates the right incentives. Making funds available to governors, however, may not be the most effective way to do so. In the Afghan state system, governors have limited power and virtually no budgetary or expenditure authority. The idea of rewarding governors appears to have developed from observation of provinces where governors with a great deal of personal influence because of their tribal or mujahid background managed to reduce poppy cultivation. These governors were able to do so, however, because of their personal power networks and links with the drug trade, not because of the powers of the governor's office.

It might be more effective to target such incentives to communities through programs organized like the National Solidarity Program, which provides block grants to community councils to carry out development projects chosen by the communities themselves. The Independent Directorate for Local Governance (IDLG) in the office of the president is developing plans for the reintegration of communities into the national and provincial administration and state structure through long-term agreements between the state and communities. These agreements may include measures for the gradual elimination of poppy cultivation and trafficking as part of a package of public services provided. Experience has shown that tying aid closely to reductions in cultivation does not give a sustainable counternarcotics outcome, but linking communities to the state through public services does create capacities for monitoring and incentives to comply. This subnational approach to incentives could work better than one solely focused on governors.

The IDLG program provides for gradual reduction of cultivation where it exists. Such transitional measures are essential. Farmers cannot reasonably be expected to abandon a pivotal part of their livelihood strategy as soon as a foreign government official decides that they have alternative livelihoods (perhaps because an office called "Alternative Livelihoods Program" has been established in the province). The risk-averse Afghan peasant and the foreign official under pressure from a capital to show quick results have differing definitions of when alternatives to poppy cultivation are available.

Management of this risk during the transition to alternative livelihoods poses a challenge to counternarcotics policy. One example courtesy of Mansfield: an aid organization provided funding to enable farmers in Kandahar to plant fruit trees. The farmers planted the trees in their poppy fields and continued to grow poppy among the saplings. As the trees matured over several years, their shade would prevent the poppy from growing, while their increasing yield of fruit would provide cash income as well as advance payments from traders in due course. By growing poppy the farmers could still earn a return on their land while the trees were maturing. Both farmer and development practitioners saw this process as a rational way to manage the transition from opium to another crop (and other cropping options could be seen as part of the transition in other parts of the country). However, those involved in drug control saw this as unacceptable and argued that now that farmers were in receipt of assistance and growing other crops they should cease their opium poppy cultivation immediately. They suggested the aid should be ceased and made conditional on the elimination of opium poppy even though farmers were not yet gaining an income from the new crop they had planted. These drug controllers failed to recognize that there is an inevitable process of diversifying into other activities and only gradually abandoning poppy as farmers develop greater confidence in other economic activities.[46]

The current counternarcotics strategy has no explicit plan for managing the transition, sequencing the different policy tools, or building the state institutions simultaneously with trying to use them. These are, however, the key questions for counternarcotics strategy. The one exception is the statement that eradication should be carried out "where access to alternative livelihoods is available," a principle with no mechanism for implementation.

Interdiction: High on the Supply Chain

Several policy instruments address higher parts of the value chain.

Interdiction of the trade: mainly destruction of the product, including raids on opium bazaars, police seizures of drugs found in vehicles or in storage, and destruction of heroin or morphine laboratories. Though these actions are carried out by law enforcement institutions, they entail more enforcement than law. Once a banned substance is seized, the government can destroy it without additional legal procedure or referral to a court. Needless to say, this is not what always happens. There is a system for how much traffickers must pay the police to recover a portion of their goods. Instead of destroying the captured substance, Afghan police sometimes claim they have to transport it to their superiors for "evidence." What happens to it afterward is not always well documented.[47]

Arrest of traffickers: the number of such cases is on the rise, according to the U.S. *Strategy*, but such arrests mainly target small traffickers or smugglers.[48] The incapacity and corruption of the Afghan justice system is such that few of the reported 562 arrests and prosecutions lead to fair trial and conviction. Instead arrests lead to detention and bribery for release. In response, the U.S. Drug Enforcement Agency (DEA) is working to compile cases against major traffickers that can be presented for extradition to the United States. The total number of such cases so far is only two or three and cannot increase quickly enough to have any appreciable impact on the largest sector of the Afghan economy.[49]

Arrests of corrupt officials: such arrests are rare in the extreme, since the police and courts are the main object centers of corruption. Although officials of the National Directorate of Security (NDS), the intelligence agency, have allegedly been arrested, tried, and punished for accepting bribes from traffickers, we are not aware of any such prosecutions in the Ministry of the Interior.

Building institutions for interdiction and law enforcement: just as foreign donors have supported the formation of the Central Poppy Eradication Force (CPEF), they have also supported the formation of the Counternarcotics Police Force (CNPF) for interdiction and law enforcement. The United States is also supporting the creation of special prosecutors, courts, and prisons for drug offenses. These institutions will be resourced and trained better than the rest of the Afghan justice system, since foreigners think they are important.

Measures against money laundering: these are not mentioned in the public version of the *U.S. Counternarcotics Strategy*, but they are reportedly part of the classified version. A World Bank–UNODC study of money laundering for drug trafficking in Afghanistan estimated (very approximately) that in 2004–05 actors in the opium economy imported $1.7 billion into Afghanistan using the informal *hawala* system of money transfer.[50] The author of the study could not estimate the amount of drug profits transferred out of Afghanistan in the same way, but it is likely of the same order of magnitude.

Removal from or prevention of the appointment to senior positions of officials suspected of drug-related corruption: all ministers and senior officials of the government serve at the pleasure of the president and may (in principle if not in practice) be removed from office at his discretion. Hence counternarcotics policy is closely related to the benchmark in the Afghanistan Compact requiring that "A clear and transparent national appointments mechanism will be established . . . for all senior level appointments to the central government and the judiciary, as well as for provincial governors, chiefs of police, district administrators and provincial heads of security."[51]

Interdiction also includes measures for strengthening institutions through funding, equipment, and training. Properly designed, implemented, and sequenced, these are needed components of a counternarcotics policy. But they cannot succeed without building a state to implement the policies and exercise command and control over the strengthened institutions.

Interdiction that is implemented fairly and effectively would directly contribute to the goals of the Afghanistan Compact. No study has estimated the varying effects of different types of interdiction on the narcotics value chain, but the World Bank argues that interdiction would lower the farmgate price of opium.[52] By raising the cost of trafficking, interdiction would lower the demand curve of traffickers. It would reduce the demand for opium, thus making poppy cultivation less attractive and rendering legal livelihoods more competitive, and it would do so invisibly over the entire opium market, without the political discrimination that eradication entails.

Harjit Sajjan, a reserve major in the Canadian Army, observed the contrasting political effects of interdiction and eradication while serving with the Canadian NATO deployment in Kandahar:

> Interdiction is the key. Eradication impacts the farmers who are trying to feed their families but interdiction impacts the drug lords, or what the local Afghans call "Dhakoos" (Bandits). The emphasis should be against the drug labs and transportation routes. This interdiction method is more efficient and has greater impact on the drug lords. Plus, it does not disrupt the farmers. This will allow the International agencies, NGOs, and military time to work on alternative programs.[53]

The political risk of trying to implement interdiction under current conditions is that it is more likely to concentrate and integrate the opium industry than to destroy it. As the state lacks autonomy from power holders, the latter compete to gain control over the foreign-funded counternarcotics programs to use them against rivals. Control over interdiction can be a powerful tool for crushing competitors.[54]

Hence without the necessary political institutions, international training and funding does not have the desired results. Training teaches people and institutions *how* to accomplish a mission; it cannot make them loyal or committed to risking their lives or fortunes for that mission. It is not possible to create effective institutions for counternarcotics enforcement when such a high proportion of a society's power holders are directly or indirectly beholden to the drug trade and can see no way to move out of it. A political solution and transitional arrangement for the upper end of the drug value chain is as essential as a political solution for the insurgency.

A Political Strategy for Counternarcotics and State Building

At a 2007 meeting on counternarcotics and peace building, the deputy minister of defense of Colombia, Sergio Jaramillo, emphasized that the essential condition for implementing counternarcotics policies was "a state that works."[55] The state is a political organization enjoying a degree of legitimacy and sovereignty, not just a set of technical bodies, however well trained, equipped, and funded. The state is only one of several contending authorities in most of Afghanistan, and its reach is particularly weak in areas where opium production is concentrated. The state's weakness does not result solely or even primarily from a lack of technical capacities, but from a lack of resources and consent to a common institutional framework on the part of the country's key power holders. The divergent views and interests of these power holders regarding the drug economy and their relative strength compared to the state are the main reasons the drug economy has continued to grow.

Training people in the technical skills required for counternarcotics is necessary, but it is not a substitute for the political (and sometimes military and economic) work of building a state whose incumbents exercise a degree of autonomy from the socially powerful, who in Afghanistan include drug traffickers. As a result, frustrated foreign advisors increasingly press for more control over operations and autonomy from the governmental apparatus, which leaves officials the choice of being perceived as foreign puppets or of engaging in some form of resistance, whether covert (corruption) or overt (insurgency). A 2007 account of a U.S.-supported eradication effort in Uruzgan province documented the challenge faced by a former DEA agent employed by a private contractor of getting Afghan forces to equitably eradicate poppy fields belonging to a local power holder. Yet, even if the field was eradicated (the outcome in the account is uncertain), an operation carried out under foreign coercion does not strengthen the authority of the state or prevent future poppy cultivation in a sustainable way.[56] Forcing the Afghan authorities to carry out eradication programs they do not believe in demonstrates not the strength of the state but its weakness in the face of foreign pressure.

Hence the problem confronted by the policies labeled as interdiction, law enforcement, or anticorruption are pieces of the same daunting task: consolidating at least a minimal state structure in the face of the enormous resources available to unofficial (and sometimes, but not always, criminal) power holders.

For the foreseeable future, the government and its international supporters will be able to accomplish little in Afghanistan without the support or neutrality of de facto power holders. These are leaders who combine functions as politicians, tribal or ethnic leaders, businessmen, landowners, commanders of armed groups of varying degrees of legality, parliamentarians, and government officials. Many families combine these functions by a division of labor among brothers or cousins.

Members of this stratum have various political orientations, their most consistent one being support for their own interests. Many have mastered several rhetorical repertoires for different audiences, and they manifest considerable pragmatism in their actions. These leaders have a healthy respect for effective use of force, money, and rhetoric. Conversely, they hold in contempt wasteful and ineffective use of force, money, and rhetoric, which, rightly or wrongly, is what most of them see in the actions of the international community in Afghanistan, especially in counternarcotics.

Many of them derive much of their resources directly or indirectly from the opiate industry, sometimes without ever actually seeing, handling, or even mentioning the substance in question. Afghanistan's extensive, dense, and opaque family networks enable some of the powerful to denounce or oppose the drug economy while simultaneously (and invisibly) benefiting from it.

These leaders, however, are less committed to narcotics than they are to other allegiances they have made from time to time. In private, they often agree that drugs are harmful and that profiting from the trafficking is not praiseworthy, but they see no alternative way to raise the funds they need to keep up their social and political standing. In several cases, members of this group have decided that their interests are served best by banning or preventing poppy growing, and virtually all decreases in poppy cultivation have been due to their efforts, rather than to the international community's counternarcotics programs.

State building requires a combination of co-opting, neutralizing, or defeating these elites. Those engaged in or supporting military or terrorist action against the government should be targets of military action themselves. Among those not actively fighting the government, targeted sanctions (removal from office, asset seizure, arrest, exile) against the most recalcitrant of this group are necessary if the effort is to succeed. But such efforts can at most provide pressure for the core task: co-opting as many of this group as possible into the state-building and development process. Economic, social, and political change will transform elites and create new ones, as these processes create new avenues for licit pursuit of wealth and power.

Hence, whatever scarce enforcement means can be mustered should be concentrated against narcotics trafficking and protection. Intelligence collection should focus on understanding the power relations among drug traffickers and specific power holders. The international community should use this intelligence to press for the exclusion of the patrons of traffickers from high office. They need not be arrested or tried; even removing some from office and sending them far from the country would send a clear message.

NATO troops should be authorized to provide needed support to Afghan operations to interdict convoys carrying drugs across the borders and destroy heroin laboratories, while minimizing loss of civilian life. International narcotics police should be embedded with Afghans at border posts and airports. Major traffickers and their protectors, once identified by reliable intelligence, should be subject to travel bans and seizure of assets under sanctions approved by the Security Council, which in December 2006 voted in Resolution 1735 to extend the antiterrorist sanctions of Resolution 1376 to drug traffickers as well.

But law enforcement cannot defeat an elite consensus. And the elite consensus in Afghanistan right now is that foreigners have offered no credible alternative to the opium economy. Law enforcement suppresses and controls deviant behavior with the consent of a society's key elites, who make governing possible by cooperating with the law enforcement apparatus. An activity that constitutes about one third of the country's total GDP, however, is not socially deviant behavior, whatever international agreements may say. Though drug trafficking is not honored, people see it as a result of the demand for narcotics from foreign markets, which the developed countries with all their resources are unable to suppress, and an effect of the annihilation of Afghanistan's former state and economy by decades of war. Counternarcotics policy has become another risk to be managed by pseudocompliance and covert (or overt) resistance, above all by maintaining asymmetries in information, which the Afghan elite finds relatively easy to do.

Ending or reducing both the insurgency and the drug economy requires a political settlement on how Afghanistan is to be ruled and developed, not just the implementation of policies by a state that still barely exists.[57] Such a transition might provide amnesty for past trafficking while allowing traffickers to invest their money in legal enterprises plus forfeiting some assets to public purposes. The ulama (learned clergy) could be consulted about appropriate forms of restitution.

At present, there is no program to help the major entrepreneurs and power holders in the opiate business in Afghanistan transition out of the trade. On the contrary, when entrepreneurs grown rich from the trade seek help from aid organizations in creating licit enterprises, they are turned away. As already noted, such a prohibition prevented implementation of a counternarcotics agreement with the major commander in Helmand in 1988. In 2006, the provincial director of one ministry in Helmand walked into the USAID-funded Alternative Livelihoods Program compound with $800,000 in cash, offering to share the costs for setting up a wheat mill. USAID overruled local program staff who wanted to accept the offer, on the grounds that it would have constituted negotiation with a trafficker and money laundering. USAID contracts prohibit working with anyone who has a history of involvement in narcotics—even though the house rented by its major alternative livelihoods contractor in Lashkargah was owned by someone reputed to be a major drug trafficker. Rules could be bent to solve the problems of U.S. contractors, but not those of Afghanistan.

The international community recognizes that after decades of armed conflict in one of the poorest countries of the world, it is not possible to administer justice for all the wrongs that were committed in the past. The process of establishing peace and stability forgoes such justice and seeks, at best, "transitional justice." Transitional justice may enable a society to confront its past truthfully, perhaps punish a few and make amends with most, while laying the foundation for a system of government and justice that will prevent reversion to armed conflict. It is no less unrealistic to expect that Afghanistan, whose economy and polity depend more on narcotics than any other state, can move from an illicit to a licit economy without an acknowledged transition not only for farmers but also for elites that have sustained their power through the profits of trafficking.

Successful negotiations require leverage. Interdiction aimed at the high end of the value chain combined with political measures against traffickers well connected to the state are essential. The government and international community should seek to avoid perverse outcomes by seeking some measure of reparations from those who have accumulated wealth in the narcotics trade, such as contributing to the capitalization of rural development banks or microcredit institutions. Enabling traffickers to bring their funds into the open by investing in financial institutions, as well as other programs that produce social good, would offer some degree of compensation to those in the society who do not benefit from the drug trade.

This approach to Afghan traffickers and their protectors, based on a combination of counterinsurgency, interdiction, and negotiation, should proceed simultaneously with development efforts to put in place the essential economic services now provided by the narcotics industry.

Rural communities should be offered a legitimate transition from dependence on opium poppy, rather than a premature choice between eradication and resistance when they are not confident in alternative livelihoods. If the international community and Afghan government accept, as they say they do, that the society's transition from dependence on narcotics production must be gradual, then they should accept that continuation of diminishing amounts of poppy cultivation is not criminal but inevitable. Licensing or legalizing opium cannot provide a single-bullet, comprehensive solution to Afghanistan's drug problem; some transitional measures should be considered to support communities that diminish their production of opium, even if they do not move immediately to zero cultivation.

Crop eradication can be carried out most fairly and effectively by communities themselves. The Afghan state has never had the capacity or legitimacy to police village communities directly. Every time it has tried to do so with force augmented by foreigners, it has faced collapse and defeat. Counternarcotics policy that escalates forced eradication where communities do not feel confident in alternatives could do for the current Afghan government what forced land reform did for the Afghan Communist government in 1978–79: face the government's international supporters with a choice of military escalation or defeat. There is no need to learn that lesson again.

An alternative strategy follows:

- Launch a public information campaign—the first part of the existing Afghan National Drug Control Strategy—stating that the purpose of counternarcotics is not to attack but to enhance the livelihoods of the people of Afghanistan. Afghans cannot build a stable future on the basis of a criminal enterprise that is against Islam. But they also cannot build a stable future on empty stomachs. Therefore, any alternative livelihoods program must work together with the

98 percent of Afghan poppy cultivators who, according to UNODC, say that they are willing to abandon poppy cultivation if they can count on earning at least half as much from legal crops.[58] Eradication should be reserved for the other 2 percent. But first the rural population has to have confidence in the alternative.

- Ask for voluntary restraint in planting while actually delivering (not just announcing, funding, or launching) much larger development livelihood programs that have integrated counternarcotics analysis and objectives, including National Priority Programs such as the National Solidarity Program. These programs must go first of all to provinces that are not planting poppy or that are reducing it. Otherwise, there will be perverse incentives for increasing cultivation. Alternative livelihood programs should go to poppy-producing provinces as a second priority.

- Livelihood programs must provide all the services currently provided to farmers by drug traffickers: futures contracts, guaranteed marketing, financing, and technical assistance (extension services). Microfinance, some programs of which have already started, must be made easily available so that poor farmers and regions can avail themselves of new opportunities. In the last year or two, such programs have finally started, but it will take several years before they start to yield returns and people have confidence in them. Alternative livelihoods will become successful only when Afghans themselves believe they can rely on them.

- Delivering livelihood programs *without* forcible eradication will make it easier for the government and international forces to gain access to areas from which the population has thus far excluded them.

- Simultaneously, the Afghan government, NATO, and the coalition should undertake enhanced interdiction efforts. These should start with political measures at the top, consisting of removing high officials who receive narcotics money, even if their operational involvement with narcotics is distant. Intelligence assets should be directed to obtain information about which high-ranking officials are connected to the drug economy. NATO and the coalition should provide military support to attacks by Afghan national security forces on smuggling convoys and heroin laboratories, with due regard for avoiding civilian casualties. The Ministry of the Interior must be reorganized (not just reformed) from top to bottom (in that order). Precursor interdiction must be enhanced.

- The major traffickers, many of whom have residences outside of Afghanistan, should be arrested or made extremely unwelcome in those countries where they reside. As recommended by UNODC, UN member states should "take full advantage of Security Council Resolution 1735 by adding the names of a dozen drug traffickers to the United Nations al-Qaeda/Taliban list in order to seize their assets, ban their travel and facilitate their extradition."[59]

- According to analyses by both the World Bank and UNODC, interdiction efforts will lower the farmgate price of opium, sending the right price signals to farmers and making alternatives more viable. This will reinforce containment of cultivation.
- As legal livelihoods are strengthened and interdiction proceeds, a program is needed to manage the transition of both farmers and traffickers from the narcotics economy to licit economic activity. Measures are needed for the reconciliation and reintegration of cultivators and traffickers who are willing to support the government, move out of their illicit occupations, and join the development process. Traders and traffickers have valuable experience in marketing cash crops and providing services to farmers. Those not affiliated ideologically or organizationally to the armed opposition should be retrained to link other agro-based export industries to the countryside.

Introducing enhanced eradication simultaneously with interdiction and alternative livelihood efforts will lead to a decrease in security and strengthen antigovernment forces, while rendering interdiction and alternative livelihoods more difficult. The political purpose of counternarcotics is to win the support of most of those involved with the drug economy by providing them with better security and links to markets than have drug traffickers, corrupt officials, and the Taliban. This does not require replacing every dollar, as the quality of licit income can be better. Income and crop diversification also reduces risk. Expanding licit livelihoods cannot mean trying to push Afghan farmers who are now used to commercial agriculture back to subsistence farming. It requires linking farmers to licit markets and agro-based industries.

The state in Afghanistan can be built only by using the limited force available in a highly targeted and economical way against hard-core opponents, while greatly expanding the incentives (where international actors should have a decisive advantage) to win people over to the side of the government and its international supporters. Done the wrong way, counternarcotics could do to this effort what land reform did to the communists; a good idea gone bad destroyed any hope of popular support. Counternarcotics done properly is exactly what Afghans have been asking for: removing criminal power holders and bringing security and development.

Notes

1. The JCMB, including all the major donors and troop contributors, is the body responsible for monitoring the implementation of the Afghanistan Compact. In January 2006, more than sixty states and international organizations adopted the compact as the framework for their assistance to Afghanistan over the coming five years.
2. UNODC, *Afghan Opium Survey*, August 7, 2007, p. 20.

3. It is a fallacy to call areas where poppy is not grown "opium-free." Trafficking continues through such areas.

4. David Mansfield and Adam Pain, "Evidence from the Field: Understanding Changing Levels of Opium Poppy Cultivation in Afghanistan," Afghanistan Research and Evaluation Unit Briefing Paper Series (November 2007)," p. 14.

5. Barnett R. Rubin, "The Political Economy of War and Peace in Afghanistan," *World Development*, Vol. 28, No. 10, 2000: 1789–93.

6. Charney Research survey in Afghanistan, November 2007. Our thanks to Craig Charney for providing this data. The reliability of polling in Afghanistan remains to be determined. The results of Charney's polls, however, are frequently cited by U.S. officials.

7. *U.S. Counternarcotics Strategy* (August 2007), p. 13.

8. UNODC, *Afghanistan Opium Survey 2004*, p. 1, http://www.unodc.org/pdf/afg/afghanistan_opium_survey_2004.pdf.

9. It is not accurate to add the gross profits of narcotics to licit GDP to obtain a figure for total (licit and nonlicit) GDP. The gross profits would have to be transformed to value added by including changes in stocks held, subtracting costs of inputs to manufacture (e.g., precursors), and including the net international flow of capital from the industry, among other adjustments. See Edouard Martin and Steven Symansky, "Macroeconomic Impact of the Drug Economy and Counter-Narcotics Efforts," in Doris Buddenberg and William Byrd, eds., *Afghanistan's Drug Industry: Structure, Functioning, Dynamics, and Implications for Counter-Narcotics Policy* (UNODC and World Bank, 2006).

10. Colombian Deputy Minister of Defense Sergio Jaramillo at the conference, "Fighting Drugs and Building Peace: Toward Policy Coherence," New York City, May 14–15, 2007. For a conference summary, see Barnett R. Rubin and Alexandra Guaqueta, "Fighting Drugs and Building Peace: Towards Policy Coherence between Counter-Narcotics and Peace Building," Friedrich Ebert Stiftung: New York, November 2007.

11. According to Richard Holbrooke, the former U.S. ambassador to the UN, "even without aerial eradication, the [U.S. counternarcotics] program . . . may be the single most ineffective program in the history of American foreign policy. It's not just a waste of money. It actually strengthens the Taliban and al-Qaida, as well as criminal elements within Afghanistan." See "Still Wrong in Afghanistan," *Washington Post*, January 23, 2008, p. A19.

12. See David Mansfield, "Beyond the Metrics: Understanding the Nature of Change in the Rural Livelihoods of Opium Poppy Growing Households in the 2006/07 Growing Season," Report for the Afghan Drugs Interdepartmental Unit of the UK Government, May 2007; David Mansfield and Adam Pain, "Opium Poppy Eradication: How to Raise Risk When There Is Nothing to Lose?" AREU Briefing Paper, August 2006.

13. U.S. Ambassador William Wood described the seizure as worth $500 million in "street value," that is, if it had been sold in Amsterdam or London. Musa Qala, however, is rather distant from Amsterdam and London, and the prices there are correspondingly different.

14. Mansfield and Pain, "Opium Poppy Eradication."

15. Bonn Agreement, V (3), http://www.un.org/News/dh/latest/afghan/afghan-agree.htm.

16. Constitution of the Islamic Republic of Afghanistan of 2004/1382, Article 7(2), unofficial translation.

17. Mark Shaw, "Drug Trafficking and the Development of Organized Crime in Post-Taliban Afghanistan," in Buddenberg and Byrd, *Afghanistan's Drug Industry*. See also Adam Pain, "Opium Trading Systems in Hilmand and Ghor Provinces," in same volume.

18. Misha Glenny, "The Lost War," *Washington Post*, August 19, 2007, p. B01, http://www.washingtonpost.com/wp-dyn/content/article/2007/08/17/AR2007081701716.html.

19. This summary can give only a general idea. Drug trafficking involves many routes, techniques, and modes of transport.

20. Interviews with intelligence and law enforcement officials in Kabul.

21. On the border police, see Gretchen Peters, "Heroin Found in Car Allegedly Owned by Top Afghan Border Official." ABC News, August 7, 2007, http://blogs.abcnews.com/theblotter/2007/08/heroin-found-in.html. On corruption in Ariana Airlines, see Jason Straziuso, "Afghan Airline Set to Collapse," Associated Press, March 30, 2007, http://www.afghanistannewscenter.com/news/2007/march/mar302007.html#1.

22. Single Convention on Narcotic Drugs, 1961 (Article 36), https://www.incb.org/incb/en/convention_1961.html.
23. Research on eradication by genetic modification has not yet created usable technologies.
24. Charney Research survey in Afghanistan, November 2007.
25. This effect might be offset by a sufficient increase in interdiction, which lowers the amount demanded at a given price. However, we know of no analysis giving quantitative estimates of the effect of both eradication and interdiction on prices. Such an analysis would indicate what level of interdiction is necessary to ensure that eradication does not increase the overall value of the opium economy.
26. Barnett R. Rubin, *The Fragmentation of Afghanistan*, 2nd ed. (New Haven and London: Yale University Press, 2002).
27. UNODC, *Afghanistan Opium Survey 2004*, p. 3.
28. David Mansfield, personal communication on file with the authors, January 23, 2008; Alastair Leithead, "Poverty Feeds Afghan Drugs Trade," BBC News, January 22, 2008, http://news.bbc.co.uk/2/hi/south_asia/7201085.stm.
29. David Mansfield, "Water Management, Livestock, and the Opium Economy," AREU Case Study Series, 2006, p. 28. Mansfield notes that increased prices after the Taliban-imposed ban were not alone responsible for the movement of poppy cultivation into new areas.
30. UNODC, *Afghanistan Opium Survey 2007*, p. 20.
31. Harjit Sajjan, a Vancouver police detective who served as an army reserve major in Canada's NATO contingent in Kandahar, described this scenario to Barnett Rubin in an electronic mail message dated August 31, 2007.
32. For conceptual shortcomings of "alternative livelihoods" and attempts to redefine the term, see David Mansfield, "Anti-Narcotics Mainstreaming in ADB's Activities in Afghanistan, 2002–2006," Asian Development Bank, January 2007, pp. 12–15.
33. Mansfield, "Water Management, Livestock, and the Opium Economy," p. 10.
34. Ibid., p. 11, emphasis added.
35. Ibid., pp. 11–12.
36. Ibid., p. 12.
37. Charney Research survey in Afghanistan, November 2007.
38. World Bank, "Afghanistan Drug Industry: Focus on Drug Trading & Processing: World Bank," http://web.worldbank.org/WBSITE/EXTERNAL/COUNTRIES/SOUTHASIAEXT/0,,contentMDK:21466423~pagePK:2865106~piPK:2865128~theSitePK:223547,00.html.
39. Islamic Republic of Afghanistan, *Afghanistan National Development Strategy: An Interim Strategy for Security, Governance, Economic Growth, and Poverty Alleviation*, Vol. I, p. 82, http://siteresources.worldbank.org/INTPRS1/Resources/Afghanistan_PRSP(May2008).pdf.
40. Asian Development Bank, UNAMA, UNDP, World Bank, Securing Afghanistan's Future, March 2004, http://www.effectivestates.org/Papers/Securing%20Afghanistan's%20Future.pdf.
41. Daneswar Poonyth, Alexander Sams, Ramesh Sharma, and Shangnan Shui, "The Impact of Domestic and Trade Policies on the World Cotton Market," UN Food and Agriculture Organization, Commodity and Trade Policy Research Working Paper, No. April 8, 2004, ftp://ftp.fao.org/docrep/fao/007/j2731e/j2731e00.pdf.
42. Troy Schmitz and Daniel Voica, "Global Welfare Implications of U.S. Cotton Subsidies," presentation at the American-Greek-Romanian Opportunities, Trade, and Development Symposium, November 2006.
43. See Edmund Phelps and Graciana del Castillo, "A Strategy to Help Afghanistan Kick Its Habit," *Financial Times*, January 3, 2008.
44. The organization Roots for Peace, for example, is supporting the restoration of grape and raisin vineyards under USAID's Rebuilding Agricultural Markets in Afghanistan Program.
45. Section 513(b) of the FY2006 Appropriations Act.
46. David Mansfield, presentation to the International Institute for Security Studies, London, June 20, 2007.
47. In part because of such problems, NATO is now considering an enhanced role for ISAF in interdiction.

48. *U.S. Counternarcotics Strategy*, pp. 58–59.
49. Interviews with U.S. officials, Washington and Kabul.
50. Edwina Thompson, "The Nexus of Drug Trafficking and Hawala in Afghanistan," in Buddenberg and Byrd, *Afghanistan's Drug Industry*, p. 161.
51. Afghanistan Compact, http://www.nato.int/isaf/docu/epub/pdf/afghanistan_compact. pdf.
52. William Byrd and Christopher Ward, "Drugs and Development in Afghanistan," World Bank SASPR Working Paper Series, December 2004, http://siteresources.worldbank.org/ INTCPR/214578-1111996036679/20482462/WP18_Web.pdf.
53. Sajjan, "Panjwai, Kandahar," electronic message of August 31, 2007, to Barnett R. Rubin.
54. Mansfield documented the low cost of opium trading during the Taliban period; http:// www.davidmansfield.org/data/Field_Work/UNODC/strategic_study_2.doc. Adam Pain has shown how the introduction of interdiction and other counternarcotics policies has raised barriers to entry for traders without powerful political protection; see also Pain, "Opium Trading Systems in Hilmand and Ghor Provinces," in Buddenberg and Byrd, *Afghanistan's Drug Industry*.
55. Fighting Drugs and Building Peace: Toward Policy Coherence," New York City, May 14–15, 2007. For a conference summary, see Rubin and Guaqueta, "Fighting Drugs and Building Peace."
56. Jon Lee Anderson, "Letter from Afghanistan: The Taliban's Opium War," *New Yorker*, July 9, 2007, http://www.newyorker.com/reporting/2007/07/09/070709fa_fact_anderson.
57. One of the leading patrons of trafficking reportedly suggested just such an approach. According to one minister, this man, who was at that time governor of an opium-producing province, suggested that President Karzai negotiate with the major traffickers. According to the account, he told the president that he knew who the major traffickers in his province were and that they might be interested in discussing a transition to a different economy. The government could not touch them, as they were too powerful, but these individuals were not against the government in principle.
58. UNODC, Afghanistan Opium Survey 2007, p. 15.
59. UNODC, "UNODC Reports Diverging Trends Between Opium-free North and Lawless South of Afghanistan," August 27, 2007.

17

Afghan Dilemmas

Defining Commitments

Thomas Lynch has done a service by stating forthrightly that the United States is currently headed for "strategic failure" in Afghanistan, and by focusing attention on the still-undefined long-term U.S. strategic objective there. He rightly criticizes analyses that focus on tactical military victories, reminding us that the main determinants of success or failure will be political. He also offers a welcome corrective to the superficial transatlantic blame game going on lately when he asserts that neither insufficient NATO troops nor imposed national operational constraints on troop missions are the principal reasons for current problems.

Lynch accurately identifies, too, the failure of U.S. policy to address two major sources of instability: Afghanistan's inability to sustain national security forces adequate to the current threat environment; and a regional environment driven principally by a Pakistani military doctrine determined by its estimate of the threat from India, and that reads its strategic interests as precluding a full-scale offensive against the Taliban and al-Qaeda. Lynch rightly proposes that international actors, particularly the United States, guarantee Afghanistan's security, ensure that Afghanistan can finance its own security forces, and undertake diplomacy to address the broader sources of instability in the region.

However, the primary means Lynch proposes to accomplish these objectives—a binding, long-term, bilateral defense treaty between the United States and Afghanistan—would be self-defeating. The reason is one that Lynch himself cites as afflicting current policy: the failure to take into account the political effects of military deployments. Lynch argues that instability in the region results from the lack of a credible U.S. commitment to stay. But a public commitment (or a private determination) to maintain U.S. military bases in a Muslim country on the Asian landmass will also generate—indeed, has already generated—resistance

Originally published as a response to Thomas Lynch, "Afghan Dilemmas: Staying Power," in *The American Interest* 3:5 (May–June 2008).

from Afghans, their neighbors (mainly Iran and Pakistan), and Asian powers such as Russia, China, and India. Such a commitment will also invariably affect their assessments of U.S. goals. Long-term unilateral dependence on the United States will also undermine the legitimacy of any Afghan government, and no amount of money or number of foreign troops will sustain an Afghan government's security forces under such circumstances.

The United States does need to make a long-term commitment to Afghanistan, but that commitment can succeed only if it is made to an independent national government embedded within a multilateral framework that gives its neighbors and other powers a stake in its stability. Absent those conditions, no clever tactical innovations, great speeches, or defense treaties will make a difference.

The Geopolitical Imperative

The belief that the United States will not remain in Afghanistan for the duration is certainly one factor that Afghans and others in the region take into account in making political decisions. But so is the belief that the United States has goals in the region other than peace and stability in Afghanistan. It is critical that U.S. policymakers understand the reason for this belief, for if they do not it will prove impossible to define coherently and achieve U.S. goals in Afghanistan. As in the United States, hardliners abroad argue that capabilities are more reliable indicators of threat than intentions, and they often win the day in national security planning. It is therefore unwise to base U.S. strategy on the assumption that everyone else thinks our intentions are benign. Let us consider how others see regional dynamics and their stakes.

Before 1989, the war in Afghanistan was entangled with the Cold War: Pakistan joined the U.S.-led anti-Soviet alliance in order to arm itself against India. Afghanistan, which originally contested the legitimacy of Pakistan's creation and has never explicitly recognized the border between the two countries, followed India into a form of nonalignment tilted toward its northern neighbor. The United States saw the Soviet-Afghan war of the 1980s as part of its containment (and then rollback) strategy; Pakistan saw it as a way to gain strategic depth against India.

As long as the Soviet Union had troops in Afghanistan, Iran supported Shia resistance fighters there, but after the Red Army withdrew, Iran counseled its allies to move closer to Moscow, for it feared the formation of a Sunni extremist (Wahhabi) Afghanistan backed by the United States, Pakistan, and Saudi Arabia. This fear explains why Iran sponsored the formation of the Northern Alliance, which was eventually aided also by India and Russia, while Pakistan instead supported first the Hizb-i-Islami of Gulbuddin Hikmatyar and, later, the Taliban, with the help of the mainly Arab salafi jihadists we now know as al-Qaeda. In 1990, after the Soviet withdrawal from Afghanistan, the United States imposed sanctions against Pakistan's nuclear program. Though the United States had repeatedly warned Pakistan of the consequences of its program, Islamabad perceived U.S. sanctions as an act of abandonment and a signal of U.S. alignment with India, all this despite Pakistan's help in defeating the Soviets in Afghanistan.

In the 1990s, Iran and Russia saw the Taliban (like the previous U.S. policy tilt toward Saddam Hussein) as part of a U.S.-Pakistani-Saudi plan to encircle Iran. The strengthening of links between the Taliban and al-Qaeda, and the consequent worsening of relations between the United States, on the one hand, and Pakistan and the Taliban, on the other, culminated in a temporary realignment after September 11. Despite some jockeying for relative advantage, Russia, Iran, India, and the United States ultimately cooperated to defeat the Taliban and al-Qaeda in Afghanistan, and to establish the new Afghan government. Not only did Iran cooperate with the United States, Russia actively helped it establish support bases in Central Asia. Pakistan was politically marginalized in the process.

Since then, however, old alignments have reemerged thanks in part to missteps in U.S. policy. The Bush administration responded to Iranian cooperation by placing Iran in the Axis of Evil and naming Pakistan its most important non-NATO U.S. ally. Northern Alliance figures close to Iran and Russia have been eased out of power. In May 2005, Afghanistan and the United States signed a Declaration of Strategic Partnership, and, largely in response, in July 2005 the heads of state of the Shanghai Cooperation Organization (Russia, China, and all the Central Asian countries except Turkmenistan) asked the United States to set a date for closing its bases in Central Asia. They have charged that the United States is exploiting cooperation against terrorism to project power into oil-rich Central Asia.

What does all this have to do with Afghanistan and the present U.S. quest to stabilize that country? Virtually everything, for the United States cannot achieve its policy goals in Afghanistan without understanding regional dynamics, and how Afghanistan has always fit within them.

When Ahmed Shah Durrani was chosen as shah of the Afghans at a jirga in Kandahar in 1747, he led the Pashtun tribes first to conquer several territories that form part of today's Afghanistan, and then to plunder India in a series of raids. (His predecessor, Mirwais Khan Hotaki, had plundered Iran instead.) This immediate turn to conquest did not arise from some supposedly innate violent and xenophobic Afghan character but from the fact that the territory of Afghanistan did not produce enough wealth to finance a state. When the expansion of European imperial powers (Britain and Russia) into the region made external raiding impossible, Afghanistan went through a period of instability and war. The country stabilized in its current de facto borders (never accepted de jure by any Afghan government, including the Taliban), but only as a subsidized buffer state.

Bilateral agreements between Afghanistan and Britain formalized the subsidy, and a bilateral agreement between Britain and Russia formalized the country's status as a buffer state. The subsidy enabled the amir to build army and police forces that gained and administered (incomplete) control of the territory. The agreement between Britain and Russia ensured that neither imperial power would use Afghanistan against the other. The subsidy provided the Afghan state with a domestic preponderance of resources, and the diplomatic agreement among regional powers ensured that none of them would use their resources to subvert the state.

The two necessary ingredients for the stability of a state within the borders of today's Afghanistan have not changed: international aid or subsidies provided to a legitimate Afghan state; and political consent by those capable of subverting that state (mostly neighbors and great powers) to political arrangements inside Afghanistan. Rapid economic growth that would provide a tax base for adequate security forces is, at best, a very long-term scenario. The cost of security depends on the threat environment: the more domestic legitimacy and the less international opposition to the Afghan state, the fewer subsidies it needs to maintain power.

What has changed is that, where once Russia and Britain dominated Afghanistan's regional environment, today the disputatious successors to the Raj—Pakistan and India—play major roles, as do Russia and other successor states to the USSR, an independent revolutionary Iran, the Arab kingdoms and emirates of the Persian Gulf, such powers as the United States, China, NATO, the EU, the UN, and international financial institutions to boot. Under such complicated circumstances, no international consensus on political arrangements in Afghanistan has emerged to replace the one that broke down in 1978–79, and the political and military mobilization of broad sectors of the Afghan population has meant that Kabul requires even more power to rule. That power has to be generated by some combination of coercion and legitimacy, and it follows that if regional diplomacy bolsters the legitimacy of the Afghan government, it will require fewer resources.

Two ingredients for stability of a state:
1. international aid
2. political consent by those capable of subverting the state → neighbors + major powers

Inside and Out

With this background in mind, it is now possible to see why a U.S.-Afghanistan defense treaty will distort relations between the Afghan state and its own people, as well as harming relations between the Afghan state and its neighbors. It also suggests better ways to pursue U.S. goals.

Only two kinds of Afghans appear in Lynch's analysis: Taliban, "a bedrock partner" of al-Qaeda; and the Afghan government, which "covets a strategic partnership with America." In truth, Afghans corresponding to either of these stereotypes are rare. Those who join the insurgency are a more diverse group than one might think, and those who want a partnership with America are increasingly coming to the conclusion that America as it actually exists is quite different from the one with which they would like to ally.

The most common Afghan attitude toward foreign troops is like that of the restaurant customer who complains that not only is the food terrible, but the portions are too small. Lynch is right that Afghans think the portions are too small, but he forgets that they don't much like the food, even if it is the only food they can get right now. Afghans don't like their country being occupied by foreign soldiers any more than did their ancestors. However, after the experience of 1978–2001, many concluded that being occupied by the United States was the only alternative to being destroyed by their neighbors. At least the United States would improve their standard of living.

But that has not happened. The deterioration of security and the failure of the foreigners to improve the living standard of the poor majority of Afghans, especially in areas affected by insurgency, have decreased support for the international presence. Surveys provide evidence of this, as do anecdotes. Young men, largely from the most anti-Taliban group in Afghanistan, rioted against the foreign presence in Kabul in May 2006 after a brake failure on a U.S. vehicle led to a fatal traffic accident. Another incident also involved a brake failure. As the sixteen-year-old cousin of an Afghan who sometimes works with me in Kabul approached a U.S. checkpoint on his bicycle, the soldiers shouted for him to halt. This Afghan bicycle had no brakes, so the cousin started to drag his feet on the ground to slow the bike. This wasn't slow enough for the U.S. soldiers, who shot and killed the boy. The Americans then took the body and kept it for three days (a grave offense in Islam), while the family camped outside the base. After the body was finally returned, the village elders met and decided to join the Taliban to fight the Americans. They also told my Afghan colleague that as long as he worked for the government in Kabul, he could not return to the village. So this entire village joined the Taliban, though it would be a stretch to characterize it as a "bedrock partner" of al-Qaeda.

The U.S. soldiers may have feared that the bicycle rider was a suicide bomber and obeyed both their rules of engagement and the international laws of war. Nonetheless, their act generated hatred and resistance. There have been many such incidents, each of which is amplified by rumor and propaganda. American soldiers are usually as humane as heavily armed young soldiers can be when their lives are threatened in alien surroundings. There is no way to eliminate such incidents, and most measures to reduce them involve greater risk for U.S. soldiers. This suggests that a political approach to the "Taliban" insurgency may require decreasing the U.S. and other foreign military presence rather than increasing it.

The international civilian presence also undermines the legitimacy of the Afghan government. Restaurants that serve alcohol or function as covers for brothels, neighborhoods blockaded for security, and the skyrocketing cost of living partly due to the cash spent by foreign residents are symbols of Afghan powerlessness no less than civilian casualties. These symbols, in turn, diminish the Afghan state's legitimacy through mechanisms often invisible to outsiders. As Afghan clergy increasingly preach that the foreign presence is an illegitimate occupation threatening Islam, some are reportedly refusing Muslim funeral rites to Afghan soldiers killed fighting the insurgency alongside the United States or NATO. Few things could be more damaging to morale and recruitment than that.

The Bush administration, however, has managed to find another way to use the U.S. presence to undermine the Afghan National Army. It is now applying heavy pressure, including threats that Congress will cut off aid, to force the Afghan government not only to engage in opium poppy eradication in hostile areas but also to use the Afghan National Army in support of such operations. Afghan defense officials believe that using the army for such operations will seriously damage the young force, while distracting it from its core security mission.

Of course, an ideal U.S. presence would not pressure the Afghan government to act against its own national interests. The current presence, however, does so not only in domestic policy but also in its relations to its neighbors, who know the history of geopolitical competition in the area, even if we do not.

Lynch claims that a unilateral, open-ended commitment to Afghanistan by the United States "is certain to generate some regional controversy, but its positive potential outcomes outweigh the risks from vocal but likely temporary Russian, Pakistani or Iranian unhappiness." He misidentifies the problem. The problem is not persuading others that American goodwill will not flag; it is making them see that American interests align with their own, which they often objectively do not. Therefore, just as most Afghans no longer credit the purity of American motives or the competence of American officials inside their country, regional actors do not and will not believe that the United States is committed to Afghanistan; they are far more inclined to believe instead that the United States will make Afghanistan committed to America.

The Shanghai Cooperation Statement of July 2005 illustrates this perception, as do Iranian actions. The closest the United States has come to Lynch's proposal is the aforementioned May 2005 Declaration of Strategic Partnership. Tehran responded by asking President Karzai to sign a declaration of strategic partnership with Iran that, among its provisions, committed Afghanistan not to permit its territory to be used for military or intelligence operations against Iran. The message was clear: Iran will accept Afghanistan's strategic partnership with the United States, but only if it is not directed against Iran.

President Karzai responded that he would like to sign such a declaration, but his government was not in a position to prevent the United States from using its territory against Iran. The Iranians said that they knew this but would like such a statement anyway, and that without such a declaration President Karzai would not be welcome in Tehran for the August 2005 inauguration of President Mahmoud Ahmadinejad. A phone call to President Karzai from a cabinet officer in Washington forbade the Afghan president from signing any such declaration or attending the inauguration. A few months later, in January 2006, another phone call forbade Karzai to travel to Tehran to sign economic agreements.

In early 2007, Washington reported that Iran had started to supply sophisticated arms to the Taliban. That summer, as calls for "regime change" and a preemptive attack on Iran's nuclear program escalated in Washington, Tehran made a formal declaration: if Iran were attacked by the United States, it would respond fully against U.S. forces in Afghanistan and Iraq, regardless of its bilateral interests in those two countries. What this shows is that Iranian responses to threats posed by a larger and permanent U.S. presence in Afghanistan will be more than "vocal." Iran can respond asymmetrically—and potentially devastatingly—against the United States in Afghanistan. How Iran would respond to a U.S. commitment to a long-term military presence in Afghanistan depends on U.S. policy toward Iran, a point Lynch does not address.

The core issue with regard to Afghanistan, however, is not Iran but Pakistan. Lynch accurately diagnoses much of the situation but underestimates the difficulty of changing it. His analysis of Pakistan also leans too far in favor of military factors to the relative neglect of the critical political context.

Lynch is correct that Pakistan's policy in Afghanistan has had at least two tracks, and that the policy has mainly been determined by the Pakistani military's security concerns about India. Lynch calls these concerns "paranoid," as if they might be alleviated through the right combination of medication (more aid and training) and talk therapy (assurances from U.S. diplomats that the Indian elite attitudes toward Pakistan have undergone a sea change). Alas, the malady from which the Pakistani security establishment suffers is endemic worldwide, and it is not amenable to quick courses of treatment. Is it not "paranoid" to build a missile defense system in eastern Europe (one that will probably not work) against nonexistent Iranian missiles with nonexistent nuclear warheads at the cost of relations with Russia? Is it more "paranoid" for Pakistan to be concerned about a nuclear-armed neighbor eight times its size, with which it has a serious territorial dispute and has fought three conventional wars?

The "cure" for the Pakistani military's self-aggrandizing definition of national security is not U.S. assurances or "insistence" on an end to duplicity. [In a Council on Foreign Relations report—Chapter 12 in this book—I once proposed that the administration "should insist on the Pakistani government's full cooperation in isolating and ending the neo-Taliban insurgency." CFR President Richard Haass inquired in a marginal comment, "What if we insist and they still don't do it?"] The Pakistan government will also not readily accept "mediation" of the Durand Line dispute because there is no such dispute, according to the government of Pakistan. There is just a domestic political problem inside Afghanistan that prevents the Afghan state from openly accepting a border it has implicitly recognized many times.

Lynch has correctly identified the problem, but the solution is not greater "commitment," firmer "insistence," or any other form of interpersonal communication. The security complex in South Asia can only be transformed by political change, the centerpiece of which must be the democratization of Pakistan, to include civilian control of its national security strategy. The Pakistani military will not consent to a stable Afghanistan under U.S. hegemony because it fears that the United States will reduce military aid to Pakistan the moment it no longer needs Pakistan to address terrorism or instability in Afghanistan. The Pakistani military cannot agree to a definition of Pakistani national security that is not based on the Indian threat, because this threat, in addition to being founded on the reality of Indian capabilities, provides the rationale for the military's domination of Pakistan's state, society, and economy.

Fortunately, many forces in Pakistan contest the military's definition of national security. But these forces have been powerless over national security issues in the face of military dominance—and that goes even for elected prime ministers. Unfortunately, the Bush administration has worked against these forces by supporting the autocratic rule of Pervez Musharraf. The administration hoped and believed that Pakistan under military rule would act as an effective proxy in the War on Terror, but it has not. By insisting that Pakistan's poorly conceived and counterproductive counterterrorist operations be pursued more vigorously, the administration has made things worse, as Lynch points out. U.S. policy has had the collateral effect of keeping the Pakistani military semiautonomous under U.S. oversight rather than accountable to Pakistani civilian authorities. This ensures exclusion from Pakistani national security policy of those most interested in changing it in ways that align with actual U.S. interests.

As Lynch and others have noted, a strategic approach to addressing the long-standing hostility between Afghanistan and Pakistan is essential to success in Afghanistan. Anything that reduces Indo-Pakistani tension and threat perceptions will help. The key, however, is to be found inside Pakistan. If Pakistan will not respect a border that Afghanistan does not recognize, Afghanistan cannot recognize a border for which Pakistan does not take responsibility. Improving relations between Afghanistan and Pakistan thus requires the political and administrative integration of the Federally Administered Tribal Areas with Pakistan. This is now possible: all the parties that form part of the new governing coalition in the Pakistani parliament support such integration, as do the two parties that will form the government of the Northwest Frontier Province and that dominated the nominally nonparty February 2008 elections in the tribal areas.

The Pakistani military and presidency have opposed such integration, however, although they have done so indirectly. They claim that it is impossible, or too difficult, or contrary to Pakistan's constitution (though the latter proved easy to modify when it conflicted with the immediate interests of President Musharraf). They do this because they use the tribal areas as a staging ground for asymmetrical warfare, which forms part of the Pakistani military's security doctrine. The problems posed by this doctrine can be addressed only by a civilian government, and only a civilian government seeking to extend Pakistani democracy to the tribal areas, rather than a military one that feigns implementation of the War on Terror, will ever truly overcome resistance there. This is exactly what the United States should want to happen, especially since this is where the global headquarters of a revived al-Qaeda is now located.

Five Elements of Commitment

Lynch proposes that the United States solve the Afghan security puzzle by combining two approaches. The first approach is to compensate for Afghanistan's inability to finance and sustain adequate security forces by unilaterally guaranteeing Afghanistan's security through a treaty and continuing to fund Afghan security forces at whatever level the threat environment requires, whether Afghanistan can afford them or not. The second approach is to reduce the threat level by a commitment so strong that all will conclude resistance is futile, and then to cure Pakistan's "paranoia" through talk therapy (diplomacy) and medication (train and equip the military). As I have suggested, unilateral policies based on an Afghan government dependent on the United States and the chimera of unchallengeable U.S. military hegemony will not work. But what will?

To answer that question we must decide not only what our goals are but also what it will take to achieve them. We can never stabilize Afghanistan and then make a victorious exit without coming to some understanding with Afghanistan's neighbors. So the first thing we must do is show that we understand regional realities by engaging the neighbors on their genuine interests; otherwise they will continue to wage asymmetrical warfare against us until we get the message.

We should therefore launch regional consultations to develop a common understanding of the future of Afghanistan in the region with all neighbors, including Iran, Russia, China, India, and the Persian Gulf countries. Both the UN and regional organizations offer forums to pursue these objectives. Afghanistan can no longer be an isolated buffer state, but it can serve as a connector of a wider region through trade, transit, energy transmission, and labor migration, as long as it is not a source of threats. Integrating Afghanistan as a focal point for regional cooperation, however, is not compatible with making it a base for U.S. power projection in the region. The long-term U.S. presence in Europe is enabled by the substantial overlap in membership between the security alliance (NATO) and the framework for economic and political cooperation (the European Union). Without a similar overlapping of security and economic frameworks in South Asia, a U.S. presence will be destabilizing, not stabilizing.

 Second, we must crack the Pakistani nut. The absence of U.S.-Iranian cooperation in Afghanistan (which was essential to our initial military success in 2001) and growing tensions with Russia and China in Central Asia give Pakistan monopoly control of U.S. access to landlocked Afghanistan. It follows that as long as the Pakistani military is calling the shots, Afghanistan will remain roiled no matter how many battles NATO forces win. To change this dynamic, the United States must relinquish, not strengthen, the privileged relationship between the United States and the Pakistani military. It must instead support civilian control over the government and the military alike, even by parties that oppose U.S. objectives openly (rather than covertly, like the military).

 Third, the United States must also invest far more in Afghanistan's economy and civilian institutions, especially those that are important for rule of law. This requires a far more effective set of policies than we have had so far. It also requires a reversal of much of the Bush administration's counternarcotics policy. Strengthening the legitimacy of the Afghan government works best when pursued through a multilateral framework, not because multilateralism is always superior to unilateralism but because regional realities in South Asia render unilateral efforts futile. The Afghan government formed at the UN Talks on Afghanistan in Bonn (where I was a member of the UN delegation) enjoyed far greater legitimacy than either the Coalition Provisional Authority in Iraq or its elected successors.

 Fourth, as a component of strengthening civilian institutions, we should fully support efforts by the Afghan government to negotiate and reconcile with insurgents, making it clear that we are concerned about threats to international security, not weakening Islamic political forces for its own sake. Most of those fighting the Karzai government are not "bedrock partners" of al-Qaeda, though the resources provided by and through al-Qaeda and its partners make the insurgency far more deadly. They can be weaned away from al-Qaeda, but this must happen Afghan-style, and only Afghans can make the deals necessary to do that. We need to let them.

Fifth, external support for Afghan security forces and for civilian parts of the budget must be institutionalized. It would be preferable to make such support more multilateral and to devise a scenario for eventual self-sufficiency. Such a scenario would combine threat reduction, economic development, and state building. At the very least, funding for Afghan security forces should be delinked from Iraq and integrated into the regular U.S. defense budget; no country can build institutions on the basis of a foreign country's supplemental appropriations. A smaller but reliable commitment is better than a huge but unpredictable one. Together with consultations on Afghanistan's role in the region's security, the United States should structure Afghan forces to act independently rather than as auxiliaries of the United States and NATO, so that they do not appear to threaten the region on behalf of external powers.

Lynch rightly refers to Clausewitz on the relationship of politics to war. He might also recall Sun Tzu's statement, "If you know the enemy and know yourself, you need not fear the results of one hundred battles." Who is the enemy? As I see it, the most serious threat to security in the region derives from al-Qaeda's transnational campaign against the integration of the Islamic world into the current international order. The way to defeat al-Qaeda is to deprive it of a base by strengthening legitimate governance throughout the territories of Afghanistan and Pakistan, while ending policies (such as the occupation of Iraq) that act as recruiting tools for the enemy.

But who are we? The United States is the most powerful state in the world, yet its power has limits. We deceive ourselves if we expect others to respond to our exercise of power as a disinterested pursuit of "stability." We have neither the strength nor the knowledge to shock and awe all opposition in an environment we understand poorly. But we do have the capacity to define and mold common interests, and to build coalitions of the truly willing in defense of those interests.

1. Regional consultation
2. pakistan
3. Afg civilian consultation
   - Rule of law

18

The Transformation of the Afghan State

Had I written an essay on the next ten years of the Afghan state in 1998, I would have proposed several scenarios. Notably lacking would have been the one that actually occurred. The events since then have made accurate prediction even more difficult. The history of Afghanistan over the last thirty-five years has been that of the end of the country's status as an isolated buffer state. Rather than separating conflicts, Afghanistan now links them. Ten years ago Afghanistan, besides having a low-intensity conflict between the Taliban and the Northern Alliance, was also the scene of India-Pakistan and Sunni-Shia conflicts and, to a certain extent, U.S.-Iranian-Russian competition over pipeline routes. All of those conflicts have only become more intense. In addition, today Afghanistan is the theater for the War on Terror, the ill-defined confrontation between the United States and global Islamist movements; the conflict between NATO and Russia; the confrontation between the United States and Iran; the struggle within Pakistan over that country's future; and a transnational insurgency spanning Afghanistan and Pakistan and linked to al-Qaeda. Finally, there is a higher level of mobilization around the ethnic, tribal, regional, and sectarian cleavages that have always marked Afghan politics.

If it seems unlikely that Afghanistan can return to its days of isolation, it is because all of the elements that enabled Afghanistan to survive in relative stability for nearly a century have disappeared: a population largely isolated in remote valleys with few links to the outside world, some small arms, and no political organization on a scale that could challenge the state; a government subsidized by great powers and accepted as legitimate by all neighbors; and an economy largely based on subsistence farming, pastoralism, limited pockets of commercial agriculture, and trade.

The territory of today's Afghanistan has never sustained a state without international aid to the security forces, and it has repeatedly collapsed in the face of invasion or contestation. The stability of such a state would require, at a minimum, a level of income and legitimacy sufficient to recruit and maintain security

Originally published in Alex Thier, ed., *The Future of Afghanistan* (Washington, DC: United States Institute of Peace, January 2009).

forces adequate to defend from the level of threat faced by the state. In the current environment, that is a tall order indeed.

Evolution of the State

The territory of today's Afghanistan more or less corresponds to the Eastern Iranian world (Khurasan), which remained Sunni despite the conquest of Persia by the Shia Safavids in the sixteenth century. This area (Kabul and its dependencies) became a kingdom of the Afghans (Pashtuns) only from the eighteenth century, when both the Ghilzai and Durrani Pashtun tribal confederations sought to establish empires as the Safavids collapsed. The empire founded in 1747 by Ahmad Shah Durrani survived by raiding Punjab, Kashmir, and Iran, and dividing the taxes (booty) among the tribes.

The arrival of Russian and British imperialism on the Asian landmass confined Afghan rule to a demarcated territory, which came to be known as the state of "Afghanistan." In the nineteenth century that state underwent a series of upheavals and invasions until finally becoming stable as a buffer state after the Treaty of Gandamak (1879). The Anglo-Russian Convention of 1907 recognized Afghanistan's new borders and its status as a buffer state under British suzerainty enjoying full domestic autonomy. From 1879 to 1919, British India controlled Afghanistan's foreign relations and provided a yearly subsidy in cash and weapons to enable the emir to control the territory. The emir established a centralized administration to ensure security and sharia courts for justice, while leaving local governance and dispute settlement to tribes and communities.

The key elements of stability were

- Agreement among the great powers (which were also regional powers) not to interfere inside Afghanistan or use Afghanistan's weakness against one another, leading to a low degree of international contestation of the Afghan state and the separation of rival powers by a neutralized Afghanistan;
- A disarmed, demobilized, and isolated population without large-scale political organization and largely engaged in subsistence activities, resulting in a low degree of domestic demand on and contestation of the state; and
- An international subsidy exclusively to the state to enable it to finance security forces adequate to the low-threat environment.

The Anglo-Russian Convention expired in the wake of the Russian Revolution and the Third Anglo-Afghan War (1919), in which Afghanistan won full independence. Nonetheless, an informal agreement on nonintervention continued until 1978. The British continued to support the army through the end of the

British Empire in India; when the United States, allied with Pakistan, refused to take up where the British left, Kabul turned to Moscow. As the educational system and road network expanded, and as capital flowed into the Persian Gulf after the 1973 oil embargo, more Afghans left their villages, entered the cash economy, and became politicized. The state financed its development programs through foreign aid and hence did not need to confront the rural society over the legitimacy of revenue extraction. The rural areas remained untaxed and largely self-regulating, so long as they posed no threat.

The coups in 1973 and 1978 and then the Soviet invasion in 1979 destroyed what remained of international agreement over Afghanistan, and the country became a theater of the Cold War, which overshadowed the regional and sectarian conflicts. When the Soviet Union dissolved and the United States disengaged, they left behind an Afghanistan that had become a cockpit for regional competition, a shattered state with no functioning security forces or civilian political process, a highly mobilized and armed population increasingly dependent on international organizations and cash for livelihood (including through the drug trade), and a multiplicity of armed groups linked transnationally to both state and nonstate patrons.

In addition to these general conditions, Afghanistan's relations with Pakistan had also led to the blurring of the lines between the two states. Since Pakistan's independence, the Federally Administered Tribal Agencies (FATA) had been a buffer between Afghanistan and the core of Pakistan. Now FATA was settled with miliions of Afghan refugees, and FATA tribes had been mobilized to fight in Afghanistan's "civil war." The Pakistani directorate of Inter-Services Intelligence (ISI), at first with U.S. and Saudi support, had turned the border region into a militarized platform for asymmetrical power projection using jihadi groups in Afghanistan, Kashmir, and beyond. FATA and Karachi also constituted markets and transit points for goods smuggled into and out of Afghanistan. In many respects the countries came to intermingle and overlap rather than border on each other like two states.

The events of September 11, 2001, illustrated that the Afghan state was both weak and no longer integrated into the global community and that its territory now included the center for a highly organized global network of political violence. The U.S. response was to destroy the weak government of the Taliban and call on the United Nations to try to resurrect the Afghan state. But resurrecting the previous Afghan state under current conditions may be doomed to failure.

Transformation by War

The relationship of Afghanistan to the international system has changed decisively since 1978 and cannot be restored to its former status. After September 11, it appeared that a grand coalition had formed to support the new government and that, just as in the early twentieth century, great powers might reach an agreement to support the government and to not compete in Afghanistan. But this time, virtually every major international and regional actor decided to become involved in Afghanistan with no restraining rules of the game. The result has been the importation into Afghanistan of innumerable other conflicts, making the original one harder to solve.

The following international issues and actors are now linked to the conflict in Afghanistan:

- The War on Terror: as defined by the Bush administration, it includes as a goal not only the destruction of al-Qaeda but also the destruction of organizations and states that harbor or support "terrorists," including both the Taliban and Iran (not Pakistan, for some reason). Although the War on Terror is not the sole policy framework for U.S. involvement in Afghanistan, it constrains others.
- The India-Pakistan conflict: Pakistan seeks to exclude Indian influence from Afghanistan, which it considers part of its security perimeter; India considers a presence in Afghanistan important to gain a back window into Pakistan. Both countries' intelligence agencies are active there.
- Sunni-Shia conflict: Saudi Arabia and Iran are competing for leadership of the Islamic world; both have proxies in Afghanistan.
- U.S. relations with its NATO allies: NATO allies who opposed the war in Iraq agreed to send troops to Afghanistan to reduce strain on their relations with Washington. Now that same commitment is further straining relations.
- Russia's relations with the United States and NATO: Russia supports the war and sanctions against the Taliban and al-Qaeda, but one of its principal security preoccupations is the expansion of NATO to the former Soviet space and its borders. Russia does not want to see a permanent NATO deployment in Afghanistan or U.S. bases in Central Asia.
- U.S.-Iran conflict: the United States and Iran worked together to overthrow the Taliban and bring the current Afghan government to power, but the Bush administration rebuffed Iran's overtures and has placed limits on the relations Afghanistan has with Iran. Iran has also begun providing limited support to insurgents to warn of the consequences of attacking Iran.

This is only a list of the most evident problems and stakeholders, the sheer number of which is prohibitively high to reach an agreement.

The Afghan population is no longer isolated and quiescent. Every group in the population has been mobilized militarily and politically and enjoys some patronage from foreign powers or movements. Every village has been penetrated by armed militants competing to mobilize young men. Afghans have been heavily politicized and listen incessantly to international news. One of the results of this has been the increased recruitment of Afghans into national ethnic or ideological politics.

At least half of Afghans have suffered war displacement and perhaps a third traveled abroad (largely as refugees), exposing them to life outside the extended family. The subsistence economy has been largely destroyed, and Afghanistan relies on imports of food and exports of agro-based commodities—opium and heroin. Afghans are participating in global labor, commodity, and capital markets and in global politics and warfare, all at the same time. The expansion of cash transactions has empowered ideological groups, including the ulama and islamists, who rely on cash contributions for power rather than solely on ownership of productive assets. Without a cash economy that can be taxed by an armed organization, the Taliban regime, composed of clerics who do not directly control productive assets, would not have been possible.

As community coping mechanisms have become less reliable and cash more necessary, families and communities are increasingly looking to the state for livelihood and public services, including education, the demand for which has mushroomed. Afghanistan has become the most rapidly urbanizing society in Asia, with resultant escalating demands for public services and political participation. The demands placed on the state are far greater and the task of legitimation far more demanding than at any time in the past. Hence, the type of weak state that encapsulated a quiescent Afghan society is no longer feasible or effective; yet the state is still structured and resourced to maintain control, not provide services.

Under these conditions of increasing external and transnational threat, plus mounting domestic demand, stability would require a state and security forces with substantially more resources and capabilities than at any time in the past. Currently the Afghan government extracts about 7 percent of licit GDP in revenues (or $960 million), which is not sufficient even to cover its recurrent nondefense costs. The entire defense and development budget is paid for by foreign assistance; an even greater amount is spent directly by aid donors outside of the government budget for projects of every description. As the estimated size of the security forces Afghanistan needs continues to rise, there is no realistic scenario under which the country would be able to finance even the recurrent costs of security.

Does the Afghan State Have a Future?

The Afghan state is now well advanced along an unsustainable trajectory. Its army and, increasingly, its police depend for their salaries and equipment on supplemental appropriations of the U.S. Congress, which cannot be projected from year to year. There was no supplemental appropriation in 2006. A massive devaluation of the U.S. dollar or a prolongation of the economic crisis in the United States could eventually prevent the Afghan National Security Forces

(ANSF) from being paid. Furthermore, the increase in expenditures by aid organizations outside the Afghan government budget and the disbursement of huge amounts of cash through the dozens of uncoordinated financial systems used by various aid agencies generates a tsunami of corruption, which both undermines the legitimacy of the system and prevents the assistance from achieving its objectives.

Of the three trends—the rise in conflict among powers involved in Afghanistan, the increasing mobilization of the population, and the proliferation of funding channels outside the government—the one that is most clearly irreversible is the increase in mobilization, politicization, and urbanization of the Afghan population. One may add to that the rapid increase in education without any comparable increase in the amount of licit employment, and all the ingredients are present for a chronic social crisis, expressed in ethnic and Islamic politics, violence, criminalized economic activity, and increased efforts to emigrate in search of work.

It is difficult but not impossible to imagine the mounting external tensions becoming less threatening. If, for instance, the coalition apprehended or killed the top leadership of al-Qaeda in Pakistan, leading to an end of the pressure of the War on Terror doctrine on operations, a political settlement with elements of the insurgency in Pakistan and Afghanistan might become more feasible. U.S.-Iran relations might warm slightly above their current frozen state. It is more difficult to imagine a deescalation of the India-Pakistan conflict, but if elected government does start to take hold in Pakistan, and civilians with a primarily economic program remain in power, we might see a shift in emphasis in India-Pakistan relations from confrontation to competition and even economic cooperation.

Such trends might make it possible to reduce the size and sophistication of security forces and thus move in a direction toward sustainability. The reduction of the level of threat would also favor investment and economic activity, which is strongly dependent on security in a landlocked country. Such growth might make it possible to increase the tax base as well as the government's share of GDP to pay for public services.

These do not, however, seem to be the most likely trends. Although the next administration may seek less confrontational and militaristic ways of coping with the threat from global terrorism and competition with Iran, the persistence of al-Qaeda in the Pakistan border region and, covertly, in cities could continue and create pressure for broader intervention in Pakistan, destabilizing that country and its neighbor further. The loss of legitimacy to rule by the Pakistan Army combined with the continued incapacity and corruption of civilian political parties could lead to a prolonged crisis or collapse of governance, with more space being occupied by armed extremist groups also active in Afghanistan. Any number of unpredictable events—another large attack by al-Qaeda in the United States, a riot in Kabul or another Afghan city, the collapse of a regional center (most likely

Kandahar) under Taliban assault—could precipitate a rapid crisis, although all the capabilities put in place in the past several years might prove themselves able to surmount even such a crisis.

The most important lines of policy to cope with these threats include:

- Increasing regional diplomacy and economic cooperation to lower regional tensions.
- Expanding higher education and employment opportunities to absorb more of the educated youth.
- Developing a plan for stable financing of Afghan security forces by putting them on a recurrent budget (Afghan or U.S.) or creating a trust fund.
- Phasing out the most intrusive and kinetic counterterrorism parts of the international mission.
- Strengthening the foundational legitimacy of the government through elections and measures against corruption.

If Afghanistan is to meet even a fraction of the new demands placed on it, the state will have to be restructured to provide for more accountability to citizens and communities, but this cannot happen in isolation. As long as the existence of the state is under threat from a combination of domestic and international challenges, rulers will resist decentralization of authority. The state is simply too weak to manage decentralized service provision, which would require some kind of budgetary process in each province and perhaps district, even if it were based solely on grants from the central government. There is little organizational capacity to carry out the required monitoring and implementation. A few provinces (Herat, for instance) could probably do a better job of managing their own finances and service provision than the central government, but such an arrangement would appear to threaten the control of the central government and its ability to redistribute resources among provinces and regions. This redistributionary function is highly political: non-Pashtuns charge that the state has historically allocated resources from north Afghanistan to Pashtuns and southern Afghanistan. There is some, though inadequate, evidence for this claim, but certainly all members of ethnic groups have not been affected equally, and the beneficiaries of government patronage have been much smaller groups than entire ethnicities. Nonetheless, the seemingly technical issue of decentralization of service provision is closely related to the most potentially divisive issue, namely the relation of the state to different ethnic groups and in particular to Pashtuns and non-Pashtuns.

Over the past few years, the government has experimented with methods to reach communities through national programs that bypass the dysfunctional administrative structure. The best-known example is the National Solidarity

Program, which provides communities with block grants of up to $20,000 for development projects chosen and implemented by elected Community Development Councils (CDCs). Financial management and transparency is ensured by implementing the funding through international agencies and NGOs, while leaving actual implementation in the hands of the communities.

The program appears to work well in delivering projects to the village level, but it has not sparked any major institutional change. The CDCs exist in parallel to the historically rooted local institutions (for example, village shura, or local councils, meeting in the mosque) and have not displaced them. Afghans understand that the NSP depends on yearly aid appropriations of foreign donors and is not sustainable. Therefore, they treat it as a windfall rather than as an institution. Attempts by the Ministry of Rural Rehabilitation and Development (MRRD) to have the CDCs recognized as representatives of communities within the administrative structure have met stiff resistance. Other national programs implemented in the same way will meet the same response as long as they are dependent on foreign aid and are not integrated into the communities' permanent institutional structure. Nor will any central government be willing to delegate genuine authority over mobilization and use of resources to localities as long as the state remains vulnerable to subversion by much larger foreign countries.

There is no foreseeable trajectory under which the Afghan state will become a self-sustaining member of the international community at peace with its neighbors in the coming ten years. It might be possible, however, to approach rather than recede from that goal. The highest priority should be to reduce the level of threat through both regional diplomacy and domestic reconciliation with insurgents who renounce al-Qaeda. By reducing threats, the level of security forces needed will be more manageable, and it will be more practical to call on Afghanistan's neighbors to provide the economic cooperation and integration needed to turn an isolated former buffer state into a connector state in a rapidly growing Asia. Once Afghanistan no longer fears for its own disintegration, it will become more feasible for the state to experiment with forms of local governance and decentralization of the administration in order to provide the public services that the Afghan people are now demanding.

19

From Great Game to Grand Bargain

Ending Chaos in Afghanistan and Pakistan

WITH AHMED RASHID

The Great Game is no fun anymore. The term was used by nineteenth-century British imperialists to describe the British-Russian struggle for position on the chessboard of Afghanistan and Central Asia—a contest with a few players, mostly limited to intelligence forays and short wars fought on horseback with rifles, and with those living on the chessboard largely bystanders or victims. More than a century later, the game continues. But now, the number of players has exploded, those living on the chessboard have become involved, and the intensity of the violence and the threats it produces affect the entire globe. The Great Game can no longer be treated as a sporting event for distant spectators. It is time to agree on some new rules.

Seven years after the U.S.-led coalition and the Afghan commanders it supported pushed the leaderships of the Taliban and al-Qaeda out of Afghanistan and into Pakistan, an insurgency that includes these and other groups is gaining ground on both the Afghan and the Pakistani sides of the border. Four years after Afghanistan's first-ever presidential election, the increasingly besieged government of Hamid Karzai is losing credibility at home and abroad. Al-Qaeda has established a new safe haven in the tribal agencies of Pakistan, where it is defended by a new organization, the Taliban Movement of Pakistan. The government of Pakistan, beset by one political crisis after another and split between a traditionally autonomous military and assertive but fractious elected leaders, has been unable to retain control of its own territory and population. Its intelligence agency stands accused of supporting terrorism in Afghanistan, which in many ways has replaced Kashmir as the main arena of the still-unresolved struggle between Pakistan and India.

Originally published in *Foreign Affairs* (November–December 2008): 2–16.

For years, critics of U.S. and NATO strategies have been warning that the region was headed in this direction. Many of the policies such critics have long proposed are now being widely embraced. The Bush administration and both U.S. presidential campaigns are proposing to send more troops to Afghanistan and to undertake other policies to sustain the military gains made there. These include accelerating training of the Afghan National Army and the Afghan National Police; disbursing more money, more effectively for reconstruction and development and to support better governance; increasing pressure on and cooperation with Pakistan, and launching cross-border attacks without Pakistani agreement to eliminate cross-border safe havens for insurgents and to uproot al-Qaeda; supporting democracy in Pakistan and bringing its Inter-Services Intelligence (ISI) under civilian political control; and implementing more effective policies to curb Afghanistan's drug industry, which produces opiates equal in export value to half of the rest of the Afghan economy.

Cross-border attacks into Pakistan may produce an "October surprise" or provide material for apologists hoping to salvage George W. Bush's legacy, but they will not provide security. Advancing reconstruction, development, good governance, and counternarcotics efforts and building effective police and justice systems in Afghanistan will require many years of relative peace and security. Neither neglecting these tasks, as the Bush administration did initially, nor rushing them on a timetable determined by political objectives can succeed. Afghanistan requires far larger and more effective security forces, international or national, but support for U.S. and NATO deployments is plummeting in troop-contributing countries, in the wider region, and in Afghanistan itself. Afghanistan, the poorest country in the world but for a handful in Africa and with the weakest government in the world (except Somalia, which has no government), will never be able to sustain national security forces sufficient to confront current—let alone escalating—threats, yet permanent foreign subsidies for Afghanistan's security forces cannot be guaranteed and will have destabilizing consequences. Moreover, measures aimed at Afghanistan will not address the deteriorating situation in Pakistan or the escalation of international conflicts connected to the Afghan-Pakistani war. More aid to Pakistan—military or civilian—will not diminish the perception among Pakistan's national security elite that the country is surrounded by enemies determined to dismember it, especially as cross-border raids into areas long claimed by Afghanistan intensify that perception. Until that sense of siege is gone, it will be difficult to strengthen civilian institutions in Pakistan.

U.S. diplomacy has been paralyzed by the rhetoric of "the war on terror"—a struggle against "evil," in which other actors are "with us or with the terrorists." Such rhetoric thwarts sound strategic thinking by assimilating opponents into a homogeneous "terrorist" enemy. Only a political and diplomatic initiative that distinguishes political opponents of the United States—including violent ones—from global terrorists such as al-Qaeda can reduce the threat faced by the Afghan and Pakistani states and secure the rest of the international community from the international terrorist groups based there. Such an initiative would have two elements. It would seek a political solution with as many of the Afghan and Pakistani insurgencies as possible, offering political inclusion, the integration of Pakistan's indirectly ruled Federally Administered Tribal Areas (FATA) into the mainstream political and administrative institutions of Pakistan, and an end to hostile action by international troops in return for cooperation against al-Qaeda. And it would include a major diplomatic and development initiative addressing the vast array of regional and global issues that have become intertwined with the crisis—and that serve to stimulate, intensify, and prolong conflict in both Afghanistan and Pakistan.

Afghanistan has been at war for three decades—a period longer than the one that started with World War I and ended with the Normandy landings on D-day in World War II—and now that war is spreading to Pakistan and beyond. This war and the attendant terrorism could well continue and spread, even to other continents—as on September 11—or lead to the collapse of a nuclear-armed state. The regional crisis is of that magnitude, and yet so far there is no international framework to address it other than the underresourced and poorly coordinated operations in Afghanistan and some attacks in the FATA. The next U.S. administration should launch an effort, initially based on a contact group authorized by the UN Security Council, to put an end to the increasingly destructive dynamics of the Great Game in the region. The game has become too deadly and has attracted too many players; it now resembles less a chess match than the Afghan game of *buzkashi*, with Afghanistan playing the role of the goat carcass fought over by innumerable teams. Washington must seize the opportunity now to replace this Great Game with a new grand bargain for the region.

The Security Gap

The Afghan and Pakistani security forces lack the numbers, skills, equipment, and motivation to confront the growing insurgencies in the two countries or to uproot al-Qaeda from its new base in the FATA, along the Afghan-Pakistani border. Proposals for improving the security situation focus on sending additional international forces, building larger national security forces in Afghanistan, and training and equipping Pakistan's security forces, which are organized for conflict with India, for domestic counterinsurgency. But none of these proposals is sufficient to meet the current, let alone future, threats.

Some additional troops in Afghanistan could protect local populations while the police and the administration develop. They also might enable U.S. and

NATO forces to reduce or eliminate their reliance on the use of air strikes, which cause civilian casualties that recruit fighters and supporters to the insurgency. U.S. General Barry McCaffrey, among others, has therefore supported a "generational commitment" to Afghanistan, such as the United States made to Germany and South Korea. Unfortunately, no government in the region around Afghanistan supports a long-term U.S. or NATO presence there. Pakistan sees even the current deployment as strengthening an India-allied regime in Kabul; Iran is concerned that the United States will use Afghanistan as a base for launching "regime change" in Tehran; and China, India, and Russia all have reservations about a NATO base within their spheres of influence and believe they must balance the threats from al-Qaeda and the Taliban against those posed by the United States and NATO. Securing Afghanistan and its region will require an international presence for many years, but only a regional diplomatic initiative that creates a consensus to place stabilizing Afghanistan ahead of other objectives could make a long-term international deployment possible.

Afghanistan needs larger and more effective security forces, but it also needs to be able to sustain those security forces. A decree signed by President Karzai in December 2002 would have capped the Afghan National Army at 70,000 troops (it had reached 66,000 by mid-2008). U.S. Secretary of Defense Robert Gates has since announced a plan to increase that number to 122,000, as well as add 82,000 police, for a total of 204,000 in the Afghan National Security Forces (ANSF). Such increases, however, would require additional international trainers and mentors—who are, quite simply, not available in the foreseeable future—and maintaining such a force would far exceed the means of such a destitute country. Current estimates of the annual cost are around $2.5 billion for the army and $1 billion for the police. Last year, the Afghan government collected about 7 percent of a licit GDP estimated at $9.6 billion in revenue—about $670 million. Thus, even if Afghanistan's economy experienced uninterrupted real growth of 9 percent per year, and if revenue extraction nearly doubled, to 12 percent (both unrealistic forecasts), in ten years the total domestic revenue of the Afghan government would be about $2.5 billion a year. Projected pipelines and mines might add $500 million toward the end of this period. In short, the army and the police alone would cost significantly more than Afghanistan's total revenue.

Many have therefore proposed long-term international financing of the ANSF; after all, even $5 billion a year is much less than the cost of an international force deployment. But sustaining, as opposed to training or equipping, security forces through foreign grants would pose political problems. It would be impossible to build Afghan institutions on the basis of U.S. supplemental appropriations, which is how the training and equipping of the ANSF are mostly funded. Sustaining a national army or national police force requires multiyear planning, impossible without a recurrent appropriation—which would mean integrating ANSF planning into the budgets of the United States and other NATO members, even if the funds were disbursed through a single trust fund. And an ANSF funded from those budgets would have to meet international or other national, rather than Afghan, legal requirements. Decisions on funding would be taken by the U.S. Congress and other foreign bodies, not the Afghan National Assembly. The ANSF would take actions that foreign taxpayers might be reluctant to fund. Such long-term international involvement is simply not tenable.

If Afghanistan cannot support its security forces at the currently proposed levels on its own, even under the most optimistic economic scenario, and long-term international support or a long-term international presence is not viable, there is only one way that the ANSF can approach sustainability: the conditions in the region must be changed so that Afghanistan no longer needs such large and expensive security forces. Changing those conditions, however, will require changing the behavior of actors not only inside but also outside of the country— and that has led many observers to embrace putting pressure on, and even launching attacks into, Pakistan as another deus ex machina for the increasingly dire situation within Afghanistan.

Borderline Insecurity Disorder

After the first phase of the war in Afghanistan ended with the overthrow of the Taliban in 2001 (and as the United States prepared to invade Iraq), Washington's limited agenda in the region was to press the Pakistani military to go after al-Qaeda; meanwhile, Washington largely ignored the broader insurgency, which remained marginal until 2005. This suited the Pakistani military's strategy, which was to assist the United States against al-Qaeda but to retain the Afghan Taliban as a potential source of pressure on Afghanistan. But the summer of 2006 saw a major escalation of the insurgency, as Pakistan and the Taliban interpreted the U.S. decision to transfer command of coalition forces to NATO (plus U.S. Secretary of Defense Donald Rumsfeld's announcement of a troop drawdown, which in fact never took place) as a sign of its intention to withdraw. They also saw non-U.S. troop contributors as more vulnerable to political pressure generated by casualties.

The Pakistani military does not control the insurgency, but it can affect its intensity. Putting pressure on Pakistan to curb the militants will likely remain ineffective, however, without a strategic realignment by the United States. The region is rife with conspiracy theories trying to find a rational explanation for the apparently irrational strategic posture on the part of the United States of supporting a "major non-NATO ally" that is doing more to undermine the U.S. position in Afghanistan than any other state. Many Afghans believe that Washington secretly supports the Taliban as a way to keep a war going to justify a troop presence that is actually aimed at securing the energy resources of Central Asia and countering China. Many in Pakistan believe that the United States has deceived Pakistan into conniving with Washington to bring about its own destruction: India and U.S.-supported Afghanistan will form a pincer around Pakistan to dismember the world's only Muslim nuclear power. And some Iranians speculate that in preparation for the coming of the Mahdi [Messiah], God has blinded the Great Satan to its own interests so that it would eliminate both of Iran's Sunni-ruled regional rivals, Afghanistan and Iraq, thus unwittingly paving the way for the long-awaited Shia restoration.

The true answer is much simpler: the Bush Administration never reevaluated its strategic priorities in the region after September 11. Institutional inertia and ideology jointly ensured that Pakistan would be treated as an ally, Iran as an enemy, and Iraq as the main threat, thereby granting Pakistan a monopoly on U.S. logistics and, to a significant extent, on the intelligence the United States has on Afghanistan. Eighty-four percent of the materiel for U.S. forces in Afghanistan goes through Pakistan, and the ISI remains nearly the sole source of intelligence about international terrorist acts prepared by al-Qaeda and its affiliates in Pakistan.

More fundamentally, the concept of "pressuring" Pakistan is flawed. No state can be successfully pressured into acts it considers suicidal. The Pakistani security establishment believes that it faces both a U.S.-Indian-Afghan alliance and a separate Iranian-Russian alliance, each aimed at undermining Pakistani influence in Afghanistan and even dismembering the Pakistani state. Some (but not all) in the establishment see armed militants within Pakistan as a threat; but they largely consider it one that is ultimately controllable, and in any case secondary to the threat posed by their nuclear-armed enemies.

Pakistan's military command, which makes and implements the country's national security policies, shares a commitment to a vision of Pakistan as the homeland for South Asian Muslims and therefore to the incorporation of Kashmir into Pakistan. It considers Afghanistan as within Pakistan's security perimeter. Add to this that Pakistan does not have border agreements with either India, into which Islamabad contests the incorporation of Kashmir, or Afghanistan, which has never explicitly recognized the Durand Line, which separates the two countries, as an interstate border.

That border is more than a line. The frontier between Pakistan and Afghanistan was structured as part of the defenses of British India. On the Pakistani side of the Durand Line, the British and their Pakistani successors turned the difficulty of governing the tribes to their advantage by establishing what are now the FATA. Within the FATA, these tribes, not the government, are responsible for security. The area is kept underdeveloped and overarmed as a barrier against invaders. (That is also why any ground intervention there by the United States or NATO will fail.) Now, the Pakistani military has turned the FATA into a staging area for militants who can be used to conduct asymmetric warfare in both Afghanistan and Kashmir, since the region's special status provides for (decreasingly) plausible deniability. This use of the FATA has eroded state control, especially in Pakistan's Northwest Frontier Province, which abuts the FATA. The Swat Valley, where Pakistani Taliban fighters have been battling the government for several years, links Afghanistan and the FATA to Kashmir. Pakistan's strategy for external security has thus undermined its internal security.

On September 19, 2001, when Pakistani President Pervez Musharraf announced to the nation his decision to support the U.S.-led intervention against the Taliban in Afghanistan, he stated that the overriding reason was to save Pakistan by preventing the United States from allying with India. In return, he wanted concessions to Pakistan on its security interests.

Subsequent events, however, have only exacerbated Pakistan's sense of insecurity. Musharraf asked for time to form a "moderate Taliban" government in Afghanistan but failed to produce one. When this failed, he asked that the United States prevent the Northern Alliance (part of the anti-Taliban resistance in Afghanistan), which had been supported by India, Iran, and Russia from occupying Kabul; the appeal failed. Now, Pakistan claims that the Northern Alliance is working with India from inside Afghanistan's security services. Meanwhile, India has reestablished its consulates in Afghan cities, including some near the Pakistani border. India has genuine consular interests there (Hindu and Sikh populations, commercial travel, aid programs), but it may also in fact be using the consulates against Pakistan, as Islamabad claims. India has as well, in cooperation with Iran, completed a highway linking Afghanistan's ring road (which connects its major cities) to Iranian ports on the Persian Gulf, potentially eliminating Afghanistan's dependence on Pakistan for access to the sea and marginalizing Pakistani's new Arabian Sea port of Gwadar, which was built with hundreds of millions of dollars of Chinese aid. And the new U.S.-Indian nuclear deal effectively recognizes New Delhi's legitimacy as a nuclear power while continuing to treat Islamabad, with its record of proliferation, as a pariah. In this context, pressuring or giving aid to Pakistan without any effort to address the sources of its insecurity cannot yield a sustainable positive outcome.

Big Hat, No Cattle

Rethinking U.S. and global objectives in the region will require acknowledging two distinctions: first, between ultimate goals and reasons to fight a war; and, second, among the time frames for different objectives. Preventing al-Qaeda from regrouping so that it can organize terrorist attacks is an immediate goal that can justify war, to the extent that such war is proportionate and effective. Strengthening the state and the economy of Afghanistan is a medium-to-long-term objective that cannot justify war except insofar as Afghanistan's weakness provides a haven for security threats.

This medium-to-long-term objective would require reducing the level of armed conflict, including by seeking a political settlement with current insurgents. In discussions about the terms of such a settlement, leaders linked to both the Taliban and other parts of the insurgency have asked, What are the goals for which the United States and the international community are waging war in Afghanistan? Do they want to guarantee that Afghanistan's territory will not be used to attack them, impose a particular government in Kabul, or use the conflict to establish permanent military bases? These interlocutors oppose many U.S. policies toward the Muslim world, but they acknowledge that the United States and others have a legitimate interest in preventing Afghan territory from being used to launch attacks against them. They claim to be willing to support an Afghan government that would guarantee that its territory would not be used to launch terrorist attacks in the future—in return, they say, for the withdrawal of foreign troops.

The guarantees these interlocutors now envisage are far from those required, and Afghanistan will need international forces for security assistance even if the current war subsides. But such questions can provide a framework for discussion. To make such discussions credible, the United States must redefine its counterterrorist goals. It should seek to separate those Islamist movements with local or national objectives from those that, like al-Qaeda, seek to attack the United States or its allies directly—instead of lumping them all together. Two Taliban spokespeople separately told the *New York Times* that their movement had broken with al-Qaeda since September 11. (Others linked to the insurgency have told us the same thing.) Such statements cannot simply be taken at face value, but that does not mean they should not be explored further. An agreement in principle to prohibit the use of Afghan (or Pakistani) territory for international terrorism, plus an agreement from the United States and NATO that such a guarantee could be sufficient to end their hostile military action, could constitute a framework for negotiation. Any agreement in which the Taliban or other insurgents disavowed al-Qaeda would constitute a strategic defeat for al-Qaeda.

Political negotiations are the responsibility of the Afghan government, but to make such negotiations possible the United States would have to alter its detention policy. Senior officials of the Afghan goverament say that at least through 2004 they repeatedly received overtures from senior Taliban leaders, but they could never guarantee that these leaders would not be captured by U.S. forces and detained at Guantánamo Bay or the U.S. air base at Bagram, in

Afghanistan. Talking with Taliban fighters or other insurgents does not mean replacing Afghanistan's constitution with the Taliban's Islamic Emirate of Afghanistan, closing girls' schools, or accepting other retrograde social policies. Whatever weaknesses the Afghan government and security forces may have, Afghan society—which has gone through two loya jirgas and two elections, possesses more than five million cell phones, and has access to an explosion of new media—is incomparably stronger than it was seven years ago, and the Taliban know it. These potential interlocutors are most concerned with the presence of foreign troops, and some have advocated strengthening the current ANSF as a way to facilitate those troops' departure. In November 2006, one of the Taliban's leading supporters in Pakistan, Maulana Fazlur Rahman, publicly stated in Peshawar that the Taliban could participate as a party in elections in Afghanistan, just as his party did in Pakistan (where it recently lost overwhelmingly), so long as they were not labeled as terrorists.

The End of the Game

There is no more a political solution in Afghanistan alone than there is a military solution in Afghanistan alone. Unless the decision makers in Pakistan decide to make stabilizing the Afghan government a higher priority than countering the Indian threat, the insurgency conducted from bases in Pakistan will continue. Pakistan's strategic goals in Afghanistan place Pakistan at odds not just with Afghanistan and India, and with U.S. objectives in the region, but with the entire international community. Yet there is no multilateral framework for confronting this challenge, and the U.S.-Afghan bilateral framework has relied excessively on the military-supply relationship. NATO, whose troops in Afghanistan are daily losing their lives to Pakistan-based insurgents, has no Pakistan policy. The UN Security Council has hardly discussed Pakistan's role in Afghanistan, even though three of the permanent members (France, the United Kingdom, and the United States) have troops in Afghanistan; the other two are threatened by movements (in the North Caucasus and in Xinjiang) with links to the FATA; and China, Pakistan's largest investor, is poised to become the largest investor in Afghanistan as well, with a $3.5 billion stake in the Aynak copper mine, south of Kabul.

The alternative is not to place Pakistan in a revised "axis of evil." It is to pursue a high-level diplomatic initiative designed to build a genuine consensus on the goal of achieving Afghan stability by addressing the legitimate sources of Pakistan's insecurity while increasing the opposition to its disruptive actions. China, both an ally of Pakistan and potentially the largest investor in both Afghanistan and Pakistan, could play a particularly significant role, as could Saudi Arabia, a serious investor in and ally of Pakistan, former supporter of the Taliban, and custodian of the two holiest Islamic shrines.

A first step could be the establishment of a contact group on the region authorized by the UN Security Council. This contact group, including the five permanent members and perhaps others (NATO, Saudi Arabia), could promote dialogue between India and Pakistan about their respective interests in Afghanistan and about finding a solution to the Kashmir dispute; seek a long-term political vision for the future of the FATA from the Pakistani government, perhaps one involving integrating the FATA into Pakistan's provinces, as proposed by several Pakistani political parties; move Afghanistan and Pakistan toward discussions on the Durand Line and other frontier issues; involve Moscow in the region's stabilization so that Afghanistan does not become a test of wills between the United States and Russia, as Georgia has become; provide guarantees to Tehran that the U.S.-NATO commitment to Afghanistan is not a threat to Iran; and ensure that China's interests and role are brought to bear in international discussions on Afghanistan. Such a dialogue would have to be backed by the pledge of a multiyear international development aid package for regional economic integration, including aid to the most affected regions in Afghanistan, Pakistan, and Central Asia, particularly the border regions. (At present, the United States is proposing to provide $750 million in aid to the FATA but without having any political framework to deliver the aid.)

A central purpose of the contact group would be to assure Pakistan that the international community is committed to its territorial integrity—and to help resolve the Afghan and Kashmir border issues so as to better define Pakistan's territory. The international community would have to provide transparent reassurances and aid to Pakistan, pledge that no state is interested in its dismemberment, and guarantee open borders between Pakistan and both Afghanistan and India. The United States and the European Union would have to open up their markets to Pakistan's critical exports, especially textiles, and to Afghan products. And the United States would need to offer a road map to Pakistan for achieving the same kind of nuclear deal that was reached with India, once Pakistan has transparent and internationally monitored guarantees about the nonproliferation of its nuclear weapons technology.

Reassurances by the contact group that addressed Pakistan's security concerns might encourage Pakistan to promote, rather than hinder, an internationally and nationally acceptable political settlement in Afghanistan. Backing up the contact group's influence and clout must be the threat that any breaking of agreements or support for terrorism originating in the FATA would be taken to the UN Security Council. Pakistan, the largest troop contributor to UN peacekeeping operations, sees itself as a legitimate international power, rather than a spoiler; confronted with the potential loss of that status, it would compromise.

India would also need to become more transparent about its activities in Afghanistan, especially regarding the role of its intelligence agency, the Research and Analysis Wing. Perhaps the ISI and the RAW could be persuaded to enter a dialogue to explore whether the covert war they have waged against each other for the past sixty years could spare the territory of Afghanistan. The contact group could help establish a permanent Indian-Pakistani body at the intelligence and military levels, where complaints could be lodged and discussed. The World Bank and the Asian Development Bank could also help set up joint reconstruction programs in Afghanistan. A series of regional conferences on economic cooperation for the reconstruction of Afghanistan have already created a partial framework for such programs.

Then there is Iran. The Bush administration responded to Iranian cooperation in Afghanistan in 2001 by placing Tehran in the "axis of evil" and by promising to keep "all options on the table," which is understood as a code for not ruling out a military attack. Iran has reacted in part by aiding insurgents in Afghanistan to signal how much damage it could do in response. Some Iranian officials, however, continue to seek cooperation with the United States against al-Qaeda and the Taliban. The next U.S. administration can and should open direct dialogue with Tehran around the two countries' common concerns in Afghanistan. An opening to Iran would show that the United States need not depend solely on Pakistan for access to Afghanistan. And in fact, Washington and Tehran had such a dialogue until around 2004. In May 2005, when the United States and Afghanistan signed a "declaration of strategic partnership," Iran signaled that it would not object as long as the partnership was not directed against Iran. Iran would have to be reassured by the contact group that Afghan territory would not be used as a staging area for activities meant to undermine Iran and that all U.S. covert activities taking place from there would be stopped.

Russia's main concern—that the United States and NATO are seeking a permanent U.S.-NATO military presence in Afghanistan and Central Asia—will also need to be assuaged. Russia should be assured that U.S. and NATO forces can help defend, rather than threaten, legitimate Russian interests in Central Asia, including through cooperation with the Shanghai Cooperation Organization. Russia and the Central Asian states should be informed of the results of legitimate interrogations of militants who came from the former Soviet space and were captured in Afghanistan or Pakistan.

To overcome the zero-sum competition taking place between states, ethnic groups, and factions, the region needs to discover a source of mutual benefit derived from cooperation. China—with its development of mineral resources and access roads in Afghanistan and Pakistan, the financial support it gave to build the port of Gwadar, and its expansion of the Karakoram Highway, which links China to northern Pakistan—may be that source. China is also a major supplier of arms and nuclear equipment to Pakistan. China has a major interest in peace and development in the region because it desires a north-south energy and trade corridor so that its goods can travel from Xinjiang to the Arabian Sea ports of Pakistan and so that oil and gas pipelines can carry energy from the Persian Gulf and Iran to western China. In return for such a corridor, China could help deliver much-needed electricity, and even water, to both countries. Such a corridor would also help revive the economies of both Afghanistan and Pakistan.

More Than Troops

Both U.S. presidential candidates are committed to sending more troops to Afghanistan, but this would be insufficient to reverse the collapse of security there. A major diplomatic initiative involving all the regional stakeholders in problem-solving talks and setting out road maps for local stabilization efforts is more important. Such an initiative would serve to reaffirm that the West is indeed committed to the long-term rehabilitation of Afghanistan and the region. A contact group, meanwhile, would reassure Afghanistan's neighbors that the West is determined to address not just extremism in the region but also economic development, job creation, the drug trade, and border disputes.

Lowering the level of violence in the region and moving the global community toward genuine agreement on the long-term goals there would provide the space for Afghan leaders to create jobs and markets, provide better governance, do more to curb corruption and drug trafficking, and overcome their country's widening ethnic divisions. Lowering regional tensions would allow the Afghan government to have a more meaningful dialogue with those insurgents who are willing to disavow al-Qaeda and take part in the political process. The key to this would be the series of security measures the contact group should offer Pakistan, thereby encouraging the Pakistani army to press—or at least allow—Taliban and other insurgent leaders on their soil to talk to Kabul.

The goal of the next U.S. president must be to put aside the past, Washington's keenness for "victory" as the solution to all problems, and U.S. reluctance to involve competitors, opponents, or enemies in diplomacy. A successful initiative will require exploratory talks and an evolving road map. Today, such suggestions may seem audacious, naïve, or impossible, but without such audacity there is little hope for Afghanistan, for Pakistan, or for the region as a whole.

All handbooks of war recommend
"Divide the enemy", WAR ON TERROR"
Did the opposite ‖ 20 ‖

The Way Forward in Afghanistan

End the War on Terror explicitly Renounce war on terror

The situation in Afghanistan has turned so far against the United States, NATO, the international community, and those Afghans who originally hoped that the post–September 11 intervention would finally bring them a chance for normal lives that it will be very difficult to salvage. Al-Qaeda has established a new safe haven in the Federally Administered Tribal Agencies of Pakistan, from which it supports insurgencies in Afghanistan and Pakistan and continues its global planning against the United States and its allies. Its press releases are so frequent that they are hardly newsworthy unless they feature video of Usama Bin Laden himself. [The Obama administration refocused efforts on al-Qaeda, severely degrading its capabilities and ultimately killing Bin Laden himself in his home in Abbottabad, Pakistan, on May 2, 2011.] Negative trends in Afghanistan include the deterioration of security, Afghan governance, and regional stability. The stability of Pakistan, a nuclear weapons state that has been the main source of proliferation over the past two decades, is now at serious risk. Rising India-Pakistan tensions further exacerbate the regional risk, as do tensions over Iran's nuclear program and its relations with Hizbullah and Hamas.

The task in Afghanistan would have been difficult under any circumstances. The Bush administration's unique record of incompetence, fecklessness, and criminality has ensured that the Obama administration inherits its responsibilities under the worst possible circumstances, not only for the region but globally as well. Still, as President Obama's chief of staff Rahm Emmanuel said of the economic situation, "You never want a serious crisis to go to waste."

This serious crisis may finally force equally serious thinking about the goals of the international intervention in Afghanistan and the means required to have any serious hope of attaining or approaching them. Rather than proclaim objectives

---

Originally published in *Survival* 51 (February–March 2009), no. 1: 83–96.

limited only by the audacity of our imaginations (an Islamic democratic, stable, gender-sensitive, and prosperous Afghanistan) and the paucity of our means (fewer resources per capita than any other such operation), we need to align objectives with reality, and means with objectives.

The most important change in the definition of U.S. objectives is to explicitly renounce the War on Terror. Instead the United States is engaged in a war against al-Qaeda, which attacked the United States and its allies. Al-Qaeda, a nonterritorial transnational network, can obtain a safe haven only through alliance with groups such as the Taliban, which have a national or ethnic base connected to a territory and population. Such alliances are inherently unstable, however, insofar as any territorialized political movement has objectives related to the territory and population where it is based, objectives that are necessarily different from al-Qaeda's global goals of reestablishing the Islamic caliphate throughout Muslim territory.

The "war on terror," which amalgamated all Islamist groups that used violence into a common threat, thus strengthened its primary target, al-Qaeda, by creating incentives for local groups treated as "terrorists" to ally themselves with al-Qaeda. All handbooks of war, dating back at least to Sun Tzu, have recommended dividing the enemy. The War on Terror did the opposite.

Counterterrorism requires military and intelligence tools, but only a drastic strategic reorientation can provide those with their required political complement. In the Afghan context, such a clear, public reorientation of counterterrorism policies should lead the United States and its partners in Afghanistan to offer political negotiations to any Taliban and other insurgents who are willing to separate themselves from al-Qaeda. Such a policy has been in effect formally for several years, but related policies on sanctions, detention, and reintegration have not been restructured to reflect that stance. Political accommodation with groups that accept effective guarantees against the creation or protection of terrorist sanctuaries will require reciprocal U.S. guarantees against detention or sanctions for any leader willing to enter into such an agreement. Thus far the United States has no mechanism to ensure that such a guarantee is observed by the multitude of agencies involved in the counterterrorism effort.

The same shift in counterterrorism policy should apply to Pakistan, though it will take a different form. The United States should support efforts by the elected government of Pakistan to separate Pakistani insurgents from al-Qaeda and other foreign fighters, in particular by supporting programs to reform the status of the Federally Administered Tribal Agencies to address the grievances and isolation of the population there.

Separating Afghan or Pakistani Islamic insurgents from al-Qaeda would constitute a serious political setback for the latter that would damage its claims to legitimacy and its recruitment capacity in the Islamic world. Much of the diffuse international sympathy for al-Qaeda (now on the decline) derives from resistance to "occupations" of Afghanistan and Iraq. Any political settlement with Afghan insurgents, especially the Taliban leadership, would deprive al-Qaeda of that claim.

Inclusion of Taliban leadership and other insurgents in a political settlement does not mean returning Afghanistan to Taliban rule or abandoning the broad portion of the Afghan political spectrum that has worked with the international community and welcomed liberation from Taliban rule. Nor is it meant as a quick fix to replace policies aimed at the regional factors behind the insurgency or the corruption and abuse that have so weakened the Afghan government. A political settlement cannot succeed without policy changes by the Taliban's regional sponsors, and insurgents cannot be reintegrated unless the government becomes more credible.

What the United States should ask of its Afghan partners is that any political agreement be based on recognizing the authority of the Afghan government and its security forces throughout the territory of Afghanistan. Participation in power among (more or less) disarmed political groups through coalition or cooptation is acceptable; division of the country into spheres of influence under the control of multiple authorities or security forces is not. Power sharing in the latter sense permits formation of safe havens.

This is what the U.S. and Afghan governments should mean when they state that negotiating partners must accept the Afghan constitution. This should not mean passage of an ideological test requiring agreement with every article but recognition of the sovereignty of the government established by the constitution. Many issues dealt with (often ambiguously) by the constitution will remain contentious for a long time, and not only to insurgents. Insurgents who lay down arms will have the same rights as other Afghans to disagree with and seek to change the constitution through peaceful means.

Such a declaratory policy is already in effect, but no one takes it seriously, since the existing policies on detention and sanctions send the other message. Taliban and al-Qaeda are detained together in Guantánamo and sanctioned together by the UN Security Council. Closing Guantánamo is a first step. Afghan and Pakistani detainees (except for those closely linked to al-Qaeda leadership, which includes no Afghans) should be transferred to national custody or released. The international community will have to fund generous reintegration packages in both countries.

Both national and international sanctions regimes should be changed to guarantee security and integration of insurgents who join the political process. Russia has thus far opposed removal of anyone from the sanctions list, for reasons that should be explored further. The main reason is probably its concern that the purpose of integrating former Taliban is to consolidate a NATO base in its near abroad. Diplomatic efforts to overcome these objectives could serve common Russian and Western interests in the elimination of the threat from al-Qaeda.

Such a policy change will not work by itself. To succeed, it must be accompanied by military, security, and governance efforts that enable the Afghan government to present a more credible alternative than it has. The Afghan Taliban leaders are dependent on their Pakistani sponsors and supporters, including the country's military and security apparatus, for their safe haven, and regional diplomacy aimed at changing Pakistan's security calculus remains essential. The core of such a policy is firm support for the efforts of the elected government of Pakistan to gain control of the country's security policy and define the national interest as the welfare of the citizens of Pakistan.

Within Pakistan, integrating FATA into what Pakistanis call the "mainstream" is also not a quick fix. It will require a strategy that will take many years. There will be armed resistance by al-Qaeda and many other armed groups whose existence depends on the isolated nature of these areas. But gaining control of national territory in order to protect the rights of Pakistani citizens will certainly provide a more legitimate mission for the country's security forces than assisting the United States in its "War on Terror."

No single policy change can solve any problem, let alone a set of problems so complex and interdependent as those of this region. But such a bold, clear announcement, followed by concrete public steps, can go a long way toward transforming the poisonous environment we all have inherited.

A Tribe Apart

Afghan Elites Face a Corrosive Past

The Asia Society stands out from its neighbors on New York's Park Avenue. The façade, constructed in a spirit of cross-cultural cooperation, mixes Oklahoma's red granite with Rajasthan's red sandstone, the stone from which the medieval emperors of Delhi, descendants of conquerors from Afghanistan and Central Asia, hewed the Red Fort of Delhi. Like traditional Persian forts, the Asia Society has both public and private audience rooms (*diwan-i aam* and *diwan-i khas*). Several times I have heard Afghanistan's President Hamid Karzai speak in the public auditorium, but in September 2008 I took the elevator to a small, private room, where Dr. Abdullah Abdullah, Afghanistan's former minister of foreign affairs, was briefing a few colleagues.

As Abdullah somewhat bitterly recounted how the international community had prematurely declared victory in Afghanistan, he reminded me of a fall 2002 conference we both attended in the United Kingdom. A British deputy minister had just finished a self-congratulatory speech about success in Afghanistan. I asked for the floor and reported complaints from colleagues in the Afghan government. They were spending half their time trying to make up for the political harm done by coalition military actions, there was neither a plan nor adequate funding for economic recovery, and armed commanders were consolidating control of all the provinces and borders. The distinguished British official responded, "Well, I've just heard the voice of doom!"

Since 2002 I have often encountered variations on this theme when expressing concern that the international project in Afghanistan is out of touch with local realities, sometimes disastrously so. A tolerant German diplomat allowed that I saw a half-full glass as half-empty; an avuncular American NATO official explained that I was losing credibility in international gatherings because my analysis was distorted by a partisan domestic agenda. Officials always claim to be better informed, more

Originally published in *Boston Review* (January/February 2009): 21–27.

practical, and less partisan than outside experts. The most bizarre case, I suppose, was when a Bush political appointee accused me of being an "expert from Washington."

With chaos in Afghanistan impossible to deny, U.S. officials have increasingly sought my views. Most of the solutions they propose, such as increasing troop levels, might have worked several years ago, but my sense of the society—the same sense that led to my previous skepticism—now makes me suspect that it is too late to save the enterprise we began after September 11. But this does not mean Afghanistan will go back to what it was under the Taliban. If I have learned anything from experience, it is that Afghanistan defies expectations.

I have studied Afghanistan, its region, and many other zones of conflict around the world for decades, but it is true that I have little experience as a practitioner. The apogee of my practical-political career was a stint as a UN official at the UN Talks on Afghanistan (the "Bonn Negotiations") in November–December 2001. Lakhdar Brahimi, Special Representative of the UN Secretary-General on Afghanistan, asked me to assist him in the mission he had hurriedly assembled at the Bush administration's request. Having driven out al-Qaeda and destroyed the Taliban regime that had harbored it, the administration realized that the United States would have to do something about Afghanistan itself and turned to the United Nations, a sign that it considered this task relatively unimportant. The Russian UN Representative (now foreign minister) Sergei Lavrov repeatedly objected to my role. He was disturbed by an interview I had given to *Le Monde* before taking up my UN duties. In that interview, I declared Russia "irresponsible" for trying to preempt the negotiations by lavishing funds on its preferred candidate for leader of Afghanistan. My official service proved exceedingly brief.

I remained until the end of the Bonn Negotiations, and, after returning home, I launched work on an independent project on the reconstruction of Afghanistan that my longtime friend and colleague Ashraf Ghani, then a World Bank official and later minister of finance of Afghanistan, and I had designed. This project took me to the country three times in 2002 and has brought me there dozens more times since. On these trips I have observed the grand projects of the War on Terror and reconstruction of Afghanistan as they meet the fractious realities of a society traumatized by generations of conflict. I have divulged my formal sources in footnotes, mainly taken from documents and interviews on political, economic, and military matters. But it is my experiences outside of formal meetings—Personal Intelligence Estimates, you might call them—that have prompted the reservations that my official interlocutors interpret as groundless or politically motivated pessimism.

Under the more open conditions that have prevailed since the fall of the Taliban, I have seen clearly more of what I had only sensed on visits in previous decades. The human effect of decades of war: how the collapse of even a relatively weak state authority forced people back to their kin, clan, or tribal groups; how violence, which could erupt at any moment, from any direction, quickly rekindled memories of earlier traumas. Over the years, with violence and its legacy a constant presence, the trust that institutional cooperation demands had been blown to bits as surely as the Buddhas of Bamiyan. Afghans returning from prolonged exile found a society they did not recognize; they often commented that there was no trust between people. Against that corrosive background, every effort to reconnect the scattered fragments of the former national elites— or to reconnect returning elites with those who had remained—could be undermined with a careless word, a careless dollar, or a careless bomb.

* * *

In March 2002, on my first night in Kabul after the December 2001 defeat of the Taliban, I drove through a bone-chilling rain to a freezing house in the Wazir Akbar Khan neighborhood. The area was once—and would become again—the diplomatic quarter and home to Kabul's wealthy and high officials. The hero of Khaled Hosseini's best-selling novel *The Kite Runner* spent his childhood here, playing under the pomegranate trees as violence gradually overtook the city and the country.

I had arrived just days before Nawruz the ancient Persian New Year celebrated each spring in Afghanistan, Iran, and neighboring regions. There were no signs of any festivities. And though the end of a four-year drought would bring crops— licit or otherwise—to relieve some of the country's hunger, now the rain only turned dust to mud. U.S. military vehicles churned unpaved streets into rutted tracks, splashing the new uniforms of a few men on foot patrol. Former resistance fighters from the Panjshir Valley now serving in a fledgling Afghan army, they nonchalantly fingered their Kalashnikovs.

In a barely lit room I greeted my hosts, Qayum Karzai and Ghani. A few months earlier, in Bonn, we had worked around the clock with many others for eight days to outline a political settlement for Afghanistan. We had hoped to seize what Ghani called the "open moment" created for Afghanistan—if unintentionally—by the U.S. military response to September 11. After years of failure at promoting "intra-Afghan dialogue" to create a "broad-based government," the United Nations had brought together Afghans (minus the recently defeated Taliban) to form a new government in a country without a functioning army or administration. Brahimi convened four Afghan groups: the United Front (known as the Northern Alliance), which had occupied Kabul and the North as the Taliban fled; the Rome group, which included exiles supporting the former king, Muhammad Zahir Shah, who had lived in Rome since a 1973 coup and who represented the historical continuity (now broken) of the Afghan state and its elites; and two other exile groups—called Peshawar and Cyprus, after the places they had gathered to discuss the country's future—which were supposed to represent the concerns of Pakistan and Iran.

The gathering was unrepresentative, but, Brahimi explained, if the four groups made good decisions, no one would remember how unrepresentative they were. The Tajik-led Northern Alliance, the largest resistance alliance, included groups that had fought the Afghan communists, the Soviets, and then the Taliban under the brilliant and charismatic command of Ahmad Shah Massoud, as well as some militias formerly allied with the communist government. In December 2001, the Northern Alliance leaders were using the leverage provided by the American military intervention and the prestige of the ex-king to turn their presence on the ground into at-least-temporary control over the centers of coercive power, including the army, police, administration, intelligence, and foreign affairs. In return they accepted a political process to broaden the government, making it more representative and effective through an Emergency Loya Jirga— a Great Council, bringing together indirectly elected representatives of all districts plus special seats for women, minorities, and prominent individuals— opened by the former king. They agreed as well to the adoption of a constitution and national elections.

By March 2002, Hamid Karzai, Qayum's brother and a member of the Rome group, had become Afghanistan's president. Ghani and Qayum were presidential advisors, and I had come for a series of meetings to launch the Afghanistan Reconstruction Project, a modified version of the plan that Ghani and I had designed in the United States before Bonn. We initially hoped to convene Afghans and independent experts to generate proposals to help a new government managing a vast transformation. When change arrived with surprising suddenness, Ghani moved to Kabul (first with the United Nations, then as an Afghan official, eventually as finance minister), and I redirected the program toward research and analysis in support of the UN-monitored transitional process outlined in the Bonn Agreement.

Qayum Karzai and Ghani, like many returning Afghan exiles, had been living outside the country for decades. Both were studying in the United States when communist army officers seized power in a 1978 coup d'état. They had spent the succeeding years involved in Afghanistan's struggles largely from their American homes. Although they personally escaped, their families suffered in the violence of those years. The post-'78 regime was led by the Khalq (People) faction of the People's Democratic Party of Afghanistan (PDPA). The Khalqis, dominated by recently educated rural Pashtuns from the south and east of Afghanistan, moved quickly to avenge themselves on the urban elites whom they blamed for the country's backwardness, starting with the royal family and those groups closest to them. Among thousands of others, they arrested all male members over fifteen years old of both the Karzai and Ghani families, including both men's fathers. Detainees were routinely tortured and executed in the crowded prison of Pul-i-Charkhi, where more than ten thousand disappeared.

Ghani's family managed to bribe officials to hide the fact that most of his relatives had not been killed; only his father's first cousin Shahpur Ahmadzai, commander of the Kabul Military Academy, was executed. Karzai's father, Abdul Ahad, former deputy speaker of the Afghan parliament, came out alive, only to be assassinated in 1999 one Friday in Quetta, Pakistan, while walking home after prayers. He had been trying to unite Southern Afghanistan's tribes to resist the Taliban and propose a national solution to Afghanistan's conflict.

Although no overall statistics were available, Afghan intellectuals exiled in Peshawar, Pakistan, in the 1980s estimated that 60 percent of the faculty of Kabul University (the country's leading higher education institution) had fled, died, or been arrested. Virtually all Afghans with international degrees or training fled the country or were killed.

In 1979 Hamid Karzai was studying in India when the Soviet Union invaded Afghanistan to replace a defiant communist leader with one who was more moderate and pliable. Karzai went to Pakistan, where he worked in the political office of one of the moderate nationalist resistance parties during the ten-year Soviet occupation of Afghanistan. Over the years, the Karzais campaigned with increasing intensity against the favor shown by Pakistan, with U.S. complicity, to the radical Islamists at the expense of the more traditionalist or nationalist parties in the resistance movement. Pakistan associated the nationalists with Afghanistan's territorial claims against it: no government in Kabul has recognized the 1893 Durand Line, drawn by the British through the middle of Pashtun lands, as an international boundary dividing Afghanistan and Pakistan. The Islamists claimed to care nothing for national borders, and Pakistan told the Americans that radical Islamists killed more Russians.

When the formerly Soviet-supported regime fell in April 1992, Hamid Karzai returned as deputy minister of foreign affairs in the mujahidin government, while Qayum stayed in the United States. Hamid's stay was short-lived. He fell victim to factional rivalry in what would escalate into a nine-year civil war. He escaped from detention thanks to a rocket attack and returned to Pakistan. Hamid went back to Afghanistan one more time before September 11, 2001, after the 1999 assassination of his father. He buried his father in Taliban-controlled Kandahar; the power of the Popalzai tribe, which the Karzais led, and the neutral status of funerals in the tribal code of Pashtunwali guaranteed his safety.

Qayum, who worked out of the public eye, formulated much of the family's strategic thinking. I met him in 1990 at a meeting on Afghanistan at the United States Institute of Peace in Washington, D.C., where his brother Hamid was posing tough questions to Zalmay Khalilzad, then an official of the first Bush administration's Department of Defense and serving under Paul Wolfowitz. Hamid challenged Khalilzad about the U.S. failure to support Afghan nationalists rather than Islamist clients of Pakistan.

Ghani, too, was drawn deeper into Afghan politics in the 1980s and 1990s. His own family and Ahmadzai tribe had suffered repeatedly at the hands of the royal dynasties they had served as ministers, administrators, and military commanders. (And the dynasties had their bill of particulars against these troublesome retainers.) Such powerful allies, of course, could be more dangerous than any enemy. But, for Ghani, these concerns were only the starting point for a critique of his society. He had studied every province of the country and scoured the archives and bookstores for documents explaining how the Afghan state had been built. Ghani became an anthropologist, and after 1983, when he moved to Baltimore to teach at Johns Hopkins University, he became a fixture at Washington meetings on Afghanistan. Drawing on his unparalleled knowledge of the society, he opposed the Soviet invasion, the American obsession with arming radical Islamists to kill Russians, and what he saw as the venality and opportunism of so many of his fellow exiles.

Ghani soon started work as a senior social scientist at the World Bank, gaining the experience and networks he later deployed as the principal architect of Afghanistan's post-2001 reconstruction program. He traveled extensively, to China, India, even to Russia—where he helped to rescue the coal industry—but only once, in 1994, to his own country.

* * *

Eight years later, Ghani was back. With Hamid Karzai in the palace, Ghani, Qayum Karzai, and I settled on thin pillows on the scanty carpet with the other guests: Craig Karp of the U.S. embassy, who had been with us in Bonn; Anthony Richter of the Open Society Institute (a patron of the Afghanistan Reconstruction Project); and our research associate, Helena Malikyar, an Afghan-American with close family ties to the monarchy. We wrapped ourselves in blankets against the chill and began to sip our tea. "Everyone is failing us," Ghani said.

Ghani often seemed to be in pain in those days. He was still recovering from cancer, which had required the removal of most of his stomach. But that night his pain seemed to come from another source. The UN political mission was virtually alone in pressing for the political changes the Bonn process was supposed to bring about, in particular the broadening of the government at the upcoming Emergency Loya Jirga. Kabul's streets were still dominated by the militias that should have been withdrawn under the Bonn Agreement. The Rumsfeld-led Defense Department was intent on bolstering militias to pursue terrorists, not disciplining them to create space for national politics. The International Security Assistance

Force, authorized by the UN Security Council under the Bonn Agreement, operated in parallel to the militias in the city. It prevented factional fighting and provided public security, but it could not prevent the armed groups from turning into predatory gangs.

Rumsfeld had vetoed expansion of the security force, and the militias were consolidating their hold on Afghanistan's assets and customs revenue. Without waiting for the new Afghan authorities to set priorities, international aid agencies had presented gross underestimates of reconstruction costs, while a U.S. administration opposed to "nation building" had allocated no new funding. Rather than delivering a coherent aid package to the new government, the aid bazaar opened with a rush of contractors and NGOs.

As early as March 2002, Ghani saw time slipping away, and so it did, even that night. Karp earned a reprimand from the Embassy for returning well after curfew, while Malikyar and I circled the darkened alleys, as our Pashto-speaking driver from a village south of Kabul asked the Persian-speaking militia men from Tajik villages to the north how to find the house where we were staying. Neither the driver nor the soldiers, all of them strangers to the city, knew the streets of Wazir Akbar Khan.

A few days later, during a lull in our program, Malikyar and I drove across the Kabul River to the hillside where the founder of the Mughal Empire, Babur, lies buried in the garden that he built to celebrate the beloved, cosmopolitan city and that bears his name, Bagh-i Babur. In accordance with his wishes, Babur's son, the Emperor Humayun, had his father, who had died in Agra, reburied there in 1544.

I had visited Bagh-i Babur during a trip to Kabul in June 1998, when it was under Taliban rule. Four years of fighting among mujahidin factions had left the city in ruins, and although now safe under the Taliban, there seemed little of hope of return to past glory. Bagh-i Babur's enclosure was locked and abandoned, the grand caravanserai entrance with a sweeping upward view of the garden and its flower beds, which had long since replaced Babur's central watercourse, destroyed. The garden itself had become an expanse of arid rubble. The exquisite white marble mosque that Shah Jahan, builder of the Taj Mahal, commissioned in honor of his great-grandfather Babur, was pockmarked with shrapnel from rockets, which had shattered one corner. As a guard in threadbare clothes unlocked a remaining side gate, an unveiled nomad woman, holding the metal scythe with which she cut grass for her animals, looked on, too humble even to merit the Taliban's chastisement.

When I returned in March 2002 with Malikyar, the only change was that the gate was open, and the ruined garden was animated by a gang of boys, gambling and hanging out next to Babur's tomb. This was Malikyar's first visit to Kabul since she had fled to Pakistan with her family in 1978 at the age of fifteen, when one of her father's employees, a member of the Parcham (Banner) faction of the

PDPA, had warned him he was targeted for execution. A few weeks earlier, after the coup that had overthrown President Muhammad Daoud Khan and put the PDPA in power, Malikyar rushed to the hospital to see her friend and second cousin Hila, Daoud's granddaughter. Malikyar learned that Hila had been killed, along with her father—Daoud's son Omar—and Hila's younger sister, Ghizal.

Like many Afghans who returned after decades of exile, Malikyar was shocked by the destruction of Kabul. One day, as we drove from the relatively intact east of the city, where the government offices and embassies were located, to the Intercontinental Hotel in the northwest, we passed through entire neighborhoods pulverized by the factional fighting of 1992–1996. When we later met her uncle, a Voice of America reporter, Malikyar sobbed, "We never should have left! We should have stayed with the people!"

In Babur's Garden, Malikyar approached the boys and greeted them. They asked where we were from, and we told them; they told us they were from Panjshir, the valley north of Kabul whose mountain Tajiks had resisted the Afghan communists, the Soviets, and the Taliban under the leadership of Massoud and the Northern Alliance.

The Valley withstood eight Soviet offensives between 1980 and 1984, when the KGB negotiated a truce directly with Massoud. For his followers, the truce was recognition of his strength and capacity for strategic planning. He used the security of his Panjshir base to lay the foundations of a regionwide organization, a move that enabled his Northern Alliance to take control of Kabul twice: after the fall of the ex-communist regime in 1992, and after the fall of the Taliban in 2001. For other Afghans, especially Pashtuns living south of Kabul, the truce was the mark of Massoud's treachery. They accused him of securing his base at their expense, letting Soviet convoys reach Kabul through the Salang pass. Massoud claimed he had never agreed to a truce in Salang, but that he was not able to block the highway consistently. Despite his victories against the Soviets, he lost a lifelong battle to match his national vision with a national following. Upon his death in 2001, Afghans, especially Pashtuns, firmly perceived him as a Tajik leader, a role he had never sought.

I had not visited Panjshir during the jihad against the Soviet occupation, so I never saw the devastation firsthand. But I had a glimpse of it in 1984 in Peshawar, the capital of Pakistan's northwest frontier province, at a packed clinic exclusively devoted to caring for the child amputees of Panjshir.

On that 1984 trip, Massoud's men in Peshawar brought me to meet a defector from Kabul who had been assigned by Afghanistan's KGB-trained intelligence service to kill Massoud. His masters failed in their mission, but others succeeded years later. Massoud was assassinated on September 9, 2001, by al-Qaeda. Two Moroccan immigrants to Europe posing as journalists detonated their camera in Afghanistan's first suicide bombing. Bin Laden had hoped to decapitate the

Northern Alliance earlier, enabling the Taliban and al-Qaeda to eradicate the last foothold of resistance on Afghan territory before September 11 and the reprisals that would follow. The al-Qaeda leader had never shared with his Afghan hosts his plans to attack the United States, and killing Massoud was his peace offering to the Taliban leader, Mullah Mohammed Omar, who would soon suffer the consequences. The assassination was delayed by the usual Afghan logistical problems, and the anti-Taliban resistance only had to hold from September 9 until shortly after September 11, when Marshall Muhammad Qasim Fahim, Massoud's successor as military commander, began to work with the CIA and U.S. Special Operations forces to oust the Taliban.

That is how the Tajik boys in the garden ended up in Kabul. Their fathers had entered the city with Fahim's troops and were staying in the largely Panjshiri neighborhood near the garden. The boys hailed from Bazarak, Massoud's native village. When we told them we knew many people in Afghanistan, they asked, "Do you know Amrullah Khan?" This was the first time I had heard Amrullah Saleh's name with the honorific "Khan" attached.

Saleh, also from Bazarak and barely thirty years old at the time, was head of the first directorate of the National Directorate of Security, the national intelligence agency, which he would later lead. He had served as Massoud's liaison with the CIA when Massoud decided to cooperate with intelligence gathering after the 1998 al-Qaeda attacks on the U.S. embassies in Kenya and Tanzania. I first met him in the northern Afghan city of Kunduz in January 1996, when he was deputy spokesman of the Afghan Ministry of Defense, then led by Massoud. (The Taliban already controlled Afghanistan's south and west, but not Kabul, although they would capture it later that year.) My colleagues and I had all been impressed by the intellect and eloquence of this man in his early twenties.

So when the boys asked if we knew him, I answered, "Yes, I know him."

"*Az qawm-i maast*" (he is from our clan), they said proudly.

Earlier that day, Malikyar and I had lunched with Saleh in a private room in the rear of the Marco Polo restaurant, where Malikyar's father had run a nightclub in Kabul's swinging sixties. It was Saleh who complained that he spent half his time trying to compensate for the "mistakes" of the coalition—a euphemism for killing civilians and arbitrarily detaining and abusing "terrorist" suspects.

Saleh had his own stories of loss. When the PDPA took power in 1978, they arrested and killed five of his mother's brothers, Islamic scholars from a respected family of Panjshir. During the Soviet occupation, his father, a laborer in Kabul, was found mysteriously dead, and two of his brothers had died in the jihad, in battle or in prison. One relative refused to leave his house near Bagh-i Babur when the Taliban settled scores with the Pansjhiris there in the 1990s; they killed the man's twenty-three-year-old son.

After we told the boys we knew Saleh, one of them, a blue-eyed tough wearing a black and white kafiya tied as a scarf, stepped forward as the group's spokesman. He began telling us how the garden was destroyed. "The mujahidin were up there," he said, pointing to the bomb-wracked heights above the garden, "and Hizb-i Islami was down there." He pointed to the ruined houses below. Malikyar and I looked at each other: only Massoud's forces were "mujahidin"? Hizb-i Islami, the Islamic Party, was one of the several officially recognized mujahidin parties, but its leader was Massoud's main rival in the anti-Soviet resistance, Gulbuddin Hikmatyar—the favorite of the Pakistani intelligence agency. "Mujahidin," once a near-sacred term, had become another factional category.

Far below, on the road at the foot of the ruined garden, several Kamaz trucks rumbled past, their ancient diesel motors grinding. "Those are Russian trucks," the boy said. "*Rus khub mardum hastand*" (Russians are good people). Malikyar was taken aback: "What kind of mujahid are you, praising the Russians?" Russia, together with Iran, had supported Massoud in the fight against the Taliban.

He paused and looked Malikyar in the eye. "Do you know why the Americans can't find Usama Bin Laden?" he asked. We had some idea but wanted to hear his view. "Because Bin Laden is sitting safely in America. The Americans sent Arabs to kill our King (*padishah-i ma*), because they knew that if Massoud was alive, they could never enter Afghanistan."

Seeing that this young man was political, Malikyar recognized a kindred spirit. Her very existence was due to politics: her mother was the descendant of Amir Habibullah Khan (who ruled Afghanistan from 1901 until he was assassinated in 1919) from one of the wives he took from the Pamir Mountains of Badakhshan in the far northeast of the country, on the border of what is now Tajikistan. Afghanistan's rulers took wives from all major tribes and ethnic groups of the country, using kinship and patronage to ensure dynastic loyalty. Daughters of the royal house in turn married into other prominent families. Many of Malikyar's relatives, like those murdered in the 1978 communist coup, had married into the royal Pashtun clan, the Muhammadzais and she was something of a favorite "niece" of Zahir Shah. She recalled sitting with the king at his country retreat north of Kabul as a seven-year-old child in 1970, listening to radio broadcasts of the parliamentary debate over the vote of confidence for Prime Minister Abdul Zahir, in accordance with Afghanistan's 1964 "New Democracy" constitution.

In recent years, after finishing a master's degree at New York University, Malikyar had worked for Zahir Shah at his exile office in Rome. She managed the ex-king's schedule and arranged a network of contacts with tribal leaders who came to Rome or sent their representatives as Zahir Shah and his entourage campaigned for a loya jirga to establish a new government in Afghanistan, an idea the ex-king had first proposed in 1983. The term *loya jirga* seems to have entered Afghan vocabulary in the constitution of Malikyar's great-uncle,

Amanullah Khan. It played the role of a symbolically representative body to provide a form of popular legitimation to the government. Afghanistan's ruling elite retroactively redefined many past gatherings as loya jirgas, creating a mythical history of nation building through consultation and consent. Although the institution was contested by Afghans who saw it as a means of cooptation by the royal family, it had also entered the discourse, especially among Pashtuns, as the expression of Afghan-style democracy. The Bonn Agreement had incorporated elements of this proposal, notably the convening of the Emergency Loya Jirga to broaden the interim government after its first six months.

In March 2002, Zahir Shah was scheduled to return to Afghanistan for the first time since 1973, when he had been overthrown by his cousin Daoud. I had first met Zahir Shah during a 1991 visit to Rome. After a relatively uneventful discussion, his nephew and son-in-law, General Abdul Wali, drove me back to my hotel in the historic center of the city. As the Castel Sant'Angelo, scene of the bloody finale of *Tosca*, came into view, we turned left toward the Piazza Navona, and General Wali described a past that could rival any opera in drama and blood. During his Italian vacation in the summer of 1973, Zahir Shah left General Wali in charge of the Kabul garrison. When Daoud Khan ousted his cousins in a coup, he imprisoned General Wali in a fortress. And then the torture began. Nearly twenty years after his ordeal, General Wali still shook as he told the story.

Wali's daughter Humaira, a close friend of Malikyar's, was also to return to Afghanistan with the royal family in April 2002, and that imminent arrival was on Malikyar's mind in March. She asked the boys' spokesman what he thought about Zahir Shah. He shot back, "Zahir Shah should stay where he is. Also, Hamid Karzai should leave the country, and Rabbani should become president." (Burhanuddin Rabbani was a Tajik from Badakhshan and had been president of the mujahidin-controlled Islamic State of Afghanistan in the mid-1990s. He continued to hold the title through the Taliban period and symbolically handed over authority to Hamid Karzai.) Malikyar asked why they were against Zahir Shah. "Because he oppressed us," the boy answered. "He oppressed us, and now we will oppress them. You'll see."

"How did he oppress you?" Malikyar asked.
"He took our women."

That evening, I had dinner with two Pashtun elders I had known for years. After the other guests left, I recounted the conversation in Bagh-i Babur. When I told them the boy's claim, they looked at each other as if a family secret had just been revealed. The boy might have been referring to Zahir Shah's playboy youth, when he was said to favor the women of Panjshir. But my hosts knew that he also referred to the very real casualties in Afghanistan's violent political history, to an especially crucial episode in the struggle to build and control state power in which both Ashraf Ghani's and Qayum Karzai's grandfathers had played prominent roles.

After a while one of the elders asked me, "Do you know what they say in Paktia? They say Massoud told his men, 'Go down to Paktia and rescue your nephews.'" Paktia is an area including several provinces in southeastern Afghanistan whose tribes brought Zahir Shah's father to power in 1929 after a battle with forces based in the north. The elder was not accusing Massoud of mobilizing his people around past injury; rather he repeated the saying to demonstrate how the people of Paktia recall their own history. The saying revealed the fear, guilt, and deeply rooted mutual mistrust that Afghans of different origins felt as they returned to Kabul to try to rebuild—or build—their country.

* * *

For the past quarter-century, Afghanistan's surviving elites were dispersed around the world, while the people who stayed behind suffered round after round of violence. For years Afghan leaders and people had communicated largely at a distance, lacking a common national political space. In this gap had grown many divergent memories of pre-war Afghanistan, memories filtered through the daily perceptions of violence and attack. Although facing common threats, the different parts of Afghanistan's population had become more disunited than ever, rehearsing among themselves conflicting versions of their common history.

For Afghan elites and for the United Nations and other internationals, violence and oppression began in 1978 with the communist coup; continued through the Soviet invasion, occupation, and withdrawal; took on a new form with the factional wars under mujahidin rule; and continued through the harsh dictates of the Taliban. In keeping with this history, international human rights organizations called for "transitional justice," an accounting for the abuses committed since the 1978 coup. In 2004 I was asked by UN High Commissioner for Human Rights Louise Arbour to help compile all available accounts of human rights violations in Afghanistan since the wars began. When I described this project, which involved parsing documentation from international organizations and NGOs, to one of my oldest Afghan friends, he asked me, "Why do you start with 1978? You know, the Afghan state was not built with roses."

In 1928 Malikyar's great-uncle, King Amanullah Khan, fled Kabul in the face of a growing revolt against his attempt to advance a "developmental state," committed to building the infrastructure and human capital needed for rapid economic growth. He refused to use his tiny air force to attack the tribal forces opposing him, and, as Zahir Shah later would, he lived out his days in Roman exile.

The revolt had started among the Pashtun tribes of Eastern Afghanistan, including Paktia, mobilized by mullahs' warnings that the king was a threat to Islam. But the tribes remained leaderless and uncoordinated.

Tajiks from the plains and mountains to the north, including Panjshiris, were the first rebels to reach Kabul. They were led by Habibullah Kalakani, an army deserter who filled perfectly the role of the bandit king. Some Islamic leaders ratified his military victories, installing him in January 1929 as Amir Habibullah, *"Khadim-i Din-i Rasul Allah"* ("Servant of the Religion of the Messenger of God"). Others, especially Habibullah's Pashtun foes, dismissed him as *"Bacha-i Saqaw,"* the son of the water carrier. But this humble birth also formed part of his legend. He was the first Tajik to sit on the throne of Kabul since the Afghan monarchy moved there from Kandahar in 1775. His brief reign recalled the long history of Persian-speaking rulers in the land that was known as Khurasan before it became Afghanistan.

The British in neighboring India were glad to see the back of Amanullah Khan, but they wanted a reliable Pashtun dynasty in Kabul, not Habibullah or any other Tajik guerrilla. Even though they no longer controlled Afghanistan's foreign relations, they still considered Afghanistan a key part of the strategic defense of the British Empire. They seized an opportunity to support a contender who could stabilize the country, especially the Pashtun areas bordering on India, which were in a state of turmoil.

That contender was Nadir Khan, father of Zahir Shah. Nadir had commanded the Afghan forces in the Third Anglo-Afghan War of 1919 but later fallen out with Amanullah. He and his brothers came from a branch of the royal Muhammadzai clan that had ruled Peshawar before the city fell to the Sikh kingdom of Ranjit Singh in 1826, and they were known as the "Peshawar sardars."

In 1929 the Peshawar sardars returned to Peshawar. With support from the British governor of the Northwest Frontier Province, they established a base in Waziristan, where they began to gather the tribes from both sides of the Durand Line: Wazir, Tani, Mehsud, Jaji, Jadran, and Ahmadzai. Among Nadir Khan's supporters was Ashraf Ghani's grandfather, Abdul Ghani Khan Ahmadzai. He had served in Amanullah Khan's army as a colonel and also fought in the 1919 war of Afghan independence, along with Qayum Karzai's grandfather.

The lashkar (tribal militia) commanded by Abdul Ghani Khan inflicted the first defeat on the forces of Habibullah in Logar province, where, today, the Taliban sit at the gates of Kabul. In September 1929 Nadir Khan's lashkars captured Kabul. Since Nadir had no money to pay his troops, he permitted them to loot the city. A jirga of his fighters proclaimed him Nadir Shah, King of Afghanistan. He and his brothers formed the new royal family, and Abdul Ghani Khan became mayor of the capital and later commander of the Second Corps. Nadir Shah captured and hanged Habibullah.

But the 1929 battle did not end with Habibullah's execution. Tribal lashkars moved north to take control of Shamali and the valleys to the north, where the Tajik revolt had been based. As the tribes looted these areas, they took young women as booty—the mothers and grandmothers of the lost "nephews" of Paktia. The dynasty of Nadir Shah exempted these tribes from taxation and conscription in recognition of their services. Many entered the officer corps; some of those officers were among those who launched the coup that brought the Khalq faction of the PDPA to power in 1978, ending more than two hundred years of rule by Durrani Pashtuns from Kandahar and more than 150 years of rule by the Muhammadzai clan of the Durrani Barakzai tribe, interrupted only by the brief rule of Amir Habibullah in 1929. The 1978 coup broke the Muhammadzai monopoly on the state, opening the political arena to a free-for-all, with militias linked to different communities in contention for power.

The tribes that had looted the north saw their ties to the dynasty of Nadir Shah as their link to the state; others saw themselves as victims of that dynasty, their women stolen and nephews still in need of rescue.

* * *

In May 2002, after the former king's return to Afghanistan, I attended a jirga he was hosting in the garden of his residence in Kabul. A delegation from the Jaji tribe in Khost (formerly part of Paktia) was addressing him, and I saw firsthand the persistence of the loyalty to the dynasty of Nadir Shah.

There I ran into an old friend, Sayyid Naim Majrooh. I had met Majrooh during my trip to Peshawar in 1984, when he was working for the International Committee of the Red Cross. He was the descendant of a distinguished family of Sufis and intellectuals from the Kunar Valley in northeastern Afghanistan. In November 1987 Naim Majrooh's father—Professor Said Bahauddin Majrooh, who fled to Peshawar after the Soviet invasion—published survey results showing that Afghan refugees in Pakistan (mostly Pashtuns from Eastern Afghanistan) overwhelmingly supported Zahir Shah rather than any of the mujahidin leaders as their future leader. On February 11, 1988—as the agreement on the Soviet withdrawal from Afghanistan was being finalized in Geneva and rumors of the formation of a transitional government, perhaps involving Zahir Shah, began to spread—gunmen probably sent by Hikmatyar shot down Professor Majrooh in his home. The message: those who try to restore the king will share this fate.

After his father was killed, Naim Majrooh moved to California, and I saw him occasionally in the United States, including at a State Department brainstorming session soon after the start of the air war in Afghanistan in October 2001. In May 2002 Majrooh was back in Kabul, preparing for his job as chief rapporteur of the

Emergency Loya Jirga. Majrooh and I greeted each other, and I asked him what the Jajis were saying in Pashto. He leaned over with a half-smile and whispered, "They are offering to drive the militias out of Kabul for Zahir Shah as they did for his father. But Zahir Shah is asking them to work for peace."

Malikyar and I continued our rounds, meeting with UN officials to discuss plans for the Emergency Loya Jirga, aid monitoring, judicial reform, and civil service training. We met leaders of the new Ministry of Women's Affairs, newly arrived Western journalists, and dozens of returning exiles. The government took me and several other guests on a tour of the areas north of Kabul where the Taliban and al-Qaeda had destroyed nearly every building and uprooted or cut down every tree or vine in what had been a base area for Massoud and the Northern Alliance, and previously for the supporters of Amir Habibullah. Local officials, mostly former fighters, claimed that hearing my interviews on the BBC had given them hope during the resistance to the Taliban. I celebrated Nawruz with a dinner at the palace with President Hamid Karzai and U.S. Presidential Special Envoy (later Ambassador) Zalmay Khalilzad and dined with the new Interior Minister Yunus Qanooni, now speaker of the lower house of the National Assembly. I gave a lecture at Kabul University on the future of Afghanistan; a group of Islamist students walked out when I dedicated my talk to the late Professor Majrooh.

Malikyar had a few other tasks to accomplish before we could leave for home. In the center of the city, we stopped by the imposing tomb of Amir Abdul Rahman Khan, her great-great-grandfather, who had ruled Afghanistan—conquering even areas that had never submitted to Kabul—from 1880 to 1901. Rudyard Kipling wrote poems about his ruthlessness, and he died of natural causes in his bed. In March 2002 the shrine and the walled garden around his tomb were locked.

Not far away, in a small alleyway of Shahr-i Naw, we found Malikyar's father's house, where she had lived as a child. The family had learned that it had been occupied over the years by communist officials, then mujahidin, and then used as a guest house by the Taliban. No one was home when we arrived, but the neighbors said that the new occupant was a *saranwal*—prosecuting magistrate—from Panjshir.

Toward the end of our trip, we made one last visit, to the Qabristan, or graveyard, at the western edge of Kabul, behind the hill of Bala Hisar, the fifth-century Upper Fort and the seat of power in Kabul since ancient times. On this Friday afternoon, the sabbath, families were picnicking in the graveyard where Malikyar's aunts, daughters of the royal household of Amir Habibullah Khan, were buried. After praying at her aunts' tomb, Malikyar walked to the main shrine in the graveyard, Shuhada-i-Salahin, which, according to tradition, was the tomb of two Arab mujahidin who had been martyred bringing Islam to Afghanistan.

Such shrines to martyrs mark all of Afghanistan; a new shrine sprung up in 2002 below the mountains of Tora Bora in Khugiani district of Nangarhar Province. Here were buried the Arab fighters of al-Qaeda who died in the American bombardments of December 2001. Now women of the tribes visited the shrine to pray for fertility and health, a practice those buried there had condemned as paganism. Malikyar entered the shrine and circled the tomb clockwise, until she noticed that, unlike the practice she remembered from childhood, there was now a separate entrance for women.

Outside the shrine, a one-eyed beggar sat with a pot, surrounded by street children. They wore rags, their faces were dirty, and many had sores or other wounds. They had none of the bravado of the boys in Babur's garden. These were the abandoned orphans of decades of war. In the 1980s Afghans had told me in hushed tones of a Soviet program to form future elites by placing Afghan children in orphanages and sending them, sometimes by force, to be educated in the Soviet Union. At a 1988 meeting, the late Soviet Orientalist Yuri Gankovsky explained that this program was aimed at caring for the abandoned orphans of Kabul. Whatever the truth about the program to take Afghan children into orphanages and then the Soviet Union, a boarding school in Soviet Tajikistan might have been attractive compared to how the children in the Qabristan were living.

As we conspicuously walked past them—a foreign man and an obviously foreign-returned Afghan woman, modestly covered from head to toe in elegant clothes (some whispered that she must be Iranian)—the children began to follow us and ask for money. At first we followed the international protocol for dealing with beggars—ignore—but finally Malikyar could not. These were the children orphaned in the battles that devastated western Kabul, the ones whom the refugees like her had abandoned. She opened her purse and started to take out some money. Suddenly dozens, seemingly hundreds, of ragged, needy children ran toward us, demanding money. As they surrounded us, we ran to the car and managed to push them away enough to close the door. But before we did, one child shouted something. After we pulled away in silence, Malikyar said, "The child cursed us. He said, 'May God dry up your hand! By God, may you never see good.'"

* * *

Several months later, back in New York, when the stress of the previous few months finally took its toll on me and I had to rest for some weeks, Malikyar reminded me of the child's curse. When I heard boasts from Western governments about our good work in Afghanistan, I wondered if it did any more good than Malikyar's attempt to help those children.

The day the Bonn Accord was signed, someone asked me what would happen in Afghanistan. I replied that the only certainty was that we would not see flawless enactment of the scenario it envisioned. On this question, I was right. The Afghan government met the formal benchmarks of the Accord (loya jirga, Constitution, elections), but, along with its international supporters, it failed to stabilize and secure the country.

That is not the whole story, certainly not its end. Ashraf Ghani joined the government and became finance minister, enacting a series of bold reforms that stabilized the currency and started the state-building process. He bruised a lot of feelings in the process, and many were relieved that he did not join the government formed by President Karzai after his election in 2004. Amrullah Saleh set out to reform the Afghan intelligence service and make it into an organization that would make Afghans secure rather than vulnerable. As he joined the new national elite, he spent long hours discussing his country with Ghani, overcoming the years of mistrust and division. Qayum Karzai was elected to the National Assembly from Kandahar in 2005. He resigned for health reasons in early 2008 but has taken on reconciliation with the Taliban as a major task. He led the Afghan delegation that engaged in preliminary dialogue in Mecca during Ramadan in 2008.

Malikyar remarried and had a son. Today [2009] she lives in Prague, working for the Afghan reporting desk of Radio Liberty. On my visit to Kabul in May 2008, I heard that she was there and called her. She told me her son was thrilled to be home, and that she was the only person she knew who actually went to Afghanistan for R&R. It has become hard for her to live outside of Afghanistan—almost as hard as it is to live in it.

Afghans were back at war. That war was also engulfing northwest Pakistan; among its victims was Benazir Bhutto, assassinated by terrorists based in Pakistan's tribal areas on December 27, 2007. Everywhere Afghans had lost faith in the government, the international community, and the United States and feared the future. Pervasive insecurity fueled corruption and opportunism, as people stashed away what they could against an uncertain future. As I had predicted, the future of Afghanistan was not the happy ending promised in the Bonn Agreement. But the future was not the past either. Decades, indeed centuries, of strife had marked the society; but so, just as irreversibly, had seven years of revival.

On that same visit I had another chance to see Babur's garden with my friend Jolyon Leslie, who had worked in Afghanistan for UN agencies since the 1990s. Now he was using his training as an architect to oversee the reconstruction of historical sites in Kabul for the Aga Khan Trust for Culture. Babur's garden is one of their major projects.

Several of the rooms around the courtyard surrounding the reconstructed caravanserai entrance hosted a small exhibition describing the history of

Bagh-i Babur and its place in the tradition of Persian and Central Asian gardens. It ended with a photograph of the ruined garden as the Taliban found it on their entry into Kabul. Leslie described how, not long before our visit, Afghanistan's First Vice-President Ahmad Zia Massoud, brother of Ahmad Shah Massoud, had visited the exhibition and, pausing at the photo of the ruined garden, proclaimed to the nearly empty room, "We must not forget that we did this—we must take responsibility for it."

Small family groups ambled along the stone paths that flank the newly restored marble watercourse, as gardeners planted new rosebushes. A reconstructed marble enclosure now surrounded Babur's grave. As we walked, Leslie recounted how a few days earlier he received a text message warning that a suicide bomber had entered the garden. The gardeners, mostly residents of the surrounding communities, which the Aga Khan Trust had helped to rebuild, searched the entire garden with only their shovels and hoes for weapons, looking for the thankfully nonexistent threat. Leslie mentioned that some of the Afghan colleagues who had supervised the restoration, though proud that the garden is now visited by many international dignitaries, were wary of being filmed with these guests. The Taliban are watching, they explained, and they feared being seen on television with foreigners.

As we strolled up the hill from Babur's tomb to a rebuilt pavilion, we passed a terrace of newly replanted plane trees. Leslie said his Afghan colleagues had saved the trees from Presidential Palace security guards who wanted to cut them down to allow a helicopter to land with "important guests." So far they were still growing in a garden above the Kabul River.

WORKS CITED

Abizaid, General John. "Update on the Global War on Terrorism in the U.S. Central Command Area of Responsibility." Testimony before the U.S. House of Representatives Armed Services Committee (March 3, 2004), http://www.globalsecurity.org/military/library/congress/2004 hr/040304abizaid.pdf.

Abolfathi, Farid. "A Reassessment of the Afghan Conflict, 1978–1988." Prepared under contract for the U.S. government, Fairfax, VA, March 1989.

Afghan Independent Human Rights Commission (AIHRC). "A Call for Justice: A National Consultation on Past Human Rights Violations in Afghanistan." Kabul, January 28, 2005, http://www.aihrc.org.af/rep_29_eng/rep29_1_05call4justice.pdf.

AIHRC. "Monitoring Human Rights." http://www.aihrc.org.af/mon.inv.htm. AIHRC. *Annual Report 2003–04.*

Afghan Peace Accord (Islamabad Accord), http://www.incore.ulst.ac.uk/services/cds/agreements/ pdf/afgan1.pdf.

"Afghanistan's Regional Economic Cooperation: Central Asia, Iran and Pakistan." Report of a conference in Bishkek, May 10–12, 2004, Kabul: UNDP, 2004, http://www.undp.org.af/Does/ Bishkek report.pdf.

Aizenman, N. C. "Afghan Crime Wave Breeds Nostalgia for Taliban." *Washington Post*, March 18, 2005.

Anderson, Benedict. *Imagined Communities: Reflections on the Origin and Spread of Nationalism.* London: Verso, 2006.

Anderson, John Lee. "The Man in the Palace." *New Yorker*, June 6, 2005.

Anderson, Jon W. "There Are No Khans Anymore: Economic Development and Social Change in Tribal Afghanistan." *Middle East Journal* 3 (1978): 167–83.

Ansari, Hamied N. "The Islamic Militants in Egyptian Politics." *International Journal of Middle East Studies* 16 (1984): 140.

Anthony, Ian, Agnes Courades Ailebeck, Gerd Hagmeyer-Gaverns, Paolo Miggiano, and Herbert Wulf. "The Trade in Major Conventional Weapons." In *SIPRI Yearbook 1991: World Armaments and Disarmament.* Oxford: Oxford University Press, 1991, 199–208.

"Arab Veterans of Afghanistan Lead New Islamic Holy War." Federal News Service. October 28, 1994.

AREU. "Subnational Administration Update, Initial Findings and Conclusions from the Provincial Visits." (Kabul, 2003).

Asian Development Bank. "Afghanistan: Comprehensive Needs Assessment in Education." Final draft report, July 2002.

Aubron, Arnaud. "L'éradication précipitée du pavot peut avoir un coût humain catastrophique." Interview with Pierre Arnaud Chouvy, *Libération*, March 12, 2005.

Barnard, Anne, and Farah Stockman. "US Weighs Role in Heroin War in Afghanistan." *Boston Globe*, October 20, 2004.

Barnett, Michael. "The New United Nations Politics of Peace: From Juridical Sovereignty to Empirical Sovereignty." *Global Governance* vol. 1 no. 1 (Winter 1995): 79–97.

Basic Education Coalition. "Education in Emergencies: Afghanistan and Other Hot Spots." March 2004, http://www.basiced.org/facts/afghanistan.pdf.

BBC News. "Bush Praises Pakistan Terror Role." March 4, 2006.

Bhatia, Michael, Kevin Lanigan, and Philip Wilkinson. *Minimum Investments, Minimum Results: The Failure of Security Policy in Afghanistan.* Kabul: AREU, 2004.

Blank, Stephen. "The Arming of Central Asia." *Asia Times Online*, August 23, 2002, http://www.atimes.com/atimes/South_Asia/DH24Df02.html.

Boyce, James. "Introduction." In James K. Boyce and Madalene O'Donnell, eds., *Peace and the Public Purse: Economic Policies for Postwar Statebuilding.* Boulder, CO: Lynne Rienner, 2007.

Buddenberg, Doris, and William Byrd, eds., *Afghanistan's Drug Industry: Structure, Functioning, Dynamics, and Implications for Counter-Narcotics Policy.* UNODC and World Bank, 2006.

Bush, President George W. "Remarks on War Effort." Address delivered to the George C. Marshall ROTC Award Seminar on National Security at Cameron Hall, Virginia Military Institute. Lexington, VA, April 17, 2002, http://www.whitehouse.gov/news/releases/2002/04/20020417-1.html.

Byrd, William, and Christopher Ward. "Drugs and Development in Afghanistan." *Social Development Papers, Conflict Prevention and Reconstruction* paper no. 18. World Bank: December 2004, http://Inweb18.worldbank.org/ESSD/sdvest.nsf/67ByDocName/DrugsandDevelopmentinAfghanistan/SFILE/WPi8_web.pdf.

Byrne, Karen. "Aid Agencies Take on the Taliban." UPI (Islamabad), October 13, 1996.

Call, Charles T. "Conclusion." In *Constructing Justice and Security After War.* Washington, DC: United States Institute of Peace Press, 2007, 25–27.

Cardozo, Barbara Lopes, et al. "Mental Health, Social Functioning, and Disability in Post-war Afghanistan." *Journal of the American Medical Association* (2004): 292:575–84.

CARE and Center on International Cooperation. "Too Early to Declare Success: Counter-Narcotics in Afghanistan." Afghanistan policy brief, March 2005.

Castells, M. *End of Millennium, The Information Age: Economy, Society, and Culture*, vol. 3. Oxford: Blackwell, 1998.

Center on International Cooperation, http://www.cic.nyu.edu/conflict/conflictproject4.html//Aid and CARE, http://www.careusa.org/newsroom/specialreport/afghanistan/a policy positions.asp.

Chesterman, Simon, Michael Ignatieff, and Ramesh Thakur. *Making States Work: From State Failure to State-Building.* International Peace Academy/United Nations University, July 2004.

Chipaux, Françoise (cédille). "Des mines d'émeraude pour financer la résistance du commandant Massoud." *Le Monde* (Paris), July 17, 1999.

CIA. *The World Fact Book: Afghanistan.* July 2004 est., www.cia.goWcia/publications/factbook/gcos/af.html.

Cicero, M. Tullius. "The Fifth Philippic of M. Tullius Cicero Against M. Antonius." In *Cicero Philippics*, trans. Walter C. A. Kerr. Cambridge, MA: Harvard University Press, 1951, V. ii.5

Cohen, Stephen P. *The Pakistan Army.* Berkeley: University of California Press, 1984.

Colburn, Marta. "Water Conservation and Scarcity in Afghanistan." In *The Many Faces of Afghanistan Curriculum Guide.* Mercy Corps International, http://www.mercycorps.org/pdfs/1081988010.pdf.

Coll, Steve. "The Stand-off." *New Yorker*, February 13, 2006.

Collier, Paul. "Doing Well out of War." Washington, DC: World Bank (1999), http://siteresources.worldbank.org/INTKNOWLEDGEFORCHANGE/Resources/491519-1199818447826/28137.pdf.

Collier, Paul., with V. L. Elliott, Havard Hegre, Anke Hoeffler, Marta Reynal-Querol, and Nicholas Sambanis. *Breaking the Conflict Trap: Civil War and Development Policy*. New York: Oxford University Press, 2003.

Collier, Paul, and Anke Hoeffler. "Justice-seeking and Loot-seeking in Civil Wars." Washington, DC: World Bank (1999), http://www-wds.worldbank.org/external/default/WDSContentServer/WDSP/IB/2004/03/18/000265513_20040318171154/Rendered/PDF/28151.pdf.

Collier, Paul, Anke Hoeffler, and Måns Söderbom. "On the Duration of Civil War." Washington, DC: World Bank (1999), later published under the same title in *Journal of Peace Research* May 2004, 41:3, 253–73.

Communiqué of Meeting Between Foreign Minister Boris Pankin and Secretary of State James Baker. Moscow, September 13, 1991.

Cooney, Daniel. "Karzai Wants End to U.S.-Led Operations." Associated Press Online, September 20, 2005.

Cordovez, Diego, and Selig Harrison. *Out of Afghanistan: The Inside Story of the Soviet Withdrawal*. New York and Oxford: Oxford University Press, 1995.

Crocker, Chester A. "Peacemaking and Mediation: Dynamics of a Changing Field." *Coping with Crisis: Working Paper Series*. International Peace Academy, March 2007.

Cronin, Richard. *Afghanistan After the Soviet Withdrawal: Contenders for Power*. Washington, DC: Congressional Research Service, May 1989.

Deen, Thalif. "UN-Afghanistan: UN Warns Taliban over Treatment of Women." InterPress Service (New York), October 9, 1996.

"Development Backlog in FATA." *Dawn*, November 22, 2005.

Dobbins, James, Keith Crane, Seth G. Jones, Andrew Rathmell, Brett Steele, and Richard Teltschik, "The UN's Role in Nation-Building: From the Congo to Iraq," RAND, 2005.

Hussain, Zahid. "Musharraf's Other War." *Newsline Magazine* (Karachi), January 2006.

Hussain, Zahid. "Terror in Miran Shah." *Newsline Magazine* (Karachi), April 2006.

International Center for Agricultural Research in Dry Areas (ICARDA). "Seed and Crop Improvement Situation in Afghanistan," http://www.icarda.org/Afghnistan/NA/Full/Physical_F.htm.

International Monetary Fund (IMF). "IMF Executive Board Concludes 2004 Article IV Consultation with the Islamic State of Afghanistan." January 27, 2005, http://www.imf.org/external/np/sec/pn/2005/pn0509.htm.

International Monetary Fund (IMF). "Islamic State of Afghanistan, Third Review Under the Staff Monitored Program—Concluding Statement." February 3, 2005, http://www.imf.org/external/np/ms/2005/020305.htm.

International Monetary Fund (IMF). "Islamic State of Afghanistan: First Review Under the Staff-Monitored Program."

International Peace Academy/Center on International Cooperation. "Post-Conflict Transitions: National Experience and International Reform." Meeting Summary, Century Association, New York, March 28, 2005.

IRI and Williams & Associates. "Afghans Most Concerned About Security." March–April 2004. National poll.

IRIN Afghanistan. "New School Year Opens on Optimistic Note." March 22, 2004.

IRIN. "Pakistan: Afghan Refugee Returns Top 100,000 in 2004." May 10, 2004.

IRIN. "Bittersweet Harvest: Afghanistan's New War." IRIN web special on the threat of opium to Afghanistan and the region. July 2004, http:www.plusnews.org/webspecials/opium/regOvr.asp.

IRIN. "Afghanistan: Struggle to Raise HIV Awareness as First Official AIDS-related Deaths Reported." December 1, 2004.

IRIN. "Afghanistan: IDPs Willing to Settle in South." December 27, 2004, www.irinnews.org.

Islamic Government of Afghanistan. "Terms of Reference for the Combined Force Command and ISAF PRTs in Afghanistan." January 27, 2005.

Islamic State of Afghanistan—Second Quarterly Review Under the Staff-Monitored Program and the 2004 Article IV Consultation Concluding Statement. November 3, 2004, http://www.imf.org/external/np/ms/2004/110304.htm.

Ivanov, Sergei, Russian minister of defense. Remarks in New Delhi, December 1, 2004, Radio Free Afghanistan, http://www.azadiradio.org/en/weeklyreport/2004/12/08.asp.

Jackson, Robert, and Carl G. Rosberg. "Why Africa's Weak States Persist: The Empirical and the Juridical in Statehood." World Politics 35(1), (1982): 1–24.

Jacoby, Lowell E., vice admiral U.S. Navy, director, Defense Intelligence Agency. "Current and Projected National Security Threats to the United States." Statement for the Record, Senate Select Committee on Intelligence, February 24, 2004.

Jalali, Ali A. "The Future of Afghanistan." *Parameters* (Spring 2006), 6.

Jean, F., and J. Rufin. *Économie des guerres civiles.* Paris: Hachette, 1996.

Johnston, Tim. "Despite Taliban, Women Are Back Working." Reuters (Kabul), October 30, 1996.

Johnston, Tim. "Red Cross Hands out Food to Disabled Afghan Veterans." Reuters (Kabul), November 13, 1996.

Jones, Seth G. "Averting Failure in Afghanistan." *Survival* vol. 48 no. 1 (Spring 2006).

"Kabul's War-Battered Airport Beats the Millennium Bug." Agence France-Press, June 29, 1999.

"Kabul's Money Market Burgled." Agence France-Press, January 13, 2000.

Kaldor, M. *New and Old Wars: Organized Violence in a Global Era.* Cambridge: Polity Press, 1999.

Karzai, Hamid. "Address to the Closing Session of the Constitutional Loya Jirga." January 4, 2004, http://www.kabul-reconstructions.net/images/KarzaiCLJClosingAddress.pdf.

Keen, D. *The Economic Functions of Violence in Civil Wars*, Adelphi Paper 320. London: Oxford University Press, 1998.

Kelly, John. Assistant Secretary's Testimony Before the Sub-Committees on Europe and the Middle East and Asia and the Pacific, Committee on Foreign Affairs, House of Representatives. March 7, 1990.

Kepel, Gilles. *Le Prophète et le Pharaon: Aux Sources des Mouvements Islamistes*, 2nd ed. Paris: Editions du Seuil, 1993.

Khan, Fulzar Ahmed. "Bajaur Raid Killed Five Foreigners: Musharraf." *Dawn*, February 12, 2006.

Khan, Riaz Mohammad. *Untying the Afghan Knot: Negotiating Soviet Withdrawal.* Durham, NC: Duke University Press, 1991.

Khashoggi, Jamal. "Arab Youths Fight Shoulder to Shoulder with Mujahedeen." *Arab News*, May 4, 1988, 9.

Khashoggi, Jamal. "Arab Mujahedeen in Afghanistan-II: Masada Exemplifies the Unity of Islamic Ummah." *Arab News*, May 14, 1988, 9.

Kothari, Miloon. "Adequate Housing as a Component of the Right to an Adequate Standard of Living." Report by the Special Rapporteur, E/CN.4/2004/48/Add.2, UN Commission on Human Rights, March 4, 2004.

Laber, Jeri, and Barnett R. Rubin. *"A Nation Is Dying": Afghanistan Under the Soviets, 1979–1987.* Evanston, IL: Northwestern University Press, 1988.

Leslie, Jolyon, and Chris Johnson. *Afghanistan: The Mirage of Peace.* London: Zed Books, 2004.

Lister, Sarah. "Caught in Confusion: Local Government Structures in Afghanistan." Kabul: AREU, 2005, http://www.areu.org.af/publications/Local%20Governance%20Briefing%20Paper.pdf.

Majrooh, S. "End of a Sojourn in the Abode of Refugees: Gul andam [body like a flower], or, The Story of Laughing Lovers." Translated by Ashraf Ghani. In *Izhda-yi Khudi (The Ego Monster)*, book 1, vol. 5. Peshawar: Unpublished manuscript, 1984.

Maley, W. *Fundamentalism Reborn? Afghanistan and the Taliban.* New York: St. Martins, 1998.

Mansfield, Edward D., and Jack Snyder. "Democratic Transitions and War: From Napoleon to the Millennium's End." In *Turbulent Peace: The Challenges of Managing International Conflict*, ed. Chester A. Crocker, Fen Osler Hampson, and Pamela R. Aall. Washington, DC: United States Institute of Peace Press, 2001, 113–26.

Maram-i Hizb-i Islami-yi Afghanistan [Program of the Islamic Party of Afghanistan]. Peshawar? n.p., 1986–1987, vi.

Médecins Sans Frontières. "After 24 Years of Independent Aid to the Afghan People MSF With-draws from Afghanistan Following Killing, Threats and Insecurity." Transcript of press con-ference, Kabul, July 28, 2004.

Naqvi, Z. F. *Afghanistan-Pakistan Trade Relations.* Islamabad: World Bank, 1999.

Nazif, Shahrani M. "Afghanistan's Presidential Elections: Spreading Democracy or a Sham?" *MERIP Reports,* October 7, 2004.

Nunn, S., N. Lubin, and Barnett R. Rubin. *Calming the Ferghana Valley: Development and Dialogue in the Heart of Central Asia, Preventive Action Reports,* vol 4. New York: Council on Foreign Relations, 1999.

"The Other Taliban." *Economist,* March 16, 2006.

Ottaway, Marina, and Anatol Lieven. "Rebuilding Afghanistan: Fantasy Versus Reality." *Carnegie Endowment for International Peace: Policy Brief* 12 (2002): 1–7.

Our Global Neighborhood: The Report of the Commission on Global Governance. Oxford: Oxford University Press, 1995.

"Pakistan Opposition Barred from U.S. Air-Strike Village." Reuters, January 23, 2006.

Paris, Roland. *At War's End: Building Peace After Civil Conflict.* Cambridge: Cambridge University Press, 2004.

Patterson, M. *The Shiwa Pastures 1978-2003: Land Tenure Changes and Conflict in Northeastern Afghanistan.* Kabul: AREU, 2004.

Pincus, Walter. "Growing Threat Seen in Afghan Insurgency: Defense Intelligence Agency Chief Cites Surging Violence in Homeland." *Washington Post,* March 1, 2006.

Piquard, Patrice. "Pourquoi le Chaos Afghan Peut Faire Exploser L'Asie Centrale." *l'Evènement du Jeudi,* January 13, 1993, 7.

"Policies of the Pakistan Military with Respect to Afghanistan: Human Rights Concerns." News from Asia Watch. February 27, 1989.

Putnam, Robert D. *The Comparative Study of Political Elites.* Englewood Cliffs, N.J.: Prentice-Hall, 1976.

Qureshi, Ahmad, and Ihsan Sarwaryar. "Suicide Attack at Herat PRT Kills Two, Injures Nine." Pajhwok Afghan News, April 8, 2006, http://www.pajhwok.com/en/2006/04/08/suicide-attack-herat-prt-kills-two-injures-nine.

Rashid, Ahmed. "Pakistan and the Taliban." In *Fundamentalism Reborn? Afghanistan and the Tali-ban,* edited by W. Maley, 72–89. New York: St. Martins, 1998.

Rashid, Ahmed. "Afghanistan Develops New Trade Routes Beyond Pakistan." *Nation* (Pakistan), January 23, 2003.

Rashid, Ahmed. "He's Welcome in Pakistan." *Washington Post,* February 26, 2006.

Rastegar, Farshad. "Education and Revolutionary Political Mobilization: Schooling Versus Up-rootedness as Determinants of Islamic Political Activities Among Afghan Refugee Students in Pakistan." Ph.D. diss., University of California, Los Angeles, 1991.

ReliefWeb. "Special Rapporteur on Adequate Housing Expresses Concern over Forced Evictions in Kabul." September 10, 2003, http://www.reliefweb.in/rw/rwb.nsf/db900SID/SKAR-647G9Y?OpenDocument.

Reno, W. *Warlord Politics and African States.* Boulder, CO: Lynne Rienner, 1998.

Report of the Panel on United Nations Peace Operations (the Brahimi Report). United Nations (A/55/305 S/2000/809), 2000.

Reuters. "Students Take Afghan City, Free Pakistani Caravan." November 5, 1994.

Reuters. "UN Says New Afghan Ceasefire Plan Drawn Up." (Peshawar, Pakistan), November 13, 1996.

Reuters. "UN Says Afghan Meeting Sent 'Resounding Message.'" (New York), November 19, 1996.

Reuters. "Afghan Taliban Asks Members Not to Be Harsh." (Kabul), December 3, 1996.

Ritter, Don, and Saad Mohseni. "Privatizing Afghanistan." *Washington Times,* March 17, 2005.

Roy, Olivier. *Islam and Resistance in Afghanistan.* Cambridge: Cambridge University Press, 1986. Originally published in French as *L'Afghanistan: Islam et modernité politique.* Paris: Editions du Seuil, 1985.

Roy, Olivier. *L'Echec de L'Islam Politique.* Paris: Editions du Seuil, 1992.

Roy, Olivier. *The Civil War in Tajikistan: Causes and Implications: A Report of the Study Group on the Prospects for Conflict and Opportunities for Peacemaking in the Southern Tier of Former Soviet Republics*. Washington, DC: United States Institute of Peace, December 1993.

Rubin, Barnett R. "Afghanistan: The Next Round." *Orbis* 33 (Winter 1989): 57–72.

Rubin, Barnett R. "Political Elites in Afghanistan: Rentier State Building, Rentier State Wrecking." *International Journal of Middle East Studies* 24 (1992): 77–99.

Rubin, Barnett R. "Post-Cold-War State Disintegration: The Failure of International Conflict Resolution in Afghanistan." *Journal of International Affairs* 46 (Winter 1993): 469–92.

Rubin, Barnett R. "The Fragmentation of Tajikistan," *Survival* 35 (Winter 1993/94): 71–91.

Rubin, Barnett R. *The Fragmentation of Afghanistan: State Formation and Collapse in the International System*. New Haven, CT: Yale University Press, 1995.

Rubin, Barnett R. *The Search for Peace in Afghanistan: From Buffer State to Failed State*. New Haven, CT: Yale University Press, 1995.

Rubin, Barnett R. "Afghanistan: The Forgotten Crisis." *Refugee Survey Quarterly* 15 (1996): 1–35, http://www.unhcr.org/refworld/country,,WRITENET,,AFG,,3ae6a6c0c,0.html.

Rubin, Barnett R. "Afghanistan: The Last Cold-War Conflict, the First Post-Cold-War Conflict." In *War, Hunger and Displacement: The Origins of Humanitarian Emergencies*, eds. E. Wayne Nafziger, Frances Stewart, and Raimo Väyrynen. Oxford: Oxford University Press, Vol. II, 2000, pp. 23–52.

Rubin, Barnett R. "The Political Economy of War and Peace in Afghanistan." *World Development* 28 (2000), no. 10, pp. 1789–1803.

Rubin, Barnett R. *Blood on the Doorstep: The Politics of Preventive Action*. New York: Century Foundation Press and Council on Foreign Relations, 2002.

Rubin, Barnett R. "Road to Ruin: Afghanistan's Opium Economy." Center for American Progress and Center on International Cooperation, NYU, 2004, http://www.cic.nyu.edu/pdf/RoadtoRuin.pdf.

Rubin, Barnett R. "Constructing Sovereignty for Security." *Survival* vol. 47 no. 4 (Winter 2005), 93–106.

Rubin, Barnett R. "The Wrong Voting System." *International Herald Tribune*, March 16, 2005.

Rubin, Barnett R. "Afghan Dilemmas: Defining Commitments." (Response to Thomas Lynch, "Afghan Dilemmas: Staying Power.") *American Interest* 3:5 (May–June 2008).

Rubin, Barnett R. "The Transformation of the Afghan State." In Alex Thier, ed., *The Future of Afghanistan*. Washington, DC: United States Institute of Peace, January 2009.

Rubin, Barnett R., and Andrea Armstrong. "Regional Issues in the Reconstruction of Afghanistan." World Policy Journal vol. 20 no. 1 (Spring 2003): 37–48.

Rubin, Barnett R., Ashraf Ghani, William Maley, Ahmed Rashid, and Olivier Roy. "Afghanistan: Reconstruction and Peacebuilding in a Regional Framework." *KOFF Peacebuilding Reports* 1/2001. Berne: Swiss Peace Foundation, 2001.

Rubin, Barnett R., with Vanessa T. Wyeth. "The Politics of Security in Postconflict State Building." In Charles T. Call, ed., *Building States to Build Peace*. Boulder, CO: Lynne Rienner, 2008.

Rubin, Barnett R., and Omar Zakhilwal, "War on Drugs or War on Farmers?" *Wall Street Journal*, January 11, 2005.

Saba, Daud. "Environment and Human Development in Afghanistan." Background paper for UNDP, *Afghanistan National Human Development Report 2004: Security with a Human Face*, February 2004.

Saba, Daud, M. E. Najaf, A. M. Musazai, and S. A. Taraki, "Geothermal Energy in Afghanistan: Prospects and Potential," http://www.cic.nyu.edu/pdf/Geothermal.pdf.

Salamé, Ghassan. *Appels d'empire: ingérences et résistances a l'âge de la mondialisation*. Paris: Fayard, 1996.

Schmitt, Eric, and David S. Cloud. "United States May Start Pulling out of Afghanistan Next Spring." *New York Times*, September 14, 2005.

Securing Afghanistan's Future: Accomplishments Aid the Strategic Path Forward. A report prepared by the government of Afghanistan in collaboration with the ADB, IMF, United Nations Development Program, and the World Bank, March 2004.

"Senior al-Qaida Operative Struck by Predator Missile." ABC News, May 13, 2005.

Shahzad, Raza. "Civil, Military Man to Be Political Agents." *Daily Times* (Lahore), May 10, 2006.

"Sheikh Abdullah Azzam Is Martyred." *Mujahideen Monthly* 4 (January 1990): 10–11.

Siddique, Abubakar, and Iqbal Khattak. "War on Terror Highlights Development Needs in FATA." *Friday Times* (Lahore), January 23, 2004.

Skocpol, Theda. *States and Social Revolutions: A Comparative Analysis of France, Russia and China.* Cambridge: Cambridge University Press, 1979.

Starr, S. Frederick. "A Partnership for Central Asia." *Foreign Affairs* (July/August 2005).

Stedman, Stephen John. "Spoiler Problems in Peace Processes." *International Security* 22, no. 2 (Autumn 1997): 5–53.

Stockman, Farah. "Afghan Women Pay the Price for War on Drugs." *Boston Globe*, September 29, 2005.

Swedish Committee for Afghanistan (SCA). *The Agricultural Survey of Afghanistan: First Report.* Peshawar: Swedish Committee for Afghanistan, 1988.

Synovitz, Ron. "Afghanistan: Are Militants Copying Iraqi Insurgents' Suicide Tactics?" Radio Free Europe/Radio Liberty, January 17, 2006, http://www.rferl.org/content/article/1064791.html.

Talk of the Town. *New Yorker.* January 10, 1994. Interview by Marianne Weaver.

Tarzi, Amin. "Afghan Demonstrations Test Warlords-Turned-Administrators." Radio Free Afghanistan, March 9, 2005.

Tawana, Sayyed Musa. "Glimpses into the Historical Background of the Islamic Movement in Afghanistan: Memoirs of Dr. Tawana, Part 1." *AFGHANews* 5, April 1, 1989, 6–7.

Tawana, Sayyed Musa. "Glimpses into the Historical Background of the Islamic Movement in Afghanistan: Memoirs of Dr. Tawana, Part 4." *AFGHANews* 5 (May 15, 1989): 5ff.

Tilly, Charles. *Coercion, Capital, and European States: AD 990–1992* (Studies in Social Discontinuity). Cambridge: Blackwell, 1992.

Tomsen, Peter. "Untying the Afghan Knot." *Fletcher Forum on World Affairs* 25 (Winter 2001): 17.

Torabi, B. "Entretien avec Mollah Mohammad Omar." *Politique internationale* 74 (1996–1997): 135–143.

Transitional Islamic Government of Afghanistan Ministry of Health. "A Basic Package of Health Services for Afghanistan." March 2003.

Travers, James. "Smart Move to Sidestep Afghanistan Prison Controversy." *Hamilton Spectator* (Ontario, Canada), March 4, 2006.

Trives, Sebastien. "Afghanistan: Tackling the Insurgency, the Case of the Southeast." *Politique étrangère*, January 2006.

Under-Secretary-General for Political Affairs, United Nations. Press briefing. New York, September 26, 1996.

United Nations. "Supplement to An Agenda For Peace: Position Paper of the Secretary-General on the Occasion of the Fiftieth Anniversary of the United Nations." (1995), A/50/60.

United Nations. *Report of the Independent Inquiry into the Actions of the United Nations During the 1994 Genocide in Rwanda.* UN Doc. S/1999/1257 (1999).

United Nations. *Report of the Secretary-General Pursuant to General Assembly Resolution 53/35: The Fall of Srebrenica.* UN Doc. A/54/549 (1999).

United Nations. *Statement by the Secretary-General on Report of the Independent Inquiry into the Actions of the United Nations During the 1994 Genocide in Rwanda.* UN Doc. SG/SM/7263 (1999).

United Nations. "A More Secure World: Our Shared Responsibility." In *Report of the Secretary-General's High-level Panel on Threats, Challenges and Change* (2004), A/59/565.

United Nations. "In Larger Freedom: Towards Development, Security and Human Rights for All." *Report of the Secretary-General on the Implementation of the Recommendations of the High-level Panel* (2005), A/59.

United Nations. "Security Council Extends UN Mission in Afghanistan for Additional 12 Months, Unanimously Adopting Resolution 1589" (2005). UN Press Release SC/8341 (March 24, 2005), http://www.un.org/News/Press/docs/2005/sc8341.doc.htm.

United Nations Assistance for Afganistan: Weekly Update no. 187, October 8, 1996, and no. 193, November 20, 1996.

United Nations Assistance Mission in Afghanistan (UNAMA) and Afghan Independent Human Rights Commission (AIHRC). "Joint Verification of Political Rights." Third report, 24 August–30 September 2004, http://www.aihrc.org.af/jvoprtr.htm.

United Nations Department of Public Affairs. "Secretary-General Restates United Nations Policy on Gender Equality in Response to Concerns About Status of Women in Afghanistan." New York, October 8, 1996.

UNDP. *Afghanistan: National Human Development Report 2004*, http://hdr.undp.org/docs/reports/national/AFG-Afghanistan/afghanistan-2004-en.pdf.

United Nations General Assembly. "Emergency International Assistance for Peace, Normalcy and Reconstruction of War-Stricken Afghanistan." A/RES/48/208, December 21, 1993.

United Nations General Assembly. *Report of the Independent Expert of the Commission on Human Rights on the Situation of Human Rights in Afghanistan*. A/59/370, September 21, 2004, http://daccessdds.un.org/doc/UNDOC/GEN/N04/518/00/PDF/N0451800.pdf.

UNICEF. "Afghanistan Is Among Worst Places on Globe for Women's Health, Say UNICEF and CDC." Joint press release, November 6, 2002, http://www.uniccf.org/newsline/02pr59afghanmm.htm.

UNICEF and UNDP. Human Development Index. http://hdr.undp.org/statistics/data.

United Nations Integrated Regional Information Networks. "Central Asia: HIV/AIDS Growing Rapidly." October 2, 2002.

United Nations International Drug Control Program (UNDCP), Afghanistan Program. *Annual Opium Poppy Survey 1998*. Islamabad, 1998.

UNDCP, Afghanistan Program. *Strategic Study #1: Analysis of the Process of Expansion of Opium Poppy Cultivation to New Districts in Aghanistan, Preliminary Report*. Islamabad, 1998.

UNDCP, Afghanistan Program. *Strategic Study #2: The Dynamics of the Farmgate Opium Trade and the Coping Strategies of Opium Traders, Final Report*. Islamabad, 1998.

UNDCP, Afghanistan Program. *Annual Opium Poppy Survey 1999*. Islamabad: UNDCP, 1999.

UNDCP, Afghanistan Program. *Strategic Study #3: The Role of Opium as a Source of Informal Credit, Preliminary Report*. Islamabad: UNDCP, 1999.

UNDCP Afghanistan Program. *Strategic Study #4: Access to Labour: The Role of Opium in the Livelihood Strategies of Itinerant Harvesters Working in Helmand Province, Afghanistan, Final Report*. Islamabad: UNDCP, 1999.

UNDCP, Afghanistan Program. *Strategic Study #5: An Analysis of the Process of Expansion of Opium Poppy to New Districts in Afghanistan, Second Report*. Islamabad: UNDCP, 1999.

United Nations Office for Drug Control and Crime Prevention. *Global Illicit Drug Trends*. New York: United Nations, 2002.

United Nations Office on Drugs and Crime. *Afghanistan: Opium Rapid Assessment Survey*. Vienna, March 2005a.

United Nations Office on Drugs and Crime. *Afghanistan: Opium Survey 2005*. Government of Afghanistan Counter Narcotics Directorate, 9, http://www.unodc.org/pdf/afg/afg_survey_2005_exsum.pdf, 2005b.

United Nations Office of the Coordinator of Humanitarian Affairs for Afghanistan (UNOCHA). *Afghanistan Consolidated Appeal for Assistance 1997*. Islamabad: UNDCP, 1996.

United Nations Security Council. "Security Council Welcomes Acceptance by Afghan Parties of Phased National Reconciliation Process." S/PRST/77, November 30, 1994.

United Nations Security Council. "The Situation in Afghanistan and Its Implications for Peace and Security: Report of the Secretary-General." S/2005/183, March 18, 2005.

United Nations Security Council Resolution 1386, December 20, 2001.

UPI. "UNHCR Suspends Programs in Kabul." (Islamabad), November 20, 1996.

U.S. Department of Energy. "Afghanistan Fact Sheet." June 2004, http://www.eia.doe.gov/emeu/cabs/afghan.html.

U.S. Department of State. USAID. "Afghanistan Health Program." Presentation (2004), http://www.maqweb.org/miniu/present/2004/afganistan.

Verstegen, Suzanne, Luc van de Goor, and Jeroen de Zeeuw. *The Stability Assessment Framework: Designing Integrated Responses for Security, Governance and Development*. The Hague: Clingendael Institute, 2005.

Walter, Barbara F., and Jack Snyder, eds. *Civil Wars, Insecurity, and Intervention*. New York: Columbia University Press, 1999.

Wantchekon, Leonard. "The Paradox of 'Warlord' Democracy: A Theoretical Investigation." *American Political Science Review* vol. 98 no. 1 (2004), 17–33.

"Wanted Al-Qaida Militant Killed." *Dawn*, April 21, 2006.

Wardak, Ali. "Jirga, Human Rights and Building Post-War Justice System in Afghanistan." http://bgalatzer.de/arp/wardak.pdf.

Weinbaum, Marvin G. "Legal Elites in Afghan Society." *International Journal of Middle East Studies* 12 (1980): 39–57.

White House. "Joint Declaration of the United States-Afghanistan Strategic Partnership." May 23, 2005, http://www.state.gov/p/sa/rls/pr/2005/46628.htm. Press Release.

White House, Office of Management and Budget. "Request to Congress for Fiscal Year 2005 Supplemental Appropriations." February 14, 2005, http://www.whitehouse.gov/omb/budget/amendments/supplemental_2_14_05.pdf.

Wily, L. Alden. *Land Relations in Bamyan: Findings from a 15 Village Case Study*. Kabul: AREU, 2004.

Wily, L. Alden. *Land Relations in Faryab Province: Findings from a Field Study in 11 Villages*. Kabul: AREU, 2004.

Woodward, Bob, and Charles R. Babcock. "U.S. Covert Aid to Afghans on the Rise: Rep. Wilson Spurs Drive for New Funds, Anti-aircraft Cannon for the Insurgents." *Washington Post*, January 13, 1985.

World Bank. "Afghanistan Border States Development Framework." Discussion draft, November 12, 2001.

World Bank. *Afghanistan: Managing Public Finances for Development, Main Report*, vol. 1. Washington, DC: World Bank, November 27, 2005, 24.

World Bank. *Afghanistan: State Building, Sustaining Growth and Reducing Poverty*. September 2004, http://sisteresources.worldbank.org/INTAFGHANISTAN/News%20and%20Events/20261395/AfghanistanEconomicReportfinalversion909.pdf.

World Bank, Asian Development Bank, United Nations Development Program. *Afghanistan: Preliminary Needs Assessment for Recovery and Reconstruction*. January 2002.

Yousaf, Mohammad, and Mark Adkin. *The Bear Trap: Afghanistan's Untold Story*. London: Mark Cooper, 1992.

Zakaria, Fareed. *The Future of Freedom: Illiberal Democracy at Home and Abroad*. New York: Norton, 2003.

INDEX

Inside the Ministry of the Interior, September 7, 2003. I took this picture on the way to a memorial service for the UN staff killed in the bombing of UN headquarters in Baghdad on August 19, 2003. It shows one of the many photos of Ahmad Shah Massoud in Kabul and especially the offices of the security services. Massoud, the military commander of the United Front (Northern Alliance), was killed by al-Qaeda suicide bombers on September 9, 2001.

The executive committee of the constitutional commission takes a break for lunch on October 7, 2003. Center three, from left to right: Commission Chairman and third Vice-President Nematullah Shahrani, now minister of Hajj and Islamic foundations; Musa Marufi, later ambassador to Italy; and Abdul Salam Azimi, deputy chairman, now chief justice of the Supreme Court. At left, foreground, Musa Ahmadi, professor at private university in Kabul; and Kawun Kakar, political officer, UN Assistance Mission in Afghanistan, now CEO, Alokozay Group.

Abdul Rashid Dostum greets his followers on the campus of the Kabul Polytechnic as he arrives for the Constitutional Loya Jirga, December 13, 2001.

Author (right) with UN Special Representative for Afghanistan Lakhdar Brahimi (center) and Pakistani journalist Ahmed Rashid at the Constitutional Loya Jirga, December 14, 2003. Photo by Ambassador Enrico de Maio. I worked closely with Brahimi from the preparation for the Bonn Talks to the end of his tenure as Special Representative to the Secretary-General in January 2004.

At the Constitutional Loya Jirga on December 14, 2003, CLJ chairman Hazrat Sibghatullah Mojaddedi (right) confers with Marshall Muhammad Qasim Fahim, minister of defense, now first vice-president (left); and Abdul Rabb al-Rasul Sayyaf, now chairman of the foreign affairs commission of the Wolesi Jirga (lower house of parliament).

Just before the opening session of the Constitutional Loya Jirga on December 14, 2003, Minister of the Interior Ali Ahmad Jalali (center) jokes with former President Burhanuddin Rabbani (right) and Ayatollah Asif Mohseni. Jalali declared his candidacy for president of Afghanistan in the scheduled 2014 elections on April 9, 2012. Rabbani, whom President Karzai appointed as head of the High Peace Council, was assassinated by a suicide bomber on September 20, 2011. Mohseni is a prominent Shia political and religious leader.

December 18, 2003, at the Constitutional Loya Jirga: Ahmad Wali Massoud (left), brother of the late Ahmad Shah Massoud (assassinated September 9, 2001) and Salahuddin Rabbani, son of Burhanuddin Rabbani (assassinated September 20, 2011). Rabbani, who was appointed ambassador to Turkey, succeeded his father as chairman of the High Peace Council.

This photo, taken on December 21, 2003, shows a working group at the Constitutional Loya Jirga. The fifteen-hundred-member body split into fifty-member working groups, each of which reviewed the entire text. This picture shows the group chaired by Momina Yari, the only woman chair. Yari was appointed chair after a group of non-Pashtun delegates protested against the original chair, who, they claimed, showed Taliban sympathies by trying to eliminate references in the preamble to the "resistance" against the Taliban.

December 23, 2003: General Muhammad Daud Daud (right) speaks to Constitutional Loya Jirga delegates from Northern Afghanistan. General Daud, then commander of the garrison in Kunduz and later deputy minister of the interior for counternarcotics, was assassinated by a suicide bomber in Kunduz on May 28, 2012. The attack killed six others, including two German military officers.

Dr. Ashraf Ghani, minister of finance and former chief social scientist at the World Bank, addresses a plenary session of the Constitutional Loya Jirga on December 25, 2003. Ghani, a coauthor of Chapter 1, later headed the security transition effort for President Karzai's government. He ran for president in 2004.

December 25, 2003, at the Constitutional Loya Jirga: Deputy Chairman Mawlawi Qiamuddin Kashaf confers with chief of secretariat newscaster Jamila Mujahed. Mujahed, removed from her job at Afghan TV by the Taliban, was the first newscaster to broadcast the announcement of the fall of the Taliban after they fled Kabul. Kashaf is today the chairman of the Council of Ulama and a member of the High Peace Council.

On December 26, 2003, a ceremony at the Ministry of Foreign Affairs in Kabul marked completed reconstruction of the Kabul-Kandahar road (Highway 1), which the United States had made a key deliverable. After the dinner, President Karzai dons a cowboy hat given to him by a representative of the Louis Berger American construction company. At the table in front, Foreign Minister Dr. Abdullah Abdullah and UN Special Representative of the Secretary-General Lakhdar Brahimi provide visual commentary. Berger was widely criticized for its performance in Afghanistan.

On November 30, 2004, Deputy Minister of Finance Ghulam Jilani Popal reviews the border police at the customs post on the Iranian border at Islam Qala, Herat province. In the course of this visit, Popal tried to take control of customs revenue on behalf of the central government. This visit took nine months of preparation after the removal of former commander and "Amir of Herat" Muhammad Ismail Khan as governor of Herat on March 3, 2004.

April 2, 2005: an arms handover by a militia commander in Bagram district of Kapisa province. The commander had to prove he was not leader of an "illegal armed group" in order to become a candidate for the provincial assembly. The top photo shows the ceremony inside the district headquarters of the National Directorate of Security: the uluswal (district governor) is addressing representatives of the central government, the UN, and Japan, which together financed this program. In the background, former fighters wonder what they will do next, as they spent their lives fighting rather than getting an education and cannot even pass the minimum qualification to join the police.

The second picture shows some of the arms being handed over against the background of the Hundu Kush mountains, as a mixed group of government officials and former fighters look on.

On August 5, 2006, I traveled to Gardez, Paktia, to visit an old friend, Professor of Sociology Abdul Hakim Taniwal, then governor of Paktia, as recounted in the Preface to Part Three. After meeting in his office, we had lunch at the governor's official residence, where Center on International Cooperation research associate (and later President Karzai's official spokesman, deputy minister of finance, and coauthor of Chapter 13) Humayun Hamidzada took this picture. Taniwal was killed by a suicide bomber forty-one days later, on September 10, 2006, as he left his office to drive home for lunch.

The author with U.S. Special Representative for Afghanistan and Pakistan Richard Holbrooke during an official visit to Afghanistan's Presidential Palace on January 16, 2010. Together with U.S. Ambassador to Afghanistan Karl Eikenberry (not shown), they had just finished a meeting with President Karzai. The official cable reporting on the discussion (classified as secret) was later disclosed by WikiLeaks. Holbrooke died of a ruptured aorta on December 13, 2010. Photo credit: Morgan O'Brien.

I visited Jalalabad on April 8, 2005, for the annual Orange Blossom Festival of Pashto Poetry. The picture above shows a portion of the Kabul-Jalalabad road; this is a secondary road, as the main one was shut down while being reconstructed. The two pictures on the left are at the festival, with the first showing the crowd from the podium, where I was seated. The most popular poems denounced the behavior of U.S. military forces in Eastern Afghanistan. The second shows the podium, with Governor Haji Din Muhammad (in turban) and, to his left, Minister of Information and Culture Sayed Makhdoom Raheen. Din Muhammad, later the governor of Kabul, hails from one of the most powerful tribal families of Eastern Afghanistan. Raheen, a scholar of Persian literature and Sufism from Kabul, received a warm welcome when he addressed the crowd in Dari.

Stability of a state:

a. international aid, in security to legitimate state.

b. political _____ _____ _____ _____ of _____

→ domestic legitimacy

→ less international opposition

⇓ less international aid or subsidy to
  stabilize the state